PLUTARCH'S *LIVES*
Exploring Virtue and Vice

PLUTARCH'S *LIVES*
Exploring Virtue and Vice

TIM DUFF

CLARENDON PRESS · OXFORD

OXFORD
UNIVERSITY PRESS

Great Clarendon Street, Oxford OX2 6DP
Oxford University Press is a department of the University of Oxford.
It furthers the University's objective of excellence in research, scholarship,
and education by publishing worldwide in
Oxford New York
Athens Auckland Bangkok Bogotá Buenos Aires Cape Town
Chennai Dar es Salaam Delhi Florence Hong Kong Istanbul Karachi
Kolkata Kuala Lumpur Madrid Melbourne Mexico City Mumbai Nairobi
Paris São Paulo Shanghai Singapore Taipei Tokyo Toronto Warsaw
with associated companies in Berlin Ibadan

Oxford is a registered trade mark of Oxford University Press
in the UK and in certain other countries

Published in the United States
by Oxford University Press Inc., New York

© T. E. Duff 1999

The moral rights of the author have been asserted
Database right Oxford University Press (maker)

First published 1999

All rights reserved. No part of this publication may be reproduced,
stored in a retrieval system, or transmitted, in any form or by any means,
without the prior permission in writing of Oxford University Press,
or as expressly permitted by law, or under terms agreed with the appropriate
reprographics rights organization. Enquiries concerning reproduction
outside the scope of the above should be sent to the Rights Department,
Oxford University Press, at the address above

You must not circulate this book in any other binding or cover
and you must impose this same condition on any acquirer

British Library Cataloguing in Publication Data
Data available

Library of Congress Cataloging in Publication Data
Duff, Tim.
Plutarch's lives : exploring virtue and vice / Tim Duff
p. cm.
Originally presented as the author's thesis (doctoral—Cambridge,
1994).
Includes bibliographical references.
1. Plutarch. Lives. 2. Biography (as a literary form) 3.
Greece—Biography—History and criticism. 4.
Rome—Biography—History and criticism. 5.
Plutarch—Knowledge—History. 6. Greece—Historiography. 7.
Rome—Historiography. 8. Rhetoric, Ancient. 9. Virtue in
literature. 10. Vice in literature. I. Title.
PA4385 .D84 1999 920.038-ddc21 98-40794
ISBN 0-19-815058-X

3 5 7 9 10 8 6 4 2

Typeset by Regent Typesetting, London
Printed in Great Britain on acid-free paper by
Biddles Ltd,. www.Biddles.co.uk

For my friends

Εἰς Εἰκόνα Πλουτάρχου

Σεῖο πολυκλήεντα τύπον στῆσαν, Χαιρωνεῦ
Πλούταρχε, κρατερῶν υἱέες Αὐσονίων,
ὅττι παραλλήλοισι βίοις Ἕλληνας ἀρίστους
Ῥώμης εὐπολέμοις ἤρμοσας ἐνναέταις.
ἀλλὰ τεοῦ βιότοιο παράλληλον βίον ἄλλον
οὐδὲ σύ γ' ἂν γράψαις· οὐ γὰρ ὅμοιον ἔχεις.

TO A PORTRAIT OF PLUTARCH

The sons of the mighty Italians set up your renowned form, Plutarch of Chaironeia, because in your *Parallel Lives* you brought together excellent Greeks with warlike citizens of Rome. But not even you could write another life parallel to your own. For you have no equal.

Agathias Scholastikos (AD 531–c.580), *Palatine Anthology* 16. 331.

. . . there is no prophane studye better than Plutarke. All other learning is private, fitter for Universities than cities, fuller of contemplacion than experience, more commendable in the students themselves, than profitable unto others. Whereas stories are fit for every place, reache to all persons, serve for all tymes, teache the living, revive the dead, so farre excelling all other bookes, as it is better to see learning in noble mens lives than to read it in Philosophers writings.

From Thomas North's Preface to his English translation of the *Parallel Lives* (1579).

Preface

THIS book is a revised version of my Cambridge Ph.D. dissertation, which was completed in June 1994 under the supervision of Richard Hunter. I thank him warmly for his guidance and encouragement. I am also grateful to Paul Cartledge and Christopher Pelling who have read and offered insightful criticism on more drafts of this work than they would care to remember. Whatever mistakes or muddled thinking remain are, of course, all my own responsibility.

I am grateful to the institutions which have supported this work. The dissertation was completed while I was a graduate student at Christ's College, and the book in two summers spent there. I am grateful to the present and previous Masters and to the Fellows of the College for their hospitality on those occasions. I also thank the members and staff of the Cambridge Faculty of Classics for continuing use of its exceptional library. I acknowledge the support of the British Academy, the Deutscher Akademischer Austauschdienst, the Jebb Fund of Cambridge University, and, especially, of my parents. I am grateful to my colleagues in the Department of Classics at the University of Reading for allowing me the time to bring this project to completion. It is a pleasing coincidence, and one which Plutarch would have enjoyed (see *Sertorius* 1.1–8), that the last monograph to be written in English on Plutarch's *Lives* was by one of my predecessors at Reading (Wardman 1974).

Finally, my thanks to those who read parts or the whole of this book and offered advice or help: in particular, to Christopher Kelly and Tim Whitmarsh, from whose incisive criticism and wise conversation I continue to benefit; also to John Moles and Jan Opsomer; to Tao-Tao Huang, who proof-read the thesis; to Jeremy Duff, Anthea Harris, Pantelis Michelakis, and Rebecca Preston, who proof-read and offered suggestions on the book; and to those others without whom the writing of this book would have been a less pleasant task: in particular Maria-Stella Aloupie, Maria Antoniou, Peter and Rebecca Clarke, Rosemary Evetts, Yuri Hara, Amalia Karamitrou, Maria Kiniari, Brent

Kinman, Hwa-Yong Lee, Helen Raphtopoulos, Vicky Sgardoni, Marina Terkourafi, and Yan-Jing Wang.

Shorter, earlier versions of Chapters 6 and 7 have appeared respectively in Mossman (1997), 169–87, and Fernández Delgardo and Pordomingo Pardo (1996), 333–49 [see p. 352]. An earlier version of Chapter 8 is to appear in *Rhetorical Theory and Praxis in Plutarch* (Collection d'Études Classiques), edited by L. Van der Stockt. In all cases, the version that appears here is to be preferred.

T.D.

Reading–Cambridge
April 1999

Contents

Editions and Abbreviations   xiii
Introduction   1

I. THE MORALIZING PROGRAMME

1. The Programmatic Statements of the *Lives*   13
2. Moralism in Plutarch's *Lives*   52
3. The Soul of a Plutarchan Hero   72

II. EXPLORING VIRTUE AND VICE: THE CASE STUDIES

4. The Lives of Pyrrhos and Marius   101
5. The Lives of Phokion and Cato Minor   131
6. The Lives of Lysander and Sulla   161
7. The Lives of Coriolanus and Alkibiades   205

III. WRITING IN PARALLEL

8. *Synkrisis* and the *Synkriseis* in the *Parallel Lives*   243
9. The Politics of Parallelism   287

Appendix 1: Plutarch and Ancestors   310
Appendix 2: Plutarch and Chronology   312

Bibliography   315
Indices   353

Editions and Abbreviations

Plutarch's works have been consulted in the Teubner editions: for the *Lives* those of Cl. Lindskog and K. Ziegler, *Plutarchus: Vitae Parallelae* (three volumes, Leipzig, 1914–39; second edition, K. Ziegler, 1957–71); for the *Moralia*, those of M. Pohlenz et al., *Plutarchus: Moralia* (five volumes, 1925–78, some in a second edition).[1] Manuscripts of Plutarch, and earlier editions, are referred to using the abbreviations of Ziegler. References to the *Lives* follow the Teubner editions in using the chapter and verse divisions of the edition of Sintenis (1852–5); readers should note that these verse divisions do not correspond to those of the Loeb edition (see below). References to the *Moralia* use, as is conventional, the page numbers of the Frankfurt edition of the text of Stephanus (1599). References to the 'formal' *synkriseis* which close many pairs of *Parallel Lives* are by both titles of the two Lives which they follow (e.g *Per.-Fab.* 1. 4).

All translations are my own, although B. Perrin's translation of the *Lives* (*Plutarch's Lives*, Cambridge, Mass., and London, 1914–26) and those of the *Moralia* by various hands (*Plutarch's Moralia*, Cambridge, Mass., and London, 1927–69),[2] all in the *Loeb Classical Library* and numerously reprinted, have been consulted throughout. Also consulted was D. A. Russell (1993), *Plutarch. Selected Essays and Dialogues* (The World's Classics: Oxford).

I have not adopted the conventional Latinized forms of Greek names but have preferred to transliterate as precisely as is possible. This is more than personal preference: to Latinize the Greek would be a reversal of Plutarch's cultural programme, which functioned to *Hellenize* the Roman.[3] In a few cases, and most

---

[1] Some recent Italian studies have argued that the Teubner editions have imposed a level of atticism not present in Plutarch's original nor preserved in the manuscripts: e.g. Giangrande (1988; 1991; 1992a and b); Gallo (1992a). On Plutarch's style in general, see Weissenberger (1895); Schmid (1887–97), iv. 635–85; Ziegler (1951), 931–8 (= 1964, 293–301); Ambrosini (1991); Brenk (1992), 4426–57; Yaginuma (1992); Torraca (1998). Cf. also Russell (1973), 18–41.

[2] F. C. Babbitt, W. C. Helmbold, P. H. de Lacy, B. Einarson, P. A. Clement, H. B. Hoffleit, H. Cherniss, E. L. Minar, F. H. Sandbach, H. N. Fowler, and L. Pearson.

[3] Hence Plutarch talks of Broutos (Βροῦτος), Kassios (Κάσσιος), and Kikeron (Κικέρων), the Greek versions of Brutus, Cassius, and Cicero. It would be attractive to retain, as Frederick Brenk does (Brenk 1992), these Greek spellings of Roman names in order to capture a sense of Plutarch's appropriation of Roman history into a Greek cultural world-view. I have not been so brave. On Greek and Roman in Plutarch, see below, Ch. 9.

notably in the case of Plutarch himself (in Greek, Ploutarchos: Πλούταρχος), I have retained the conventional Latinized or Anglicized form, where it is considered too well-known to admit change (for example, Thucydides, Plato, Aristotle).

PARALLEL LIVES

Theseus and Romulus	Thes.	Rom.
Lykourgos and Numa	Lyk.	Num.
Solon and Publicola	Sol.	Pub.
Themistokles and Camillus	Them.	Cam.
Perikles and Fabius Maximus	Per.	Fab.
Coriolanus and Alkibiades	Cor.	Alk.
Aemilius Paulus and Timoleon	Aem.	Tim.
Pelopidas and Marcellus	Pel.	Marc.
Aristeides and Cato Major	Arist.	Cato Maj.
Philopoimen and Flamininus	Phil.	Flam.
Pyrrhos and Marius	Pyrrh.	Mar.
Lysander and Sulla	Lys.	Sulla
Kimon and Lucullus	Kim.	Luc.
Nikias and Crassus	Nik.	Crass.
Sertorius and Eumenes	Sert.	Eum.
Agesilaos and Pompey	Ages.	Pomp.
Alexander and Caesar	Alex.	Caes.
Phokion and Cato Minor	Phok.	Cato Min.
Agis and Kleomenes and Tiberius and Caius Gracchus	Ag./Kleom.	Gracchi
Demosthenes and Cicero	Dem.	Cic.
Demetrios and Antony	Demetr.	Ant.
Dion and Brutus	Dion	Brut.

OTHER LIVES

Aratos	Arat.
Artaxerxes	Art.
Galba	Galba
Otho	Otho

MORALIA

Ad Princ. Inerud.	Ad principem ineruditum: To an uneducated ruler (Πρὸς ἡγεμόνα ἀπαίδευτον: 779d–782f)
Adv. Col.	Adversus Colotem: Against Kolotes (Πρὸς Κωλώτην: 1107d–1127e)
Amat.	Amatorius: Dialogue on love (Ἐρωτικός: 784e–771e)
An Seni	An seni sit gerenda res publica: Whether an elderly man should engage in politics (Εἰ πρεσβυτέρῳ πολιτευτέον: 783a–797f)
An Virt. Doc.	An virtus doceri possit: Whether virtue can be taught (Εἰ διδακτὸν ἡ ἀρετή: 439a–440c)
Ap. Lac.	Apophthegmata Laconica: Spartan sayings (Ἀποφθέγματα Λακωνικά: 208a–242d)
Bellone an Pace	Bellone an pace clariores fuerint Athenienses: Were the Athenians more glorious in war or in wisdom? (Πότερον Ἀθηναῖοι κατὰ πόλεμον ἢ κατὰ σοφίαν ἐνδοξότεροι: 345d–351b)
Brut. Anim.	Bruta animalia ratione uti: On the fact that beasts are rational (Περὶ τοῦ τὰ ἄλογα λόγῳ χρῆσθαι: 985d–992e)
Con. Praec.	Coniugalia praecepta: Marriage advice (Γαμικὰ παραγγέλματα: 138a–146a)
De Alex. Fort.	De Alexandri Magni fortuna aut virtute: On the fortune or virtue of Alexander (Περὶ τῆς Ἀλεξάνδρου τύχης ἢ ἀρετῆς: 326d–345b)
De Am. Prol.	De amore prolis: On the love of offspring (Περὶ τῆς εἰς τὰ ἔκγονα φιλοστοργίας: 493a–497e)
De An. Procr.	De animae procreatione in Timaeo: On the creation of the soul in the Timaios (Περὶ τῆς ἐν Τιμαίῳ ψυχογονίας: 1012a–1030c)
De Aud. Poet.	Quomodo adulescens poetas audire debeat: How a young man should listen to the poets (Πῶς δεῖ τὸν νέον ποιημάτων ἀκούειν: 14d–37b)
De Cap. ex Inim.	De capienda ex inimicis utilitate: How to benefit from one's enemies (Πῶς ἄν τις ὑπ' ἐχθρῶν ὠφελοῖτο: 86b–92e)
De Cohib. Ira	De cohibenda ira: On lack of anger (Περὶ ἀοργησίας: 452e–464d)
De Comm. Not.	De communibus notitiis adversus Stoicos: Against the Stoics on common conceptions (Περὶ τῶν κοινῶν ἐννοιῶν πρὸς τοὺς Στωικούς: 1058e–1086b)
De Cup. Divit.	De cupiditate divitiarum: On the love of wealth (Περὶ φιλοπλουτίας: 523c–528b)

De Defect. Orac.	De defectu oraculorum: On the obsolescence of oracles (Περὶ τῶν ἐκλελοιπότων χρηστηρίων: 409e–438e)
De Esu Carn.	De esu carnium: On the eating of meat (Περὶ σαρκοφαγίας: 993a–999b)
De Exil.	De exilio: On exile (Περὶ φυγῆς: 599a–607f)
De Facie	De facie quae in orbe lunae apparet: On the face which appears in the circle of the moon (Περὶ τοῦ ἐμφαινομένου προσώπου τῷ κύκλῳ τῆς σελήνης: 920a–945e)
De Fort.	De fortuna: On chance (Περὶ τύχης: 97c–100a)
De Fort. Rom.	De fortuna Romanorum: On the fortune ⟨or virtue⟩ of the Romans (Περὶ τῆς Ῥωμαίων τύχης ⟨ἢ ἀρετῆς⟩: 316b–326c)
De Frat. Amore	De fraterno amore: On brotherly love (Περὶ φιλαδελφίας: 478a–492d)
De Garrul.	De garrulitate: On idle talk (Περὶ ἀδολεσχίας: 502b–515a)
De Gen. Soc.	De genio Socratis: On the sign of Sokrates (Περὶ τοῦ Σωκράτους δαιμονίου: 575a–598f)
De Herod. Malig.	De Herodoti malignitate: On the malice of Herodotos (Περὶ τῆς Ἡροδότου κακοηθείας: 854e–874c)
De Ipsum Laud.	De se ipsum citra invidiam laudando: On inoffensive self-praise (Περὶ τοῦ ἑαυτὸν ἐπαινεῖν ἀνεπιφθόνως: 539a–547f)
De Is. et Osir.	De Iside et Osiride: On Isis and Osiris (Περὶ Ἴσιδος καὶ Ὀσίριδος: 351c–384c)
De Lat. Viv.	An recte dictum sit latenter esse vivendum: Whether 'live unknown' is a good doctrine (Εἰ καλῶς εἴρηται τὸ λάθε βιώσας: 1128a–1130c)
De Prim. Frig.	De primo frigido: On the first cold (Περὶ τοῦ πρώτως ψυχροῦ: 945f–955c)
De Pyth. Orac.	De Pythiae oraculis: Why does the Pythia no longer give oracles in verse? (Περὶ τοῦ μὴ χρᾶν ἔμμετρα νῦν τὴν Πυθίαν: 394d–409d)
De Sera Num.	De sera numinis vindicta: On why the gods are so slow to punish (Περὶ τῶν ὑπὸ τοῦ θείου βραδέως τιμωρουμένων: 548a–568a)
De Stoic. Repugn.	De Stoicorum repugnantiis: On Stoic contradictions (Περὶ Στωικῶν ἐναντιωμάτων: 1033a–1057c)
De Superstit.	De superstitione: On superstition (Περὶ δεισιδαιμονίας: 164e–171e)
De Tranq. An.	De tranquillitate animi: On tranquillity of mind (Περὶ εὐθυμίας: 464e–477f)
De Tuenda Sanit.	De tuenda sanitate praecepta: Advice on health (Ὑγιεινὰ παραγγέλματα: 122b–137e)
De Virt. Moral.	De virtute morali: On moral virtue (Περὶ τῆς ἠθικῆς ἀρετῆς: 440d–452d)

De Vit. Pud.	De vitioso pudore: On compliancy (Περὶ δυσωπίας: 528c–536d)
Max. cum Princ.	Maxime cum principibus philosopho esse disserendum: On the fact that the philosopher ought most of all to converse with leaders (Περὶ τοῦ ὅτι μάλιστα τοῖς ἡγεμόσι δεῖ τὸν φιλόσοφον διαλέγεσθαι: 776a–779c)
Mul. Virt.	Mulierum virtutes: Virtues of women (Γυναικῶν ἀρεταί: 242e–263c)
Non Posse	Non posse suaviter vivi secundum Epicurum: It is not possible even to live pleasantly according to Epikouros (Ὅτι οὐδὲ ζῆν ἔστιν ἡδέως κατ' Ἐπίκουρον: 1086c–1107c)
Plat. Quaest.	Platonicae quaestiones: Platonic questions (Πλατωνικὰ ζητήματα: 999c–1011f)
Praec. Ger.	Praecepta gerendae reipublicae: Political precepts (Πολιτικὰ παραγγέλματα: 798a–825f)
Prof. in Virt.	Quomodo quis suos in virtute sentiat profectus: How to recognize that one is making progress in virtue (Πῶς ἄν τις αἴσθοιτο ἑαυτοῦ προκόπτοντος ἐπ' ἀρετῇ: 75a–86a)
Quaest. Conv.	Quaestiones convivales: Table talk (Συμποσιακὰ προβλήματα: 612c–748d)
Quaest. Graec.	Quaestiones Graecae: Greek questions (Αἴτια Ἑλληνικά: 291d–304f)
Quaest. Rom.	Quaestiones Romanae: Roman questions (Αἴτια Ῥωμαϊκά: 263d–291c)
Quomodo Adult.	Quomodo adulator ab amico internoscatur: How to tell a flatterer from a friend (Πῶς ἄν τις διακρίνειε τὸν κόλακα τοῦ φίλου: 48e–74e)
Terrest. an Aquat.	Terrestriane an aquatilia animalia sint callidiora: Which are cleverer: land animals or sea animals? (Πότερα τῶν ζῴων φρονιμώτερα, τὰ χερσαῖα ἢ τὰ ἔνυδρα: 959a–985c)

OTHER WORKS

Barigazzi	Barigazzi, A. (1966) (ed.), Favorino di Arelate. Opere (Florence)
Bernardakis	Bernardakis, G. N. (1888–96) (ed.), Plutarchi Chaeronensis Moralia, 7 vols. (Leipzig)
Blass	Blass, F. (1996) (ed.), Antiphonis Orationes et fragmenta, 2nd edn. edited by T. Thaleim (Leipzig)
CIL	Corpus Inscriptionum Latinarum (1896–) (Berlin)
Diano	Diano, C. (1974) (ed.), Epicuri Ethica et Epistulae (Florence)

Diels–Kranz	Diels, H., and Kranz, W. (1972) (eds.), *Die Fragmente der Vorsokratiker*, 2 vols. (Berlin)
Di Marco	Di Marco, M. (1989) (ed.), *Timone di Fliunte* (Rome).
Dindorf	Dindorf, W. (1829) (ed.), *Georgius Syncellus et Nicephorus* (Bonn)
E–K	Edelstein, L. and Kidd, I. G. (1972) (eds.), *Posidonius: the Fragments*, 3 vols. (Leipzig)
FGrH	Jacoby, F. (1923–58) (ed.), *Die Fragmente der griechischen Historiker*, 3 vols. (Berlin, 1923–30; Leiden, 1940–58)
Förster[a]	Förster, R. (1893) (ed.), *Scriptores Physiognomonici Graeci et Latini*, 2 vols. (Leipzig)
Förster[b]	Förster, R. (1903–27) (ed.), *Libanii Opera*, 12 vols. (Leipzig)
Gernet–Bizos	Gernet, L., and Bizos, M. (1955) (eds.), *Lysias: Discours* (Collection des Universités de France: 3rd edn., Paris)
Giannantoni	Giannantoni, G. (1990) (ed.), *Socratis et Socraticorum Reliquiae*, 4 vols. (Naples)
Heinze	Heinze, R. (1892) (ed.), *Xenokrates: Darstellung der Lehre und Sammlung der Fragmente* (Leipzig). Reprinted Hildersheim, 1965
Hense	Hense, O. (1889) (ed.), *Teletis Reliquiae* (Freiburg im Breisgau)
Hilgard	Hilgard, A. (1901) (ed.), *Grammatici Graeci*, iii (Leipzig)
Hobein	Hobein, H. (1910) (ed.), *Maximi Tyrii Philosophumena* (Leipzig)
IG	*Inscriptiones Graecae* (1913–) (2nd edn., Berlin)
ILS	H. Bessau (1892–1914) (ed.), *Inscriptiones Latinae Selectae* (Berlin)
Jocelyn	Jocelyn, H. D. (1967) (ed.), *The Tragedies of Ennius: The fragments* (Cambridge)
Kassel–Austin	Austin, C., and Kassel, R. (1989) (eds.), *Poetae comici Graeci*, vii. *Menecrates–Xenophon* (Berlin and New York)
Kühn	Kühn, C. G. (1821–33) (ed.), Κλαυδίου Γαληνοῦ Ἅπαντα. *Claudii Galeni Opera Omnia*, 22 vols. (Leipzig). Reprinted 1964–5, Hildesheim
Littré	Littré, E. (1839–61) (ed.), *Oeuvres complètes d'Hippocrate*, 10 vols. (Paris)
LSJ	Liddell, H. G., Scott, R., and Jones, H. S. (1925–40), *Greek-English Lexicon* (9th edn., Oxford)
Maehler	Maehler, H. (1987–9) (ed.), *Pindari carmina cum fragmentis*, 2 vols. (Leipzig)
Marcovich	Marcovich, M. (1978) (ed.), *Eraclito: Frammenti* (Florence). A revised version of English edition, *Heraclitus: Greek Text with a Short Commentary* (Mérida, 1967).

Mayer	Mayer, A. (1910) (ed.), *Theophrasti Περὶ Λέξεως Libri Fragmenta* (Leipzig)
Meineke	Meineke, A. (1855–7) (ed.), *Ἰωάννου Στοβαίου Ἀνθολόγιον. Ioannis Stobaei Florilegium*, 4 vols. (Leipzig)
Migne	Migne, J.-P. (1844–65) (ed.), *Patrologia Latina* (Paris)
Nauck, *Aristoph.*	Nauck, A. (1963) (ed.), *Aristophanis Byzantii Grammatici Alexandrini Fragmenta* (Hildersheim)
Nauck, *TrGF*	Nauck, A. (1926) (ed.), *Tragicorum Graecorum Fragmenta* (2nd edn.) (Leipzig)
OGIS	Dittenberger, W. (1903–5) (ed.), *Orientis Graeci Inscriptiones Selectae*, 2 vols. (Leipzig)
Page	Page, D. L. (1962) (ed.), *Poetae Melici Graeci* (Oxford)
Pfeiffer	Pfeiffer, R. (1949) (ed.), *Callimachus* (Oxford)
Rabe[a]	Rabe, H. (1913) (ed.), *Hermogenes: Opera* (Leipzig)
Rabe[b]	Rabe, H. (1906) (ed.), *Scholia in Lucianum* (Leipzig)
RE	Pauly, A. F. von, Wissowa, G., and Kroll, W. (1894–1980) (eds.), *Real-Encyclopädie der Classischen Altertumswissenschaft* (Stuttgart)
Sandbach	Sandbach, F. H. (1969) (ed.), *Plutarch's Moralia*, xv. *Fragments* (Loeb Classical Library: Cambridge, Mass., and London)
Schöne	Schöne, R. (1911) (ed.), *Aeneae Tactici de Obsidione toleranda Commentarius* (Leipzig)
SEG	*Supplementum Epigraphicum Graecum.* Hondius, J. J. E., and Woodhead, A. G. (eds.), vols. 1–25 (Leiden, 1923–71); Pleket, H. W., and Stroud, R. S. (eds.), vols. 26–7 (Alphen, 1979–80), and vols. 28– (Amsterdam, 1982–)
SGDI	Collitz, H., and Bechtel, F., *et al.* (1884–1915) (eds.), *Sammlung der griechischen Dialekt-Inschriften*, 4 vols. (Göttingen)
SIG³	Dittenberger, W. (1915–24) (ed.), *Sylloge Inscriptionum Graecarum* (3rd edn.)
Spanheim	Spanheim, E. F. (1696) (ed.), *Ἰουλιανοῦ αὐτοκράτορος τὰ σωζόμενα. Καὶ τὰ ἐν ἁγίοις Κυρίλλου . . . πρὸς τὰ τοῦ ἐν ἀθέοις Ἰουλιανοῦ λόγοι δέκα. Iuliani imp. opera quae supersunt omnia. Et S. Cyrilli . . . contra impium Iulianum libri decem* (Leipzig)
Spengel	Spengel, L. (1853–6) (ed.), *Rhetores Graeci*, 3 vols. (Leipzig)
SVF	Arnim, I. von (1903–24) (ed.), *Stoicorum Veterum Fragmenta*, 4 vols. (Leipzig)
TrGF II	Kannicht, R., and Snell, B. (1981) (eds.), *Tragicorum Graecorum Fragmenta*, ii. *Fragmenta adespota; testimonia volumini 1 addenda; indices ad volumina 1 et 2* (Göttingen)

TrGF III	Radt, S. (1985) (ed.), *Tragicorum Graecorum Fragmenta*, iii. *Aeschylus* (Göttingen)
TrGF IV	Radt, S. (1977), *Tragicorum Graecorum Fragmenta*, iv *Sophocles* (Göttingen)
Usener	Usener, H. (1963) (ed.), *Epicurea* (Rome)
Us.–Rad.	Usener, H., and Radermacher, L. (1899–1929) (eds.), *Dionysii Halicarnasei Opuscula* (Leipzig)
Voss	Voss, O. (1896) (ed.), *De Heraclidis Pontici Vita et Scriptis* (Rostock)
West	West, M. L. (1971) (ed.), *Iambi et Elegi Graeci ante Alexandrum Cantati. Volumen I. Archilochus, Hipponax. Theognidea* (Oxford)
Wimmer	Wimmer, F. (1854–62) (ed.), *Theophrasti Eresii Opera quae supersunt omnia*, 3 vols. (Leipzig)

Introduction

The *Parallel Lives* of L. Mestrius Plutarch (*Πλούταρχος*) were written in the early decades of the second century AD. They have since been widely read and, after a sharp decline in their fortunes in the middle years of the twentieth century, are once again at the forefront of interest in the ancient world. This book is an attempt to explore two related aspects of the *Parallel Lives*: their moralizing purpose and the comparative structure through which Plutarch's moralism is so often mediated. It will look at the ways in which the *Parallel Lives* explore issues of right and wrong, good and evil; the ways in which they cause us to question or to understand our world.

Much is known about Plutarch's own life from his writings. He was born sometime between AD 40 and 50 to a wealthy family in the small city of Chaironeia in central Greece. An inscription tells us that he gained Roman citizenship through his friend the consular Mestrius Florus, whose name he took. He travelled widely: certainly to Asia Minor, to Rome and Italy, and to Alexandria. He mentions many important figures, both Greek and Roman, as personally acquainted with him. But most of his life was spent in or near his home town of Chaironeia. He held several municipal offices there; he was also a priest at Delphoi, which was not far distant.[1] He died early in the reign of the Emperor Hadrian, who acceded in AD 117.[2]

It is not, however, as a local politician that Plutarch is known, but as a philosopher and a writer. His output was enormous: over seventy works of a miscellaneous nature survive, known collectively as the *Moralia* (*Ἠθικά*); the so-called Lamprias Catalogue, a list of works attributed to Plutarch and probably dating from the third or fourth

---

[1] Cf. *Ant.* 68. 6–8; *Dem.* 2. 1–4; *Praec. Ger.* 811c. On Plutarch's life, see Ziegler (1949), 4–60 (= 1951, 639–96); Jones (1971), 3–64. On his family, cf. also Babut (1981). For Plutarch's Roman citizenship: *SIG*³ 829A.

[2] Possibly around 120: Jones (1966), 63–6. Flacelière (1971) pushes the date as late as 125, but as Swain (1991), 319–22, demonstrates, this is unlikely.

centuries AD, records the titles of about double that number.³ The surviving works range in content from a commentary on Plato's *Timaios* to political treatises, such as the *Political precepts* and *To an uneducated ruler*, and moral and scientific works, such as *On lack of anger* or *On the first cold*.

This book concerns another part of Plutarch's literary *oeuvre*, probably the last to be written: his biographies, known in ancient terminology as Lives (Βίοι). A series of Lives of Roman emperors from Augustus to Vitellius, of which only the *Galba* and *Otho* survive, was followed by a series of paired *Parallel Lives* of earlier Greek and Roman figures. The *Parallel Lives* were written between about AD 96, when the Emperor Domitian died, and Plutarch's own death sometime around 120.⁴ Twenty-two out of the twenty-three books known of *Parallel Lives* survive. The first pair of *Parallel Lives*, that of Epameinondas and one of the Scipios, is no longer extant; but it probably contained a dedication to Sosius Senecio, who is addressed frequently in the surviving Lives;⁵ Senecio's consulship in AD 96 may well have provided the occasion for the publication of the first pairs. Each book of *Parallel Lives* contains a pair of parallel biographies, Greek and Roman, welded together by a common introduction and a closing comparison. They were probably worked on, and published, in bundles.⁶ Together the surviving *Parallel Lives* cover a vast span of Greek and Roman history, from the 'mythical' period of the *Lives of Theseus and Romulus*, to the Hellenistic and late Republican worlds of the *Demetrios and Antony*.⁷

---

³ On the Lamprias Catalogue, see Ziegler (1908), 239–44; (1927), 20–1; (1949), 60–6 (=1951, 696–702); Irigoin (1982–3; 1986); ead. in Flacelière and Irigoin (1987), pp. ccxxviii–ccxxix and ccciii–cccx.

⁴ We know that the *Dem.-Cic.* was the fifth pair (*Dem.* 3. 1), *Per.-Fab.* the tenth (*Per.* 2. 5), and *Dion-Brut.* the twelfth (*Dion* 2. 7). On the relative and absolute chronology of the Lives, see, in particular, Jones (1966), 66–74, based partly on Stoltz (1929). Cf. also Ziegler (1949), 71–82 and 262–5 (=1951, 708–19 and 899–903); Theander (1958); Brożek (1963); Geiger (1981), esp. 89–94. For reflections on the relationship between the relative chronology of the Lives and their content, see Van der Valk (1982); Stadter (1983–4), 358–9; (1989), pp. xxvii–xxix; (1992a), 48–51.

⁵ *Thes.* 1. 1; *Dem.* 1. 1; 31. 7; *Dion* 1. 1; *Aem.* 1. 6; *Ag./Kleom.* 2. 9.

⁶ See Mewaldt (1907). Piccirilli (1977), 999–1004; (1980), 1753–5, argues that the *Lyk.-Num.*, *Thes.-Rom.*, *Them.-Cam.*, and *Lys.-Sulla* were composed together (as numbers 6 to 9 in the collection). Pelling (1979), demonstrates that the *Ages.-Pomp.*, *Nik.-Crass.*, *Alex.-Caes.*, *Phok.-Cato Min.*, *Dion-Brut.*, and *Demetr.-Ant.*, together with their Greek parallels, were composed together; cf. Pelling (1995b), 312–18, answering the criticism of Hillard (1987) and Steidle (1990).

⁷ Two other Lives survive, which are part of neither series: the *Aratos* and *Artaxerxes*. The Lamprias Catalogue records the titles of a number of others: *Herakles*, *Hesiod*, *Pindar*, *Krates*, *Daïphantos*, and *Aristomenes* (nos. 34–9; cf. fr. 6–12 Sandbach).

THE INFLUENCE OF THE *PARALLEL LIVES*

The *Parallel Lives* seem to have been an almost instant success. In the late second century, the Latin writer Aulus Gellius quotes from them frequently.[8] Shortly afterwards, Athenaios in his *Sophists at Dinner* seems to borrow from them, although without acknowledging his debt.[9] Menander Rhetor, late in the third century, advises would-be rhetoricians to read them (2. 392. 28–31). In the fourth century Sopatros the Sophist uses the *Moralia* and the Lives of Demetrios and Brutus for his *Miscellaneous Extracts*.[10] In Byzantine times, the twelfth-century writer Ioannes Zonaras makes use of, or possibly composes, a summary of at least some of the *Parallel Lives* in order to write his own *Epitome of Histories*.[11]

The preservation into modern times of such a large part of the Plutarchan corpus is chiefly owed to the Byzantine scholar Maximos Planoudes (c.1255–1305), who commissioned the production of several large codices incorporating both *Lives* and *Moralia*.[12] Latin translations of the *Lives* began to appear in the West from the fifteenth century; by the sixteenth century a host of vernacular translations was becoming available.[13] The most important of these was perhaps the French translation of Jacques Amyot published in 1559.[14] Not long after, the first critical edition of the Greek text was published in Paris in 1572 by Stephanus. Amyot's French translation was itself translated into English by Thomas North, whose *Lives of the noble Grecians and Romanes* appeared in 1579[15] and was subsequently read by Shakespeare, who used the Lives of the Roman statesmen Coriolanus, Julius Caesar, and Mark Antony as sources for the plays which bear their names.[16] A new English

---

[8] e.g. *Attic Nights* 1. 26. 4. He also quotes from the *Moralia* frequently, sometimes in Greek (for example, 2. 8. 1 and 4. 11. 12) and sometimes in Latin paraphrase (3. 6. 1–3; 4. 11. 13).   [9] See Sansone (1988), 311–12.

[10] According to Photios, *Bibliotheca* 161, 104a23–633.

[11] Manfredini (1992b and 1993). Cf. Pelling (1973).

[12] Manfredini (1992a). For discussions of the textual tradition of the *Lives*, see Ziegler (1907); Manfredini (1987).

[13] Cf. Federici (1828); Teza (1902–3); Giachetti (1910); Weiss (1953); Lasso de la Vega (1961–2); Resta (1962); Bergua Cavero (1995). On Plutarch's popularity, see Burke (1966). Bibliographies on the reception of Plutarch are given by Criniti (1979) and Harrison (1992a), 4675–8. See also the forthcoming proceedings of the VII Convegno Plutarcheo held in Milan and Gargnano in May 1997.

[14] Cf. Blignières (1851); Aulotte (1965).

[15] On North's translation, see Denton (1993).

[16] Cf. Shackford (1929); Spencer (1964); D. C. Green (1978); Miola (1983), 76–205.

translation by a team of scholars working under the direction of Dryden appeared in several volumes between 1684 and 1688. In the seventeenth and eighteenth centuries few Classical works were more highly regarded.[17]

One can suggest several reasons why the *Lives* were so popular in the seventeenth and eighteenth centuries. First, the *Lives* offered a complete conspectus of the Classical world, both Greek and Roman, from Theseus to the emperors Galba and Otho. For Plutarch, the world of Republican Rome and the Greek city-states was already a thing of the past. He shared with his readers an interest in, and nostalgia for, the Classical age. Secondly, his taste for moralizing was congenial to the sensibilities of the age. It was self-evident for people of this time, as for Plutarch, that the function of history and biography was to inculcate moral values in the reader.[18] Biography, often written explicitly in imitation of Plutarch, became popular.[19] Thirdly, Plutarch's beliefs and values found favour in this age: in particular his stress on the virtues of humanity and of calmness in the face of adversity, and his preference for enlightened monarchy. For example, Plutarch's analysis of the rights and wrongs of tyrannicide in the *Julius Caesar* found particular resonance in the discourse of Shakespearian England.[20] Similarly, his supposed opposition to despotism made the Lives of Timoleon, Dion, and Cato the Younger particularly popular with the liberals and revolutionaries of the eighteenth and nineteenth centuries.[21] The founders of the United States saw in some Plutarchan Lives, notably the *Cato Minor*, *Brutus*, and *Cicero*, powerful symbols of their own Republicanism.[22]

The influence of Plutarch's *Lives* on the development of biography as a separate literary genre can hardly be exaggerated. Boswell, in the introduction to his *The Life of Samuel Johnson, LL.D.* (1791), claims allegiance

---

[17] Cf. Scardigli (1987b), 5–9.

[18] See e.g. Francis Bacon's *Advancement of Learning* (1605).

[19] The 15th-c. Florentine scholar Donato Acciaivoli even added a pair of Lives, those of Hannibal and Scipio Africanus, composed by himself, to one of the early Latin editions. These Lives found their way into subsequent editions, including those of Amyot and North: see Affortunati and Scardigli (1992). On Plutarch's lost Lives of the Scipios, see below, Ch. 1, n. 4.

[20] Miola (1985).

[21] On Plutarch's influence in later centuries, see Hirzel (1912), 74–206; Barrow (1967), 162–76; Gossage (1967), 67–70; Gianakaris (1970), 129–50; Russell (1973), 143–63. For his influence specifically in the 17th and 18th cents., see Berry (1961), esp. 1–34; Howard (1970), with the review of Barthelmess (1977); on Plutarch and Montaigne, see Norton (1906); Konstantinovic (1989). For Plutarch and Cavafy, see Lavagnini (1989); Harrison (1992b); González González (1994); for Plutarch and Nietzche, see Ingenkamp (1988).

[22] Reinhold (1975), 39–41; (1984); Sellers (1994), 77–82.

to the Plutarchan model. Lytton Strachey, in the preface to his *Eminent Victorians* (1918), puts forward a case for a very Plutarchan selectivity.[23] Despite the recent trend to so-called 'exhaustive' biography, the main stream of modern biography, with its interest in character as revealed in deed, can still meaningfully be said to be Plutarchan.[24] For Plutarch, the chief object of the biographer was to reveal his subject's character. This might often be achieved through a recounting of his deeds on the grand stage of politics, statesmanship, and war: Plutarch, like most ancients, believed character was revealed most of all through what a man *did*. But he also held that anecdotes and details about the subject's family life, or his education, about his 'off-duty' moments, or other apparently minor matters, could be just as revealing (see pp. 13–17). But Plutarch's biographical programme had a second, complementary aim. *Understanding* the subject's character was a preliminary to *judging* his moral qualities. Character, for Plutarch, as in ancient Greek thinking in general, had a strong moral dimension. To this concern with moral character, Plutarch added a third dimension to his task, a dimension familiar to ancient readers of historical narrative: the improvement of the reader. Reading about a statesman of the past and making judgements on his conduct and character would lead to that kind of self-examination which brings moral improvement. To this extent, the *Lives* were an extension of his concern with morality, with the formulae for correct living, which we see in so many of his non-biographical essays preserved in the *Moralia*. There is an essential unity between *Moralia* and *Lives*, between, on the one hand, works of moral theory and, on the other, works in which the theory is examined—and questioned—in practice.[25]

PLUTARCHSTUDIEN

Despite the continuing influence of Plutarch's *Lives* on the genre of biography, his standing in academic circles has, for much of the twentieth century, been at a markedly low ebb. The ebb and flow of

---

[23] Cf. the titles of J. Spence's *A Parallel in the Manner of Plutarch* (1759), W. C. Taylor's *The Modern British Plutarch* (1846), S. C. Chitty's *The Tamil Plutarch* (1859), and J. Cournos' *A Modern Plutarch* (1928).

[24] For example, Conquest (1991), p. xv, makes direct claim to Plutarchan influence in his biography of Stalin, citing Plutarch's *Alexander* prologue as a justification for not giving an 'exhaustive chronicle' of Stalin's life, but rather 'a portrait', for which the criterion for selection is 'to illuminate Stalin's nature'. See also Vukobrat (1995).

[25] On the unity of *Lives* and *Moralia*, cf. Barthelmess (1986), 61–4; Valgiglio (1992).

Plutarch's fortunes have reflected changes in modern conceptions of the writing of history and of the relationship of historical writing to the events it claims to represent. Nineteenth-century conceptions of history as a science, in which the historian's duty was to collect 'facts' which would 'speak for themselves', were particularly damaging for Plutarch. The denial by historians of their own creative role in writing history led them to ignore, or at least play down, the creative role of ancient historians or biographers in composing their narratives. Such ancient writers were viewed as mines for 'facts' ripped from their literary and sociological context. Most of Plutarch's biographies concern periods of history hundreds of years before his own, and so were considered, with some justification, less reliable than earlier, more contemporary ancient texts. So the study of Plutarch became, in the nineteenth and early twentieth centuries, a search for sources; the unity of his texts as literary works, and their value for throwing light on the concerns of their author and his age, were ignored. In the same way, the study of the four canonical Gospels was dominated by a concern for sources.[26]

In this period Plutarch was denied not only a creative role as author, but even the more mechanical role of compiler of disparate sources. Scholars of the nineteenth and early twentieth centuries assumed, almost certainly incorrectly, that Plutarch's *Lives* were based on pre-existing political biographies. The literally hundreds of earlier authors to whom Plutarch refers, including the great classics, were known, it was argued, only at second-hand via these intermediaries; each Life was, it was claimed, written from only a single source; all references to other sources were copied from this source. So each Life was reduced to a series of unconnected fragments inherited from earlier writers through an intermediary, whose work, it was assumed, Plutarch had used almost unchanged.[27] Scholarly attention was, as with the Gospels, to focus on the passage through time and via successive intermediaries of these individual blocks of text.

Frederick Leo, the author of the first major work on biography in antiquity (1901), argued most clearly the case for Plutarch's dependence on earlier biographies. He also attempted to explain the differences in

[26] The source-critical approach to the Gospels, and its extension, form-criticism, is most clearly seen in Dibelius (1919) and Bultmann (1921). Cf. Eduard Meyer's source-critical analysis of the *Kimon* in Meyer (1899), 1–87, and of the Gospels in id. (1921–3). On the Gospels as ancient biographies (βίοι), see Burridge (1992).

[27] e.g. Strasburger (1938) on *Caes.*; Westlake (1938) on *Tim.*; Smith (1940; 1944) on *Flam., Aem.*, and *Cato Maj.*; Fuhrmann (1960), 264–9, Townend (1964), Mittelstadt (1967) on *Galba* and *Otho*; Ferrarese (1974; 1975) on *Per.*; Hillard (1987) on *Luc.*

form, emphasis, and preoccupation between Plutarch's *Lives* and the *Lives* of his near contemporary Suetonius, by reference to the literary pedigree of the two writers. The structure of Plutarch's biographies is chronological, that of Suetonius' thematic; as a result, Plutarch characterizes his subjects indirectly, Suetonius directly.[28] This Leo explained by positing two distinct biographical traditions, supposedly emerging in the Hellenistic period, of which Plutarch and Suetonius were merely the end points. 'Plutarchan' chronological biography was assigned to the Aristotelian or 'Peripatetic' school, while 'Suetonian' topical biography was seen as descended from Alexandrian work on the lives of poets and philosophers.

Leo's theories, which deny Plutarch any creative role in constructing his texts, are based almost entirely on arguments from silence and on assumptions of the derivative nature of post-Classical Greek literature. There is no evidence for biographies on either Plutarchan or Suetonian lines before Plutarch or Suetonius,[29] and no grounds for the assumption of Plutarch's wholesale copying of such works. Works of a broadly biographical nature were certainly being written from the fourth century BC onwards, and the production of works focusing on great individuals surely continued in the Hellenistic age. But the form or range of forms which such works took is impossible to recover. At any rate, the evidence is against there being merely two biographical traditions. A fragment of a Life of the playwright Euripides by Satyros, dating from the early second century BC and discovered in 1912, is, significantly, in dialogue form, and so fits neither of Leo's two types of biography.[30] Cornelius Nepos' *Lives of illustrious men*, written in Latin in the late first century, were known by Plutarch and certainly influenced him, but even Nepos' work, a series of short biographies, several to a book, does not easily fit into one or other supposed type.[31] The differences between Plutarch and Suetonius should be assigned not to the influence of literary traditions or

---

[28] Cf. the later assumptions of Weizsäcker (1931), that the rare passages in Plutarch of explicit characterization (the *eidologische*) must be derived from sources different from those of the narrative passages (the *chronographische*). See the criticisms of Gomme (1945), 57–8; Momigliano (1971), 16–17; Polman (1974), 172–3.

[29] Geiger (1985), 30–65; though equally there is insufficient evidence to conclude, as Geiger does, that political biographies of this kind did *not* exist in the Hellenistic age: Moles (1989).

[30] Gallo (1967); Momigliano (1971a), 80–1. For criticism of Leo, see Gallo (1967), 152–4; Momigliano (1971b), esp. 8–13; Polman (1974), 169–70. For further bibliography on this question, see Swain (1989c), 328 n. 52; Rosenmeyer (1992), 206 n. 6. Cf. Piccirilli (1985).

[31] Ramón Palerm (1994). Possibly Oppius' work on his contemporary Julius Caesar provided some sort of model for Suetonius: Townend (1987), esp. 341–2.

sources which they blindly followed, but to their own choice, their own conception of the biographer's task and their own cultural identity.³²

Over the last half-century, there has been a sea-change in the study of ancient historiography, and of Plutarch in particular, coinciding with, and encouraged by, theoretical advances in the study of history. From the 1920s some scholars were challenging the idea of Plutarch as simply summarizing or elaborating a single source.³³ Konrat Ziegler in his influential 1949 monograph, reprinted in Pauly's *Real-Encyclopädie* (1951), emphasized Plutarch's creativity: his *Lives* are the product of his own reading and of his own creative design.³⁴ Of course, it would be foolish to maintain that *every* writer whom Plutarch mentions, particularly in the Roman Lives, where he was on less familiar territory, has been directly consulted.³⁵ It is also probable that, given the technology of book-production in antiquity, Plutarch was only able to have open one source at any one time: for other writers, he would most likely rely on his memory or on the services of secretaries.³⁶ But later studies have tended to confirm that Plutarch did know at first hand a vast range of earlier Greek writers, and that he moulded this material to suit his own purposes.³⁷ Historical theory, furthermore, has laid stress on the importance of the process of writing itself as interpretation and emphasized the historian's own role in creating history.³⁸ The priorities which he gives to

³² It seems likely that the form and content of Suetonian biography are derived as much from the contemporary ideology of the Principate and from the Roman rhetorical tradition as from any background in Greek *enkomion* or biography: see Stuart (1928), 189–220; Wallace-Hadrill (1983), 66–72 and 142–58; Lewis (1991a). Suetonius' use of a topical format may well also have something to do with his background as a scholar or bureaucrat (Townend [1967], 84–6).

³³ Wilamowitz-Moellendorf (1926): 64–8 in the translation of 1995; Klotz (e.g. 1934; 1935a; 1935b; 1938; 1941); Zimmerman (1930); Gomme (1945), 81–4; Theander (1959).

³⁴ Ziegler (1949), 273–91 (= 1951, 911–28). Also emphasized by Theander (1951), 2–66.

³⁵ See e.g. Pelling (1984b), 88–9; Delvaux (1988), 37–48. For mistakes in translating Latin sources, cf. Hardy (1890), 185–6; Holden (1886), p. xv n. 15; Rose (1924), 16–18; Russell (1973), 54 n. 27; Townend (1987), 332 and 339; Gamberale (1995). But claims by e.g. Jones (1971), 76–7, that Plutarch's Latin was too poor to allow him to consult a Latin source directly are unconvincing: cf. Rose (1924), 11–19; Jones (1971), 81–7; Babut (1975), 208; Flacelière (1980), 114–16; Rosalia (1991). Plutarch's protestations in *Dem.* 2. 2–4 are part of a *recusatio* for not writing about Demosthenes and Cicero as *literary* figures, and should not be taken seriously as indications of his knowledge of Latin. I have not been able to see Strobach (1997) (see p. 352). ³⁶ Pelling (1979).

³⁷ Wide-reading: Erbse (1956), 420–4 (=1979, 501–5); Stadter (1965); Jones (1971), 81–7; Geiger (1985), 58–62; Piccirilli (1990b); Walsh (1992), esp. 231–3; Buckler (1993). Reshaping source material: Russell (1963); Pelling (1979; 1980; 1985; 1990b; 1992; 1996); de Romilly (1988a) with the criticisms of Pelling (1992), n. 29; Stadter (1965), esp. 125–40. Flacelière (1968), 491–8, and Delvaux (1988), 27–37, give summaries of the history of scholarship on this issue.

³⁸ e.g. Collingwood (1946); Carr (1961), esp. 1–24; White (1978); Tosh (1991), 130–51.

different sorts of material are themselves revealing of the assumptions and values of the writer and of his society. Plutarch's construction of Classical Athens or Republican Rome can throw as much light on his own society as it does on those he writes about. Plutarch as a writer has re-emerged.[39]

THE SCOPE OF THIS BOOK

This book is an attempt to read Plutarch's *Lives* not as mines for history but as an area of study in their own right, and one which throws light on the intellectual climate of Plutarch's own day. It is less concerned with the 'truth-status' of Plutarchan narrative, more with how that narrative is constructed and how it would have been read in its original context.

The focus of this book is on the ethical discourse of Plutarch's *Parallel Lives*. Plutarch claims that a study of his work will instil virtue. What would this mean to an ancient reader? How does this moral purpose affect a reading of any individual pair of *Parallel Lives*? My main contention, discussed in Part I and demonstrated in the case studies of Part II, is that the moralism of many *Parallel Lives* is not one which simply affirms the norms of Plutarch's society; rather it is complex, exploratory, and challenging. Like the best tragedies, the *Parallel Lives* invite the reader to consider and ponder.[40] They do not, or at least not always, simply expound a set of values. They throw questions back to the reader. Some core values are unchallenged, but many Lives intrude a thought-provoking doubt and uncertainty about morality and virtue.

Part I, then, discusses Plutarch's moral programme. Chapter 1 consists of a detailed reading of the surviving programmatic statements. Chapter 2 explores the programme set out in these statements, particularly the theory of 'great natures', and assesses if and how Plutarch fulfils his declared aim of improving the reader. Chapter 3 examines Plutarch's assumptions about human psychology and the value-system which informs his moral outlook. In Part II, a series of case-studies of individual pairs of Lives are used to examine Plutarch's moral and literary programme in practice. Chapter 4 consists of a study of the *Pyrrhos–Marius*, Chapter 5 of the *Phokion–Cato Minor*, Chapter 6 of the *Lysander–Sulla* and Chapter 7 of the *Coriolanus–Alkibiades*. The

[39] Cf. the similar recognition of the artistic unity of Xenophon's *Hellenika*: Gray (1989); Lévy (1990); Diodoros' *Universal History*: Sacks (1990; 1994); Dionysios' *Roman Antiquities*: Fox (1993); *Luke–Acts*: Barrett (1961); Stein (1991).
[40] See pp. 61–2, 69–70, 221, and 284.

Pyrrhos–Marius has a fairly straightforward moral lesson at its core; the other three pairs are all in some way challenging and problematic.

In Part II, I aim also to demonstrate a second contention, that each pair of *Parallel Lives* must be read as a complete book, not as individual biographies: no one Life can be understood without its partner, and without the other components—prologue and comparison—which go to make up a whole Plutarchan 'book'. The importance of the parallel structure of the aptly named *Parallel Lives* has been argued by others. Both Erbse in 1956, and more recently Pelling in 1986,[41] have demonstrated that the parallel structure encourages comparison and contrast between paired Lives, a process which itself illuminates and clarifies the moral questions at their core. The need to read the *Parallel Lives* 'in parallel' is a lesson which is, however, still only sporadically applied. The modern tendency, therefore, to print paired Lives separately, begun by Adamantios Koraes in his edition of 1809–1815 (Paris), is to be deplored.[42] My understanding of Plutarchan *synkrisis*, however, involves more than a recognition of the literary and thematic unity of paired biographies. In my reading, as will become apparent, the paired structure also contributes to the ethical uncertainty and complexity which inform many pairs of Lives.

Part III of the book looks more closely at two aspects of the Plutarchan parallel programme or *synkrisis*. Chapter 8 examines the formal comparisons (*synkriseis*) which end most pairs of *Parallel Lives* and is perhaps the most controversial part of this book. In my reading, the formal comparisons are seen as increasing the moral complexities of the Plutarchan book to which they are attached; they provide a sometimes striking revision of the preceding narrative and of the moral judgements which had been implied. Thus, in moral effect as well as in structure, they are firmly welded to the books which they close. Chapter 9, finally, examines the cultural and political implications of Plutarch's programme of writing in parallel. The *Parallel Lives* are seen as documents of a Greek reaction to Roman power, a Greek attempt to absorb Roman history into the orbit of Greek values and Greek historiographical tradition. In this respect Plutarch is a forerunner of the champions of the Greek 'Second Sophistic', men such as Dion of Prousa, Lucian, Ailios Aristeides, and Arrian.

---

[41] Erbse (1956); Pelling (1986*b*).

[42] For example, the translations in the *Penguin Classics* series and those forthcoming from *Oxford World Classics*. Editions of whole books are being produced by the *Biblioteca Universale Rizzoli*, and in the more recent volumes of the *Fondazione Lorenzo Valla*.

PART I
The Moralizing Programme

1

The Programmatic Statements of the *Lives*

χρησιμώτατοι δὲ πρὸς λαλιὰν καὶ οἱ Πλουτάρχειοι βίοι, ὥσπερ εἰς ἄλλην πολλὴν καὶ παντοδαπῆ παίδευσιν· καὶ γὰρ πλήρεις εἰσὶν ἱστοριῶν καὶ ἀποφθεγμάτων καὶ παροιμιῶν καὶ χρειῶν.

Plutarch's Lives too are very useful for the 'talk', as for many other varied educational purposes. For they are full of narratives, sayings, proverbs, and maxims.

Menander Rhetor, II. 392. 28–31 (late 3rd-c. AD).

Plutarch claims, through his *Parallel Lives*, to reveal his subjects' character and thereby improve his readers' character. In this chapter, I shall consider Plutarch's conception of the moralizing function of his biographies.[1] We should note first, however, that the concept of moralism, like its content, is not transcultural. Ancient Greek has no term equivalent to our abstract 'moralism' or 'morality'. The nearest equivalents are terms relating to character, such as ἦθος ('character') or ἠθικὴ ἀρετή ('character-virtue').[2] In Greek thought, character had an ethical element, conceived in terms of right and wrong, virtue and vice, in terms of conformity to or divergence from moral norms, and this was revealed by deeds. Ancient conceptions of character were therefore less centred on the private, inner world of the individual; more with actions, and their evaluation.[3] The link in ancient Greek thought between

---

[1] The moral function of the *Lives* asserted as unproblematic: Ziegler (1949), 266–8 (=1951, 903–5); Averincev (1965); Wolman (1972); Frost (1980); Nikolaidis (1982–4); Schneeweiss (1985); Rose (1988).

[2] Normally translated, slightly inaccurately, as 'ethical' or 'moral' virtue. Cf. below, pp. 72–6 on Plutarch's treatise *On moral virtue* (Περὶ ἠθικῆς ἀρετῆς).

[3] Gill (1983 and 1990) sees most ancient works, including Plutarch's *Lives*, as written from a 'character-viewpoint', in which the appropriate response to individuals is to *evaluate* them. The 'personality-viewpoint', in which the appropriate response is *understanding*, is more characteristic of modern writing (though also present in varying degrees in Homer and Greek tragedy: Gill 1986; 1990, 9–31). Gill (1996) revises this distinction to one between 'objective-participant' and 'subjective-individualist' conceptions of personality. In ancient works, then, audience enagagment is invited not through identification

character and action is seen in the very word for virtue (ἀρετή), which has connotations also of excellence and success: military and political success or failure was, for many Greeks, a central feature of character. For Plutarch, then, understanding character was less about what somebody was like, more about recognizing right and wrong deeds; its consequence was a desire to judge and evaluate.

There is no surviving formal preface to the *Parallel Lives* as a whole, but at a number of points, usually the prologues to individual pairs, Plutarch makes clear statements about the way in which he conceived his undertaking.[4] The extent to which he fulfilled these claims will be the subject of Chapter 2. In this chapter, however, the five most important of these subtle and nuanced 'programmatic statements' will be examined. They will be considered here not in the order in which they were published,[5] but in an order which allows us best to apprehend Plutarch's conception and presentation of his task as biographer.

1. THE *ALEXANDER—CAESAR*

A claim for the ethical-pedagogic purpose of the *Lives* is seen clearly in the introduction to the *Lives of Alexander and Caesar*. This prologue is one of the most famous passages of Plutarch, and is often taken, wrongly, as Plutarch's manifesto for the *Parallel Lives* as a whole:

(1. 1) Τὸν Ἀλεξάνδρου τοῦ βασιλέως βίον καὶ τὸν Καίσαρος, ὑφ' οὗ κατελύθη Πομπήϊος, ἐν τούτῳ τῷ βιβλίῳ γράφοντες, διὰ τὸ πλῆθος τῶν ὑποκειμένων πράξεων οὐδὲν ἄλλο προεροῦμεν ἢ παραιτησόμεθα τοὺς ἀναγινώσκοντας, ἐὰν μὴ πάντα μηδὲ καθ' ἕκαστον ἐξειργασμένως τι τῶν περιβοήτων ἀπαγγέλλωμεν, ἀλλ' ἐπιτέμνοντες τὰ πλεῖστα, μὴ συκοφαντεῖν. (1. 2) οὔτε γὰρ ἱστορίας γράφομεν, ἀλλὰ βίους, οὔτε ταῖς ἐπιφανεστάταις πράξεσι πάντως ἔνεστι δήλωσις ἀρετῆς ἢ κακίας, ἀλλὰ πρᾶγμα βραχὺ πολλάκις καὶ ῥῆμα καὶ παιδιά τις ἔμφασιν ἤθους ἐποίησε μᾶλλον ἢ μάχαι μυριόνεκροι καὶ παρατάξεις αἱ μέγισται καὶ

with a protagonist's quest for individual self-realization, but through recognition of the ethical stances underlying his action.

[4] A prologue which set out more fully the way in which Plutarch conceived his undertaking may have stood at the beginning of the lost *Epameinondas–Scipio* (Lamprias Catalogue no. 7; cf. fr. 1–2 Sandbach). On this pair, see Herbert (1957); Sandbach (1969), 74–5; Tuplin (1984); Stadter (1989), p. xxviii n. 12.

[5] Thirteen out of the twenty-two extant pairs have a formal prologue: see below, Ch. 8, n. 46. Of those discussed in detail in this chapter, the *Per.-Fab.* is probably the first; the *Alex.-Caes.* and *Aem.-Tim.* are next and roughly contemporary; then, towards the end of the series, the *Nik.-Crass.* and *Demetr.-Ant.* See Jones (1966), 66–70, and above, Introduction, n. 4.

πολιορκίαι πόλεων. (1. 3) ὥσπερ οὖν οἱ ζωγράφοι τὰς ὁμοιότητας ἀπὸ τοῦ προσώπου καὶ τῶν περὶ τὴν ὄψιν εἰδῶν οἷς ἐμφαίνεται τὸ ἦθος ἀναλαμβάνουσιν, ἐλάχιστα τῶν λοιπῶν μερῶν φροντίζοντες, οὕτως ἡμῖν δοτέον εἰς τὰ τῆς ψυχῆς σημεῖα μᾶλλον ἐνδύεσθαι, καὶ διὰ τούτων εἰδοποιεῖν τὸν ἑκάστου βίον, ἐάσαντας ἑτέροις τὰ μεγέθη καὶ τοὺς ἀγῶνας.

(1. 1) As we begin in this book to write the life of Alexander the King and the life of that Caesar by whom Pompey was overthrown, we shall, because of the number of deeds which are in prospect, make no other preface than to beg our readers not to complain, if we do not report all of their famous deeds and do not even report exhaustively on any of them, but do the majority in summary. (1. 2) For it is not so much histories that we are writing but lives, and there is not always in the most outstanding deeds a revelation of virtue or vice, but often a little matter like a saying or a joke hints at character more than battles where thousands die, huge troop deployments, or the sieges of cities. (1. 3) So, just as painters get likenesses from the face and the appearance of the eyes, by which character is hinted at, paying very little attention to the other parts of the body, so we must be allowed to penetrate rather the signs of the soul, and through these to shape the life of each man, leaving to others the magnitudes and battles. (*Alex.* 1. 1–3)

Plutarch here distinguishes the *Lives of Alexander and Caesar* from what he terms 'history' (ἱστορία) both in their subject-matter and in their purpose. The object of his writing this pair of Lives is—in apparent contrast with that of the historiographers with whom he compares himself—an understanding of character in its moral aspect, with the 'revelation of virtue and vice' (δήλωσις ἀρετῆς καὶ κακίας). It was generally assumed in antiquity that character could best be understood by examining men's actions (πράξεις)—that is, at least for statesmen, the 'outstanding deeds' of politics and war (cf. *Dem.* 11. 7). As a result, the analysis of character was most often conducted as part of a narrative of deeds. But Plutarch claims here that, for him, the deeds most revealing of character are not the great deeds of state, but the smaller matters of everyday life and interaction with others. His narrative, then, will be less concerned with the great deeds with which historiography is traditionally associated; these he will narrate in summary form only. He will instead concentrate on the minor details of history, on the subject's 'off-duty' moments, his words and jokes.[6] Such details, he

---

[6] Cf. *Cato Min.* 24. 1; 37. 10. This idea goes back at least as far as Xen. *Symp.* 1. 1; cf. Plato, *Laws*, 649d–652: what a man does while drunk reveals his character. On this topic, see also Moles (1989), 231–2. For words revealing character better than deeds, cf. *De Alex. Fort.* 330e; ps.-Plut. *Reg. et Imp.* 172d; cf. also *Phok.* 5. 10 and *Dem.-Cic.* 1. 4, where style of speaking is related to character. The stress on word and jest is particularly appropriate to the *Alex.*,

claims, best give an impression (ἔμφασις) of the character of the subject.[7]

Plutarch compares his concern to reveal his subject's character, or, as he puts it, 'the signs of his soul' (τὰ τῆς ψυχῆς σημεῖα), to that of a portrait painter.[8] It is a common motif in biographies and *enkomia* to compare a literary work to the plastic arts, on the grounds that the written word, unlike any painting or statue, can reveal character.[9] But it is also a common belief that appearance can reflect character. This is the sense here: Plutarch claims that his biography of Alexander can, just like a good portrait, reveal character.[10] The metaphor was one Plutarch would return to in the *Life of Cato the Younger* (24. 1), when he justifies the inclusion of an anecdote about Cato with the words: 'Since I should not pass over even the little signs of character (τὰ μικρὰ τῶν ἠθῶν σημεῖα), as though sketching an image of the soul (ὥσπερ εἰκόνα ψυχῆς ὑπογραφομένους).' Portrait painters were thought to concentrate on the eyes and face, in which character could be seen most clearly, ignoring, or at least treating less carefully, the rest of the body. So Plutarch claims that he will concentrate on the apparently insignificant details which have eluded other writers but which hint at character; in doing so he will (1. 3) 'leave to others the magnitude and the battles' (ἐάσαντας ἑτέροις τὰ μεγέθη καὶ τοὺς ἀγῶνας). The rather strange use of μέγεθος ('size, magnitude, stature') takes us back to the comparison with the portrait

which is rich in revealing sayings: e.g. *Alex*. 4. 10; 5. 4; 14. 5; cf. Hamilton (1969), p. xlii. Cf. Pelling (1997*b*), 231 n. 10 on sayings in the *Caes*., and *Lys*. 22. 1–5; *Flam*. 17. 3–8; *Phok*. 9. 1–10.

[7] Cf. *Kim*. 2. 2; Demetr. *On Style* 171 (Spengel iii, 299–300): 'there is also an impression of character (τοῦ ἤθους τις ἔμφασις) to be gained from a man's jokes, that is, from either their playfulness or their licentiousness'. Ἔμφασις ('impression') has the sense, primarily, of making something clear, and often means no more than 'indication' or 'expression'. But it is often used for *indirect* communication, and so can carry the sense of the 'suggestion' or 'impression' of a latent truth. In this sense it was recognized as a rhetorical technique or trope. Quintilian defines it (*Inst. Orat*. 8. 3. 83) as ' . . . providing a deeper meaning different from that which the words themselves express'; cf. 8. 2. 11. Tiberius defines it (*De Fig*. 14, Spengel iii, 65, 28–9) as 'when someone does not say the thing itself, but hints at it (ἐμφαίνῃ) by saying other things'; cf. also *Rhet. ad Herenn*. 4. 53, 67; ps.-Tryphon 746–7, Spengel iii, 199, 15–20 = Theophrastos, *On Style* 139 Mayer. See Lausberg (1960), i. 450–3; Grube (1961), 137–8; Schenkeveld (1964), 129–31; Sacks (1981), 36–7; Ahl (1984), 176–9.

[8] For 'signs of the soul', cf. Sext. Empeir., *Pyrrh*. 2. 99–101 and *Adv. Dogm*. 2. 148–158; Aristotle, *Politics* 1340a32–5. Cf. *Arist*. 25. 10: τῆς ἐπιεικείας σημεῖα.

[9] e.g. Isok. *Evag*. 73; Cic. *Pro Arch*. 30; Tac. *Agric*. 46. 3; Plut. *Kim*. 2. 2–3; cf. Isok. *Ad Nicocl*. 36. Such comparisons go back as far as Pindar (*Nem*. 5. 1ff.). Hence statues do not give true honour: Dem. *Or*. 23, 197; Plut. *Praec. Ger*. 820b–f. Words as more revealing than looks: *Cato Maj*. 7. 3.

[10] For 'sketching' a man's character with words: cf. Lucian, *Imag*. 3; *Alex*. 3. On εἰκών ψυχῆς, see also below, pp. 163–4.

painter: the word is often used of the size or 'stature' of people, as well as of size in general. Just as the portrait painter does not concentrate on the stature or size of his subjects, preferring their faces, so Plutarch will not concentrate on the 'magnitude' of their deeds or on their military achievements.[11]

By concentrating on revealing details, Plutarch claims that he will 'shape the life of each man'. 'Life' (βίος) here has a double reference. Primarily it is a literary work, a biography, for which the Greek term was simply 'life'. Plutarch presents himself as, like a painter, 'shaping' the biographies he is writing, through careful attention to details. But 'life' also refers to the real lives of Plutarch's readers, whom he hope to influence and morally improve ('shape') by his work. By carefully 'shaping' his literary lives, Plutarch claims to be 'shaping' the lives of his readers. This double meaning of 'life', as will become clear, is one which Plutarch will exploit elsewhere.[12]

The prologue to the *Alexander–Caesar*, with its stress on the selection of revealing details rather than the narration of political and military events, has been very influential in determining modern approaches to the *Lives*. It is often elevated into a general statement about the generic differences between history and biography in ancient thought. This is mistaken. The terms which Plutarch uses, while revealing in themselves, should not be taken as implying a widely accepted ancient definition of any distinction between history and biography. The boundaries between history, political biography, and related forms of writing such as *enkomion* and the so-called historiographical monograph, were never clearly drawn; rather, generic differences were open to construction by individual authors in order to distinguish their work from those of rivals.[13] The term ἱστορία, here used in a particular sense of 'large-scale' history, could be used in a general sense to mean any kind of narrative.

[11] The idea that a good portrait can convey its subject's character (ἦθος) is common: e.g. Xen. *Mem.* 3. 10. 1–8; Aristotle, *Poet.* 1450a27–9; Aelian, *VH* 4. 3; Pliny, *NH* 35. 100. Cf. also Diod. 26. 1. 1; Petron. *Sat.* 88; Pliny, *NH* 34. 58, 70; Lucian, *Imag.* 6. See below, Ch. 6, n. 11. On the eyes as especially revealing of character, cf. ps.-Aristotle, *Physiogn.* 806a30; 814b1–9. The analogy of the portrait painter is particularly suited to its context within the *Alex.*, as it prepares for 4. 1–7 (cf. ἐμφαίνουσιν in 4. 1), where Alexander's appearance, especially his eyes, is described in terms which suggest a link with character. On that passage, see Evans (1935), 57–8; Sansone (1980), esp. 64–8; its physiognomic content is ignored by Hamilton (1969) ad. loc., and played down by Georgiadou (1992b), 4622–3. Cf. also, in the paired Life, *Caes.* 4. 9 and 17. 2, which may also invite a physiognomic reading.

[12] For the ambiguities of βίος, see below, pp. 33–4.

[13] On the blurred distinctions between history and biography, see Gentili and Cerri (1978), 7–14 and 27 (= 1988, 61–8 and 84–5); Geiger (1985), esp. 18–25; Burridge (1992), 65–9. Desideri (1995a) adds little.

Plutarch on other occasions seems to refer to his own biographical work as 'history' in this broader sense. At the beginning of his *Lives of Theseus and Romulus*, for example, he declares (1. 2) 'I have traversed in my writing of the *Parallel Lives* that period of time which is accessible to probable reasoning (εἰκότι λόγῳ) and forms a basis for a history of facts (ἱστορίᾳ πραγμάτων).' 'I have decided', he continues, 'that it would not be unreasonable to go back further to Romulus, now that we have come close to his times in our history (or *research* or *narrative*: τῇ ἱστορίᾳ).' 'May it therefore be possible', he goes on a little later (*Thes.* 1. 4–5), 'for me to cleanse the mythic (τὸ μυθῶδες) and make it obey reason and take on the appearance of history (ἱστορίας ὄψιν).' His own *Lives of Theseus and Romulus* are, he implies, or at least, have 'the appearance of', history.[14]

The distinction which Plutarch draws in the prologue to the *Theseus–Romulus*, then, is not one between 'history' and 'lives' but one drawn long before by Thucydides (1. 22. 4) between 'history' and 'myth'. Of course this does not imply a universally valid distinction any more than the claims of the prologue to the *Alexander–Caesar* implied a universally valid distinction between 'history' and 'lives'. The breadth of ancient conceptions of history can be seen most clearly in the formulation of the first-century BC grammarian Asklepiades of Myrleia, as quoted by Sextos Empeirikos (*Against the Grammarians* 1. 252–3). Asklepiades divides 'the historical' (τὸ ἱστορικόν) into three types: 'true history' (ἀληθὴς ἱστορία), which is 'about deeds' (πρακτική); 'false history' (ψευδὴς ἱστορία), which is 'about fictions and myths' (περὶ πλάσματα καὶ μύθους); and 'apparently true history' (ὡς ἀληθὴς ἱστορία), which he seems to link with comedy and mime, though the text is corrupt at this point. Asklepiades goes on to distinguish narrative concerned with individuals from that concerned with great events or exploits (πράξεις), both as subdivisions of 'true history' (*Adv. Gramm.* 1. 253).[15] Other

---

[14] For Plutarch's own work as 'history', cf. also *Nik.* 1. 5; *Kim.* 2. 5; *Fab.* 1. 1; *Per.-Fab.* 1. 1; *Aem.* 1. 1; *Aem.-Tim.* 1. 1; *Gracchi* 1. 1; and possibly *Aem.* 5. 10. Ἱστορία and the related verb ἱστορῶ are also used by Plutarch to indicate the research done for his *Lives*: *Thes.* 1. 4; *Aem.* 1. 5; *Flam.* 21. 15; probably *Dem.* 2. 1. For ἱστορία as research in general: cf. *Quaest. Conv.* 642d; *De Stoic. Repugn.* 1047c; cf. *Per.* 13. 16. For ἱστορῶ as 'narrate', cf. *Dem.* 4. 1; *Dem.-Cic.* 1. 1; *Lys.* 30. 8; *Pel.-Marc.* 1. 1; *Eum.* 1. 1; *Pyrrh.* 1. 1. In *Demetr.* 1. 6 ἀνιστορήτως perhaps draws on both these ideas. On the meaning of ἱστορία, see Mazzarino (1966), 136–9; Valgiglio (1987), 50–62; (1991), 27–35. It is a pity that Plutarch's work *How to judge true history* (Lamp. Cat. 124), does not survive. On *Thes.* 1, cf. Ampolo (1990), 221–3.

[15] He divides 'true history' into three types: 'one concerns the persons of gods, heroes and illustrious men (πρόσωπα θεῶν καὶ ἡρώων καὶ ἀνδρῶν ἐπιφανῶν); one concerns places and times (τόπους καὶ χρόνους); and one concerns deeds (πράξεις).' Cf. Dion, *Ant. Rom.* 5. 48. 1.

critics generally do not use the term 'history' (ἱστορία) when talking of narratives which are acknowledged to be false, preferring the more usual terms 'myth' (μῦθος) or 'fiction' (πλάσμα); but they placed within the orbit of history (Asklepiades' 'true history') narrative both of events which actually happened and of events which were traditionally held to have happened.[16]

The general fluidity of terms such as 'history' and 'lives' is seen in the variations in the labels attached to individual works. Cicero, for example, (*Brutus* 112) refers to Xenophon's *Education of Kyros* as 'Kyros' life and teaching' (*Cyri vita et disciplina*), whereas Diogenes Laertios refers to it as an *enkomion* (6. 84). Josephus variously refers to the work we know of as the *Jewish War* as the 'Jewish War' (*Jewish Antiquities* 1. 11, 203), the 'Jewish Wars' (13. 3. 3, 72), 'On the Jewish War' (*Life* 74, 412), the 'Jewish Matter' (ἡ Ἰουδαϊκὴ πραγματεία: *Jewish Antiquities* 13. 5. 9, 173),[17] and the 'Jewish Affairs' (τὰ Ἰουδαϊκά: 13. 10. 6, 298). Jerome (*Comm. in Zach.* 3. 14. 47, 1522 Migne) later describes Tacitus' *Annals* and *Histories* as 'Lives of the Caesars' (*vitas Caesarum*).[18] Particularly significant is the list of works which Plutarch groups together under the general terms 'history and narrative' (ἱστορία καὶ διήγησις) in his polemic *It is not possible even to live pleasantly according to Epikouros* (1093b–c): 'the Greek Affairs' (τὰ Ἑλληνικά) of Herodotos (that is, the *Histories*); 'the Persian Affairs' (τὰ Περσικά) of Xenophon (that is, the *Education of Kyros*); the work of Homer; Eudoxos' 'Circumnavigations' (Περίοδοι); Aristotle's 'Foundations and Constitutions' (Κτίσεις καὶ Πολιτεῖαι); and Aristoxenos' 'Lives of Men' (Βίοι ἀνδρῶν). All these works narrate, Plutarch says, in a way pleasurable for the reader, 'fine and great deeds' (πράξεις καλαὶ καὶ μεγάλαι).

Plutarch's own *Lives of the Caesars* are a case in point. If we insist on strict genre distinctions, it becomes impossible to classify this work without a separate category for it. Should it be seen as 'history', a collection of 'Lives', or, a category invented by modern critics, 'historiographical monograph'? The individual texts are intended to be read as a

---

[16] e.g. the scholiast on Dionysios Thrax (449. 11 Hilgard): an interesting adaptation of Aristotle, *Poetics* 9; cf. Sext. Empeir. *Adv. Gramm.* 263. Other critics define true ἱστορία as a narrative of events of the distant past: e.g. Cic. *De Inv.* 1. 27; ps.-Cic. *Rhet. Ad Herenn.* 1. 8, 13; Aphthonios 2, Spengel, ii, 22, 6–7. See Ritzenstein (1906), 90–1; Meijering (1987), 76–82; Bowersock (1994), 7–11.

[17] Presumably πραγματεία here implies πραγματικὴ ἱστορία, on which see below, n. 47.

[18] There is likewise no firm distinction discernible in the use of the singular or plural of ἱστορία: Rutilius Rufus' historical work is called 'history' by Athenaios (168e; 274c), 'histories' by Plutarch (*Pomp.* 37. 4). See Valgiglio (1987), 61.

series rather than on their own or in consort with a paired Life, and probably therefore owe much in their conception to the monographs on series of rulers which existed from Hellenistic times, such as Phainias of Eresos' work on the Sicilian tyrants. Such series probably included a number of Lives per book, as is certainly the case, for example, in Nepos' *Lives of illustrious men* and in Suetonius' *On the life of the Caesars* (*De vita Caesarum*); this partially explains the comparatively short length of the surviving Lives, those of Galba and Otho, in comparison with the *Parallel Lives*. It is most likely that these two surviving Lives, together with a lost *Life of Vitellius*, formed a discrete group; the prologue to the *Galba*, with its discussion of the dangers of mutinous soldiers, is appropriate to all three Lives; the mention of four emperors being ushered onto and off the stage in ten months (1. 8) confirms that the comments of the prologue provide a way of reading the Lives of all three of the emperors of AD 68–9. Accordingly, there is no prologue to the *Otho* and there was, we may presume, none to the *Vitellius*.[19] Furthermore, the *Galba* and *Otho* are less autonomous in content than the later *Parallel Lives*. Unlike Suetonius' versions, Plutarch's *Galba* and *Otho* do not narrate the subject's life from birth to death, at least not in a single Life. Otho and Vitellius are both introduced in the *Galba*; it is here that their characters are described and their early careers briefly sketched (at *Galba* 19–21 and 22. 7–23. 1 respectively). Thus the *Otho* begins not with Otho's early life but after his assumption of power.[20] If this series of linked texts can be categorized as biography, it is of a markedly different kind from that of the *Parallel Lives*.

The distinction, then, between biography and history drawn by Plutarch at the start of the *Alexander* is not a universal one and does not apply equally to all Plutarch's works.[21] It belongs specifically to the *Life of Alexander*; it is tailored to this context and to Plutarch's rhetorical agenda at this point. Indeed, the concerns of some other *Parallel Lives*

---

[19] Cf. Georgiadou (1988), 354–5. Neither the manuscripts nor the Lamprias Catalogue (32–3) seem to have listed the three as one unit, as the Catalogue does with paired Lives; the latter may, however, have listed Galba and Otho together (Γάλβας Ὄθων Βιτέλλιος Parisinus gr. 1678; Γάλβας καὶ Ὄθων Βιτέλλιος Neapolitanus IIIB29). See Ziegler (1973), pp. xiv–xxi. Suetonius' *Galba*, *Otho*, and *Vitellius* formed a single book.

[20] The prediction of Galba's future greatness made by Tiberius (Dio Cassius 57. 19. 4; Tac. *Ann.* 6. 20) or Augustus (Suet. *Galba* 4. 1) is not recorded in Plutarch's *Galba*, even though in the *Parallel Lives* prophecies about, or indications in childhood of, the subject's future adult career are not uncommon (e.g. *Alex.* 5. 1–6; 6. 1–8; *Cic.* 2. 1–5; *Alk.* 2. 1–7; *Them.* 2. 1–3; *Cato Min.* 1. 3–3. 10). It may have occurred in the lost *Tiberius* (Lamp. Cat. 27).

[21] It is drawn occasionally elsewhere: *Fab.* 16. 6; Nepos, *Pel.* 1. 1 (cf. Geiger 1985, 114–15); *Atticus* 11. 3.

seem very close to those of historiography as presented here: there is a variety of approaches within the corpus.[22] The *Life of Caesar*, which is paired with and immediately follows the *Life of Alexander*, is a good example.[23] In this Life, the narration of political and military events, and the analysis of the processes—especially the popular support for Caesar—which led to the establishment of monarchy at Rome, are much more prominent than the revelation of character.[24] Plutarch, in contrast to Suetonius, narrates the Gallic Wars at some length (*Caes.* 15–27), even though, as a large-scale military narrative, it was apparently ruled out in this prologue.[25] Plutarch's words in the *Alexander* prologue, then, are tailored specifically to the Life which they introduce. In writing about Alexander the Great, one of the most hackneyed themes in antiquity, Plutarch had to find some way of differentiating his narrative from that of others. So he indulges in a form of staged refusal or 'recusatio', a well-known literary form which also serves to bring greater glory to Alexander, his subject. The claim that there is too much material to write down all the great deeds of the subject is an enkomiastic *topos*, recommended, for example, by Menander Rhetor.[26]

So the formulation at the start of the *Alexander* represents one of the means open to Plutarch by which to distinguish his *Alexander* from other historiographical works on the same theme. It is not a universally valid definition of biography. Thus Polybios seems to use the same criterion, that of selectivity, with a rather different end. His separate work, he claims, on the Achaian general Philopoimen is much more selective than his treatment of him in the *Histories* (10. 21. 2–8). In the work dedicated solely to Philopoimen, Polybios claims to have dealt with the general's 'boyhood upbringing and outstanding deeds' (τὴν τε παιδικὴν ἀγωγὴν . . . καὶ τὰς ἐπιφανεστάτας πράξεις), but to have given only a summary of 'the achievements of his prime' (τοῖς . . . κατὰ τὴν

---

[22] On the variation in the levels of historical and ethical interest in the six late-Republican Lives which were composed together, see Pelling (1980), 131–9; (1985), 322–9; (1986a), 159–63; (1990b), 29–35. On the closeness of many Lives to what Plutarch presents here as the concerns of historiography, that is, great deeds rather than character, see Wardman (1971), 257–61; (1974), 2–10, 154–61; Moles (1988), 33–5; Piccirilli (1989), 20; Valgiglio (1992), 4014. Cf. the description of Britain in Tac. *Agric.* 10–17, which has marked similarities to what we find in standard histories: see Ogilvie and Richmond (1967), 164–6; Goodyear (1970), 4–5. [23] Wardman (1971), 257–61.
[24] Pelling (1980), 136–7; (1985), 325–6.
[25] Pelling (1984b), esp. 90–1.
[26] Il. 368. 10–12 and 368. 23–369. 2. For the *topos* in use, cf. Xen. *Ages.* 1. 1; Thuc. 2. 35; Dem., *Or.* 60. 15; Isok. *De Bigis* 39; John 20: 30; 21: 25; Lucian, *Demon.* 67; *Alex.* 61; ps.-Aristeides, *Or.* 35. 1–2; Libanios, *Antiochikos* 6; Julian, *Or.* 1. 1 Spanheim. Cf. Norden (1898), 595 n. 1.

ἀκμὴν αὐτοῦ . . . ἔργοις). In his historical work, he will narrate these great deeds in detail. But the distinction Polybios is making here is not between history and biography, but between, in his terms, history and *enkomion*.[27] As has been argued, the boundaries between different forms of writing about the past, and the labels applied to them, remained fluid.

2. THE *NIKIAS–CRASSUS*

In writing the Life of the Athenian statesman Nikias, Plutarch was faced with the same problem as he had been with Alexander: how to differentiate his treatment from those of his predecessors. The earlier writers against whom Plutarch sets himself in the opening words of the *Alexander* are shadowy, unnnamed figures. Near the start of the *Life of Nikias*,[28] however, Plutarch names those whom this time he has in mind: the great fifth-century Athenian historian Thucydides and the Syracusan historian Philistos (c.430–356 BC), whose portraits of Nikias could be considered definitive. He will not, Plutarch declares, try to rival these writers. Another historian, Timaios, had already tried this: he had attempted to improve on the diction of Thucydides and Philistos, and had failed miserably. Plutarch seeks to justify his account on other grounds (1. 5):

ἃς γοῦν Θουκυδίδης ἐξήνεγκε πράξεις καὶ Φίλιστος ἐπεὶ παρελθεῖν οὐκ ἔστι, μάλιστά γε δὴ τὸν τρόπον καὶ τὴν διάθεσιν τοῦ ἀνδρὸς ὑπὸ πολλῶν καὶ μεγάλων παθῶν ⟨ἀπο⟩καλυπτομένην περιεχούσας, ἐπιδραμὼν βραχέως καὶ διὰ τῶν ἀναγκαίων, ἵνα μὴ παντάπασιν ἀμελὴς δοκῶ καὶ ἀργὸς εἶναι, τὰ διαφεύγοντα τοὺς πολλούς, ὑφ᾽ ἑτέρων δ᾽ εἰρημένα σποράδην ἢ πρὸς ἀναθήμασιν ἢ ψηφίσμασιν εὑρημένα παλαιοῖς πεπείραμαι συναγαγεῖν, οὐ τὴν ἄχρηστον ἀθροίζων ἱστορίαν, ἀλλὰ τὴν πρὸς κατανόησιν ἤθους καὶ τρόπου παραδιδούς.

καλυπτομένην codd: ἀποκαλυπτομένην U²: ἀνακαλυπτομένην Jones

At all events, in order not to appear totally careless or lazy, I have run through briefly and without unnecessary detail those deeds which Thucydides and Philistos described, since it is impossible to pass them by, containing as they do indications of the man's character and disposition, revealed as it is by many great sufferings. I have also tried to bring together those incidents which escape the

---

[27] Pédech (1951) and Walbank (1967), 221–2, discuss the date and likely contents of Polybios' lost *enkomion*. It seems likely that Plutarch's *Phil.*, which is rather laudatory in tone, was influenced by it, whether directly or indirectly. Cf. Pelling (1997c), 154–66.

[28] In fact, the very first sentence of the *Nik.* seems odd as an opening and may be corrupt.

majority and which have been mentioned in scattered locations by others, or have been found either on votive offerings or in old decrees, not collecting a useless narrative but handing on one that contributes to an understanding of character and manner.

Plutarch claims that he will deal in brief with the main events or deeds (πράξεις) of Nikias' life, even though they have already been fully treated by Thucydides and Philistos. He will not, however, simply summarize their accounts, but will also use other material which 'escapes the notice of the majority' (τὰ διαφεύγοντα τοὺς πολλούς). This is a reference once again, and not a particularly flattering one, to Plutarch's literary predecessors: probably not just to Thucydides and Philistos, but also to other writers.[29] Plutarch will include material which 'the common herd' (οἱ πολλοί) neglect: a claim with a long history.[30] A similar claim is made at the start of the *Demosthenes–Cicero*, where Plutarch says that his narrative (ἱστορία) is composed from 'readings which are not at hand nor even at home, but many of them in foreign countries and scattered about among different owners' (*Dem.* 2. 1).[31] Plutarch's self-presentation is the same at the start of his treatise *Virtues of women*, where he claims that he will pass over stories which are commonly known 'except for any stories worthy of hearing which have escaped the notice of those before me who narrated the common, well-publicized tales' (243d).[32]

But Plutarch may be doing more than simply claiming to be record-

---

[29] If Plutarch were referring to material which had been left out by Thucydides and Philistos specifically, we would expect not διαφεύγοντα but διαφυγόντα as at *Dem.* 2. 1 (cf. below, n. 31); cf. also here ἐξήνεγκε.

[30] Most notably in Hellenistic literary polemic: e.g. Kallim. *Epigram* 28 Pfeiffer; *Hymn to Apollo* 105–12, with Hopkinson (1988), 86–7. Citti (1983), 100–5, rightly stresses the possible negative implications of the term οἱ πολλοί, which is often in Plutarch contrasted with 'the right-minded' (οἱ σώφρονες) or similar (e.g. *Ant.* 9. 5; *Dem.* 11. 3; *Crass.* 27. 6; *Non Posse* 1101d; 1102d). For the language, cf. Plut. *Thes.* 1. 1: in their geographical works, 'scholars (οἱ ἱστορικοί) squeeze regions which escape their knowledge (τὰ διαφεύγοντα τὴν γνῶσιν αὐτῶν) into the outer edges of their maps . . . '

[31] He goes on to undercut the claim, however, with typical Plutarchan self-effacement: it would be necessary, he continues, to live in a great city so that one might come into possession of 'such details as have escaped writers but are preserved with more conspicuous fidelity in the memories of men' (ὅσα τοὺς γράφοντας διαφυγόντα σωτηρίᾳ μνήμης ἐπιφανεστέραν εἴληφε πίστιν). He, however, has chosen to stay in Chaironeia, in order that his 'small town' might not 'become smaller' (*Dem.* 2. 1–2).

[32] πλὴν εἰ μή τινα τοὺς τὰ κοινὰ καὶ δεδημευμένα πρὸ ἡμῶν ἱστορήσαντας ἀκοῆς ἄξια διαπέφευγεν. Cf. Phil., *Apoll.* 1. 2–3 for the claim to have gathered together scattered source-material in order to combat 'the ignorance of the many'. On Plutarch's use of non-literary sources, see Ewbank (1982); Podlecki (1988), 236–7; Buckler (1992); Desideri (1992a).

ing events which previous writers missed. His claim is also that those events, which he alone has located by careful research, are particularly important, because they cast special light on his subjects' character. We have already noted how in the introduction to the *Alexander–Caesar* Plutarch presents himself as including revelatory material which was passed over by other writers (cf. also *Pomp*. 8. 7). The claim to see beyond or behind great events to the character of the participants is not unique to Plutarch. A passage of Dionysios of Halikarnassos provides an illuminating parallel (*Ad Pomp*. 6. 7 = *FGrH* 115 T 20a).[33] Here Dionysios commends the fourth-century historian Theopompos for a quality which sets him apart from other writers and which he describes in the following terms:

τί δὲ τοῦτό ἐστι; τὸ καθ' ἑκάστην πρᾶξιν μὴ μόνον τὰ φανερὰ τοῖς πολλοῖς ὁρᾶν καὶ λέγειν, ἀλλ' ἐξετάζειν καὶ τὰς ἀφανεῖς αἰτίας τῶν πράξεων καὶ τῶν πραξάντων αὐτὰς καὶ τὰ πάθη τῆς ψυχῆς, ἃ μὴ ῥᾴδια τοῖς πολλοῖς εἰδέναι, καὶ τὰ πάντα ἐκκαλύπτειν τὰ μυστήρια τῆς τε δοκούσης ἀρετῆς καὶ τῆς ἀγνοουμένης κακίας.

What is this quality? Concerning each and every deed not only to see and to tell what is obvious to the majority, but to examine also the hidden motivations of the actions and of their agents and the passions in their souls—things which it is not easy for the majority to discern—and to reveal all the mysteries of apparent virtue and undetected vice.

What sets Theopompos apart, according to Dionysios, is that he records not just what is obvious to 'the majority' but seeks out 'the hidden motivations of the actions and of their agents and the passions in their souls'. These things are difficult for 'the majority' to know. The implication is that casual observers of historical events, and inferior historians, see only the events, the externals; it requires a particularly talented historian to bring out the inner psychology of the actors. By investigating such matters Theopompos 'reveals' (ἐκκαλύπτειν) the realities of virtue and vice: in other words, he digs beyond events and actions and lays bare the real character of the men he writes about. Dionysios goes on to compare the sort of searching investigation which Theopompos practises to the examination (ἐξετασμός) of souls which is said to go on in Hades.

Plutarch claims, then, as Dionysios does for Theopompos, that he reveals what 'the majority', that is, ordinary observers and other writers, pass by: material which contributes 'to an understanding of character and manner' (πρὸς κατανόησιν ἤθους καὶ τρόπου). He claims that he will

[33] I am indebted to Franco (1991), 125–7, for this passage.

not totally ignore the material of Philistos and Thucydides on Nikias, but will summarize it: partly because such major events cannot be ignored by anyone who wants to be seen as a serious writer, but more particularly because such great events contain 'indications of the man's character and disposition, ὑπὸ πολλῶν καὶ μεγάλων παθῶν ⟨ἀπο⟩καλυπτομένην'. If we accept the manuscript reading (καλυπτομένην), Plutarch would be claiming that great sufferings or experiences (πάθη) hide, rather than reveal, character. This would make little sense in this context, where Plutarch is justifying the inclusion of events already narrated by his predecessors. It seems sensible, therefore, that we should emend the text.[34] In the *Alexander* prologue, Plutarch had claimed that great events or exploits (πράξεις) often do not reveal character; here he seems to be claiming that they can and do, if they involve great sufferings, if they are emotionally disturbing: it is through observing Nikias and Crassus in the midst of such stressful experiences that a true appreciation of their character will emerge.[35] Plutarch perhaps has in mind most of all the final days and deaths of Nikias and Crassus. But it is clear that he is tailoring his argument to suit the requirements of each Life. There would, one must assume, be little for Plutarch to say about Nikias if he were not to recount the battles and campaigns, especially the Sicilian expedition, in which he was involved, and which Thucydides and the now lost Philistos had treated at length.[36] In fact, it is noticeable that in practice Plutarch does, like Thucydides and like, one assumes, Philistos, concentrate much of his narrative about Nikias on the Sicilian expedition.[37] Where Plutarch

---

[34] Two emendations are possible, both giving the meaning 'revealed': either ἀνακαλυπτομένην, the suggestion of Jones (1971, 104 n. 4), or ἀποκαλυπτομένην, the suggestion of the second hand of U.

[35] Cf. Plutarch's claim in *Dem.-Cic.* 3. 2 that power and authority (ἐξουσία καὶ ἀρχή) most test and reveal a man's character (τρόπος), 'rousing every passion and revealing (ἀποκαλύπτουσα) all wickedness'; *Pomp.* 31. 1, where Pompey's 'deeds' (ἔργα) 'revealed' him (ἀπεκάλυπτε). In *Sulla* 30. 5–6, Plutarch debates, in view of Sulla's cruelty in the civil wars and their aftermath, whether power caused a change in, or a revelation of, his character. But power reveals Perikles' character to be, paradoxically, better than it had seemed (*Per.* 15. 1). Cf. also *Thes.-Rom.* 3. 1; *Eum.* 9. 1–2.

[36] Plutarch's protestations are probably at least partly motivated by a desire for polemic against an earlier historian, Timaios, a traditional feature of the establishment of authorial competence in a historiographical prologue: cf. Hekataios, *FGrH* 1 F 1; Thuc. 1. 20–1; Theopompos, *FGrH* 115 F 24; Dion., *Ant. Rom.* 1. 4. 1–1. 6. 2. See Lieberich (1898), 16; Martin and Woodman (1989), 170–1; Moles 1993b, especially 98–103). Polybios criticizes Timaios at length in 12. 3–16; 23–8.

[37] In the *Alk.*, however, Plutarch seems to conform to his programme much more closely, dealing briefly with episodes on which Thucydides was fullest, and adding details not in Thucydides. Pelling (1992) argues that Plutarch expected his readers to be familiar with Thucydides and so to notice his own changes of emphasis.

differs from those writers, and indeed from most writers about Nikias, is in his treatment of, and judgement of, Nikias' character. We know little of Philistos' attitude to Nikias. But the treatment of Nikias by Thucydides and by Timaios—as far as we can tell from the account of Diodoros (Books 12–13), which used Timaios as its main source on the Sicilian expedition—is much more favourable than Plutarch's. Plutarch seems to depart from the main classical tradition in painting Nikias in a rather unfavourable light. He is, for Plutarch, the man of fear, superstition, and hesitation.[38]

So Plutarch bases his claim to be different from his predecessors in the prologues to both the *Alexander* and the *Nikias* on two elements. One is his access to alternative sources, not used by the standard accounts. The other is his focus on character rather than deeds. Tacitus, writing in his *Annals* at roughly the same time, makes similar claims. In Book Four of the *Annals* he seeks to set his work apart from those historians who had written about Republican Rome: Livy may have been particularly in his mind. Tacitus announces (4. 32) that his *Annals* may seem 'little things, too trifling to record' (*parva forsitan et levia memoratu*). This is a paradoxical reversal of the standard historiographical claim that one's material is 'worthy of record' or 'noteworthy'.[39] Normally, by 'noteworthy' historians meant that the events concerned had a large political and military significance, and probably involved sufferings or upheavals on a large scale: the stuff of history from Homer onwards. This is what Thucydides implies when he says that he expects the Peloponnesian War to be more 'noteworthy (ἀξιολογώτατον) than any that had preceded it' (1. 1. 1–3; 1. 21. 1).[40] Tacitus himself had made a similar claim about the greatness of the events he was describing at the start of the *Histories* (1. 2).[41] Part of the rationale for choosing 'great deeds' was that a historian's own character was thought to be somehow reflected in his choice of subject matter; a trivial subject might imply a trivial mind.[42] Plutarch, and Tacitus in *Annals* 4. 32, subvert this standard historio-

---

[38] Piccirilli (1990*b* and *c*); (1993*b*), pp. ix–xvi. See below, p. 56 n. 16 and pp. 62–3.

[39] In Greek often ἀξιόλογος: e.g. Xen. *Hell.* 2. 3. 56; 4. 8. 1; 7. 2. 1; 7. 5. 21; Diod. 4. 5; Dion., *Ant. Rom.* 1. 1. 2; 11. 1. 5; Appian, *BC* 4. 16. See Martin and Woodman (1989), 170. Plutarch often claims, at the end of the narrative section of a pair of Lives, to have recorded what is memorable (ἄξια μνήμης): *Thes.-Rom.* 1. 1; *Cor.-Alk.* 1. 1; *Arist.-Cato Maj.* 1. 1; *Dem.-Cic.* 1. 1; *Sert.-Eum.* 1. 1; cf. also *Fab.* 1. 1.

[40] Livy makes a similar claim in the preface to his account of the Hannibalic War (21. 1. 1–3).

[41] Cf. Martin and Woodman (1989), 169–70, who argue for a parallelism between the two Tacitean passages.   [42] See below, pp. 56–8.

graphical criterion for inclusion. In a subtle, but revolutionary, move, 'noteworthy' for them does not imply large-scale events—wars and the like—but those events, however apparently trivial, which reveal character.

Tacitus invites his reader to 'compare' (*contendere*) his history with those of historians who had written about Republican Rome. He will not record great events, as his predecessors had done; his is 'inglorious toil in a narrow field' (*nobis in arto et inglorius labor*),[43] as there were no wars or great events to describe, or so he claims, in the period with which he was dealing. This is in itself a political point: a criticism of the period of the emperor Tiberius' reign, when, he implies, no truly great deeds, no deeds worthy of record by the historian, were done. It is also, paradoxically, a claim for his own special work as a historian, as becomes clear from the following sentence. 'But', he continues, 'it may not be unprofitable (*sine usu*) to look beneath the surface (*introspicere*) of those incidents, trivial at first sight, which so often set in motion the great events of history.' Tacitus' subject matter is 'trivial' (*levia*). Any historian, such is the implication, can record great deeds; Tacitus' special claim, like Plutarch's, is that he can 'look beneath the surface' of these trivial events to find the causes from which great events arise. And Tacitus makes clear in the next chapter (4. 33) that the cause of events, the focus of his work, is the character of the participants. His claim, therefore, is not that this work contains 'great deeds', but that he— unlike the historians against which he sets himself—can look beyond actual events, to discover the character of the participants, in his case, that of the emperors about whom he will write and of those with whom they deal. And it is in knowing about the character of past emperors and their associates that the value, the utility, of history for Tacitus lies.[44]

These passages from Theopompos and Tacitus illuminate the train of thought in Plutarch's prologues, and show that Plutarch's arguments in his prologues use well-tried conventions for building up the value of his historical narrative. Notably, both Plutarch and Tacitus (*Annals* 4. 33. 1) associate, in a claim familiar to many ancient writers, this concentration on character with the 'usefulness' of the narrative they are writing.[45] The

[43] The reversal of another standard historiographical claim, that the historian would gain glory by his work: see Martin and Woodman (1989), 172.
[44] Already Xen. *Hell.* 5. 1. 4 had protested that the popularity of Teleutias and the conduct that had inspired it were 'the work of a man, more noteworthy (ἀξιολογώτερον) than much money and many dangers'.
[45] 'Useless' (ἄχρηστος) narrative is for Plutarch that which does not contribute to a knowledge of character (cf. *Tim.* 15. 11 and *Dion* 21. 9).

usefulness of the *Nikias–Crassus* lies in the fact that Plutarch's choice of material will help the reader understand the character of the subject, and will therefore, it is implied, contribute to his own moral improvement. This train of thought, moving from understanding of a subject's character to improvement of one's own, is made explicit in the prologue to the *Aemilius–Timoleon*, to which we shall turn in a moment.

Before that, however, it may be worth looking briefly at two passages where Plutarch justifies his narrative and sets it apart from accounts by previous writers. Both passages come from Lives which were composed before Plutarch embarked on the principle of parallel composition. The first passage is drawn from the prologue to the *Life of Galba*, part of Plutarch's collection of *Lives of the Caesars*. As noted earlier, the prologue to the *Galba* seems to function as the prologue to the Lives of Galba, Otho, and Vitellius. In the final sentence of this prologue Plutarch attempts to justify his selection of material in the three Lives which follow:

τὰ μὲν οὖν καθ' ἔκαστα τῶν γενομένων ἀπαγγέλλειν ἀκριβῶς τῆς πραγματικῆς ἱστορίας ἐστίν, ὅσα δ' ἄξια λόγου τοῖς τῶν Καισάρων ἔργοις καὶ πάθεσι συμπέπτωκεν, οὐδ' ἐμοὶ προσήκει παρελθεῖν.

To report in detail[46] each of the events which occurred belongs to the sort of history which deals with exploits; but it is not right even for me to omit such noteworthy things as have occurred through what the Caesars did and what was done to them.   (*Galba* 2. 5)

Plutarch differentiates the *Galba–Otho–Vitellius* from 'pragmatic history', that is, a work of history which deals primarily with great political and military exploits (πράξεις).[47] The implication is that his work is concerned with character rather than with the great events *per se*. He will limit himself to describing 'such noteworthy things as have occurred through what the Caesars did and what was done to them'. Once again, Plutarch uses the vague term 'noteworthy' without qualification. And once again it appears, though this is not made explicit, that it is the

[46] ἀκριβῶς is 'in a detailed way' (as at Isok. *Ad Phil.* 46; *De Bigis* 22; Aristotle, *NE* 1104a2; 1107b14–16; Diod. 1. 5. 2; Dion., *Ant. Rom.* 1. 5. 4; 7. 66. 5; 11. 1. 5; Plut. *Kim.* 2. 3: ἐξακριβοῦν) as well as 'accurately' (cf. Thuc. 1. 22. 1).

[47] This is the only occurrence of the phrase 'pragmatic history' (πραγματικὴ ἱστορία) outside Polybios, except in some late authors (but note ἡ Ἰουδαϊκὴ πραγματεία in Jos. *Ant. Jud.* 13. 5. 9, 173, of the *Jewish Wars*). This and related terms are used by Polybios (e.g. 3. 57. 4; 6. 5. 2; 9. 2. 4; 12. 25e1) to differentiate his subject matter, military and political events (πράξεις), from that of other historians, who write of genealogies, the founding of cities, and colonization: the sort of wide-ranging history for which Theopompos is commended by Dion. *Ad Pomp.* 6. See Pédech (1964), 21–32; Sacks (1981), 178–86 and 188–9.

uncovering of character, and the moral value that this brings, that he claims as his task and as the *raison d'être* of his narrative. There may, furthermore, be in the *Galba* prologue an attempt to engage with Aristotle's judgement on history in the *Poetics* (9, 1451b4–11). For Aristotle history was less philosophical than poetry because it dealt with the particular (τὰ καθ' ἕκαστον; cf. τὰ ... καθ' ἕκαστα) rather than the universal (τὰ καθόλου), with 'what Alkibiades did or what experiences he had' (τί Ἀλκιβιάδης ἔπραξεν ἢ τί ἔπαθεν; cf. ἔργοις καὶ πάθεσι). Plutarch's Lives of Galba and Otho, which in fact focus on the danger of passion when not controlled by reason, will indeed show how history can convey universal, moral, truths.[48]

Similar concerns seem to lie behind a statement in the free-standing Life of Artaxerxes II, king of Persia from 404 to 359 BC. This statement comes immediately before Plutarch's discussion of Artaxerxes' decisive victory at Kounaxa (401). In dealing with this episode, Plutarch was faced with the same problem as he had been in writing the Lives of Alexander and Nikias: namely, a predecessor—in this case Xenophon in his *Anabasis*—who had already treated the incident at some length (*Anab.* 1. 8). Plutarch describes the vividness of Xenophon's account in terms standard in ancient literary criticism; it is, he maintains, not to be rivalled. His response is to claim, once again, that he will add an element which his predecessor failed to include, and which he denotes, once again, with the vague term 'noteworthy'.

τὴν δὲ μάχην ἐκείνην πολλῶν μὲν ἀπηγγελκότων, Ξενοφῶντος δὲ μονονουχὶ δεικνύοντος ὄψει καὶ τοῖς πράγμασιν ὡς οὐ γεγενημένοις, ἀλλὰ γινομένοις ἐφιστάντος ἀεὶ τὸν ἀκροατὴν ἐμπαθῆ καὶ συγκινδυνεύοντα διὰ τὴν ἐνάργειαν, οὐκ ἔστι νοῦν ἔχοντος ἐπεξηγεῖσθαι, πλὴν ὅσα τῶν ἀξίων λόγου παρῆλθεν εἰπεῖν ἐκεῖνον.

Many have reported that battle, and Xenophon brings it almost before our eyes, by the vividness of his account making the reader share the passion and danger of the actors, fixing his attention on the events as though they had not happened in the past, but were happening in the present. In view of this it would not be sensible to recount it all again, except for those noteworthy events which escaped Xenophon's mention. (*Art.* 8. 1)

Although he does not spell it out so clearly here, Plutarch's claim for uniqueness, as revealed in the narrative which follows, is based on familiar grounds. First, he will use a source which Xenophon knew (cf.

---

[48] On Plutarch's engagement with the *Poetics*, see below, pp. 44–5. On the *Galba-Otho*, see Ash (1997).

Anab. 1. 8. 26–7) but neglected: the *Persika* of Ktesias, a Greek writer who was actually present in Artaxerxes' camp. Plutarch introduces this source to give a version of Kyros' death different from the one Xenophon narrates (*Art.* 11. 1–11), but Ktesias' account seems, in fact, to lie behind much of Plutarch's Life, and is probably the sole source for chapters 12–19. Secondly, Plutarch's account focuses on character. His description of the battle itself (8. 2–11. 11) examines the characters of Kyros, Artaxerxes' rebel brother and pretender to his throne, and of Kyros' Greek mercenary commander, the Spartan Klearchos. Kyros is criticized for his rashness (e.g. 8. 3–6; 11. 4), which led him to plunge headlong into the enemy's ranks and so eventually, and after some considerable success, lose his life. In other Lives Plutarch severely disapproves of such conduct on the part of a general, regarding it as a distasteful triumph of the passions over reason. Klearchos too is criticized for letting, explicitly, his passions overrule his reason (λογισμοί).[49] The problem, as Plutarch diagnoses it, was his cautiousness (8. 6: εὐλάβεια), which led him to refrain from engaging the king's forces directly.

In the prologue to the *Nikias–Crassus* Plutarch lays stress on the revelation of character, rather than the magnitude of the events described, as the distinguishing feature of his work. He aims to select material, perhaps material unknown to other writers, which will lay bare the characters of the participants and will therefore be 'useful' to the reader. But how is a knowledge of the characters of the great men of the past to be useful? We turn now to the third major passage in which Plutarch discusses the purpose and value of the *Parallel Lives*, or at least of one pair of Lives.

3. THE *AEMILIUS–TIMOLEON*

In the prologue to the *Lives of Aemilius and Timoleon* (*Aem.* 1. 1–4),[50] Plutarch presents himself as a paradigmic reader of his own *Lives*:[51]

(1. 1) Ἐμοὶ [μὲν] τῆς τῶν βίων ἅψασθαι μὲν γραφῆς συνέβη δι' ἑτέρους, ἐπιμένειν δὲ καὶ φιλοχωρεῖν ἤδη καὶ δι' ἐμαυτόν, ὥσπερ ἐν ἐσόπτρῳ τῇ ἱστορίᾳ

---

[49] See below, Ch. 3 *pass.*, and esp. p. 82.

[50] Unusually here the Roman Life precedes the Greek Life. Such a reversal also occurs in the *Sert.-Eum.* and *Cor.-Alk*: for the reasons, see below, p. 206 n. 3. The Aldine edition, followed by the Loeb edition (Perrin 1918), reverses the manuscript order in a misguided wish for consistency.

[51] On the passage, see Desideri (1989), 199–202 and 212–13; Den Boer (1985), 380–2.

πειρώμενον ἀμῶς γέ πως κοσμεῖν καὶ ἀφομοιοῦν πρὸς τὰς ἐκείνων ἀρετὰς τὸν
βίον. (1. 2) οὐδὲν γὰρ ἀλλ' ἢ συνδιαιτήσει καὶ συμβιώσει τὸ γινόμενον ἔοικεν,
ὅταν ὥσπερ ἐπιξενούμενον ἕκαστον αὐτῶν ἐν μέρει διὰ τῆς ἱστορίας
ὑποδεχόμενοι καὶ παραλαμβάνοντες ἀναθεωρῶμεν "ὅσσος ἔην οἷός τε", τὰ
κυριώτατα καὶ κάλλιστα πρὸς γνῶσιν ἀπὸ τῶν πράξεων λαμβάνοντες. (1. 3) "φεῦ
φεῦ, τί τούτου χάρμα μεῖζον ἂν λάβοις" (1. 4) ⟨καὶ⟩ πρὸς ἐπανόρθωσιν ἠθῶν
ἐνεργότερον;

(1. 1) It befell me to begin writing the Lives for the sake of others, but now to continue it and enjoy my stay for my own sake, endeavouring somehow or other in the mirror of history to adorn life and make it like the virtues of those men. (1. 2) There is no other result than this: what happens is like spending time together and living together, whenever, receiving and inviting each of these men in turn when they visit us through history, we examine 'how great he was and of what kind' taking from his deeds the most important and most beautiful to know. (1. 3) 'Ah! What greater joy than this could you obtain', (1. 4) and what more effective for the improvement of character?   (*Aem.* 1. 1–4)

The ideal reader uses history as a mirror, 'adorning' and modelling his life on the virtues of the subjects of the *Lives*, choosing out what is most efficacious 'for the improvement of character' (πρὸς ἐπανόρθωσιν ἠθῶν).[52] In what follows, a theory ascribed to Demokritos, that men are of necessity visited by both good and bad phantoms or spirits (εἴδωλα), is used to bring out, by contrast, the freedom which history gives to turn away from whatever is bad and concentrate on the good (1. 4–5).[53] This claim is particularly suitable for the *Aemilius–Timoleon* pair, which is one of the most enkomiastic; its subjects are explicitly (1. 5–6) 'the best of examples' (τὰ κάλλιστα τῶν παραδειγμάτων).[54] The reference to spirits, and the opening metaphor in which Plutarch's writing about his subjects is compared to the entertaining in person of such great men, lends a mystical quality to Plutarch's claim here: the men of the past are more than just examples to be followed; they are, in some sense, living presences.

A parallel to this passage is seen in Plutarch's own moral tract *How to recognize that one is making progress in virtue*. Here Plutarch warns, employing a contrast standard in ancient historical theorizing, that philosophy, poetry, and history should not be studied merely for pleasure but for the benefit that they can bring (79c–e). Such benefit

[52] For πρὸς ἐπανόρθωσιν + genitive, compare *Quomodo Adult.* 73e; *Prof. in Virt.* 79c; Polyb. 10. 21. 4; 15. 36. 3.
[53] Cf. *Kim.* 2. 3–5; *Per.* 1. 1–3; *Demetr.* 1. 1–3.
[54] Cf. *Tim.* 24. 3 and 37. 4. On the *Tim.* as a particularly enkomiastic Life, see Talbert (1974), 1–16; Geiger (1981), 102–3; Swain (1989c), 319–23.

consists, he says, in the improvement of character (ἐπανόρθωσις ἤθους). Imitation (ζῆλος), he argues a little later (84b), and a desire 'to do what we admire', is the proper response to virtuous men; similarly, one should abhor evil men (cf. *Cato Min.* 9. 10). That these good men are to be seen, to some extent at least, as great figures from the past soon becomes clear from the examples Plutarch cites (84e–85a). We should love good men, even when they suffer misfortune, admiring Aristeides even when he is exiled, Sokrates even though he is poor, and Phokion even when condemned to death. 'For that inspiration (ἐνθουσιασμόν) which holds true even to the point where one is not appalled at apparent disaster but still admires and emulates (θαυμάζειν καὶ ζηλοῦν), this no-one can ever turn away from what is good' (85a). Before undertaking any action, Plutarch tells his readers that they should 'set before their eyes good men of the present or the past and ask, "What would Plato have done in this circumstance, what would Epameinondas have said, what sort of a man would Lykourgos have showed himself, or Agesilaos?", as though before mirrors, adorning and refashioning themselves' (85a–b: οἷον πρὸς ἔσοπτρα κοσμοῦντας ἑαυτοὺς καὶ μεταρρυθμίζοντας).

Plutarch's use of the mirror comparison in these passages serves to set his work in a tradition of moralizing literature, where the lives of virtuous men are sometimes presented as a mirror in which to shape one's own life.[55] In Cicero's *Republic*, the ideal statesman is said to improve himself, urge others 'to imitate him' (*ad imitationem sui*) and 'furnish in himself, as it were, a mirror (*speculum*) for his fellow citizens by means of the supreme excellence of his life and character' (2. 69). Similarly, in the pseudo-Plutarchan *On the education of children*, fathers are advised to make themselves an example (παράδειγμα) to their children, 'in order that, through looking at their fathers' life as at a mirror, they may turn away from base deeds and words' (14a). In Seneca (*De Clem.* 1. 1) and Epiktetos (in Arrian, *Discourses* 2. 14. 21), the philosopher's advice serves as a mirror to reveal the listener to himself. Elsewhere, moral self-inspection is compared to looking in a mirror (Plut. *De Aud.* 42b; Bias in Stob. *Flor.* 21. 11, i, 317 Meineke).[56]

[55] On the varied use of the image of the mirror in Latin and Greek literature, see Mayor (1910), 71–2; Fantham (1972), 68–9; W. McCarty (1989), esp. 168–9.

[56] Seneca (*NQ* 1. 17. 4), presents real, natural (as opposed to man-made) mirrors as having been provided by nature: 'that a man may know himself' and that the ugly man may know 'that whatever he lacks in body can be made up in virtues'. Terence, *Adelph.* 414–16, probably based on a Menandrian original, seems to be a humorous exploitation of the idea. Anything which reveals the true nature of a man can be compared to a mirror: wine (Aisch. *TrGF* III F 393; Alkaios fr. 333 Page; Theopompos Com. fr. 33. 3 Kassel–Austin); song

But there is also an additional ambiguity in the image of the mirror as used here, part of a nexus of subtle ambiguities that runs through the opening of the *Aemilius*. The mirror here is, on the one hand, the lives of virtuous men, in accordance with which Plutarch amends his own life. But, for his readers, the mirror is Plutarch's own literary work. The ambiguities of the terms 'history' and 'life' reinforce this double meaning. 'History' (ἱστορία) can, in Greek as well as in English, refer both to the events of the past (e.g. Dionysios, *Ant. Rom.* 1. 2. 1) and to research into the past or a work of literature recording the past;[57] as has been seen, Plutarch calls his own work 'history' on several occasions. Similarly 'life' (βίος) can refer both to the character and career of a man, and to the written record of such; here the reference is to the lives of the virtuous men on whom Plutarch is modelling his life, and to the work of literature which Plutarch is writing, *and* to the lives of the readers and of Plutarch himself, which are thereby improved.[58] These ideas are combined when Plutarch talks of 'receiving and inviting each of these men in turn when they visit us through history (διὰ τῆς ἱστορίας)'.[59] Plutarch presents himself as meeting these virtuous men personally;[60] but he does this 'through history' (or possibly, 'through research'). For the reader, the two meanings dovetail; one reads of the virtuous lives of the great men of the past through Plutarch's own *Lives*. But the purposeful confusion between, on the one hand, the actual lives and virtues of his subjects, and, on the other, Plutarch's own literary representation of them, allows him to make a subtle claim for the worth of his writings: his *Lives* invite the reader to model himself *as it were directly* on the lives of virtuous men. Furthermore, by comparing his own work to a mirror, Plutarch seems to suggest that the *Lives* share the mirror's mimetic qualities: the image of the mirror is often used to describe anything which gives a good representation of reality.[61] The implication is that the

(Pindar. *Nem.* 7. 14); time (Eur. *Hipp.* 428–30); the Jewish scriptures (Philo, *De Vit. Cont.* 78, 483–4 M; Ep. James 1: 23); sayings and utterances, rather than deeds and experiences (ps.-Plut. *Reg. et Imp.* 172d); cf. Plaut. *Epidic.* 383–6; Clem. Alex. *Paid.* 1. 88, 150 Potterius.

[57] e.g. Polyb. 12. 28. 1–28a10; 2. 14. 7; 9. 14. 1–4; 9. 25. 2.

[58] Cf. *Demetr.* 1. 5–7 and *Tim.* 15. 11, which also contain ambiguities. For βίοι as Plutarch's literary work, see *Per.* 2. 5. Plutarch calls his work παράλληλοι βίοι at *Dem.* 3. 1; *Dion.* 2. 7; *Thes.* 1. 2; and *Kim.* 2. 2.

[59] For διὰ τῆς ἱστορίας, cf. pseudo-Plut. *Consol. ad Apoll.* 119d.

[60] Cf. *Prof. in Virt.* 85c–d, where the student of virtue is urged to entertain contemporary good men in his house; and Seneca's advice in *Ep. Moral.* 11. 8–10 (quoting Epikouros, fr. 210 Usener).

[61] Cf. Plato, *Laws* 905b; *Phaidros* 255d; Plut. *Terrest. an Aquat.* 967d; Lucian, *De Hist.* 51. Of a work of literature, cf. Alkidamas' praise of the *Odyssey* as a 'mirror of life' in Cic. ap. Don. *De Com.* 5.

reason why Plutarch's literary *Lives* are almost indistinguishable from the real lives of the men he wrote about is precisely their mirror-like reflective quality.[62]

4. THE *PERIKLES–FABIUS*

In the prologue to the *Aemilius–Timoleon* Plutarch sets out the moral improvement of his readers as a goal of the *Lives*. He does not, however, make it clear in that passage how such improvement is to take place. This question is raised in the introduction to another pair of Lives, the *Perikles–Fabius*. Here it becomes clear that the correct response on the part of the reader is *imitation*.

Plutarch begins the *Perikles–Fabius* with a *bon mot* of the Emperor Augustus who, on seeing certain non-Romans lavishing affection on pet dogs and monkeys, asks whether the women of their land did not bear children—implying, Plutarch explains, that our natural 'love of affection' should be concentrated not on animals but on humans (1. 1).[63] This anecdote provides Plutarch with the starting point for his discussion. Just as we are by nature affectionate, so our souls have a natural 'love of learning and seeing' (1. 2: φιλομαθές τι κέκτηται καὶ φιλοθέαμον), and this love should not be wasted on sights and sounds 'worthy of no study' (τὰ μηδεμιᾶς ἄξια σπουδῆς). Unfortunately, our physical senses (ἡ αἴσθησις) must receive every impression which strikes them; but our intellect (ὁ νοῦς) may be turned away from the unhelpful and directed at what is useful (cf. *Demetr.* 1. 1–3). Already it is clear that what Plutarch has in mind is the reading of history, traditionally advertised as 'useful', and as 'worthy of study' or 'worthy of note'. He continues, in language which is subtle and ambiguous:

(1. 4) ταῦτα δ' ἔστιν ἐν τοῖς ἀπ' ἀρετῆς ἔργοις, ἃ καὶ ζῆλόν τινα καὶ προθυμίαν ἀγωγὸν εἰς μίμησιν ἐμποιεῖ τοῖς ἱστορήσασιν· ἐπεὶ τῶν γ' ἄλλων οὐκ εὐθὺς ἀκολουθεῖ τῷ θαυμάσαι τὸ πραχθὲν ὁρμὴ πρὸς τὸ πρᾶξαι, πολλάκις δὲ καὶ

---

[62] Perhaps here the meaning of βίος as 'real life, reality' would be in the reader's mind. Βίος and its cognates are sometimes used in this sense by the scholiasts when discussing the difference between comedy and tragedy, e.g. the scholiast on Dionysios Thrax (173. 3–4 Hilgard): 'Tragedy contains narrative and report of deeds that took place (πράξεων γενομένων); comedy comprises fictional real-life (or daily-life) affairs (πλάσματα βιωτικῶν πραγμάτων)'; cf. Meijering 1987, 88–9. Cf. also, the comment of Aristophanes of Byzantion on Menander (249 Nauck = Syrian, *In Hermog.* 2. 23. 10–11 Rabe[a]): 'O Menander and life, so which of you imitated which?'

[63] The subject of another of Plutarch's works, *On the love of offspring*. For parallels to Augustus' saying, cf. *De Cohib. Ira* 462e; *De Frat. Amore* 482c.

τοὐναντίον χαίροντες τῷ ἔργῳ τοῦ δημιουργοῦ καταφρονοῦμεν, ὡς ἐπὶ τῶν μύρων καὶ τῶν ἁλουργῶν τούτοις μὲν ἡδόμεθα, τοὺς δὲ βαφεῖς καὶ μυρεψοὺς ἀνελευθέρους ἡγούμεθα καὶ βαναύσους . . . (2. 1) . . . οὐ γὰρ ἀναγκαῖον, εἰ τέρπει τὸ ἔργον ὡς χαρίεν, ἄξιον σπουδῆς εἶναι τὸν εἰργασμένον. (2. 2) ὅθεν οὐδ' ὠφελεῖ τὰ τοιαῦτα τοὺς θεωμένους, πρὸς ἃ μιμητικὸς οὐ γίνεται ζῆλος οὐδ' ἀνάδοσις κινοῦσα προθυμίαν καὶ ὁρμὴν ἐπὶ τὴν ἐξομοίωσιν. ἀλλ' ἥ γ' ἀρετὴ ταῖς πράξεσιν εὐθὺς οὕτω διατίθησιν, ὥσθ' ἅμα θαυμάζεσθαι τὰ ἔργα καὶ ζηλοῦσθαι τοὺς εἰργασμένους. (2. 3) τῶν μὲν γὰρ ἐκ τύχης ἀγαθῶν τὰς κτήσεις καὶ ἀπολαύσεις, τῶν δ' ἀπ' ἀρετῆς τὰς πράξεις ἀγαπῶμεν, καὶ τὰ μὲν ἡμῖν παρ' ἑτέρων, τὰ δὲ μᾶλλον ἑτέροις παρ' ἡμῶν ὑπάρχειν βουλόμεθα. (2. 4) τὸ γὰρ καλὸν ἐφ' αὑτὸ πρακτικῶς κινεῖ καὶ πρακτικὴν εὐθὺς ὁρμὴν ἐντίθησιν, ἠθοποιοῦν οὐ τῇ μιμήσει τὸν θεατήν, ἀλλὰ τῇ ἱστορίᾳ τοῦ ἔργου τὴν προαίρεσιν παρεχόμενον.

1. 4 ἱστορήσασιν Amyot, Reiske: ἱστορήμασιν codd. 2. 2 ὁρμὴν Reiske: ἀφορμὴν codd. ἅμα θαυμάζεσθαι: either ἅμα τῷ θαυμάζεσθαι or ἅμα θαυμάζεσθαί τε Ziegler.

(1. 4) These things are found in works done out of virtue, which implant in those that investigate them a sort of emulation and desire which leads to imitation. For in the case of other works an impulse to do them does not immediately follow upon an admiration for what has been done. Often, in fact, it is the opposite which happens: we enjoy the work but despise the artist. This happens, for example, in the case of perfumes and purple clothes: we enjoy the items themselves, but think the dyers and perfumers servile labourers. . . . (2. 1) . . . For it is not a necessity that, if the work pleases you as graceful, the one who worked it is worthy of attention. (2. 2) Hence such works do not even benefit those who look at them, as in response to them there arises no eagerness for imitation nor any uplift which arouses enthusiasm or an impulse to equal them. But virtue immediately so disposes one towards actions that at the same time one admires the works and emulates those who worked them. (2. 3) The good things which come by way of chance, we love to possess and enjoy, while the good things which result from virtue we love to perform. And the former we want to receive from others, while the latter we want rather others to receive from us. (2. 4) For the good stirs one actively towards itself and implants immediately an active impulse, forming the spectator's character not so much by imitation but by the investigation of the work, providing him with character. (*Per.* 1. 4–2. 4)

The argument here has parallels with the less explicitly developed sequence of thought at the start of the *Aemilius*: Plutarch claims that the study of virtuous deeds—in action or in writing—has, unlike the study of other works of art, the effect of implanting an impulse (ὁρμή) to imitation.[64] The first-person verbs here (2. 3: we love, we want) provide

[64] Cf. Plato, *Alk.* I. 133c ff.; *Gorg.* 509d–510a; Plut. *De Alex. Fort.* 334d. For ζῆλος as 'emulation', cf. *De Lat. Viv.* 1129b–c; Polyb. 15. 36. 3–7: there are two objects in the study of

paradigms for how the reader—called here the spectator—should think; as in the *Aemilius* opening, Plutarch presents himself as the ideal reader, modelling himself on the virtues of the great men of the past. A contrast between pleasure and utility, standard in discussions of the theory of history, runs throughout this passage.[65] Similarly, there is an underlying contrast between the senses and the intellect.[66] Thus in 1. 2, the senses have to react to everything, whether useful (χρήσιμον) or not, whereas the mind can concentrate on those subjects which will 'nourish' (τρέφειν) it. Similarly, works of art delight (1. 4: χαίροντες . . . ἡδόμεθα; 2. 1: τέρπει . . . ὡς χαρίεν), but bring no benefit (2. 2: οὐδ' ὠφελεῖ); deeds of virtue 'through pleasure (τῷ χαίρειν) invite the intellect towards its own good' (1. 3) and encourage imitation.

The contrast between other works of art and the exercise of virtue, which runs through this passage, rests on the Platonic conception of virtue as an art (τέχνη).[67] In this respect, Plutarch exploits two senses of the word 'work' (ἔργον). In 2. 1 it means 'work of art', and τὸν εἰργασμένον ('the one who worked it') is 'the artist'; in 2. 2, however, 'the works' (τὰ ἔργα) are the great deeds of heroes, who are referred to as τοὺς εἰργασμένους ('those who worked them').[68] But a second and more subtle double reference exists alongside this one: it is through Plutarch's own literary work that deeds of virtue are brought to the attention of the observer. Plutarch makes no distinction here between the virtue of his heroes and his own representation of it; in this way, he again makes an unspoken claim for the importance and mimetic qualities of his work, which presents the virtues of the past to the reader as if directly: his work *is* the virtue of his subjects.[69] Furthermore, by aligning his own literary activity in writing the *Lives* with the deeds of virtue of his subjects rather than with other works of art, he makes a subtle claim for the uniqueness of the *Lives*. They are qualitatively different from other works of art, in

history, utility (ὠφέλεια) and enjoyment (τέρψις); therefore 'what is said must be something either to be emulated (ζηλωτόν), or pleasing (τερπνόν)'. On ζηλωτόν, see Walbank (1967), 496. For μίμησις and ζῆλος together, cf. also Polyb. 10. 21. 4; Plut. *Cato Min.* 9. 10 (see below, p. 148); *Gracchi* 4. 5.

[65] Cf. also *Prof. in Virt.* c–e, above, pp. 31–2; *Mul. Virt.* 242f–243e with Stadter (1965), 9–12, and my discussion on pp. 247–8.

[66] Familiar from Plato: e.g. *Rep.* 580d–583a; cf. Aristotle, *NE* 1117b30–1118a7; 1176a1–3.

[67] On this concept in Plato, see Gould (1955), 3–46. It is taken up by Plutarch in *An Virt. Doc.* (especially 440a–b); cf. also *Dem.* 1. 3; *Demetr.* 1. 4; *Mul. Virt.* 243a–b; *De Alex. Fort.* 335f.

[68] For ἔργον in Herodotos as a monument (e.g. 1. 51. 3; 1. 93. 2; 3. 41. 1) as well as a deed, see Immerwahr (1960).

[69] Cf. the comparable claim implied in Herodotos' first preface by the repetition ἀπόδεξις . . . ἀποδεχθέντα; on which, see Moles (1993b), 94.

that they benefit the viewer as well as giving pleasure, that is, they encourage imitation, not just observation or admiration.[70]

The final sentence of this section of the prologue continues the contrast between pleasure and benefit (*Per.* 2. 4). This sentence has been much misunderstood and much mistranslated and so requires closer study.[71] The *Lives* are here assimilated not simply to the virtues of their subjects, but to the Platonic 'form' of *the good* (τὸ καλόν).[72] That 'the good' is in fact the *Lives*, appears clearly from the play on the participle ἠθοποιοῦν, which draws on two senses of ἠθοποιΐα. The primary reference of ἠθοποιοῦν here is to the positive 'moulding of character' which *the good*, discernible in the virtues of good men, will produce in the reader of Plutarch's work.[73] In the language of literary criticism, however, ἠθοποιΐα usually has the meaning of 'character portrayal', in particular the giving to a speaker of words which are appropriate to him or her.[74] The presence of this second sense of the word encourages the reader to see the activity of 'the good' as being within the realm of literature: the *Lives* mould the character of the reader (ἠθοποιΐα) by accurate character portrayal (ἠθοποιΐα). The second sense of the word ('character-portrayal') also continues the subtle claims to vividness, which, as shall become clear, are reinforced here by the use of the term *mimesis*.

We now move to the most controversial part of this sentence. Plutarch maintains that *the good* (τὸ καλόν), to which the *Lives* are assimilated, forms character οὐ τῇ μιμήσει . . ., ἀλλὰ τῇ ἱστορίᾳ τοῦ ἔργου τὴν προαίρεσιν παρεχόμενον. At first reading, the meaning seems to be that morally improving narrative such as the *Lives* improves character *not* by

---

[70] The argument of Valgiglio (1992, 4014–15), that Plutarch in this passage insists that he is not engaged in a work of art, misses its multi-layered quality.

[71] Stadter (1989), in his introduction (pp. xxix–xxx), captures some of the complexities: '. . . not merely building character in the observer through a *representation* but producing a moral choice by a reasoned account of the action . . .' (my italics). His gloss in the note ad loc., and the suggestion of Martin (1992), 299, are less satisfactory.

[72] Plutarch seems to have accepted the Platonic doctrine of forms (seen e.g. in *Rep.* 478e–480a; cf. Ross 1951). It is discussed briefly at *Plat. Quaest.* 1001e and *De An. Procr.* 1023c. In the Lamprias Catalogue, we find works entitled, *Where are the Forms* (no. 67) and *How has matter participated in the Forms, that it makes the first bodies?* (no. 68). See Schoppe (1994) and Ferrari (1996).

[73] Ἠθοποιΐα and ἠθοποιός mean 'moulding or determining character' in ps.-Aristotle, *Problems* 30. 1, 955a32; Plut. *De Virt. Moral.* 450f; *Praec. Ger.* 799a–b; 814b; *De Stoic. Repugn.* 1053d. As at *Numa* 16. 4, the positive aspect of ἦθος as 'good character' is in view.

[74] Quint. *Inst. Orat.* 9. 2. 58 defines ἠθοποιΐα, along with μίμησις, as 'imitation of other people's character' (*imitatio morum alienorum*). Hermog. *Prog.* 9 (Spengel ii, 15) defines it as 'imitation of the character of a set person (μίμησις ἤθους ὑποκειμένου προσώπου), for example, the words that Andromache would say to Hektor'.

imitation *but* by 'the investigation of the deed'. This is surprising, given the stress earlier in this same passage on the imitation (*mimesis*) which virtue, and the narrative of virtuous deeds, encourages: the impulse to imitation which deeds of virtue, and by implication the *Lives*, instil in the observer has been contrasted with the lack of any corresponding impulse produced by other forms of art. Those works of art produce no 'eagerness for imitation' (μιμητικὸς ζῆλος) nor any 'uplift which arouses enthusiasm or an impulse to equal them' (ἀνάδοσις κινοῦσα προθυμίαν καὶ ὁρμὴν ἐπὶ τὴν ἐξομοίωσιν). In contrast, Plutarch has told us, virtue makes one 'admire the works and emulate those who worked them'. The final sentence (2. 4) seems, then, to pick up these themes, once again referring to the reader as an observer or spectator (θεατήν). We would expect from the whole logic of the passage that 'imitation' of the virtues observed in the subjects of the *Lives* is just what Plutarch intends. But the phrase οὐ τῇ μιμήσει seems to deny this. Perhaps the best response to this apparent contradiction is to emend the text by the addition of μόνον before τῇ μιμήσει.[75] This would yield the sense 'forms character *not only* by imitation but also by the investigation of the deed'.[76] It is just possible, however, that this emendation is unnecessary. Several examples appear to demonstrate the use of the phrase οὐκ . . . ἀλλά to privilege the second clause while not denying the first; in other words, the sense may be 'not so much . . . but more . . . '.[77]

At any rate, whether we opt to emend the text or not, Plutarch must, it seems, be arguing that the reader of the *Lives* will be improved *not just* by imitation (*mimesis*) of the virtuous actions which he reads about, *but also* by 'investigating the deed'. The relationship between 2. 2 and 2. 4 can now be understood more clearly. Other works of art do not instil in the reader any 'eagerness for imitation' (μιμητικὸς ζῆλος) nor any 'uplift which arouses enthusiasm or an impulse to equal them'. His *Lives* will do this, but not just this. They will not only provoke in the reader a desire

[75] Jones (1971), 103 n. 4.

[76] Such an emendation would not require the further addition of καί before τῇ ἱστορία: the phrase οὐ μόνον . . . ἀλλά is not uncommon in the sense 'not only . . . but *also*' (e.g. Xen. *Mem.* 1. 6. 2; Plato, *Phaidros* 233e; Isok. *Ad Phil.* 146; Dem. *De Corona* 26): Kühner (1904), 257; Denniston (1966), 3.

[77] For example, Mark 9: 37: '. . . and whoever receives me, receives *not so much* me but the one who sent me' (. . . καὶ ὃς ἂν ἐμὲ δέχηται, οὐκ ἐμὲ δέχεται ἀλλὰ τὸν ἀποστείλαντά με); cf. John 12: 44; Matt. 10: 20. Cf. also 1 Cor. 15: 10: 'I have worked harder than all these; *not so much* I but the grace of God with me' (. . . περισσότερον αὐτῶν πάντων ἐκοπίασα, οὐκ ἐγὼ δὲ ἀλλὰ ἡ χάρις τοῦ θεοῦ σὺν ἐμοί). This sentence is glossed by Augustine as *nec gratia Dei sola, nec ipse solus, sed gratia cum illo*. Robertson and Plummer paraphrase (1911, 342): '*So far from its being I (alone)* who did all this, it was the grace of God with me' (my italics). Cf. *Praec. Ger.* 819f.

to imitate those great men of the past whom he sees represented in the *Lives*; the *Lives* will also provoke in him a reasoned attitude, a desire for imitation which follows upon full moral knowledge, or, as Plutarch puts it, 'the investigation of the deed' (τῇ ἱστορίᾳ τοῦ ἔργου). In essence, we have here, as throughout the whole prologue, a contrast between sense and intellect, between passion and reason. The *Lives* arouse not simply an 'eagerness' or 'uplift' to imitate the subjects delineated. That could be merely an unreflective aping of the great men of the past, and as such on a much lower plane of moral usefulness and intellectual worth. Imitation is involved, and is indeed central. But there is more. The *Lives*, Plutarch claims, not only instil a desire for imitation but actually change or 'mould' character (ἠθοποιοῦν). This is achieved by the observer not simply looking, but also investigating, considering, testing; applying, as Plutarch might have put it, philosophy and reason.

The *Lives* have this powerful, character-changing, effect 'by providing a προαίρεσις'. The word προαίρεσις means literally 'choice', but in Plutarch's work it commonly involves aspects of character, which he, like Aristotle, saw partly in terms of choice.[78] At one level the reference could be to the characters of the subjects of the *Lives*, and the moral choices they make, which are 'provided' for the benefit of the reader, the spectator. But as with ἠθοποιοῦν there is a double reference: the *Lives* also 'provide' the reader with character, help him to make correct moral choices. The reader's character, then, is moulded, as he observes and investigates the character of the great men of the past. By doing this, he gains προαίρεσις, gains the ability to make correct moral choice. This naturally leads to or involves imitation. Plutarch, in accordance with much ancient thought, related character (ἦθος) with habituation (ἔθος). So imitation would naturally have an important role in any theory of character formation or improvement.

An illuminating parallel with Plutarch's argument here is provided by a passage from his *Life of Coriolanus*. Plutarch is discussing the reason for Coriolanus' sudden change of heart in calling off his war on his own country. Perhaps, he muses, it was divine intervention. To believe in such divine intervention, he continues, is not to believe that the gods take away our power of reasoned choice (32. 5: τὸν ἑκάστου λογισμὸν τῆς

---

[78] Προαίρεσις is a key Aristotelian term: see, for example, *NE* 1111b4–1112a17 and *Poetics* 1450b8–10 with Sherman (1989), 56–117, esp. 57–8, 79–86, and 107–17. Plutarch was himself familiar with Aristotle's work (e.g. Babut 1969a; cf. Scardigli 1995b, 6 n. 42), though perhaps not with the *Nikomachean Ethics* (Sandbach 1982). On Plutarch and προαίρεσις, see Wardman (1974), 107–15; Pérez Jiménez (1995). In *Dion* 2. 1 and *De Sera Num.* 551e προαίρεσις retains its primary meaning of 'choice'.

προαιρέσεως). Rather, the god 'moves our choice' (32. 7: κινοῦντα τὴν προαίρεσιν) by creating 'conceptions which lead to impulses' (φαντασίας ὁρμῶν ἀγωγούς); by these conceptions the god does not 'make action involuntary' but, if we so wish it, provides a 'beginning' (ἀρχήν) and adds courage and expectation. The gods do not work on us physically, but they rouse or check 'that part of our soul which is active and makes choices' (32. 8: τῆς ψυχῆς τὸ πρακτικὸν καὶ προαιρετικόν). It seems, then, that in the *Perikles* prologue Plutarch is presenting *the good*, working through or consisting in the *Lives*, as having an effect on readers similar to that of the gods in moments of divine intervention. The reader's powers to make choices are not taken away; rather the *Lives* provide an impulse, a beginning, a conception, to reasoned moral choice leading to action.[79]

It is noticeable how, throughout this passage, Plutarch subtly assimilates his own *Lives* with the actual events of the past which they narrate, and the activity of the writer with that of the reader. Such a double reference is embedded also in Plutarch's use of the term *mimesis* (literally, 'imitation'). *Mimesis* in this passage is primarily the 'imitation' by the observer of the deeds narrated in the *Lives*. But Plutarch's implicit claim here, that a reading of the *Lives* will encourage *mimesis* in the reader, also subtly exploits existing concepts of literary *mimesis*. In Platonic and Aristotelian thought, as in ancient historical theory, it was the artist who engaged in *mimesis* (representation).[80] For Plutarch, the effect of the *Lives* is such that it encourages *mimesis* (imitation) in the reader himself. But the observation of these deeds comes about through

---

[79] Cf. *Max. cum Princ.* 776c: 'The message of philosophy . . . wants to make whatever it touches effective (ἐνεργά), active (πρακτικά), and alive (ἔμψυχα); it implants men with impulses which spur them on, with judgements which lead them to what is useful, with characters which love the noble . . .' (κινητικὰς ὁρμὰς ἐντίθησι [Reiske: ἐπιτίθησι] καὶ κρίσεις ἀγωγοὺς ἐπὶ τὰ ὠφέλιμα καὶ προαιρέσεις φιλοκάλους . . .)

[80] On *mimesis* in historical theory, see Gray (1987a), who gives examples of its use in Dionysios and ps.-Longinos. This application of the term probably arose in the Peripatetic school, and is seen in the criticisms made of Ephoros and Theopompos by Theophrastos' pupil, Douris (*FGrH* 76 F 1 = Phot. *Bibl.* 176, 121a41–63): 'For they did not engage in any *mimesis* at all nor took any pleasure in the way they expressed themselves, but took care only about the actual writing' (οὔτε γὰρ μιμήσεως μετέλαβον οὐδεμιᾶς οὔτε ἡδονῆς ἐν τῷ φράσαι, αὐτοῦ δὲ τοῦ γράφειν μόνον ἐπεμελήθησαν). The precise meaning of this passage has been much debated. Gray claims that the criticism is that Theopompos and Ephoros used language inappropriate to what they were describing—the opposite of *mimesis*, which seeks to re-create reality. The traditional interpretation of *mimesis* is of narrative designed to arouse strong emotional reactions in the reader: Walbank (1972), 34–7; Sacks (1981), 144–70; Fornara (1983), 124–34. Cf. Gentili and Cerri (1988), 14–33. Walbank (1990), 258–9, follows Gray.

reading Plutarch's own *mimesis* (representation) of them.[81] *Mimesis* in historical theory seems to imply vivid and probably emotive representation by the use of a style appropriate to the subject matter. So the contrast between utility and pleasure is continued: the goal of Plutarch's work is not simply, or not only, 'vivid representation' (*mimesis*); it is primarily the improvement of the character of the reader, which is attained, as we have seen, through 'imitation' (another sort of *mimesis*).

A similar double reference to the activity of the writer and that of the reader is present in the phrase 'the investigation of the work' (τῇ ἱστορίᾳ τοῦ ἔργου). Both writer and reader are involved in the investigation (ἱστορία) of deeds of virtue (one sense of ἔργον).[82] But the reader investigates the deeds of the heroes through reading the writer's narrative, another of the meanings of ἱστορία. And that narrative is, of course, the *Lives* (another ἔργον).[83] This stress on the investigation which the reader must perform picks up the emphasis, noted earlier in the prologue, on reason, as opposed to simple sense-perception (1. 2).

This contrast between reason and sense-preception is continued in Plutarch's references to the reader as a 'spectator' or 'viewer' (θεατής): the more usual Greek term is ὁ ἀναγιγνώσκων ('the reader'). The use of the word 'spectator', a metaphor from the stage, continues the imagery of vision which is prominent in these chapters (colours and statues), and underlines the contrast between works of art which do not benefit those who view them (2. 2: τοὺς θεωμένους) and virtuous deeds which do benefit 'the viewer' (τὸν θεατήν). But there may be something more at stake in Plutarch's choice of this word. A feature of the kind of emotive historiography to which Plutarch seems to be alluding by his use of the word *mimesis* is its emphasis on vividness (ἐνάργεια) and its use of visual imagery. According to practitioners of this kind of history, which is sometimes referred to by modern critics as 'tragic history', the historian, like the orator, should aim to describe events so vividly that

---

[81] For these two meanings of *mimesis* (imitating someone 'in order to do the same thing myself' and producing a 'toy or model of the activity'), cf. Russell (1981), 100–1.

[82] Cf. 1. 4, τοῖς ἱστορήσασιν ('those who investigate'), Amyot's emendation of τοῖς ἱστορήμασιν ('the narratives').

[83] Thucydides similarly implies that both historian and reader are involved in the same act of investigation (σκοπεῖν) into the past (historian: 1. 1. 3; 1. 22. 2–3; reader: 1. 21. 2; 1. 22. 4). As Moles puts it (1993b, 110), 'Thus the historian's *mimesis* of events, the product of his 'seeing' and 'looking', is like a mirror, at which he invites his readers to look'. For ἱστορία as 'research' or 'investigation', see above, n. 14. Ἱστορία in the sense of 'research' is on several occasions elsewhere linked with the idea of sight (*De Defect. Orac.* 419e; *Cato Min.* 12. 2; cf. *De Aud. Poet.* 44b): Valgiglio (1991), 27–8.

the reader seems actually to 'see' them happening before his eyes.[84] Plutarch, by himself using this imagery, and by employing the term *mimesis*, reinforces his message in this sentence, that he is not, or at least not only, engaged in the kind of emotive and vivid narrative which many historians of the school of so-called 'tragic history' deployed.[85] His narrative, he would like us to believe, has a higher purpose: the improvement of character.

To sum up, in this multi-layered, complex, and subtle sentence, Plutarch claims that his reader's character will be improved by reading his *Lives*. This will be achieved, he says, not only by their imitating the virtuous deeds they read about (one sort of *mimesis*), nor just by the vivid qualities of the narrative itself (another sort of *mimesis*), but also by ἱστορία, that is, by his narrative, his research, and the reader's diligent attention and thought.

Plutarch claims, then, a very different value for his own literary endeavour than for other forms of, or other writers', literature. This is seen more clearly if we compare this passage with a passage fom the *How a young man should listen to the poets*. Similar ideas and imagery are there used to stress the *danger* of imitating the actions and characters presented in literature. Poetry is compared (17e–18f) to painting; it is 'painting which speaks' (ζωγραφία φθεγγομένη),[86] an 'imitative' or 'representational' art (μιμητικὴ τέχνη). The sensible reader, however, will admire the 'representation' (*mimesis*)—the poet's skill at re-creating reality—but not the base acts or characters represented:[87] 'let him learn to admire the ability and the art which imitates these things, but to repudiate and reproach the dispositions and actions which it imitates' (18c–d).[88] The special value of the *Lives*, then, is that, unlike the other

---

[84] e.g. ps.-Longinus, *Sublime* 15. 2; Dion., *Lys.* 7, 1. 14. 17 Us.-Rad.; Quint. *Inst. Orat.* 6. 2. 29. Cf. Borzák (1973). The Greek word is often θεᾶσθαι: a cognate of θεατής; cf. Plut. *Artax.* 8. 1. On 'tragic history', see Kebric (1977), 14–18; Sacks (1981), 144–70; Fornara (1983), 120–34; Gentili and Cerri (1988), 14–33.

[85] In fact, vivid description, sudden twists of fortune, and tragic patterning—all features of the so-called tragic history—are not eschewed in Plutarch's works, despite his criticisms of the 'tragic' (e.g. *Them.* 32. 4; *Per.* 28. 2; *Alex.* 75. 5) in historians such as Douris and Phylarchos. On elements of 'tragic' history in the *De Gen. Soc.*, see Desideri (1984), 583–5. Mueller (1995) argues for the high frequency of visual imagery in the *Perikles*.

[86] Plutarch calls the comparison 'oft-repeated' (17f: θρυλούμενον). At *Bellone an Pace* 346f and *Quaest. Conv.* 748a he ascribes it to Simonides. It is alluded to at *Quomodo Adult.* 58b; ps.-Cic. *Rhet. ad Herren.* 4. 28, 39; ps.-Plut. *De Vita et Poesi Homeris* 2. 216, 7. 460 Bernardakis.

[87] On Plutarch's views of *mimesis*, cf. Van der Stockt (1990); (1992), 21–55.

[88] διδασκέσθω τὴν μιμουμένην ταῦτα δύναμιν καὶ τέχνην ἐπαινεῖν, ἃς δὲ μιμεῖται διαθέσεις καὶ πράξεις προβάλλεσθαι καὶ κακίζειν.

arts, they inspire not just admiration, but also imitation; the *mimesis* is not simply the author's but also the reader's.

A parallel to the argument of the *Perikles* prologue, and an example of the kind of reader of history which Plutarch wants, is constructed by him at the start of the *On the sign of Sokrates*. This work combines an exciting narrative of the overthrow of Thebes' tyrants and their Spartan garrison with reports of philosophical and ethical discussions held by the protagonists: a combination, so central to the *Lives*, of military-political narrative with moral exploration. In the prologue to this work, the viewing of art is used as a parallel to the reading of history. The speaker Archidemos maintains that there are two sorts of 'viewers' (θεαταί) of painting: one sort just gets a general impression of the paintings they look at; the other sort looks carefully at all the details, noticing the good and the bad. 'I think it is similar', he continues, 'with real deeds. Someone of a rather slow intellect is content with history if he learns the chief point and the result of the matter. But someone who loves honour and beauty (τὸν δὲ φιλότιμον καὶ φιλόκαλον), when he views works done by virtue as by great art (τῶν ὑπ' ἀρετῆς ὥσπερ τέχνης μεγάλης ἀπειργασμένων θεατήν), is more delighted in the detail (τὰ καθ' ἕκαστα). For, since the outcome has much in common with chance, he observes in the motives and the deeds themselves the struggles of virtue against whatever comes along and sane acts of daring in the midst of peril, when reason is mingled with crisis and passion' (575b–c).[89]

One further note. By claiming that his work has a serious moral purpose Plutarch places it within a well-established historiographical tradition. It is possible, however, that he is also engaging directly with the Platonic and Aristotelian views of *mimesis*. Platonic criticism of poetry in Book Ten of the *Republic* was framed in terms of *mimesis*. First, poetry is a poor imitation (*mimesis*) of reality, being 'third from the truth' (602c2: τρίτον . . . ἀπὸ τῆς ἀληθείας): an imitation of real life, which is itself an imitation of the world of Forms (595a1–602c3). Secondly, it appeals to the lower, irrational part of the soul (602c4–605c5: τὸ ἀλόγιστον), thus stirring up the emotions of the audience and thereby harming them (605c6–b).[90] Plutarch is usually heavily influenced by the views of Plato,[91] but he seems to have differed in his valuation of literature. He disagrees with Plato's exclusion of most types of poetry

---

[89] The text is very corrupt, though its sense is clear enough. On this passage, see the brief remarks by Desideri (1984), 570–1.
[90] Cf. also *Rep.* 392c–398b for the exclusion of mimetic arts from the state.
[91] See below, Ch. 3.

from his ideal state:[92] as we have seen, in the *How a young man should listen to the poets*, Plutarch argues that the young *can* be taught to read Homer and the tragedians without being morally damaged; indeed, it can actually be profitable (15d–16a).[93] In taking up the language of *mimesis*, Plutarch seems to be correcting Plato by using Platonic terms.

Plutarch's view of literature seems more in line with Aristotle's. In the *Poetics*, Aristotle had attempted to answer the Platonic criticisms of poetry. For Aristotle, all poetry was 'mimetic' (*Poetics* 1447a13–1448a25), but this meant not simply an attempt to mimic in poetry the events or emotions of real life, as it did for Plato; poetry offered images of possible reality; it was a form of idealized representation. Indeed, this, for Aristotle, was what distinguished poetry from history: poetry represented universal truths, history the particular. Poetry was for this reason 'more philosophical' than history (*Poetics* 1451b5–7). It could represent 'one of three things: things such as they once were or now are, things such as men say and believe that they are; or things such as they ought to be' (*Poetics* 1460b8–11).[94] Tragedy presented men as 'better' than they are (1454b8–10).[95] It is noticeable that Aristotle does not attempt to defend poetry on moral grounds, that is, in terms of any beneficial effect it might have on the listener. He does suggest that emotional engagement with the protagonist and his situation might have some 'purificatory' effect (κάθαρσις), but it is unclear quite what he meant by this. We may, however, be able to reconstruct what Aristotelian beliefs about the moral benefit of poetry may have been from his comments on music in the *Politics* (1339b11–1340b19). Virtue, Aristotle argues, is to do with 'feeling delight, love, and hatred rightly'.[96] 'Nothing is of more importance than to learn and become accustomed to judging correctly and rejoicing in noble characters and fine deeds' (cf. *Ethics* 1104b12–13; 1105a10–12). Music contains representations (ὁμοιώματα) and imitations (μιμήματα) of character and emotion and so can be a good training in how to feel pain and delight at reality itself; it can therefore benefit character and soul (ἦθος and ψυχή). Aristotle may well have put forward a similar argument for the benefit of poetry, which after all would be more suitable for

---

[92] Cf. Plutarch's verdict at *De Alex. Fort.* 328d–e that Plato's ideal state never became a reality because of its forbidding nature (τὸ αὐστηρόν). For Plutarch's views on the educational use of literature, cf. Korus (1977).

[93] Cf. Isok. *Ad Nicocl.* 35; *Ad Demon.* 34.

[94] On this passage, cf. Ste Croix (1975).

[95] On the Platonic and Aristotelian views of *mimesis*, see Russell (1981), 99–113; Gentili and Cerri (1988), 29–31; Murray (1996), 3–6.

[96] *Politics* 1340a15–16; cf. also *Ethics* 1104b4–1105a13.

training the listener to feel the right emotions in that, as Aristotle emphasized (*Poetics* 1450a15–21), it represented character in the context of action: the narrative element of tragic poetry would allow one to see the causes of the emotion being portrayed on the stage.[97] Be that as it may, the Aristotelian defence of literature as it stands in the *Poetics* specifically excluded history; it had also criticized poems whose unity rested on their being centred around a single man's life rather than a single deed (πρᾶξις: 1451a16–35). Plutarch seems to go one step further than Aristotle in his 'correction' of the Platonic views of *mimesis*: biography, like tragic poetry, can have a morally positive function.[98]

5. THE *DEMETRIOS–ANTONY*

In the *Perikles* and *Aemilius* prologues, the reader is urged to imitate the real lives which are narrated in the literary *Lives* that follow. One implication of this is that the men whose careers will be narrated are worthy of imitation, and, therefore, by definition, good. In fact, Plutarch revises this programme in the prologue to the *Demetrios–Antony*. Here he justifies the inclusion in the *Lives* of bad men, examples of vice as well as of virtue.

In this prologue, in contrast to what was argued at the start of the *Perikles*, Plutarch's *Lives* are aligned, rather than contrasted, with other arts. But as in the *Perikles* prologue, there is an underlying antithesis between reason and sense-perception (αἴσθησις). This time, however, reason is assimilated with the arts (τέχναι). Both reason, Plutarch claims, and the arts, that is, the practioners of the arts, have powers of discernment. The senses, on the one hand, register equally all impressions which strike them, being as equally open to black as to white, cold as to hard:

αἱ δὲ τέχναι μετὰ λόγου συνεστῶσαι πρὸς αἵρεσιν καὶ λῆψιν οἰκείου τινός, φυγὴν δὲ καὶ διάκρουσιν ἀλλοτρίου, τὰ μὲν ἀφ' αὑτῶν καὶ προηγουμένως, τὰ δ' ὑπὲρ τοῦ φυλάξασθαι κατὰ συμβεβηκὸς ἐπιθεωροῦσι.

But the arts in conjunction with reason operate to select and take what belongs to them and to flee and evade what does not. They contemplate the one sort of objects for their own sake and on purpose, the other sort incidentally and for the purpose of guarding against it. (*Demetr.* 1. 3)

[97] Simpson (1988), esp. 289–91.
[98] Plutarch was certainly familiar with the Aristotelian views of *mimesis* as set out in the *Poetics*, as his exploitation at *Bellone an Pace* 346f–347a of Aristotle's triple criteria for *mimesis* (*Poetics* 1447a16–18) shows: Van der Stockt (1992), 27–8.

For the arts can better be practised by understanding what is to be avoided as well as what is to be sought after. Thus students of medicine study disease and students of music, discord. Plutarch continues:

αἴ τε πασῶν τελεώταται τεχνῶν, σωφροσύνη καὶ δικαιοσύνη καὶ φρόνησις, οὐ καλῶν μόνον καὶ δικαίων καὶ ὠφελίμων, ἀλλὰ καὶ βλαβερῶν καὶ αἰσχρῶν καὶ ἀδίκων κρίσεις οὖσαι, τὴν ἀπειρίᾳ τῶν κακῶν καλλωπιζομένην ἀκακίαν οὐκ ἐπαινοῦσιν, ἀλλ' ἀβελτερίαν ἡγοῦνται καὶ ἄγνοιαν ὧν μάλιστα γινώσκειν προσήκει τοὺς ὀρθῶς βιωσομένους.

And the most perfect arts of all—temperance, justice, and wisdom—do not consist of judgements about fine, just and useful things alone, but also about harmful, shameful and unjust things. So these arts do not praise the innocence that plumes itself in its inexperience of evil, but they consider it silliness and ignorance of what those who intend to live correctly ought to know.

(*Demetr.* 1. 4)

So the practice of virtue, Plutarch maintains, is to be aided by an understanding of vice, an argument which springs naturally from the traditional Greek view which connects virtue with knowledge. Plutarch goes on, in a subtle, self-reflexive move typical of his prologues, to cite a negative example: how *not* to carry out this principle. The Spartans, Plutarch tells us, used to force helots to get drunk in order to demonstrate to their young men the dangers of drunkenness. Plutarch disapproves:

ἡμεῖς δὲ τὴν μὲν ἐκ διαστροφῆς ἑτέρων ἐπανόρθωσιν οὐ πάνυ φιλάνθρωπον οὐδὲ πολιτικὴν ἡγούμεθα, τῶν δὲ κεχρημένων ἀσκεπτότερον αὑτοῖς καὶ γεγονότων ἐν ἐξουσίαις καὶ πράγμασι μεγάλοις ἐπιφανῶν εἰς κακίαν οὐ χεῖρον ἴσως ἐστὶ συζυγίαν μίαν ἢ δύο παρεμβαλεῖν εἰς τὰ παραδείγματα τῶν βίων.

I do not consider the improvement of some through the perversion of others to be either very humane or the act of a true statesman. But perhaps it is not such a bad idea for me to insert into the paradigms of my Lives one or two pairs of men who conducted themselves in a more unreflecting way and who became in their positions of power and amid great affairs notorious for their vice.

(*Demetr.* 1. 5)

Plutarch adds that his purpose in doing this is not to please his readers or entertain them by the introduction of some variety into his writing. Rather, he compares himself to two famous flute players who used to take their pupils to see bad flautists as well as good ones.[99] He concludes:

[99] One of these flute players, Ismenias, has been mentioned, though with a different purpose, in the *Per.* prologue (*Per.* 1. 5); also at *Quaest. Conv.* 632c–d; *De Alex. Fort.* 334b;

οὕτως μοι δοκοῦμεν ἡμεῖς προθυμότεροι τῶν βελτιόνων ἔσεσθαι καὶ θεαταὶ καὶ μιμηταὶ βίων, εἰ μηδὲ τῶν φαύλων καὶ ψεγομένων ἀνιστορήτως ἔχοιμεν.

In the same way I think we will be more enthusiastic both as spectators and imitators of the better Lives, if we do not leave unexamined the base and the castigated. (*Demetr.* 1. 6)

Plutarch's rationale for introducing 'one or two pairs' of men not worthy of imitation rests here on the premiss that the reader, through the use of reason, can distinguish virtue and vice. The reader should not be in a state of innocence or ignorance about vice, but, through studying some examples of men 'notorious for vice', should learn the better to avoid it and become more enthusiastic and discerning in the study of virtuous men. The implication is, then, that Demetrios and Antony are to be seen as negative or 'deterrent' examples.[100] This prologue picks up and continues themes which have been observed in the other programmatic statements; the stress is once again on virtue and vice, and the reader's response is to be one of imitation or avoidance. Historians since Herodotos (*Preface*) had claimed that the recording of the deeds of evil men was a function of history. Tacitus, too, claims that recording vice for posterity is one function of his *Annals* (3. 65). In both these cases the aim is commemorative as well as, one assumes, salutary.[101] Perhaps the best parallel for the rationale of 'negative examples' given by Plutarch is Valerius Maximus, who had already included a book on vices to be avoided in his *Memorable Deeds and Sayings*.

In fact, however, when Plutarch actually comes to talk of the subjects of the *Lives of Demetrios and Antony* he introduces them not simply as negative examples, but rather as proofs of the Platonic doctrine of 'great natures':

(1. 7) Περιέξει δὴ τοῦτο τὸ βιβλίον τὸν Δημητρίου τοῦ Πολιορκητοῦ βίον καὶ τὸν Ἀντωνίου τοῦ αὐτοκράτορος, ἀνδρῶν μάλιστα δὴ τῷ Πλάτωνι μαρτυρησάντων, ὅτι καὶ κακίας μεγάλας ὥσπερ ἀρετὰς αἱ μεγάλαι φύσεις ἐκφέρουσι. (1. 8) γενόμενοι δ' ὁμοίως ἐρωτικοὶ ποτικοὶ στρατιωτικοὶ μεγαλόδωροι πολυτελεῖς ὑβρισταί, καὶ τὰς κατὰ τύχην ὁμοιότητας ἀκολούθους ἔσχον. οὐ γὰρ μόνον ἐν τῷ λοιπῷ βίῳ μεγάλα μὲν κατορθοῦντες, μεγάλα

Non Posse 1095f. Apollonios, in Phil. *Apoll.* 5. 32, uses the same argument to encourage Vespasian to study examples of the poor emperors who preceded him, so as to learn 'how not to rule'.

[100] Russell (1973), 135.

[101] On *Ann.* 3. 65 see Fornara (1983), 118–19, and Luce (1991), who argue that the aim is to commemorate good and bad deeds, not to present them for imitation or avoidance (cf. Quint. *Inst. Orat.* 10. 1. 31). But the two need not be mutually exclusive.

δὲ σφαλλόμενοι, πλείστων δ' ἐπικρατοῦντες, πλεῖστα δ' ἀποβάλλοντες, ἀπροσδοκήτως δὲ πταίοντες, ἀνελπίστως δὲ πάλιν ἀναφέροντες διετέλεσαν, ἀλλὰ καὶ κατέστρεψεν ὁ μὲν ἁλοὺς ὑπὸ τῶν πολεμίων, ὁ δ' ἔγγιστα τοῦ παθεῖν τοῦτο γενόμενος.

(1. 7) This book will contain the life of Demetrios the Besieger and that of Antony the Imperator, men who most bear witness[102] to Plato's assertion that great natures produce great vices as well as great virtues. (1. 8) Both became equally addicted to sex and drink, they behaved like troopers, they became munificent, extravagant, and arrogant, and they gained similarities in fortune accordingly. For not only in the rest of their lives did they continually win great successes, but suffer great failures, make huge conquests, but suffer huge losses, stumble unexpectedly, but against hope once again recover, but they also met their ends in a similar way, one captured by the enemy, the other coming very near to suffering this fate. (*Demetr.* 1. 7–8)

Plutarch is probably alluding here to a passage in Plato's *Republic*, in which Plato discusses the nature of the true philosopher (491b–492a).[103] The philosophical nature, he maintains, is rare and is often corrupted and diverted from philosophy by those qualities of nature which are often praised, such as manliness and self-control, and by so-called good things, such as beauty, wealth, strength of body, and a powerful family (491b–c). In the plant and animal worlds, the most vigorous seeds or growths suffer most from deprivation of their proper nurture. Plato continues:

ἀγαθῷ γάρ που κακὸν ἐναντιώτερον ἢ τῷ μὴ ἀγαθῷ. Πῶς δ' οὔ; Ἔχει δή, οἶμαι, λόγον, τὴν ἀρίστην φύσιν ἐν ἀλλοτριωτέρᾳ οὖσαν τροφῇ κάκιον ἀπαλλάττειν τῆς φαύλης. Ἔχει. Οὐκοῦν, ἦν δ' ἐγώ, ὦ Ἀδείμαντε, καὶ τὰς ψυχὰς οὕτω φῶμεν τὰς εὐφυεστάτας κακῆς παιδαγωγίας τυχούσας διαφερόντως κακὰς γίγνεσθαι; ἢ οἴει τὰ μεγάλα ἀδικήματα καὶ τὴν ἄκρατον πονηρίαν ἐκ φαύλης, ἀλλ' οὐκ ἐκ νεανικῆς φύσεως τροφῇ διολομένης γίγνεσθαι, ἀσθενῆ δὲ φύσιν μεγάλων οὔτε ἀγαθῶν οὔτε κακῶν αἰτίαν ποτὲ ἔσεσθαι; Οὔκ, ἀλλά, ἦ δ' ὅς, οὕτως. Ἥν τοίνυν ἔθεμεν τοῦ φιλοσόφου φύσιν, ἂν μέν, οἶμαι, μαθήσεως προσηκούσης τύχῃ, εἰς πᾶσαν ἀρετὴν ἀνάγκη αὐξανομένην ἀφικνεῖσθαι, ἐὰν δὲ μὴ ἐν προσηκούσῃ σπαρεῖσά τε καὶ φυτευθεῖσα τρέφηται, εἰς πάντα τἀναντία αὖ, ἐὰν μή τις αὐτῇ βοηθήσας θεῶν τύχῃ.

'For bad is more contrary to the good, than to the not good.' 'Of course.' 'It makes sense, I think, that the best nature comes off worse than the poor nature in conditions of nurture which are more alien to it.' 'That is so.' 'So,' I said, 'Adeimantos, should we not say that, in the same way, those souls which have the

---

[102] For the phrase, cf. *Cor.* 1. 3; *Dion* 1. 3; 32. 8; *Galba* 1. 4.

[103] The idea of 'great natures' is also seen in Xen. *Mem.* 4. 1. 4; Plato, *Kriton* 44d; *Hipp. Min.* 375e; *Gorgias* 525e; ps.-Aristotle, *Problems* 30. 1, 953a10–32.

best natural endowment but which have had a bad education become especially bad? Or do you think that great crimes and unmixed evil stem from a poor nature and not from a vigorous one which has been corrupted by nurture? Do you think that a weak nature would ever be responsible for either great good or great evil?' 'No,' he replied, 'that is correct.' 'So I think that the nature which we posited for the philosopher, if it receives the proper teaching, must grow and reach complete virtue; but if it is sown, planted, and brought up in an unsuitable environment, the opposite will happen—unless one of the gods happens to help it!' (*Republic* 491d–492a)

Plato goes on to discuss the sort of man who, though he has a great nature might be drawn away from the pursuit of virtue by the praise of the mob; his younger contemporary Alkibiades is clearly in his mind. He concludes:

καὶ ἐκ τούτων δὴ τῶν ἀνδρῶν καὶ οἱ τὰ μέγιστα κακὰ ἐργαζόμενοι τὰς πόλεις γίγνονται καὶ τοὺς ἰδιώτας, καὶ οἱ τἀγαθά, οἳ ἂν ταύτῃ τύχωσι ῥυέντες· σμικρὰ δὲ φύσις οὐδὲν μέγα οὐδέποτε οὐδένα οὔτε ἰδιώτην οὔτε πόλιν δρᾷ.

From these men come both those who do the greatest evil to their cities and to individuals—and those who do the greatest good, if they happen to flow in that direction. For a little nature never does anything great, either to an individual or to a city. (*Republic* 495b)

'Great natures', then, exhibit great vices as well as great virtues: men with great natural potential can use that potential for great good or great ill. Demetrios and Antony are presented by Plutarch as examples of men whose great natural potential, whose 'great natures', have been perverted through a bad environment.[104] More will be said about this theory, and its importance for understanding Plutarch's 'deterrent' Lives, in the next chapter. It has relevance for our reading of all the pairs of Lives which we shall deal with in the course of this book.[105]

6. CONCLUSION: PLUTARCH ON THE VALUE OF HISTORY

It is clear, then, from an analysis of the programmatic statements to the *Lives* that for Plutarch, at least in theory, the purpose of writing or of reading about the statesmen of the past was twofold. First, one should

---

[104] In fact, Plutarch twice refers to Demetrios' good natural qualities (εὐφυΐα: 4. 5; 20. 2).
[105] Plutarch himself repeats the theory of great natures, in very similar language to Plato's, in *De Sera Num.* 551d–552d: see pp. 207–8. He also employs the notion at *Lys.* 2. 5 and *Ag./Kleom.* 23(2). 6; *De Gen. Soc.* 575b–c; *Non Posse* 1092e–f (cf. Paus. 7. 17. 3 on Nero). The concept underlies all four of the pairs examined in the case studies of this book.

come to an understanding of the character of the subject. This involves both knowledge of the subject, in off-duty moments as well as in speeches and battles, and an evaluation of him: in what ways was he good or bad? Secondly, and more importantly, Plutarch thought that a knowledge of the character of the great men of the past should lead the reader in his own life to imitate the good and abhor the bad; the study of the past was—or at least should be—a morally improving activity.[106] Plutarch puts this doctrine into practice in his own non-biographical works, where historical incidents and figures are used as *exempla* to back up instruction.[107] For example, in the *On tranquillity of mind* he urges his reader to imitate (μιμεῖσθαι) the men of the past who bore changes of fortune with indifference (467d). In the midst of misfortune one should look attentively (ἀποθεωρεῖν) at the famous who suffered similar misfortunes to one's own (467e): he quotes the examples of the kings of Rome, and of Epameinondas, Fabricius, and Agis; elsewhere in the essay he uses, amongst others, Alexander and Aemilius Paullus as examples to follow. In the *On inoffensive self-praise* he uses Perikles, Cato the Elder, Alexander, Agesilaos, Phokion, Demosthenes, and Themistokles; in *Marriage advice*, each piece of instruction is backed up by an example drawn from history, poetry, or proverbial wisdom. Perhaps the clearest use of incidents drawn from the past to teach lessons to the reader—in this case largely political lessons—is to be found in Plutarch's *Political precepts*. Most of the incidents narrated are also told in the *Lives*. But here the arrangement is not chronological; there is no attempt to narrate events within their historical contexts. Rather they are used explicitly and exclusively as examples or models (παραδείγματα: 798b–c) of behaviour to be imitated or avoided, as evidence to back up a programme of politico-moral instruction.[108]

Plutarch believed, then, that one should imitate virtuous men, whether one observes them in the flesh, in the mind's eye, or through reading his own literary work. By dint of this, he argues, one becomes a better person. It is no surprise, therefore, that in the *Lives* themselves

---

[106] In *De Defect. Orac.* 410b, Kleombrotos is said to be 'collecting history to serve as material for philosophy' (ἱστορίαν οἷον ὕλην φιλοσοφίας). On this passage, see Flacelière (1974); Brenk, (1977), 90–1. Cf. *De Lat. Viv.* 1129b–c: why, Plutarch asks sarcastically, should a great man like Themistokles, Camillus, Plato, or Epameinondas follow the Epicurean doctrine of 'living unknown': 'in order to educate nobody, to inspire no one with his virtue, not to be a fine example?' (ἵνα μηδένα παιδεύσῃ, μηδενὶ ζηλωτὸς ἀρετῆς μηδὲ παράδειγμα καλὸν γένηται;).

[107] See Valgiglio (1992), 3965–79.

[108] On the use of historical examples in speeches, cf. Aristotle, *Rhet.* 1393a23–1393b4. On this aspect of the *Praec. Ger.*, see Desideri (1991), 225–8.

Plutarch often stresses that a protagonist began his virtuous works as a result of observing—and desiring to imitate—a contemporary or predecessor. Thus Philopoimen as a young man wanted to be an 'imitator' of Epameinondas (*Phil.* 3. 1: ζηλωτής). In fact, Plutarch tells us, he did imitate (ἐμιμεῖτο) Epameinondas' military virtues and incorruptibility, but, because of his anger and love of strife (φιλονεικία), he was not able to maintain Epameinondas' 'gentleness, gravity, and humanity in political disputes' (cf. 4. 8). In the *Life of Pelopidas*, the protagonist urges the Theban exiles to take the daring and virtue of Thrasyboulos, leader of the Athenian democratic exiles, as their 'example' (*Pel.* 7. 2: παράδειγμα). Later on we are told that Pelopidas thought that brave men were more useful when they inspired each other to action (19. 5)—just like horses when they are yoked together, 'because mutual rivalry and love of victory inflame the spirit'.[109] The young Demosthenes 'envied' (ἐζήλωσε) the glory of the orator Kallistratos and admired the power of his speech, and so devoted himself to oratory (*Dem.* 5. 1–5). The young Theseus is inspired to great deeds by the achievements of Herakles (*Thes.* 6. 8–9; 25. 5). In a similar way, the young Themistokles is inspired by Miltiades' success at Marathon (*Thes.* 6. 9; *Them.* 3. 4–5); in the treatise *How to recognize that one is making progress in virtue* (84b–c) Plutarch uses Themistokles as an example of how praise and admiration (ἐπαινεῖν and θαυμάζειν) should lead to emulation and imitation (ζηλοῦν and μιμεῖσθαι). Similarly the young Tiberius Gracchos is inspired by his commander, Scipio Aemilianus, whose nature is said to provide 'many great incentives towards emulation and imitation in action' (*Gracchi* 4. 5).[110]

Reading about the men of the past will, then, be useful to the reader, who will use the examples of such men as inspiring models of what to imitate and what to avoid. Indeed, as we have seen, some of Plutarch's protagonists themselves provide a paradigm for how a knowledge of virtuous men should work on the soul of the viewer. Plutarch has declared a very utilitarian view of the value of history. But how might Plutarch's moralism work in practice? This is the subject of the next chapter.

[109] ὅτι συνεκκαίει τὸν θυμὸν ἡ μετ' ἀλλήλων ἅμιλλα καὶ τὸ φιλόνικον.

[110] πολλὰ καὶ μεγάλα πρὸς ζῆλον ἀρετῆς καὶ μίμησιν ἐπὶ τῶν πράξεων. More examples of heroes inspired to emulation of others are given by Valgiglio (1992), 4011–13; Frazier (1995), 148–9.

2
Moralism in Plutarch's *Lives*
Didacticism and Exploration

In the programmatic statements which we have examined, Plutarch seems to claim that the subjects of his *Lives* could be understood, taking their careers as a whole, as paradigms of either virtue or vice, and that, at the level of detail, individual actions could be understood as either virtuous or the reverse. For this reason the *Lives* would lend themselves to the extraction of practical moral lessons for the reader's own implementation and edification. In this chapter I attempt to assess whether these claims are substantiated in the *Lives* themselves and how Plutarch's original readers might have reacted to his works. The next chapter will examine the moral value-system which informs the *Lives*. Part II will constitute a series of case studies of the moral texturing of a number of different pairs of *Lives*.

Plutarch's claims for a moral purpose to his *Lives*, while unusual in their subtlety and depth of meaning, were not, of course, novel in their conception of the moral function of history. The claim for some higher purpose for historiography was an old one, going back to Thucydides, and often expressed in terms of a contrast between utility (ὠφέλεια) and pleasure (τέρψις). The relative weight to be given to these two facets of historiography was one of the main areas of debate in historical theory, often conceived in terms of allegiance to the Herodotean or Thucydidean model.[1] Utility was often conceived by historians and theorists in terms of 'examples' of virtue or vice (παραδείγματα or *exempla*).[2] The historian should guide his readers towards the correct response to these examples by allotting praise and blame where appropriate.[3]

---

[1] Cf. Avenarius (1956), 22–9; Fornara (1983), 104–34; Gentili and Cerri (1988), 10–33. On moralism in historiographers in general, see also Brunt (1979), 312–13 (=1993, 182–3).

[2] e.g. Diod. 1. 1. 4; 16. 70. 2; Josephus, *Ant. Jud.* 17. 3. 3, 60; Livy, pref. 10; Tac. *Hist.* 1. 3; 3. 51; Justin, *Praef.* 4.

[3] Cf. Dion. *Ad Pomp.* 3. 15; Cic. *Ad Fam.* 5. 12. 4; *De Fin.* 1. 10, 36. On Tac. *Ann.* 3. 65, see above, Ch. 1, n. 101.

Plutarch's programmatic statements, then, exploit *topoi* standard in ancient literature, especially in historiography. They set his work in the tradition of historiography that stresses 'utility' rather than 'pleasure' as its main aim, a utility which is moral rather than political or military. Behind the belief in the utility of history lay the belief that at some level history repeats itself: it is in identifying these repeated patterns that the benefit of studying history lies (e.g. Thuc. 1. 22. 4; Polyb. 9. 2. 5–6). Plutarch sets himself within this tradition by his use of a parallel structure, which invites the reader to identify similarities between Lives lived in different *milieux*.[4] The programmatic statements should also be seen as an important means of manipulating audience expectation. Proemial statements in ancient works must be seen as part of the 'negotiation' between narrator and reader at the beginning of the work, which governs the way in which the text is approached. They play a major role, together with other features of the opening, such as title, indication of subject matter, and allusion to predecessors, in setting the generic expectations of the reader.[5] Each prologue, then, with all its own individual twists, prepares the reader to approach the Life or pair of Lives which follow. But are these theoretical pronouncements reflected in Plutarch's actual practice? How much of the declared ethical-pedagogic aim is visible in the texts themselves?

1. PRAISE AND BLAME: POSITIVE AND NEGATIVE LIVES

A question which poses itself immediately is how moralism was expected to function within ancient texts. Moralism may be implicit or explicit. Explicit moralism involves direct narratorial intervention, characterized in ancient criticism as 'praise' or 'blame', in which the deeds or characters of actors in the narrative are assessed on a moral scale, and sometimes a lesson drawn for the reader.[6] Many examples of this are found in the writers of '*exempla*' literature, who use historical material for explicitly didactic purposes. Valerius Maximus, for instance,

---

[4] Cf. repeated cycles of *hubris* and *nemesis* in Herodotos; the repeated patterns in the structure of Thucydides: see Rawlings (1981), esp. 38–57; Moles (1993b), 107–8. Plutarch refers to the repetition of events as a possibility in *Sert.* 1. 1–2—the other possibility being that the universe is totally random—but it is difficult to judge the tone of this passage. Cf. *Dem.* 3. 3–5: the similarities in the nature of the two subjects and in the events that befell them were fashioned by ὁ δαίμων (God, or perhaps providence).

[5] Cf. Fowler (1982), 106.

[6] e.g. Xen. *Hell.* 5. 4. 1; Polyb. 1. 35. 1–10; Nep. *Thras.* 1. 1–2; *Eum.* 8. 1–3.

lists historical incidents to illustrate particular virtues or vices.[7] The second form of moralism involves narrative without direct narratorial comment; but moral issues are highlighted and often presented in such a way as to encourage in the reader a particular attitude of praise or blame. Generally, moralism in ancient historiographical works is of the second sort. Livy, for example, constructs the narrative of the Gallic sack of Rome and its subsequent recapture (5. 32. 6–55. 5) in such a way as to show implicitly that defeat was to due to moral collapse, and victory to virtue.[8] In the same way, Sallust gives his Catiline many of the features of the stock villain, introduced as an *exemplum* of Rome's moral decline. In the *Jugurthan War*, as David Levene has argued, the moralism is a little more complex. The underlying theme is that of moral degeneration; this is seen in Rome itself (especially in 1–4), but also in the increasing corruption of the leading figures: Jugurtha, Metellus, Marius, and Sulla. Each is given a favourable portrait when introduced, but each shows a moral decline worse than his predecessor. The work breaks off with the full extent of Marius' and Sulla's vices remaining in the future (cf. especially 95. 4): the cycle of vice and corruption continues.[9]

In the body of the *Lives* themselves—as opposed to the formal *synkriseis*[10]—moralism is almost invariably of the second sort. But it is often far from simple. As has been noted, some Lives concentrate much more than others on the great events and deeds with which history is traditionally associated, with the result that the emphasis on the character and disposition ($\mathring{\eta}\theta os$ and $\tau\rho\acute{o}\pi os$) of the subject is rather small, thus reducing the opportunity for critical evaluation. Some Lives do seem to have been written at least partly with moral lessons deliberately in mind; for example, the *Aristeides–Cato Major, Lykourgos–Numa*, and *Nikias–Crassus*, whose subjects conform, to some extent, to well-known paradigms. Generally, however, Plutarch's characters are more individuated; they are rarely assimilated to stock types.[11] As we shall see, some of the *Lives* do not seem obviously to teach moral lessons. The focus of much of the rest of this book will be on such complex and challenging Lives.

A number of factors stand in the way of an approach to the *Parallel Lives* which looks for the kind of easily extractable moral lessons that

[7] e.g. 3. 1. 2–3. 2. ext. 9, all explicitly illustrating the virtues of *fortitudo*.
[8] Luce (1971), 273–6.
[9] Levene (1992).
[10] My analysis here will concentrate on the values seen in the *Lives* themselves; the formal *synkriseis* present their own problems and are dealt with separately in Ch. 8.
[11] *Pace* Bucher-Isler (1972). Cf. Ingenkamp (1992*b*), 4624–31.

Plutarch seems to promise. First, most Lives provide very little explicit guidance as to how to understand the moral position of their subjects or of the actions narrated. Plutarch rarely intervenes into the narrative to point out where right and wrong lie. Where he does intervene, such as to discourse on justice in the *Aristeides* (6. 1–5) or *Demetrios* (42. 8–11), or on the dangers of the love of honour in the *Lysander* (23. 3; cf. *Ages.* 8. 5), or to point out a moral message about contentment and frugality in the *Aemilus* (*Aem.* 5. 10), the effect is striking.[12] Occasionally authorial judgement is inserted into the narrative as the thoughts of protagonists or 'sensible' onlookers.[13] But on the whole, moral judgements are left implicit: Plutarch expects his reader to recognize, and to question, where an action is to be commended, and where blamed. He shapes his *Lives* in a way which draws on a set of moral doctrines, though it is not clear whether and on what level the audience would share these moral doctrines. To what extent does the value-system of the *Lives* overlap with those of the reader, and to what extent is it a construct of Classical Greek values and therefore itself part of the historical programme? Given the renewed interest in the Classical world in this period, Plutarch's readers would certainly have had some familiarity with such Classical values and perhaps even some sympathy; but they would share them in a much less direct way, and perhaps not expect to imitate them. At any rate, the reader is more often than not expected to see for himself the moral categories being invoked and to recognize for himself how he should judge the conduct and lives of Plutarch's protagonists. Often, the moral categories which are being invoked would be so uncontroversial, and the implications so clear, that the reader's reaction is predictable and the moral message unproblematic. But, as we shall observe in later chapters, some Lives are so full of incidents whose moral value is in doubt, that it is not clear how the reader is meant to judge the protagonists.

This phenomenon seems to contradict Plutarch's words at the start of the *Demetrios–Antony*, where he seems to promise a set of paired Lives which were clearly divisible into two types: good Lives, which should be imitated, and bad, which should provide salutary warnings of what not to be.[14] On the basis of this prologue, modern commentators have understandably tried to classify individual pairs of Lives as either negative or positive. But the difficulties involved in such a classification, unsurprising given Plutarch's own admission that human nature is never

---

[12] Cf. Martin (1995), 13–14.
[13] See below, p. 120.
[14] See above, pp. 45–9.

wholly good (*Kim.* 2. 4–5),[15] are apparent from the lack of agreement as to which Lives should be seen as negative. The *Demetrios–Antony* is the only pair explicitly said to be an example of vice; as we shall see, there are problems even with this. Other suggested negative pairs are the *Nikias–Crassus*,[16] *Coriolanus–Alkibiades*,[17] and *Pyrrhos–Marius*.[18] There is agreement on none. The *Philopoimen* has also been suggested as a negative example, with, unusually, its partner, the *Flamininus*, providing a positive paradigm.[19]

In fact, the attempt to classify Lives as being either negative or positive is not only difficult but probably misguided. It is based on programmatic passages which, as has been argued, should be seen as cohering most closely with the Lives to which they are attached and cannot be taken unproblematically as guides to the whole collection. But even for those few pairs of Lives whose prologues suggest that the Lives which follow should be seen as exemplars of virtue or vice, it is impossible in practice to see the protagonists as wholly good or bad. Few protagonists live wholly blameless or blameworthy Lives; they are not stock examples of virtue or vice.

It is certainly true that Plutarch is generally more prepared to commend than to criticize. Such a practice would be consistent with his *persona* of tolerance and understanding for the foibles of human nature—his own $\phi\iota\lambda\alpha\nu\theta\rho\omega\pi\iota\alpha$—which we see displayed in his non-biographical work. It would also be in keeping with a common ancient view of literature, which associated the material about which an author, especially a historian, chose to write with that author's own character.[20] Dionysios of Halikarnassos states this doctrine very clearly at the

---

[15] Cf. Ag. /*Kleom.* 37(16). 8; *An. Virt. Doc.* 439b; *De Aud. Poet.* 25b–d; 26a; *Terrest. an Aquat.* 964d–e; *De Ipsum Laud.* 545e.

[16] Nikias is criticized for his cowardice, hesitation, and superstition (2. 4–6; 4. 3; 4. 8; 8. 2; 10. 8; 22. 2; ; *Nik.-Crass.* 1. 2; 2. 4; 2. 6), but has many virtues too (e.g. 9. 6; 12. 5; 14. 1; 16. 3; 16. 9; 17. 1; 21. 6–11; *Nik.-Crass.* 3. 6; 5. 1). Some have seen the negative as outweighing the positive: Marasco (1976), 22; Nikolaidis (1988), esp. 331–2; Piccirilli (1989), 14–16; (1990b and c); (1993b), pp. ix–xvi; Titchener (1991); Martin (1995). Pelling (1992), 35 n. 28 disagrees, arguing that, for example, Nikias' indecisiveness *is* emphasized in the early chapters to a greater extent than it had been in Thucydides, but, in contrast, it is not made a major issue in the defeat in Sicily.

[17] Russell (1966b), 37 n. 2; (1973), 108; (1982), 30; Aalders (1982), 9; Marasco and Nikolaidis (see previous n.).

[18] Also suggested by Nikolaidis (see n. 16).

[19] Walsh (1992), esp. 217–18. He sees *Phil.-Flam.* as demonstrating the importance of harmony and the dangers of 'love of strife' ($\phi\iota\lambda\omicron\nu\epsilon\iota\kappa\iota\alpha$).

[20] The notion is seen clearly in some passages of Aristophanes, in particular the contest between Aischylos and Euripides in the *Frogs* 830–1481: cf. also *Ach.* 410–13; *Thesm.* 149–50. See Muecke (1982), 51–3.

opening of his *Roman Antiquities* (1. 1. 2–1. 1. 4). He also uses this theory of literary criticism in his assessment of various historians in the second half of his *Letter to Pompey* (3–6, a summary of the second book of his earlier, now lost, treatise *On Imitation*).[21] Herodotos is judged far superior to Thucydides because of his choice of subject matter: Herodotos wrote about a glorious war, whereas Thucydides, ignobly, wrote about one which brought suffering on the Greeks. Furthermore, Herodotos chose to start and stop his history at points which gave the narrative an uplifting moral message: Persian aggression is traced from its beginning to its final punishment. Thucydides' whole narrative, on the other hand, is a depressing tale of warfare between Greeks. The most significant point of Dionysios' analysis of these two historians is the way he links their different choice of subject matter and starting- and stopping-points with their own disposition ($\delta\iota\acute{a}\theta\epsilon\sigma\iota s$): Herodotos quite properly rejoices at the good and is grieved at the bad. Thucydides, on the other hand, records Athens' mistakes 'in too much detail' and never, or only reluctantly, mentions its successes; he thus reveals, Dionysios argues, his grudge against his country (*Letter to Pompey* 3). In another work, his essay *On Thucydides*, Dionysios gives the Melian Dialogue as an example of what he considers Thucydides' maliciousness against his country, born of his grudge against it. In the Melian Dialogue the Athenians are made to say things which, according to Dionysios, they could not have said. The criteria is appropriateness ($\tau\grave{o}\ \pi\rho o\sigma\hat{\eta}\kappa o\nu$; $\tau\grave{o}\ \pi\rho\acute{\epsilon}\pi o\nu$): the liberators of Greece, the heroes of the Classical past, should not be represented as having said such arrogant things. To present them in this way reveals Thucydides' own maliciousness.

In the *Letter to Pompey* (4–5), Dionysios goes on to make a similar link between the virtuous character of Xenophon and the noble subjects which he chose for his histories, and, in contrast, the evil character of the historian Philistos, revealed by his choice as subject of Dionysios I, tyrant of Sicily. Philistos thus shows himself to be flattering, mean, petty, and a tyrant-lover.[22] Dionysios' comments on the historians Theopompos and Ephoros are particularly interesting. As was noted in the discussion of the *Nikias* prologue, he commends Theopompos for his perceptiveness in revealing hidden motives, exposing 'apparent virtue and undetected vice'.[23] This, says Dionysios, has made Theopompos appear malicious ($\beta\acute{a}\sigma\kappa a\nu o s$)—for reasons his comments on the other historians have

---

[21] On Dionysios' statement of this doctrine, see Fox (1993), 37–8.
[22] $\mathring{\eta}\theta\acute{o}s\ \tau\epsilon\ \kappa o\lambda a\kappa\iota\kappa\grave{o}\nu\ \kappa a\grave{\iota}\ \phi\iota\lambda o\tau\acute{u}\rho a\nu\nu o\nu\ \grave{\epsilon}\mu\phi a\acute{\iota}\nu\epsilon\iota\ \kappa a\grave{\iota}\ \tau a\pi\epsilon\iota\nu\grave{o}\nu\ \kappa a\grave{\iota}\ \mu\iota\kappa\rho o\lambda\acute{o}\gamma o\nu$.
[23] See above, p. 24.

made clear.[24] But Dionysios defends Theopompos: he is like a doctor who treats only the diseased parts of the body and leaves the healthy parts alone. In other words, Theopompos' criticisms of his subjects are just and not excessive.

It is probably this strand of ancient literary critical thinking, with its inherent belief that the classical past was glorious and nothing should be suggested otherwise, that influenced Plutarch to avoid criticizing the protagonists of his *Lives*. As Dionysios' comments on Theopompos and Herodotos have made clear, criticism of bad men can and should be part of the good historian's repertoire. But excessive criticism, and criticism of good men or of men who had become by the second century representatives or 'icons' of Hellenism and its glorious past, anything which might impugn the image of Classical Greece in general, opened the historian to accusations of malice, that is, bias against those criticized. This conception of the historian's task lies behind some words of Josephus in his own *Life* (65, 339). Here he explains his silence in the *Jewish War* about matters that would have redounded to the discredit of Justus by claiming that, although the historian must tell the truth, yet it is permissible for him not to scrutinize the crimes of individuals 'too bitterly'—not, he adds, because of bias in their favour, but because of his own 'moderation'.[25] Plutarch himself uses this approach in attacking Herodotos, thereby disagreeing with Dionysios' positive judgement of him, in the treatise *On the malice of Herodotos*. Here Plutarch uses the fact that Herodotos recorded versions of events unfavourable to some Greek cities as evidence of Herodotos' own evil character (κακοήθεια); Herodotos is, in a memorable formulation, a barbarian-lover (857a: φιλοβάρβαρος).[26] Plutarch thus presents himself, of course, by implication, as philanthropic and Hellenic.[27]

So it is almost certain that Plutarch felt that the task of a virtuous historiographer was to record, as far as possible, good and uplifting events. Where criticism is made, it must, like that of Theopompos, be fair and deserved. But criticizing basically good men, particularly the

---

[24] Nepos expresses surprise that Theopompos, like Timaios, praises Alkibiades: both are normally 'very abusive' (Nep. *Alk*. 11. 1: *maledicentissimi*). Plut. *Lys*. asserts that Theopompos' complimentary words should be taken particularly seriously: 'for he prefers to criticize than to praise' (*Lys*. 30. 2). Lucian, *De Hist*. 59 attacks Theopompos for excessive criticism.

[25] οὐ διὰ τὴν πρὸς ἐκείνους χάριν ἀλλὰ διὰ τὴν αὐτοῦ μετριότητα.

[26] At *De Alex. Fort*. 344b the same word is applied to fortune. It appears nowhere else in extant Greek literature.

[27] Luce (1989), 21–3; Marincola (1994), 192–3. On Plutarch's unfavourable view of Herodotos, see also Hershbell (1993).

heroes of the Classical Greek past, is to be avoided. Writing about bad men is difficult without either giving the impression that one shares or sympathizes with their vices, or producing a miserable and far from uplifting indictment. Hence it is, in all probability, that Plutarch did not write about men like Pausanias, the fifth-century regent of Sparta, and Philip II of Macedon, father of Alexander, or Philip V. This understanding of the task of the historiographer seems to lie behind and to be summed up in Plutarch's words in the prologue to the *Kimon–Lucullus*. Here he declares that no man's life is blameless or pure (ἀμεμφῆ καὶ καθαρὸν). Mistakes (or sins?: ἁμαρτίας) or defects which occur in a man's life—whether through passion or 'political necessity' (πολιτικῆς ἀνάγκης)—he will regard as 'shortcomings in a particular virtue rather than the wickednesses of vice' (ἐλλείμματα μᾶλλον ἀρετῆς τινος ἢ κακίας πονηρεύματα). These will not be delineated too clearly, 'as though out of respect for human nature, since it cannot produce anything absolutely good, nor any character which is indisputably turned to virtue' (*Kimon* 2. 3–5; cf. *De Herod. Malig.* 855c–856d). If a keenness to record vice could be seen as an indication of the malicious character—the κακοήθεια—of the historian who records it, Plutarch is here laying claim to the opposite quality: 'humanity' (φιλανθρωπία)—the generosity and sympathy towards his fellow human beings which are appropriate for an educated man. Plutarch almost says as much directly when in the same passage he talks of 'respecting human nature' (αἰδουμένους ὑπὲρ τῆς ἀνθρωπίνης φύσεως). Humanity is a virtue which recurs in the heroes of the *Lives* themselves and which, as we have noted, is an important part of Plutarch's own *persona*.

Now it is true that this passage from the prologue to the *Kimon–Lucullus* should, as with other programmatic statements, be seen as applying, first and foremost, to the paired Lives which it introduces. In fact, Plutarch's claim here—that moral failure should be seen as a shortcoming in virtue, rather than as vice—probably applies most specifically in the first instance to Lucullus. This passage comes immediately after a long, laudatory introduction sketching Lucullus' benefit to Plutarch's own city of Chaironeia at a time when it was arraigned before the Roman governor over the murder of some Roman soldiers (cf. *Kim.* 1. 1–2. 2). The passage develops out of a description of a marble statue of Lucullus and of thoughts on the correct way to represent a man in the plastic arts or in biography. Plutarch implies, then, that he is writing the *Life of Lucullus* as a tribute to the latter's kindly intervention on behalf of Plutarch's home town. Plutarch may also have felt that he ought to play down Lucullus' faults out of a desire for balance with the very positive *Life of Kimon*. Later on, in Lucullus' Life itself, Plutarch does indeed give him a more favourable treatment than he might have done. Lucullus provided an obvious opportunity for outraged moralism. In other writers, and elsewhere in Plutarch, he is presented as a paradigm of excess and luxury in old age.[28] But in this Life, Plutarch has chosen to play down Lucullus' most well-known feature. It is discussed in 39–41,[29] but in the following chapter he is rehabilitated (42. 1–4); his house becomes a centre not for pleasure and extravagance but for Greek learning, fitting in with a theme present from the start of the Life.[30]

So, one can suggest several reasons particular to this text why Plutarch was concerned to play down Lucullus' faults: his words at the start of the *Kimon–Lucullus* should, as with his other prologues, be taken most closely with the Lives which they introduce. But the general tone of sympathy for the subject of a Life which informs this passage does seem to be one which is found in all Lives. Plutarch is not as strict or stern a moralist as some of his other programmatic statements may have led us to expect. This is important. Plutarch is unwilling to point out explicitly, or dwell too heavily on, the vices and failures of his heroes. The conception of vice as a 'shortcoming in virtue',[31] is an underlying brake on the impulse to condemn vice which other programmatic statements had seemed to imply. Plutarch does not write wholly negative Lives, such as Suetonius' *Nero* or Lucian's *Alexander*. It is significant in this respect that, in introducing the single extant pair of Lives which is explicitly said to be a negative example, Plutarch appeals to the Platonic doctrine of 'great natures'. This doctrine, which, as we have seen, is most clearly set out in *Republic* 491d–492a, and which is repeated in Plutarch's treatise *On why the gods are so slow to punish* (551e–552d), presents great vice as

[28] Other writers: Vell. 2. 33. 4; Athen. 274e–f; 543a. Plutarch: *An Seni* 785f–786a; 792b–c.
[29] Cf. Lavery (1994), 267–70.
[30] e.g. 1. 6–8; 29. 6. See Swain (1990b), 143–5; (1992b); Pelling (1997a), 239–42. If Jones's understanding (1982) of ἀντετάττετο (42. 3) as 'opposed' is correct, Plutarch seems to have imagined Lucullus as actively engaging in philosophical debates with leading philosophers (cf. Barnes 1989, 90–2). Earlier, the Senate is said to have envisaged Lucullus as an 'opposition' (ἀντίταγμα) to the tyranny of Pompey (38. 2): as Christopher Pelling has pointed out to me, Lucullus abandons one sort of opposition for another. Cf. Lucullus' beneficence in throwing open his house as a 'Greek *prytaneion*' (πρυτανεῖον Ἑλληνικόν) for learned Greeks (*Luc.* 42. 2), which is parallel to Kimon's throwing open of his house as a 'public *prytaneion*' (πρυτανεῖον κοινόν) for the Athenians (*Kim.* 10. 7). For the metaphor, cf. Plato, *Protag.* 337d. For the parallels between these Lives, see Fuscagni (1989), 43–52.
[31] See Martin (1995). On the rather different sense of *Nik.-Crass.* 1. 4, where vice is described as 'a sort of inequality and incongruity of character' (ἀνωμαλίαν εἶναί τινα τρόπου καὶ ἀνομολογίαν), see below, pp. 270–1.

having its roots in the same sort of people—those with great natural endowments—as great virtues.[32] The difference is determined by education and environment. By associating Demetrios and Antony with this paradigm, Plutarch not only implies their inherent greatness but also suggests a less negative way of viewing their vice. Be that as it may, they are, still, as Plutarch himself implies in the prologue to the *Demetrios–Antony*, to be viewed as bad, as examples of 'vice' (κακία). Plato himself seems to imply, in the passage from the *Republic* to which Plutarch refers us, that for great natures the choice is stark, either good or bad: 'bad [bad nurture, bad education] is more contrary to the good, than to the not good' (491d: ἀγαθῷ γάρ που κακὸν ἐναντιώτερον ἢ τῷ μὴ ἀγαθῷ). Demetrios and Antony are, then, in Plutarch's view, evil men, examples of vice. But they are good men gone wrong, not innately evil. They are men of great natural potential, but whose potential is perverted by their environment and by their own weaknesses.

This, then, is one way into an understanding of the moral content of the *Demetrios–Antony*. As we have seen, it is the one pair introduced explicitly as an example of vice. But, as Christopher Pelling has demonstrated, it does not seem in practice to be wholly negative.[33] In the early chapters of the *Antony* there are a number of instances where the narrative is couched in terms of moral evaluation; for example, in 6. 6–7 Antony is said to neglect the wronged, listen angrily to those who consult him, and have a reputation for adultery,[34] all activities carrying an implicit moral criticism; in contrast in 14. 4–5 he is said to handle the crisis after Caesar's death 'very shrewdly and like a true politician' (ἐμφρονέστατα . . . καὶ πολιτικώτατα), but to be led astray by the desire for glory immediately afterwards. Plutarch is particularly outspoken in making a moral judgement when it comes to the proscriptions, where the three triumvirs, Antony included, barter over who is to be murdered. In a rare first-person intervention, he declares 'I do not think anything could be crueller or more savage than this exchange' (19. 4). Later in the Life, however, particularly after the introduction of Kleopatra (25. 1), the tone of praise and blame fades. The interest is in the fall of a great man and the traits which lead to it; by the end, the reader's sympathy lies wholly with Antony and Kleopatra, caught up in the pathos of their fall.

[32] Cf. *Praec. Ger.* 819f, where 'love of honour' is said to be innate 'not so much in lazy and humble characters but in very strong and impetuous ones'. See pp. 45–9 and 207–8.
[33] Pelling (1980), 138; (1988*b*), 10–18.
[34] κακῶς ἐπὶ γυναιξὶν ἀλλοτρίαις ἤκουε; cf. the parallel in *Demetr.* 14. 4, and also *Demetr.–Ant.* 1. 4.

The impression is one of tragedy—a great man is ruined by the very qualities which made him great; a sense of impending doom hangs over the actions on stage, as the reader watches the hero unwittingly working out his own downfall.[35] There is no simple moral lesson here. This is surprising, given the possibilities which Antony's association with Kleopatra provided for the presentation of a simple moral paradigm.

Luigi Piccirilli has suggested that we should add to the two categories of Lives to which Plutarch himself makes reference, 'positive' and 'negative' (that is, the *Demetrios–Antony*), a third intermediate category: Lives, which, while not explicitly said to be 'negative', give rather an unfavourable picture of their protagonists.[36] Into this category he would put the *Nikias–Crassus* and *Coriolanus–Alkibiades*. This is an unnecessary refinement. The *Demetrios–Antony* is not wholly negative. Its subjects belong to the class of Lives of men of 'great natures', whose great natures swung, on the whole, in the direction of vice rather than virtue. All Plutarch's characters are to be regarded, we may assume, as having 'great natures', but Plutarch introduces the doctrine to explain those whose careers were particularly blemished. This rubric is explicitly applied to several other characters whose moral status is dubious. The youthful Themistokles is described in this way, though here it is implied that he improved later in life. He was 'uneven and unstable, since his nature was unadulterated (τῇ φύσει καθ' αὑτὴν χρώμενος). This nature, without reason or education (ἄνευ λόγου καὶ παιδείας), produced great changes of habit to both good and bad, and often degenerated for the worse, as he himself later used to admit, saying that even the most intractable colts become excellent horses, when they get the education and discipline (παιδείας καὶ καταρτύσεως) they require.' (*Them.* 2. 7). As so often, instability or wickedness of character are linked with poor education. As we shall see, a similar link is invoked in Plutarch's discussions of other 'great natures' turned bad, which form the case-studies of this book. Coriolanus and Alkibiades, and Lysander, are explicitly such. So it is implied is Pyrrhos, and presumably also Marius and Sulla. The

[35] Cf. the use of stage imagery in the *Demetr.-Ant*: De Lacy (1952), 168–71; Pelling (1988b), 21–2; Mossman (1992), 100 and 103; Andrei (1989), 78–82 and below, p. 125. As Pelling points out, the primary effect is to reinforce the air of theatricality which surrounds the two flamboyant figures, but it also suggests the coming disaster. Swain (1992a) also draws attention to the many features in the *Ant.* which are normally associated with the ancient novel: Antony and Kleopatra are, in one sense, the heroes of a love story; moralizing is largely absent. Such variation in the generic register is a feature of Plutarch's *Lives*: in the *Mar.*, Marius' flight into exile contains many novelistic elements (*Mar.* 35. 8–40. 14).

[36] Piccirilli (1990a), pp. xxix–xxxiv. But later Piccirilli (1993b), pp. xiii–xiv, labels the *Nik.* simply as a negative Life.

subjects of the other pair discussed in this book, Phokion, and especially Cato, also have something of the 'great nature' about them.[37]

It may well be, however, that Plutarch became more willing to introduce more negative elements into the portraits of his heroes as the writing of the Lives progressed. Piccirilli suggests that the distribution of Lives in his three categories may be related to the order in which they were written. Although Piccirilli's tripartite classification is unnecessary, it is certainly true that all the Lives which Plutarch seems to consider as examples of great virtues gone wrong, or which have significant negative elements, that is, the *Coriolanus–Alkibiades, Nikias–Crassus, Demetrios–Antony*, and *Pyrrhos–Marius*, seem to have been written towards the end of Plutarch's programme. According to C. P. Jones, these four pairs of Lives (and possibly also the *Philopoimen–Flamininus*, another pair which has been noted for its negative elements) were amongst the last seven of the surviving Lives to be written by Plutarch.[38] It is surely no coincidence that all but one of the pairs of Lives in which the moralism is of a challenging kind, and which form the case-studies for this book (the *Pyrrhos–Marius, Phokion–Cato Minor, Lysander–Sulla*, and *Coriolanus–Alkibiades*), were written towards the end of Plutarch's programme.[39] It is surely also no coincidence that the majority of these challenging pairs of Lives, whose subjects have something of the great nature turned bad in them, are of men who lived outside of what Plutarch would have considered the golden age of their countries, in ages in which he considered the exercise of virtue was more difficult or the temptations of power very great. Lysander is a proto-Hellenistic king; Pyrrhos the real thing: Plutarch considered Hellenistic kings particularly vulnerable to the temptations of overconfidence and *hybris*.[40] Sulla and Marius, their partners, lived in the age when Roman commanders were obtaining exceptional personal power: it is not hard to see why Plutarch paired these men with their Hellenistic counterparts. Phokion and Cato both witness the death-throws of their own states, periods which Plutarch admits were antipathetic to the exercise of virtue (*Phok.* 1–3). Coriolanus dates from an early period of Roman history before the arrival of civiliz-

---

[37] See Chs. 4–7.
[38] Jones (1966), 66–8. See also Andrei (1989), 39.
[39] The exception seems to be *Lys.-Sulla*, dated to before AD 114 by a reference to the Battle of Orchomenos (86 BC) as having taken place 'almost two hundred years' earlier (*Sulla* 21. 8), and placed by cross-references (*Lys.* 17. 11; *Per.* 22. 4) to between the seventh and ninth pair in order of composition: see below, p. 2 n. 6.
[40] See below, pp. 115–16.

ing Greek influence (*Cor.* 1. 6);⁴¹ his incomplete education and moral degeneracy is not surprising. Only Alkibiades comes from the Classical age of his country, and Plutarch shows how unique and unpredictable he is, even to his own contemporaries.

So Demetrios and Antony are not to be seen as purely negative examples. They are rather great natures turned bad—not simply paradigms of evil. This must, partly at least, be a result of Plutarch's desire to seem humane rather than malicious. But it cannot be just that. For just as an explicitly 'bad example' is not wholly bad, so the 'good examples', men like Perikles and Alexander, appear not wholly good. Even in these Lives, where Plutarch is most favourable to the protagonist, there is still implicit criticism.⁴² Thus Perikles, whose Life opens with Plutarch's famous disquisition on the importance of imitation and who gets one of the most positive treatments of all Plutarch's protagonists, appears to fall below par on several occasions, in particular in his handling of the dispute with Megara (*Per.* 30. 1–32. 6).⁴³

The difference is surely one of degree, degrees of good and bad. Plutarch's *Lives* do not after all—and as will be argued in the course of subsequent chapters—provide comfortably black or white characters. So why did Plutarch choose to present his Lives in this antithetical way? Why did he introduce his *Demetrios–Antony* as belonging to a separate category of 'negative' Lives, men of great natures? The answer must be the same as to the related question of why in some Lives, notably the *Perikles–Fabius* and *Aemilius–Timoleon*, Plutarch chose to imply—and in the latter case to state directly (*Aem.* 1. 5–6)—that their subjects were examples of virtue. These two claims are different sides of the same coin. What is important, and what deserves our attention, is what the two claims have in common. First, both claims invite the reader to focus on issues of morality, on issues of right and wrong. This is the lens through which Plutarch's narratives of the past are to be read. In effect, Plutarch's claims in the *Demetrios–Antony* prologue are the same as in the other programmatic statements. He emphasizes that morality is at the core of this text. Plutarch gives a twist to his previous programmatic changes, focusing now on evil and its deterrent value. But the programme has not changed: the subjects' moral character and the reader's moral response

---

⁴¹ Plutarch seems to have dated the beginning of significant Hellenic influence to the sack of Syracuse in 211 BC (e.g. *Marc.* 21. 7). See Swain (1990*b*), 131–2.

⁴² Piccirilli (1989); (1990*a*), pp. xxxi–xxxii.

⁴³ Martin (1995), 15–16.

remain central.[44] Secondly, the prologue to the *Demetrios–Antony* shares with that to the *Perikles–Fabius* and *Aemilius–Timoleon* an emphasis on the reader's practical response. The sensitivity to moral issues which the reader is to bring to all these Lives is, Plutarch makes clear, to have a practical end. The reader's response, as Plutarch puts it, is to imitate in his own life the examples of virtue which he sees displayed before his eyes, and to learn to avoid repeating the deeds of vice. The phraseology and conceptualization are simple and stark.

It is possible to argue that in writing the *Lives*, he gravitated first to the positive, but became aware, as his writing progressed, that he would be forced to write more negative Lives: it would be difficult to present Mark Antony, Coriolanus, or Marius as paradigms of virtue.[45] But Plutarch, in introducing the concept of 'great natures', is doing more than simply providing himself with a justification to write Lives of dubious characters. These men, the focus of this book, allowed Plutarch to explore complex questions of right and wrong. His programmatic statements place him in the main stream of ancient historiographical theory, in reducing the past to a dichotomy of virtue and vice. But as will emerge in the course of this study, in practice the body of Plutarch's own work belies this simple reduction. Morality—virtue and vice—is central to the *Lives*, and must be central to a reading of them. But the *Lives* will demonstrate that, very often, the question of where good and evil lie, of what is the best course of action, is not as simple or easy to discern as Plutarch's theorizing would suggest. The Alexander of Plutarch's Life is not simply the champion of Greek culture (παιδεία), the ideal philosopher-king, as he is in the speeches *On the fortune or virtue of Alexander*;[46] nor is he a paradigm of the dangers of drink and despotism as he is in Curtius Rufus and in Stoic writers such as Seneca. The *Life of Alexander* presents a complex picture. A dark side, often signalled by tragic associations, coexists alongside the more positive and more usual Greek presentation of Alexander as the epitome of all things Hellenic.[47] The picture is thought-provoking, manipulating and pulling the reader's sympathy in contradictory directions.

---

[44] Cf. Andrei (1989), 38–9.
[45] Cf. Brenk (1992), 4381.
[46] Cf. Humbert (1991), 175–81.
[47] On the two sides of Alexander in Plutarch's Life, see Wardman (1955), 100–7; Mossman (1988). For the Alexander of the Life as civilizer and devotee of Greek culture, cf. *Alex.* 5. 7–8; 7. 1–8. 5; 26. 1–7; 47. 6.

2. IMITATION AND EXPLORATION

Another factor which adds to the problems involved in a moralizing reading of the *Lives* is the question of imitation: how does the reader 'imitate' the virtues which he sees in the heroes whose Lives he reads? The *Lives* without exception have as their subjects statesmen and soldiers. Plutarch had the option of including philosophers or literary figures; there was a long tradition of biographical writings concerning such men, often associated with the Aristotelian school (the Peripatos).[48] But he chose, instead, men of action. Perhaps Plutarch thought that the stress of great events and crises provided a better arena for the analysis of character.[49] He certainly seems to have shared the Greek tradition of prioritizing the public over the private sphere. The treatise *On the fact that the philosopher ought most of all to converse with men in power* (776a–779c) is a particularly clear statement of his belief that philosophy should have a practical aim.[50] He seems also to have believed that true virtue is possible only when one lives a life of 'action', that is a life of political involvement (ὁ πρακτικὸς βίος), as opposed to a life of contemplation (ὁ θεωρητικὸς βίος). This is certainly the emphasis in the *Were the Athenians more glorious in war or in wisdom?* Furthermore, it seems reasonable to suppose that one of Plutarch's purposes in writing the *Lives* was to provide a political and military history of the Greek and Roman world, which can be viewed within the tradition of the 'universal histories' which set the past and destiny of Greece and Rome side by side. For such a programme, it was natural that the great men of action of the past would be chosen.

But where does this leave the contemporary reader? In what sense would imitation of the lives of the great men of the past have been possible for him? It is true that, for some Greeks of the early second century, high positions in the Roman administration were becoming open, some carrying with them considerable military responsibility. It is also possible that some Romans beyond Sosius Senecio, Plutarch's dedicatee, read the *Lives*: men to whom such positions might be a matter of course. So for these men there may well have been something to imitate in the political and military deeds of a Perikles or a Fabius.

---

[48] Cf. Momigliano (1971a), 66–73.
[49] See above, p. 25. Cf. Jones (1971), 103–4.
[50] See also *An Seni, Non Posse*, and *De Lat. Viv.* In *De Tranq. An.* 465c–466a Plutarch criticizes the Epicurean ideal of avoiding public life (ἀπραξία).

But, for the majority of Plutarch's readers, times had changed. In several passages of the *Political precepts*, Plutarch shows himself very much aware that the modern statesman's role in a Greek *polis* was far different from that of his classical counterpart. The reality of Roman power meant, for example, that matters of war and peace were no longer within his control (805a, 813d–814c, 824c–d). So, even if Plutarch did conceive of his readers as local magnates and statesmen, imitation of the political and military deeds of the subjects of the *Lives* was in one sense impossible.[51] One might contrast the much more up-to-date and immediately applicable moralism of Plutarch's speeches and tracts, texts where the 'message' is never in doubt.

But the problem goes deeper than this. Plutarch often seems deliberately to *avoid* drawing parallels with contemporary life.[52] For example, the great stress on benefaction as a virtue in the world of the Greek cities in the first and second centuries AD is not reflected in the *Lives*.[53] In fact, despite Plutarch's belief that warfare was no longer a concern of most of his readers, the stress in many Lives is uncompromisingly military: compare, for example, the relative space given to Julius Caesar's campaigns in Suetonius' *Divus Julius* and Plutarch's *Caesar*. Plutarch's avoidance of contemporary reference is particularly clear in the *Philopoimen*, as Christopher Pelling has pointed out.[54] Here, despite his harsh words on Greek contentiousness and disharmony, put into the mouths of Greek bystanders as Flamininus declares freedom for Greece in 196 BC (*Flam*. 11. 3–7), Plutarch avoids making a link between Greek contentiousness and Roman intervention. Such a suggestion would have chimed well with Plutarch's advice in the *Political precepts*, where the danger of Roman intervention is cited as a major reason why such contentiousness must be avoided (*Praec. Ger.* 814e–815b). At just one point in the *Philopoimen* is this link made: when Philopoimen urges Diophanes not to attack Sparta because of the dangers of intervention from Rome or from Antiochos (*Phil.* 16. 2). But, in fact, Plutarch goes on to deliberately disassociate Philopoimen's attacks on Sparta (*Phil.* 16. 1–8) from the Roman intervention for which it was, partly at least, responsible (17. 1–7); 16. 9, which talks of Sparta's later succession from the Achaian League with Roman permission is strangely detached from

---

[51] Cf. Gossage (1967), 49.

[52] See Pelling (1995*a*). Contrast the contemporary relevance of Nepos (e.g. *Eum*. 8. 2–3): Dionisotti (1988); Millar (1988).

[53] Though cf. the suggestion of Moles (1992), 293–4, that the *Per*. contains an implied plea to the Emperor Trajan to engage in building works to rival Perikles' in Athens.

[54] Pelling (1995*a*), 213–17.

the narratives both of Philopoimen's attack which precedes it and of Roman intervention which follows.

The Life of Aratos of Sikyon (third century BC) is a case in point. This Life is not one of the *Parallel Lives*: like the *Artaxerxes*, it stands alone. Its place outside the corpus of the *Parallel Lives* probably accounts for its unusual opening. Plutarch addresses by name a certain Polykrates, a contemporary descendant of Aratos. He assures Polykrates that he is not sending him the Life of his famous ancestor because he does not know about Aratos already. Far from it, Plutarch flatteringly assures him; Polykrates has always 'tried to model his life on the most noble of examples drawn from his own family' (1. 3).[55] Rather, Plutarch is sending him the Life for the benefit of his sons (1. 5): '. . . in order that your sons Polykrates and Pythokles may be nurtured on their own examples (ὀκείοις παραδείγμασιν ἐντρέφωνται), as they hear and they read what it befits them to imitate (ἅπερ αὐτοὺς μιμεῖσθαι προσήκει).'[56] The direct address to Polykrates and the naming of those apparently intended to learn from the paradigm provided by this Life are unusual. But the claims for a didactic moralism are familiar from elsewhere: this Life will improve its readers when they 'imitate' the 'examples' which it contains. And indeed the Life has some strongly moralistic elements. The last chapter gives the retribution which was visited on Philip V for his evil deeds: he himself was humiliated, and his line became extinct on his son's execution; in contrast, 'the descendants of Aratos have remained in Sikyon and Pellene to this day' (54. 7–8). The message seems to be that good ultimately triumphs. But how were two sons of a member of the Sikyonian élite, two descendants of Aratos living under the Roman Empire, supposed to 'imitate' a man whose fame rested on his military exploits as leader of the Achaian League? How, in other words, is a moral programme based on imitation of models supposed to work, when there exists such a gulf between the circumstances of the reader and the subject, between the (supposed) imitator and imitated?

Christopher Pelling has suggested one possible approach to this problem by proposing two distinct models for the way a moralistic text might work. One he calls 'protreptic' moralism, the other 'descriptive' moralism. Texts which employ 'protreptic' (from προτρέπειν, to urge), or expository, moralism explicitly or implicitly carry some sort of advice or injunction to be put into effect. 'Descriptive', or exploratory, moralism occurs in discourse which raises moral issues without

---

[55] πρὸς τὸ κάλλιστον ἀφομοιοῦντι τῶν οἴκοθεν παραδειγμάτων τὸν βίον.
[56] For the exhortation to imitate an ancestor, cf. Isok. *Evag*. 77.

attempting to guide conduct. So, as Pelling argues, the moralism in the *Antony*, at least in the second part, and in parts of other Lives such as the *Pompey*, is less concerned with explicit praise and blame, more with 'pointing an ethical truth about human nature'.[57] It is this kind of gentle exploration of the realities of human life and the moral dilemmas which it raises—much more gentle and more nuanced and complex than, say, Theophrastos' *Characters*—which is at the heart of Plutarch's *Lives*, and constitutes their most valuable feature. 'Moralism' is probably not the best English term to describe Plutarch's practice, implying as it does a protreptic, sermonizing, second-person discourse. As was noted at the very start of this book, the Greeks spoke instead of character, which itself had a moral dimension. So to sketch character, even without explicit moral exhortation, or 'praise and blame', would be to invite the kind of ethical interest which Plutarch expects. Tragedy provides, as Pelling suggests, a good parallel with this sort of moralism. Sophokles' *Antigone* is about moral issues; even though it does not contain imperatives, it provides food for reflection, a reflection which may, ultimately, affect the audience's behaviour.[58]

The moral texturing, then, of Plutarch's *Parallel Lives* is, very often, of this subtle and implicit kind. Thus the sensitive interest which we see in the *Antony* in a great man's psychology and frailty fits much better this model of Plutarch's moralism. There are no imperatives or explicit narratorial judgements in the second part of the *Antony*. But though Antony is not made into a paradigm of virtue or vice, there is still material here for moral reflection, something for the reader to learn from for his own life. Furthermore, Plutarch does, even in this Life, construct the world, partly at least, in terms of a 'timeless' set of moral categories: the control of passion by reason, the dangers of ambition or contentiousness, the need to control 'the people' in the right way. All these moral issues may have struck a chord with Plutarch's readers, even though their own circumstances were very different from those of the subjects about whom they were reading. The *Antony* reads more like a tragedy or a novel than a moral treatise. It raises profound moral issues, but it is as much concerned with *understanding* the protagonists as with

---

[57] Pelling (1988b), 10–18, especially 15–16.
[58] Pelling (1995a), 206–8. Thucydides' history contains this kind of moralism too. As Rutherford (1994) has pointed out, Thucydides' reader would gain more than practical lessons in statesmanship: he would also gain an increased understanding of human nature, the workings of politics, and the vicissitudes of war, lessons which might not have an obvious practical application (e.g. 2. 47; 3. 82).

judging them. The interest, to use Gill's terminology, is as much in 'personality' as in 'character'.[59]

It appears, then, that Plutarch's programmatic statements are a little misleading in the kind of texts which they give the reader to expect. Whether Plutarch was himself aware of this gap between his pronouncements and his actual practice is impossible to tell. We should remember that programmatic statements should perhaps be taken more closely with those Lives to which they are attached; their general applicability is rather more limited than sometimes supposed. But, more importantly, the programmatic statements function, as we have seen, to set the *Lives* within a particular historiographical tradition; perhaps it is natural that in practice the exploration of moral issues is sometimes more nuanced than advertised. This is one of the strengths of Plutarch's work. His moralism is not a set of prescriptions; it is more interesting, more various, and more challenging than that.

There are some values, drawn from the classicizing philosophic currency of contemporary intellectual life, that are consistently reinforced and little challenged: in particular, the priority of reason over the passions in the soul of a statesman, which will be the subject of the next chapter. Some Lives, too, are rather straightforward in the issues they raise. Such is the *Pyrrhos–Marius*, the subject of the first case study of this book. One of Plutarch's last pairs, it is a fine moralizing text, which shows the thoroughness with which Plutarch reworks and integrates the narratives of two historically unconnected figures into a single unit illuminating the dangers of the vice of discontent to those who, like the subjects of these Lives, had 'great natures'.

Other Lives cause us to reflect more deeply on the difficulties and contradictions which arise in practice when one attempts to judge great men on a moral scale. It is these challenging and difficult Lives which are the focus of subsequent chapters. They share with the *Pyrrhos–Marius* their chronological position late in Plutarch's corpus and the fact that their subjects are all regarded as being, like Pyrrhos and Marius, men of 'great natures'. They are all, with the exception of Alkibiades, drawn from periods in which Plutarch considered the exercise of virtue to be difficult or problematic. Is not compromise sometimes necessary in the less than ideal conditions of political life? This is the question that Plutarch invites us to ask in the *Phokion–Cato Minor*. What is the relationship, furthermore, between the strict demands of morality and the interests of the state? Lysander, Sulla, and Alkibiades all appear to

[59] See above, Ch. 1, n. 3.

break moral codes in order to serve their country. As detailed studies will demonstrate, there are few easy moral lessons to be drawn from the *Lysander–Sulla* and *Coriolanus–Alkibiades*. On the contrary, these Lives seem to threaten to overturn any moral system applied: Sulla is more successful than Lysander because of his use of greater violence; the Athenian people do not know how to judge Alkibiades, whose very bad points—his versatility and ability to flatter—win victories for Athens. In these Lives we see Plutarch at his best: gently questioning the conventional boundaries between right and wrong. Moralism is a major feature of many of the *Lives*, and provides the explicit *raison d'être* of the corpus. But it is a challenging moralism. Plutarch invites us to address moral issues, but simple answers, simple paradigms, are not always forthcoming.

3

The Soul of a Plutarchan Hero

Plutarch and Platonic Psychology

Before we begin our case studies of pairs of Lives in which moral values are explored and challenged, it is worth pausing to consider some aspects of the value-system which informs Plutarch's work, the overall moral framework running through the *Lives* as a whole. This framework functions to reinforce certain key values which are implicit in all the *Lives*: transgression of, or adherence to, these norms both determines the moral status of the subject and reinforces the norms themselves. The value system implicit in the *Lives* can be related to Plutarch's background in Platonic thought: in particular, Platonic conceptions of human psychology.[1]

Plutarch's dependence on Plato in his conception of the human soul is set out most clearly in his treatise *On moral virtue* (Περὶ ἠθικῆς ἀρετῆς).[2] The aim of this work is to attack the Stoic notion of the unitary nature of the soul, and the Stoic insistence on insensibility to emotions, or rather the extirpation or abolition of emotion (*apatheia*), as an ideal. The language and ideas of the text are chosen with this polemical aim in mind,[3] but despite this it gives a good picture of the psychological assumptions which Plutarch brought to his writing of the *Lives*. The theme Plutarch sets out to investigate at the start of the work (440d–e) is the nature of 'moral' or 'character' virtue (ἠθικὴ ἀρετή) as opposed to 'contemplative' virtue (θεωρητικὴ ἀρετή). Moral virtue, he states at the very start of the treatise, 'has passion as its material (τὸ μὲν πάθος ὕλην

---

[1] The issue is very complex: Plutarch was certainly influenced also by the contemporary Platonic and Peripatetic schools, as well as by the Platonic and Aristotelian texts themselves (on which cf. his *Plat. Quaest.* and *De An. Procr.*, and Jones 1916). See next n.

[2] The precise nature of the philosophic influences in this text is debated. Babut (1969*a*), 61–76, and Opsomer (1994) argue for Plato as the main inspiration, despite some striking similarities with Aristotle's *NE*. Donini (1974), 63–125; Becchi (1975; 1978; 1981; 1990*b*, 27–49) stresses the place of this work within contemporary Peripatetic and Middle-Platonic thought, especially in the light of its emphasis on the doctrine of the mean between opposing passions (μετριοπάθεια) and of its polemic against Stoic *apatheia*.

[3] Babut (1969*a*), esp. 2–43 and 54–80.

ἔχειν) and reason as its form (τὸν δὲ λόγον εἶδος)'. Which part of the soul, Plutarch enquires, is involved in the exercise of this virtue; is it rational or irrational? He concludes, after running through and dismissing the views of some Stoic philosophers (440e–441d), that Pythagoras, Plato, and Aristotle were correct in thinking that the soul is divided into two, a rational part (τὸ λογιστικόν) and an irrational or passionate part (τὸ ἄλογον or τὸ παθητικόν); the rational should lead and guide the irrational (441d–442c). The irrational, he notes, was further subdivided by Plato into the appetitive (τὸ ἐπιθυμητικόν) and the spirited (τὸ θυμοειδές). Plutarch is thinking here of Plato's tripartite division of the soul in the *Republic*. For Plato, the 'appetitive' is the purely irrational part of the soul and capable only of responding to bodily instincts. The 'spirited' part of the soul (τὸ θυμοειδές), or the 'spirit' (θυμός), is for Plato that part which reacts emotionally to a sense of right and wrong, especially to a sense of being wronged; it is the 'spirit' which causes anger, indignation, shame, and ambition, all of which, if manifested in the right circumstances, are good and indeed necessary. But if the 'spirit', which is irrational by nature, is not properly subordinated to reason, then the emotions to which it gives rise will get out of control and be harmful.[4] Plutarch defends this doctrine: the spirit gives rise to the emotions necessary, for example, to fight or to make love; though essentially irrational, it can be trained to obey the rational (442c–443d). In fact, Plutarch tends not to refer to the 'spirited' part of the soul in the rest of the treatise, talking instead simply of the passions or the irrational.[5] But he is clear in this treatise that the passions, when strictly controlled by reason, are necessary for the exercise of virtue. For the rest of the treatise, the Platonic terminology of the three parts of the soul is eclipsed by the more fundamental distinction between reason and passion. Virtue consists in the attainment of the right 'mean' between opposing passions, that is, when passions are harmonized through the order or direction imposed by reason.

At 443c–d Plutarch outlines how character is formed and what the role of education is:

Διὸ καὶ καλῶς ὠνόμασται τὸ ἦθος· ἔστι μὲν γάρ, ὡς τύπῳ εἰπεῖν, ποιότης τοῦ ἀλόγου τὸ ἦθος, ὠνόμασται δ' ὅτι τὴν ποιότητα ταύτην καὶ τὴν διαφορὰν ἔθει λαμβάνει τὸ ἄλογον ὑπὸ τοῦ λόγου πλαττόμενον, οὐ βουλομένου τὸ πάθος

---

[4] See esp. *Rep.* 439e–440d; 442a–c. Cf. Gill (1985), esp. 6–12.

[5] Plutarch's collapsing of the 'spirited' and the 'appetitive' into a single 'irrational' is characteristic of Peripatetic and Middle-Platonic philosophy: see Vander Waerdt (1985), esp. 379–80.

ἐξαιρεῖν παντάπασιν (οὔτε γὰρ δυνατὸν οὔτ' ἄμεινον), ἀλλ' ὅρον τινὰ καὶ τάξιν ἐπιθέντος αὐτῷ καὶ τὰς ἠθικὰς ἀρετάς, οὐκ ἀπαθείας οὔσας ἀλλὰ συμμετρίας παθῶν καὶ μεσότητας, ἐμποιοῦντος·

Therefore, character (*ēthos*) too is well named. For character is, to sketch in outline, a quality of the irrational. It is so named because the irrational gets this quality and differentiation by habit (*ĕthos*) as it is moulded by reason. Reason does not want to do away with passion totally (for that is neither possible nor better), but places some boundary and order on it, and implants the ethical virtues, which are not absences of passion (*apatheia*) but proportionalities and means of passions. (*De Virt. Moral.* 443c)

Character (ἦθος), he argues, is a 'quality' of the irrational part of the soul; it is acquired through habituation (ἔθος), as the irrational part of the soul is moulded, or fails to be moulded, by reason (λόγος).[6] In other words, a man's character (ἦθος), his ability to exercise 'moral virtue' (ἠθικὴ ἀρετή), depends on the extent to which the rational part of his soul is able to influence and change, through habit, the irrational in him. Throughout this text, as elsewhere, Plutarch observes the common ancient distinction between nature (φύσις) and character (ἦθος). A person's nature is what he is born with; a person's character is related to his nature, but is affected, for better or worse, by the kind of life he or she habitually leads, and by the extent to which reason acts upon it.[7] The soul, he goes on, has capacity (δύναμις), passion (πάθος), and acquired state (ἕξις). This latter is a result of habituation: 'The acquired state (ἕξις) is a strong and settled condition of the capacity of the irrational (τὸ ἄλογον), which is engendered by habit (ἔθος): vice, if the passion has been poorly schooled (παιδαγωγηθῇ) by reason, virtue, if it has been well schooled' (443d).[8] The most vital period for the formation of character is in childhood: hence the importance of good education in Plutarchan as in Platonic thought. Ethical virtues are implanted in the irrational, when the passions are kept within proper bounds (444b–c).

---

[6] Both Plato and Aristotle had argued that character (ἦθος) is formed by habituation (ἔθος): e.g. Plato, *Laws* 792e (ἐμφύεται . . . τὸ πᾶν ἦθος διὰ ἔθος); Aristotle, *NE* 1103a11–b25 (esp. 1103a17–18: ἡ δ' ἠθικὴ [ἀρετή] ἐξ ἔθους περιγίνεται, ὅθεν καὶ τοὔνομα ἔσχηκε μικρὸν παρεκκλῖνον ἀπὸ τοῦ ἔθους); *EE* 1220a38–1220b7; *MM* 1185b38–1186a8. Cf. ps.-Plut. *De Lib. Educ.* 2f–3b; Plut. *De Garrul.* 511e.

[7] But see below, pp. 119 and 230. On nature and character, cf. *De Sera Num.* 551d; 562b. See Dihle (1956), 63–4 and 84–7; Bergen (1962), 62–94; Russell (1966a), 144–7 (=1995, 83–6); Wardman (1974), 132–7; Brenk (1977), 171–81; Gill (1983), 473–4; 478–81; Swain (1989a).

[8] Compare the argument in the *De Cohib. Ira.* Anger is a passion (πάθος) which is particularly hard for reason (λόγος) to control once it is roused (453d–454b); in the long term, it produces a bad state (ἕξις) in the soul (454b). Most of the treatise (454c ff.) contains advice on how to habituate oneself to avoid anger (see below, pp. 87–9.)

At the end of the treatise (451b–452d), Plutarch returns to the theme of education and habituation.⁹ The irrational is an indispensable part of human nature, not to be done away with, but requiring nurture and education: 'So man too has a share in the irrational (τὸ ἄλογον), and has innate within him the source of passion (πάθος), not as a chance possession but as a necessity and which should not be done away with totally but which requires care and education (θεραπείας καὶ παιδαγωγίας δεομένην).' The passions, Plutarch maintains, when controlled by reason, are necessary for the exercise of the virtues: 'reason (ὁ λογισμός) makes use of the passions (τὰ πάθη) when they have been tamed and made tractable, not hamstringing or cutting away that part of the soul which is its servant' (451d).¹⁰ Much more useful than trained animals are 'the animals of the passions (τὰ τῶν παθῶν θρέμματα), when they work in tandem with reason and strive alongside the virtues: spirit (θυμός), if it is moderate, with courage, hatred of evil with justice . . .' (451d–e). For this reason, Plutarch continues, lawgivers instilled in their states the passions of love of honour (φιλοτιμία) and emulation (ζῆλος), and for this reason too educators make use of the pain and pleasure of rebuke and commendation to improve the young men under their charges (452b).¹¹ Education (παιδεία) is the proper acting of reason (λόγος) and custom or law (νόμος) on the emotions of the young (452c–d).

The *On moral virtue* reveals some of Plutarch's most characteristic and important concerns in the *Lives*. His interest in 'moral virtue', in the virtue which involves correct action, rather than in the more theoretical 'contemplative virtue', is clearly demonstrated in the *Lives*, which are about virtue in action. Indeed, it is the conflict between virtue in theory and the demands of practice in the world of affairs that is at the heart of many of the Lives which form the case-studies of this book. The *On moral virtue* also reveals some key elements in Plutarch's conception of human psychology as manifested in the *Lives*. First, he sees the human soul as a site of potential conflict between reason and passion. He argues, against Stoic views of the unitary nature of the soul, that conflicting impulses arising from reason and passion can exert their influence simultaneously on the soul (cf. 446f–448c). This analysis leads naturally

---

⁹ Cf. Babut (1969a), 38–43, who sees contradictions between *De Virt. Moral.* 451b–452d and the preceding chapters.
¹⁰ καὶ τοῖς πάθεσι δεδαμασμένοις χρῆται καὶ χειροήθεσιν ὁ λογισμός, οὐκ ἐκνευρίσας οὐδ' ἐκτεμὼν παντάπασι τῆς ψυχῆς τὸ ὑπηρετικόν. ἐκνευρίσας is a clear allusion to Plato, *Republic* 411b, which is quoted more explicitly at 449f.
¹¹ He is surely thinking here of Lykourgos in particular (cf. *Lyk.* 25. 5; ps.-Plut. *Inst. Lac.* 238a–b).

to some of the most important themes in the *Lives*. In particular, the extent to which a hero held fast to reason and controlled his passions is a question in which Plutarch is always interested and which carries an implicit moral charge. Secondly, Plutarch argues that the passions are necessary for the exercise of virtue but must be strictly controlled by reason. In the *Lives*, Plutarch concedes, as we shall see, that emotions such as ambition or rivalry are necessary spurs to action. Occasionally, as most notably in the case of Alexander the Great, he takes up the Platonic terminology of the 'spirited element' of the soul, which provides the impulse to virtuous action, but can easily lead to pride and violence. But in general in Plutarch's *Lives*, the emphasis is on the need for control; the passions are dangerous forces, necessary perhaps when the subject is a young man, but with little or no role in the life of a mature statesman. Hence, where the Platonic terminology of 'spirit' is used, it is usually of spirit out of control, rarely spirit acting in consort with virtue. The reason for this difference in emphasis must, partly at least, be one of literary context. The anti-Stoic nature of the *On moral virtue* makes Plutarch disposed to argue against the Stoic doctrine of *apatheia*, which states that all emotions are to be avoided.[12] In the *Lives*, Plutarch's attitude to the passions is in fact closer to the Stoic position.

Thirdly, the *On moral virtue* demonstrates the link in Plutarch's thought between failure to control the passions and deficient education, a prominent theme in the *Lives* (e.g. *Solon* 21. 2). The thought is Platonic; education is necessary to train the 'spirited' part of the soul (τὸ θυμοειδές) to be obedient to reason. Much of Books Two and Three of the *Republic* are spent in a discussion of the appropriate moral education for the imagined defence force of Plato's state, men who are characterized by their 'spirited' nature (374d–417b).[13] But the great emphasis on education is Plutarch's own, an emphasis which reflects the important role which *paideia* (education, culture) plays in the way Greeks defined themselves in the second century AD. For Plutarch, this emphasis is especially apparent where Roman heroes are concerned: education

[12] On Plutarch and Stoic *apatheia*, see Babut (1969b), 319–33, and Spanneut (1994), 4704–7.

[13] On Platonic conceptions of education, see Gill (1985); cf. also *Rep.* 441e–444a; 548b–c; 549a–b; 606a. In *Cic.* 32. 7, in criticizing Cicero for dejection in exile, which is presented as a failure of his philosophic principles, Plutarch says that 'public opinion (δόξα) has great power to wash away reason, like a dye, from the soul': a clear reference to Plato's comparison of *education* to dye in *Rep.* 429b–430b: see Moles (1988), 180–1. The presentation of Cicero's depression in Platonic terms underlines his failure to live up to his philosophic ideals, a theme of the *Cicero* (on which, see Swain 1990c, 194–7). For the metaphor, cf. *Lyk.-Num.* 4. 9.

(παιδεία) is for him, as for other writers of this period such as Dion of Prousa (e.g. *Or.* 32. 3; 48. 8) and Ailios Aristeides (e.g. *Panath.* 225–31), a particularly Greek phenomenon.[14] For Plutarch, it seems to involve knowledge of the Greek language and reading of the Greek classics. Greek subjects, then, are generally assumed to have had the benefit of a good Greek education; where Plutarch does enlarge on the education of a Greek figure,[15] he shows little interest in its actual effects. There is much more interest, as Christopher Pelling and Simon Swain have so well demonstrated, in the extent to which Romans acquired Greek education or culture.[16] Where Romans are concerned, levels of Greek education are used as an explanation for successes and failures to assert reason over the passions: for example, Lucullus' success in controlling his love of honour (*Luc.* 1. 5–6) and Cicero's failure (*Cic.* 32. 5–7). A Roman's attitude to Greek education is also used as an item of moral evaluation in its own right (e.g. *Cato Major* 23. 1–3).[17] This is seen particularly well in the *Coriolanus* and *Marius*, as later chapters will demonstrate.

For Plutarch education, and the resultant ability to control the passions, brings to the individual that broad set of virtues which de Romilly has described as *douceur*.[18] This loose grouping of qualities is expressed by a number of words, the most common of which are 'gentleness' or 'calmness' (πραότης) and 'humanity' (φιλανθρωπία). The general idea of the former is basically 'self-restraint', that is, the control of passions (cf. *Cor.* 21. 1); it carries with it the ideas variously of calmness, temperance (σωφροσύνη), forbearance, the use of legal as opposed to violent measures.[19] The meaning of φιλανθρωπία for Plutarch is the quality of kindness and compassion for other members of humanity which is appropriate to a cultured state or man; this implies the benefit of Greek *paideia* (*Flam.* 5. 6–7), and, for a society, the existence of Greek institutions (*Pyrrh.* 1. 4; *Phil.* 8. 1). In particular it carries the sense of

---

[14] The self-conscious display of Hellenic literary culture is a notable feature of the second century: cf. Reardon (1971), 3–11; Bowie (1991); Frézouls (1991), 143–5; Anderson (1993), *pass.*

[15] Cf. the central place of Greek philosophical education in Plutarch's Lykourgan Sparta (e.g. 14. 1), itself a 'city practising philosophy' (*Lyk.* 31. 3: πόλις φιλοσοφοῦσα): see Schneeweiss (1979).

[16] At least for those who lived after the sack of Syracuse, when Plutarch considered Hellenic influence to have properly begun: see above, Ch. 2, n. 41.

[17] On education in the *Lives*, see Pelling (1989); Swain (1989a), 62–6; (1990b): partly summarized in id. (1996a), 140–4.

[18] de Romilly (1979), esp. 275–307.

[19] Martin (1960). See also, on πραότης in the *Per.*, Stadter (1975), 81–5. I have followed Ziegler's text in printing πραότης (but see below, n. 62); Nikolaidis (1980) argues rather for the orthography πραότης.

affability, kindness, and generosity.[20] Very often these two qualities are linked by the occurrence of the two terms or their equivalents together.[21] The quality of *douceur* is often reflected in physical appearance, just as are its opposites, harshness and anger.[22] This is one of the areas of human activity in which Plutarch shows most interest, and which he judges most obviously from a moral point of view; it is a value which not only dominates his view of the heroes of the *Lives*, but is also evident in his own *persona* throughout the *Moralia*.[23]

1. REASON AND PASSION IN CONFLICT

In fact, the discourse of reason and passion is more pervasive in the *Lives* than even this analysis makes clear. The contrast between reason and passion is clearly important for the *Life of Antony*. Antony abandons his conciliatory stance with Caesar's murderers because of ambition, the most common passion in the *Lives* : 'But from these reasonings (λογισμῶν) he was soon shaken by the glory he got from the mobs (ἡ παρὰ τῶν ὄχλων δόξα), hoping to be the unchallenged first man, once Brutus had been removed' (*Ant*. 14. 5). Later it is his passionate love (ἔρως) for Kleopatra which ruins him:

(36. 1) Εὕδουσα δ' ἡ δεινὴ συμφορὰ χρόνον πολύν, ὁ Κλεοπάτρας ἔρως, δοκῶν κατευνάσθαι καὶ κατακεκηλῆσθαι τοῖς βελτίοσι λογισμοῖς, αὖθις ἀνέλαμπε καὶ ἀνεθάρρει Συρίᾳ πλησιάζοντος αὐτοῦ. (36. 2) καὶ τέλος, ὥσπερ φησὶν ὁ Πλάτων τὸ δυσπειθὲς καὶ ἀκόλαστον τῆς ψυχῆς ὑποζύγιον, ἀπολακτίσας τὰ καλὰ καὶ σωτήρια πάντα, Καπίτωνα Φοντήιον ἔπεμψεν ἄξοντα Κλεοπάτραν εἰς Συρίαν.

(36. 1) That awful curse, his love for Kleopatra, slept for a long time, apparently lulled and charmed by his better reasonings, but then it flared up and regained its confidence as he was approaching Syria. (36. 2) Finally, like the disobedient and stubborn beast of the soul, as Plato puts it, having kicked away all the fine plans which would bring him salvation, he sent Fonteius Capito to bring Kleopatra to Syria. (*Ant*. 36. 1–2)

This passage uses Platonic terminology, and in fact makes specific mention of Plato as the source of the image of passion as an animal. The reference is surely to a passage of Plato's *Phaidros* (253c–254e),[24] where

[20] Martin (1961).
[21] e.g. *Cato Min*. 23. 1; *Arist*. 23. 1.
[22] *Douceur*: *Per*. 5. 1; *Fab*. 17. 7; *Gracchi* 2. 2; *Phil*. 20. 3; *Pomp*. 2. 1; *De Cohib. Ira* 455b. Harshness: *Mar*. 2. 1.   [23] Cf. de Romilly (1988b).
[24] Cf. *Rep*. 588e–591d for the passions as a beast which may, in good men, be lulled (591b).

the attempt of reason to control the irrational part of the soul is compared to a charioteer's attempt to control a disobedient horse (cf. 255e–256a), a passage which Plutarch evidently knew well, judging from his references to it elsewhere.[25] His passion for her ruins his preparations for his Parthian campaign, as he is eager to return to spend the winter with her; he was, Plutarch tells us, 'not master of his own reasonings (οὐκ ὄντα τῶν ἑαυτοῦ λογισμῶν), but as though under the influence of drugs or sorcery' (37. 6). In the campaign which follows, Antony in fact performs well and regains some of his moral stature; notably he asserts reason over passion after the desertion of his Armenian ally Artavasdes:

ἅπαντες οὖν ὀργῇ παρώξυνον ἐπὶ τὴν τιμωρίαν τοῦ Ἀρμενίου τὸν Ἀντώνιον. ὁ δὲ λογισμῷ χρησάμενος, οὔτ' ἐμέμψατο τὴν προδοσίαν οὔτ' ἀφεῖλε τῆς συνήθους φιλοφροσύνης καὶ τιμῆς πρὸς αὐτόν, ἀσθενὴς τῷ στρατῷ καὶ ἄπορος γεγονώς.

Now everyone in anger urged Antony to take revenge on the Armenian. But he employed reason, and neither blamed him for his treachery, nor withdrew his usual friendliness and respect for him, because he himself had become weak in his forces, and was without resources. (*Ant.* 50. 5)

There are numerous other parallel passages; the question of whether, in the face of disturbing circumstances, a man was able to retain his reason (λογισμοί) or was overwhelmed by passion (πάθος) is an important moral indicator for Plutarch. For example, one of the few points at which the psychology of Julius Caesar is probed is at the crossing of the Rubicon; here the discussion is framed once again in the discourse of reason and passions.[26] Clearly Plutarch regarded the crossing of the Rubicon as a vital moment. As he neared the Rubicon 'reasoning (λογισμός)', as Plutarch puts it, 'came to him even more as he approached the terrible event and was agitated by the magnitude of his ventures'. He slows down and eventually halts: 'He was greatly divided within himself (πολλὰ μὲν αὐτὸς ἐν ἑαυτῷ διήνεγκε), in silence

[25] *Ant.* 36. 1–2; *De Virt. Moral.* 445b–c; *De Gen. Soc.* 588f; *Plat. Quaest.* 1008c–d; 1009b; cf. *Galba* 6. 4; *De Tuenda Sanit.* 125b; *De Cohib. Ira* 453c. The metaphor of the horse to represent the passions is a common one in Plutarch: cf. *De Aud.* 31d; *Prof. in Virt.* 83a–b; *De Virt. Moral.* 442d; and possibly *De Cohib. Ira* 459b. Cf. Fuhrmann (1964), 141–3; Opsomer (1994), 46–7. Plutarch's readers could be expected to understand the allusion given the high degree of knowledge of the *Phaidros* (Trapp 1990) and of Plato in general (De Lacy 1974) discernible in many writers of this period. The *Phaidros* is Plutarch's model for *Amat.* to which he makes direct allusions in 749a; 751d–e; 764a (Brenk 1995a), and for *De Defect. Orac.* 419a–e (Dušanić 1996). Within the *Demetr.-Ant.* Plutarch also refers to Plato explicitly at *Demetr.* 1. 7; 32. 8; *Ant.* 29. 1.

[26] Significantly Plutarch on two occasions calls Caesar's epilepsy (cf. Benediktson 1994) a πάθος (17. 2 and 53. 6), an emphasis not present in Suetonius (*Div. Jul.* 45. 1) or Appian (*BC* 2. 16. 110).

changing his resolution back and forth, and his purpose then suffered change after change' (32. 6). He adds up (ἀναλογιζόμενος) the evils the crossing would cause for all mankind, and how greatly these evils would augment his fame (32. 7). The invasion of Italy is here presented as an immoral act done through desire for glory; Caesar's uncertainty about what he is about to do, recorded also in Suetonius and Lucan and perhaps originating from a source common to all three,[27] is interpreted by Plutarch as a struggle between his reason and his desires or passions; a struggle of the kind envisaged in *On moral virtue* 446f–448c. The stress is not on what Caesar's motives were, but on the fact of his hesitation and disquiet which reveals his inner moral struggle. Compare the uneasiness of Pyrrhos at the prospect of invading Italy (*Pyrrh.* 14. 14): although he knew 'how much happiness he was leaving behind' (ὅσην ἀπέλειπεν εὐδαιμονίαν), he was unable to abandon his plans. For Pyrrhos, as for Caesar, the passion of love of honour (φιλοτιμία) overrules reason.[28] This negative view is confirmed in the following sentence (32. 8) when Plutarch, as often in other Lives, applies the terms of Platonic moral philosophy to Caesar's action: 'Finally, with a certain passion (μετὰ θυμοῦ τινος), as though giving himself up from reasoning to the future (ἀφεὶς ἑαυτὸν ἐκ τοῦ λογισμοῦ πρὸς τὸ μέλλον) . . . he rushed to cross the river . . .' Caesar's passions get the better of his reason—a damning statement in Plutarch's eyes.[29]

Λογισμοί must often be translated 'plans', but it always carries with it connotations of reason and reasoned behaviour.[30] In the *Artaxerxes*, Kyros' mercenary commander, Klearchos, is criticized for failing to engage the enemy's main force at Kounaxa: 'He was like one who, through fear of the present, casts off his reasoned plans for the success of all (τοὺς περὶ τῶν ὅλων λογισμοὺς) and abandoned the purpose of the expedition' (*Art.* 8. 4). There is a close parallel with the criticism of

[27] *Div. Jul.* 31–3; Lucan, *BC* 1. 185–203. See Tucker (1988).

[28] On the rarity of such scenes of hesitation in Plutarch, see Frazier (1995), 151–4.

[29] Plutarch goes on to report a dream of incestuous intercourse with his mother on the night before the crossing (32. 9). Plutarch has moved this episode from the earlier position it occupied in his source, probably Oppius (cf. Suet. *Div. Jul.* 7. 2; Dio Cassius 37. 52. 2), and, more significantly, avoided mentioning the favourable interpretation which Suetonius gives it (conquest of the world); for Plutarch, as is often his practice elsewhere with dreams and oracles, this dream is used not to predict events but to illuminate psychology and character: Caesar's self-doubt at invading his country erupts in this disturbing dream in which he invades another sort of forbidden territory. It underlines the extent of his ambition for power, and his moral disquiet. See Brenk (1975), 346; (1977), 225–7. Perhaps the dream is also suggestive of his coming murder: cf. *Dion* 55. 1–4.

[30] e.g. *Cato Min.* 55. 4; 68. 6. Occasionally only the translation 'plans' seems appropriate: e.g. *Demetr.* 44. 7. On the paradox of *Cor.* 34. 3, see below, p. 215.

Timoleon for falling into despair because of popular disapproval of the assassination of his brother, the tyrant Timophanes:

Οὕτως αἱ κρίσεις, ἂν μὴ βεβαιότητα καὶ ῥώμην ἐκ λόγου καὶ φιλοσοφίας προσλάβωσιν, ἐπὶ τὰς πράξεις σείονται καὶ παραφέρονται, ῥᾳδίως ὑπὸ τῶν τυχόντων ἐπαίνων καὶ ψόγων ἐκκρουόμεναι τῶν οἰκείων λογισμῶν.

In this way unless a man's decisions gain additional firmness and strength from reason and philosophy, they are shaken and swept away when it comes to deeds, being easily forced by casual praises and blame from his own reasoned plans. (*Tim.* 6. 1)[31]

Standing by one's plans is a mark of virtue and abandoning them a mark of moral weakness. Pompey, for example (*Pomp.* 61. 4), was swayed from his own λογισμοί in the war with Caesar—a weakness for which he is roundly criticized in the *synkrisis* (*Ages.-Pomp.* 4. 3–11);[32] the prime meaning here of λογισμοί is 'plans', but the full context makes clear that there is an underlying antithesis between reason and passion (cf. *Pomp.* 67. 7; *Caes.* 33. 6):

οὐ γὰρ ἦν παῦσαι τὸν φόβον οὐδ' εἴασέ τις χρῆσθαι τοῖς ἑαυτοῦ λογισμοῖς Πομπήϊον, ἀλλ' ᾧ τις ἐνετύγχανε πάθει, φοβηθεὶς ἢ λυπηθεὶς ἢ διαπορήσας, τούτου φέρων ἐκεῖνον ἀνεπίμπλη.

For it was not possible to check the general fear, and no-one allowed Pompey to use his own reasoned plans, but whatever passion anyone fell in with—fear, distress, despair—he would bring it and infect Pompey with it. (*Pomp.* 61. 4)

This sort of expression is particularly common in the *Perikles–Fabius*, where the calm (πρᾳότης) with which the two statesmen resist the attacks of their opponents is a particular theme. Thus when Perikles disregards the distress of the people at the invasion of Attike and the resulting attacks on him by demagogues, he is said to have 'used his own reasoned plans' (λογισμοί) and refrained from fighting (33. 6). In the *Fabius*, the report of the defeat at the Trebia in 218 BC caused such consternation that 'reasoned plans (λογισμοί) could not stand firm or endure in the face of such great shock' (*Fab.* 3. 6). Hannibal tries unsuccessfully to force Fabius to fight, 'wishing to force him from his reasoned plans concerning safety' (5. 4). Fabius, despite the discontent of

---

[31] Cf. *Mar.* 28. 2 (quoted on pp. 118–19). Cf. *Caes.* 66. 3, where the passion caused by great events banishes Cassius' supposedly (cf. Alfinito 1992) Epicurean principles.

[32] In *Ages.-Pomp.* 4. 8 Agesilaos is successful because, unlike Pompey, he followed his own 'best reasonings' (τοῖς ἀρίστοις ὡς ἐβούλετο λογισμοῖς).

his troops and the attacks of his Master of the Horse, Minucius, in a passage obviously parallel to *Per.* 33, claims that he would seem an even greater coward 'if through fear of jests and abuse I were to be shaken from my own reasoned plans' (5. 7). Aemilius Paullus does engage Hannibal at Cannae, with predictable results. His last words, though, are to ask Cornelius Lentulus to report (16. 8) that 'he remained in his own reasoned plans to the end'. In 19. 3 Fabius, despite the very different and aggressive tactics of Marcellus, is said to cling to his first reasoned plans. Finally, in the comparison to the *Perikles–Fabius*, the magnitude of Rome's difficulties in the time of Fabius is said to reveal him to be 'strong in his resolution . . . and a great man, who was not confused nor did he abandon his own reasoned plans' (*Per.-Fab.* 1. 5).

Passions, then, must be controlled by reason. Plutarch is particularly concerned to examine his heroes' conduct in this respect in two circumstances. The first is at the death of a relative.[33] The second is in the heat of battle. We have already noted the disapproval which Plutarch expressed for Kyros' rashness in battle. In the *Life of Pelopidas*, Plutarch expresses this disapproval in terms drawn more explicitly from the discourse of reason and the passions (*Pel.* 32. 9):[34]

ὡς δ' εἶδεν . . . οὐ κατέσχε τῷ λογισμῷ τὴν ὀργήν, ἀλλὰ πρὸς τὴν βλέψιν ἀναφλεχθείς, καὶ τῷ θυμῷ παραδοὺς τὸ σῶμα καὶ τὴν ἡγεμονίαν τῆς πράξεως, πολὺ πρὸ τῶν ἄλλων ἐξαλλόμενος ἐφέρετο, βοῶν καὶ προκαλούμενος τὸν τύραννον.

When Pelopidas saw him [Alexander of Pherai] . . . he could not hold his anger back by reason, but inflamed at the sight and handing over his body and his leadership of the enterprise to his spirit, he jumped out far in front of the others and rushed forward, shouting and challenging the tyrant.

It is under the pressure of such potentially disturbing circumstances that a man's true virtue can be seen; this may be one of the reasons why it suited so much more Plutarch's conception of virtue to examine the lives of statesmen rather than of poets or philosophers.[35]

---

[33] e.g. *Sol.* 7. 5–6; *Per.* 36. 7–9; *Brut.* 15. 5–9; *Aem.* 36. 1–9; *Aem.-Tim.* 2. 10. Cf. Plato, *Rep.* 387d–388a; 603e–604d.
[34] Cf. *Pel.-Marc.* 3. 6–8; *Lys.–Sulla* 4. 3–5; *Phok.* 6. 2; *Phil.-Flam.* 1. 7; cf. Arrian, *Anab.* 6. 13. 4.
[35] See above, p. 66.

2. AMBITION AND ANGER

Of all the passions which the hero must control, that of ambition receives the most consistent attention.[36] Ambition, for Plutarch, is an ambiguous quality. The concept is expressed by a number of related words and their cognates, such as 'love of honour' or 'status' (φιλοτιμία), the most common; also 'love of victory' (φιλονικία) and 'love of coming first' (τὸ φιλόπρωτον). In a more negative sense, Plutarch uses words which carry a stronger critical flavour, such as 'love of strife' (φιλονεικία), 'love of glory' (φιλοδοξία), or even 'madness for glory' (δοξομανία) and 'boastfulness' (μεγαλαυχία). The ambiguity of this set of concepts is seen most clearly in the ambiguity over the words 'love of victory' (φιλονικία) and the more negative 'love of strife' (φιλονεικία).[37] It is unclear whether these two were considered different words in Plutarch's time, and what the orthographic conventions were. The manuscripts of Plutarch, as of other writers, seem to use these two words as synonyms; as early as the third century BC, ει and ι were being pronounced the same.[38] It is therefore often unclear whether Plutarch intends associations with victory or, more negatively, with strife. The ambiguity may be deliberate.

Plato saw love of honour as arising from the 'spirited' part of the soul, that part which, though irrational, can be trained by the rational to act in consort with it: love of honour, then, is both a necessary spur to action, and a dangerous passion which must be strictly controlled.[39] It is characteristic of the 'spirited' (θυμοειδής) man (*Rep.* 548c),[40] and of the

---

[36] On φιλοτιμία in Plutarch, cf. Wardman (1955), 105–7; (1974), 115–24; Bucher-Isler (1972), 12–13, 31, 41, 58–9; Frazier (1988a). Cf. also Walsh (1992), 219–20, on its ambiguous moral status.

[37] Often φιλον[ε]ικία and φιλοτιμία occur together: e.g. *Fab.* 25. 3; *Aem.* 22. 4; *De Vit. Pud.* 532d; cf. Pelling (1996), p. xlix. Unusually in *Phil.* 3. 1 and *Phil.-Flam.* 1. 4 φιλον[ε]ικία is contrasted with a less reprehensible φιλοτιμία.

[38] Cf. Allen (1987), 66. Aulus Gellius (*NA* 7. 8. 1) has a pun on -νικ-/-νεικ-. Associations with νίκη are apparent in Classical Attic writers (but cf. Xen. *Lac. Pol.* 4. 1–6). By Plutarch's time, however, associations with νεῖκος are common, often displacing the earlier νίκη associations (cf. Schmidt 1882, i. 386–91). This is certainly the case in *Ages.* 5. 5 where the necessity for νεῖκος and ἔρις in the universe is used as an analogical justification for the introduction of τὸ φιλότιμον καὶ φιλόν[ε]ικον into Sparta. *Phil.* 17. 7 is similar. See Adam (1902), ii. 343; Nikolaidis (1980). It may be that, as Pelling (1997c), 130–1, argues, there was in Plutarch's time only one word—probably to be spelt φιλονικία—which was able to draw on either or both senses. Ziegler opts to retain both words (and to print, e.g. both ἀνδρεία and ἀνδρία). I disagree with Ziegler's choice at *Alk.* 21. 6; *Per.* 31. 1; *Cam.* 40. 1; *Ages.* 5. 5; *Ages.-Pomp.* 1. 7; *Phil.* 3. 1; *Phil.-Flam.* 1. 4; *Quaest. Conv.* 724b.

[39] Similarly in Aristotle: e.g. *NE* 1107b21–1108a2 and 1125b1–25.

[40] Plutarch takes up this terminology: e.g. *Cor.* 15. 4 (see pp. 210–11); *Alex.* 26. 14.

state which places status and competition as the highest goal, of which Sparta was for him the archetype (545a). In Greek society of Plutarch's own time, ambition seems also to have had an ambiguous status; in contemporary honorific inscriptions, 'love of honour' and related terms such as 'love of glory' (φιλοδοξία), occur frequently in a positive sense;[41] but Dion of Prousa (*Or.* 4, 16–32) is able to attack the 'the lover of honour' (τὸν φιλότιμον).

For Plutarch, too, love of honour is an ambiguous quality. He does on occasion recognize its positive aspect in providing a motivation for virtuous action, especially where the young are concerned.[42] It is viewed as a necessary psychological force and can carry a positive or neutral moral value, as in the cases of Themistokles and Theseus who are inspired by the achievements of predecessors.[43] Like Plato, Plutarch sees it as a special feature of the Spartan state and of Spartan education;[44] it is a key characteristic of Agesilaos and Lysander.[45] Most often ambition is seen as a negative force; when out of control it is destructive for both the individual and society.[46] In the prologue to the *Agis/Kleomenes–Gracchi*, where Plutarch expounds the benefits of love of honour for the young (*Ag./Kleom.* 1. 1–2. 8), he also points out the dangers of excessive political ambition, when men 'refuse to regard what is honourable as glorious, but consider that what is glorious is good' (2. 3).[47] At the start of the *Agesilaos* Plutarch discusses the claim that, just as strife and rivalry (νεῖκος . . . ἔριν) are necessary principles in the cosmos, so, in a state, love of honour and strife (τὸ φιλότιμον καὶ φιλόνεικον) is a necessary incentive to virtue (ὑπέκκαυμα τῆς ἀρετῆς). But, he concludes, excessive love of strife is 'troublesome for states and carries many dangers' (*Ages.* 5. 5–7). The two sides of ambition are well demonstrated in the narrative which follows. Agesilaos' rivalry with Lysander nearly

---

[41] Frézouls (1991), 141.

[42] e.g. *De Virt. Moral.* 451b–452d; *Cor.* 4. 1–2. Love of honour is, conversely, out of place for the old: *Luc.* 38. 3; *Marc.* 28. 6, *Flam.* 20. 1–2; *Mar.* 2. 4; 34. 6; 45. 10–12. Plutarch criticizes overambition in older politicians in *An Seni* 785c–d; 791c; 793d; 794a.

[43] See above, p. 51. Cf. *Pel.* 31. 6, where Pelopidas is said to be inspired by a desire for glory to attempt the liberation of the Greeks of Thessaly from Alexander of Pherai. He is also, however, motivated by anger (31. 5), which leads him to die recklessly on the field (32. 9–11).   [44] *Lys.* 2. 2–4; cf. *Ag./Kleom.* 23(2). 3–5; *De Virt. Moral.* 452d.

[45] e.g. *Ages.* 2. 3; 7. 4; 8. 5; *Lys.* 2. 4; 19. 1–2; 23. 3, 7. See also pp. 177–80 and 194.

[46] It is described in *Kim.* 17. 9 as 'predominant of all passions' (πάντων ἐπικρατοῦσα τῶν παθῶν). Love of honour particularly effects 'vigorous and youthful (or impetuous: νεανικαῖς) characters' in *Praec. Ger.* 819f.

[47] Glory is merely 'as it were an image of virtue' (τῆς ἀρετῆς ὥσπερ εἰδώλῳ), like the cloud which Ixion tried to embrace, thinking it was Hera (*Ag./Kleom.* 1. 1–2). Ixion is a symbol of excessive love of honour also in Dion of Prousa, *Or.* 4. 123, 130–1.

proves disastrous (*Ages.* 7. 1–8. 7).⁴⁸ But his glorious and successful expedition to Asia is undertaken out of a desire for glory (9. 2), and his resistance of sexual temptation in Asia—for Plutarch a highly commendable act—is also put down to his love of victory (φιλονικία), which causes him to fight 'like a young man' (νεανικῶς) against his desires (11. 6). However, it is his rivalry with Thebes which finally does bring disaster on his city (23. 11–24. 3; 28. 1–8).

Alexander and Caesar, whose Lives form a single Plutarchan book, are paradigms of the benefits and dangers of ambition. Alexander's character is (4. 7) specifically 'spirited' (θυμοειδής). It is no surprise, then, that we find in him (4. 8) a 'love of honour' (φιλοτιμία), which is illustrated by a series of anecdotes about his precocious behaviour in childhood (e.g. 4. 8–9. 4). One such anecdote is his taming of the horse Boukephalas, who is described (6. 6) as being, like him, 'full of spirit' (πληρούμενον θυμοῦ). This anecdote leads into a discussion of Alexander's own education. Philip saw, Plutarch tells us, 'that Alexander's nature (φύσιν) was difficult to defeat (δυσνίκητον), since he strove against compulsion, but was easily led by reason (λόγου) to duty'. So he summoned Aristotle to be Alexander's teacher, because he understood that Alexander's training was 'as Sophokles says, *a task requiring many bits and rudders*' (7. 1–2). The use of equestrian imagery makes clear the link between Boukephalas' 'spirited' nature, and its need for proper education, and that of Alexander. It also encourages the reader to see Alexander's education in terms of the training of the 'spirited horse' in Plato's *Phaidros* which seems to have influenced Plutarch so much (253c–254e).⁴⁹ Alexander's good education channels his ambition into an honourable course: it is his ambitious and spirited nature which propels him to his great conquests and to pursue his civilizing mission.⁵⁰ 'For fortune (τύχη)', Plutarch tells us, 'yielding to his onsets, was making his purpose strong and the spirited part of his soul (τὸ θυμοειδὲς) was making his love of victory (τὴν φιλονικίαν) invincible even in impossible tasks, so that it subdued not only enemies but also times and places' (26. 14).

But Alexander's spirited and ambitious nature is never fully controlled. This is apparent early on when he sacks Thebes, an act which is put down (13. 2) to 'spirit' (θυμός). In particular, his ambition causes

---

⁴⁸ Cf. the parallel in Pompey's rivalry with Metellus and Lucullus in the paired life: *Pomp.* 29. 1–7; 30. 3–31. 13, on which, see Hillman (1994), 273–7.

⁴⁹ See above, pp. 78–9.

⁵⁰ For Alexander's devotion to Greek *paideia* and his civilizing mission in the Life, see above, Ch. 2, n. 47.

Alexander to turn against his friends. As Plutarch puts it 'the many accusations brought before him made him thoroughly harsh . . . and most of all, when he was criticized himself, he lost his reason (ἐξίστατο τοῦ φρονεῖν) and was cruel and inexorable, because he had become more fond of glory (δόξαν) than of life or kingship (42. 3–4)'. It is his ambitious and spirited nature which leads him to kill his friend Kleitos (51. 10), to degenerate into tyranny at the end of his life, and to have delusions of divinity.[51] Ambition, then, can lead to great deeds, but also to disaster.

The ambiguous status of ambition is seen also in the career of Julius Caesar. Caesar's craving for power is introduced early in the Life (3. 2–3; 4. 7–8; 5. 8–9; 7. 1–4, especially 7. 2) and forms a leitmotif which runs throughout. In illustration of his ambition, Plutarch quotes Caesar's comments on passing through a small Gallic town, that he would rather be first (πρῶτος) there than second in Rome (11. 3–4).[52] Significantly, he is inspired to emulate the deeds of Alexander, the protagonist of the paired Life (11. 5–6).[53] It is his ambition which lies behind his performance in Gaul (17. 2; 22. 6; 23. 2), and which provides the motivation for his plans, building-works, and achievements after he had attained supreme power.[54] 'His many successes', Plutarch tells us, 'did not turn his natural spirit of enterprise and love of honour (τὸ φύσει μεγαλουργὸν αὐτοῦ καὶ φιλότιμον) to the enjoyment of his achievements, but were fuel (ὑπέκκαυμα) and courage for what was to come and instilled in him plans for greater achievements and a love of new glory (καινῆς ἔρωτα δόξης), as though he had used up what was at hand. This passion (πάθος) was none other than rivalry (ζῆλος) with himself as with someone else, and a sort of competition (literally, love of victory/strife: φιλονικία) on behalf of what was to come against what had been achieved' (58. 4–5). But it is this same trait, ambition, which motivates his striving for supreme power and leads to his downfall. Notably the phrase 'love of new glory' is echoed a little later in the 'love of kingship' (60. 1: ὁ τῆς βασιλείας ἔρως), which Plutarch sees as the cause of Caesar's eventual unpopularity and assassination.[55] The theme of Caesar's ambition is

[51] On the moral decline of Plutarch's Alexander and Caesar, see Harris (1970), 193–7.

[52] This anecdote is noted by no other author but may, like the following anecdote, derive from Oppius: Townend (1987), esp. 338.

[53] The same motif is found in Suetonius (*Div. Jul.* 7. 1), and so probably derives from one of Plutarch's sources.

[54] Significantly also Caesar's acts of largesse to the *plebs* are called φιλοτιμίαι (6. 1; 6. 3; cf. 5. 9). On φιλοτιμίαι as acts of benefaction, cf. Frazier (1988a), 114–16 and 125–6.

[55] For ἔρως τῆς δόξης in a disparaging sense, cf. Lucian, *Peregrinus* 1 and 38 (μόνος οὗτος ὁ ἔρως ἄφυκτος).

stated most clearly towards the end of the Life when Plutarch briefly sums up his view of Caesar: '. . . of that domination and rule which he just about achieved after pursuing it all his life and through so many dangers, he enjoyed nothing but the name and the glory (δόξαν) which awoke the citizens' envy' (69. 1). On one level, then, Caesar stands as a model for the delusion and false promise of glory.[56]

Anger is another of the passions which Plutarch considers most dangerous (e.g. *On brotherly love* 481b–c). For Plato, anger arises from the 'spirited' part of the soul and is one of its most characteristic traits; indeed, θυμός is often used by Plato to mean anger.[57] Although anger is often destructive and irrational, Plato concedes it a legitimate role in the soul of a virtuous man; there are times when reason demands that a man be angry, such as when he is unjustly ill-treated or when he must fight. At these times the spirit, in alliance with the reasoning part of the soul, may struggle against the appetitive (e.g. *Republic* 439e–441c). For Plato, then, 'spiritedness' and the anger to which it gives rise, are necessary qualities for those involved in warfare and essential for bravery (ἀνδρεία),[58] though they must always be tempered (*Rep.* 375b–c) by calmness or self-restraint (πραότης). Aristotle too is willing to concede that there are circumstances when it is right to get angry. He defines that quality in a man which leads him to use anger only at the right time as 'calmness' (πραότης), which he defines as 'a mean concerning anger' (μεσότης περὶ ὀργάς: *NE* 1125b26), the correct middle course between 'irascibility' (ὀργιλότης) and an excessively meek 'lack of anger' (ἀοργησία)—a term which Aristotle coined.[59]

In the *On moral virtue*, Plutarch admits the possibility in theory of just and reasonable anger (e.g. 448d). Significantly in this passage he uses the rarer word θυμός, with its Platonic associations. But elsewhere in his work, and especially in the *Lives*, anger (ὀργή) is for him almost always wrong, implying a loss of control of the passions; the correct middle course for him is the quality of 'lack of anger' (ἀοργησία): not a blameworthy inability to get angry, but a praiseworthy absence of the passion of anger. It is, as far as the passion of anger is concerned, identical with the broader 'calmness' (πραότης): the ability to keep one's passions in check, whatever the circumstances.[60] Plutarch actually wrote a work

---

[56] Cf. Steidle (1951), 13–24.
[57] For the link, cf. *Rep.* 439e: τὸ δὲ δὴ τοῦ θυμοῦ καὶ ᾧ θυμούμεθα . . .
[58] e.g. *Rep.* 375a; 410b–412a; 441e–442a.
[59] See Nikolaidis (1982); cf. also Galinski (1988), 328–38.
[60] Becchi (1990a) argues that Plutarch is not correcting the Aristotelian position, but

entitled *On lack of anger* (Περὶ ἀοργησίας), a dialogue in which he holds this quality out as the ideal, and which has many similarities with the Stoic Seneca's treatise *On anger*.[61] The subject is how to use reason to control destructive outbursts of anger. Plutarch uses here the Platonic terminology of θυμός, meaning both the spirited part of the soul and more specifically its tendency to anger, but sees its role as wholly negative. One of the speakers, Sulla (not the dictator), comments on the reduction he has noticed in his friend Fundanus' susceptibility to anger. His comments are couched in the familiar Plutarchan discourse of reason and the passions :

τὸ μὲν ἐξ ὑπαρχόντων δι' εὐφυΐαν ἀγαθῶν ἐπίδοσιν γεγονέναι τοσαύτην καὶ αὔξησιν οὐ πάνυ θαυμαστὸν ἡγοῦμαι· τὸ δὲ σφοδρὸν ἐκεῖνο καὶ διάπυρον πρὸς ὀργὴν ὁρῶντί μοι πρᾶον οὕτω καὶ χειρόηθες τῷ λογισμῷ γεγενημένον ἐπέρχεται πρὸς τὸν θυμὸν εἰπεῖν "ὢ πόποι, ἦ μάλα δὴ μαλακώτερος".

I do not consider it altogether surprising that the virtues which are yours because of your good nature have grown and increased so much. But when I see that your vehement and fiery inclination to anger has become so calm and obedient to reason, it occurs to me to say to your spirit: 'Goodness, how much softer you have become! [Iliad 22. 373]' (*De Cohib. Ira* 453a–b)[62]

Fundanus' soul, Sulla goes on, is like land which has been cultivated (κατειργασμένη), so that it has gained a 'smoothness and depth which are productive of deeds (ἐνεργὸν ἐπὶ τὰς πράξεις)'. He continues with a medical metaphor:

διὸ καὶ δῆλόν ἐστι οὐ παρακμῇ τινι δι' ἡλικίαν τὸ θυμοειδὲς οὐδ' αὐτομάτως ἀπομαραινόμενον, ἀλλ' ὑπὸ λόγων τινῶν χρηστῶν θεραπευόμενον.

Therefore, it is obvious that the spirited part of your soul is not fading away through any decay caused by age, nor of its own accord, but that it is being treated by some good reasons.[63] (*De Cohib. Ira* 453b)

Sulla asks Fundanus (453c) to explain what 'remedy' he used to make his spirit (τὸν θυμόν) 'so obedient to the rein and tender, so mild and

rather later peripatetic views which allowed anger a role in providing an impetus to the activity of the soul.

[61] The *De Cohib. Ira* was probably completed before any of the *Parallel Lives* were begun: see Jones (1966), 61–2. On this text, cf. Ingenkamp (1971), 14–26; Becchi (1990a).

[62] For passion, especially that of anger, linked to heat, see also *De Cohib. Ira* 457a; *An Seni* 788f; and the repeated association of Alexander's temperament with heat: see below, p. 187. I follow the Teubner text here in printing πραότης (see above, n. 19).

[63] The Greek λόγων carries connotations of both words, reasoned thoughts, and rationality; as Jan Opsomer pointed out to me, the contrast with αὐτομάτως, a term of distinct Epicurean flavour, is standard (e.g. *De Is. et Osir.* 369c; *De Pyth. Orac.* 398b; *De Defect. Orac.* 420b; 426d; 435e).

obedient to reason' (οὕτως εὐήνιον καὶ ἀπαλὸν καὶ τῷ λόγῳ πρᾷον καὶ ὑπήκοον)—probably an allusion to the famous passage of Plato's *Phaidros* (see above). Sulla, after a show of reluctance, explains (453d–454a) that the key is that people should remain under 'treatment' all their life (θεραπευομένους βιοῦν). Reason (λόγος) should not be used like a drug, which one takes only when one is ill, but like good food, which engenders, in the long term, an excellent 'state' (ἕξις) for those who have become habituated to it (οἷς ἂν γένηται συνήθης). For, Fundanus argues, once the spirit is roused it is difficult to subdue with reason; so we must take care to stock our soul well in advance with the precepts of philosophy. Even for the exercise of bravery, anger (θυμός, ὀργή) has no place (458d–e). As we shall see, the *Life of Coriolanus*, which can be seen as the practical counterpart to the theoretical *On lack of anger*, demonstrates what happens when anger is allowed free rein, unrestrained by reason or education.

3. THE METAPHORS OF HARMONY AND MIXING

Ambition and anger, then, are some of the commonest and most deadly passions of the *Lives*. Plutarch sees ambition as carrying particular moral dangers because it can cause rifts in society and destroy the harmony of the state, one of Plutarch's chief concerns both in the *Parallel Lives* and in his own *Political precepts* (e.g. 823f–825f), and also a preoccupation of the second century.[64] Plutarch places great value on the co-operation of statesmen,[65] and the harmony of all classes. For example, the most valuable result of Numa's wise and just methods was the harmony he established amongst all the citizens of Rome (*Lyk.-Num.* 4. 15). He is at his most outspoken when criticizing those whose personal ambition leads to a rivalry which is harmful for the state.[66] Plutarch was certainly aware of the realities of continual inter- and intra-city warfare in classical times, but he seems to have had as an ideal the harmony of the Greek world, thus reflecting the strong sense of cultural identity seen in the Hellenic world of the second century AD.[67] Harmony within the state

[64] On harmony in Plutarch, cf. Wardman (1974), 57–63. On harmony as a contemporary concern, see Jones (1971), 111–19; Sheppard (1984–6), 241–52.
[65] e.g. *Praec. Ger.* 809b–810a; 816a–817c; cf. *Them.* 11. 1; 12. 6–8; *Kim.* 17. 9.
[66] e.g. *Lys.* 23. 3; *Sulla* 4. 6; *Ages.* 8. 5–7; *Pomp.* 29. 4.
[67] *Them.* 6. 5; *Kim.* 19. 3–4; *Flam.* 11. 3–7; *Phil.-Flam.* 1. 2; *Ages.* 15. 2–4; cf. *Arat.* 24. 5–6 (on the Achaian League) and *De Pyth. Orac.* 401c–d. In *Kim.* 3. 1 and 18. 1 wars between Greek *poleis* are described as civil wars (ἐμφύλιαι στάσεις or ἐμφύλιοι πόλεμοι). For Plutarch's panhellenism, see also Aalders (1982), 18–19. The Panhellenic ideal had, of

meant the proper relationship not only of statesmen towards each other, but also of people and statesman. The best scenario seems to be where the people is submissive to its statesman, and he in turn governs mildly, but also firmly, resisting the attacks of demagogues.[68] For Plutarch, a good example of this firm rule was that of Perikles. After an early and uncharacteristic use of 'demagogic' methods to gain power (*Per.* 7–14),[69] Perikles adopts what Plutarch calls an aristocratic and kingly policy (15. 1: ἀριστοκρατικὴ καὶ βασιλικὴ πολιτεία; cf. 9. 1). Plutarch is here, as in many other Lives, less interested in forms of government than in the moral qualities of the ruler,[70] qualities in which Perikles excels, as is stated explicitly in what follows (15. 1–3).[71] In *Dem.* 14. 3–6 Plutarch likewise describes the firm rule of a statesman as 'aristocratic', a Platonic and Aristotelian usage referring to the rule of the best people, whatever the exact form of government.[72]

As well as harmony within the state, Plutarch places a high value on harmony within the soul of the individual. A passage which hints at the link between these two different levels of harmony, as well as illustrating the importance which Plutarch attaches to education as a means to control the passions, is *Numa* 3. 6–7:

(3. 6) ἦν δὲ πόλεως μὲν ὁ Νομᾶς ἐπιφανοῦς ἐν Σαβίνοις τῆς Κυριτῶν, ἀφ' ἧς καὶ Κυρίτας Ῥωμαῖοι σφᾶς αὐτοὺς ἅμα τοῖς ἀνακραθεῖσι Σαβίνοις προ-

course, been exploited from Classical times: e.g. Hdt. 8. 144. 2; Isok. *Paneg.* 81; *Philip* 127; cf. Dillery (1995), 41–98. For inter-*polis* war as στάσις, see Hdt. 8. 3. 1; Plato, *Rep.* 470b–471c. See also Walbank (1951), 51–4 (= 1985, 11–13).

[68] e.g. *Phok.* 2. 6–9; *Ag./Kleom.* 1. 3–4; 2. 5–6; *Per.* 2. 5. On Plutarch's views on political leadership, see Carrière (1977), 238–41; Aalders (1982), 28–36; De Blois (1992), 4600–11. *Num.* 20. 7–12 provides a picture of the ideal leadership, in which 'the power of a king is united with the insight of a philosopher': such a ruler is an example (παράδειγμα) of virtue, and the people submit to him without compulsion (cf. *Lyk.* 30. 4). The thought is Platonic (*Laws* 711d–712a; *Rep.* 473c–e; cf. Polyb. 12. 28. 2).

[69] On the demagogic period of Perikles' career, cf. Breebaart (1971); Stadter (1987), 258–60.

[70] Cf. Aalders (1982), 28–36. There is little real constitutional debate elsewhere in the literature of this period (e.g. the speeches on kingship by Dion of Prousa); the stress is on the moral character of the monarch: De Blois and Bons (1992), 172–3.

[71] An elaboration of Thucydides 2. 65. 6–9; cf. Stadter (1989), 90–1.

[72] e.g. Plato, *Rep.* 544e; *Menex.* 238c–d; Aristotle, *Pol.* 1293b30–1294a25. At *Rep.* 445d, Plato says that the constitution of the ideal state is to be labelled either 'kingship' or 'aristocracy' depending on how many men are in charge; it was of no importance to Plato whether one man ruled or, as is normally assumed in the *Rep.*, several men (540d; 587c–d). For Plutarch, furthermore, as for Aristotle (*Pol.* 1288b1–2), 'kingliness' (τὸ βασιλικόν) can refer primarily to *character* without any reference to constitutional position, e.g. *Num.* 20. 8–12; *Ag./Kleom.* 34(13). 3; 34(13). 9; 45(24). 3; *Sulla* 12. 11; *Pomp.* 2. 1; *Crass.* 2. 8 (reading βασιλικὴν with the codices: cf. Xen. *Oik.* 21. 10, ἤθους βασιλικοῦ); *Cato Min.* 9. 5 (reading βασιλικὸν with the codices).

σηγόρευσαν· . . . (3. 7) φύσει δ' εἰς πᾶσαν ἀρετὴν εὖ κεκραμένος τὸ ἦθος, ἔτι μᾶλλον αὐτὸν ἐξημέρωσε διὰ παιδείας καὶ κακοπαθείας καὶ φιλοσοφίας, οὐ μόνον τὰ λοιδορούμενα πάθη τῆς ψυχῆς ἀλλὰ καὶ τὴν εὐδοκιμοῦσαν ἐν τοῖς βαρβάροις βίαν καὶ πλεονεξίαν ἐκποδὼν ποιησάμενος, ἀνδρίαν δ' ἀληθῆ τὴν ὑπὸ λόγου τῶν ἐπιθυμιῶν ἐν αὐτῷ κάθειρξιν ἡγούμενος.

ἀνακραθεῖσι Auratus: ἀνακηρυχθεῖσι codd.: ἀναμειχθεῖσι Cobet

(3. 6) Numa came from a conspicuous Sabine city called Cures. It was from this city that the Romans derived one of their names for themselves and for the Sabines who had been mixed in: Quirites . . . (3. 7) By nature he was well-mixed in his character and he had softened himself even more through education, endurance of hardship, and philosophy, getting rid not only of the despised passions of the soul but also of the violence and greed which were in good repute among the barbarians, and counting true manliness to be the confinement within oneself of one's passions through the use of reason.

Here we see a properly functioning state, where harmony—or more specifically 'mixing'—works both within the soul of the leader and within the city. This emphasis on correct mixing is derived ultimately from Plato, whom Plutarch also follows in presenting the state as at some level the macrocosm of the human soul: an idea seen most clearly in Plato's tripartite division of both soul and state, which lies behind much of the discussion of the soul in the *Republic*.[73] Plutarch has also been influenced by Plato's *Timaios*, where the metaphors of mixing and musical harmony—blending together the rational and irrational—are used to describe the creation of both the world-soul and the human soul. Plutarch takes up this terminology of the 'mixing' and 'harmony' of the soul in his commentary *On the creation of the soul in the Timaios*, as he does also in the *On moral virtue*.[74] In the latter, Plutarch declares that, in the soul of a temperate man, 'the irrational is fitted and mixed (συγκέκραται) with reasoning, which is adorned with persuasion and amazing calmness' (*De Virt. Moral.* 446d); virtue is a mean between opposing passions, like a harmony of high and low notes (444e). In the *Lives* Plutarch frequently presents the proper 'mixing' (κρᾶσις) of the soul as an important determinant of good character; it functions as a moral index. Sometimes a man's character (ἦθος) is said simply to be 'mixed' or 'well-mixed',[75] or conversely 'unmixed' (ἄκρατος), a term of

[73] Especially 435ff. Cf. Neu (1971).
[74] e.g. *De Virt. Moral.* 440d; 441d–442a; 451d–f; *De Procr. An.* 1025a–c; 1026a–c. Jan Opsomer, whose advice I gratefully acknowledge, argues for the unity of Plutarch's (Platonic) thought in these two works (Opsomer 1994).
[75] e.g. *Tim.* 3. 5; *Dion* 52. 6; *Brut.* 1. 3.

moral criticism.⁷⁶ A man's character may even be compared to 'unmixed wine'.⁷⁷ Some of these passages present the proper mixing of the soul and its reverse as the result of education;⁷⁸ the thought is, once again, Platonic.⁷⁹ A state is also said to be well or badly mixed on the analogy of human character.⁸⁰ When Plutarch speaks, therefore, at *Kim*. 15. 12 of 'unmixed democracy' (ἄκρατος δημοκρατία), the tone is negative.⁸¹

Many of these features are seen together in a passage in the *Life of Pelopidas* (19. 1–5). The early Theban law-givers (19. 1), wishing to mollify their subjects' 'spirited and unmixed natures' (τὸ φύσει θυμοειδὲς αὐτῶν καὶ ἄκρατον), 'mixed in (ἀνεμείξαντο) the flute' and reared them to love the wrestling-ground, thus 'blending (συγκεραννύντες) the dispositions of the young men'. For this reason they honoured 'the daughter of Ares and Aphrodite' (that is, Harmony),⁸² because:

ὅπου τὸ μαχητικὸν καὶ πολεμικὸν μάλιστα τῷ μετέχοντι πειθοῦς καὶ χαρίτων ὁμιλεῖ καὶ σύνεστιν, εἰς τὴν ἐμμελεστάτην καὶ κοσμιωτάτην πολιτείαν δι' ἁρμονίας καθισταμένων ἁπάντων.

where the fighting and warlike quality are particularly associated and have to do with one who partakes of persuasiveness and charm, then all things in the city are brought into the most melodious and orderly state through harmony. (*Pel*. 19. 2)

A digression follows (19. 3–5) on the Theban Sacred Band, which is presented as a model for harmonious co-operation.⁸³

In fact, Plutarch's emphasis on the benefit of a 'well-mixed' character springs from his understanding of human physiology: the term is sometimes to be taken as referring to a physical mixing of elements, not to a metaphysical or metaphorical harmony of rational and irrational in the soul. Plutarch argues in the *On moral virtue* for the influence of the body on the irrational; the body may thus determine the dispositions of

---

⁷⁶ e.g. *Phok*. 6. 1; *Mar*. 2. 1; *Quomodo Adult*. 49e; *Con. Praec*. 142b; cf. *Cor*. 15. 4. It may be that when Plutarch uses the term ἄκρατος, he has in mind the associations both of ἀκρασία (lack of mixing) and of the much more common moral term ἀκρασία (lack of self-control: the opposite of ἐγκράτεια). ⁷⁷ e.g. *Cato Min*. 46. 1: οἶνον ἄκρατον.
⁷⁸ e.g. *Brut*. 1. 3; *Mar*. 2. 1; *Cor*. 15. 4.
⁷⁹ e.g. *Rep*. 412a; 441e–442a; 443d–444a; 549b; 591c–d. Cf. Gill (1985), 12–15; 21–4.
⁸⁰ e.g. *Aem*. 4. 4; *Lyk*. 7. 1; 7. 5; *Per*. 3. 2; cf. *Phil*. 8. 3; Cic. *Rep*. 2. 69. Note that the idea of the 'mixed constitution' is not prominent in Plutarch's political thought: Aalders (1968), 124–6; Carsana (1990), 47–55. It occurs as an ideal form of government (cf. Aristotle, *Pol*. 1273b37–8), but one confined to the distant past (e.g. at *Sol*. 18. 1; *Lyk*. 5. 11; 7. 1), or an unattained ideal (*Dion*. 53. 4).
⁸¹ Cf. Plato, *Rep*. 410d; 491e; 545a; Aristotle, *Pol*. 1296a2–3; 1312b35–6; but cf. 1273b37–8.
⁸² Cf. Hesiod, *Theog*. 933–7; 975–7.
⁸³ On *Pel*. 19, see also Wardman (1974), 59–61.

men and animals (450e–451b). Here he is following Platonic, Aristotelian, and Poseidonian thought,[84] but is also in line with contemporary thinking as seen in the humoral theories of Galen and the interest in physiognomics exemplified by Polemon of Laodikaia.[85] These humoural theories lie behind Plutarch's frequent use of medical metaphors to describe the activity of the good statesman, metaphors themselves related to the Platonic notion of the state as the macrocosm of a man.[86] The sickness within the state which needs the attention of the statesman/doctor is commonly division and disharmony;[87] this corresponds to the humoral disharmony which causes sickness in a human. The link in Plutarch's thought between harmony in the body and in human relationships is particularly clear at *On brotherly love* 478f–479b. Here the value of fellow-feeling (ὁμοφροσύνη) within a family is illustrated by comparison with the importance of the concord (ὁμόνοια and συμφωνία) of the elements in the body, which are said to engender 'the best and sweetest mixing and harmony' (τὴν ἀρίστην καὶ ἡδίστην κρᾶσιν ... καὶ ἁρμονίαν). Conversely, he argues that sickness is caused by disharmony in the body, which is described with words usually found in political contexts (πλεονεξία καὶ στάσις).[88]

Sometimes, then, the mixing of different elements within a man is to be taken as something physical. The mixing (κρᾶσις) of Alexander's body, which is said to be hot and fiery (πολύθερμος and πυρώδης), explicitly provides an explanation (*Alex*. 4. 5–7) for Alexander's character: he was prone to drink (ποτικός) and full of spirit (θυμοειδής).[89] At other times mixing is used in a more metaphorical sense to suggest the harmonious mixing of potentially opposite character-traits, another factor carrying a high moral charge. In *Phok*. 2. 6–9, for example, wise government is described as a good mixture of austerity (τὸ σεμνόν) and reasonableness (τὸ ἐπιεικές).[90] Here, as in many other examples, the

---

[84] e.g. Plato, *Tim*. 69b–71d; 88b; Aristotle, *Prior An*. 2. 27, 70b1–37; Poseidonios fr. 153 E–K (= Galen, *De Plac. Hipp. et Plat*. 5. 464 Kühn). See Babut (1969*a*), 54–62.

[85] On physiognomics, see Evans (1935; 1941; 1945; 1969); Barton (1991); Gleason (1995).

[86] e.g. *Sol.-Pub*. 3. 2; *Lyk*. 4. 4; *Kim.-Luc*. 2. 7; *Cam*. 9. 3; *Per*. 7. 7 (see Sansone 1988, 312); 15. 1; *Cato Min*. 20. 1; 47. 2; *Brut*. 55. 2; *Dion* 37. 7; *Dion.-Brut*. 2. 2; *Ages*. 30. 2; *Pomp*. 55. 4; *Ages.-Pomp*. 2. 3; *Marc*. 24. 2; *Caes*. 28. 6; *Ag./Kleom*. 31(10). 7; *Ag./Kleom.-Gracchi* 4. 3; cf. Fuhrmann (1964), 238–40; Quet (1979), 64; Boulogne (1996), 2775. The image goes back to Plato: cf. Dodds (1959), 327–8 (on *Gorgias* 503d5–505b12); Jouanna (1978), 82–91.

[87] e.g. *Cor*. 12. 5; *Phil*. 18. 2; *Praec. Ger*. 815a–b; 818b; 818d–e; 824a; 825d.

[88] On Plutarch's medical theories, cf. Tsekourakis (1989); Boulogne (1996). The qualitative link between the human soul and the state is one which recurs elsewhere in Plutarch's work, in particular in the *Galba-Otho*: e.g. *Galba* 1. 1–7; 6. 4. See Ash (1997).

[89] Cf. Sansone (1980).

[90] Cf. *Galba* 1. 3; *Arat*. 4. 1.

metaphor of musical harmony (ἐμμελής and related words) is combined with the notion of mixing (κρᾶσις).[91] For Plutarch the ideal character seems to be one that is a mixture of 'hard' and 'soft' elements. This is the way in which, as we shall see, Phokion is presented throughout his Life.[92] The proper subordination of the irrational to the rational is sometimes also described metaphorically in terms of mixing (De Virt. Moral. 446c–d). Many of these points are illustrated in De Virt. Moral. 451f, where the proper relationship of the rational and the irrational is illustrated by comparison with musical harmony and medicine, which aims at the proper 'mixture' of high and low, heat and cold.

4. SEX

A subject's sex-life, where it is dealt with, is fitted into the nexus of ideas associated with reason and passion.[93] In fact, however, Plutarch is generally uninterested in sex—that is, as far as concerns the subjects of his Lives. This is surprising. Sexuality has, since the work of Freud, been considered an essential component of a person's nature and therefore an essential theme of modern biography. Plutarch himself declares at the start of the Life of Alexander that anecdotes of the subject's 'off-duty' moments will be considered particularly useful in building up a picture of his character. Furthermore, Plutarch himself, in his non-biographical work, was profoundly interested in the valuation of sex, both within and outside marriage, both heterosexual and homosexual, and in relations between the sexes. This interest is revealed most clearly in his *Dialogue on love* (Ἐρωτικός) and his *Marriage advice* (Γαμικὰ παραγγέλματα).[94]

Comparison with Plutarch's younger Roman contemporary Suetonius is instructive. In narrating Julius Caesar's life, Suetonius records accusations that, while sojourning abroad during Sulla's dictatorship, Caesar became the homosexual partner of Nikomedes, king of Bithynia (*Div. Jul.* 2). Later on, in the analytical section of his *Divine Julius* (49. 1–52. 3), Suetonius discusses this and similar allegations concerning Caesar's sex-life at length. Plutarch, in contrast, does not

---

[91] e.g. *Pel.* 19. 2; *Brut.* 1. 3; *Galba* 1. 3; *De Vit. Pud.* 529a. The thought is once again Platonic; see the examples in n. 79 above, and in Dodds (1959), 260.

[92] See also *Sol.* 15. 1; *Cor.* 15. 4; *Nik.* 2. 4 (making a virtue out of Nikias' cowardice?).

[93] Self-control in the face of great sexual temptation is seen in this light in *De Virt. Moral.* 442e–f.

[94] On these texts, cf. Brenk (1988 and 1995a); Aguilar (1990–1); Foucault (1986), 193–210; Montano (1991); Patterson (1992); Goldhill (1995), 144–61.

mention it in his *Life of Caesar*. This omission points to a major difference between the two biographers. Suetonius commonly records and discusses anecdotes about emperors' sexual conduct (e.g. *Div. Aug.* 68–69. 2; 71. 1; *Tib.* 43. 1–45); Plutarch, in contrast, almost never comments on sexual matters. How is this to be explained?

For Suetonius, inclusion of sexual material does not spring from mere curiosity or scandal-mongering. He assesses each emperor and his fitness to rule according to a series of topics, topics which reflect contemporary Roman constructions of the virtues required in a ruler.[95] Amongst these moral categories is that of sexual self-control; a key site for assertions or denials of claims to proper male virtue. Accusations of immorality made use of two different sets of associations. First, violent or unlawful fulfilment of sexual lusts carried with them in antiquity associations of tyrannical behaviour; lust was a stock attribute of the stereotypical king or tyrant of the stage or the rhetorical schools.[96] Secondly, assertions that a rival was guilty of heterosexual or active homosexual excess, or of homosexual passivity, associated him with a set of qualities seen as suitable only for women and opposed to traditional male Roman qualities, such as self-control, courage, and *gravitas*; sexual passivity and a lack of sexual self-control were linked with cowardice and luxury as qualities associated with the feminine, the subject and the inferior: wholly inappropriate to a member of the Roman élite.[97]

Suetonius' regular inclusion of anecdotes of sexual misconduct is to be explained by their central role in assessing an emperor's regime and his suitability for rule; they stand against the backdrop of the traditional Roman constructions of masculinity and marriage.[98] Notably, in all but the *Divus Augustus*, these anecdotes occur in the section on 'public' rather than on 'private' life. Thus Suetonius, like Tacitus, is often careful to record the high status of those women whom the emperor seduced (e.g. *Div. Jul.* 50); the sexual act itself is not what is at stake but the

---

[95] See Wallace-Hadrill (1983), esp. 126–74.

[96] e.g. Cicero, *In Verr.* 1. 14; 2. 1. 82: tyrannum libidinosum crudelemque; *Prov. Cons.* 6; *Respub.* 2. 45–6. See Dunkle (1967), esp. 161–9; (1971–2), 15–19; Seager (1967), 7, 15. The Greek association of the tyrant with lust was clearly influential here; cf. Hdt. 3. 80. 5 (with Fisher 1992, 346–8); Eur. *Supp.* 447–55; Plato, *Rep.* 573d; Aristotle, *Pol.* 5. 1314b30–6 (with Fisher 1992, 27–31); Polyb. 6. 7. 7–8.

[97] Thus Cicero accuses Clodius both of heterosexual excess (*Harr. Resp.* 9; 38; *Dom. Sua* 92; *Pro Sest.* 16–17) and of homosexual passivity (*Harr. Resp.* 42; *Dom. Sua* 49). See Edwards (1993), esp. 3–32 and 63–97. For accusations of immorality as a *topos* of invective, see also Süss (1910), 249–50; Krenkel (1980); Morgan (1979) on Cat. 112. For the routine association of cowardice with femininity, see Cicero, *Pro Mur.* 31; Suet. *Otho* 12. 1; Tac. *Ann.* 13. 30. 2.

[98] See Bradley (1985).

affront caused to the élite by such 'tyrannical' behaviour. Similarly, Suetonius and Tacitus are interested in recording examples where emperors played a sexually passive role. Such behaviour demonstrates the unfitness to rule men of a man who adopted the feminine sexual role. In those Lives, such as the *Nero*, where Suetonius mounts a concerted attack on the subject, this kind of material was indispensable.[99]

Plutarch's general lack of interest in the sex-lives of his subjects is particularly surprising given his words in the *Alexander* prologue on the value of anecdotal material. His unwillingness to include such material is probably to be explained partly by his avowed intent not to criticize unnecessarily (*Kim*. 2. 3–5), his *persona* of humanity and understanding. Or, to put it another way, Plutarch's *Lives* perhaps display most clearly the generic roots of political biography in *enkomion* in this refusal to dig the dirt on the subjects: though their moral status is often far from simple, none of his *Lives* is a concerted attack. Some of the most extended treatments of sexuality, then, are in cases where a subject's self-control (ἐγκράτεια) overcame his passions rather than the opposite: most notably Alexander (*Alex*. 21. 1–22. 6) and Agesilaos (*Ages*. 11. 6–10; cf. *Prof. in Virt*. 81a).[100]

But Plutarch's reluctance to include sexual material cannot be explained simply by the fact that he preferred not to criticize his subjects. After all, men like Nikias, Coriolanus, or Marius are not presented, in general, in a particularly favourable light. It could be that Plutarch did not think sex was particularly revealing of a subject's character. But given his attention to reason and passion elsewhere, and given Greek tendencies to associate transgressional sexuality with tyrants or with women or barbarians, this seems unlikely. Probably it is because he considered sexual material as unsuitable for historical narrative.[101] So, where sexual material is discussed, it is generally because such conduct has a direct bearing on the subject's career on the grand stage of war and politics. This is the point of the references to Antony's passion for Kleopatra,

---

[99] Tyrannical lust: 28. 1–2; prostituting himself: 29; cf. Tac. *Ann*. 15. 37. 4. See Wallace-Hadrill (1983), 142–74; on the *Nero*, see Barton (1994).

[100] The incident narrated in *Ages*. 11. 6–10 may be intended to recall the similar incidents in *Alex*. 21. 1–22. 6 (probably composed just before the *Ages*.: Jones 1966, 67) and so to present Agesilaos as a proto-Alexander, a theme prominent throughout the Life (especially at 15. 3–4).

[101] Cf. Nepos' preface to his book on foreign generals, where he appears to apologize for including anecdotes unconnected with the political or military conduct of his subjects: some people, he predicts, may find 'this kind of writing frivolous and insufficiently worthy of the characters of great men' (*hoc genus scripturae leve et non satis dignum summorum virorum personis*). On the interpretation of this sentence, see Geiger (1985), 113. Cf. p. 66.

or, in the paired Life, to Demetrios' debaucheries. The conceptual framework is still that of reason and the passions (e.g. *Ant.* 36. 1–2), but it is the devastating effect which their sexual passions have on their careers which seems the criterion for inclusion.[102] Perikles' affair with Aspasia is discussed in the *Life of Perikles* (24). But here the issue is not what it reveals about Perikles' character, that he lacked self-control, for example, but its political effect. Aspasia is thought to be the cause of the declaration of war on Samos in 440 BC; this in itself carries the negative implications that Perikles' foreign policy was influenced by a woman, and a foreign one at that.[103] Similarly, Plutarch mentions the youthful passion ($\pi\acute{a}\theta os$) of Aristeides and Themistokles over the favours of a certain Stesilaos of Keos; but he uses it not as an item of interest in its own right, but as an explanation for their rivalry ($\phi\iota\lambda o\nu\epsilon\iota\kappa\acute{\iota}a$) later in life (*Arist.* 2. 3–4; cf. *Them.* 2. 2). Sexual conduct is rarely included as an indicator of character in its own right; it does not itself play a very large role in Plutarch's estimation of a statesman's worth in the *Lives*. What matters more is how he conducted himself with regard to his peers and to the people, and in war as well as in peace. Hence the importance of the traditional stereotypes of the tyrant or demagogue, and the emphasis on military campaigns. It is on these that the emphasis falls in the *Life of Caesar*, not on the stuff of gossip which Plutarch may have considered unsuitable for a historiographical narrative and motivated by a spirit of malice.

5. EPILOGUE: MORALITY AND SUCCESS

The last section has argued that, although analysis of a subject's sexual conduct could be made to fit in so well to the discourse of reason and the passions, Plutarch subordinates it to a concern with the success or failure of the subject's conduct as statesman or general. This is important. Running in parallel to Plutarch's concern for the subject's psychology, and sometimes conflicting with it, is a concern for the success or failure, the importance and consequences, of the subject's actions on the grand stage of politics and war. Plutarch's admiration for military success is at its clearest in the treatise *Were the Athenians more glorious in war or in wisdom?*, where he argues that the military achievements of Classical Athens should be praised before the artistic and cultural.[104] Of

---

[102] e.g. *Demetr.* 1. 8; 9. 5–7; *Ant.* 36. 1–7; 53. 5–11; *Demetr.-Ant.* 3. 1–5.
[103] Cf. Blomqvist (1997).
[104] See Frazier (1990), 168–77. The preference for action over artistic endeavour is Platonic (e.g. *Rep.* 598d–602b).

course, this work is a display-speech and as such need not reflect Plutarch's considered views: he may have been equally capable of arguing the opposite case. But in fact the attitude evinced there, the positive evaluation of military success, is one seen clearly in the *Lives*, in which much space is devoted to the narration of campaigns and battles. Sometimes, it is true, such military narrative serves the purpose of revealing a subject's character, particularly when youthful exploits are being described; for example, the narrative of Cato the Elder's successes in Spain and at Thermopylai (*Cato Major* 10–14) implicitly characterizes him as brave, decisive, incorruptible, and a little boastful.[105] But warfare is not always used in this way. For Plutarch virtue (ἀρετή) still retained its inescapably military associations: military skill and success are things to be admired in their own right. So, for example, he devotes much more attention than Suetonius does to Caesar's military campaigns, especially the Gallic Wars (*Caes.* 15–27).[106] The tone of Plutarch's long account of this period is enkomiastic, particularly the opening chapter of the section, which announces a new beginning, and where Caesar's greatness is brought out by explicit comparison with other generals: a well-known enkomiastic trope (15). Anecdotes follow, showing Caesar as the ideal general (16–17).[107] This admiration for military success is particularly clear in the formal *synkriseis*, where success is often treated as a moral positive, inversely proportional to the scale of the resources which a hero had at his disposal.[108] It is this high valuation of success, a success achieved sometimes at the cost of strict morality or without the benefit of a correct psychological configuration, which makes some Lives so interesting and so problematic. It is to case-studies of such problematic Lives that we now turn.

[105] Cf. also *Pel.* 4. 5–8; *Gracchi* 4. 5–6; 23(2). 1–3.

[106] Suetonius deals with Caesar's conquests in Gaul only briefly in *Div. Jul.* 24. 3–25. 2; *Div. Jul.* 57–70 deal with Caesar's personal qualities as commander; they do not narrate his campaigns. His short account presents Caesar's wars as unnecessary, and concentrates on the extent to which Caesar extended the empire: a concern of Suetonius elsewhere: *Div. Aug.* 21. 1–3; *Cal.* 43–7; *Div. Claud.* 17. 1–3; *Nero* 18; *Div. Vesp.* 8. 4. In general, Suetonius gives little space to foreign wars (e.g. *Div. Aug.* 20–3. 2; *Tib.* 16. 1–17. 1), as opposed to civil wars (*Div. Jul.* 34. 1–36; *Div. Aug.* 9–17. 3), which had direct relevance to an emperor's treatment of the élite (cf. *Div. Aug.* 19. 1–2), or to changes in military custom (*Div. Aug.* 24. 1–25. 4; *Tib.* 18. 1–19), which had relevance to his relations with the army. See Wallace-Hadrill (1983), 129–31.

[107] Many of these anecdotes illustrate stock qualities (cf. also 12. 4; 18. 5; 34. 7–8; 48. 3–4; 54. 4; 57. 8). They are probably derived from Oppius (Townend 1987), but also find a specific parallel in the behaviour of Alexander in the paired Life (e.g. *Alex.* 21. 1–7; 24. 10–14; 39. 1–13; 42. 5–10; 43. 5–7; 44. 3–5; 59. 1–5; 60. 14–15).

[108] e.g. *Pel.-Marc.* 1. 4–2. 3; *Phil.-Flam.* 2. 1–6; *Per.-Fab.* 1. 1–5; *Aem.-Tim.* 1. 1–5.

PART II
Exploring Virtue and Vice
The Case Studies

4
The Lives of Pyrrhos and Marius

The first of our case studies of the moralism of the *Parallel Lives* consists of a pair of biographies in which there is a clear and largely unproblematic moral message. The *Pyrrhos–Marius* poses few problems of overall interpretation. A single moral theme runs through both Lives. Together they form an illustration and warning of the dangers of discontent. Though Plutarch never states this explicitly, Pyrrhos and Marius should most probably be seen as 'great natures': men with great natural endowments, and indeed of great achievements, but whose characters are perverted through a bad environment or bad education. They thus fulfil the function of negative examples of that rather specific kind to which Plutarch alludes in the prologue to the *Demetrios–Antony*.

A word should be said about the sources for these two Lives, a subject which has relevance for the analysis of all Plutarch's *Lives*. In writing the *Marius*, although Plutarch plainly made some use of sources which were slanted in favour of Marius, for the most part he was undoubtedly using hostile sources, primarily the memoirs of Sulla and the account of Rutilius Rufus.[1] It would be reasonable to wonder, therefore, whether Plutarch's generally hostile attitude to Marius is simply a result of what he found in his sources. A similar question could be asked of his treatment of Pyrrhos. His conception of him as a man driven by discontent could—though this is far from certain—derive from the Peripatetic writer Douris of Samos, an older contemporary of Pyrrhos. Douris is certainly one of the sources, at least indirectly, of the *Life of Demetrios*, and it is noticeable that Plutarch's picture of the character of Demetrios has some similarities with that of Pyrrhos.[2] So has Plutarch simply

---

[1] Plutarch perhaps knew Rutilius Rufus' work at second-hand through reading Poseidonios. On the sources for the *Mar.*, see Corbellini (1976); Scardigli (1977); Sordi (1991).

[2] On the moral characterization of Demetrios, see below, pp. 116–18. On Douris as an indirect source for the *Demetr.*, see Sweet (1951), 179–81; Kebric (1977), 55–60; Andrei (1989), 43–4 and 47–8. On Douris as a possible source for the *Pyrrh.*, see Kebric (1977), 59 n. 31, and below p. 125. Douris was also a source for the *Eum.*, the other Hellenistic Life: see *Eum.* 1. 1.

'lifted' the emphases of his sources into his own narrative? There must be a modicum of truth in this. But, as much of the recent work on the *Lives* has asserted, Plutarch does not, where we can observe, simply follow the emphasis of his sources; his creativity as a literary artist should not be forgotten.³ It seems, furthermore, that he exercises his own creativity in the very choice of which sources to use. This is particularly clear in his works on Alexander the Great, where he chooses different sources for works with different purposes.⁴ In fact, it is clear from the unified moral focus of the *Pyrrhos–Marius* that Plutarch was not a victim of his sources: he has chosen to explore the morality of happiness and discontent, and this he consistently does through his presentation of both Pyrrhos and Marius. It is in his creation of a unified whole of the separate careers of his two protagonists—careers pursued in different milieux and recorded by different sources—that Plutarch's originality most clearly lies. Notably, the concluding philosophical reflection of *Marius* 46. 1–5 (see below), which sets out the moral of these Lives, is not paralleled in any other source on Marius and springs almost certainly from Plutarch's own concerns.

These two Lives, then, must be read as a pair, a contention which holds true for all Plutarch's *Parallel Lives* and which is a major theme of this book. Together the two Lives, composed and published together, form a single book, and function, like all pairs of Plutarchan *Parallel Lives*, as a literary and moral unit. This technique of paired composition, in which the same themes are explored through the Lives of two protagonists separated in time, place, and culture—one Greek and one Roman—is one of Plutarch's most original contributions to the art of biography. It is also a key feature of his moralizing craft. By looking at the same moral issue in two different manifestations, a greater understanding is gained.⁵ In this case, the two Lives, taken together, explore the theme of happiness: where does true happiness lie?

Many pairs of Plutarchan Lives are preceded by a 'formal' prologue which introduces themes relevant to both Lives and most are followed by a 'formal' comparison, or *synkrisis*, in which the two subjects are weighed against each other for their moral virtue or vice and their practical success or failure. This pair, unusually, does not contain either

---

³ See pp. 8–9, and, of particular relevance to the *Demetr.*, and hence to the *Pyrrh.*, Andrei (1989), 61–71.

⁴ The 'vulgate' tradition alone for the speeches, the vulgate and the tradition derived from Aristoboulos and Kleitarchos for the Life. Cf. Rubina Cammarota (1992), 120–4.

⁵ On the importance of *synkrisis* in the *Parallel Lives*, cf. Erbse (1956); Pelling (1986*b*). This topic is discussed in Ch. 8 below.

of these two elements. The lack of a formal introduction is not unusual; only twelve out of the surviving twenty-two pairs possess such an opening. But it is not clear why this pair, along with only three others (*Themistokles–Camillus, Coriolanus–Alkibiades*, and *Alexander–Caesar*), lacks a formal 'comparison'. Either Plutarch for some reason chose not to write one, or it has dropped out of the manuscript tradition. This is a question to which we shall return.[6]

Despite the lack of a prologue and comparison, the unity of this pair as a single book should not be in doubt.[7] These two Lives both teach the same message: happiness lies in being content with what one has, not in straining after more. Happiness (εὐδαιμονία) was the philosophical theme *par excellence*: Aristotle had asked the same question, what is happiness?, in his *Nikomachean Ethics* (1095a14–1102a4); the answer to this question was one of the major goals of all Hellenistic philosophical enquiry.[8] At the heart of both Lives is the theme of discontent with present blessings, a discontent which leads to greed and immoderate hopes for the future, and in the cases of Marius and Pyrrhos, to an inability to cease from warfare: greed (πλεονεξία), hope (ἐλπίς) and the desire for new or great deeds (καινὰ or μεγάλα πράγματα) are leitmotifs of this pair.

1. THE ETHICAL BACKGROUND: DISCONTENT

The moral-philosophical concerns of this particular pair seem to have been drawn from the commonplaces of popular philosophy rather than the specifically Platonic tradition. The vice of discontent with one's lot is a common theme in many Hellenistic 'diatribes', written by Cynics and others. The discontented man (μεμψίμοιρος)[9] already occurs in the fourth century as one of the *Characters* of Theophrastos; Theophrastos defines discontent (μεμψιμοιρία) as 'unsuitable fault-finding with what

---

[6] See below, pp. 252–5. On how pairs of Lives begin, see Stadter (1988); Rosenmeyer (1992) is less useful.

[7] Erbse (1956), 404–5 (=1979, 485) noted briefly the unity of themes in this pair, consisting in the subjects' ambition and restlessness, their personal courage, and their hostility to cultural pursuits; Costanza (1956), 153–4, gives a similar list; he puts down the lack of prologue and comparison, unconvincingly, to a supposed lack of final revision. Other studies on the *Pyrrh.* by Kuhn (1976), 23–4, and Mossman (1992), and on the *Mar.* by Carney (1958; 1960; 1961b; 1962 *pass.*; 1967, 9–13) have not noted the unity of themes in these Lives. [8] See e.g. Annas (1993).

[9] Literally, 'one who blames his fate'. Fate plays a large part in the *Pyrrh.-Mar.*: cf. *Pyrrh.* 16. 14; 30. 2; *Mar.* 39. 6; 40. 9; 45. 12; 46. 9, and pp. 123–4, below.

has been given' (*Char.* 17).[10] In those surviving diatribes and treatises which deal with the vice of discontent, it is often linked with πλεονεξία, which can carry the sense of both greed and competitive envy of others (cf. Plato, *Republic* 349b–350c). The link is one of cause and effect: greed, especially for money, causes discontent.

All this can be seen in the Cynic Teles' diatribe *On self-sufficiency* (Περὶ Αὐταρκείας; late third century BC), which seems to draw heavily on the writings of the eclectic philosopher Bion of Borysthenes, himself a contemporary of Pyrrhos. Of particular relevance to the *Pyrrhos–Marius* are the injunctions to make use of present blessings and (particularly important for the *Marius*) to accept old age with good grace: 'Act according to what is at hand (τὰ παρόντα). You have become old: do not seek a young man's life' (p. 6. 13–15 Hense).[11] Also of relevance to the concerns of this pair of Lives is Teles' diagnosis: 'we are unable to be content with what is at hand (τοῖς παροῦσιν), when we actually give much to luxury' (p. 7. 7–8 Hense).[12] The spurious seventeenth letter of Hippokrates again links greed and discontent as cause and effect. In a long discussion of men's activities on 'unimportant' matters (περὶ τὰ ἀσπούδαστα) the writer includes two activities of relevance for Plutarch's picture of Pyrrhos: repeated marriage and divorce, and unnecessary warfare (ix. 362, 8–11 Littré):

γαμεῖν σπεύδουσιν, ἃς μετ' ὀλίγον ἐκβάλλουσιν, ἐρῶσιν, εἶτα μισέουσι, μετ' ἐπιθυμίης γεννῶσιν, εἶτ' ἐκβάλλουσι τελείους. τίς ἡ κενὴ σπουδὴ καὶ ἀλόγιστος, μηδὲν μανίης διαφέρουσα; πολεμοῦσιν ἔμφυλον, ἠρεμίην οὐχ αἱρετίζοντες . . .

They hurry to be married to women whom they cast off after a short time; they love, then they hate; with desire they beget children, then they cast them off when they are grown up. What is this empty and unreasoning hurry, no different from madness? They wage civil war, not choosing rest . . .

Maximos of Tyre similarly sees greed for wealth as the cause of discontent (*Discourses* 15. 1a–d Hobein). The same combination is seen in Horace's first *Satire*.[13] For Horace, as becomes clear towards the end of the *Satire* (108–21), greed is the cause of such discontent; desire for wealth and the related desire to have more than others leads men to discontent with their present blessings.

Such is the background in Greek ethical thought to Plutarch's concern with greed (πλεονεξία) in the *Pyrrhos–Marius*. A distinctly Plutarchan

[10] ἐπιτίμησίς τις παρὰ τὸ προσῆκον τῶν δεδομένων.
[11] καὶ σὺ πρὸς τὰ παρόντα χρῶ. γέρων γέγονας· μὴ ζήτει τὰ τοῦ νέου.
[12] ἡμεῖς οὐ δυνάμεθα ἀρκεῖσθαι τοῖς παροῦσιν, ὅταν καὶ τρυφῇ πολὺ διδῶμεν.
[13] Discontent: 1–40; 108–21; greed: 41–107. See Fraenkel (1957), 90–5; Rudd (1966), 20–1.

practice is his ascribing of the cause of such greed, at least in the case of Marius, to lack of reason in his soul, which itself was a result of lack of education.[14] In fact, all these themes are set out clearly in another, probably earlier, work of Plutarch, his treatise *On tranquillity of mind* (Περὶ εὐθυμίας).[15] This work almost certainly draws material from Epicurean sources, such as the work of the same title by Demokritos of Abdera,[16] and possibly from the Stoic Panaitios' work also of the same title.[17] But, significantly, it also has many similarities of presentation and subject matter with Cynic diatribes.[18] As its moral concerns are so close to those of the *Pyrrhos–Marius* it is worth exploring in a little detail. After an epistolary introduction, Plutarch sets out his theme:

πόθεν γε δὴ πρὸς ἀλυπίαν ψυχῆς καὶ βίον ἀκύμονα χρημάτων ὄφελος ἢ δόξης ἢ δυνάμεως ἐν αὐλαῖς, ἂν μὴ τὸ χρώμενον εὐχάριστον ᾖ τοῖς ἔχουσι καὶ τὸ τῶν ἀπόντων μὴ δεόμενον ἀεὶ παρακολουθῇ; τί δὲ τοῦτ' ἐστὶν ἄλλο ἢ λόγος εἰθισμένος καὶ μεμελετηκὼς τοῦ παθητικοῦ καὶ ἀλόγου τῆς ψυχῆς ἐξισταμένου πολλάκις ἐπιλαμβάνεσθαι ταχὺ καὶ μὴ περιορᾶν ἀπορρέον καὶ καταφερόμενον ἀπὸ τῶν παρόντων;

What use is money or fame or power at court to give one an untroubled mind or a calm life, unless employing them is pleasant to those who have got them, and unless desire for them when they are absent is never a consequence. What other solution is there except reason, which has been accustomed and trained quickly to hold back the passionate and unreasoning part of the soul, when it so often breaks out, and not to allow it to flow away and be swept downstream away from what is present.   (*De Tranq. Anim.* 465a–b)[19]

As so often in the *Pyrrhos–Marius*, the imagery of a river in flood or a storm at sea is used in connection with the dangers of love for what is absent (τὰ ἀπόντα): the image of the contented mind as a 'waveless' sea gives way to the image of the passionate part of the soul being 'swept' away by desire for what is absent—if it were not for the restraining influence of a well-trained reason. The comparison of the soul to a calm

---

[14] Swain (1990b), 138–9.
[15] Jones (1966), 62–3, argues that the *De Tranq. An.* was published after AD 107. The *Pyrrh.-Mar.* seems to have been composed amongst the last of the *Parallel Lives* (ibid. 68; cf. the unfulfilled promise in *Mar.* 29. 12 to write about Metellus Numidicus) and so probably post-dates the *De Tranq. An.*
[16] Hershbell (1982), 84–9; Tsekourakis (1983), 77–9.
[17] Gill (1994), 4624–31.
[18] Heinze (1890), 507–9; Tsekourakis (1983), esp. 77–117. Compare e.g. 470b with Teles 43 Hense and 470f–471a with Teles 12–13 Hense.
[19] Plutarch touches on the same theme in *Sert.-Eum.* 2. 1–5, where he criticizes Eumenes for his inability to live at peace: 'one who prefers greed to safety is', he says (2. 5), 'fond of war' (φιλοπόλεμος μὲν οὖν ὁ τῆς ἀσφαλείας τὴν πλεονεξίαν προτιμῶν); cf. *Nik.-Crass.* 4. 1–2.

or a stormy sea is a common way of talking about contentment and discontent.[20] One must, Plutarch concludes, pay attention in advance to our reasonings (λόγοι), so that they are adequately trained to control the wild dogs of our passions (465b–c).

Plutarch goes on: discontent is not to be cured by changing one's lifestyle, by getting married, or gaining more influence at court (466a–d): such changes do not relieve the soul of the true causes of its grief, which are: 'inexperience of affairs, unreasonableness (ἀλογιστία), and not being able, nor knowing how, to use what is present (τοῖς παροῦσιν) properly' (466c). The key to contentment is rather reason, that is, a correct estimation of the value of things. Reason allows one to bear both good and bad fortune with indifference (466d–467a; 474c–475c). One must, as Plato urged, not be too much elated by the one or cast down by the other—after all even great men like the kings of Rome, and like Epameinondas, Fabricius, Agis of Sparta, and Stilpo the philosopher suffered misfortune (467a–468a). One should, even in misfortune, concentrate on the good things that are still at hand, rather than on what has been lost (468f–469d). The example of the philosopher Antipatros of Tarsos is quoted: when counting up his blessings at the end of his life he did not omit even the good voyage he had from Kilikia to Athens (469d–e). In the same way, one should appreciate blessings when they are present, not just when they are absent; we should remind ourselves of how valuable health is to the sick and peace to those at war (469e–470a). One should avoid jealously dwelling on the blessings enjoyed by others (470a–471c). One should also (471d) control one's impulses so as not to 'aim in our hopes at things too great for us' (μειζόνων ἐφιεμένους ταῖς ἐλπίσιν). Men attempt the impossible because of self-love (φιλαυτία), which 'makes them love being first and being victorious in everything and makes them engage in everything insatiably (πάντων ἐπιδραττομένους ἀπλήστως)'. Happiness is of the individual's own making: everyone has within his own soul the 'store-rooms' (ταμιεῖα) of contentment and discontent (473b). Plutarch continues:

οἱ μὲν γὰρ ἀνόητοι καὶ παρόντα τὰ χρηστὰ παρορῶσι καὶ ἀμελοῦσιν ὑπὸ τοῦ συντετάσθαι πρὸς τὸ μέλλον ἀεὶ ταῖς φροντίσιν, οἱ δὲ φρόνιμοι καὶ τὰ μήκετ'

---

[20] e.g. *De Virt. Moral.* 446d; *Brut. Anim.* 989c: part of a sermon on contentment delivered to Odysseus by a pig. See Diog. Laert. 10. 37 (ἐγγαληνίζων τῷ βίῳ), quoting Epik. *Ad Herod.* p. 4 Usener, and 10. 83 (γαληνισμός), p. 32 Usener. Cf. Thévenaz (1938), 120–1; Clay (1972), esp. 64–5. The philosopher can remain calm (γαληνός) even in a storm, like a pig (Poseidonios fr. 278 E–K = Diog. Laert 9. 68). Cf. also Diog. Laert. 9. 45 (quoting Demokritos) and Timon fr. 63–4 Di Marco (= Sext. Empeir. *Adv. Eth.* 141).

ὄντα τῷ μνημονεύειν ἐναργῶς ὄντα ποιοῦσιν ἑαυτοῖς. τὸ γὰρ παρὸν τῷ ἐλαχίστῳ τοῦ χρόνου μορίῳ θιγεῖν παρασχὸν εἶτα τὴν αἴσθησιν ἐκφυγὸν οὐκέτι δοκεῖ πρὸς ἡμᾶς οὐδ' ἡμέτερον εἶναι τοῖς ἀνοήτοις·

For the foolish overlook and neglect good things even when they are present because in their thoughts they are always straining towards the future. But the wise, by remembrance, make even those good things which are no longer present appear vividly before their eyes. For the present good, which allows us to touch it for the smallest portion of time and then flees our perception, seems to the foolish to be no longer connected with us nor even to be ours any more. (473b–c)

It is forgetfulness which strips us of appreciation of present or past blessings:

οἱ δὲ τῇ μνήμῃ τὰ πρότερον μὴ στέγοντες μηδ' ἀναλαμβάνοντες ἀλλ' ὑπεκρεῖν ἐῶντες ἔργῳ ποιοῦσιν ἑαυτοὺς καθ' ἡμέραν ἀποδεεῖς καὶ κενοὺς καὶ τῆς αὔριον ἐκκρεμαμένους, ὡς τῶν πέρυσι καὶ πρῴην καὶ χθὲς οὐ πρὸς αὐτοὺς ὄντων οὐδ' ὅλως αὐτοῖς γενομένων.

Those who do not contain within their memory nor recollect past good things but allow them to flow away, actually make themselves each day deficient and empty and dependent on tomorrow, as though the good things of last year and of the day before yesterday and of yesterday itself have no connection with them and did not happen to them at all. (473d–e)

The contrast between good things which are present (τὰ παρόντα) and those which are absent (τὰ ἀπόντα), a feature of the Epicurean tradition on contentment,[21] recurs frequently in this essay (e.g. 469e–f; 474d), as indeed it will in the *Pyrrhos–Marius*, to which we now, finally, turn.

2. PYRRHOS AND MARIUS: PLUTARCH'S DIAGNOSIS

There is, as we have noted, no formal prologue to the *Pyrrhos–Marius*, nor a formal *synkrisis* at the end; but the moral message of the two Lives is set out clearly in the final chapter of the *Marius* (46) which forms a coda to both Lives; the presence of this final passage may well go some of the way towards explaining the lack of a 'formal' *synkrisis*. It is structured around an implicit *synkrisis* between the wise and the foolish—a contrast familiar from the *On tranquillity of mind* (473b–c). Two philosophers, Plato and—significantly—Antipatros, are introduced to provide the positive paradigm: they appreciated and enumerated the

[21] e.g. Demokritos, frs. 191 and 202 Diels–Kranz; Cic. *De Fin.* 1. 17–19, 57–63 and *Tusc.* 5. 95, both discussing Epicurean theory. See Gill (1994), 4611.

blessings which fortune gave them (46. 1–2). Characteristically, Plutarch associates the good and bad paradigms of this section with the presence or absence of reason: among the blessings which Plato is said to enumerate are 'first that he had been born a man not an animal, unreasoning by nature; then that he had been born a Greek not a barbarian' (46. 1).[22] Antipatros has already occurred in the *On tranquillity of mind*; significantly, the same anecdote is used, that of the philosopher counting his blessings on his death-bed (469d). The similarity in language between the two passages strongly suggests that the same source lies behind both, or that Plutarch was in the *Pyrrhos–Marius* re-using material which he had first met in researching the *On tranquillity of mind*. Antipatros was behaving, Plutarch explains, as though every gift of fortune calls for gratitude and should be stored in the memory, the 'store-room' (ταμιεῖον) of the mind.

In contrast to the two philosophers, stand 'the forgetful and foolish':

(46. 3) τοὺς δ' ἀμνήμονας καὶ ἀνοήτους ὑπεκρεῖ τὰ γιγνόμενα μετὰ τοῦ χρόνου· διὸ μηθὲν στέγοντες μηδὲ διατηροῦντες, ἀεὶ κενοὶ μὲν ἀγαθῶν πλήρεις δ' ἐλπίδων, πρὸς τὸ μέλλον ἀποβλέπουσι τὸ παρὸν προϊέμενοι. (46. 4) καίτοι τὸ μὲν ἂν ἡ τύχη κωλῦσαι δύναιτο, τὸ δ' ἀναφαίρετόν ἐστιν· ἀλλ' ὅμως τοῦτο τῆς τύχης ὡς ἀλλότριον ἐκβάλλοντες, ἐκεῖνο τὸ ἄδηλον ὀνειρώττουσιν, εἰκότα πάσχοντες. (46. 5) πρὶν γὰρ ἐκ λόγου καὶ παιδείας ἕδραν ὑποβαλέσθαι καὶ κρηπῖδα τοῖς ἔξωθεν ἀγαθοῖς, συνάγοντες αὐτὰ καὶ συμφοροῦντες, ἐμπλῆσαι τῆς ψυχῆς οὐ δύνανται τὸ ἀκόρεστον.

τύχης: ψυχῆς Ziegler

(46. 3) Forgetful and foolish people, on the other hand, let what happens flow away with time. Therefore since they contain and hold nothing, always empty of good things but full of hopes, they look away to the future and reject the present. (46. 4) And yet, fortune could prevent the former, whereas the latter cannot be taken away. Nevertheless, they cast off what fortune gives in the present as though it belonged to someone else, but they dream of the future with all its uncertainties. The consequences which they suffer are what might be expected (46. 5) For before they have laid a base and foundation for their external blessings, a base made from reason and education, they gather these blessings together and heap them up, and are, even so, unable to fulfil the insatiable appetite of their soul. (*Mar.* 46. 3–5)

The imagery of blessings as liquids which should be preserved in one's memory is, as we have seen, used in exactly the same way and in almost identical language in the *On tranquillity of mind* (473b–e).[23] Plutarch has

[22] This saying is attributed to Thales by Diog. Laert. 1. 33 (Thales fr. A. 1 Diels–Kranz).
[23] ταμιεῖον, ὑπεκρεῖν, στέγειν, κενός. 'Empty' (κενός) is also a term commonly associated

added to it here the image of the discontented as 'full of hopes' (πλήρεις ἐλπίδων). Plutarch uses πλήρης ('full') rarely when discussing human psychology; when he does, it usually refers to the negative influence of passions.[24] Passions which are out of control are, for Plutarch, usually the result of poor education and lack of reason, and this is the case here:[25] before the foolish have 'laid a base and foundation for their external blessings, a base made from reason and education',[26] their unstable souls are swamped by blessings for which they are ill-prepared and which lead them to discontent. The implication is that lack of education has been an important factor in the discontent and greed of Pyrrhos and Marius. In fact, as often, the theme of defective education, while present in the Greek Life,[27] is not developed nor any link made between defective education and the failings of the subject; but the link between poor education and moral shortcomings is clear in the *Marius*:

(2. 2) λέγεται δὲ μήτε γράμματα μαθεῖν Ἑλληνικὰ μήτε γλώττῃ πρὸς μηδὲν Ἑλληνίδι χρῆσθαι τῶν σπουδῆς ἐχομένων, ὡς γελοῖον γράμματα μανθάνειν ὧν οἱ διδάσκαλοι δουλεύοιεν ἑτέροις· . . . (2. 4) οὕτως εἴ τις ἔπεισε Μάριον θύειν ταῖς Ἑλληνικαῖς Μούσαις καὶ Χάρισιν, οὐκ ἂν ἐκπρεπεστάταις στρατηγίαις καὶ πολιτείαις ἀμορφοτάτην ἐπέθηκε ⟨τελευτήν⟩, ὑπὸ θυμοῦ καὶ φιλαρχίας ἀώρου καὶ πλεονεξιῶν ἀπαρηγορήτων εἰς ὠμότατον καὶ ἀγριώτατον γῆρας ἐξοκείλας. ταῦτα μὲν οὖν ἐπὶ τῶν πράξεων αὐτῶν εὐθὺς θεωρείσθω.

ἀμορφοτάτην ἐπέθηκε ⟨τελευτήν⟩L²: ἀμορφοτάτην ἐπέθηκε ⟨κορωνίδα⟩ Aldine edition[28]

(2. 2) He is said neither to have learnt Greek literature nor to have used the Greek language for anything important, saying that it was ridiculous to learn a literature whose teachers were other people's slaves. . . . (2. 4) So if anyone had persuaded Marius to sacrifice to the Greek Muses and Graces, he would not have put a most ugly ending on to his most illustrious career as general and politician, when he ran himself aground on a most premature and savage old age under the

---

with the love of false glory in passages on discontent: e.g. Epik. fr. 422 Usener, and repeatedly in *Brut. Anim.* 989b–f.

[24] e.g. *Cor.* 31. 5; *Fab.* 5. 5; *Flam.* 7. 4; *Pomp.* 69. 7; *Alex.* 6. 6; 75. 2 (δίκην ὕδατος . . . ἀναπληροῦν ἀβελτερίας καὶ φόβου τὸν Ἀλέξανδρον, apparently making clear that the image is one of vessels and liquids, but the text is seriously in doubt). Cf. also Plato, *Gorg.* 493d–494c.

[25] Cf. *De Tranq. An.* 465b–c; 466d; 466f; 474d; 475a.

[26] Cf. *Lyk.-Num.* 4. 12 for education as cement within the building of a state. Cf. also *Ad Princ. Inerud.* 780a–b: 'Uneducated generals and leaders are often tossed and overturned by their inner ignorance. For they build up their power high on an uneven base (βάσει οὐ . . . κειμένῃ πρὸς ὀρθὰς) and so they totter with it (συναπονεύουσι).'

[27] *Pyrrh.* 1. 4; 2. 6; 6. 7 and esp. 8. 6–7.

[28] For ἐπιθεῖναι τελευτήν in this sense, see *Them.* 31. 5: ἐπιθεῖναι τῷ βίῳ τὴν τελευτὴν πρέπουσαν. But cf. also χρυσῷ βίῳ χρυσῆν κορώνην ἐπιθεῖναι at Lucian, *Peregr.* 33.

influence of passion, an untimely love of office and uncontrollable greeds. These things should be immediately discernible in his actual deeds. (*Mar.* 2. 2–4)

The image is a strong one: Marius 'ran himself aground on a most premature[29] and savage old age', a metaphor which looks forward to the shipwreck imagery at the end of his life (45. 10: ἐξοκεῖλαι),[30] and which indicates the way in which Marius' life is to be understood, as the last sentence makes clear.[31] Once again, flood imagery is used of discontent. But the image here is particularly striking as it reverses a traditional comparison of old age to a harbour (λιμήν) or anchorage (ὅρμος).[32] The cause of his shipwreck is, it is implied, that his soul was piloted not by reason or education, but by passion.[33] The message is clear, and, for Plutarch, unsurprising: lack of education and reason in the soul leads to greed, excessive ambition and, ultimately, disaster. We shall find a similar emphasis in the *Life of Coriolanus*.

Greed, as this last passage makes clear, is not in these *Lives* greed for *wealth*, but the competitive desire for success, victory, and honour. It is this which leads Pyrrhos and Marius to unnecessary and ultimately disastrous warfare and conflict. The *Lives* of Pyrrhos and Marius, then, reinforce the value-system which we have traced running through all Plutarch's *Lives*, a value-system in which ambition is highly dangerous, if to some extent necessary.[34] A similar preoccupation with the dangers of greed and overconfidence runs throughout Thucydides' history. As is

---

[29] ὠμότατον. ὠμός means 'raw, unripe, uncooked', and by extension often 'savage, cruel'. But Homer once (*Od.* 15. 357) talks of ὠμὸν γῆρας, as does Hesiod (*Erg.* 705), which seems to mean 'premature' old age, a different metaphorical extension of the root meaning 'unripe' (of fruit etc.). Plutarch probably intends both senses to be in view here: savage is confirmed by the second half of the couplet ἀγριώτατον (such tautology is common in Plutarch: cf. Brenk 1992, 4446–7); and Plutarch does indeed present Marius as dying prematurely, at least in his own eyes (45. 12).

[30] Cf *Luc.* 38. 3, where Marius is cited as an example of a statesman who, unlike Lucullus, continued in politics too long: 'through an insatiable desire for glory and office (ἀπληστίᾳ δόξης καὶ ἀρχῆς), though an old man he competed in politics with young men, and ran himself aground (ἐξώκειλε) on terrible deeds and on sufferings (πάθη) more terrible than the deeds.' For ἐξοκέλλω εἰς (literally, 'run aground on'): Hdt. 7. 182; Aristotle, *Hist. Anim.* 631b2) as a metaphor, cf. also Isok. *Areopag.* 18 (with φερομένην); Polyb. 7. 1. 1; ps.-Plut. *De Lib. Educ.* 5b.

[31] For similar references forward to the narrative itself to back up an initial moral characterization, see *Per.* 2. 5; *Kim.* 3. 3; *Pomp.* 23. 6 and 46. 4, with Hillman (1994); *Ag./Kleom.* 2. 9; *Arat.* 10. 5; cf. *Quaest. Conv.* 697e.

[32] Herakleitos, *Hom. Prob.* 61. 5; Epikouros, *Frag. et Sent.* 108 Diano; cf. Plut. *An Seni* 785e.

[33] Cf. Plato, *Phaidros* 247c; 253c–254e; 255e–256a.

[34] The actual terms φιλοτιμία and φιλονικία/φιλονεικία (on which, see above, p. 83) are not central in the *Pyrrh.-Mar.*, though they do occur: *Pyrrh.* 30. 1; *Mar.* 2. 4; 10. 9; 34. 6; 45. 10–11.

characteristic of both writers, the analysis is applied by Thucydides primarily to states, and by Plutarch primarily to individuals:[35] success can lead to overconfidence; the overconfident overreach themselves and fall prey to the vicissitudes of war ($τύχη$). It is a conventional piece of wisdom, familiar from tragedies. Archidamos (Thuc. 1. 80. 1–1. 81. 6) warns the Spartans against it (cf. 1. 78. 1–2; 1. 83. 3; 1. 84. 2).[36] Both Kleon (3. 39. 3–4) and Diodotos make a similar point about the Mytileneans (3. 45. 1–7); as in Plutarch's *Pyrrhos–Marius*, greed, arrogance, unrealistic hope, and love ($πλεονεξία$, $ὕβρις$, $ἐλπίς$, and $ἔρως$) are linked as the causes of elation ($τὸ\ ἐπαίρεσθαι$), overambitious behaviour, and therefore defeat.[37] The Spartan ambassadors in Book Four warn the Athenians of this.[38] For Thucydides, the result of Athenian hope ($ἐλπίς$) was the disastrous Sicilian expedition; as we shall see, Plutarch in the *Life of Pyrrhos* goes on to exploit these Thucydidean associations of Sicily with overconfidence and disaster.

3. THE *PYRRHOS*

The theme of ambition and greed is introduced early on in the *Pyrrhos*. The Epeirotes urge him (5. 14) to kill the usurper Neoptolemos 'and not to be content with having a small share of the kingdom, but to use his nature and undertake greater matters' ($μειζόνων\ πραγμάτων$). The opportunity to indulge his hopes is soon presented by events in Makedonia (6. 2). Before long, Pyrrhos finds himself at war with Demetrios, who has annexed much of the area; the cause is, in Plutarch's words, 'that disease innate in despotisms, greed' (7. 3: $τὸ\ σύμφυτον\ νόσημα\ ταῖς\ δυναστείαις,\ ἡ\ πλεονεξία$). A little later (9. 6), when Pyrrhos declares that he will leave his kingdom to whichever of his sons has the sharpest sword, Plutarch comments again on the dangers of greed

[35] Thus Thucydides' emphasis on civil strife ($στάσις$) finds its counterpart in Plutarch's interest in the rivalry ($φιλονικία/φιλονεικία$) of individuals, and in the presence or absence of agreement ($ὁμόνοια$) between them.

[36] Cf. the words of the Korinthian ambassadors at 1. 42. 2–4 and 1. 120. 3–4.

[37] Cf. esp. 3. 45. 5–6: $ἥ\ τε\ ἐλπὶς\ καὶ\ ὁ\ ἔρως\ ἐπὶ\ παντί,\ ὁ\ μὲν\ ἡγούμενος,\ ἡ\ δ'\ ἐφεπομένη$ . . . $καὶ\ ἡ\ τύχη\ ἐπ'\ αὐτοῖς\ οὐδὲν\ ἔλασσον\ ξυμβάλλεται\ ἐς\ τὸ\ ἐπαίρειν$.

[38] 4. 17. 4 ($αἰεὶ\ γὰρ\ τοῦ\ πλέονος\ ἐλπίδι\ ὀρέγονται\ διὰ\ τὸ\ καὶ\ τὰ\ παρόντα\ ἀδοκήτως\ εὐτυχῆσαι$); 4. 18. 2–4. The Athenians reject this advice: 4. 21. 2 ($τοῦ\ δὲ\ πλέονος\ ὠρέγοντο$); 4. 41. 4 ($οἱ\ δὲ\ μειζόνων\ τε\ ὠρέγοντο$); 4. 65. 4 ($ἡ\ παρὰ\ λόγον\ τῶν\ πλεόνων\ εὐπραγία\ αὐτοῖς\ ὑποτιθεῖσα\ ἰσχὺν\ τῆς\ ἐλπίδος$). Many of these passages are discussed by Hunter (1973), 74–82; cf. Proctor (1980), esp. 68–9. On Thucydides and Athenian *hubris*, cf. de Romilly (1977), 46–62; Fisher (1992), 386–411. On $ἐλπίς$ in Thucydides as usually unrealistic hope rather than reasonable expectation, see also Huart (1968), 141–51 and 334–5.

(πλεονεξία). After Demetrios has been removed, Pyrrhos comes into conflict with his new neighbour, Lysimachos. How, Plutarch asks, could men on whose greed even the greatest natural boundaries were unable to set a limit (ὁρίζειν),[39] ever remain at peace (ἀτρεμεῖν), when now they were in such proximity? Plotting and jealousy were innate (ἔμφυτον) in them (12. 2–5). The point could not be clearer; Pyrrhos was, in Plutarch's words, 'not well-suited to peace and quiet' (12. 8: οὐκ εὖ πρὸς ἡσυχίαν πεφυκώς; cf. *Mar.* 31. 3). Finally, when Pyrrhos is driven back into Epeiros, Plutarch comments:

(13. 1) ἡ μὲν τύχη παρεῖχε χρῆσθαι τοῖς παροῦσιν ἀπραγμόνως καὶ ζῆν ἐν εἰρήνῃ, βασιλεύοντα τῶν οἰκείων· (13. 2) ὁ δὲ τὸ μὴ παρέχειν ἑτέροις κακὰ μηδ' ἔχειν ὑφ' ἑτέρων ἄλυν τινὰ ναυτιώδη νομίζων, ὥσπερ ὁ Ἀχιλλεὺς οὐκ ἔφερε τὴν σχολήν . . .

(13. 1) Fortune gave him the opportunity to enjoy what he had without trouble and to live in peace, ruling his own territory. (13. 2) But thinking that it was sickeningly boring not to do evil to others or have it done to him by them, just like Achilles[40] he could not bear the leisure . . . (13. 1–2)

Plutarch's diagnosis of Pyrrhos' problem was, as this passage shows, *ennui*: he found inactivity 'sickeningly boring' (ἄλυν τινὰ ναυτιώδη). As we have noted, discontent with one's lot was a theme of Hellenistic diatribe, though it is not known whether this theme was ever applied to Pyrrhos before Plutarch.[41] The concept of boredom as such does not seem to appear in the extant literature until the first century BC.[42]

So, Plutarch continues (13. 3), Pyrrhos seeks 'new undertakings' (πράγματα καινά), which he finds in the Roman war with the people of Tarentum, who invite him to help, and who believe him to have the most leisure (σχολὴν . . . πλείστην) of any of the kings and to be the best general (13. 4). The inability of Pyrrhos to endure peace is most clearly

---

[39] Neither Pyrrhos nor Marius knows where to set a ὅρος to his ambition: *Pyrrh.* 12. 3; 30. 3; *Mar.* 34. 6. Crossing natural barriers could be seen as an act of *hubris*: Hdt. 7. 24; 8. 28; Thuc. 6. 13. 1. Cf. Cornford (1907), 204.

[40] On Achilles as a paradigm for Pyrrhos in this Life, see Mossman (1992).

[41] A fragment of a play entitled *Pyrrhos* by the Attic comedian Philemon preserved in Stobaios (*Fl.* 55. 5, ii, 332–3 Meineke = fr. 74 Kassel-Austin) may possibly be an example of the life of Pyrrhos being used as a vehicle for reflection on the true nature of happiness. But it is by no means certain that the Pyrrhos of the title is the same as the subject of Plutarch's Life.

[42] Lucret. 3. 1060–7; Hor. *Ep.* 1. 8; 1. 11; cf. Sen. *Ep.* 24. 26. Epikouros (fr. 496 Usener/103 Diano = Sen. *Ep.* 24. 22) and Ennius (fr. 99, 195–202 Jocelyn) *may* have used the concept of boredom; it is also possible that Zeno (*SVF* 1. 246) intended ἄλυς to convey this sense. For ναυτιώδης, cf. Sen. *Ep.* 24. 26. On all this, see Toohey (1987; 1988). On the history of the concept of boredom, see Kuhn (1976), esp. 23–4 on the *Pyrrhos*.

demonstrated in the following chapter (14. 1–14), the dialogue between Pyrrhos and his official Kineas. The effect of Kineas' questions is similar to that of the Sokratic questioning; Pyrrhos experiences a kind of confused perplexity or *aporia*: he cannot refute Kineas' argument that more conquests will not increase his happiness, but, says Plutarch (14. 14) 'although he realized how much happiness he was abandoning, he was unable to let go of his hopes for what he desired (ὧν δ' ὠρέγετο τὰς ἐλπίδας)'. Furthermore, this scene has many of the features of the traditional stories of the meeting of the wise man and the tyrant. Many such meetings feature in Herodotos, the most well-known and influential being that between Solon and Kroisos (1. 30–3; cf. Plut. *Sol.* 27. 1–9). In the traditional story, which is usually told, as here, in dialogue form,[43] the wise man gives advice to the tyrant on the subject of what constitutes true happiness. This is usually ignored, through the hybristic arrogance and greed of the tyrant, leading to later disaster: Kroisos is driven by the gods' envy to attack Kyros. Similarly, Artabanos warns Xerxes not to attack Greece (7. 10–18), which he ignores to his peril.[44] The effect of the inclusion of these traditional motifs in the narrative at this point is three-fold. First, Pyrrhos is shown to be, like the tyrants of the story, unaware of where true happiness lies (an important theme of the Life as a whole). His association with the tyrant of these stories reinforces Plutarch's repeated association of him with excessive ambition and greed, and suggests a tyrannical *hybris*. Secondly Kineas' role as the 'wise adviser' here, combined with the good pen picture which he is given at the start (14. 1–3), suggests that his views are to be taken, to some extent at least, as the authorial comment of Plutarch, providing an authoritative diagnosis of Pyrrhos' deficiencies of character, and a statement of the moral themes which this pair of Lives explores.[45] Thirdly, the traditional form of the story encourages the reader to expect disaster to follow, as indeed it does. An instructive comparison can be made with

---

[43] Dialogue is also a feature of the diatribe, a form of writing which regularly dealt with the key issue at stake here: the importance of contentment. See Tsekourakis (1983), 30–1.

[44] For the motif of the wise man and the tyrant, see Lattimore (1939) and Gray (1986), esp. 118–22 (on Xen. *Hieron*). The adviser often warns of the dangers of *hubris* or arrogance in general (Hdt. 7. 10. ε. 2; 7. 16. α. 2); of being 'lifted up' (ἐπαίρεσθαι) by hopes or success (Hdt. 7. 10. ε. 2; 7. 18. 4; Thuc. 6. 11. 6; 6. 12. 2); of desiring too much or what is absent (Hdt. 7. 16. α. 2; 7. 18. 2; Thuc. 6. 9. 3; 6. 10. 5; 6. 13. 1). On the immediate sources of the Kineas episode, see Garoufalias (1979), 315–16 n. 43, and Marasco (1983), 226–9; the latter, remarking on the similarity of the thoughts expressed by Kineas here and by Demetrios in *Demetr.* 52. 3–4 (see below), argues that both passages are derived from Douris of Samos. It also has elements common in the diatribe (despite Lévêque 1957, 276 n. 7): Tarn (1913), 237 n. 53, links it with Teles 32. 5ff Hense.   [45] *Pace* Garoufalias (1979), 64–5.

Livy's treatment of Hannibal. He is characterized as hubristic, and finally comes to recognize that his own greed and overconfidence has been the cause of his destruction (Livy 30. 23–30). Hanno, who plays the part of the wise adviser, tries to warn him against invading Italy—but to no avail (21. 3; 21. 10).[46]

Suffering heavily in Italy, Pyrrhos 'falls into new hopes' (ἐλπίδας . . . καινάς), which 'divide his purpose' (22. 1). Messengers arrive offering him the chance of conquest in both Sicily and Makedonia. He berates Fortune (τύχη) for having given him two opportunities for 'great deeds' at once, and 'thinking that the presence of both meant the loss of one, he wavered in his reasonings for a long time' (22. 3–4: διηνέχθη τοῖς λογισμοῖς πολὺν χρόνον). Once again Pyrrhos experiences an *aporia*, a paralysis of judgement; such moments of doubt and hesitation are rare in Plutarch's *Lives*,[47] and normally signal some sort of moral breakdown.[48] Finally, he invades Sicily, because it appears to offer 'greater matters' (μειζόνων . . . πραγμάτων). There 'what he hoped for at once fell securely into his lap' (22. 6), and, 'desiring greater things' (πλειόνων ἐφιέμενος), he refuses peace terms with Carthage (23. 2). It is his grandiose schemes which lead him to behave like a tyrant in Sicily and earn him the enmity of its inhabitants:

εὐτυχίᾳ δὲ καὶ ῥώμῃ τῶν παρόντων ἐπαιρόμενος, καὶ διώκων τὰς ἐλπίδας ἐφ' αἷς ἀπ' ἀρχῆς ἔπλευσε, πρώτης δὲ Λιβύης ἐφιέμενος . . . ἤγειρεν ἐρέτας, οὐκ ἐπιεικῶς ἐντυγχάνων οὐδὲ πρᾴως ταῖς πόλεσιν, ἀλλὰ δεσποτικῶς καὶ πρὸς ὀργὴν βιαζόμενος καὶ κολάζων.

Lifted up by good fortune and by strength in what he had at hand, and pursuing the hopes for which he had set sail from the start, desiring first Libya . . . he collected rowers, not dealing reasonably or gently with the cities, but like a master, angrily using force and punishment against them. (*Pyrrh.* 23. 3)

Finally driven out of both Sicily and Italy, Plutarch gives as the thoughts of an unnamed observer his own conclusion on Pyrrhos' career:

καὶ νομισθεὶς ἐμπειρίᾳ μὲν πολεμικῇ καὶ χειρὶ καὶ τόλμῃ πολὺ πρῶτος εἶναι τῶν καθ' αὑτὸν βασιλέων, ἃ δὲ ταῖς πράξεσιν ἐκτᾶτο ταῖς ἐλπίσιν ἀπολλύναι, δι' ἔρωτα τῶν ἀπόντων οὐδὲν εἰς ὃ δεῖ θέσθαι τῶν ὑπαρχόντων φθάσας.

He was considered to be much superior to the other kings of his time in political skill, strength of arm, and daring; but what he won by his deeds he lost by his hopes, since through love of what was absent he succeeded in establishing adequately none of things which he had. (*Pyrrh.* 26. 1)

[46] Mader (1993). [47] Frazier (1995), 151–4.
[48] Compare in particular, *Caes.* 32. 6–8 (see above, pp. 79–80).

The phrase 'love of what is absent' (ἔρως τῶν ἀπόντων: cf. *Marius* 45. 11) may have been proverbial.⁴⁹ The narrative of Pyrrhos' overambitious designs on Sicily would probably also bring to mind the Athenian expedition to Sicily in Thucydides: a *locus classicus* for military overconfidence.⁵⁰ Similar language recurs.⁵¹ In fact, Thucydides seems to have presented Nikias in his two speeches to the Assembly as a wise adviser,⁵² thus assimilating the overambitious people to a tyrant.⁵³

After returning from Sicily and Italy, Pyrrhos wins a success in Makedonia, but we are told (26. 14) that 'before his affairs were securely and firmly established, he was lifted up again in his thoughts towards other hopes' (ἠωρεῖτο τῇ γνώμῃ πάλιν πρὸς ἑτέρας ἐλπίδας). Thus begins his campaign in the Peloponnese, which results in his death. At the end of his life (30. 2–3), he is described as marching on Argos, where he is 'fated' to die, because he always 'piled hope on hope' (ἐλπίδας ἐξ ἐλπίδων ἀεὶ κυλίνδων), always seeking new successes and allowing 'neither defeat nor victory to put a limit (ὅρον) to his troubling himself and others' (τοῦ ταράττεσθαι καὶ ταράττειν).⁵⁴

In fact, Plutarch's picture of Pyrrhos as a man destroyed by greed and discontent seems to be a picture which he saw as particularly characteristic of the Hellenistic kings as a group. He presents the Hellenistic age as a decline from the heights of Hellenic power and internal harmony supposedly achieved by Alexander: an emphasis one might have expected, given Plutarch's distaste for strife and rivalry between Greek states (cf. *Flam.* 11. 3–7; *Ages.* 15. 2–4). Neighbouring Hellenistic kings were always in a state of conflict, like elements in the universe (*Demetr.* 5. 1; cf. *Pyrrh.* 7. 3).⁵⁵ The Hellenistic kings are characterized as a group by their desire for what Plutarch sometimes

---

⁴⁹ e.g. Pind. *Pyth.* 3. 19–23; Thuc. 6. 13. 1; Lysias 12. 78; Theok. 10. 8.

⁵⁰ The idea that Pyrrhos desired to conquer Libya may have been found in Dionysios of Halikarnassos, one of Plutarch's sources (cf. Stephen of Byzantion, s.v. Ὠκεανός, citing Dionysios Book 16).

⁵¹ Cf. Thuc. 6. 6. 1: ἐφιέμενοι τῆς πάσης ἄρξαι; 6. 8. 4: τῆς Σικελίας ἁπάσης, μεγάλου ἔργου, ἐφίεσθαι; 6. 13. 1: δυσέρωτας τῶν ἀπόντων (cf. 6. 11. 5–6; *Pyrrh.* 26. 1); 6. 15. 2 (cf. 6. 90. 2); 6. 24. 3: ἔρως ἐνέπεσε τοῖς πᾶσιν ὁμοίως ἐκπλεῦσαι (a very strong metaphor: cf. 6. 13. 1; 3. 45. 5); ἐν . . . τῆς . . . ἀπούσης πόθῳ ὄψεως καὶ θεωρίας; εὐέλπιδες; 6. 24. 4: διὰ τὴν ἄγαν τῶν πλεόνων ἐπιθυμίαν; 6. 31. 6: ἐπὶ μεγίστῃ ἐλπίδι τῶν μελλόντων πρὸς τὰ ὑπάρχοντα (cf. 6. 30. 2). ⁵² Marinatos (1980).

⁵³ Athenian rule had twice earlier been called a 'tyranny': 2. 63. 2 (by Perikles); 3. 37. 2 (by Kleon).

⁵⁴ Cf. 13. 2; 14. 13.

⁵⁵ Significantly, in *De Fort. Rom.* 316e–317c Plutarch justifies Rome's conquest of the world using a similar simile, adapted from Plato, *Tim.* 28b and 31b–32b. See below, pp. 300–1.

calls 'false glory': excessive honours, usually given by an unwilling populace.[56] He compares the assumption of kingly dress and bearing by the successors of Alexander to the donning of royal costume by tragic actors.[57] Plutarch is particularly critical of the assumption of divine honours and grandiose titles by Hellenistic kings.[58] In the *On tranquillity of mind* he uses such megalomaniac tendencies amongst some kings as a warning against discontent: people always compare themselves with those who are superior, he explains; thus kings compare themselves with the gods, almost wishing they could produce thunder and lightning (cf. *Ad Princ. Inerud.* 780f). 'Thus', he concludes, 'because they always bemoan the lack of things which are out of their reach, they are never thankful for what is within it' (*De Tranq. An.* 470b).[59]

It is no surprise, then, that Plutarch's Demetrios Poliorketes, another Hellenistic king, fits a similar pattern to Pyrrhos.[60] He begins well. When as a young man he defeats a Ptolemaic army under Killes he frees the prisoners to repay an obligation to Ptolemy. Plutarch comments with admiration that 'he rejoiced in his victory not so much because of what he would have (οἷς ἕξειν), but because of what he was going to give away' (*Demetr.* 6. 4). He seeks 'to free the whole of Greece' (8. 1; cf. 10. 1–2; *Demetr.-Ant.* 2. 3). But Demetrios is, as Plutarch had declared in the prologue to his Life, and as we may assume Pyrros and Marius are, a 'great nature', whose good natural qualities are, in the course of his career, perverted (1. 7–8).[61] Success leads to *hybris*, which he demonstrates in sexual violence and excess. As Plutarch points out in both the prologue and *synkrisis* of the book, *hybris* is one of the qualities shared by both Demetrios and Antony, as is an immoderate propensity to sexual indulgence (*Demetr.* 1. 8; *Demetr.-Ant.* 3. 1–2).[62] He assumes the

---

[56] e.g. *Arist.* 6. 1–5; *Demetr.* 10. 2–13. 3; 25. 6–8; *Ag./Kleom.* 34(13). 2–3; *Ad Princ. Inerud.* 799f–780b.   [57] e.g. *Demetr.* 18. 1–7; 41. 5–7; *De Alex. Fort.* 337d–e.

[58] *Demetr.* 10. 2–13. 3; *Ag./Kleom.* 34(13). 3; 37(16). 7; *De Alex. Fort.* 338a–c. In *De Is. et Osir.* 360c–d, Plutarch associates the desire for shortlived divine honours with, amongst other things, the recipients' overconfidence (ἐξαρθέντες), folly (ἄνοια), and emptiness (κενότης). See above, n. 23.

[59] Cf. Aalders (1982), 22–3. In the *Pomp.*, Plutarch extends this analysis to the Republican dynasts Pompey and Caesar. Fortune could not satisfy their desire (ἐπιθυμία), even with a half-share in the Roman Empire; they could not, unlike the gods, share power (*Pomp.* 53. 10). Before Pharsalos, sensible bystanders reflect on the greed (πλεονεξία) and love of rivalry (φιλονεικία) which had prevented Pompey and Caesar from enjoying in peace the best part of the earth (70. 1–3).

[60] On Demetrios' moral decline, cf. Andrei (1989), 68–71. For Plutarch's generally unfavourable view of Hellenistic history, see *De Alex. Fort.* 336f–337a, *Cato Maj.* 8. 12–14 and *Eum.* 13. 5–6, all cited by Geiger (1995b), 183–5.   [61] See pp. 45–9.

[62] For Demetrios' sexual antics, cf. also *Demetr.* 2. 3; 9. 5–7; 19. 4–5; 19. 10.

title and dress of king from his father Antigonos, leading the other successors of Alexander to follow suit (18. 1–4). Plutarch comments that this change 'stirred the spirits (φρονήματα) of the men and lifted up (ἐπῆρε) their opinions and introduced into their lives and their dealings with others pride and ostentation just as tragic actors adapt to their costumes also their walk, voice, way of reclining and way of addressing others' (*Demetr.* 18. 5).[63] When he is proclaimed commander-in-chief in Greece he is 'lifted up (ἐπαιρόμενος) by his present good fortune and power', even considering himself superior to Philip and Alexander (25. 4–5). Similarly Seleukos I, with whom Demetrios concludes an alliance but later, typically, falls into conflict, is described in terms familiar from our study of Pyrrhos. Despite possessing huge domains of his own, Seleukos still considered himself so poor and beggarly that he demanded the surrender of Tyre and Sidon by Demetrios (32. 7). Plutarch concludes with a paraphrase of Plato's *Laws* 736e: 'He provided clear support (λαμπρὰν . . . μαρτυρίαν) for Plato's insistence that the man who wants to be truly rich should not enlarge his property but reduce his insatiability (ἀπληστία), since the man who does not put an end to his love of wealth is never free of poverty or want' (*Demetr.* 32. 8). Seleukos is made into a paradigm of the dangers of greed, and it is to this paradigm that Demetrios will increasingly conform. Failure follows success, as the prologue had predicted, making Demetrios explicitly an example of the unreliability of fortune (35. 3–6). But when news of defeat arrives, he is filled with 'other hopes of new and great matters' (35. 6: ἑτέρας πραγμάτων καινῶν καὶ μεγάλων . . . ἐλπίδας). Later he rejects the chance of peace, being, like Pyrrhos, 'not well suited to peace' (41. 1).

Finally, in captivity at the end of his life, Demetrios falls into drinking and playing dice. Plutarch gives two possible reasons for this (52. 2–4), both of which reveal his own moral conceptions, and both of which have at their centre the contrast between future hopes and present reality which are so central to the *Life of Pyrrhos*. The first possibility, Plutarch explains, is that Demetrios was drinking to 'avoid his sober reflections about the present (ἀναλογισμοὺς τῶν παρόντων) and cover over his thoughts by drunkenness', a damning statement in view of Plutarch's concern for the priority of reason (52. 3). As the second possibility,

---

[63] This led them, Plutarch concludes, to become harsher in their judgements (18. 6–7); Plutarch later comments on the sham of Demetrios' kingship in that he neglected the most kingly duty of all, the dispensing of justice (42. 8–11). Tatum (1996), 141–3, also notes the contrast implicit in Plutarch's narrative between Demetrios' kingly physical appearance and his unkingly character.

Plutarch states as his own authorial view on Demetrios a version of the judgement on Pyrrhos which he had put into the mouth of Kineas:

(52. 3) . . . εἴτε συγγνοὺς ἑαυτῷ τοῦτον εἶναι τὸν βίον, ὃν ἔκπαλαι ποθῶν καὶ διώκων ἄλλως ὑπ' ἀνοίας καὶ κενῆς δόξης ἐπλάζετο καὶ πολλὰ μὲν ἑαυτῷ, πολλὰ δ' ἑτέροις πράγματα παρεῖχεν, ἐν ὅπλοις καὶ στόλοις καὶ στρατοπέδοις τὸ ἀγαθὸν ζητῶν, ὃ νῦν ἐν ἀπραγμοσύνῃ καὶ σχολῇ καὶ ἀναπαύσει μὴ προσδοκήσας ἀνεύρηκε. (52. 4) τί γὰρ ἄλλο τῶν πολέμων καὶ τῶν κινδύνων πέρας ἐστὶ τοῖς φαύλοις βασιλεῦσι, κακῶς καὶ ἀνοήτως διακειμένοις, οὐχ ὅτι μόνον τρυφὴν καὶ ἡδονὴν ἀντὶ τῆς ἀρετῆς καὶ τοῦ καλοῦ διώκουσιν, ἀλλ' ὅτι μηδ' ἥδεσθαι μηδὲ τρυφᾶν ὡς ἀληθῶς ἴσασιν.

(52. 3) Or he realized that this was the life which he had so long desired and pursued, but which he had foolishly missed through folly and empty glory. He had brought many troubles on himself and many troubles on others, as he sought the good in arms and fleets and camps, the good which he had now unexpectedly discovered in lack of action, leisure, and rest. (52. 4) For what other end to wars and dangers is there for worthless kings, whose characters are base and foolish?—not just because they pursue luxury and pleasure instead of virtue and the good, but also because they do not even know how to enjoy and luxuriate properly.   (*Demetr.* 52. 3–4)

4. THE *MARIUS*

Marius, like Pyrrhos, is characterized by an inability to remain inactive, a result of discontent and an ambition which, as Plutarch underlines, shockingly did not abate in old age (*Mar.* 2. 4; 34. 6).[64] In the case of Marius, this failing is linked to deficient education. These themes are spelt out most clearly, as has been seen, at the start of the Life, in a passage which explicitly provides a way of reading the deeds which follow (*Mar.* 2. 1–4: see p. 00). Plutarch's picture of Marius is particularly negative. A remark of Scipio encourages the youthful Marius on a political career, 'lifted up by hopes' (4. 1: ἐπαρθέντα ταῖς ἐλπίσιν; cf. 8. 8). Marius wins tremendous prestige for victories in wars against Jugurtha and against the German invaders of Italy, and crowns an unprecedented five consulships held in succession with a triumph. But, Plutarch makes clear, at the height of his career, he was not content.

(28. 1) Πέμπτην μὲν οὖν ὑπατείαν διεῖπε· τῆς δ' ἕκτης ὡς οὐδ' εἰς πρώτης ὠρέγετο, θεραπείαις τε τὸν δῆμον ἀναλαμβάνων καὶ πρὸς χάριν ἐνδιδοὺς τοῖς

---

[64] In *Luc.* 38. 3, Marius is contrasted with Lucullus, who did retire when old: see above, n. 30.

πολλοῖς, οὐ μόνον παρὰ τὸν ὄγκον καὶ τὸ κοινὸν ἀξίωμα τῆς ἀρχῆς, ἀλλὰ καὶ παρὰ τὴν αὑτοῦ φύσιν ὑγρός τις εἶναι βουλόμενος καὶ δημοτικός, ἥκιστα τοιοῦτος πεφυκώς. (28. 2) ἀλλ' ἦν ὡς λέγουσι πρὸς πολιτείαν καὶ τοὺς ἐν ὄχλοις θορύβους ὑπὸ φιλοδοξίας ἀτολμότατος, καὶ τὸ παρὰ τὰς μάχας ἀνέκπληκτον καὶ στάσιμον ἐν ταῖς ἐκκλησίαις ἀπέλειπεν αὐτόν, ὑπὸ τῶν τυχόντων ἐπαίνων καὶ ψόγων ἐξιστάμενον.

(28. 1) So he brought his fifth consulship to an end. But he desired a sixth more strongly than anyone desired a first, attempting to court the favour of the people and giving in to the multitude in order to win favour, acting not only contrary to the dignity and rank of his office but also contrary to his own nature, in that he wanted to be easy-going and one of the people, when he was by nature not at all like this. (28. 2) He was, so they say, because of his love of glory, very cowardly when facing political life or the disturbances of the rabble; his imperturbability and steadfastness in battles deserted him in assemblies, as he was driven out of his wits by chance praise and blame. (*Mar.* 28. 1–2)

In his desire to be re-elected consul, Plutarch's Marius demeans his office and himself by courting the favour of the people. Marius' action is described in terms which associate him with the Greek 'types' of the flatterer and the demagogue, as the use of the terms θεραπεία and χάρις imply. Marius, until now the fearless commander and firm politician (4. 6–7), here trembles at the disapprobation of the common people. In the treatise *How to tell a flatterer from a friend* Plutarch argues that the most important diagnostic of a flatterer is his instability of character, the way in which he adapts himself to suit the character of the one into whose affections he is trying to wheedle (51a–53b); he is 'supple to change' (*Quomodo Adult.* 51c: ὑγρὸς . . . μεταβάλλεσθαι). Marius' action is, then, flattery; what is worse, it is flattery of the common people, an activity which Plutarch considered particularly reprehensible.[65] For Plutarch, Marius was not merely acting out of character, he was acting 'contrary to his own nature' (παρὰ τὴν ἑαυτοῦ φύσιν), a rather startling formulation given ancient views on the immutability of nature.[66] The cause of his disgraceful behaviour is discontent fed by love of glory. As Plutarch continues, 'he fled for refuge to the good will and favour of the multitude, rejecting the possibility of being best in order to become the greatest' (28. 5). He thus runs into collision with the 'aristocrats' (οἱ ἀριστοκρατικοί) and especially Metellus Numidicus 'who had

[65] On this theme in the Roman Lives, see De Blois (1992), 4590–9. Plutarch's account ignores the reality of the Roman political system, which involved popular election for the consulship: the historical Marius had to win some measure of popular support. On such distortions of Roman history, see below, pp. 302–3.

[66] As opposed to character (ἦθος). On this topic, see above, p. 74.

experienced his ingratitude and who, by nature, because of his genuine virtue, was at war with those who wickedly tried to insinuate themselves into the favour of the masses and used pleasure as a means of demagogy' (28. 6). Marius is thus forced to side with the unscrupulous Saturninus, and so begins the decline of his fortunes.

After his humiliation in the Saturninus affair (29–30), Marius tries to stir up war with Mithridates. Plutarch explains (31. 3), 'He was unsuited by nature for peace and not fitted for public affairs (ἀφυὴς . . . πρὸς εἰρήνην καὶ ἀπολίτευτος), having risen through war. And now, thinking that his influence and reputation were gradually fading away again because of inactivity and quiet (ὑπ' ἀργίας καὶ ἡσυχίας), he sought opportunities for new affairs (καινῶν πραγμάτων ἀρχάς).' A little later, despite his age, Marius attempts unsuccessfully to gain the command in the war against Mithridates. Plutarch presents as the thoughts of bystanders, as they watch Marius attempting to train in the Campus Martius, two different reactions and two contrasting valuations of his action; as often, he expects the reader to share the judgement of those whom he styles the 'best people':[67]

ἐνίοις μὲν οὖν ἤρεσκε ταῦτα πράττων, καὶ κατιόντες ἐθεῶντο τὴν φιλοτιμίαν αὐτοῦ καὶ τὰς ἁμίλλας, τοῖς δὲ βελτίστοις ὁρῶσιν οἰκτίρειν ἐπῄει τὴν πλεονεξίαν καὶ τὴν φιλοδοξίαν, ὅτι πλουσιώτατος ἐκ πένητος καὶ μέγιστος ἐκ μικροῦ γεγονὼς ὅρον οὐκ οἶδεν εὐτυχίας, οὐδὲ θαυμαζόμενος ἀγαπᾷ καὶ ἀπολαύων ἐν ἡσυχίᾳ τῶν παρόντων, ἀλλ' ὥσπερ ἐνδεὴς ἁπάντων εἰς Καππαδοκίαν καὶ τὸν Εὔξεινον Πόντον ἄρας ἐκ θριάμβων καὶ δόξης ἐκφέρει τοσοῦτον γῆρας.

Some people were pleased to see him doing this, and they used to go down and watch his competitiveness and struggles. But the best people, when they saw him, were moved to pity at his greed and love of glory, because, although he had become very rich from being poor and very powerful from being powerless, he did not know how to set a bound to his good fortune. He was not content to be admired and to enjoy in peace and quiet what was present. Instead, as though lacking everything, he was setting out for Kappadokia and the Black Sea and dragging along his great old age after triumphs and glory. (*Mar.* 34. 6)

Marius, like Pyrrhos (*Pyrrh.* 12. 3; 30. 3), does not know how to set a bound (ὅρος) on his good fortune, even in old age. What some regard as a healthy 'love of honour' is really the much more negative 'craving for more' and 'love for glory' (πλεονεξία and φιλοδοξία).

Finally, at the end of his life, on his deathbed, Marius suffers from the delusion that he has obtained the Mithridatic command (45. 10).

[67] e.g. *Thes.* 17. 1–2; *Flam.* 11. 3–7; *Nik.* 26. 4–6; *Crass.* 27. 6; *Phok.* 37. 1–2; *Cato Min.* 26. 5; *Pomp.* 70. 1–7; *Pyrrh.* 26. 1; *Mar.* 34. 6–7. See also p. 55 and Pelling (1988*b*), 40.

Plutarch comments again on that particular mix of ambition and discontent which characterizes Marius, and has characterized Pyrrhos too (45. 11–12):

(45. 11) οὕτως δεινὸς αὐτῷ καὶ δυσπαραμύθητος ἐκ φιλαρχίας καὶ ζηλοτυπίας ἔρως ἐντετήκει τῶν πράξεων ἐκείνων· (45. 12) διό, ἔτη μὲν ἑβδομήκοντα βεβιωκώς, ὕπατος δὲ πρῶτος ἀνθρώπων ἑπτάκις ἀνηγορευμένος, οἶκόν τε καὶ πλοῦτον ἀρκοῦντα βασιλείαις ὁμοῦ πολλαῖς κεκτημένος, ὠδύρετο τὴν ἑαυτοῦ τύχην ὡς ἐνδεὴς καὶ ἀτελὴς ὢν ἐπόθει προαποθνῄσκων.

(45. 11) Such a terrible and inconsolable passion for those actions had sunk into him, as a result of his love of office and his sense of rivalry. (45. 12) So, having lived for seventy years, having been the first man to be declared consul seven times, having gained possession of a house and wealth which sufficed many kingdoms at once, he lamented his own fate, claiming that he was dying in want before his time and had not completed what he desired. (*Mar.* 45. 11–12)

5. MILITARY VIRTUES IN THE *PYRRHOS–MARIUS*

Like all the subjects of Plutarch's *Lives*, Pyrrhos and Marius have great potential, 'great natures'. But this potential is not fully realized in Pyrrhos and Marius, but translated into virtue in only one sphere of their character: the military. As is the case also with Philopoimen, Flamininus, and Coriolanus, the education of both men is purely military.[68] Like Coriolanus, Marius does not know how to act in peace time or politics (cf. *Pyrrh.* 12. 8), a danger which Plutarch saw as facing all successful generals after their time of office (*Pomp.* 23. 5–6).[69] Plutarch underlines the two men's personal bravery, which shows itself at a very young age: Marius wins Scipio Africanus' regard on his first campaign at Numantia (3. 2), just as Pyrrhos had won Demetrios' while fighting at Ipsos (4. 3–7). Both men fight and win single combats.[70] In the first of these combats (*Pyrrh.* 7. 5–9), Pyrrhos defeats Pantauchos in a formal duel, the pattern of which is reminiscent of Homeric single combats.[71] Pyrrhos enters the duel partly because of a desire 'to make the glory of Achilles his own through valour rather than blood': as so often in this Life, Pyrrhos' military successes are linked to his supposed ancestor Achilles.[72] Later

[68] *Phil.* 3. 1–5; *Flam.* 1. 4; *Cor.* 1. 3–2. 2; *Pyrrh.* 8. 3–7; *Marius* 2. 1.
[69] Cf. *Pomp.* 46. 1–4; *Cor.* 1. 4; 15. 4–7; *Mar.* 6. 3; 28. 1–5; 32. 2. See Wardman (1974), 93–100; Hillman (1992), 128–35.
[70] *Pyrrh.* 7. 5–9; 24. 4–6; 30. 9–11; cf. 34. 1; *Mar.* 3. 3.
[71] For the generic features of Homeric duels, see Fenik (1968).
[72] e.g. *Pyrrh.* 1–2; 7. 7; 13. 2; 17. 1–6. See Mossman (1992), 95 and *pass.*

he challenges his enemy Antigonos Gonatas of Macedon to single combat; Antigonos refuses (31. 3–4). This episode foreshadows the end of Pyrrhos' heroic life, and contrasts him with Antigonos, who is wiser and gentler, as the last chapter of the Life will demonstrate, and whose approach to generalship is not based on personal prowess.[73] None of the three single combats of Pyrrhos (7. 5–9; 24. 4–6; 30. 9–11) is mentioned elsewhere, and there is no independent evidence that the successors of Alexander engaged in single combat any more than their classical predecessors, for whom it is virtually unknown.[74] It seems that Plutarch has chosen to emphasize the role of single combat in the *Life of Pyrrhos* both to give his military activities epic and Achillean associations, and also to create a parallel with Marius: both men are brave soldiers.[75] For Marius too engages in single combat (3. 3). As a result of it, Scipio predicts him as the next great Roman general (3. 4–5), just as Antigonos had 'talent-spotted' Pyrrhos, and Hannibal had declared him the best general of all (8. 4–5).[76]

The bravery of the two men is often expressed with seafaring imagery. This imagery not only links the two men, but links their military greatness with the discontent which destroys them. The achievements of both men are linked to struggles with floods. Pyrrhos when a baby is carried with difficulty across a raging river to escape his pursuers (2. 3–8). On his way to Italy he is caught in a storm and demonstrates his bravery by leaping overboard and swimming ashore (15. 3–8). Similarly, storm and sea imagery is used repeatedly in the *Marius* to describe the threat posed by the German tribes, imagery which also makes use of the ship of state metaphor.[77] Furthermore, as we have noted, storm imagery is a not uncommon way of symbolizing inner discontent, so it is not surprising that it is this image which is used to mark the decline in the fortunes of the two men. In *Pyrrh.* 23. 7, Pyrrhos sails away, unable to conquer Sicily, which is described as a 'storm-tossed ship' (νεὼς ταραχθείσης). Finally,

[73] The anecdote is probably from Hieronymos, but the criticism implied of Pyrrhos' method of generalship would certainly have been one with which Plutarch concurred.

[74] Pace Hornblower (1981), 194–6.

[75] Although Marius' single combat is recorded nowhere else, there is evidence that single combat was not unusual in late 2nd-c. BC Rome, and was particularly common in warfare with northern enemies: see Oakley (1985), esp. 392–9, 404–10.

[76] The patronage Marius receives from Metellus (*Mar.* 4. 1) and his marriage into the family of the Caesars (6. 4), recall Pyrrhos' being chosen as a young man to marry Antigone daughter of Berenike, and the help he receives from Ptolemy (*Pyrrh.* 4. 6–5. 1); cf. Pyrrhos' later dynastic marriages, listed in *Pyrrh.* 9. 1–2.

[77] Ship imagery: 11. 1; 14. 1; 16. 2; 20. 9; 23. 1; 26. 2. Ship of state: 11. 1; 14. 1; 23. 1. See Carney (1960), 24–5. For the long history of the ship of state image, see Nisbet and Hubbard (1970), 179–80; Meichsner (1983).

the confusion in Argos which resulted in Pyrrhos' death is described with the words 'storm and surf' (34. 1: χειμῶνα καὶ κλύδωνα). A similar linking of Marius' greatest successes, the German Wars, with his savage old age, is achieved by the use of sea imagery in the reflective passages at the start and end of the Life.[78] Excessive ambition, old age, and seafaring imagery are thus linked.

6. TRAGIC PATTERNING IN THE *PYRRHOS–MARIUS*

There is a strong sense of fatalism in both Lives, a sense that Pyrrhos and Marius are being led by forces stronger than themselves to their appointed ends. Both men share certain traits: personal courage combined with an unwillingness to remain inactive, qualities which lead both to their successes and to their ultimate downfall. This linking of both success and failure to the same traits is indeed a feature of Plutarchan biography more generally,[79] but it is the sense of impending doom, the dramatic irony, which runs throughout these Lives which gives them their distinctive tragic quality. Pyrrhos' dialogue with Kineas encourages the reader to expect disaster. Tragic irony is at its clearest in the frequent references to *tyche*. Both men experience great changes of fortune, which are directly ascribed to the operation of *tyche*.[80] But, whereas often in the *Lives tyche* means either chance or providence, here it seems to be more like the impersonal fate which we meet in tragedy.[81] Comparison with Sophokles' *Oidipous Tyrannos* is attractive.[82] Judith Mossman has demonstrated how tragic associations are used in the *Pyrrhos* to suggest the negative features of the hero.[83] In fact, as the Life progresses, Pyrrhos is cast increasingly in the role of a tragic hero: driven by fate, which works through his own moral weaknesses, to press on to a goal which leads inevitably to disaster. The ominous statement that fate was 'inescapable' (30. 2: ἄφυκτον; cf. 16. 14) sets up a tragic irony which overshadows Pyrrhos' last venture. Portents multiply as his death

[78] 2. 4: ἐξοκείλας; 45. 1–4: reports of Sulla's successes are like a change of wind and Marius is deluged; 45. 7: he is terrified by the fresh news of a messenger who comes, significantly, 'from the sea'; 45. 10: ἐξοκεῖλαι.

[79] Pelling (1986b), 87–96; (1988b), 13.

[80] Brenk (1977), 181, lists the occurrences of *tyche* in the *Mar.* Neither Pyrrhos nor Marius is content with the good which fate brings: they are μεμψίμοιροι. See above, n. 9.

[81] On *tyche* in the *Lives*, cf. Brenk (1977), 145–83; Swain (1989b; 1989c; 1989d).

[82] Cf. Mossman (1992), 102.

[83] Mossman (1992). See also, for tragic features in other Lives, ead. (1988) on *Alex.*, Braund (1993) on *Crass.*; and in general De Lacy (1952).

approaches (29. 1–4; 30. 5; 31. 7; 32. 8–10). Pyrrhos himself, like many a tragic hero, ignores them to his peril. Tragic irony is at its strongest when Pyrrhos ignores an unfavourable interpretation of a dream and declares, adapting Hektor's words at *Iliad* 12. 243, 'One omen is best: to fight for Pyrrhos'.[84] The incident reveals his inability to refrain from war, even when the omens are bad, and marks a stage in his progression towards his fated end in the ill-conceived attack on Argos. But more significantly, the Homeric context casts a portentous shadow over his campaigns in the Peloponnese: Hektor was to regret his disregard of Polydamas' advice to withdraw; his foolhardiness led ultimately to his death at Achilles' hands. Pyrrhos has been so far in the Life consistently linked with Achilles; the change to Hektor is highly charged.

In the *Marius*, tragic patterning is even clearer. Tragic irony is set up by the reference at the start of his Life to his final end (2. 4). Fate plays a bigger part in leading Marius through his successes and reverses to his appointed end. In the Roman writer of 'exemplary' history, Valerius Maximus, the figure of Marius is a paradigm for the ups and downs of fortune. In Plutarch, this theme is linked to that of ambition and discontent. As Frederick Brenk has put it, 'Marius is continually motivated by portents which first lift him to undreamed of success, then to delusions of grandeur, and finally hurl him into the abyss of despair'.[85] His life can be seen as a series of cycles in which *hybris* (the word is used in 9. 2) is followed by disaster, which is on a number of occasions referred to as *nemesis*.[86] In 39. 6, the magistrates of Minturnae cast him out to meet his destiny (τὸ μεμορμένον) and pray that the gods will not visit them with *nemesis* for their deed. In 40. 9, he compares his own change of fortune (μεταβολή) to the fate (τύχη) of Carthage.[87]

The fortunes of Pyrrhos and Marius are reflected in the clothes they wear. In the *Pyrrhos* clothing is used as a moral indicator: Pyrrhos' valour is symbolized by his goat-horned helmet (11. 11: τῷ τε λόφῳ διαπρέποντι καὶ τοῖς τραγικοῖς κέρασιν); when, like Achilles, he swaps armour with a comrade, disaster nearly befalls his army until he puts it on again (17. 1–6). But this ostentatious headgear may also be a negative feature, suggesting a certain 'tragic' arrogance in Pyrrhos; there is probably a pun on the two meanings of τραγικός here (from τράξ, goat,

---

[84] εἷς οἰωνὸς ἄριστος ἀμύνεσθαι περὶ Πύρρου, replacing Homer's πάτρης with Πύρρου (*Pyrr.* 29. 4). The line is also quoted, in a shorter form, at *De Alex. Fort.* 333c.
[85] Brenk (1977), 192; e.g. *Mar.* 4. 1; 8. 8; 36. 7–11; 38. 9; 45. 3–12.
[86] *Mar.* 10. 2; 23. 1; 26. 5: πρᾶγμα νεμεσητόν.
[87] The instability of human affairs is a theme of these Lives: cf. *Pyrrh.* 34. 8; *Marius* 23. 1.

and τραγῳδία, tragedy).[88] For Plutarch, ostentatious display, often involving fine clothes (e.g. *Ag./Kleom.* 37[16]. 7), is sometimes compared with performances on the tragic stage to suggest pride and a gap between appearance and reality. The comparison with the tragic stage can in the usage of this period imply excessive pomp.[89] In Plutarch's *Life of Demetrios*, which, as has been noted, shares some of the moral concerns of these Lives, fine clothes mark Demetrios' pride; poor clothes mark his humbling. When Demetrios is caught in a surprise attack as he awaits a visit from the beauty Kratesipolis, he flees (*Demetr.* 9. 7) wearing a 'cheap little cloak' (χλαμύδιον εὐτελές). Later, when his troops want to desert to Pyrrhos they put on garlands; in contrast, Demetrios flees dressed in humble clothes (11. 11–13).[90] Contrast Demetrios' fine clothes in *Demetr.* 41. 5–7, which Plutarch again links with tragedy (cf. 18. 5, above). When Demetrios decides to flee again, Plutarch says that, 'he went to his tent (σκηνή: a word with stage associations), as if he were not a king but an actor, and put on a dark cloak instead of that tragic one (χλαμύδα φαιὰν ἀντὶ τῆς τραγικῆς ἐκείνης), and stole away unnoticed' (*Demetr.* 44. 9).[91] Some of this may well have come from Douris of Samos, whose account certainly influenced both the *Life of Pyrrhos* and the *Life of Demetrios*, and who was well known as a proponent of the so-called tragic history, which put a high premium on the dramatic, emotive, and sensational.[92] But, even if Plutarch did get some of his material for these Greek Lives from Douris, the application of the same principles to the Life of Marius, and indeed to that of Antony, is his own.[93] Triumphal robes mark

---

[88] For similar puns on τραγικός, cf. Plato, *Krat.* 408c; Longos 4. 17. 2 (with Hunter 1983, 89); Lucian, *Gall.* 10.

[89] Plut. *Demetr.* 41. 5–7; *Arat.* 15. 3; Lucian, *Gall.* 24; *Alex.* 5, 12; cf. Diod. 5. 31. 1; Dion. Hal. *Ant. Rom.* 6. 70. 2. On Lucian, *Gall.* 24, the scholiast explains that the cock's pomposity is called 'tragedy' 'because things in a tragedy are pompous (κομπά)' (94. 8–9 Rabe[b]). See De Lacy (1952); Kokolakis (1960), 85–7; Anderson (1976), 18–19. Tragic costume in this period, which included padded dress and huge boots (κόθορνοι or ἐμβάται), was especially grand; cf. Damis' description in Lucian, *Jupp. Trag.* 41: οἷς ἐκεῖνοι σεμνύνουσι τὴν τραγῳδίαν. See Kokolakis (1960), 100–6; cf. Phil. *Apoll.* 5. 9. Hence Plutarch's references to Demetrios' ostentatious clothes as a 'tragic' feature in *Demetr.* 41. 5–7. Plutarch compares kings or emperors who do not have real power to actors who play kings: *Galba* 1. 7–8; *De Alex. Fort.* 337d–e.

[90] Diodoros notes Demetrios' fine clothes, but does not not make the link with tragedy (19. 81. 4; 20. 92. 3).

[91] Cf. Cavafy, *King Demetrios* (published 1906), based on this passage, which captures the mood nicely. On stage imagery in the *Demetr.* cf. De Lacy (1952), 168–71; Mossman (1992), 100 and 103; Andrei (1989), 78–82. Cf. above, 62 n. 35.

[92] e.g. Kebric (1977), 14–18. On 'tragic history', see above, pp. 41–2.

[93] For a sensational description à la Douris in the *Ant.*, compare *Ant.* 26. 1–3 with the fragment of Douris preserved in *Alk.* 23. 2 (*FGrH* 76 F70).

Marius' arrogance (12. 7). His exhibiting the prophetess Martha in a doubled-over red tunic[94] with a golden clasp, and a spear crowned with garlands and ribbons (cf. *Pel.* 29. 8), probably has a similar force (17. 2–5). Significantly, this display is referred to as a play ($\delta\rho\hat{a}\mu a$) in which, as some people at least thought, Marius too acted a part ($\sigma\upsilon\nu\upsilon\pi o\kappa\rho\iota\nu\acute{o}\mu\epsilon\nu os$); we should take this as a negative judgement.[95] Marius' success is marked by fine clothes (22. 2–5); nakedness, on the other hand, marks his lowest ebb. In 38. 2 he is dragged naked and covered in slime from the pond where he had hidden himself. When he returns to Italy, it is as a savage: he presents himself to Cinna 'in mean attire with his hair uncut since the days of his flight', refusing the consular *insignia* offered him. His appearance is 'frightful' ($\phi o\beta\epsilon\rho\acute{o}s$), and, says Plutarch, 'his dejection revealed that his spirit ($\theta\upsilon\mu\acute{o}s$) had not been humbled but rather made savage by his reverse' (41. 6). This recalls Plutarch's description of his statues in 2. 1, where his appearance had reflected his harsh and bitter character.

7. SYNKRISIS IN THE *PYRRHOS–MARIUS*

As often in Plutarchan Lives, the reader is encouraged to read the second Life in the light of the first, to compare and contrast. Such a reading underscores the differences between the two men and between the two biographies, the departures of the second Life from the model of the first.[96] In this pair, the greater ruthlessness of Marius is illustrated by the way he departs from the model set by Pyrrhos. Pyrrhos sets the pattern of the great military leader who cannot cease from war and whose hopes lead him to disaster. He rules humanely (8. 8–12; 11. 8–9; 20. 10), and only towards the end of his life begins to act like a tyrant (23. 3). Marius, however, comes into conflict not only with enemies but also with his own countrymen and institutes a reign of terror. Fittingly, he dies with his mind unhinged: contrast Pyrrhos who dies bravely on the battlefield.

Several parallel episodes reinforce this distinction. One such parallel is found in their interpretation of omens. Pyrrhos, as we have seen, ignores

---

[94] According to Chamoux (1974), 83–5, Martha's $\phi o\iota\nu\iota\kappa\grave{\iota}s$ $\delta\iota\pi\lambda\hat{\eta}$ is a red cloak 'doubled over' to transform it into a *chlamys*, the Greek military garment (cf. Lyk. *Against Leokrates* 40).

[95] Elsewhere, Plutarch compares the manipulation of popular superstition to a play: *Num.* 8. 10; *Them.* 10. 1; *Lys.* 25. 2; 26. 6; *Sert.* 11. 2; 20. 1: see Berardi (1990), 148.

[96] The first Life frequently sets a paradigm which is exploited by the second: Pelling (1986*b*), 93–6.

an unfavourable interpretation of a dream (29. 4). The incident reveals his inability to cease from war and suggests the coming disaster. Contrast Marius' interpretation of the omens before Vercellae (26. 4), where the emphasis is on his rivalry with his colleague Catulus. Hints of divine disfavour follow immediately:

(26. 4) τὸν δὲ Μάριον καὶ θύσαντα λέγεται, τῶν ἱερῶν αὐτῷ δειχθέντων, μέγα φθεγξάμενον εἰπεῖν· "ἐμὴ ⟨ἡ⟩ νίκη." (26. 5) γενομένης δὲ τῆς ἐφόδου πρᾶγμα νεμεσητὸν παθεῖν τὸν Μάριον οἱ περὶ Σύλλαν ἱστοροῦσι· κονιορτοῦ γὰρ ἀρθέντος, οἷον εἰκὸς ἀπλέτου καὶ τῶν στρατοπέδων ἀποκεκρυμμένων, ἐκεῖνον μὲν, ὡς τὸ πρῶτον ὥρμησε πρὸς τὴν δίωξιν, ἐπισπασάμενον τὴν δύναμιν ἀστοχῆσαι τῶν πολεμίων . . .

(26. 4) When he had sacrificed and the victims had been shown to him, Marius is actually said to have shouted out 'The victory belongs to me'. (26. 5) But Sulla's party reports that when the assault had begun Marius had an experience brought about by the wrath of the gods [*nemesis*]. For they say that a large cloud of dust was raised and, as might be expected, the two armies were obscured; when Marius first rushed to the pursuit at the head of his force he missed the enemy. (*Mar.* 26. 4–5)

The result is that it is Catulus' forces which bear the brunt of the fighting and Catulus who claims the victory. Marius' contentiousness is such that, after the battle, a quarrel breaks out over whose was the victory (27. 6–10).

Marius' greater ruthlessness is revealed in the way the two men treat their sons. After Sulla's march on Rome, Marius takes ship at Ostia, abandoning his son to almost certain death, though through good fortune and the loyalty of a retainer he escapes to Africa (35. 8–12). Pyrrhos had lost his son, Ptolemy, in an ambush (*Pyrrh.* 30. 5–6). His grief is emphasized; in anguish he charges into battle and fights more fiercely than ever before, and 'fills himself with slaughter' (ἐνεπίμπλατο φόνου). He kills in hand-to-hand combat the Spartan Eualkos (30. 7–11), whose death is described as a sacrifice for his son as hero (ἐναγισμός).[97] Marius vents his anger later on his fellow citizens: his θυμός growing day by day and thirsting for blood, he hunts down anybody he suspects (43. 7). His brutality is brought out by showing the more conciliatory

---

[97] Probably recalling Achilles' human sacrifice at Patroklos' pyre (*Iliad* 23. 175–6) and Alexander's killing of the Kossaioi in honour of Hephaistion (*Alex.* 72. 4): Mossman (1992), 103. An ἐναγισμός is specifically a sacrifice to the heroized dead, or to the gods of the underworld, rather than to the Olympian gods; for the distinction, see Hdt. 2. 44. 5; Aristotle, *Ath. Pol.* 58. 1; Paus. 2. 10. 1; 2. 11. 7; 8. 34. 3; Heliodoros 2. 35. 2; cf. Harrison (1922), 55–65, and Casabona (1966), 204–8.

attitude of Cinna (43. 2), who becomes 'sated with slaughter' (43. 7: μεστὸς τοῦ φονεύειν).[98]

Synkrisis, as often, functions not only at the level of the pair but also within the individual Life. The subject of the Life is set against minor characters. Internal *synkrisis* within the *Marius* emphasizes the subject's moral failings. We have already noticed such *synkriseis* with Cinna and with Plato and Antipatros. In 23. 5, the comment that Catulus 'had less regard for his own reputation than for that of his fellow-citizens' brings with it an implicit censure of Marius. The most central *synkrisis* is with Metellus. The early part of the Life sketches the history of the jealousy between the two men, the blame for which is laid on Marius. After the German Wars, Marius decides to banish Metellus, because he has experienced Marius' ingratitude and because Metellus is the enemy of the flatterers of the people (28. 6). Marius uses Saturninus' agrarian law with its compulsory oath to set an 'inescapable trap' (ἀπάτην . . . ἄφυκτον) for Metellus (29. 4). In a neat twist, suggesting the *nemesis* of the gods, it is in fact Marius and his son who, like Pyrrhos, will face an 'inescapable fate' (46. 9; cf. 39. 6).[99] Metellus' firmness of purpose is emphasized. He is a steadfast man (29. 5: βέβαιον ἄνδρα), a fact emphasized by a quotation from Pindar. Metellus refuses to swear the oath to the *Lex Apuleia*, 'remaining true to his character (ἐμμένων τῷ ἤθει)', as Plutarch puts it, 'and prepared to suffer any fate rather than do something dishonourable' (29. 8). Marius' moral failings are emphasized in contrast, particularly his duplicity and flattery. In exile, significantly, Metellus spends his time in philosophical studies (29. 12)—a direct contrast to the uneducated Marius.[100]

When Marius is engaged in the blockade of Rome (42. 1–9), Plutarch once again employs comparison, though this time it is more thought-provoking. Octavius, one of his opponents, is said (42. 7) to be keeping

---

[98] It is significant that in Appian (*BC* 1. 73) the freed slaves who terrorize Rome during the Cinnan *regnum* are associated wholly with Cinna; in Plutarch, they are associated solely with Marius (43. 4–6 and 44. 9–10). Cf. Corbellini (1976).

[99] On fate, see above, pp. 103–4 and 123–4.

[100] And unlike the educated Cicero (*Cic* 32. 5–7). The good treatment of Metellus undoubtedly owes much to Rutilius Rufus, who was hostile to Marius and therefore pro-Metellus (see above, n. 1). Cicero (*Ad Fam.* 1. 9. 16) also rejects unfavourable reports of Metellus' reaction to his exile and, like Plutarch, affirms his good character. Plutarch did, however, know Sallust (at least, that is, he knew the *Cat*.: Moles 1988, 29; and the *Hist*.: Peter 1865, 61–4; 106–9; 112–14; Moreno 1992, esp. 141–2) whose *Jug.* has an unfavourable picture of Metellus. It is just possible that Plutarch read Sallust in Greek: the *Souda* (s.v. Ζηνόβιος) records that in the reign of Hadrian a certain Zenobios translated Sallust's *Hist.* into Greek; it is possible that the *Pyrrh.-Mar.* was written after Hadrian's accession: see above n. 15.

the dignity (πρόσχημα) of the consulship 'free from flattery' (ἀκολάκευτον), which directly contrasts with Marius' lowering of its dignity in 28. 1 (παρὰ τὸν ὄγκον καὶ τὸ κοινὸν ἀξίωμα τῆς ἀρχῆς). However, Plutarch demonstrates that Marius and Cinna were able to take Rome in 87 BC partly because of their opponents' refusal to budge from the letter of the law: Octavius refuses to mobilize the slaves, and Metellus destroys morale by turning down an extraordinary command which the soldiers offered (42. 4–6). Plutarch comments: 'Octavius damaged his cause not so much through lack of skill (ἀπειρίᾳ), as by a too scrupulous observance of justice (ἀκριβείᾳ τῶν δικαίων); he acted contrary to everyone's interests in neglecting what was necessary' (42. 4).[101] There may be a moral point being made here: perhaps in such circumstances legal niceties should be abandoned?[102] On this issue, Plutarch will have more to say in the Lives of Phokion and Cato Minor and of Lysander and Sulla, the subjects of the next chapters of this book.

Unusually, Marius is set not only against minor characters within his own Life, but also, implicitly, against the Romans with whom Pyrrhos comes into contact. They are men of virtue: Fabricius, for example, shows himself above threats and bribery, and refuses to act in an underhand way: he reports to Pyrrhos a plot to kill him (*Pyrrh*. 20. 1–21. 6). Against this background Marius' failings stand out.[103] Marius' own ruthlessness is also implicitly contrasted with the kindness he had received. After he is captured, he is sent under arrest to Minturnae (38. 2). A horseman is despatched to kill him. But when the assassin approaches, flames seem to shoot from Marius' eyes, and a loud voice is heard demanding 'Do you dare to kill Caius Marius?' (39. 1–4). The assassin, who is said to be 'either a Gaul or a Cimbrian' flees; the mention of his race momentarily recalls Marius' successes over the northern barbarians and his benefits to Rome. The incident is plainly parallel to the description of Pyrrhos' death, where Pyrrhos had given a 'terrible look' to his assassin: enough to put him off his stroke, but not deter him (*Pyrrh*. 34. 6). Marius fares better. Impressed by the portent, the magistrates of Minturnae experience a change of heart and set Marius free to meet 'his fate' (39. 5–9). Thus he survives. Later, in Rome, the tables are turned. Marius sends soldiers to kill a certain Antonius. When the soldiers enter the room, such are the 'enchantment and charm'

---
[101] οὐ τοσοῦτον ἀπειρίᾳ τοῦ Ὀκταβίου τὰ πράγματα βλάπτοντος, ὅσον ἀκριβείᾳ τῶν δικαίων προϊεμένου τὰ χρειώδη παρὰ τὸ συμφέρον.
[102] See below, esp. 131–3.
[103] Swain (1990*b*), 137–8.

(σειρὴν καὶ χάρις) of Antonius' words (qualities Marius lacked: 32. 2) that none of them can bring himself to do the deed (44. 6). Finally Annius, the soldiers' commander, has to hack off Antonius' head himself. Marius had received mercy in a similar position; he grants none to Antonius.[104]

The *Marius* finishes with Marius' son (46. 6–9). The brief narration of his character, his installing of a new and equally brutal tyranny, and his suicide in Praeneste to avoid falling into Sulla's hands, provides a strong closed ending to the book. This final section, a kind of addendum to the main narrative, corresponds structurally to the opening chapter of the *Marius* with its discussion of Roman names.[105] Endings of Lives often narrate a brief history of the descendants of the hero, which provides a wider perspective on his life and gives the judgement of posterity on him. The character of the younger Marius is the same as his father's: he displays cruelty (ὠμότης; cf. 2. 4) and bitterness (πικρία; cf. 2. 1), which lead him to murder the 'best and most esteemed citizens' (46. 7). Like Marius and Pyrrhos, he is fond of war; like theirs, his fate is inescapable (46. 9: ἄφυκτα).[106] His brief *regnum* and suicide mark the extinction of the family of Marius, perhaps the most pilloried of all Plutarch's heroes.

---

[104] Plutarch's narrative technique here is analysed by Carney (1960), 28–9.

[105] The mention here (46. 8) of the nickname of the younger Marius, 'son of Ares/Mars' (παῖς Ἄρεως), recalls the opening chapter with its discussion of Roman names, and reinforces the sense of closure; cf. Carney (1960), 26. Plutarch also discusses Roman names at *Cor.* 11. 2–6, and appears to have written a book entitled *On the three names, which is most important?* (Lamp. Cat. 100).

[106] Cf. *Pyrrh.* 16. 14; 30. 2; *Mar.* 39. 6.

5

The Lives of Phokion and Cato Minor

The *Pyrrhos–Marius* is a pair of Lives with a fairly straightforward moral message, which runs across both Lives of the pair. More complex, and providing more difficulties for a moral reading, is the *Phokion–Cato Minor*. Here Plutarch confronts the issue of whether there is, in the reality of political life, such a thing as absolute good and absolute evil. What happens when different imperatives conflict? What is the relationship between private morality and public interest (τὸ συμφέρον)? Plutarch seems to allow the possibility that it may be appropriate for a statesman to compromise his values. The proper functioning of virtue may depend on the right circumstances; at times of extreme crisis, a case can be made for compromise as well as for heroism.[1]

These issues are central not only to the *Phokion–Cato Minor*[2] but also, as the next chapter will demonstrate, to the *Lysander–Sulla*. They are also raised in other Lives. We know, for example, that Plutarch disapproved of superstition as a negation of reason; but we see him at times approving of a statesman's manipulation of the common people's irrational fears in order to achieve a greater end.[3] On several occasions he commends leaders for adapting the laws in order to suit the conditions of their state. Thus, while praising Lykourgos for discouraging the Spartans from practising commerce, he commends Solon for not following the same course; the economic situation of Athens, he explains, would not allow such a policy (*Solon* 22. 1–3). Similarly, he commends Agesilaos for not punishing, as the law required, those who ran away at the battle of Leuktra; as Plutarch comments, 'by bidding

---

[1] Cf. *Ag./Kleom.-Gracchi* 4. 2–3 where Plutarch condemns Kleomenes' murder of his political opponents without good reason: 'For to apply the blade (σίδηρον), except in the most dire necessity (τῆς ἐσχάτης ἀνάγκης), is the mark neither of a doctor nor of a statesman' (note the pun on scalpel/sword). The implication is that in a time of crisis such brutal behaviour *might* be justified. For ἡ ἐσχάτη ἀνάγκη, cf. *Cato Min.* 47. 2.
[2] As noted briefly by Frazier (1995), 159, 168–9.
[3] e.g. *Num.* 4. 12; *Fab.* 4. 4–5. 1; *Dion* 24. 1–10; *Non Posse* 1101d; 1104a–b; cf. *Aem.* 17. 1–13. See Berardi (1990). In his political treatises Plutarch several times approves of the ascription to the gods of responsibility for success as a device to avoid envy: *De Ipsum Laud.* 542e–543a; *Praec. Ger.* 816e.

the laws sleep for that day', he saved both his country and the laws themselves (*Ages*. 30. 2–6; *Ages.-Pomp*. 2. 3–4). The same point is made in reverse in the *Life of Marius*, where, as has been seen, Plutarch demonstrates that Marius and Cinna were able to take Rome in 87 BC partly because of their opponents' 'too scrupulous observance of justice (ἀκριβείᾳ τῶν δικαίων)'; Octavius acted, Plutarch tells us, 'contrary to everyone's interests (παρὰ τὸ συμφέρον) in neglecting what was necessary' (42. 4).[4] For such reasons, the more idealistic Dion fails to liberate Sicily, whereas the more pragmatic Timoleon succeeds.[5]

In several other instances Plutarch seems to suggest that the end may justify the means: injustice—or at least bending the rules—can be excused, if the result is beneficial for the state.[6] Plutarch takes this line in discussing Romulus' seizure of the Sabine women (*Thes.-Rom*. 6. 2–3) and Crassus' attack on Parthia (*Nik.-Crass*. 4. 3–4). In a similar way, he seems to approve of the decision of Aristeides, despite his reputation for justice (*Arist*. 2. 6; 4. 1–8; 5. 6; 6. 1–5; 7. 7), not to arrest those suspected of plotting to overthrow the Athenian democracy in 479 BC (13. 2), 'because it could not be known how many would be implicated in a test whose remit was justice (τοῦ δικαίου) rather than expediency (τοῦ συμφέροντος)'. The issue of the relationship of justice and expediency is raised again (22. 3–4) when Aristeides declares of Themistokles' plan to burn the Greek fleet (or dockyard: ναύσταθμον) 'that nothing was more expedient (λυσιτελεστέραν) and nothing more unjust (ἀδικωτέραν)'. The people reject the plan, demonstrating, Plutarch comments, their love of justice. But a little later Plutarch notes Aristeides' willingness to put expediency before justice in foreign policy, specifically in Athens' treatment of her allies. Here Aristeides encourages the Athenians actually to break their oaths and 'to use affairs to their advantage' (ᾗ συμφέρει). The morality of this is left ambiguous. 'Affairs, so it seems, demanded' we are told, 'that the Athenians rule ἐγκρατέστερον'; it is not clear whether this should be taken as 'with more control' (over the allies) or 'with more *self*-control', nor, if the former, whether the narrator shares this view or not (25. 1). Plutarch records, however, the view of Theophrastos that, although Aristeides was 'strictly just' (ἄκρως ὄντα δίκαιον) as regards his private affairs (25. 2), in public life 'he acted in accordance with his country's policy (πρὸς τὴν ὑπόθεσιν τῆς πατρίδος), saying that it

---

[4] See above, p. 129.
[5] On Timoleon and Dion, cf. De Blois (1992), 4604–5.
[6] As argued by Nikolaidis (1995), especially 311–12 and Frazier (1995), 155–60 and 165–70, who discuss some of these passages.

needed much actual injustice (ὡς συχνῆς καὶ ἀδικίας δεομένην). Plutarch goes on (25. 3) to cite the example of Aristeides' support for the transfer of the Delian League treasury to Athens in 454, which, Aristeides himself declared, was unjust, but expedient (οὐ δίκαιον μέν, συμφέρον δέ). Plutarch gives no clear authorial guidance on how to view Aristeides' policy, but, significantly, in the Life of one famed for his justice, raises the question of whether morality and the national interest are reconcilable.

The *Life of Phokion* deals with the period of Athens' loss of independence to the growing power of Macedon. An instructive parallel can be drawn with the slightly earlier *Life of Demosthenes*, which deals with roughly the same period.[7] In an important reflective passage in the *Demosthenes* (13. 1–14. 1), Demosthenes is compared favourably with other orators of his time: he did not waver from his principles, but consistently put honour (τὸ καλόν) before expediency (τὸ συμφέρον); other leaders, including Phokion, are criticized for compromising their values in order to preserve the state. In the *Phokion–Cato Minor*, however, Plutarch takes the opposite view.[8] Phokion is commended for being willing, in the interests of his state, to compromise with Philip of Macedon and successive Macedonian leaders such as Antipatros and Nikanor. In contrast to this stands Cato's disastrous policy of unbending opposition to the late-Republican triumvirs. The syncritic structure of the pair invites us to contrast and compare.

The *Demosthenes* and the *Phokion* give us two different evaluations of Athenian foreign policy in the fourth century. The fact that in the *Demosthenes* we find Phokion criticized, suggests that in the *Phokion* Plutarch has not simply been a victim of his sources. It is true that the ancient tradition on Phokion, as represented also by Diodoros Books 16–18, appears to have been extremely favourable: his anti-democratic policies were presented as those of a 'moderate', and Plutarch, as we shall see, develops this interpretation.[9] But Plutarch was certainly aware of a different tradition, pro-democratic and hostile to Phokion, which is preserved in the *Life of Phokion* by Nepos, an author whom Plutarch knew well.[10] Furthermore, the very different presentation of the fourth century in the earlier *Life of Demosthenes* shows that, although Plutarch

[7] The *Dem.-Cic.* was the fifth pair of Lives written (*Dem.* 3. 1); the *Phok.-Cato Min.* was rather late in the series: Jones (1966), 66–70.

[8] Noted by Gomme (1945), 72–3.

[9] On the ancient tradition on Phokion and the degree of its accuracy, see Bearzot (1985), 11–67, or (1993), 100–42.

[10] See below, p. 228 n. 71. On Nepos' *Phokion*, see Bearzot (1985), 50–7, or (1993), 116–19.

chose in the *Life of Phokion* to follow a tradition favourable to Phokion, he was aware of, and elsewhere prepared to follow, a contrary tradition.[11] Such a double presentation demonstrates Plutarch's tendency to present the same material or the same ethical problem from different angles. This can partly be explained by Plutarch's willingness to be more sympathetic to a figure in that figure's own Life than he is elsewhere; but it also raises some important questions, which seem to disturb or to challenge simple moral codes. Is the virtuous course of action always self-evident? Perhaps morality is not always simple or unitary; perhaps, to some extent at least, it depends on one's point of view: in some circumstances, particularly in great crises, it does not lie in one course of action alone; a case can be made for both unbending virtue and its opposite, compromise.

An interesting parallel can be found in the *Philopoimen–Flamininus* pair. Here, once again, Plutarch demonstrates his ability to look at a problem from different angles; he presents the Roman conquest of Greece from the perspectives both of a Roman commander and of a Greek who fought him. Plutarch makes it clear in these Lives that Rome's conquest of Greece was willed by the gods (*Phil.* 17. 2; *Flam.* 12. 10);[12] but he still seems to admire Philopoimen's personal courage in defence of the liberty of Greece (especially at 17. 3), even though he regarded it as ultimately futile and, partly at least, the result of love of strife (φιλονεικία).[13] Similarly, in the *Dion–Brutus* Caesar's monarchy is divinely ordained,[14] but Brutus is still commended for opposing him (*Dion–Brut.* 3. 6–11). Like Phokion before them, Philopoimen and Brutus *could* have compromised; like Cato the Younger, they refused. At the end of the *synkrisis* between Philopoimen and Flamininus (*Phil.-Flam.* 3. 4), Plutarch declares that Flamininus' generosity to the Greeks was 'noble' (γενναῖα), but Philopoimen's opposition to him, and his love of freedom, were 'more noble' (γενναιότερα): both hard-headed

---

[11] e.g. *Dem.* 14. 1: 'Phokion was the champion of a policy which was not commended; he seemed rather to favour Macedon (οὐκ ἐπαινουμένης προϊστάμενος πολιτείας, ἀλλὰ δοκῶν μακεδονίζειν)'; Plutarch goes on, however, to praise Phokion's courage and justice, in contrast to Demosthenes' cowardice, citing Demetrios of Phaleron as his source. The latter is probably Plutarch's source for many of the anti-democratic and pro-Phokionic elements in the *Phok.* (see below, n. 40). In writing the *Dem.*, then, Plutarch was already aware of the source which he was later to use for the *Phok.*, but chose in this case not to follow its emphases.

[12] Swain (1989*b*), 284–5.

[13] Walsh (1992), esp. 221–6; cf. Jones (1971), 100–2.

[14] *Brut.* 47. 7; *Dion-Brut.* 2. 2. Cf. *Kim.-Luc.* 1. 1; *Ant.* 56. 6. See also Swain (1989*b*), 288–92.

expediency and a romantic commitment to virtue at all costs have their attraction.

1. VIRTUE, VICE, SUCCESS, AND FAILURE

These two Lives adhere more closely than most to the principles set down in the programmatic statements. Indeed, the emphasis there on anecdotes and sayings as the best clues to character (e.g. in *Alex.* 1. 1–3) recurs in Plutarch's statements in these Lives (*Cato Min.* 24. 1; 37. 10); both contain a great number of anecdotes and sayings. Thus these Lives are concerned more with revealing the moral character ($\mathring{\eta}\theta o\varsigma$) of the two men than with giving a chronological narrative of the historical events in which they were involved. This lack of interest in chronology is particularly apparent in the early chapters of the *Phokion*; chronological narrative begins only in 12. 1, with the entrance of Philip II on to the scene and Phokion's dispatch to Euboia (350 BC).[15] In the *Cato Minor*, it is personal rather than political factors which are emphasized. Thus the origins of the civil wars are traced back to Cato's refusal of a marriage alliance with Pompey (30. 9–10), who then marries Caesar's daughter (31. 6); the political reasons behind the alliance of Caesar and Pompey are played down.[16] The narrative is shaped to communicate and reinforce moral lessons. Phokion and Cato are presented as good statesmen in contrast to their self-serving contemporaries (in particular Demades, and Caesar and Pompey). Thus, for example, the incident of Phokion's refusal to accept gifts from Alexander (*Phok.* 18. 1–5) is treated at length, with the memorable scene of the shock of the Macedonian emissaries at seeing Phokion's wife kneading bread while he himself draws water from his well and washes his own feet; this leads into a discourse by Phokion on the philosophical tenet that the wise man desires only what is sufficient for his needs and no more.[17] The point of the story is to demonstrate the proper attitude to wealth, and the correct way to be a 'friend' of a king. Phokion, was not, it is implied, a 'flatterer' of the Macedonians—in contrast with Demades, who is used con-

---

[15] Bearzot (1985), 17–21, or (1993), 92–6. No extant ancient account contains clear indications of Phokion's activities before this date.

[16] Pelling (1986a), 163 n. 13. This is in contrast to the very different interests in the other six late Republican Lives composed at roughly the same time (e.g. the political interests of *Caes.*). Cf. p. 21 n. 22.

[17] On the tendency of Plutarch's narrative to fragment into self-contained and dramatic scenes (e.g. the Bona Dea episode in *Caes.* 9–10), see Frazier (1992).

sistently as a foil to Phokion.¹⁸ The incident is of doubtful historicity, but the moral it exemplifies—how to behave with a king or other powerful figure—was an important one in Greek political and moral discourse of all ages. It closes with the narrator's comment, 'So the money went back again from Athens, after it had showed the Greeks that the man who did not want so great a sum was richer than the man who offered it'.¹⁹ Similarly, in the *Cato Minor*, the narrative of the Catilinarian incident (22. 1–23. 5) is shaped not towards a historical understanding of its causes or course, but towards a moral tableau, in which Cato is the hero and Caesar the villain.²⁰ Cato's total devotion to the state, which has already been revealed in the previous chapters (especially in 16–21), is exemplified in this moral tale.²¹

In narrating these two Lives Plutarch was faced with the problem—fundamental for a writer of moral lessons—that in history the good do not always win: though virtuous, both Phokion and Cato ultimately failed. Elsewhere, in the treatise *On why the gods are so slow to punish*, Plutarch discusses the related problem of why evil men often prosper. He suggests several reasons why the god does not step in to punish evil men and put a stop to their crimes: perhaps he wants to give them time to repent (551c–552d); sometimes he uses evil men to bring about unforeseen good (552d–553d); or he waits for the moment when he can punish them in a way which most fits the crime (553d–f); and, significantly, the crime itself, and the consciousness of it, is often its most powerful penalty (553f–556e). In *How to recognize that one is making progress in virtue* 84f–85a, Plutarch follows a related line to this last argument in insisting that the virtue of good men is worth imitating, whatever the circumstances.²²

In these Lives, Plutarch attempts to deal with the problem of the defeat and death of such virtuous men by showing that both received posthumous honours and that their deaths were ultimately avenged: Phokion's death causes regret in Athens, and his body is later brought back to Athens and given a public funeral; a statue is erected; his accusers

---

¹⁸ The contrast runs throughout the *Phok.*: whereas Phokion is moderate, Demades is a toady of the Macedonians (1. 1–3; 16. 5; 17. 5–10; 20. 6; 30. 4–5), though certainly no real friend of theirs (22. 5; 30. 8–10).

¹⁹ See Bearzot (1984), esp. 83–5. This incident is recounted in ps.-Plut. *Reg et Imp*. 188f; Aelian, *VH* 1. 25; 11. 9. Phokion also occurs in the *De Cup. Divit.* 525b–c, where he is contrasted with Demades, an exemplar of the avaricious man who can get no benefit from his wealth.

²⁰ Pelling (1985), esp. 326–7.

²¹ Cf. the similar treatment of the election for 55 BC in *Cato Min.* 41–2.

²² See above, p. 32.

are later killed by the people or Phokion's son, suggesting the working of divine vengeance on behalf of a virtuous man (*Phok.* 37–8).[23] Cato's death is greeted with mourning from all the people of Utica, who give him a splendid burial; even his enemy Caesar regrets his death (*Cato Min.* 71–2).[24] Such posthumous 'restitution' is not uncommon in Plutarch.[25] But such restitution, though in one sense providing a greater sense of closure, a more morally satisfying ending, in as much as good finally triumphs or is at least recognized, is in another sense highly disturbing. Rather like the final *synkriseis* which follow many pairs, such examples of posthumous 'restitution' introduce a new and discordant note with which the Life closes.

Another strategy which Plutarch uses to explain the failure of good men is the concept of *tyche*, in this case fate or the will of the gods.[26] In the lengthy prologue to this pair, both men are said to have been of great virtue but to have been unsuccessful because of the circumstances in which they lived.[27] Of Phokion, the narrator says the following:

(1. 4) τὴν δὲ Φωκίωνος ἀρετήν, ὥσπερ ἀνταγωνιστῇ βαρεῖ καὶ βιαίῳ καιρῷ συλλαχοῦσαν, αἱ τύχαι τῆς Ἑλλάδος ἀμαυρὰν καὶ ἀλαμπῆ πρὸς δόξαν ἐποίησαν.
. . . (1. 6) τοσοῦτον δὲ τῇ τύχῃ δοτέον ἀντιταττομένῃ πρὸς τοὺς ἀγαθοὺς ἄνδρας ἰσχύειν, ὅσον ἀντὶ τῆς ἀξίας τιμῆς καὶ χάριτος ἐνίοις ψόγους πονηροὺς καὶ διαβολὰς ἐπιφέρουσαν, τὴν πίστιν ἀσθενεστέραν ποιεῖν τῆς ἀρετῆς.

(1. 4) The fortunes of Greece made the virtue of Phokion dark and obscure as far as fame went, as though it had been allotted a heavy and violent opponent in the times in which it found itself. . . . (1. 6) Such great power has been granted to fate when she opposes good men that, instead of the honour and thanks which they

---

[23] On divine vengeance in the *Lives*, see Brenk (1977), 261–75. For the technique of using the fact of posthumous punishment of enemies to mark approval of the dead, cf. Xenophon's closing words after the trial of the Athenian generals who were executed after Arginousai (*Hell.* 1. 7. 35). In fact, Phokion's rehabilitation was the work of the tyrant Demetrios of Phaleron, not of the people: Bearzot (1985), 242–50, or (1993), 145–8.

[24] Both Appian (*BC* 2. 99) and Dio Cassius (43. 11. 6)—perhaps both drawing on the same source as Plutarch—later use the public funeral given to Cato by the people of Utica as evidence for his virtue.

[25] Many Lives finish by tracing a hero's descendants (e.g. *Them.* 32. 1–3, 6; *Cato Maj.* 27. 7; *Ant.* 87. 1–9; *Cato Min.* 73. 2–6), showing posthumous honours being awarded (e.g. *Them.* 32. 4–6; *Lys.* 30. 5–6; *Dem.* 30. 5) or vengeance finally being done to his enemies (e.g. *Pel.* 35. 1–12; *Cic.* 49. 2–6 with Moles 1988, 24; *Caes.* 69. 2–14, on which see below, p. 255; *Sert.* 27. 6–7; *Eum.* 19. 3). The ending of the *Phok.* (38. 1–4) combines all these elements. See also *Thes.* 36. 1–6; *Num.* 22. 1; *Pub.* 23. 4–5; *Luc.* 43. 3–4; *Fab.* 27. 3–4; *Phil.* 21. 3–9; *Dem.* 30. 5–31. 6. On some of these passages, and on Plutarch's tendency not to end a Life at the point of the protagonist's death, see Pelling (1997a), 228–36.

[26] On *tyche* in the *Lives*, see above, p. 123.

[27] Cf. *Tim.* 6. 1–5: good deeds must be done with a firm conviction and after reasoned thought, so that if unsuccessful we do not regret them. Phokion is cited as an exemplar.

deserve, she brings to some base invectives and slanders, weakening men's confidence in their virtue. (*Phok.* 1. 4–6)

Cato is said to have given fortune a long, but ultimately unsuccessful fight (3. 4: μέγαν ἀγῶνα τῇ τύχῃ περιέστησεν).[28] The same point is put into Cato's mouth in his own Life (*Cato Min.* 53. 3) when he declares that there is much inconsistency and great lack of clarity in the gods' behaviour (πολὺν ἔφη περὶ τὰ θεῖα πλάνον εἶναι καὶ ἀσάφειαν) in that, as soon as Pompey had decided to join him in fighting in defence of his country's liberty, his good fortune had deserted him (προλέλοιπε τὸ εὐτυχεῖν).[29] In *Phokion* 28, the imposition of a Macedonian garrison on Athens makes the common people wonder why the gods had deserted her. Reflections in the minds of sensible bystanders are often in Plutarch intended as a guide to how the reader should react.[30] It is less clear in this case how much weight is to be attributed to the reflections of 'the majority', but, in view of the emphasis of the prologue, we are probably to imagine Plutarch as sharing their feeling: the divine will had deserted Athens.

Plutarch seems to follow a similar line in dealing with the Lives of Dion and Brutus. In the prologue to the pair (*Dion* 1. 3), Plutarch claims that their careers are an illustration of the fact that successful political careers require wisdom and justice to be united with strength (δύναμις) and good fortune (τύχη). 'Their fortunes were the same in terms of what befell them (τοῖς συμπτώμασι) more than in their choices (τοῖς προαιρέσεσιν)', Plutarch tells us (2. 1). He goes on to discuss the apparitions which appeared to both men in the course of their lives, and concludes by reluctantly accepting the Zoroastrian doctrine that evil spirits attack good men out of envy and try to divert them from the path of virtue (2. 5–6). This passage is striking, because the doctrine is not one to which Plutarch subscribes elsewhere, and indeed is contrary to his denial of the existence of evil spirits in his polemic *On superstition*. The reason for Plutarch's introduction of this, for him, outlandish doctrine, is the same as that which led him to introduce the idea of a hostile fortune in the *Phokion–Cato Minor*: despite their acknowledged virtue, these men were, as he admits in *Dion* 2. 2, unsuccessful.

For a similar emphasis on the caprices of fortune (τύχη), despite the

---

[28] Lucan had already treated Cato as a man of virtue bravely fighting fortune and its protégé, Caesar: see Friedrich (1938).
[29] A desertion which is linked with and mirrors Pompey's own desertion (ἐκλελοιπότα) of Italy in the campaign (*Cato Min.* 53. 3).
[30] See above, p. 120.

subject's acknowledged virtue, one should compare the *Life of Aemilius*,[31] and the *Life of Sertorius*. At the beginning of the latter, Plutarch discourses on the phenomenon of coincidence in history and notes, somewhat tongue-in-cheek, that some of the most cunning generals have been one-eyed, as indeed was Sertorius. Sertorius, he continues, was superior to all these other generals; he was 'inferior in intelligence to none of them, but in fortune (τύχῃ) to all of them, which he always found much harder to deal with than his open enemies' (*Sert.* 1. 9–10).[32] Likewise, at the beginning of the *On the sign of Sokrates*, the speaker admits that fortune can have as much to do with success as virtue does.[33]

So one reading of the history of Phokion and Cato which Plutarch seems to allow is that they were brave men, who failed through the opposition of fortune. But the prologue suggests another reading. In the less than ideal conditions in which Phokion and Cato found themselves, Plutarch suggests that the correct course was moderation. When a city is in a poor state, the good statesman, he argues, must temper his frankness with gentleness, otherwise he will simply aggravate his listeners as light aggravates an inflamed eye. He must adopt a course like the sun's, which 'has neither the same motion as the sky nor is absolutely opposed to it and contrary' (ἄντικρυς ἐναντίαν καὶ ἀντιβατικήν); it has a curved course, and turns in a 'smooth, flexible, and winding spiral' (ὑγρὰν καὶ εὐκαμπῆ καὶ παρελιττομένην ἕλικα), thus preserving all things and producing 'the best mixture' (*Phok.* 2. 6). The statesman, therefore, Plutarch says, should combine a mixture of firmness and softness in dealing with the people (2. 7–9). He must not be 'harsh and cruel' (ἀπηνὴς καὶ σκληρὸς) in opposing the popular will, nor be too tolerant of their mistakes. Wise government involves yielding where necessary in order to get what is expedient for the state (τὸ συμφέρον); such wise government possesses that 'mixture of severity and reasonableness which is so difficult to get' (2. 8: τὸ σεμνὸν ἔχουσα τῷ ἐπιεικεῖ δύσμεικτον).[34] 'If that mixture is attained', Plutarch continues (2. 9), 'then this is the most concordant and musical mixing of all rhythms and

---

[31] See Swain (1989c), esp. 323–7 and 334; Desideri (1989), 204–12.

[32] Cf. *Nik.* 17. 4, where the defeat of Nikias and the Athenians in Sicily is ascribed to 'some opposition actually from the gods or from fortune' (cf. *Ag./Kleom.* 60[39]. 1).

[33] See above, p. 43. Cf. *Phil.-Flam.* 2. 2: 'Flamininus used the power of Rome when it was at its zenith (ἀκμὴν ἐχούσῃ), Philopoimen reached his zenith when Greece was already waning' (τῆς Ἑλλάδος ἤδη φθινούσης ἐπακμάσας, the reading of the codices: on the text, see Pelling [1997c], n. ad loc).

[34] On the ideal of the mixed character, see above, pp. 90–4.

harmonies (ἡ πάντων μὲν ῥυθμῶν, πασῶν δ' ἁρμονιῶν ἐμμελεστάτη καὶ μουσικωτάτη κρᾶσις), by which god is actually said to administer the cosmos, not using compulsion but by persuasion and reason introducing what is necessary.' He continues:

(3. 1) ταῦτα δὲ καὶ Κάτωνι τῷ νέῳ συνέβη. καὶ γὰρ οὗτος οὐ πιθανὸν ἔσχεν οὐδὲ προσφιλὲς ὄχλῳ τὸ ἦθος, οὐδ' ἤνθησεν ἐν τῇ πολιτείᾳ πρὸς χάριν. (3. 2) ἀλλ' ὁ μὲν Κικέρων φησὶν αὐτὸν ὥσπερ ἐν τῇ Πλάτωνος πολιτείᾳ καὶ οὐκ ἐν τῇ Ῥωμύλου πολιτευόμενον ὑποσταθμῇ τῆς ὑπατείας ἐκπεσεῖν. ἐμοὶ δὲ ταὐτὸ δοκεῖ παθεῖν τοῖς μὴ καθ' ὥραν ἐκφανεῖσι καρποῖς. (3. 3) ὡς γὰρ ἐκείνους ἡδέως ὁρῶντες καὶ θαυμάζοντες οὐ χρῶνται, οὕτως ἡ Κάτωνος ἀρχαιοτροπία, διὰ χρόνων πολλῶν ἐπιγενομένη βίοις διεφθορόσι καὶ πονηροῖς ἔθεσι, δόξαν μὲν εἶχε μεγάλην καὶ κλέος, οὐκ ἐνήρμοσε δὲ ταῖς χρείαις διὰ βάρος καὶ μέγεθος τῆς ἀρετῆς ἀσύμμετρον τοῖς καθεστῶσι καιροῖς.

(3. 1) These conditions befell also Cato the Younger. For his character was not persuasive or pleasing to the mob, nor did he bloom in his career in terms of popularity.[35] (3. 2) Now Cicero says that he was defeated for the consulship because he pursued his politics as though he was living in the Republic of Plato and not in the dregs of Romulus. But I think that the same thing happened to him as happens to fruit which appears out of season. (3. 3) For just as people look at such fruit with pleasure and admiration, but do not use it, so Cato's old-fashioned nature, which came along after many years among corrupt lives and debased habits, had great glory and fame, but did not fit what was necessary because of the weight and size of his virtue, which were out of proportion to the immediate times. (*Phok.* 3. 1–3)

Cato, Plutarch goes on, put up a good but ultimately unsuccessful fight against fortune. He was, then, both virtuous and unfortunate, certainly; but also unwise. His 'old-fashioned nature' (ἀρχαιοτροπία) was ill-suited to his times.[36] Cato did not attain that ideal blend of firmness and softness in dealing with the multitude which was necessary in the circumstances. His character was virtuous, there is no doubt of that, but his strict virtue led him into an unhelpful refusal to compromise, which was harmful both to him and to his state. It is on this question, the ability of the two men to attain the ideal mix in character and in policy, that they will be judged. This is clear from the summary of the similar characters of the two men in 3. 8–9:

[35] Cf. the parallel in *Sert.* 18. 3: ἤνθει τότε μάλιστα πρὸς δόξαν. Ἀνθέω is particularly appropriate in the present passage, given the subsequent plant metaphor. Χάρις suggests the charm which Cato sadly lacked; but the phrase πρὸς χάριν also has implication of 'ingratiation' with the mob: cf. *Cato* 5. 3; 50. 3.
[36] But Phokion's modelling of his statesmanship on that of Perikles, Aristeides, and Solon (7. 5–6, on which cf. Tritle 1987; J. T. Roberts 1987) is apparently successful.

(3. 8) τούτων δὲ τῶν ἀνδρῶν αἱ ἀρεταὶ μέχρι τῶν τελευταίων καὶ ἀτόμων διαφορῶν ἕνα χαρακτῆρα καὶ μορφὴν καὶ χρῶμα κοινὸν ἤθους ἐγκεκραμένον ἐκφέρουσιν, ὥσπερ ἴσῳ μέτρῳ μεμιγμένου πρὸς τὸ αὐστηρὸν τοῦ φιλανθρώπου, καὶ πρὸς τὸ ἀσφαλὲς τοῦ ἀνδρείου, καὶ τῆς ὑπὲρ ἄλλων μὲν κηδεμονίας, ὑπὲρ αὐτῶν δ' ἀφοβίας, καὶ πρὸς μὲν τὸ αἰσχρὸν εὐλαβείας, πρὸς δὲ τὸ δίκαιον εὐτονίας συνηρμοσμένης ὁμοίως· (3. 9) ὥστε λεπτοῦ πάνυ λόγου δεῖσθαι καθάπερ ὀργάνου πρὸς διάκρισιν καὶ ἀνεύρεσιν τῶν διαφερόντων.

(3. 8) But the virtues of these two men, right down to the minute and indivisible differences, displayed the same stamp and shape and a common mix of colour in their character, such that humanity was mixed, as it were, in equal measure with austerity, and bravery with caution; and care for others was combined with fearlessness for themselves, and avoidance of evil was combined with eagerness for justice. So we need very subtle reasoning, like an instrument, to separate and discover the differences.

It is the ability of both men to combine opposing traits which Plutarch singles out here. These traits are all picked up and exemplified in the narratives which follow,[37] thus reinforcing the parallelism of the two Lives and encouraging comparison between them. In fact, Plutarch's emphasis on the difficulty of discovering any differences between the characters of Phokion and Cato, and the need of 'subtle reasoning' to do it, is itself a subtle claim for the insight contained in his own narrative which follows immediately on from this sentence.[38] Phokion and Cato are very similar men: devoted to philosophy, austere yet kind. But Plutarch will reveal, through his comparative analysis, the vital difference: Cato's philosophy led him to an almost arrogant rigidity. In our terms, Phokion compromised; Cato did not.

2. THE SOKRATIC PARADIGM

A theme which runs through both Lives and which provides a substantive link between them is the figure of Sokrates. Comparison of both men with Sokrates emphasizes the parallels between Cato and Phokion themselves; it may well have been the Sokratic theme which provided Plutarch with the impetus to compare the two men in the first place. Plutarch had a particular interest in the figure of Sokrates and wrote three works devoted to him: the extant *On the sign of Sokrates*, and the

---

[37] Geiger (1988), 254–6.
[38] Cf. the emphasis in *Arist.-Cato Maj.* 1. 1 on the difficulty of finding differences between Aristeides and Cato the Elder.

Defence of Sokrates and *On the condemnation of Sokrates*, which are listed in the Lamprias Catalogue (nos. 189–90).[39] But the Sokratic parallels in these two Lives were probably already to be found in Plutarch's sources. For the *Phokion* the main source was probably a Peripatetic writer, such as Demetrios of Phaleron, or more speculatively Hermippos of Smyrne.[40] This source presumably influenced Nepos' *Life of Phokion*, which also connects Phokion with Sokrates (4. 3); Diodoros does not. Plutarch's source for the Sokratic elements in the *Cato Minor* was probably Thrasea Paetus, who is cited in *Cato Min.* 25. 2 and 37. 1, and who probably based his account on the memoirs of Munatius Rufus.[41] At any rate, Plutarch implicitly likens both Phokion and Cato to Sokrates at numerous points, especially in their deaths. The link is made clear in the last chapter of the *Phokion* (*Phok.* 38. 5):

Ἀλλὰ τὰ μὲν περὶ Φωκίωνα πραχθέντα τῶν περὶ Σωκράτην πάλιν ἀνέμνησε τοὺς Ἕλληνας, ὡς ὁμοιοτάτης ἐκείνῃ τῆς ἁμαρτίας ταύτης καὶ δυστυχίας τῇ πόλει γενομένης.

What had been done to Phokion reminded the Greeks[42] again of what had been done to Sokrates, for they thought that the sin and the misfortune which had happened to the city in this case was very similar to the sin and misfortune of that previous case.

The next sentence begins the *Life of Cato* with a δέ picking up the μέν here:[43] the expectation is set that he too will be similar to Sokrates. The

---
[39] On the widespread interest in Sokrates in the first and second centuries AD, see Döring (1979).
[40] Demetrios: Tritle (1992), 4290–4; Bearzot (1993), 100–6. Hermippos: Bearzot (1985), 26–34. See also Gehrke (1976), 232–6.
[41] Cf. Scardigli (1979), 136 and 139; Geiger (1993), 299–304; Delvaux (1993). Thrasea seems to have modelled his description of Cato's death on Sokrates' in order to present Cato as a martyr, although the comparison may have been common: e.g. Cic. *Tusc.* 1. 71–4; Sen. *Ep.* 67. 7; 71. 16–17; 98. 12; 104. 27–33. In addition, Thrasea may have modelled his own real death on those of Sokrates and Cato; at any rate the account of it in Tac. *Ann.* 16. 34–5, probably derived from Arulenus Rusticus (cf. Tac. *Agric.* 2. 1), contains a large number of parallels with the accounts of their deaths; cf. Tac. *Ann.* 15. 64, for a reference to Sokrates' death in Tacitus' description of Seneca's suicide. The accounts of Thrasea Paetus and Arulenus Rusticus fit into the type of writing current under Nero and Domitian in which, as a form of political opposition, the lives of great men who died under tyrannies were recounted, with special attention paid to their deaths: cf. Pliny *Ep.* 5. 5. 3; 8. 12. 4; Tac. *Agric.* 2. 1; see Geiger (1979b), 61–5. Under Nero and Domitian the figure of Cato functioned as a *locus* for opposition to the principate (cf. Cossutianus Capito's words in Tac. *Ann.* 16. 22. 2); but by the accession of Trajan it had lost its political significance: Syme (1958), i. 28.
[42] The Greeks rather than the more historically plausible Athenians. For Plutarch, Classical Athens is seen in some measure as the representative of Greece as a whole.
[43] It is not uncommon for the two Lives of a pair to be linked by μέν and δέ: e.g. *Aem.* 39. 11 and *Tim.* 1. 1; *Lyk.* 31. 10 and *Num.* 1. 1; *Lys.* 30. 8 and *Sulla* 1. 1; *Dem.* 31. 7 and *Cic.* 1.

effect of this parallelism is both to increase the stature of Phokion and Cato, and to emphasize the unfairness of their deaths. Detailed parallels are numerous. The opening pictures of the two men recall the picture of Sokrates given by Alkibiades in Plato's *Symposium*, a work with which Plutarch was undoubtedly familiar.[44] For example, Phokion is explicitly said to have been a pupil of Plato and Xenokrates in the Academy (4. 2; cf. 14. 7). Both men are said to wear fewer clothes than would be considered normal, whatever the weather, and to go about without shoes (ἀνυπόδητος: *Phok.* 4. 4; *Cato Min.* 6. 6; 44. 1).[45] The picture of Cato walking while his friend rode (5. 7) is reminiscent of Sokrates and Alkibiades in *Symp.* 221a. Furthermore, Cato's love of drink, probably a detail of the hostile tradition, is transformed into a very Sokratic tendency to discuss philosophy all night while drinking (*Cato Min.* 6. 2–3).[46] Cato's refusal of prizes for valour for his service in the Social War (8. 3) recalls Sokrates' similar refusal in *Symp.* 220e. Cato is described (25. 3) as having many 'lovers and admirers' (ἐρασταὶ καὶ θαυμασταί). This rather striking erotic image recalls the erotic subject matter of the *Symposium* and the attempts by Alkibiades to seduce Sokrates, as recounted in *Symposium* 217a–219d. The calm of both men at crises, and particularly at their deaths, is another Sokratic feature. During the violence of 59 BC, Cato's calm retreat from the forum after the other senators had fled (32. 4) is described in terms reminiscent of Sokrates' retreat after Delion in *Symp.* 221b.[47] The most obvious encouragement to compare Cato and Sokrates comes at 46. 1, where M. Favonius is said to be a friend and admirer of Cato 'just as Apollodoros of Phaleron is said to have been of Sokrates of old'.

It is in their deaths that the parallel is clearest (*Phok.* 36–7; *Cato Min.* 64–70). Like Sokrates, both men remain calm despite the emotion of

1; *Kim.* 19. 5 and *Luc.* 1. 1. In *Demetr.* 53. 10 and in *Gracchi* 1. 1 the link with the preceding Life is made explicit, though without μέν and δέ.

[44] Jones (1916), 139–42, and Helmbold and O'Neil (1959), 61, give a list of allusions to the *Symposium* in Plutarch's work. See further pp. 216–18.

[45] Cato, like Sokrates, inspires interest from the troops for his unusual habits; *Cato Min.* 5. 6, 6. 6; cf. *Symp.* 174a; 220b–d. Horace notes Cato's 'grim face and naked feet' (*Odes* 2. 1. 12). For a similar picture of Sokrates, see Aristoph. *Clouds* 102–4, 362–3; Xen. *Mem.* 1. 2. 1; 1. 3. 5–13; 1. 6. 2.

[46] Recalling Alkibiades' description of Sokrates (*Symp.* 220a), and Sokrates' drinking feat at the end of the *Symp.* (223b–d). For hostile treatments of Cato and drink, cf. Martial 2. 89; Pliny, *Ep.* 3. 13, who ascribes the tradition of Cato's drunkenness to Caesar's *Anticato*. Seneca feels the need to answer charges of Cato's drunkenness (*De Tranq. An.* 1. 9; 17. 4).

[47] Both men retreat in the midst of enemies, calmly looking around. There is perhaps also a Homeric model behind *Cato Min.* 32. 4 (ἀπῄει βάδην): cf. Idomeneus' retreat (βάδην ἀπιόντος) in *Il.* 13. 516.

others. Phokion dies, like Sokrates, by drinking hemlock (36. 3–7; cf. *Phaidon* 116b–118a).[48] Two differences from the Platonic account of Sokrates' death emphasize the increased wickedness of Phokion's execution. First, Sokrates had died surrounded by his friends, whereas Phokion is killed along with his friends. Secondly, Sokrates' death was delayed while the state galley was visiting Delos (*Phaidon* 58a–c); Phokion's was not delayed by the festival which was taking place at the time (37. 1–2). Plutarch comments: 'it was clear to all those who were not wholly savage or whose souls were not wholly corrupted by rage or jealousy that a most impious thing had been done in not halting for that day nor keeping the city pure from public murder when it was holding a festival' (37. 2);[49] as is often the case in Plutarch, the views of sensible onlookers provide a paradigm for the reader. Cato, like Sokrates, prefaces his death by philosophical discussion (67. 2–3, on the Stoic Paradoxes; 69. 1–5). He does not die by drinking hemlock, but by his own sword. But, like Sokrates, he had the chance of survival, which he refused, despite the efforts of his friends to dissuade him (they take his sword from him only to return it later: 68. 2 and 70. 1); he was intent on death (64. 4). Finally, after dinner (68. 2), and again later (70. 2), Cato reads Plato's dialogue *On the soul* (that is, the *Phaidon*), which recounts Sokrates' death and the philosophical discussions about the soul's immortality which preceded it. After reading this text a second time, Cato falls into a deep sleep, which is probably meant to recall Sokrates' deep sleep before his death which so amazed Kriton (Plato, *Kriton* 43b–c).[50]

This link with Sokrates helps both to set the moral tone of the Lives of Phokion and Cato, which is one of general admiration and respect, and to emphasize the unfairness of their deaths. It also suggests that the two men should be measured in their political conduct against the ideals of

---

[48] On Plutarch's knowledge of the *Phaidon*, see Jones (1916), 142–4.
[49] For 'public murder' (δημόσιος φόνος), cf. Soph. *Ant.* 36.
[50] There are other parallels between the *Phok.* and *Cato Min.* Both men refuse gifts (*Phok.* 18. 1–8; *Cato Min.* 11. 4). The parallel here, like that of their simple life-styles (*Phok.* 18. 1–8; *Cato Min.* 12. 2–13. 5), may be the result of the application of standard *topoi* to the two men. But notably, whereas Phokion's virtues win universal approval, Cato's appear ridiculous or annoying to his friends: a major theme of the Life. Other parallels include the refusal of personal honours for themselves, but the request for help for their clients (*Phok.* 18. 6; *Cato Min.* 39. 4); the averting of massacre through their calming influence on Alexander and on the younger Pompey (*Phok.* 17. 5–8; *Cato Min.* 55. 6; κατεπράϋνεν occurs in both contexts); both have dealings with an Antipatros; finally, both their sons are said in the last chapter of their Lives to be guilty of sexual misconduct—although Cato's redeems himself by dying bravely at Philippoi (*Phok.* 38. 3–4; *Cato Min.* 73. 2–6). See also Bearzot (1993), 85–8.

philosophy. It is the ideal blend of firmness and softness in dealing with the multitude which is singled out in the prologue and which forms the standard against which the two men are to be viewed and measured.

3. PHOKION

Phokion, an ardent opposer of democracy, is shown to conform well to the paradigm of wise government set out in the prologue. The ideal of the 'mean' between the extremes of overbearing harshness and excessive gentleness runs throughout the Life. This is brought out in 5. 1 in the contrast between Phokion's gentle and kind character (προσηνέστατος ὢν καὶ φιλανθρωπότατος) and his rather harsh frown and severe words (cf. 5. 2–10). Similarly in 6. 1–3, his even temper is revealed by an implicit comparison with the more senior general Chabrias. The latter is characterized (6. 2) with the words:

νωθρὸς γὰρ ὢν ὁ Χαβρίας καὶ δυσκίνητος ἄλλως, ἐν αὐτοῖς τοῖς ἀγῶσιν ὤργα καὶ διεπυροῦτο τῷ θυμῷ, καὶ συνεξέπιπτε τοῖς θρασυτάτοις παραβολώτερον . . .

Chabrias was in general sluggish and slow to action, but in the thick of action he grew angry and fiery in his spirit, and used to rush forward with the boldest of them at much too great a risk to himself . . .

In contrast, Phokion is described (6. 3) as 'at the same time safe and active' (ἀσφαλὴς . . . ἅμα καὶ δραστήριος), and is said both to put courage into Chabrias when he delayed and to take away the 'untimely intensity of his impulse' (τὴν ἄκαιρον ὀξύτητα τῆς ὁρμῆς). Incidents illustrating the courageous and active side of Phokion's nature follow, including his frequent opposition to the will of the Athenian people (8. 1–10. 4), especially their demands for war.

The transition to a section illustrating his humanity and lack of excess is introduced with the words (10. 5):

ἔστι δ' οἶμαι χαλεπόν, οὐ μὴν ἀδύνατον, ὥσπερ οἶνον καὶ ἄνθρωπον τὸν αὐτὸν ἡδὺν ἅμα καὶ αὐστηρὸν εἶναι·

It is, I think, difficult, but certainly not impossible, for the same human being, like wine, to be both sweet and austere.

The next chapters show his lack of personal animosity to his enemies (10. 6–9) and his popularity with the allies (11). While on campaign in Euboia he displays (in contrast to his ally Ploutarchos of Eretria) an appropriate *sangfroid* in the face of the enemy, and restrains his troops' pursuit in order to support his defeated comrades (13. 1–6). After his return from Euboia, the allies are said (14. 1) to miss his goodness (χρηστότης) and justice (δικαιοσύνη), and the Athenians his experience (ἐμπειρία) and vigour (ῥώμη). A contrast is implicitly drawn with the general Chares who, because of the fear and mistrust he inspired in Byzantion, was unable to achieve anything: when Phokion is sent out, he is welcomed gladly (14. 3–8; for the contrast, cf. 5. 2). The Athenian troops are inspired by Phokion's own virtuous blend of qualities, becoming (14. 7) 'not only blameless and temperate in their conduct but also most enthusiastic in action . . . ' (οὐ μόνον ἀνεγκλήτους ταῖς διαίταις καὶ σώφρονας, ἀλλὰ καὶ προθυμοτάτους ἐν τοῖς ἀγῶσι . . .). Significantly, Phokion's welcome into Byzantion is presented partly as a result of his friendship with Leon, who, like him, is a member of the Academy. Phokion, according to Plutarch, persuades the Athenians to seek peace with Alexander after the defeat at Chaironeia and Philip's death, and brings it about because of his personal influence with the king (16. 5–17. 9).[51] He advises Alexander either to stop the war completely, or to turn it 'against the barbarians' (17. 7).

The theme of his mixing of 'hard' and 'soft' qualities continues throughout the Life; it is particularly clear in the account of his firm but mild government of Athens after Antipatros' victory (29. 5): by ruling gently and lawfully (πράως καὶ νομίμως) he keeps the urbane and cultured (τοὺς . . . ἀστείους καὶ χαρίεντας) in power and persuades the troublesome to be content with private life. After Antipatros' death, he succeeds in making Nikanor, Kassandros' general, 'gentle and gracious' (πρᾶον . . . καὶ κεχαρισμένον) to the Athenians, and persuades him to give generously to the city as director of games (31. 3). Later, when the Athenian general Derkylos tries to arrest Nikanor, Phokion apparently allows him to escape. His own justification of his action and Plutarch's criticism of him—the only place in the Life where Plutarch seems to disapprove of Phokion—are significant. Phokion says (32. 6) 'that he trusted Nikanor and expected no harm at his hands; but in any case, he would rather be seen to be wronged (ἀδικούμενος) than to be doing wrong (ἀδικῶν)'. Plutarch comments: 'This declaration might seem to be honourable and noble for one seeking his own interests; but someone who endangers the safety of his country, and that too when he is general and magistrate, transgresses, I suspect, a greater and more venerable obligation, that of justice to his fellow citizens' (32. 7). The

[51] In fact, Diodoros makes Demades responsible for obtaining peace with Alexander (17. 15), and Plutarch appears to confirm this at Dem. 23. 4–6.

conflict between private morality and the demands of statesmanship is one which will be developed in the *Cato Minor*. This incident aside, Phokion conforms to the Plutarchan ideal of the moderate, and therefore good, ruler.[52] His fall from power in 33. 1–12 leads to the end of good order in Athens, the spectacle of slaves and foreigners in the assembly, illegal trials, and suggestions of torture (34. 3–35. 5). The effectiveness of his rule is thus implicitly emphasized.

4. CATO

The many similarities already noted between the life and character of Phokion and those of Cato encourage the reader to measure the latter against the standard set by the former. The result is to draw attention to the way in which Cato departs from the admirable model set by Phokion. Cato, like Phokion, is given a very positive treatment in his Life.[53] Like Phokion, he combines humanity and gentleness with an ability to stand up for his principles against opposition. Cato's brother Caepio, who is well-known for his self-control (σωφροσύνη) and moderation (μετριότης), avows that his own qualities are nothing in comparison to Cato's (3. 10). In his first political speech (5. 3), Cato combines harsh sentiments with 'a charm (χάρις) which invited attention', and his 'mixed character' combines 'a sort of pleasure and smile' (ἡδονήν τινα καὶ μειδίαμα) with solemnity (τὸ σεμνόν).[54] His great grief at his brother's death in Thrace, in which some people thought he acted 'with more passion than philosophy' (ἐμπαθέστερον . . . ἢ φιλοσοφώτερον), a worrying sign, is taken for the moment as an indication of 'how much tenderness and affection was in the man's inflexibility and firmness' (11. 3–4).[55] In his prosecution of Murena (21. 10), he is described as 'fierce and terrible in his defence of justice, but afterwards kind and humane to everyone'.[56]

[52] On Phokion's regime, in fact a Macedonian-backed oligarchy, see Bearzot (1985), 183–200.

[53] Valgiglio (1992), 4035–6, lists passages where Cato is explicitly praised, either directly by the narrator or by others.

[54] The picture of Cato's speech conforms well with Plutarch's recommendation of what a good statesman's speech should be like in *Praec. Ger.* 802e–803b (to which Geiger 1971, n. ad loc., refers). Plutarch goes on in the Life (5. 4) to remark upon the loudness of Cato's voice and his ability to speak all day: as Geiger points out, in *Praec. Ger.* 804b–c Plutarch notes this as a requisite for a statesman, giving Cato as an example.

[55] ὅσον . . . ἀγνάμπτῳ καὶ στερρῷ τοῦ ἀνδρὸς τὸ ἥμερον ἐνῆν καὶ φιλόστοργον.

[56] χαλεπὸς ὢν καὶ φοβερὸς ὑπὲρ τῶν δικαίων, εἶτα πᾶσιν εὐνοϊκῶς καὶ φιλανθρώπως προσφερόμενος. Cf. 46. 5. Cf. Geiger (1988), 255 (=1993, 317–18).

The description of Cato's behaviour as military tribune in Makedonia is particularly significant. He is said not to want simply to display his own virtue—a luxury into which he was to fall later in his life—but to be eager to make his men like him. So he uses both fear and reason in his dealings with them, both reward and punishment (9. 5–6). The result, Plutarch tells us, in wording which recalls Phokion's similar success while general at Byzantion (*Phok.* 14. 7),[57] was that 'it was hard to tell whether he made his men more peaceful or warlike, more zealous or just. For they appeared so terrible to their enemies, gentle to their allies, cowards at doing wrong and ambitious for praise' (*Cato Min.* 9. 7). Cato wins respect by sharing their hardships 'being more like the soldiers than those who commanded them'; but in character 'he surpassed all others who had been called general or imperator' (9. 9). Plutarch continues:

(9. 9) ἔλαθε διὰ τούτων ἅμα τὴν πρὸς αὐτὸν εὔνοιαν ἐν⟨εργασάμενος⟩ τοῖς ἀνδράσιν. (9. 10) ἀρετῆς γὰρ ἀληθινὸς οὐκ ἐγγίνεται ζῆλος ἢ δι' ἄκρας τοῦ παραδιδόντος εὐνοίας καὶ τιμῆς. οἱ δ' ἄνευ τοῦ φιλεῖν ἐπαινοῦντες τοὺς ἀγαθοὺς αἰδοῦνται ⟨μὲν⟩ τὴν δόξαν αὐτῶν, οὐ θαυμάζουσι δὲ τὴν ἀρετὴν οὐδὲ μιμοῦνται.

(9. 9) In this way, without anyone realizing, he inspired at the same time good-will in his men. (9. 10) For a true desire to emulate virtue is not engendered in any other way than through absolute good-will and respect for the one who imparts it. Those who praise good men without loving them, stand in awe of their reputation, but do not admire their virtue or imitate it. (*Cato Min.* 9. 9–10)

The good-will which Cato inspired in his troops was not, Plutarch seems to imply, simply approval for his action, but a real love which led to a desire to be like him. The terminology of this passage recalls that of the earlier *Perikles–Fabius* prologue and the language in which the usefulness of history is sometimes expressed elsewhere in Plutarch.[58] The effect, then, which Cato has on his troops appears to be a paradigm for the effect which the *Lives* are supposed to have on the reader. Furthermore, Cato himself seems to have truly loved good men. For immediately after this discussion, Plutarch describes how Cato sought out and, to his great joy, persuaded the philosopher Athenodoros to reside with him in his camp, and later in Rome (10. 1–3; 16. 1). But Plutarch also states in this discussion a negative as well as a positive truth: unless a virtuous man inspires respect in those who observe him, his virtue is useless. It is to

---

[57] Note the repetition of προθυμοτάτους (*Phok.* 14. 7)—προθυμοτέρους (*Cato Min.* 9. 6) and διαίταις (*Phok.* 14. 7)—δίαιταν (*Cato Min.* 9. 9).

[58] See above, p. 36. Cf. χάρις ἀγωγὸς ἀκοῆς in 5. 3.

this negative paradigm that Cato will later in his life increasingly conform. This rare authorial intervention on Plutarch's part anticipates the unattractive rigidity of Cato's virtue as it will appear as the Life proceeds. It forewarns the reader to be alert to ways in which Cato does not conform to the positive paradigm we might expect from one of Plutarch's protagonists. He will become a man to praise, but not to imitate. It is only in his last days at Utica, when his back is against the wall and the cause is lost, that his virtue once again wins real admirers and imitators. Then the people of Utica 'perceived and desired and admired his virtue' (64. 3),[59] and Statyllios takes on the Catonian characteristics of loftiness and rigidity ($ὑψηλός$ $ἐστι$ $καὶ$ $ἄτρεπτος$), and desires to die with him (66. 6–8).

Of course, if Plutarch had wanted to make Cato into a simply negative paradigm, he could have shown his opposition to Caesar as simply evil-spirited and jealous. Elsewhere in Plutarch's works the coming of monarchy to Rome is presented as a necessary 'cure' to the ills of the state (e.g. *Dion.-Brut.* 2. 2; *Caes.* 28. 6), and even, as was noted earlier, as providence or the will of the gods.[60] But this Life in fact concedes that Cato's opposition to monarchy is justified, even if he is fighting a battle against fate which he cannot win (*Phok.* 3. 4). Cato is, at one level, the hero; Caesar, Pompey and their subordinates are the villains. Pompey's ally, the tribune Metellus, is given all the attributes of the violent demagogue.[61]

But Cato's status is not so simple. His bold opposition to illegality is shown to stem from his philosophical commitment. Beside the parallels with Sokrates, he is frequently in this Life linked with other philosophers or philosophy.[62] In his final hours in Utica, the presence of philosophers among his companions is emphasized,[63] and the Sokratic parallels

---

[59] $σαφεστάτη$ $γὰρ$ $ὡς$ $ἔοικεν$ $αἴσθησις$ $τότε$ $παρέστη$ $καὶ$ $πόθος$ $καὶ$ $θαῦμα$ $τῆς$ $τοῦ$ $Κάτωνος$ $ἀρετῆς$.

[60] See above, p. 134.

[61] $θρασύς$: 26. 4 and 29. 1. $θρασύτης$ is a stock epithet for demagogues in Plutarch: cf. Pelling (1988*b*), n. on 2. 6; (1992), 38 n. 56. For example, Kleon: *Nik.* 2. 3; cf. *De Herod. Malig.* 855b; Stratokles: *Demetr.* 11. 5; Clodius: *Caes.* 9. 2; *Pomp.* 46. 8; 48. 8; *Ant.* 2. 6; cf. Aristoph., *Knights* 134; 193; 303–4; 637.

[62] 4. 1–2; 10. 1–3; 16. 1; 20. 2; 21. 7; 54. 8; 57. 4.

[63] 65. 11; 67. 3–4; 68. 2; 69. 1–5; 70. 1. At 65. 10–11 'Apollonides the Stoic' and 'Demetrios the Peripatetic' are mentioned, along with a Statyllios, who has to be dissuaded from dying with Cato (cf. 66. 6–8; 73. 7). The mention of Demetrios the Peripatetic provides another link with the *Phok.*, for which the famous Peripatetic Demetrios of Phaleron was a source (see above, n. 40). It is possible that Statyllios is to be identified with 'Statyllios the Epicurean', mentioned in *Brut.* 12. 3 ($Στάλλιος$ in the codices) and 51. 5–6: *pace* Babut (1969*b*), 188–9. If this is so, it is surprising that Plutarch has not in the *Cato Min.* high-

become dominant. A subject's connection with philosophy is elsewhere in Plutarch a positive moral attribute (e.g. *Num.* 20. 8–12).[64] But in the *Cato Minor*, this simple moral truth is challenged. For it is from his very philosophy that the mistakes in Cato's life spring.[65] The reader has been prepared for this by the treatment in the *Phokion* of the philosopher Xenokrates, a pupil of Plato and head of the Academy from 339 to 314 BC. In *Phok.* 27. 1–4 the presence of this virtuous man is said to inflame Antipatros against the Athenians; this is in contrast with the trust which Phokion inspires (27. 5–9; 29. 4). Later Xenokrates refuses citizenship in Athens because of his opposition on principle to the Macedonian-backed government of Phokion, though the narrative is enthusiastic about the harmony and good order which Phokion brings to the state at this time (29. 5–6). Xenokrates' high philosophic principles were out of place in the world of *Realpolitik*.

The inappropriateness of Cato's virtue, and his inability to win real admirers, have already been signalled in the prologue to the two Lives. There Plutarch tells us that the statesman should follow the example of the sun, which has a curved course, and turns in a 'smooth, flexible and winding spiral' (ὑγρὰν καὶ εὐκαμπῆ καὶ παρελιττομένην ἕλικα) (*Phok.* 2. 6). The statesman should be flexible in dealing with the people (2. 7–9). Cato's character is anything but 'flexible'. Indeed, he is characterized with the opposite characteristic: he is 'inflexible' (ἄτρεπτος: 1. 3).[66] This is elsewhere a quality of which Plutarch disapproved,[67] but in the context of this text it is even more plainly a negative characteristic.[68] As Plutarch makes clear in the rest of the prologue, Cato's inflexibility was not suited to the circumstances in which he lived. He inspired respect in his contemporaries, but not any real desire to imitate him, or take notice of him. Ultimately, then, Cato is a failure: a man of great virtue—Plutarch never denies that—but one who fails in that point that Plutarch sees so clearly illustrated in Phokion, the ability to mix sternness and gentleness and to compromise when necessary.

lighted Statyllios' connection with philosophy, given his interest in philosophy at the end of Cato's Life.

[64] Cf. Wardman (1974), 211–20. For the high value Plutarch placed on a philosophical education for a statesman, cf. *Max. cum Princ.* Alexander is portrayed in the essays devoted to him as an example of the statesman-philosopher, ultimately modelled on Plato's philosopher-kings, as are Dion and Brutus in their respective Lives.
[65] Swain (1990c), 197–8; Pelling (1989), 229–30.
[66] As, at different times, are Metellus Scipio (29. 1) and Statyllios (66. 7).
[67] See below, p. 210.
[68] On Cato's inflexibility and its probable Stoic associations, see below, pp. 155–8.

Indeed, the mixture of stern and gentle qualities, which for Plutarch is normally a mark of a well-balanced character, is never really fully attained by Cato. For Cato, sternness sometimes shows itself in outbursts of anger and passion, a trait opposed to his philosophical pretensions. We have already noted how his excessive grief at his brother's death is considered by some to sit oddly with his claims to be a philosopher. In that case, Plutarch appeals to the mixing of qualities to excuse Cato (11. 3–4). But the seed has been planted in the reader's mind. Before that, as a young man, Cato reacts with such anger against Metellus Scipio who, as Plutarch puts it, 'took his girl', that he abuses him in iambic verse (7. 1–2). Even earlier, when a boy, he had disrupted a birthday party by flying into a rage ($\mu\epsilon\tau$' ὀργῆς ἔχων) when he saw a small boy being put into prison during play (2. 6–8). The incident reveals a laudable commitment to justice, but also a rigidity and inability to discern the right moment to apply his just principles, and a difficulty in controlling his passion. In the debate over the fate of the Catilinarian conspirators, Cato launches into a denunciation of Caesar and of the 'milder and more humane' (πραότερον . . . καὶ φιλανθρωπότερον) direction in which the opinions of the Senate were flowing. He speaks (23. 1) 'with anger and passion' (μετ' ὀργῆς καὶ πάθους). At the end of his life, when Cato decides to commit suicide, he finds his sword has been hidden from him. In a rage, he hits his slave in the mouth—so hard that he bruises his hand and later has to have it bandaged (68. 5; 70. 4). This incident is significant in that it is exactly this, the hitting of a slave when in anger, which philosophical tracts on the control of anger, such as Plutarch's own or Seneca's, condemn.[69] The contradiction between this and Cato's philosophical principles is underlined by the stress on the fact that, at intervals during this episode, he sits down to read Plato. Similarly, at the end of his life, Cato ends a discussion of the Stoic doctrine that only the good man is free with a loud outburst which leaves everyone silent (67. 3–4).

Cato's philosophic principles are out of place in the world of the late Republic. Thus his obedience to the letter of the law forbidding the use of *nomenclatores* when canvassing for office (8. 4–5)[70] gives offence even to those who approve of it: 'for the more clearly they saw the rectitude (τὸ καλόν) of his practice, the more distressed they were at the difficulty

---

[69] e.g. *De Cohib. Ira* 459a–460c, where, significantly, Phokion is cited as an example of not acting in anger (that is, he prevented the Athenians taking precipitate action on Alexander's death: 459e–f); Seneca, *De Ira* 3. 5. 4.

[70] This recalls Phokion's refusal to canvass for office (*Phok.* 8. 1).

of imitating it' (τὸ δυσμίμητον). In the same way Cato fails to win election to the consulship of 51 BC because he prefers to guard his dignity (ἀξίωμα) and refuses to canvass for office (49. 6). His habit of travelling simply and alone, with only two servants going on ahead to prepare the way, leads to an undignified incident at Antioch (12–13).[71] Pompey and Curio both respect him but avoid his company (14. 1–8); Pompey is made to feel in Cato's presence (14. 5) 'like a magistrate liable to scrutiny' (ὥσπερ οὐκ ἀνυπεύθυνος ἄρχων).[72] Later in Cyprus (36. 4–5) his concern to get the best price for the state in the auction of Ptolemy's goods leads him to act as though he did not trust his friends, especially Munatius, and to embitter them. There is even a hint of pride in his failure to greet the welcoming party on his return (39. 2; cf. 44. 11).[73]

Cato's extreme virtue has important negative effects in the world of high politics. He returns to Rome to stand for the tribunate of 62 BC, despite his initial reluctance, in order to provide a check to Metellus Nepos, an ally of Pompey, who was also standing (20. 3–8). As tribune, he proposes a corn dole for the poor in 62 BC to prevent Caesar's winning over the disgruntled poor to his side. Plutarch approves of this compromise: 'clearly by this act of humanity and kindness that threat was removed' (26. 1). But Cato's moderation does not last. When the tribune Metellus proposes in 62 BC that Pompey return from the East with his forces to save Rome from Caesar, Cato opposes the measure. He declares that, while he is alive, Pompey will never enter the city in arms (26. 5). Plutarch here, as so often, presents his own judgement as the thoughts of moderate onlookers. The Senate, he tells us, thought neither Metellus nor Cato was in his right mind or using 'reasonings conducive to safety' (λογισμοῖς ἀσφαλέσιν). Metellus' policy was 'madness (μανία), which, through an excess of wickedness (δι' ὑπερβολὴν κακίας), was rushing on to the destruction and confusion of all things': the terminology invokes the idea of Aristotelian moderation, which neither Metellus nor Cato attains. For the Senate thought Cato's policy was 'a frenzy for a virtue which fought in defence of the right and just' (ἀρετῆς ἐνθουσιασμός, ὑπὲρ τῶν καλῶν καὶ δικαίων ἀγωνιζομένης). Frenzy (ἐνθουσιασμός) implies in Greek, by both etymology and usage, divine inspiration; but lack of reason seems to be in prospect here too. A little later Cato is again more moderate. When Metellus flees to join Pompey,

---

[71] On Plutarch's handling of this episode, cf. Bellemore (1995).

[72] For the phrase, cf. Plato, Laws 761e: δικαστὴν δὲ καὶ ἄρχοντα ἀνυπεύθυνον οὐδένα δικάζειν καὶ ἄρχειν δεῖ.

[73] Also in Velleius 2. 45. 5 and perhaps derived from Caesar's Anticato.

he prevents the Senate from disgracing him by deposing him from office. The majority, Plutarch tells us, thought this was an act of humanity and—significantly—moderation ($\mu\epsilon\tau\rho\iota\acute{o}\tau\eta s$); but to the sensible ($\tau o\hat{\iota}s$ $\phi\rho o\nu\acute{\iota}\mu o\iota s$) it seemed 'right and expedient' not to annoy Pompey (29. 4). But a little later Cato rejects on principle Pompey's offer to form an alliance with him by marrying one of his nieces (or possibly daughters: Plutarch tells us there was disagreement amongst his sources). He is criticized for this not only by his friends and family, but also by the narrator himself: 'None of these things would have happened [Pompey's subsequent alliance with Caesar after his rebuttal by Cato] had not Cato been so afraid of the slight transgressions of Pompey as to allow him to commit the greatest of all and add his power to that of another' (30. 9–10). In the following chapter (31), Cato's opposition to the ratification of Pompey's eastern *acta* and a distribution of land is said to lead the latter to attach himself to Clodius and bring Caesar over to his side, 'a result for which Cato himself was in a way responsible' (31. 2).[74] The arguments for compromise are put into Cicero's mouth in 32. 8–11, and repeated by Cato in 35. 1; where Cato does compromise, he is seen to be successful. Cato's initial opposition to the appointment of Pompey as sole consul—an emergency measure—is presented, typically, in terms of legality: 'Cato opposed this at first, saying that the laws ought not to derive their security from Pompey, but Pompey from the laws' (47. 1). That his subsequent change of mind should be seen as correct is suggested both by the picture the narrative paints of increasing lawlessness in Rome, and by the ascription to Cato of the language of medicine to describe the ills of the state (47. 2).[75] Cato, unlike Pompey, does see the danger of Caesar's growing power, and decides to stand in the crucial consular elections for 51 BC 'in order to deprive Caesar of his weapons or to convict him of his plot' (49. 2).[76] But, as has already been noted, his refusal to compromise his dignity in the actual canvassing results in his failure to get elected (49. 1–6). Cicero upbraids him for not trying to 'win the people over by friendly intercourse' (50. 2: $o\vec{v}\delta$' $\vec{v}\pi\hat{\eta}\lambda\theta\epsilon\nu$ $\dot{o}\mu\iota\lambda\acute{\iota}\dot{q}$

---

[74] Pelling (1989), 228–9, notes 'the clash between principle and practicality' in Cato's rejection of the marriage alliance; similarly Frazier (1995), 159.

[75] Cato is thus briefly assimilated to a doctor, a role which invariably carries a positive moral force in the *Lives*. On the metaphor, see above, p. 93.

[76] Cf. his earlier candidature for the tribuneship of 61 to deprive Metellus of it (20. 3–8). In *Nik.-Crass.* 3. 4 Cato is commended for this earlier action, along with Themistokles, who bought off an unworthy candidate for the generalship (cf. *Them.* 6. 1–2); Nikias himself is criticized for hanging back and allowing Kleon to gain the command at Sphakteria (*Nik.-Crass.* 2. 4–3. 6; cf. *Nik.* 8. 5–6). See above, pp. 271–3. On these passages, cf. Frazier (1995), 158–9.

φιλανθρώπῳ τὸν δῆμον);[77] Cato replies by recognizing that it was his manner or character (τρόπος) which displeased the people, but that no sensible man would change his character to please others (50. 3: πρὸς ἑτέρων χάριν).[78]

Finally, in Africa after the defeat at Pharsalos, Cato refuses to accept command over the remaining Republican forces from Scipio and Varus, his legal superiors, saying that he 'would not break the laws for the defence of which they were fighting the law-breaker, nor would he as pro-praetor put himself ahead of a pro-consul who was present' (57. 6).[79] Once again, Cato's action has the effect of protecting his personal virtue but damaging the Republican side. For immediately Scipio plans to massacre all the people of Utica, and decides to force a battle with Caesar 'out of obstinacy' (ὑπ' αὐθαδείας) and against Cato's advice (58. 7). Cato, we are told, regretted surrendering the command, 'considering that Scipio would not wage the war well, nor, if he were unexpectedly successful, would he behave moderately as victor towards the citizens' (58. 10). In fact Cato fears that he has created in Scipio a second tyrant: he decides, we are told, that the war is lost 'through the inexperience and rashness of the commanders'; if, however, it were by good fortune to be won, 'he would not remain in Rome, but would flee the harshness and bitterness of Scipio—who was already making terrible, arrogant threats against many' (58. 12). Scipio is of course defeated at Thapsus, and with it perishes the Republican cause, and the laws which Cato wanted to protect. There is perhaps a further irony in Cato's treatment of Scipio. It was he who had stolen the youthful Cato's bride and impelled him to anger and abuse (7. 1–2). In now allowing Scipio to retain the command in Africa, he has put respect for the laws above private grudges. Ironically, it might have been better for the Republic and the laws which Cato claimed to protect if he had acted less like a philosopher and had indulged his passions a little more.

The *Phokion–Cato Minor* is one of the most moralistic pairs of Plutarch's *Lives*. But simple moral readings are challenged. Cato is undoubtedly the hero of his Life. But he is not unconditionally a model for imitation. The question is raised of when, if ever, principles need to be sacrificed to political necessity. Although Plutarch clearly admired

---

[77] The verb ὑπέρχομαι [τὸν δῆμον] is commonly used by Plutarch to denote the winning over either by gifts or flattery (e.g. *Per.* 7. 4; *Luc.* 6. 4; cf. *Pyrrh.* 4. 7) or by deception (*Dion* 14. 5).

[78] Cf. *Phok.* 3. 1 (above) on Cato's lack of popularity and χάρις.

[79] Slightly earlier (55. 5), he has attempted to give the command to Cicero, 'as one of praetorian rank to one of consular rank'; Cicero refuses.

Cato's opposition to Caesar's autocracy as virtuous and right, he suggests that in practice he should have compromised. Phokion fights against Macedon while Athens could possibly win (e.g. 12–15, 25), and the Life clearly demonstrates his personal courage. But he accepts the fact of Macedonian dominance over Athens, once it has become inevitable (e.g. 16. 1–8). By this policy he is able to ameliorate its harsher aspects and to administer Athens well (29. 4–5). Cato, however, refuses to compromise.[80]

5. CATO AND STOICISM

It may be that Plutarch's message in this Life about the dangers of an over-rigid commitment to philosophical ideals may be related to the fact that the philosophy which Cato followed was Stoic. Indeed, Cato was regarded as an exemplar of Stoicism by Cicero, Seneca, and Lucan.[81] Plutarch on occasion elsewhere, in his non-biographical writings, attacks the Stoics for their extreme views. For example, in the treatise *How to recognize that one is making progress in virtue*, Plutarch attacks the Stoic belief that there is no gradation in virtue, that one is simply either virtuous or not: a doctrine which would cut away the very point of moral education and indeed of Plutarch's own literary programme. We have already noted his attacks on Stoic views of the soul in the *On moral virtue*. These one-sided attacks probably do not represent Plutarch's reasoned views on Stoicism.[82] A more revealing hint of Plutarch's attitude can be found in his joint *Life of Agis and Kleomenes* at the start of the section on the Spartan Kleomenes III (23[2]. 2–6). Here Kleomenes is said to have studied philosophy with the Stoic Sphairos of Borysthenes. This had the effect of 'kindling his love of honour' ($\phi\iota\lambda o\hat{\omega}$ $\tau\iota\mu\acute{\iota}\alpha$), a quality which, Plutarch implies, was particularly characteristic of Spartans. He comments: 'Stoic doctrine is somewhat dangerous and risky for great and sharp natures, but when mixed with a deep

---

[80] The final chapters of both Lives offer a disturbingly new perspective on the two men, or at least on their families: see below, p. 255.

[81] e.g. Cic. *Par. Stoic.* 2; Seneca, *De Const. Sap.* 2. 1; 7. 1; Lucan, *BC* 2. 380–91. See Goar (1987), 35–49.

[82] See above, p. 76. Other anti-Stoic tracts include: *On Stoic contradictions*, *That the Stoics say things more 'paradoxical' than the poets* (of which only an excerpt survives) and *Against the Stoics on common conceptions*. Six other anti-Stoic tracts are listed in the Lamprias Catalogue (Lamp. Cat. 59, 78, 148, 149, 152, 154). We should, however, beware of thinking that Plutarch was absolutely opposed to Stoic doctrine. On Plutarch and Stoicism, see Barrow (1967), 103–5; Babut (1969b); Cherniss (1976); Hershbell (1992).

and gentle character it contributes most to its proper good' (23[2]. 6).[83] Stoicism, then, may have a dangerous effect on those of 'great natures'. By this we should probably understand that those who by nature tend to extreme positions, whether good or bad, might be dangerously encouraged in their extremism by the extreme doctrines of the Stoa. We should probably also associate this statement with the classic Platonic picture of 'great natures' gone wrong, one which Plutarch adopted:[84] such men possess great natural abilities, but, through a poor environment, do not attain to a virtuous and settled character in keeping with their nature. Plutarch seems to imply that Stoicism was a dangerous influence on men of great nature who had not yet developed an abiding character. He is, of course, in this passage discussing the effect of Stoicism on Kleomenes, and, specifically, the young Kleomenes. But it may well be that the picture of Cato the Younger which Plutarch draws in his Life is intended to have something of the 'great nature' about it.

As we have seen, the most important philosopher to whom Cato is linked in this Life, by implication, literary echo, and parallel, is Sokrates. In fact, Plutarch is reticent about stating explicitly that Cato was a Stoic, and it seems likely that Plutarch intended this pair of Lives to be an essay on the dangers of over-rigid adherence to philosophic tenets in general, rather than an attack on Stoicism in particular. After all, Xenokrates, the rigid philosopher of the *Life of Phokion*, was an Academic not a Stoic. But it is worth noting that Stoic doctrine was in accord with Cato's commitment to private virtue whatever the consequences.[85] To Stoics, who made no distinction of degree between different sins, compromise of one's principles to achieve a lesser of two evils was unthinkable. Several other aspects of Cato's life, as recorded by Plutarch, recall Stoic doctrines.[86]

At the very beginning of the Life, Plutarch tells us that Cato's character was 'unbending, un-emotional, and steadfast in everything' (1. 3: ἄτρεπτον καὶ ἀπαθὲς καὶ βέβαιον ἐν πᾶσιν). The total absence of

---

[83] ὁ δὲ Στωϊκὸς λόγος ἔχει τι πρὸς τὰς μεγάλας φύσεις καὶ ὀξείας ἐπισφαλὲς καὶ παράβολον, βαθεῖ δὲ καὶ πράῳ κεραννύμενος ἤθει μάλιστ' εἰς τὸ οἰκεῖον ἀγαθὸν ἐπιδίδωσιν.

[84] On this phrase, see above, pp. 47–9 and 206–10.

[85] Babut (1969b), 174–5, citing Epiktetos, *Ench.* 8; *Discourses* 2. 14. 7; 3. 24. 106; 3. 26. 8; Cic. *De Fin.* 5. 7, 20. Babut suggests that Cato's choice of political life as 'the proper task for a good man' (19. 3: ἴδιον ἔργον ἀνδρὸς ἀγαθοῦ) is specifically Stoic. It is rather a commonplace of intellectual thought, seen in Plato's conception of the philosopher kings in the *Republic*. It is best exemplified in Plutarch's tract *Whether an elderly man should engage in politics*.

[86] See Babut (1969b), 169–75. Contrast the *Brutus*, where little is made of Brutus' specific philosophical allegiances; he is simply '"the *philosopher*" in action' (Pelling 1989, 222–6).

emotion (*apatheia*) was a Stoic ideal, against which Plutarch argues in his treatise *On moral virtue* (especially at 451b–452d).[87] We should note, however, that the same quality is ascribed to Phokion as he goes to his death (36. 1): certainly at that point not intended as a technical term of Stoicism. The point is probably that Cato's natural inflexibility is encouraged and reinforced by his commitment to Stoicism. The clearest reference to Cato's Stoicism occurs when, as a young man, Cato is said to have become a friend of Antipatros of Tyre, 'a Stoic philosopher'. He devotes himself to the Stoics' 'political and ethical doctrines' and is said to 'have loved exceedingly (or excessively?: ὑπερηγαπηκώς) that form of goodness which consists in justice, and which is rigid and unbending (ἀτενὲς καὶ ἄκαμπτον) to clemency or favour' (4. 2).[88] We have already noticed his devotion to the Stoic philosopher Athenodoros (10. 1–3; 16. 1). He is ridiculed in court for his devotion to Stoicism (21. 7). Once Plutarch refers to Cato's 'regime' (5. 5: ἄσκησις; cf. 4. 3)—another technical Stoic term.[89] His regime involves practising public speaking, and training himself to feats of physical endurance, and self-control in illness (4. 3–4; 5. 5–8). The primary allusion here is, as we have seen, to the physical endurance of Sokrates, famous from Plato's *Symposium*, but there may be a hint at Cato's Stoicism. The same could be said of Cato's suicide. The right of the philosopher to end his own life was a key Stoic doctrine, and Cato's suicide was to find imitators in the suicides of members of the 'Stoic opposition' under Nero. Furthermore, Cato is said to have discussed the so-called Stoic paradoxes shortly before his death, namely that the good man alone is always free, whereas all the bad are slaves (67. 2–3).[90]

There are other hints at Stoicism in Cato's conduct. One of the incidents Plutarch considered most questionable in Cato's life was the divorce of his wife, Marcia, and his giving of her in marriage to his friend

[87] For Plutarch's views of *apatheia*, see above, Ch. 3, n. 12. Geiger (1971), 130–1, identifies ἄτρεπτος (cf. Statyllios in 66. 7) and ὁρμαί (1. 4) as Stoic terms (*SVF* 2. 158; 3. 140 ff). Cato's absence of fear is a constant theme in the Life, beginning in the childhood anecdotes: 2. 1. 5; 3. 3–7; 27. 1–28. 3; 32. 4; 33. 1–2; 41. 6–8; 43. 2–7; see Geiger (1988), 251–2 (=1993, 312).

[88] τοῦ καλοῦ τὸ περὶ τὴν δικαιοσύνην ἀτενὲς καὶ ἄκαμπτον εἰς ἐπιείκειαν ἢ χάριν ὑπερηγαπηκώς. On the incorruptible judge of Stoic thought, see Clement of Alexandria, *Strom.* 7. 45. 3, 858 Potterius; *SVF* 3. 639; Cic. *Pro Mur.* 60–1. Cf. Geiger (1971), 144–5.

[89] Geiger (1971), 149, refers to two works Περὶ ἀσκήσεως by the Stoics Herillos of Carthage and Dionysios of Herakleia (see *SVF* 1. 409 and 422 respectively).

[90] As Babut (1969b), 171, points out, the terms in which the people of Utica see Cato in the final days of his Life are taken from Stoic conceptions of the true philosopher, who is always 'free' and 'undefeated' whatever external ills may befall him: cf. 60. 1; 64. 7–9; 71. 1.

Hortensius (25. 1–13). Plutarch introduces the incident with the words, 'In the drama, as it were, of his life, this part has become problematic and difficult to explain' (25. 1: προβληματῶδες[91] . . . καὶ ἄπορον). After Hortensius' death he re-marries her: now, Plutarch tells us, 'a very wealthy widow' (52. 5). Caesar accuses Cato of having given away his wife for gain (52. 6–7). Plutarch refutes that, but concludes, 'but whether in some other way the affair of his marriage was not done well is worth considering (52. 8: ἐπισκεπτέον)'. In fact, Hortensius had at first asked for Cato's daughter. The terms in which he had justified his request are those with which Stoics justified the ignoring of conventional moral codes, especially those of marriage: 'In the opinion of men, such a thing is strange, but in nature, it is honourable and statesmanlike' (25. 5).[92] Cato himself considered such an argument justified; he used to accustom himself, we have already been told, 'to be ashamed only at what is shameful but to ignore what was otherwise looked down upon' (6. 6: ἐπὶ τοῖς αἰσχροῖς αἰσχύνεσθαι μόνοις, τῶν δ' ἄλλως ἀδόξων καταφρονεῖν).

It is possible, then, that the ambiguous image of philosophy which emerges from this Life—Cato's harmful commitment to virtue at all costs—may be related to the fact that the philosophy in question is Stoic. Hatred of evil (μισοπονηρία) can, as Plutarch makes clear in passing at *De Virt. Mor.* 452a, be excessive, the extreme rather than the mean. Furthermore, people sometimes count as hatred of evil what is really simple moroseness (*De Cohib. Ira* 456f: τὸ δύσκολον), or even anger (462e–f) or hatred (*De Frat. Amore* 482c). Cato's excessive commitment to virtue, his excessive hatred of evil, blind him to the need for compromise. This Life makes an important departure from what we can surmise were the enkomiastic treatments of Cato by writers such as Thrasea Paetus, for whom he was a symbol of senatorial opposition to the Principate. Plutarch recognizes the heroism of the man who died for his principles; but from the perspective of the second century Cato has also become an example of misguided extremism.[93] Blind adherence to principle may not always be the best course.[94]

---

[91] Geiger (1971), n. ad loc., points out that the subject of Cato's divorce of Marcia was a stock theme of debate (e.g. Quint. *Inst.* 3. 5. 11); the rare word προβληματῶδες probably therefore carries the sense of 'posed as a πρόβλημα', or subject of debate.

[92] δόξῃ μὲν γὰρ ἀνθρώπων ἄτοπον εἶναι τὸ τοιοῦτον, φύσει δὲ καλὸν καὶ πολιτικόν. Cf. *De Stoic. Repugn.* 1045a: μηδὲν ἄτοπον μηδὲ παρὰ φύσιν εἶναι τῶν τοιούτων; *SVF* 3. 743–56. Geiger (1971), 236, points to *SVF* 3. 728 for evidence that community of women was a Stoic doctrine. Herakles, a hero of Stoic thought, passed on his wife to his assistant Iolaos (Plut. *Amat.* 754d–e; Diod. 4. 31. 1)   [93] See above, n. 41.

[94] A point also made by Tacitus: *Agric.* 42. 4; cf. also *Ann.* 4. 20. 2–3; 6. 10. 3; 6. 27. 4.

6. A PARALLEL: PLUTARCH ON THE EMPEROR GALBA

Plutarch had taken a similar approach to the Emperor Galba in the *Lives of the Caesars*. His presentation of Galba is a good deal more positive than that of Suetonius in his *Galba* and a good deal less positive than that of Tacitus in the *Histories*.[95] It conforms in this respect to the programme set out at the start of the *Life of Kimon* (2. 3–5) of neither hiding nor dwelling on a subject's faults.[96] Galba is for Plutarch, like Cato, a paradigm of a virtuous man whose commitment to virtue led to his own death and ruin for his state.

Plutarch, like other writers on Galba (e.g. Suet. *Galba* 12. 1–13; Tac. *Hist*. 1. 18, 20), puts down the failure of his regime to his excessive parsimony (16. 1–5). The way to read this passage is made clearer by a passage which prefigures it. In 3. 4 Plutarch says that Galba's simple lifestyle and avoidance of excess[97] as a private citizen was, when he became emperor, reckoned as 'stinginess' (μικρολογία). The avoidance of excess (τὸ περιττόν) is a key virtue for Plutarch when thinking of money and its use (e.g. *De Cup. Divit.* 523d–524a and 527a–f). But virtue must be tailored to the circumstances and the age in which one lives. For a private citizen a simple life-style is commendable; but for an emperor virtue is not so straightforward. Simplicity of life-style and carefulness over expenditure are good qualities; so particularly is the refusal to give largesse to unruly troops. But these good qualities were Galba's demise.

Plutarch signals most clearly his admiration for Galba in 21. 2, when his choice of Piso for adoption rather than his personal friend Otho is said to reveal 'that he placed the public good before his private interests (πρὸ τοῦ ἰδίου τὸ κοινὸν τιθέμενος) and that he was seeking to adopt not the man who was most agreeable to himself but the one who would be most useful to the Romans'. When ambushed in the Forum by Otho's troops, he dies calmly, saying to his assassins 'Do it, if this is better for the Roman people' (27. 1); unfavourable versions of Galba's last words, recorded as alternatives by Tacitus (*Hist.* 1. 41) and Suetonius (*Galba* 20. 1), have, we must assume, been suppressed.[98] But Plutarch's version of the obituary of Galba (29. 1–5) is more nuanced: the picture is of a good

---

[95] On Suetonius' negative treatment of Galba, see Della Corte (1967), 115–27. On Tacitus going out of his way to defend Galba, see Shochat (1981).

[96] He does not, for example, play down the ugly murders at the start of Galba's reign (*Galba* 15. 1–9).

[97] τὸ δ' εὔκολον αὐτοῦ τῆς διαίτης καὶ φειδωλὸν ἐν δαπάναις καὶ ἀπέριττον.

[98] See Townend (1964), 359–60.

man whose virtue was unsuitable for the task. He is compared favourably with the others involved in the overthrow of Nero (29. 2), and his disciplinarian style of leadership is compared to that of Scipio, Fabricius, and Camillus (29. 4): this comparison does not occur in either Suetonius or Tacitus. But unfortunately, as Plutarch goes on, despite being in military affairs an 'unmixed *imperator* of the old style' (ἄκρατος . . . καὶ ἀρχαῖος αὐτοκράτωρ), he fared no better in controlling his freedmen than Nero did (29. 5). Once again one is reminded of Cato whose 'old-fashioned nature' (ἀρχαιοτροπία) was ill-suited to the times in which he lived (*Phok.* 3. 3), and who did not ultimately gain the proper mix of 'hard' and 'soft' qualities. The *Galba*, like the *Cato Minor*, demonstrates that virtue does not always guarantee success; in the reality of political life, compromise is often necessary.

6
The Lives of Lysander and Sulla

Plutarch's treatment of Lysander and Sulla forms the second example of Lives in which Plutarch seems to problematize the moral status of the subject.¹ Christopher Pelling recognized the problem posed by these Lives when he labelled the moralism here as 'descriptive' rather than evaluative, as more concerned with pointing to a truth in human nature than with presenting a model for imitation or avoidance.² In fact, although there is no simple didacticism in the text, evaluative judgements are nevertheless encouraged; the subjects *are* viewed from an ethical perspective. But these judgements are contradictory, and the ethical status of the pair seems to remain deliberately ambiguous right through to the end.

Frederick Brenk, discussing the ambivalence in Plutarch's presentation of Sulla, attributed it to the contradictory nature of the sources, which he saw as pulling Plutarch in opposite directions:³ the moral ambiguity of the Life is the result of a lack of reflection, of an inadequate harmonization of sources.⁴ But, as we have already noted, Plutarch does not usually simply follow the emphases of his sources. The lack of moral clarity in this pair does not result from the sources; rather, Plutarch seems to be making it deliberately difficult to extract simple moral lessons from this text.

Several reasons may be suggested for this. First, the moral opacity of the Lives of Lysander and Sulla reflects both the traits of cunning and deceptiveness and the contrast between appearance and reality, which Plutarch saw as central to these two figures. The way in which these two Lives are constructed seems to be deliberately mimetic of the character and career of their subjects. Secondly, Plutarch was here dealing with figures whose lives offered fewer possibilities than many of his other

[1] On the date of the *Lysander–Sulla*, see above, p. 63 n. 39.
[2] Pelling (1988a), 274.
[3] Brenk (1977), 265–7. Cf. Stadter (1992a), 43.
[4] Compare the similar claims of Gallotta (1987), 169–72, on Tacitus' treatment of Germanicus. In fact, the presentation of Germanicus is determined by the structural role he plays in the *Annals*, as a foil to bring out Tiberius' vices: Devillers (1993); Pelling (1993).

subjects for paradigmatic treatment. As has been noted, Plutarch seems to have been unwilling, despite the rather simplistic claims made in part of the *Demetrios* prologue (*Demetr.* 1. 6), to write wholly negative Lives. By refusing to see Lysander and Sulla as wholly 'bad' (cf. *Kimon* 2. 4–5), Plutarch is forced to look for ways in which their behaviour could be seen as positive, or, at least, as open to different interpretations. In fact, as in the case of Demetrios and Antony, Plutarch seems to regard Lysander and Sulla as men of 'great natures': with great potential for both good and bad. The moral questions asked of this pair thus become more complex and challenging than some of the programmatic statements may have led us to expect. In particular, the *Lysander–Sulla*, like the *Phokion–Cato Minor*, highlights the conflict between private virtue and the national interest, between ineffective good deeds and effective bad ones.[5] Philip Stadter, in a recent study, argued persuasively that these Lives, taken together, highlight the dangers of ambition and violence. There is furthermore, as Stadter maintains, a progression, in which bad traits in Lysander are shown to reach a peak in Sulla.[6] In fact the moral message of these Lives is more complex. Moral and political success are relativized and set against each other. At the heart of this pair there is a paradox: Lysander, though more successful in virtue than Sulla, is ultimately unsuccessful in the affairs of state; Sulla, less successful morally, succeeds in the affairs of state precisely because of his greater ruthlessness.

1. THE STATUE OF LYSANDER (*LYS*. 1. 1–3)

There is no formal prologue to the *Lysander–Sulla*. The pair opens with a description of a statue of Lysander, which stood outside the Akanthian treasury at Delphoi:

(1. 1) Ὁ Ἀκανθίων θησαυρὸς ἐν Δελφοῖς ἐπιγραφὴν ἔχει τοιαύτην· "Βρασίδας καὶ Ἀκάνθιοι ἀπ᾽ Ἀθηναίων". διὸ καὶ πολλοὶ τὸν ἐντὸς ἑστῶτα τοῦ οἴκου παρὰ ταῖς θύραις λίθινον ἀνδριάντα Βρασίδου νομίζουσιν εἶναι. Λυσάνδρου δ᾽ ἐστὶν εἰκονικός, εὖ μάλα κομῶντος ἔθει τῷ παλαιῷ, καὶ πώγωνα καθειμένου γενναῖον. (1. 2) οὐ γάρ, ὡς ἔνιοί φασιν, Ἀργείων μετὰ τὴν μεγάλην ἧτταν ἐπὶ πένθει καρέντων, οἱ Σπαρτιᾶται πρὸς τὸ ἀντίπαλον αὐτοῖς τὰς κόμας ἀγαλλόμενοι τοῖς πεπραγμένοις ἀνῆκαν, οὐδὲ Βακχιαδῶν τῶν ἐκ Κορίνθου φυγόντων εἰς

---

[5] See above, Ch. 5, esp. pp. 131–3.

[6] Stadter (1992*a*). The moral lessons of the *Lys.* alone are also examined by Russell (1966*a*), 151–4 (=1995, 90–4) and Pelling (1988*a*), 268–74.

Λακεδαίμονα, ταπεινῶν καὶ ἀμόρφων διὰ τὸ κείρασθαι τὰς κεφαλὰς φανέντων, εἰς ζῆλον αὐτοὶ τοῦ κομᾶν ἦλθον, ἀλλὰ καὶ τοῦτο Λυκούργειόν ἐστι· (1. 3) καί φασιν αὐτὸν εἰπεῖν ὡς ἡ κόμη τοὺς μὲν καλοὺς εὐπρεπεστέρους ὁρᾶσθαι ποιεῖ, τοὺς δ' αἰσχροὺς φοβερωτέρους.

(1. 1) The treasury of the Akanthians at Delphoi bears the following inscription: BRASIDAS AND THE AKANTHIANS, BUILT WITH SPOILS FROM THE ATHENIANS. For this reason, many think that the marble statue standing inside the temple, by the doors, is a statue of Brasidas. But it is really a representation of Lysander, with his hair very long, in the ancient custom, and with a generous beard. (1. 2) For it is not true, as some state, that because the Argives, after their great defeat, shaved their heads in sorrow, the Spartiates on the contrary let their hair grow long in exultation over their victory; nor was it because the Bakkhiadai, when they fled from Korinth to Lakedaimon, looked mean and ugly from having shaved their heads, that the Spartiates on their part became eager to have their hair long; on the contrary, this custom too goes back to Lykourgos. (1. 3) And they say that he said that hair makes the fine more beautiful, but the ugly more terrible.

This opening alerts the reader to a number of themes which will be important in the pair as a whole. The difficulty in identifying the statue as Lysander's suggests at the outset the difficulty of coming to any conclusions about him. One must presume that Plutarch had good reason for asserting that this statue be identified with Lysander and not Brasidas,[7] but it is described here in terms which seem to make any positive identification difficult: the statue is given no individualized features at all, but is presented as a stereotypical representation of a Classical Spartan. In what way then is the statue 'a representation of Lysander' (Λυσάνδρου εἰκονικός)? Plutarch seems here to be playing with two related meanings of εἰκών ('representation'), that is, first, a physical portrait or statue, and, second, metaphorically, a likeness or simile.[8] The statue is to be read as an 'image' of Lysander in this second, broader sense: it communicates an important truth about him.[9] Plutarch does

---

[7] Cf. Bommelaer (1981), 13–14.

[8] Mossman (1991), 108–11. For εἰκών in a metaphorical sense, a Platonic usage (e.g. Plato, Symp. 215a; Laws 644c; Gorgias 493d; cf. Aristoph. Clouds 559; Frogs 905–6), cf. Plut. Demetr. 45. 3–4; Adv. Col. 1115e; De Defect. Orac. 416d; Plat. Quaest. 1001c–d; 1007c; 1029d. Εἰκονικός implies individualized representation in a portrait statue; cf. Dion-Brut. 5. 2; Pliny, NH 34. 16 (on which, cf. Hyde 1921, 54–5). For the play on the meaning of εἰκών, cf. Lucian's work the Εἰκόνες (Imagines), which suggests both the mental and verbal images of the women which are produced, the statues and sculptures which are frequently alluded to, and the comparisons made with these statues.

[9] Cf. Nikolaos of Myra, Progymn. 1, Spengel, iii, 453, 19–20: 'So a fable (μῦθος) is a false tale which, by being persuasively put together, represents (εἰκονίζων) the truth'; cf. Aphthonios 1, Spengel, ii, 21, 2–3; Theon. Progym. 1, Spengel, ii, 59, 21–2.

indeed draw on this metaphorical sense of the word in *Cato Minor* 24. 1, when he talks of 'small signs of character' (τὰ μικρὰ τῶν ἠθῶν σημεῖα) as being 'like an image of the soul' (ὥσπερ εἰκόνα ψυχῆς).[10] This would accord with Plutarch's general practice of using statues and personal appearance not for their own sake but to shed light on character: sometimes appearance is shown to be a good indication of character, sometimes it is misleading.[11] As will become clear, the moral status of Lysander is as ambiguous as his statue is hard to identify. Significantly, Lykourgos' saying (1. 3) that long hair makes the fine (καλοί) more beautiful and the ugly (αἰσχροί) more terrible raises the question of whether Lysander himself is to be regarded as good or bad: as Philip Stadter has pointed out, the words καλός or αἰσχρός can refer to moral character as well as to appearance.[12] No explicit answer is given to this question, but it underlies the whole of the Life.

The statue also suggests a tension, which becomes clearer as the Life progresses, between Lysander's unorthodox behaviour and traditional Spartan values. The statue presents him as a traditional Spartan; as the Life progresses his behaviour is shown to be very different from what is expected of a Spartan, and this is stated explicitly at 2. 4 (cf. also 8. 5; 20. 8). This tension is emphasized by means of several digressions on elements of Spartan tradition, which serve to set Lysander against the traditional background. Such is the function of the discussions about wealth in Sparta (17. 1–11) and about the Spartan method of sending secret messages (19. 8–12);[13] such is also the function of the comparison which is explicitly encouraged between Lysander and the traditional Spartan Kallikratidas (7. 5).[14] The same effect is achieved by the discussion of Spartan hairstyle in this section (1. 2–3).[15] Much of the

---

[10] For the phrase εἰκών ψυχῆς, cf. *Cic.* 49. 2; *Cato Min.* 24. 1; Demetrios, *On Style* 227, Spengel, iii, 311, 26–7. Cf. above, p. 16.

[11] Good indication: *Them.* 22. 3; *Alk.* 4. 1; *Mar.* 2. 1; *De Alex. Fort.* II. 335b. Plutarch often uses generalized and non-specific descriptions of appearance as a key to character: Georgiadou (1992b), 4617–18; cf. Le Corsu (1981), 271, and Blomqvist (1997), 83–4: only good women are beautiful. Misleading: *Phok.* 5. 1; cf. *Phil.* 2. 1–6; *Demetr.* 2. 2; 41. 5–8; 44. 9, with De Lacy (1952), 168–71, and Tatum (1996), 141–3. Ambiguous: *Ages.* 2. 1–3. 9; *Ages.- Pomp.* 2. 1–2, with Tatum (1996), 146–9. Unreliability of statues as a guide to appearance: *Alex.* 4. 1–3; *Per.* 3. 3–4. On Plutarch's use of statues and physical appearance in general, see Wardman (1967); (1974), 140–52; Mossman (1991); Georgiadou (1992b); Tatum (1996).

[12] Stadter (1992a), 42.

[13] The *skytale*: on which, see Kelly (1985).

[14] Pelling (1988a), 269–70 and 272 n. 32. Cf. also *Lys.* 2. 3–4 and 30. 7. Bernini (1988) is of less relevance.

[15] Plutarch tacitly corrects Herodotos (1. 82. 7–8), perhaps in imitation of Thuc. 1. 20. 3. On Spartan hair, cf. *Phil. Apoll.* 8. 7. 6.

Lysander is taken up with showing how unlike a traditional Spartan Lysander was.

In fact, the very existence of this personalized victory monument shows how far Lysander overstepped the norms of Spartan egalitarianism.[16] Indeed, the very mention of Brasidas in the opening words of the Life sets up a paradigm for Lysander's own behaviour; Lysander will, like Brasidas, use unorthodox methods to win great victories for Sparta. Brasidas' victories abroad led him to a position of exceptional personal prestige and power, and earned him the envy of his peers (e.g. Thuc. 4. 108. 7); Lysander conforms to this pattern.[17] When later in the Life Lysander sets up a statue of himself at Delphoi (18. 1), the full extent of his personal power becomes clear. Soon afterwards his self-aggrandizement is shown to reach such a pitch that he is granted divine honours by some of the allied states and full deification in Samos (18. 5–6).[18] Once again, it is difficult to find out the truth about Lysander: Anaxandrides of Delphoi[19] is at this point quoted (18. 3) for a report that Lysander had a secret store of money at Delphoi.[20] This is neither accepted nor denied; Plutarch simply points out that the report contradicts other evidence of Lysander's poverty (cf. 2. 2).

2. THE STATUE OF SULLA (*SULLA* 2.1–2)

The ambiguity of the moral status of Lysander and Sulla is conveyed throughout this pair of Lives by the recurrent motif of the statue. Near the start of the *Sulla*, Plutarch discusses Sulla's physical appearance (2. 1–2).[21] Sulla's statues, Plutarch tells us, did not convey the terrifying gleam of his eyes:

---

[16] See Cartledge (1987), 82–6. On the historical Lysander, see also Lotze (1964); Bommelaer (1981).

[17] Brasidas does not function simply as a representative of Spartan tradition and contrast with Lysander, *pace* Mossman (1991), 111, but also as a paradigm for the exalted position of personal prestige which Lysander attained: many of the honours granted to Brasidas prefigure those granted to Lysander.

[18] Badian (1981), 33–8 tries to show that Lysander did not receive divine honours *in his lifetime*. Contrast Habicht (1970), 3–7 (=1956, 3–7) and 243–4, who gives more credence to Plutarch's account; cf. Cartledge (1987), 82–6, on the 'Navarchs Monument' at Delphoi. For the debate, see Sanders (1991), 274–8.

[19] Anaxandrides (or -as) seems to have written a history of Delphoi, judging from *Quaest. Graec.* 292f–293a and the Scholia to Aristoph. *Wealth* 925 and to Eur. *Alk.* 1 (*FGrH* 404 F 3–5). He is perhaps to be identified with Alexandrides, a Greek historian of uncertain date.   [20] Cf. *Lys.* 25. 3, with Bommelaer (1981), 205.

[21] See Stadter (1992*a*), 42–3.

(2.1) Τοῦ δὲ σώματος αὐτοῦ τὸ μὲν ἄλλο εἶδος ἐπὶ τῶν ἀνδριάντων φαίνεται, τὴν δὲ τῶν ὀμμάτων γλαυκότητα δεινῶς πικρὰν καὶ ἄκρατον οὖσαν ἡ χρόα τοῦ προσώπου φοβερωτέραν ἐποίει προσιδεῖν. (2.2) ἐξήνθει γὰρ τὸ ἐρύθημα τραχὺ καὶ σποράδην καταμεμειγμένον τῇ λευκότητι·

(2.1) His physical appearance in general is seen in his statues; but the greyness of his eyes, which was terribly bitter and unmixed, was made even more terrible to look at by the complexion of his face. (2.2) For the redness of his skin, which was covered in sores, was coarse and intermingled with whiteness.

Sulla's statue, like Lysander's, is deceptive. The parallel with Lysander's statue is made more obvious by the statement that Sulla's complexion made the gleam of his eyes 'more terrible' (φοβερωτέραν), an echo of Lykourgos' words in *Lys.* 1. 3 (φοβερωτέρους). Once again we are faced with a gap between artistic representation and real character.[22]

The terms used to describe Sulla's real appearance, 'bitter and unmixed' (πικρὰν καὶ ἄκρατον, cf. τραχύ), relate primarily to character rather than to appearance,[23] and it is Sulla's character which is the subject of the discussion which follows. Appearance and character are here, as often in the *Lives*, implicitly connected. Both his appearance, not adequately represented by his statues, and his character, are distasteful. In fact, there may well be a physiognomic theory lying behind the description, though its meaning is far from clear; later on, in *Sulla* 5. 11, a Chaldean soothsayer does indeed give an explicitly physiognomic reading of Sulla's face. Gleaming or grey eyes (ὀφθαλμοὶ γλαυκοί) can be interpreted as a sign of cowardice (ps.-Aristotle, *Physiogn.* 812b3–4) and also of a lack of humanity (Polemon i, 246 Förster[a]). Those with a white complexion can be seen as cowardly (ps.-Aristotle, *Physiogn.* 812a13), and those with a red complexion as hasty (ὀξεῖς: ibid 812a21). For Polemon (i, 244 Förster[a]), a white complexion blotched with red indicates daring and anger.[24] The contradictions of Sulla's character are particularly clear from Plutarch's discussion of an event which occurred in the Social War. Once again appearance is related to character. Soothsayers declare that a man who is 'unique in appearance' (ὄψει διάφορος) will free the city

---

[22] Cf. *De Pyth. Orac.* 397f: at the time of Leuktra, 'the stone statue of Lysander became so covered (ἐξήνθησεν) with wild shrubs and grass as to obscure the face'. The anecdote in its present form seems ready-made for some sort of parallel with Sulla's appearance as described in 2. 1–2 (cf. especially ἐξήνθε). See below, n. 155.

[23] For 'unmixed' (ἄκρατος) of character, see pp. 91–2. For ἄκρατος and πικρός together, cf. *Terrest. an Aquat.* 964e.

[24] Evans (1941), 104–5; (1969), 56–7. On Plutarch and physiognomy, see also pp. 17 n. 11 and 92–3.

from its troubles, and Sulla declares himself to be that man (*Sulla* 6. 12–13). A little later (6. 14), Plutarch echoes this phrase by describing Sulla as being, in his *character*, 'uneven and at variance with himself' (ἀνώμαλός τις . . . καὶ διάφορος πρὸς ἑαυτόν).[25] This inconsistency in his character, implicitly linked to his appearance, is then illustrated in the discussion which follows: he bestows honours and insults without reason, is excessive in both his flattery and his brutality to others, and can be variously both cruel and indulgent in response to the crimes of his troops (6. 15–17).

The statue theme recurs elsewhere in the Life. Sulla's love of honour (φιλοτιμία) and the burgeoning quarrel with Marius are associated with his having a representation (εἰκών) of the capture of Bocchus engraved on a ring (3. 8–4. 1). The same combination of ideas is seen in 6. 1–2, when Bocchus puts up representations (εἰκόνες)[26] of the same scene on the Capitol, much to Marius' annoyance. It seems likely that the satyr which Sulla meets on his return to Italy after his eastern campaigns is to be taken as a metaphor for his character (*Sulla* 27. 2–4). The meeting takes place in a mythical landscape (27. 2), where streams of fire perpetually burn, which suggests the metaphorical tone of the scene. The satyr is described (27. 3) as 'of the kind that sculptors and painters represent' (οἷον οἱ πλάσται καὶ γραφεῖς εἰκάζουσιν), a phrase which, in view of the recurrent theme of images (εἰκόνες) throughout this pair, alerts us to the possibility of a metaphorical reading.[27] The satyr's voice is 'coarse and, furthermore, a mixture of the whinnying of a horse and the bleating of a goat' (τραχεῖάν τινα καὶ μάλιστα μεμειγμένην ἵππου τε χρεμετισμῷ καὶ τράγου μηκασμῷ): a description which recalls Sulla's coarse and blotched appearance, itself an indication of his character (2. 2). The chief features of satyrs, or seilenoi (the two names are often used interchangeably), were their love of wine and violent sexual lust, often expressed by the Greek ὕβρις: characteristics also to be found in Sulla. The satyr, who is captured while sleeping at the fountain of fire, is probably to be imagined drunk, one of Sulla's vices (*Sulla* 2. 5; 26. 4; 36. 1): satyrs and seilenoi are traditionally met at fountains and caught when they are sleeping off a drinking bout.[28] The location of the encounter, at

---

[25] Stadter (1992a), 51 n. 7 notes the play between physical and moral qualities.
[26] εἰκόνες is the reading of the codices. Cobet's emendation Νίκας (to harmonize with *Mar.* 32. 4) should be resisted in the light of the recurrent εἰκών theme in this pair.
[27] For εἰκόνα πλάττειν in a metaphorical sense, cf. also Plato, *Rep.* 588b–d.
[28] e.g. Xen. *Anab.* 1. 2. 13; Virgil, *Ecl.* 6. 13–26, according to Servius (*Comm. in Verg. Ecl.* 6. 13) based on Theopompos (*FGrH* 115 F 74–5); Ovid, *Met.* 90–9; Phil. *Apoll.* 6. 27.

a shrine of the Nymphs, an appropriate place for satyrs to be found, also suggests Sulla's sexual excesses.[29]

At the very end of this pair of Lives, a statue, is used once again to convey ambiguity and inconsistency. We are told at 38. 3 that images (εἴδωλα) of Sulla and of a lictor were moulded out of incense and cinnamon to be used at his funeral.[30] The word translated 'moulded' is πλασθῆναι, which also carries with it the connotations of forgery or fiction, a sense which cognates of this word carry in *Lys*. 14. 7, 25. 5, and 26. 5 (cf. also *Sulla* 27. 3). Monuments can be deceptive, and the pair of Lives ends where it began.

3. THE STATUE OF KALLIKRATIDAS (*LYS*. 5. 7–8)

Lysander's character is portrayed partly through implicit and (at 7. 5) explicit comparison with his successor as admiral, Kallikratidas. This use of another figure to throw into relief the qualities of the subject of the Life is not an uncommon one in Plutarch. But in this Life it is not wholly clear which of the two figures the reader is meant to admire. In 5. 7–8, Kallikratidas' arrival on the scene of operations is described, and his truly Spartan virtue (ἀρετή) is compared, significantly in view of the repeated theme of images and their ambiguity in these Lives, to the beauty of a heroic statue:

(5. 7) διὸ καὶ Καλλικρατίδαν οὔτ' εὐθὺς ἡδέως εἶδον ἐλθόντα τῷ Λυσάνδρῳ διάδοχον τῆς ναυαρχίας, οὔθ' ὡς ὕστερον διδοὺς πεῖραν ἀνὴρ ἐφαίνετο πάντων ἄριστος καὶ δικαιότατος, ἠρέσκοντο τῷ τρόπῳ τῆς ἡγεμονίας, ἁπλοῦν τι καὶ Δώριον ἐχούσης καὶ ἀληθινόν. (5. 8) ἀλλὰ τούτου μὲν τὴν ἀρετὴν ὥσπερ ἀγάλματος ἡρωικοῦ κάλλος ἐθαύμαζον, ἐπόθουν δὲ τὴν ἐκείνου σπουδήν, καὶ τὸ φιλέταιρον καὶ χρειῶδες ἐζήτουν, ὥστ' ἀθυμεῖν ἐκπλέοντος αὐτοῦ καὶ δακρύειν.

---

[29] Satyrs or seilenoi are often thought of as pursuing Nymphs (e.g. Hom. *Hymn. Aphrod.* 262–3). Apollonios' encounter (see previous note) also takes place at a shrine to Nymphs. The mention of a satyr here recalls Seilenos, the boy whom Lysander promotes as part of his plots to gain the Spartan kingship (*Lys*. 26. 1–6). The reminiscence, as so often, serves to bring out differences between the two men: Lysander engages in political machinations, Sulla in wine and women.

[30] In fact, the use of an image (εἴδωλον) in a funeral was said by Herodotos (6. 58. 3) to be one of the prerogatives of Spartan kings, if their bodies could not be recovered from the field of battle; cf. Schaefer (1957); Hartog (1980), 166–70 (=1988, 152–6). Sulla seems here to have achieved an honour which Lysander could not, despite his attempts to gain royal powers (*Lys*. 12. 1, with n. 107 below; 24. 3–26. 6; 30. 4; *Lys.-Sulla* 2. 1–4, with Bernini 1985). This reinforces one of the pair's central paradoxes, that Sulla's greater ruthlessness led to his greater 'success'.

(5. 7) Therefore, too, they were not at once pleased to see Kallikratidas, when he came to succeed Lysander in the admiralty, nor later, when he had shown by clear proofs that he was the most just and noble of men, were they pleased with the manner of his leadership, which had a certain Doric simplicity and sincerity. (5. 8) But while they admired Kalliktratidas' virtue, as they would the beauty of a hero's statue, they yearned for the eagerness of Lysander, and missed his fondness for his comrades which was so useful to them,[31] so that when he was sailing away they were dejected and began to shed tears.

The use of the statue metaphor here recalls the statue of *Lys*. 1: it is Kallikratidas, not Lysander, who is the true Spartan and who truly deserves the comparison to a Spartan statue; with him appearance and reality meet. In the following chapters Kallikratidas' high moral standards are set against Lysander's pragmatic methods.[32] He is unwilling to extort funds from the cities of Asia Minor (6. 3). He is described (6. 4) as generous and high-minded (ἐλευθέριος καὶ μεγαλόφρων); unlike Lysander, therefore, he baulks at the idea of begging the Persians for money to carry on wars against other Greeks.[33] For him, the situation is seen in terms of a simple Greek–Barbarian dichotomy; Greeks should not fight Greeks (6. 8), a sentiment with which we may presume Plutarch's readers were expected to concur.[34]

But the *Lysander* seems to work against such clear-cut moral responses. Though Kallikratidas' virtue is admired, its inefficacy is also suggested. In this respect, Plutarch follows what is hinted at in Xenophon, who remains in the *Hellenika* ambivalent in his moral responses to the noble Kallikratidas and the more sinister, but successful, Lysander.[35] Plutarch, however, makes the moral ambiguity much more explicit. This is achieved in two ways. First, the comparison of Kallikratidas' virtue to a statue, while certainly in one sense complimentary, is distinctly two-edged. In the prologue to the *Lives of Perikles and Fabius* (*Per*. 1. 2–2. 4) Plutarch argues that there is an essential difference between works of art and virtue, in that the latter elicits imitation, while the former only admiration.[36] The assimilation of

---

[31] τὸ φιλέταιρον καὶ χρειῶδες. Smits (1939), ad loc., glosses χρειῶδες as τὴν χρείαν with a reference to 2. 4, where Lysander bears oppressive authority διὰ τὴν χρείαν ('where necessary', though possibly with connotations of 'poverty': cf. 2. 2). Tim Whitmarsh has pointed out to me a parallel in *Crass*. 3. 3 (τὸ ῥητορικὸν καὶ χρειῶδες εἰς ⟨τοὺς⟩ πολλοὺς), a hendiadys which seems to mean 'rhetoric which was useful to the many'.
[32] Pelling (1988*a*), 269–70.
[33] He uses the loaded term κολακεύειν: probably following Xen. *Hell*. 1. 6. 7.
[34] See above, p. 89.
[35] Moles (1994); a rather more nuanced approach than that of Due (1987).
[36] τὸ θαυμάσαι: *Per*. 1. 4; cf. 2. 2. See above, pp. 34–5.

Kallikratidas' virtue to a work of art could thus be read as damning; the implication is made clear by the antithesis here between the 'admiration' of the allies for Kallikratidas and their 'yearning' for Lysander. Furthermore, Kallikratidas is not being compared to any ordinary work of art. An ἄγαλμα is specifically a cult statue,[37] in this case that of a deified hero. The comparison is complimentary, suggesting that his virtue seemed almost divine.[38] But it also suggests his remoteness from the world of real action, and perhaps also his unbending stiffness: as will become clear, he lacks the ability to 'cultivate' others (θεραπεία) which Lysander and Sulla share.[39] The second way in which Plutarch here challenges a simple reading of Kallikratidas as superior to Lysander is by the brief and almost off-hand mention of his death at Arginousai (7. 1), which brings into close juxtaposition his Spartan virtue and his defeat and death. His *intentions* were 'worthy of Sparta' (ἄξια τῆς Λακεδαίμονος διανοηθείς); by his 'justice, highmindedness, and bravery' (δικαιοσύνη, μεγαλοψυχία, and ἀνδρία) he ranked alongside the foremost of the Greeks. But, despite this, he was responsible for one of the major Spartan defeats of the war, and disappeared (ἠφανίσθη) from his ship just as he disappears so abruptly from the narrative.[40]

4. LYSANDER AND KALLIKRATIDAS COMPARED
(*LYS*. 7. 5–6)

A little later, on the occasion of Lysander's return to the scene of operations, a direct comparison of Lysander and Kallikratidas is put into the minds of the different groups of allies (7. 5–6):

---

[37] See Bloesch (1943). The primary sense of ἄγαλμα (Schol. Aristoph. *Thesm.* 773: πᾶν ἐφ' ᾧ τις ἀγάλλεται) may also be implied here (cf. Eur. *Her.* 357–8). On the distinction between ἄγαλμα, ἀνδριάς, and εἰκών, see Nock (1930), 3 n. 2 (= 1972, 204 n. 5); (1933), 138 n. 8 (= 1972, 346 n. 8); Kerényi (1962), 168–71.

[38] Cf. the description of Kallirhoe (Chariton 1. 1. 1–2) as the ἄγαλμα of all Sicily, 'for her beauty was not human but divine'. This begins a series of explicit and implicit references to Kallirhoe as a goddess. See Scott (1938), 383–6. Cf. also *Them.* 22. 3; *Alex.* 21. 11.

[39] e.g. *Lys.* 2. 4, 4. 3; *Sulla* 5. 4; 6. 14; 6. 17; 10. 6; 12. 12–14. Θεραπεία and its cognates are standard terms in Plutarch for flattery: e.g. *Lys.* 19. 2; *Max. Cum Princ.* 776b; 778a–b. On θεραπεία in the *Lys.-Sulla*, see Pelling (1988a), 272–3; Stadter (1992a), 44–5.

[40] Ἀφανίζεσθαι (disappear) is a usual word for being lost at sea or on a river: cf. Thuc. 8. 38. 1; Plut. *Crass.* 19. 5. Xenophon, Plutarch's source here, is a little more explicit, with ἀποπεσὼν εἰς τὴν θάλατταν ἠφανίσθη (*Hell.* 1. 6. 33). Plutarch's remarks at *Pel.* 2. 2–3 suggest that he did regard Kallikratidas' courage at Arginousai as misplaced (as did Cicero, in *De Offic.* 1. 84). For a similar brief mention of a minor character's death to undercut a preceding discussion, cf. *Demetr.* 21. 4–5.

(7. 5) τοῖς δὲ τὸν ἁπλοῦν καὶ γενναῖον ἀγαπῶσι τῶν ἡγεμόνων τρόπον ὁ Λύσανδρος τῷ Καλλικρατίδᾳ παραβαλλόμενος ἐδόκει πανοῦργος εἶναι καὶ σοφιστής, ἀπάταις τὰ πολλὰ διαποικίλλων τοῦ πολέμου, καὶ τὸ δίκαιον ἐπὶ τῷ λυσιτελοῦντι μεγαλύνων, εἰ δὲ μή, τῷ συμφέροντι χρώμενος ὡς καλῷ, καὶ τὸ ἀληθὲς οὐ φύσει τοῦ ψεύδους κρεῖττον ἡγούμενος, ἀλλ' ἑκατέρου τῇ χρείᾳ τὴν τιμὴν ὁρίζων. (7. 6) τῶν δ' ἀξιούντων μὴ πολεμεῖν μετὰ δόλου τοὺς ἀφ' Ἡρακλέους γεγονότας καταγελᾶν ἐκέλευεν· "ὅπου γὰρ ἡ λεοντῆ μὴ ἐφικνεῖται, προσραπτέον ἐκεῖ τὴν ἀλωπεκῆν".

(7. 5) To those who loved the simple and noble character of their leaders, Lysander, compared with Kallikratidas, seemed to be unscrupulous and subtle, a man who varied most of what he did in war with the different colours of deceit, extolling justice if it was at the same time profitable, but if not, employing expediency as the honourable course, and not considering truth as by nature better than falsehood, but defining the value he placed on each by the needs of the hour. (7. 6) He held up to ridicule those who demanded that the descendants of Herakles should not wage war by deceit, saying, 'where the lion's skin does not reach, it must be patched out with the fox's'.

At first sight, this comparison, which emphasizes Lysander's use of deception, might seem damning, though it is left unclear to what extent this judgement is supported by the narrator. Lysander is shown not to fight in the more open, noble way—but he is successful. Throughout this pair of Lives noble morality and success are shown not always to accompany each other.

But this passage contains more ambiguities. The use of deception and trickery in warfare was not always regarded in Greek and Roman thought as morally wrong; rather its moral status was negotiable, subject to both positive and negative valorization.[41] Indeed trickery in war is often seen as one of the marks of the good general.[42] Deception (ἀπάτη; cf. 8. 5; *Sulla* 28. 1–2) and guile (δόλος) are standard words for 'military stratagem'; their tone is defined by context. After all, deception against an enemy could be considered just.[43] The possibilities of such a positive valorization of military deceit in the fourth century are especially clear from Xenophon's advice in *The cavalry commander* 4. 7–5. 15, where words implying deception or trickery are used to characterize the shrewd cavalry commander's activities.[44] His *Education of Kyros* explores the

[41] See Hesk (1997), the most comprehensive and nuanced study. What follows was conceived independently.
[42] Wheeler (1988).
[43] Xen. *Mem.* 4. 2. 15–17; *Kyr.* 1. 6. 27–40; Andok. *Or.* 3. 33–4; Plut. *De Cap. ex Inim.* 91b–c; cf. Plato, *Rep.* 382c; 548a.
[44] These include cognates of ψεῦδος (falsehood: 4. 7, 5. 8), ἐνέδρα (ambush: 4. 10, 12),

issue of how to regard trickery at length in the dialogue between Kyros and his father Kambyses (1. 6. 1–2. 1. 1).[45] In the fourth century the epic hero Odysseus, who was characterized by his cunning and deceptiveness,[46] was a site for this debate over how trickery should be regarded.[47] Plutarch draws on this tradition when, in the humorous dialogue *On the fact that beasts are rational*,[48] a pig argues with Odysseus that animals are more virtuous than humans. At one point he upbraids Odysseus for using trickery in war, in contrast to the straightforward fighting of the animals which Odysseus derides. The behaviour for which Odysseus is accused is much the same as that of Lysander: '. . . you have led astray by deceits and devices (δόλοις καὶ μηχαναῖς) men who knew only a simple and noble method (ἁπλοῦν καὶ γενναῖον) of war and who were inexperienced in deception (ἀπάτης) and lies (ψευδῶν); you apply to your unscrupulousness (πανουργίᾳ) the name of that virtue which least admits unscrupulousness' (987c). Odysseus' use of trickery in war could, then, be presented in negative light. But it is probable that part of the humour of this passage is its paradoxical nature: Odysseus is being accused of something for which he is normally commended. At any rate, deceptiveness could be judged either way.

Cunning and trickery were considered particularly characteristic of Spartans. They could be constructed negatively: perfidy was a major plank of fifth-century Athenian attacks on Sparta in comedy and tragedy.[49] They could also be presented as non-Spartan traits, conflicting with a supposed 'Dorian' simplicity, a view which Plutarch gives as the thoughts of some of those who saw Lysander replacing the upright Kallikratidas (*Lys.* 5. 7; 7. 5–6). Ephoros presents the cunning of the Spartan general Derkylidas as conflicting with Lakonic sraightforwardness (*FGrH* 70 F 71).[50] Plutarch himself describes the deceitful tactics

κλέπτω (steal or hide: 4. 17, 5. 2, 5. 7), μηχανή (device: 5. 2–3, 5. 9–10, 5. 14), ἀπάτη (deceit: 5. 5, 5. 10–12, 5. 15), and τέχνη (skill: 5. 14). Cf. also Aineias Taktikos 39–40; fr. 52; 56–8 Schöne.

[45] Hesk (1997), 115–33.
[46] Cf. e.g. Walcot (1977).
[47] e.g. Plato's *Hipp. Min.*, and Antisthenes' debate between Ajax and Odysseus (frs. V A 53–4 Giannantoni). See Hesk (1997), 111–15. Hippias describes Achilles as ἀληθής τε καὶ ἁπλοῦς, Odysseus as πολύτροπός τε καὶ ψευδής (365b). By the end of the dialogue, Odysseus emerges wiser and better than Achilles.
[48] Περὶ τοῦ τὰ ἄλογα λόγῳ χρῆσθαι: the pun ἄλογα λόγῳ is lost in translation.
[49] e.g. Eur. *Andr.* 445–53; *Suppl.* 187; Aristoph. *Lysist.* 628–9; *Acharn* 307–8; *Peace* 622–4 and 1063–7; cf. Grossman (1950), 182 ff. (*non vidi*); Hesk (1997), 12–51; also Bradford (1994), 70–7, on duplicity as a Spartan characteristic in Thucydides (e.g. 2. 39. 1; cf. Hdt. 9. 54. 1).
[50] 'For there was nothing Lakonic (Λακωνικόν) nor straightforward (ἁπλοῦν) in his character, but much unscrupulousness and savagery (πολὺ τὸ πανοῦργον καὶ τὸ θηριῶδες).'

which the Achaian Philopoimen used against the Cretans as being specifically non-Peloponnesian: 'He did not wage any kind of straightforward or honourable warfare (ἁπλοῦν τινα καὶ γενναῖον πόλεμον), as you might expect from a Peloponnesian or Arkadian; but he put on the Cretan character (τὸ Κρητικὸν ἦθος: cf. *Lys.* 20. 2) and used their schemes (σοφίσμασι), tricks (δόλοις), wiles, and ambushes against them' (*Phil.* 13. 9; cf. *Phil.-Flam.* 2. 4).

But in other contexts cunning could be presented as the mark of a *good* Spartan. Thus in the narrative section of Xenophon's *Agesilaos*, Tissaphernes is criticized for breaking his word before the formal outbreak of hostilities (*Ages.* 1. 12); but once war is declared Agesilaos' use of deception becomes a mark of good generalship: 'when war was declared', Xenophon remarks, 'and deception became in consequence righteous and fair, he showed Tissaphernes to be a child at deception (1. 17).[51] In the survey of virtues at the end of the *Agesilaos*, under the heading of wisdom (σοφία), Xenophon commends Agesilaos for engaging in deception 'where there was opportunity' (6. 5). Plutarch, in his *Life of Agesilaos*, is equally positive about Agesilaos' use of deception: in *Ages.* 9. 3, for example, Agesilaos is said to use a 'just deception' (ἀπάτη δικαία).[52] Lysander's use of 'falsehood' in warfare (7. 5) also invites an ambivalent reading: compounds of ψεῦδος commonly describe stratagems (e.g. Polyainos 3. 9. 32), and may well have formed part of a technical vocabulary of military trickery (cf. Diod. 20. 17. 5).[53] Certainly, at any rate, it is Lysander's shrewdness, almost cunning (δεινότης),[54] along with his good planning (εὐβουλία), which led to victory at Aigospotamoi (11. 12). At the opening of the *Sertorius–Eumenes* (*Sert.* 1. 8) Plutarch notes that some of the most famous generals of antiquity won their victories by guile and shrewdness' (δόλῳ . . . μετὰ δεινότητος).[55]

So the Spartans actually called him Sisyphos'. Xenophon, Ephoros' source at this point, seems to approve of Derkylidas cunning (*Hell.* 3. 1. 8); cf. Kane (1990), 4. On Ephoros as anti-Spartan, see Tigerstedt (1965), 208–22; as a source for Plutarch, see Herbert (1958); Smits (1939), 13–19.

[51] Cf. *Hell.* 3. 4. 11–12; 5. 4. 48; *Anab.* 2. 6. 7.

[52] Cf. Plutarch's subtle alteration of Xen. *Ages.* 1. 29 (οὐκ ἐψεύσατο) to οὐκέτι ψευδόμενος (Plut. *Ages.* 10. 1), thus making explicit Agesilaos' previous use of deception. Cf. also Plato's 'noble lie' (*Rep.* 414b–c: γενναῖόν τι ἓν ψευδομένους).

[53] Cf. *Sulla* 15. 5; *Ages.* 10. 1. On δόλος and ἀπάτη, cf. Wheeler (1988), 30–2 and 105–6; on words in ψευδ-, ibid. 38–41 and 43. The description of Lysander may have reminded Plutarch's reader of the Spartan *Krypteia*, on which see Vidal-Naquet (1968), 953–5 (=1981, 153–5); Cartledge (1987), 30–2.

[54] For the association of δεινότης with trickery, cf. Polyb. 4. 8. 3 and Wheeler (1988), 36–7.

[55] Cf. Sertorius' cunning: *Sert.* 10. 3; 11. 2. Themistokles' deception of the Spartans in fortifying Athens and Alkibiades' deception of their ambassadors in 419 BC are presented

The words applied to Lysander in this passage do not, then, necessarily carry a pejorative tone; their moral status is left open to both positive or negative presentation. The description of Lysander as unscrupulous (πανοῦργος) and subtle (σοφιστής) carries similar ambiguities.[56] The pejorative sense which πανουργία bore in fifth- and fourth-century Athenian literature[57] seems to have been lost in many examples from later periods (e.g. Polyb. 5. 75. 2), though the *Souda* (s.v. πανοῦργος) states that Atticists continued to use it in that sense. The word *could* be used as a compliment.[58] What is more, Plutarch saw it as a quality which the Spartan education system encouraged (*Lyk.* 17. 5–6). The only other occurrence of the word in the *Lysander–Sulla* shares the ambiguity. The speech written for Lysander by Kleon of Halikarnassos is described by the Ephor Kratidas[59] as συντεταγμένον πιθανῶς καὶ πανούργως: 'put together persuasively and *wickedly*' or 'persuasively and *cleverly*' (30. 5)? Σόφισμα could be used for a military or political ruse.[60] Plutarch used it of Sertorius' speed, cunning, and trickery in war (τάχος, ἀπάτη, ψεύδη): he is a σοφιστὴς δεινότατος (*Sert.* 10. 3).[61] But the word σοφιστής, combined with the stress here on Lysander's preference for expediency over the strict claims of truth and falsehood, recalls the criticisms made of the sophists in the fifth and fourth centuries, that they could make the weaker or morally inferior argument seem the stronger.[62]

The report of the saying, or apophthegm, which shows Lysander implicitly comparing himself to a fox (7. 6), continues the ambiguity. Foxes were known for their cunning: Pindar (*Isthmian* 4. 45–7), for

with something approaching admiration: *Them.* 19. 1–3; *Alk.* 14. 6–15. 2; *Cor.-Alk.* 2. 1–5. Pelopidas' liberation of Thebes by stealth is commended: cf. *Pel.-Marc.* 1. 6.

[56] On πανουργία, cf. Wheeler (1988), 33–5 and 107–8; on σοφιστής, ibid. 27–8.

[57] e.g. Eur. *Alk.* 766; *Hipp.* 1400; Aristoph. *Knights* 249; Thuc. 3. 82. 7.

[58] e.g. Men. *Epitrep.* 535, with Gomme and Sandbach (1973), n. ad loc.; cf. Plut. *De Aud. Poet.* 28a: κομψὸν . . . καὶ πανοῦργον; *Quaest. Conv.* 673f.

[59] Emending Λακρατίδαν, the reading of the codices, to Κρατίδαν. In the parallel passage in the *Spartan Sayings* (*Ap. Lac.* 229f) most manuscripts have Κρατίδην, and a man of this name (Kratidas) is attested as an ephor of the Lakonian city of Kotyrta on an inscription (*SGDI* 4, 36, 34–5, p. 690); cf. Piccirilli (1993a), 28–9. Fraser and Matthews (1997), 257, give three other occurrences on inscriptions outside Lakonia. The name Lakratidas is unparalleled in Lakonia (e.g. in Bradford 1977), though it seems to occur on an inscription from Methana in the Argolid (*SEG* 37, 320: [Λ]ακρατε[ίδ]α). For a similar emendation of the Life on the basis of a reading in the *Ap. Lac.*, cf. below, n. 95 (*Lys.* 2. 8).

[60] e.g. *Sol.* 15. 2; *Fab.* 5. 4; *Ages.-Pomp.* 2. 3; *De Fort. Rom.* 320e; cf. Thuc. 5. 9. 5.

[61] Cf. σοφιστικῶς in *Sert.* 11. 2.

[62] e.g. Protagoras (Aristotle, *Rhet.* 1402a23), Euthydemos (Plato, *Euth.* 272a), Sokrates as portrayed in Aristophanes' *Clouds*: see Dover (1968), pp. xxxvii–xl, and Guthrie (1969), esp. 32–40. The term σοφιστής is often used by Plutarch and other writers of the 1st and 2nd cents. AD as a term of abuse: Stanton (1973), 351–8; Brunt (1994), 27, 42–3.

example, contrasts the bravery of lions with the cunning of foxes as here.[63] The story which follows of Lysander's murder of the Milesian democrats (8. 1–3) is highly appropriate as an illustration of this apophthegm.[64] Lysander lures them into his trap by pretending to mean them no harm; compare Oppian's description (*Halieutika* 2. 107–19) of the fox playing dead or pretending to be asleep in order to lure birds to attack it. Lysander's deceit is described with the word διεποίκιλλε (literally, 'variegate, adorn').[65] The literal meaning of words from this root (ποικιλ-) is 'multi-coloured' or 'variegated'. But they can have connotations of cunning;[66] Odysseus in Homer is frequently referred to as ποικιλομήτης.[67] Ποικίλος is, like πανοῦργος, a common epithet for the fox.[68] That Lysander's deception could be regarded as culpable is apparent from a comparison with *Alex.* 59. 6–7, where a similar act is said to be a 'stain' (κηλίς) on Alexander's military deeds. But admiration of the fox's cunning was also possible.[69]

This section on Lysander's deceitfulness is rounded off by a second apophthegm (8. 5), recorded by a certain Androkleides, otherwise unknown, showing Lysander's 'indifference' (εὐχέρεια) to oaths:

[A] ἐκέλευε γὰρ ὥς φησι τοὺς μὲν παῖδας ἀστραγάλοις, τοὺς δ' ἄνδρας ὅρκοις ἐξαπατᾶν, ἀπομιμούμενος Πολυκράτη τὸν Σάμιον, [B] οὐκ ὀρθῶς τύραννον στρατηγός, οὐδὲ Λακωνικὸν τὸ χρῆσθαι τοῖς θεοῖς ὥσπερ τοῖς πολεμίοις, μᾶλλον δ' ὑβριστικώτερον· ὁ γὰρ ὅρκῳ παρακρουόμενος τὸν μὲν ἐχθρὸν ὁμολογεῖ δεδιέναι, τοῦ δὲ θεοῦ καταφρονεῖν.

[A] It was his policy, according to Androkleides, 'to deceive boys with knucklebones, but men with oaths,' thus imitating Polykrates of Samos, [B] though it was not right for a general to imitate a tyrant, nor was it Lakonian to treat the gods as one treats one's enemies, no, it was even more outrageous; since he who

---

[63] Cf. Solon 11. 5–8 West; Aisop, *Fab.* 192; Aristoph. *Lysist.* 1269–70; *Peace* 1067–8; Plato, *Rep.* 365c; Aelian, *De Nat. Anim.* 6. 24; cf. Plut. *Them.* 21. 7. There may also be a suggestion of the 'bestializing' effect of Spartan training: cf. Aristotle, *Pol.* 1388b12 and 30–1, and Hesk (1997), 24–5.

[64] It is introduced again out of chronological sequence in 19. 3. See further below, Appendix 2.

[65] On this word, see Decker (1951).

[66] Plato, *Symp.* 218c; *Laws* 863e; Strabo 7. 3. 7, C 301; cf. Alkibiades as the chameleon who changes colour: *Alk.* 23. 3–6. See also Hesk (1997), 22–3.

[67] *Il.* 11. 482; *Od.* 3. 163; 13. 293.

[68] Ποικίλος: Aisop, *Fab.* 119; πανοῦργος: Aristotle, *Hist. Anim.* 1. 1, 488b20–1; ps.-Aristotle, *Physiogn.* 6, 812a16–17; cf. Plut. *Terrest. an Aquat.* 971a.

[69] e.g. in Archilochos, fr. 174; 185; 201 West; cf. Aisop, *Fab.* 6; Plato, *Rep.* 365c. On the associations of the fox, see Bowra (1940); Detienne and Vernant (1974), 41–5 (=1978, 34–7).

deceives his enemy by means of an oath admits that he fears him, but despises the god.[70]

The saying [A] is attributed to Lysander elsewhere (e.g. Dion of Prousa, *Or*. 74. 15). The judgement [B], that Lysander's cunning behaviour was inappropriate for a Spartan general, is perhaps designed to recall the criticisms recorded of Pausanias in Thucydides 1. 95. 3.[71] But it is unclear whether this judgement represents the views of Androkleides alone, or whether the reader is expected to share it. This has the effect of distancing the narrator from the criticism of Lysander expressed and contributes to the continuing difficulty of forming a moral judgement on Lysander's behaviour.

The theme of deception continues throughout the Life. Lysander's fall from power occurs when Pharnabazos uses deception against him (20. 1–5). After his death, his plans to overthrow the Spartan state are kept secret, despite Agesilaos' desire (30. 4) to expose 'what sort of a citizen he really was' ($οἷος\ ὢν\ πολίτης\ διαλάθοι$).[72] His death at the 'Hill of Foxes' ($Ἀλώπεκον$) near Haliartos (29. 11–12) appears as a kind of retribution for his treacherous behaviour, which he himself had associated with that of a fox.[73] Deception is a trait which is shared by Sulla (e.g. 28. 1–6). Furthermore, the continuity of the theme is marked by a recurrence of the comparison of the fox and the lion (*Sulla* 28. 6): Sulla's enemy Carbo declares that 'in making war upon the fox and the lion living in Sulla's soul, he was more annoyed by the fox'.

---

[70] Plato too suggests that deception could be associated with fear of the enemy (*Rep*. 382d). See Hesk (1997), 101–9.

[71] Cf. Theopompos' criticism of Pharax, a Spartan adviser to Dionysios I: 'Even Pharax the Spartan took up a luxurious life-style . . . and indulged in pleasures so outrageously that he was on account of his life-style taken as a Greek Sicilian far more than he was on account of his homeland taken as a Spartiate' (*FGrH* 115 F 192).

[72] The use of imagery from the tragic stage also contributes to the impression of deception surrounding Lysander: cf. Pelling (1988a), 273. On Plutarch's use of tragic imagery, see also pp. 62 n. 35, 123 n. 83, and 125.

[73] Occasionally elsewhere the place or manner in which a Plutarchan hero dies has some symbolic significance for our understanding of his character. Agesilaos, whom Plutarch links to Agamemnon (*Ages*. 6. 6–9), as he does his partner Pompey (*Pomp*. 67. 5), dies at the so-called 'Harbour of Menelaos' on the North African coast (40. 3); Cicero is betrayed by his freedman Philologos ('Scholar'), whom he is said to have brought up and educated (*Cic*. 48. 2): the final irony for the statesman who had tried to withdraw into the world of Greek culture from the realities of Roman politics: see Moles (1988), 35–6; 151; 200; Pelling (1989), 222.

5. LYSANDER'S UPBRINGING AND CHARACTER
(*LYS*. 2. 1–6)

The ambiguity inherent in Lysander's character, and the difficulty of forming moral judgements on him, can also be seen in the discussion of his upbringing and character near the start of the Life (2. 1–6):

(2. 1) Λέγεται δ' ὁ Λυσάνδρου πατὴρ Ἀριστόκλητος οἰκίας μὲν οὐ γενέσθαι βασιλικῆς, ἄλλως δὲ γένους εἶναι τοῦ τῶν Ἡρακλειδῶν. (2. 2) ἐτράφη δ' ὁ Λύσανδρος ἐν πενίᾳ, καὶ παρέσχεν ἑαυτὸν εὔτακτον ὡς εἴ τις ἄλλος πρὸς τοὺς ἐθισμούς, καὶ ἀνδρώδη καὶ κρείττονα πάσης ἡδονῆς, πλὴν εἴ τινα τιμωμένοις καὶ κατορθοῦσιν αἱ καλαὶ πράξεις ἐπιφέρουσι. (2. 3) ταύτης δ' οὐκ αἰσχρόν ἐστιν ἡττᾶσθαι τοὺς νέους ἐν Σπάρτῃ. . . . (2. 4) τὸ μὲν οὖν φιλότιμον αὐτῷ καὶ φιλόνικον ἐκ τῆς Λακωνικῆς παρέμεινε παιδείας ἐγγενόμενον, καὶ οὐδέν τι μέγα χρὴ τὴν φύσιν ἐν τούτοις αἰτιᾶσθαι· θεραπευτικὸς δὲ τῶν δυνατῶν μᾶλλον ἢ κατὰ Σπαρτιάτην φύσει δοκεῖ γενέσθαι, καὶ βάρος ἐξουσίας διὰ χρείαν ἐνεγκεῖν εὔκολος· ὃ πολιτικῆς δεινότητος οὐ μικρὸν ἔνιοι ποιοῦνται μέρος. (2. 5) Ἀριστοτέλης δὲ τὰς μεγάλας φύσεις ἀποφαίνων μελαγχολικάς, ὡς τὴν Σωκράτους καὶ Πλάτωνος καὶ Ἡρακλέους, ἱστορεῖ καὶ Λύσανδρον οὐκ εὐθὺς ἀλλὰ πρεσβύτερον ὄντα τῇ μελαγχολίᾳ περιπεσεῖν. (2. 6) ἴδιον δ' αὐτοῦ μάλιστα τὸ καλῶς πενίαν φέροντα, καὶ μηδαμοῦ κρατηθέντα μηδὲ διαφθαρέντα χρήμασιν αὐτόν, ἐμπλῆσαι τὴν πατρίδα πλούτου καὶ φιλοπλουτίας . . .

(2. 1) The father of Lysander, Aristokletos, is said to have been not of the royal house, though otherwise of the lineage of the Herakleidai. (2. 2) But Lysander was brought up in poverty, and showed himself as much as any man conformable to the customs of his people, and manly and superior to every pleasure except only the sort which fine deeds bring to those who are honoured and successful. (2. 3) To this pleasure it is no disgrace for the young in Sparta to succumb. . . . (2. 4) Love of honour and love of victory, then, were firmly implanted in him by his Lakonian training, and his nature should not be blamed too much for this. On the other hand, he seems to have been by nature more given to cultivating the powerful than was usual for a Spartiate, and content to endure the weight of authority where necessary, a trait which some make no small part of political shrewdness. (2. 5) And Aristotle, when he declares that great natures, like those of Sokrates, Plato, and Herakles, have a tendency to *melancholia*, writes also that Lysander, not immediately, but when older, succumbed to *melancholia*. (2. 6) What is most singular about him is that, though he bore poverty well, and though he was in no way mastered or corrupted by money, he filled his country with wealth and the love of wealth.

This section of direct character analysis at the start of the Life, a common feature of Plutarchan biography, here performs several functions.[74] First, it signals the character-traits which are significant in this pair of Lives:[75] 'love of honour' and 'love of victory' (2. 4), the ability to flatter, and a tendency to *melancholia* (2. 5; literally 'black bile'). Plutarch's understanding of this last trait seems to be based on that of [pseudo-]Aristotle in the *Problems* (30. 1, 953a10–955a40), to whom he makes a direct reference. It implies a temperament which inclines to violence and anger, qualities which are amply demonstrated in the Life which follows and especially in 28. 1: 'being altogether harsh in his anger owing to the *melancholia* which persisted into his old age.'[76] The specific statement (2. 1) that Lysander's father was a Heraklid but not a member of the royal family prefigures another important theme in this Life, namely, Lysander's desire for kingship.[77]

The second function of this section is to suggest the moral ambiguity of Lysander. He is said to be more 'given to cultivating the powerful than was usual for a Spartiate' (2. 4). Such a tendency to flatter others, a recurrent theme of this pair (Sulla ingratiates himself frequently with the army or the people), is a wholly negative trait elsewhere in Plutarch.[78] But any easy condemnation of Lysander is undercut by the narrator's following statement that some see this ability to court the powerful as an

---

[74] Plutarch is perhaps dependent on Theopompos. Athenaios notes that most writers recorded that Lysander became known for his luxurious life-style (*Deipn.* 543b–c). He quotes, however, the tenth book of Theopompos' *Hellenika* (*FGrH* 115 F 20) for a different view: 'he [Lysander] loved toil and was able to cultivate (θεραπεύειν) both private individuals and kings, being self-restrained (σώφρων) and above all pleasures. At any rate, although he became master of almost all Greece (cf. *Lys.* 16. 1), it will become clear that in none of the cities did he rush to enjoy sexual pleasures nor indulge in bouts of drinking and drunkenness at the wrong times.'

[75] Pelling (1988a), 269–70, describes this section as a rather crude presentation of character-traits, which are then progressively redefined as the Life continues.

[76] For Lysander's anger, cf. 19. 1–6; 22. 1–5; 24. 1–2; 27. 4. Elsewhere, Plutarch associates bile (χολή) with anger: *De Cohib. Ira* 457d; 458e; fr. 157. 2 Sandbach. On *melancholia*, see Toohey (1990); Padel (1995), 47–54. Contemporary medical writers tended to associate *melancholia* with depression. But in non-medical writers the predominant trait is madness (e.g. Plut. *Adv. Col.* 1123b: Toohey 1990, 150–1). The emendation in *Lys.* 2. 5 proposed by Cruserius of Ἡρακλέους, one of the melancholics also listed by ps.-Aristotle, to Ἡρακλείτου, well known as a depressive, is thus groundless (Flacelière 1970). Aristotle (*NE* 1150b25–8) talks of 'melancholics' (μελαγχολικοί) as being prone to 'lack of restraint' (ἀκρασία); they are 'too vehement to wait for reason' (διὰ τὴν σφοδρόδητα οὐκ ἀναμένουσι τὸν λόγον): cf. Lysander's fatal advance on Haliartos, caused by his inability 'to remain inactive' (ἀτρεμεῖν: *Lys.* 28. 6). Cf. ps.-Hippokrates, *On the sacred disease* 18 (= VI, 394 Littré); Plut. *Prof. in Virt.* 81f–82a. On *Lys.* 2. 5, cf. also Bommelaer (1981), 56–7, and Sansone (1980), 67.

[77] On Plutarch's structural use of a subject's ancestors at the start of his Life, see below, Appendix 1.   [78] On this theme in the Roman Lives, see De Blois (1992), 4590–9.

important part of political shrewdness (πολιτικὴ δεινότης). Similarly, Plutarch makes Lysander's tendency to anger cut both ways, by following [pseudo-]Aristotle's lead and relating it to *melancholia* (2. 5). Plutarch explicitly refers the reader to the classic analysis of *melancholia* in the [pseudo-]Aristotelian *Problems*. There the author associates *melancholia* with 'those who are outstanding (περιττοί) in philosophy, statesmanship, poetry, or arts', and lists as examples Herakles, Lysander, Ajax, Bellerophon, Empedokles, Plato, and Sokrates (953a14–29). The author goes on to talk of the variety of mixtures within the constitutions of those who are melancholic, which produce in them a variety of effects, mental and physical. He concludes (955a36–40) that all melancholics are by nature 'outstanding' (περιττοί). Plutarch seems to have interpreted this passage as a re-statement of the doctrine of 'great natures', and to have taken περιττός (exceptional, outstanding, even abnormal) as a synonym for 'great nature'. Some men, by virtue of their natural constitution, are exceptional in their intellect and capacity. This may lead to great good, as in the case of Plato or Sokrates, or to fits of madness, as in the case of Ajax or Herakles. By referring us to this passage in the *Problems*, Plutarch is able to associate Lysander with three of the greatest figures of the Greek past, Sokrates, Plato, and Herakles, and to relate his worst trait to his having, like them, a 'great nature'.[79] Furthermore, the good traits of Lysander's austerity and financial honesty are undercut by the paradoxical statement (2. 6) that, though incorruptible himself, he filled Sparta with wealth and the love of it. This paradox turns any ordinary moral scheme on its head.

And what of Lysander's 'love of honour and love of victory'? Elsewhere in Plutarch, ambition in young men is morally problematic: a good thing, but not without its dangers.[80] But the problem of judging Lysander is intensified by the injunction not to blame him 'too much' for this trait since it was engendered by his Spartan education (2. 4).[81] The possibility of a critical assessment of Lysander's character has already been raised by

[79] On *Problems* 30. 1, see Klibansky, Panofsky, and Saxl (1964), 18–41; Padel (1995), 55–7. Cf. *Post. An.* 2. 13 (97b15–25), where Alkibiades, Achilles, Ajax, Lysander, and Sokrates are suggested hypothetically as examples of 'greatness of soul' (μεγαλοψυχία): the first three are characterized by 'intolerance of dishonour', and the second two by 'being unaffected by good and bad fortune'. On 'great natures', see above, pp. 47–9 and 206–10.

[80] See my discussion on pp. 84–7, above.

[81] On this passage, cf. Pelling (1988a), 269 and 272–3. For Plutarch, as for Plato, ambition is particularly associated with Sparta; see my discussion (previous note). Plutarch seems here to be maintaining that Lysander's *nature* was not in itself excessively ambitious, but that it was his upbringing as a Spartan which formed his ambitious *character*. Later, however, Plutarch seems to imply that Lysander's very nature was ambitious (23. 3).

the discussion of the central place which praise and blame held in Spartan society (2. 2–3). But the results here are ambiguous—do we blame Lysander for his love of honour or not? In his dealings with Kyros, φιλοτιμία has a good sense ('disinterestedness, public-spiritedness'):[82] it is the motive behind Lysander's request for extra pay for his fleet (4. 6); significantly, Xenophon does not attribute Lysander's action to this trait (Hell. 1. 5. 2–7): it is a Plutarchan concern. Later (6. 2), Kallikratidas is said to want to prove that Lysander's φιλοτιμία is boastful and empty (ἀλαζονικὴν καὶ κενήν). It is unclear whether Kallikratidas' negative judgement is shared by the narrator or not.

The moral complexity of the picture of Lysander is further developed by a Thucydidean reminiscence. His witty reply to Kallikratidas in 6. 3 ('that it was not he but the other who was in charge of the fleet') recalls a similar reply by Thucydides' Kleon (Thuc. 4. 28. 2).[83] The context of Kleon's reply is the debate in the Athenian Assembly on operations at Pylos (Thuc. 4. 27–8), in which Kleon's criticisms of the handling of the campaign by Nikias and other generals result in his being forced against his will to take command himself. The association of Lysander with Kleon, and, by implication, Kallikratidas with Nikias, is at first sight damning to Lysander; for elsewhere Plutarch presents Kleon in an even more unfavourable light than Thucydides does.[84] But then, like Kleon at Pylos, Lysander is successful, despite his moral shortcomings. This raises once again the whole dilemma of how to judge Lysander. For he appears to put his country first: he is said later (21. 7; cf. 24. 1) to have gained a reputation (δόξα) as one who worked 'not for the sake of others, nor for theatrical display,[85] but for the good of Sparta' (οὐ πρὸς ἑτέρων χάριν οὐδὲ θεατρικῶς ἀλλὰ πρὸς τὸ τῇ Σπάρτῃ συμφέρον).[86] According to Plutarch, working for one's country's benefit is the highest good in the Spartan moral code. Agesilaos uses this as a pretext for

---

[82] For this meaning, see Robert (1940), 276–80; Frazier (1988a), 123. Cf. also Whitehead (1983), 60–70.

[83] Lys. 6. 3: ὅτι οὐκ αὐτὸς ἀλλ' ἐκεῖνος ἄρχοι τῶν νεῶν; Thuc. 4. 28. 2: οὐκ ἔφη αὐτὸς ἀλλ' ἐκεῖνον στρατηγεῖν. This Thucydidean reminiscence is not in Xen. Hell. 1. 6. 3, one of Plutarch's main sources. Xenophon does, however, put a similar phrase into the mouths of the Athenian generals addressing Alkibiades before Aigospotamoi (Hell. 2. 1. 26), where it serves to denigrate the speakers; Plutarch gives it to Tydeus alone (Lys. 10. 7).

[84] e.g. Nik. 2. 2–3; 8. 5–6; Nik.-Crass. 3. 5; Demetr. 11. 2. For Thucydides on Kleon, see Thuc. 2. 65. 10; 3. 36. 6; 4. 28. 5, with Woodhead (1960).

[85] For the negative connotations of the tragic theatre in Plutarch, see De Lacy (1952), and above, pp. 123–6.

[86] In fact, Lysander's foreign policy was aimed at building a personal hegemony: Bommelaer (1981), 115, and Cartledge (1987), 90–4.

changing sides during an Egyptian civil war (*Ages*. 37. 9–11): though such action, Plutarch tells us, would most justly be called treachery (προδοσία). But the Spartans, he goes on, understood no other form of justice than looking after the interests of the state (37. 11; cf. *Alk*. 31. 8). Xenophon's Agesilaos had used the same argument in defending the illegal and sacrilegious, but successful, surprise attack on Thebes by Phoibidas.[87] Significantly, furthermore, this sort of phrase (τὸ τῇ πόλει συμφέρον) seems standard in second-century AD laudatory inscriptions.[88] Which is preferable, a noble but defeated hero, or a trickster who takes his country to the pinnacle of its power? Lysander does not exhibit traditional Spartan values, but unlike Kallikratidas he benefits Sparta. This is one of the major moral questions raised by the *Lysander*: which is preferable, personal virtues or the ruthless championing of the national interest?

The question of how the national interest fits into the moral code is raised by two incidents where we are implicitly encouraged to compare Lysander to minor figures. Before the battle of Aigospotamoi, Philokles, one of the Athenian generals responsible for the defeat, is characterized (9. 7) as the man who persuaded the Athenian Assembly to cut off the right thumb of all enemy prisoners.[89] Like Lysander, then, he puts his country's good above the strict claims of justice. After the battle, his death is narrated in a short scene which culminates in the memorable picture of him washing, putting on a bright robe, and defiantly leading his men to their death (13. 1–2). Lysander asks him what punishment he thinks he deserves 'for having given his citizens such advice concerning Greeks'; his reply is that he is willing to suffer what Lysander would have suffered had he been the one defeated. The parallelism between the two men is unmistakable. Both are great patriots, prepared to go to any length to bring victory to their countries.[90]

Another figure to provide a comparison with Lysander is the Athenian statesman Theramenes, notorious as a political trimmer. After the capture of Athens, he defends himself against a criticism that he should not have given in to the Spartan terms of surrender and allowed Athens' walls to be razed. He replies (14. 10) that he acted 'for the safety of the citizens' (ἐπὶ σωτηρίᾳ τῶν πολιτῶν). Theramenes supposedly saves

---

[87] Xen. *Hell*. 5. 2. 32; cf. 5. 4. 32 on Sphodrias.
[88] e.g. *OGIS*, 220, 5–8; *IG* xii. 5, 278; *IG* v. 1432, 33: Robert (1927), 110.
[89] ἀντίχειρα. Correcting Xenophon (*Hell*. 2. 1. 31), who says it was the right hand (χεῖρα). On these incidents, cf. Ducrey (1968), 64–8.
[90] Both break the conventions of war; cf. ibid., esp. 289–95. Contrast Pompey's clemency: *Pomp*. 28. 4–7, *Ages.-Pomp*. 3. 2–3.

his country by sharing Lysander's willingness to put expediency before honour. Ambition, cultivation of the powerful, *melancholia*, ruthlessness in the country's interests, even financial incorruptibility: all are problematized in Plutarch's picture of Lysander. Bad traits may not be so bad, and good traits may not be so good.

6. LYSANDER AND HIS DAUGHTERS
(*LYS.* 2. 7–8 AND 30. 6–7)

The ambiguities inherent in Lysander's character, and the problem of reconciling virtue and the national interest, are central to the two anecdotes which follow (2. 7–8). These are good examples of some of the typical problems that are raised by the anecdotes in the *Lives*. They also contain an important textual crux:

(2. 7) Διονυσίου δὲ τοῦ τυράννου πέμψαντος αὐτοῦ ταῖς θυγατράσι πολυτελῆ χιτώνια τῶν Σικελικῶν, οὐκ ἔλαβεν, εἰπὼν φοβεῖσθαι μὴ διὰ ταῦτα μᾶλλον αἰσχραὶ φανῶσιν. (2. 8) ἀλλ' ὀλίγον ὕστερον πρὸς τὸν αὐτὸν τύραννον ἐκ τῆς αὐτῆς πόλεως ἀποσταλεὶς πρεσβευτής, προσπέμψαντος αὐτῷ δύο στολὰς ἐκείνου, καὶ κελεύσαντος ἣν βούλεται τούτων ἑλόμενον τῇ θυγατρὶ κομίζειν, αὐτὴν ἐκείνην ἔφη βέλτιον αἱρήσεσθαι, καὶ λαβὼν ἀμφοτέρας ἀπῆλθεν.

πρεσβευτής: Ἀρίστας or Ἀρίστας πρεσβευτής Sansone: πρεσβευτής τις Renehan

(2. 7) When Dionysios the tyrant sent Lysander's daughters some expensive Sicilian tunics, he would not accept them, saying that he was afraid rather that because of them his daughters would look shameful. (2. 8) But a little later when he was sent as ambassador from the same city to the same tyrant, and the tyrant sent him two robes and told him to choose the one he preferred and take it to his daughter, he said that she herself would choose better, and went off with both of them.

The first anecdote records a gift of dresses made to Lysander by Dionysios I, tyrant of Syracuse (405–367), for his daughters, which he refuses, 'saying that he was afraid rather that because of them his daughters would look shameful' (αἰσχραί), a pun which recalls the similar play on the physical and moral senses of being ugly (αἰσχρός) in the opening lines of the Life (1. 3). If Lysander was involved in such an incident, it must be dated after his despatch to Ephesos, which took place in late 408 or early 407 BC, even though his arrival in Ephesos is not narrated until the following chapter.[91] Accuracy concerning chronology

---

[91] Possibly the incident took place in late 405 or 404: Bommelaer (1981), 73–5; 177–8.

is, as often, sacrificed to the interests of character portrayal.[92] But it is by no means certain that the original subject of this story was Lysander. The details of anecdotes change according to the purpose for which they are told, and the names which are associated with them may change or drop out.[93] In fact, in the pseudo-Plutarchan *Sayings of kings and commanders* 218e, this anecdote is also told about Archidamos.

The text of the second anecdote (2. 8) is in doubt. As the codices record it, the subject must be Lysander; πρεσβευτής, coming at the end of the clause, is naturally taken in apposition to [Λύσανδρος] rather than as a new subject.[94] There are, however, considerable difficulties with such a reading. The phrase ἐκ τῆς αὐτῆς πόλεως ('from the same city') is redundant if the subject of both sentences is the same; furthermore, only one daughter is mentioned in the second anecdote, although two had been mentioned in the first, and the plural is used in 30. 6–7. If the text is sound, then this is another striking example of the moral ambiguity which runs throughout the Life: Lysander is here attributed a vice (greed) to which he is explicitly said in the preceding discussion (2. 6) not to have succumbed. But it seems likely that the text is corrupt, and that πρεσβευτής should refer to a second ambassador, whose behaviour is contrasted with Lysander's. Either Sansone's suggestion, on the basis of some manuscripts of Plutarch's *Spartan sayings* (*Ap. Lac.* 229a)[95] and of Diod. 14. 10. 2–3, of Ἀρίστας instead of or in addition to πρεσβευτής, or Renehan's suggestion of the addition of τις after πρεσβευτής, should be adopted.[96] This section now contains an implicit *synkrisis* between Lysander and the second, unnamed ambassador, which serves to bring out Lysander's incorruptibility. But it also reinforces the paradox (stated explicitly in 2. 6) that, despite his own personal virtue, Lysander's victories harmed his country by encouraging in his countrymen the love of wealth. Lysander was not corrupt, but (ἀλλ'), because of his behaviour, those who came after him were. Such is the implication of a later incident. Here Lysander's sending of booty back to Sparta (16. 1) is

[92] See below, Appendix 2.
[93] On the tendency of anecdotes to become detached from their original context, see Fairweather (1974), 266–70; (1984), 323–7; Saller (1980), 73–82; Dover (1988), esp. 48–9.
[94] Despite Renehan (1981).
[95] For another example of an emendation of the Life (*Lys.* 30. 5), on the basis of the *Ap. Lac.* (229f), see n. 59. In fact all printed editions of the *Ap. Lac.* misguidedly follow Bernardakis' emendation of Ἀρίστας to πρεσβευτής, in order to harmonize with the manuscript reading of *Lys.* 2. 8.
[96] Sansone (1981); Renehan (1981). Diodoros gives the name as Ἄριστος (14. 10. 12) and, later, Ἀρέτης (14. 70. 2); both are probably corruptions of Ἀρίστας. Cf. Theopompos' description of Pharax (above, n. 71).

implicitly contrasted with Gylippos' attempted theft of it (16. 2–4). The former's honesty, despite the temptations provided by his position, becomes clearer. But a discussion follows which highlights the damaging effects which the influx of wealth following Lysander's victories had on Sparta (17. 1–11).[97] Though virtuous himself, he harmed his country.

The anecdote about Lysander's daughters is picked up in the closing words of the Life. After his death, Lysander's poverty is revealed, making, as Plutarch puts it, his virtue ($ἀρετή$) more obvious (30. 2). The posthumous rehabilitation which this brought in Sparta, is, however, undercut by the discovery of his revolutionary plans (30. 3–5). Thus it is not clear how sincerely the honours paid him in Sparta after his death are to be taken: the authorities force his daughters' reluctant suitors, discouraged now that their poverty is clear, to marry them (30. 6–7). The reminiscence of the Dionysios anecdotes (2. 7–8) provides a strong ending to the Life, a sense of having come full circle. As at the start, so at the end, the issue of Lysander's moral status is raised with reference to his daughters. At first sight, the story seems to show Lysander in a good light. The inclusion of posthumous honours is a strategy Plutarch often employs to demonstrate his approval of the subject, whatever the circumstances of his death.[98] But ambiguity is not far away. Although financial incorruptibility is a virtue in Plutarch's *Lives*, exemplifed by, for example, Aristeides (e.g. *Arist.* 24. 1–7), the leaving of one's family destitute is not, as the criticism of Aristeides for doing just that shows (*Arist.-Cato Maj.* 3. 2–5).[99]

7. LYSANDER'S CAREER: GOOD OR BAD?

The chapter which describes Lysander's arrival at Ephesos (3) contributes significantly to the difficulty of evaluating him. The transition from the 'timeless' anecdotes about Dionysios in *Lys.* 2. 7–8, told out of any chronological sequence, to Lysander's entry on the scene of operations in Ionia is handled by means of a long and syntactically complex

---

[97] The narrative of these incidents, and the discussion of wealth in Sparta which follows (16. 1–17. 11), probably derive from Ephoros: Alessandrì (1985).

[98] See above, pp. 136–7.

[99] Incorruptibility is an important virtue for the statesman in Plutarchan thought: see *Sol.* 27. 3–7; *Pel.* 30. 8–13; *Per.* 15. 3; *Per.-Fab.* 3. 5–6; *Phok.* 18. 1–8; *Aem.-Tim.* 2. 8–9; *Phil.* 15. 6–12. See Wardman (1974), 79–86; Panagopoulos (1977), 205–7 and 225; Desideri (1985). Cf. Demosthenes, whose bribing by Harpalos leads to shame and exile (*Dem.* 25. 1–26. 4; cf. Pecorella Longo 1995, 130–4); Cicero's 'contempt for wealth' ($ὑπεροψία\ χρημάτων$) contrasts with Demosthenes' venality (*Dem.-Cic.* 3. 2–4. 1).

sentence (3. 1–2). This sentence culminates in the word Λύσανδρον, marking out Lysander's arrival as an important and dramatic moment. More significant is the flavour of *enkomion* given to this section of narrative. The sufferings of Ephesos before Lysander's arrival are elaborated; this is the kind of thing which Menander Rhetor recommends (II. 378. 17–26) for a speech of praise greeting the arrival of a dignitary (a λόγος ἐπιβατήριος). Lysander brings new prosperity to a city in decline. Significantly, many of the details here occur also in Isokrates' enkomiastic account of Evagoras' return to Salamis, often in quite similar language (*Evag.* 47–50). Salamis was reduced to a state of 'barbarism' (*Evag.* 47: ἐκβαρβαρωμένην), that is, losing its Greekness; Ephesos was in danger of being reduced to such a state (*Lys.* 3. 3: κινδυνεύουσαν ἐκβαρβαρωθῆναι).[100] Salamis was ignorant of skills (τέχναι) and possessed neither trading port (ἐμπόριον) nor harbour (λιμήν); Lysander revived Ephesos' harbours with trade (*Lys.* 3. 4: ταῖς μὲν ἐμπορίαις τοὺς λιμένας αὐτῶν ἀνέλαβεν) and filled the houses and the workshops (literally, skills: τέχνας) with business (cf. also *Luc.* 2. 4–5). Evagoras built triremes (τριήρεις ἐναυπηγήσατο) and strengthened the city with other 'preparations' or 'constructions' (ἄλλαις κατασκευαῖς); Lysander is described (*Lys.* 3. 4) as having 'prepared the construction of triremes there' (ναυπηγίαν τριήρων ἐκεῖ κατασκευασάμενος). Both passages refer to the present-day prosperous state of the cities which is directly attributed to the hero (*Evag.* 50; *Lys.* 3. 4): a variation on the enkomiastic practice of showing the hero to be the 'cause' of many good things (πολλῶν αἴτιος).[101]

What is the effect of these reminiscences of *enkomion*?[102] Once again, as in the reference to Thucydides' Kleon (6. 3), a literary allusion contributes to the overall moral complexity of the *Lysander*. The enkomiastic *topoi* encourage a positive response from the reader towards Lysander. The chapters following continue this uncritical presentation, showing him successfully responding to the situation for which he was despatched. He wins Kyros over to Sparta and ends Alkibiades' career by

[100] On preventing barbarization, cf. Plato, *Laws* 692e–693a. For Plutarch, the bringing of Greek culture (παιδεία) to those who lack it is especially commendable. It is a key theme in the presentation of Alexander, especially in the two speeches *De Alex. Fort.* (Humbert 1991), and is seen also in the *Timoleon* (e.g. 35. 1).
[101] e.g. ps.-Aristotle, *Rhet. ad Alex.* 3, 1426b7.
[102] It is possible that Plutarch is here engaging in *direct* imitation of Isokrates' *Evagoras* (cf. *Lys.* 11. 8). Plutarch was certainly familiar with some of Isokrates' writings; the influence of the *Panathenaicus*, for example, is discernible at *Lyk.* 16. 10 and 17. 5–6 (cf. Manfredini and Piccirilli 1980, 263–5); *Bellone An Pace* 350d refers explicitly to *Panegyricus* 86. See also Helmbold and O'Neil (1959), 49; De Blois and Bons (1992 and 1995).

beating the Athenians at Notion (4. 1–5. 4). But immediately afterwards is described his ruthless support for the oligarchic factions in the cities (5. 5–6). In the rest of the Life, Lysander is not presented as a figure for praise. For example, unfavourable elements of the Lysander tradition which Xenophon missed out have been included.[103] This initial deception of the reader—the Life appears at first to present him in a positive light—fits into the picture painted of Lysander as a man whose stock-in-trade was deception, and about whom it is difficult to come to any firm moral evaluation.

Unquestionably enkomiastic is the section after the narrative of Aigospotamoi. After the battle, Lysander's success is summed up in a passage notable for its superlatives (11. 11–12): in a single hour he ended by his good planning and shrewdness ($εὐβουλία$ and $δεινότης$) a war unsurpassed in length and intensity. The effect of this hyperbolic passage is to mark clearly the end of the initial section of the narrative: the following section (12–18) shows Lysander at the height of his power, before his fall is narrated in 19 ff.[104] This passage recalls in its content and language Thucydides' praise of Themistokles in 1. 138. 2–3, a passage likewise notable for its superlatives.[105] It is perhaps also deliberately reminiscent of Thucydides 1. 1. 1–3 and 1. 23. 1–3, where Thucydides expands on the unsurpassed greatness of the war he is describing. The Thucydidean reminiscences serve to emphasize the importance of Lysander's achievement. It also suggests a way to read the striking digression on meteorites which follows (11. 13–12. 9). This is introduced by the statement (11. 13) that some considered Lysander's victory to be 'divine' ($θεῖον$; cf. the divine honours paid him in 18. 4–6). After a report that some said[106] that the two Dioskouroi were seen accompanying

---

[103] Breaking of oaths: 8. 4–5 (also Diod. 10. 9. 1; Polyain. 1. 45. 3); establishing the Thirty at Athens: 15. 6 (also Aristotle, *Ath. Pol.* 34. 2–3; Lysias 12. 71–6; Diod. 14. 3. 4–7). Neither is mentioned by Xenophon. See Krentz (1989), nn. on Xen. *Hell.* 2. 1. 15; 2. 1. 28; 2. 3. 2; 2. 3. 7. On the origins of the negative tradition on Lysander, see Keen (1996), who suggests an attempt by Agesilaos to blacken Lysander's name after his death.

[104] For superlatives as a mark of closure (cf. Thuc. 3. 86; 7. 87), see Smith (1968), 183. On closure in general, cf. Fowler (1989).

[105] And possibly well-known; at any rate, it is cited by Dionysios in *Ad Amm.* 4.

[106] $ἦσαν δέ τινες οἱ$ . . . $λέγοντες$. Plutarch uses such phrases to introduce reports the truth of which he does not guarantee (cf. Pauw 1980, 90–1): e.g. $λέγεται$ (*Alex.* 2. 2; 21. 6; *Caes.* 8. 3–4; *Thes.* 12. 5); $λέγουσι$ (*Rom.* 18. 6; 21. 5; *Per.* 30. 1); $ὡς λέγουσι$ (*Lyc* 4. 4); $ἔνιοι λέγουσι$ (*Rom.* 17. 2); $φασι$ (*Sol.* 5. 5; *Sulla* 27. 3); $ἔνιοι φασι$ (*Sol.* 7. 2); $ὡς ἔοικε$ (*Alk.* 17. 5; *Per.* 30. 2; *Cic.* 48. 2). See also Pelling (1992), 32 n. 4, for more examples. The use of 'dicitur' in Livy is similar (e.g. 1. 35. 2; 1. 55. 5; 9. 3. 9; 22. 43. 4). Occasionally such phrases may signal the introduction of an item from a source other than the main one being followed for that section (Townend 1987, 332–41, on *Caes.* 15–17).

Lysander's ship in battle (12. 1),[107] there follows (12. 2–9) a long discussion of the various explanations given for meteorites such as the one said to have fallen at Aigospotamoi at the time of the campaign. At the end of the discussion (12. 9), the narrator himself raises the question of its relevance, with the words 'But a detailed discussion of these matters belongs to another form of writing' (ταῦτα μὲν οὖν ἑτέρῳ γένει γραφῆς διακριβωτέον).[108] So what is the function of this apparent digression? Thucydides had suggested (1. 23. 3) that the greatness of the Peloponnesian War was marked by a coincidence of many natural disasters.[109] Is the import of this chapter similar?

There are a number of other instances in the *Lives* where the narrative is interrupted by discussions of topics which have apparently little relevance to the subject matter of the Life. On one level, this phenomenon can be seen as a manifestation of the widespread interest in antiquarian learning in this period, of which Plutarch's *Roman questions* and *Greek questions* and his lost work on the calendar, are examples.[110] Digressions are also not infrequently used by Plutarch as structural markers, dividing one section of the narrative off from the rest,[111] and this is certainly one of the functions of this digression. However, David Sansone's analysis of the digression on naphtha in the *Alexander* (35. 1–16) shows that an apparently gratuitous description of a novel substance is in fact closely bound up with Plutarch's presentation of Alexander's fiery temperament and character (4. 5–7); it fits into a nexus of passages linking Alexander with fire (e.g. 2. 3; 3. 5–6; 38. 4–8).[112] So is there any similar link between the discussion of rival views about the meteorite and the rest of the Life?

Plutarch does not in general seem to have considered astronomical phenomena as reflecting divine will; for example, he seems to approve of Agesilaos for ignoring an eclipse (*Ages.* 17. 4–5) and of Anaxagoras for

[107] Continuing the ambiguity by suggesting that Lysander's aspirations after monarchy or divinity were not wholly unfulfilled: it was a prerogative of each Spartan king to be accompanied by an image of one of the Dioskouroi (Hdt. 5. 75 with Cartledge 1987, 109).

[108] For similar apologies after digressions, see e.g. *Sol.* 20. 8; *Lyk.* 15. 8; *Arist.-Cato Maj.* 4. 4; *Cor.* 11. 6; *Alex.* 35. 16; *Dion* 2. 7; 21. 9; *Tim.* 15. 1; cf. *Cic.* 1. 6. Cf. Leo (1901), 152–3; Van der Valk (1982), 322–4.

[109] Perhaps aiming to outdo Herodotos' claim for the surpassing number of evils which befell Greece in the Persian wars, as demonstrated by the earthquake on Delos in 490 BC (Hdt. 6. 98. 2).

[110] On antiquarianism, see Rawson (1972); (1985), 233–49. Plutarch's Περὶ ἡμέρων is cited in *Cam.* 19. 6 (Lamp. Cat. 150).

[111] Pelling (1996), p. xxix. In the unpublished English version of his paper, Pelling notes other examples: *Cor.* 11. 2–6; 14. 2–6; 32. 4–8; 38. 1–7; *Alk.* 16 and 23; *Ant.* 4; 24; 70; *Caes.* 15–17; *Demetr.* 19–20.   [112] Sansone (1980).

teaching Perikles not to be amazed at 'the things up in the air' (τὰ μετέωρα); a correct understanding of science (ὁ φυσικὸς λόγος) prevents one from seeing natural phenomena as portentous (*Per.* 6. 1; cf. *Aem.* 17. 7–13). But he was prepared in some cases to see a prophetic explanation for such phenomena coexisting with a scientific one.[113] Furthermore, Plutarch elsewhere links events in the human political world to events in the cosmos, either at the level of analogy[114] or by showing that great changes in the human world are reflected or foretold in the heavenly world. Thus heavenly portents *do* seem to accompany Timoleon's conquest of Sicily (*Tim.* 8. 1–8; 28. 2–4) and Caesar's victory at Pharsalos (*Caes.* 43. 3–6), where, significantly, the portent is related immediately after a prophecy that there will be a great change and revolution (μεταβολή and μετάπτωσις) in human affairs. Heavenly portents also accompany Caesar's death (*Caes.* 69. 4–5). In these events Plutarch did, unusually, see the workings of divine will.[115] One might also think of the earthquake which Cicero experienced at Dyrrachion (*Cic.* 32. 4), which is interpreted by the soothsayers as a sign of change (μεταβολή). In fact, it is a passage in the *Sulla* which gives the clearest encouragement to read the meteorite here as an image for the vast change in human affairs which Lysander's victory over Athens brought. In *Sulla* 7. 3, the civil wars which began with the tribunate of Sulpicius, and Sulla's march on Rome, are described with the words:

καὶ τοῦ Σύλλα πρὸς τὰς ἐπιλιπεῖς πράξεις ὁρμήσαντος εἰς τὸ στρατόπεδον, αὐτὸς [Marius] οἰκουρῶν ἐτεκταίνετο τὴν ὀλεθριωτάτην ἐκείνην καὶ ὅσα σύμπαντες οἱ πόλεμοι τὴν Ῥώμην οὐκ ἔβλαψαν ἀπειργασμένην στάσιν, ὡς καὶ τὸ δαιμόνιον αὐτοῖς προεσήμηνε.

And when Sulla had set out for his camp on the business that remained, Marius himself stayed at home and contrived that most destructive civil war, which did Rome more harm than all her wars together had done, as indeed the heavenly powers showed them in advance.

[113] e.g. *Per.* 6. 2–5; *Dion* 24. 1–10; cf. *Pel.* 31. 3–4, where it is unclear whether or not Plutarch endorses the prophetic explanation. See Brenk (1977), 38–48; Berardi (1990), 155–62; Desideri (1992c), 80–4; Pérez Jiménez (1992). In *Nik.* 23. 1–9 Nikias is criticized for superstition in not knowing the correct physical causes of an eclipse; Plutarch has it both ways by then adding that, in any case, the prophetic interpretation which Nikias gave to it was incorrect. For ambiguity over Brutus' visions, see *Dion* 2. 2–6; *Brut.* 36. 1–7; 37. 7; 48. 2–5, with Moles (1985b). On Plutarch's use of visions to characterize, see Brenk (1977), 214–35.

[114] e.g. *De Fort. Rom.* 316e–317c; *Phok.* 2. 6–9; *Demetr.* 5. 1; *Ages.* 5. 5; cf. also *De Defect. Orac.* 416d.

[115] Brenk (1977), 163–9; Swain (1989b), 279–92; (1996a), 151–61.

The stress which is placed in this passage on the unprecedented destructiveness of the civil war is an encouragement to link it with the passage in the *Lysander* (11. 11–12). The *Sulla* passage continues with a list of portents, the interpretation of which as offered by some Etruscan soothsayers is given: they mark (*Sulla* 7. 7) 'a change of generation and a new age' (μεταβολὴν ἑτέρου γένους . . . καὶ μετακόσμησιν). History, say the soothsayers, is divided into eight ages or 'great years'; the change from one age to the next is marked by a sign.[116] This theory also occurs in the teachings of Kleombrotos' unnamed informant in the dialogue *On the obsolescence of oracles* (421c); a little earlier in the same work (419e–420a), the death of a 'deity' (δαίμων) is said to be accompanied by lightning and other heavenly portents. Perhaps the phenomena discussed in *Lysander* 12 are to be viewed as marking an important change in human events—presumably the end of Classical Athens' hegemony. The image of the meteorite may also suggest the speed and dynamism of Lysander's conquests; in a remarkable passage in Plutarch's *On the fortune or virtue of the Romans*, Alexander the Great is compared to a star shooting from East to West (326a–b).

Military success combined with brutality and deception dominates the picture of Lysander up to chapter 18. There then follows a section of static character analysis (18. 4–19. 6), where Lysander is portrayed at the height of his power.[117] Plutarch introduces the characterization with the words (18. 4):

Τότε δ' οὖν ὁ Λύσανδρος, ὅσον οὐδεὶς τῶν πρόσθεν Ἑλλήνων δυνηθείς, ἐδόκει φρονήματι καὶ ὄγκῳ μείζονι κεχρῆσθαι τῆς δυνάμεως.

So at this time Lysander was more powerful than any Greek before him had been, and seemed to be endowed with a haughtiness and pride that were even greater than his power.

Much of the characterization which follows is negative; the love of honour prefigured in 2. 4 recurs, but now combined with haughtiness and cruelty (19. 1–6). The divine worship Lysander receives presents him as a forerunner of the Hellenistic kings, whose pomposity and posturing Plutarch seems to have so despised. But the picture is once again in places ambiguous. The φρόνημα and ὄγκος which he displays (18. 4), translated here as 'haughtiness and pride', are ambiguous qualities. They

---

[116] On this theory, see Brenk (1977), 187 n. 3.

[117] Plutarch often includes an important characterization of an individual at the height of his success (his ἀκμή): Polman (1974). On the cycle of a political figure, see *Luc.* 38. 3–4. Cf. below, Appendix 2.

could be seen as positive. Perikles, for example, is said with approval to have gained φρόνημα and ὄγκος ('high-mindedness and dignity') from his association with Anaxagoras;[118] ὄγκος is, according to Plutarch (*Praec. Ger.* 803b), important in a statesman's speeches.[119] Furthermore, in giving a benefaction to the poet Antilochos (18. 7), Lysander certainly fulfils the paradigm set down for how kings should behave to poets in *On the fortune or virtue of Alexander* 333d–335e. However, the next anecdote (18. 8–9), which shows him awarding a prize to 'a certain Nikeratos of Herakleia' (Νικηράτου τινὸς Ἡρακλεώτου),[120] rather than to Antimachos of Kolophon, should be seen as critical of Lysander. It is true that Antimachos' *Lyde* was criticized by Kallimachos (e.g. fr. 398 Pfeiffer); but it was praised by Plato (Herakleides Pontikos fr. 91 Voss; Cic. *Brut.* 191) and by other third-century BC poets such as Asklepiades (*A.P.* 9. 63), who seem to have rated him as second only to Homer, though he was criticized for his prolixity; Plutarch himself seems elsewhere to reflect these views of Antimachos (*Tim.* 36. 3; *De Garrul.* 513a–b). Hadrian, furthermore, is said to have liked Antimachos' work (*Vita Hadriani* 16. 2; Dio Cassius 69. 4. 6).[121] The mention here of Plato's support for Antimachos (18. 9) suggests that Lysander's decision should be seen as a bad one; Lysander is to be seen as one of 'the ignorant' to whom Plato alludes: he lacks the sense to recognize a genius and instead backs a loser. The incident involving Aristonous the harpist (18. 10) seems less clear. He declares that, if he won again, he would 'declare himself as Lysander's' (Λυσάνδρου κηρύξειν ἑαυτόν). He seems to be suggesting that he have himself named in the official proclamation as Lysander's son. Lysander's reply 'As my slave?' (ἦ δοῦλον;), wilfully misinterprets the patronymic genitive as that designating the owner of a slave.[122] Is this arrogance, or the cutting of a flatterer down to size?

It is possible that another particularly subtle example of moral ambiguity is seen in the comparison of Lysander to a horse in 20. 8. Denounced in Sparta by Pharnabazos, Lysander declares that he must

---

[118] *Per.* 4. 6; cf. *Per.* 7. 6; *Fab.* 4. 3.
[119] Cf. *Cam.* 7. 1; *Alex.* 48. 3. On these words, see also Bucher-Isler (1972), 16–18.
[120] τινὸς here probably expresses scorn: cf. Soph. *Phil.* 442.
[121] Vessey (1971); Knox (1985), 112–16. Cf. Krevans (1993), on Antimachean influence on Kallimachos; Alan Cameron (1995), 303–38.
[122] Robert (1967), 21–2, quotes several instances from papyri and inscriptions of the imperial age where victorious athletes, in a show of loyalty, have another figure, particularly the emperor, proclaimed as victor instead of themselves. Herodotos' Miltiades the Elder had Peisistratos proclaimed victor in the Olympic chariot race (Hdt. 6. 103. 2). But as Robert notes, the use of the genitive in *Lys.* 18. 10 is unparalleled.

leave Sparta in order to makes a sacrifice to the god Ammon.[123] Plutarch continues:

τοῖς δὲ πλείστοις ἐδόκει πρόσχημα ποιεῖσθαι τὸν θεόν, ἄλλως δὲ τοὺς ἐφόρους δεδοικώς, καὶ τὸν οἴκοι ζυγὸν οὐ φέρων οὐδ' ὑπομένων ἄρχεσθαι, πλάνης ὀρέγεσθαι καὶ περιφοιτήσεως τινός, ὥσπερ ἵππος ἐκ νομῆς ἀφέτου καὶ λειμῶνος αὖθις ἥκων ἐπὶ φάτνην, καὶ πρὸς τὸ σύνηθες ἔργον αὖθις ἀγόμενος.

But the majority believed that he made the god an excuse, and feared the Ephors besides, and, not being able to bear the yoke at home nor endure being ruled, longed for some wandering and roaming, just like a horse which comes back from unrestricted pasture and meadow to his stall and is put once more to his accustomed work.

This comparison is presented as the thoughts of 'the majority': once again, Plutarch seems to distance himself from a particular value-judgement of Lysander, though in other Lives he does often use 'the majority', that is, the sensible majority, as a mouthpiece for his own views.[124] The image of Lysander as a horse which 'cannot endure being ruled' (οὐδ' ὑπομένων ἄρχεσθαι) presents him as unlike a traditional Spartan. For in Ages. 1. 2–3, for example, the Spartan education system (agoge) is said to 'train youths to be ruled' (παιδεύουσαν . . . τοὺς νέους ἄρχεσθαι); for this reason, Plutarch continues, Simonides called Sparta 'subduer of men' (δαμασίμβροτος, fr. 111 Page), because it made its citizens obedient, 'like horses that are subdued right from the start' (ὥσπερ ἵππους εὐθὺς ἐξ ἀρχῆς δαμαζομένους).[125] Lysander, then, is unlike a traditional Spartan in not being able to bear the yoke. But the refusal to endure slavery was central to Classical Greek self-representation. Most notably, Aischylos has Atossa in Persians liken Greece to a beatiful woman who throws off the yoke of slavery (181–99). The implications, then, of the comparison of Lysander to an unruly horse are ambiguous. Furthermore, the image also recalls the Homeric similes, in which Paris (Iliad 6. 506–11) and Hektor (15. 263–8) are compared to horses; νομός/νομή and φάτνη occur in both the Homeric and Plutarchan passages; σύνηθες recalls the Homeric εἰωθὼς λούεσθαι and ἤθεα. Ancient commentators were struck by the fact that the same Homeric simile was applied to both Hektor and Paris:[126] the reader of Plutarch is left to decide which paradigm, Paris or Hektor, is more

---

[123] On this episode, cf. Malkin (1990).
[124] See above, p. 120 n. 67.
[125] Cf. Lyk. 22. 1, for another generic comparison of Spartans to horses.
[126] Aristonikos on Il. 6. 506–11. He thought (comment on 15. 263–4) that the simile was less appropriate for Hektor than for Paris.

appropriate for Lysander. Once again two conflicting ways of reading him are presented.¹²⁷

When the narrative resumes (21. 1), Lysander is said to have 'procured his release (ἀφεθῆναι) with difficulty and sailed away'; ἀφεθῆναι echoes the νομῆς ἀφέτου of the simile: the horse goes back to his pasture. A reversal of the terms of the simile then takes place. Pausanias' attempt to undermine Lysander's power in Athens leads, as Plutarch presents it, to complete emancipation of Athens from Spartan control (21. 2–7).¹²⁸ Lysander's policy is vindicated. Pausanias is accused (21. 7) of 'letting loose the *demos*, when it was bridled by the oligarchy, to grow insolent and powerful again'.¹²⁹ Lysander was the Spartan horse which could not be tamed; here he is the one who succeeded in 'bridling' the Athenian *demos*. Later, again at the height of his influence after the failure of Pausanias' policy in Athens, Lysander is once more characterized, this time by a collection of apophthegms (22. 1–5). They are introduced (22. 1) to show that he was 'harsh in what he said and struck fear into those who contradicted him' (τῷ λόγῳ θρασὺς καὶ καταπληκτικὸς πρὸς τοὺς ἀντιτείνοντας). But this is not necessarily a criticism. Lysander's outspoken championing of his country's cause is implicitly contrasted with Pausanias' disastrous double-dealing in the previous chapter.¹³⁰

This raises an interesting question and one which is particularly significant as we assess the reader's moral reaction to Lysander. For it was over Athens that he won his victories. Athens was regarded in the second century AD as being in a special sense the centre of Hellenism.¹³¹ The way in which a man treats Athens has particular importance; this is stated explicitly in the final comparison to these Lives (*Lys.-Sulla* 5. 5). The

---

¹²⁷ For another example of comparison with Hektor, see *Brut.* 23. 3–7. The implicit parallelism there between Brutus and Hektor is part of the favourable presentation of Brutus throughout his Life.

¹²⁸ In fact, Athens still had to contribute troops for Thibron's expedition in Asia in 400/399; in the jargon of the time, it had gained 'autonomy' (αὐτονομία) but not independence (ἐλευθερία).

¹²⁹ ἐγκεχαλινωμένον τῇ ὀλιγαρχίᾳ τὸν δῆμον ἀνεὶς αὖθις ἐξυβρίσαι καὶ θρασύνασθαι. For bridling the people, cf. *Per.-Fab.* 1. 4 and *Cato Maj.* 27. 3, in both of which the reference is, as here, to the control of the 'audacity' (θρασύτης) or 'outrageousness' (ὕβρις) of a *demos* (cf. also *Per.* 7. 8) which has transgressed its natural station: Fuhrmann (1964), 141–3. For the image, cf. Tac. *Ann.* 5. 3. 1.

¹³⁰ Cf. Wardman (1974), 153.

¹³¹ Bowie (1970), 28–30 (=1974, 195–7); Spawforth and Walker (1985); Frazier (1990), 175–7; Swain (1997), 175–87 on Plutarch's view of Athens as a centre of Platonism; cf. Bowersock (1969), 17–18. Cf. also the periegetical works on Athens by e.g. a certain Diodoros and Heliodoros (*FGrH* 372 and 373 respectively). On Plutarch's knowledge of Athens, see Podlecki (1988).

emotional charge which the defeat of Athens carries is reflected in the brief changes of scene which momentarily transport the reader from the victorious Spartan side to the defeated Athenian: such changes are seen in the anecdotes about Theramenes (14. 9–10) and about Autolykos (15. 7–8). The *Lysander* also focuses on the issue of 'freedom for the Greeks'. The hollowness of Lysander's use of this piece of traditional propaganda[132] is clearly stated in 13. 8–9. Here Plutarch tells us that the comic poet Theopompos[133] was thought to be talking nonsense in comparing the Spartans to barmaids who, after first giving the Greeks 'a very sweet drink of freedom', then added vinegar ($ἥδιστον\ ποτὸν\ τῆς\ ἐλευθερίας\ γεύσαντες\ ὄξος\ ἐνέχεαν$); in fact, Plutarch says, 'the taste was harsh and bitter from the start' ($εὐθὺς\ γὰρ\ ἦν\ τὸ\ γεῦμα\ δυσχερὲς\ καὶ\ πικρόν$).[134] This is recalled and emphasized in 15. 5 where, with obvious irony, the thoughts of the allies are recorded, 'that that day was the beginning of freedom' ($ὡς\ ἐκείνην\ τὴν\ ἡμέραν\ ἄρχουσαν\ τῆς\ ἐλευθερίας$), a paraphrase of Xen. *Hell.* 2. 2. 23. The enkomiastic presentation of Lysander's victory is subtly subverted. Military success in Plutarch is in general seen as a positive moral achievement in its own right.[135] But the reader is reminded that it was over Athens and over Greeks that Lysander's victory was won. A tension is created, which increases the ambiguity of Lysander's moral status.

8. SULLA: MORE IMMORAL BUT MORE SUCCESSFUL?

One of the features of the *Lysander–Sulla* noted by Philip Stadter is the way in which bad features in the character and behaviour of Lysander reach a peak in Sulla.[136] The careers of Lysander and Sulla have many similarities: both rose from a poor background to become successful generals; both fought in the areas of Asia Minor and, more importantly, Plutarch's own region Boiotia;[137] both captured Athens; both treated

---

[132] Cf. Seager and Tuplin (1980).
[133] Bruce (1987), 3–4, suggests the deletion of $κωμικός$, so that the Theopompos in question is the historian not the poet: on the historian Theopompos see above, n. 74, and below, n. 161.
[134] For freedom as a drink, cf. Plato, *Rep.* 562c–d and Plut. *Per.* 7. 8, an extension of the use of $ἄκρατος$ ('unmixed', hence 'absolute') when describing political systems. See pp. 91–2. [135] See my discussion on pp. 97–8.
[136] See above, p. 162.
[137] This may be the reason why Plutarch paired these two figures. On his special interest in Boiotia, cf. Flacelière (1946); Jones (1971), 3–12; Aalders (1982), 14–17; Buckler (1992), 4801–8. The Lamprias Catalogue indicates the existence of biographies by Plutarch of three

their enemies harshly and both returned home to attempt to revolutionize the state. Sulla's greater brutality is emphasized by implicit comparison with Lysander. This *synkrisis* has some far-reaching implications for our moral evaluation of the two men; for, as Plutarch makes clear by drawing deliberate parallels between key events in the two men's careers, Sulla was successful despite, and indeed because of, his greater immorality.

Particular characteristics of Lysander's behaviour are carried to an extreme in Sulla. One of these characteristics is love of honour ($\phi\iota\lambda o\tau\iota\mu\iota\alpha$). In itself it is not an unusual trait in Plutarch's *Lives*, but it is stressed as particularly destructive in this pair (especially at *Lys*. 23. 3; *Sulla* 4. 6; 7. 2). Another such characteristic is the paradoxical combination of arrogance and subservience in the two men: their ability to flatter those from whom they wanted some benefit, and their cruelty to those in their power. Lysander's love of honour is such that it leads him to deception and violence: he flatters Kyros, quarrels with a rival, Agesilaos, tries to bribe the Delphic oracle, becomes arrogant in power, and attempts to change the constitution. Sulla goes beyond this. His very appearance suggests a harsher disposition. He uses brutality on a wider scale and fights a civil war against his rivals. In contrast to Lysander's personal incorruptibility, he indulges in luxury and disgraceful love affairs. He actually robs the shrine at Delphoi. His flattery is directed not towards an allied prince but towards the *demos* and his own men, and is combined with vulgarity and a love of low company.

Sulla's brutality is much worse than Lysander's. The latter's massacres were carried out against the enemy; Sulla's against his own countrymen, and the people of Athens. Sulla's greater brutality is made clear by two close verbal parallels: the description in *Lys*. 19. 4 of Lysander's 'uncountable slaughter' of democratic opponents in the cities of the Aegean ($\phi\acute{o}\nu os\ o\grave{\upsilon}\kappa\ \dot{\alpha}\rho\iota\theta\mu\eta\tau\acute{o}s$) is recalled during Sulla's sacking of Athens (*Sulla* 14. 5: $\H{\omega}\sigma\tau'\ \dot{\alpha}\rho\iota\theta\mu\grave{o}\nu\ \mu\eta\delta\acute{\epsilon}\nu\alpha\ \gamma\epsilon\nu\acute{\epsilon}\sigma\theta\alpha\iota\ \tau\hat{\omega}\nu\ \dot{\alpha}\pi o\sigma\phi\alpha\gamma\acute{\epsilon}\nu\tau\omega\nu$) and during the proscriptions (31. 1: $\phi\acute{o}\nu\omega\nu\ o\H{\upsilon}\tau'\ \dot{\alpha}\rho\iota\theta\mu\grave{o}\nu\ o\H{\upsilon}\theta'\ \H{o}\rho o\nu\ \dot{\epsilon}\chi\acute{o}\nu\tau\omega\nu$). His brutality is also brought out by the recurrence of two images: that of flood ($\hat{\rho}\epsilon\hat{\upsilon}\mu\alpha$) and disease ($\nu\acute{o}\sigma\eta\mu\alpha$). These metaphors occur initially to characterize Sulla's lax and immoral life (2. 6):

Boiotian poets (nos. 35–7: Hesiod, Pindar, and Krates; cf. fr. 9–10 Sandbach) as well as of works on the oracle of Trophonios at Lebadeia (no. 181) and on the Festival of Images at Plataia (no. 201; cf. frs. 157–8 Sandbach). On Plutarch's apparent knowledge of local Boiotian sources, cf. also Westlake (1939), 12–15; (1985c), 121–3; Hamilton (1994). Westlake argues, however, that Plutarch knew the Boiotian historical sources which lie behind *Lys*. 28. 1–30. 1 only second-hand through reading Theopompos.

ταύτης δὲ τῆς ἀνέσεως ἔοικε γεγονέναι νόσημα καὶ ἡ πρὸς τοὺς ἔρωτας εὐχέρεια[138] καὶ ῥύσις αὐτοῦ τῆς φιληδονίας, ἧς οὐδὲ γηράσας ἐπαύσατο·

The diseased result of this laxity seems to have been his propensity to love affairs and his flood of voluptuousness, from which he did not refrain even in his old age.

The result of his dissolute life-style is described as a disease (νόσημα).[139] The prime sense of this is metaphorical: Plutarch often uses metaphors from medicine to describe the state of a man's soul or of a city.[140] But there is also a suggestion that Sulla's disreputable life actually caused the physical disease from which he suffered and to which allusion has just been made (2. 2). Later this link will be confirmed (36. 1–4). In any case, disease and debauchery are here clearly linked in Sulla's character, and this link is reinforced by the presence of two other metaphors drawn from the world of medicine. Ἄνεσις ('laxity') means literally 'slackening' (e.g. Phil. Apoll. 5. 28), and metaphorically 'indulgence' or 'licence' (e.g. Aristotle, Pol. 1269b41; Phil. Apoll. 5. 32); it can also be a technical medical term ('remission'; cf. Galen 7. 424. 3; 7. 463. 9 Kühn).[141] 'Ρύσις (flow) is more clearly metaphorical. It suggests perhaps unrestrained emotion or passion.[142] It may well also have medical connotations.[143] It also serves to introduce the imagery of flood, which recurs in contexts of the violent bloodshed which characterizes Sulla's life. Mithridates' general Archelaos, in his advance through Boiotia, is said (11. 7) to come 'like a flood' (δίκην ῥεύματος). In the description of the massacre after Athens' capture (14. 5–6), the metaphor is used to convey the scale of the slaughter.[144] After the battle of Orchomenos, blood fills the marshes (21. 8), as it had the suburbs of Athens; as at Athens, traces of the slaughter could still be seen in Plutarch's own time. In the interview with

[138] Cf. Lysander's 'indifference to oaths' (Lys. 8. 4: περὶ τοὺς ὅρκους εὐχέρεια).

[139] The translation, which takes νόσημα as the complement, is based on the interpretation of Holden (1886), 60. Perrin (1916), 329 translates: 'It was this laxity, as it seems, which produced in him a diseased propensity to amorous indulgence ...' This would require the article with νόσημα.

[140] See above, p. 93.

[141] Cf. Durling (1993), 54.

[142] Cf. Non Posse 1093b: ἀκρασία τις εἶναι καὶ ῥύσις ἐκβιαζομένη τὸν λογισμόν; Cor. 34. 3.

[143] Cf. αἵματος ῥύσις in Hippok. Aphor. 3. 27. 5 = IV, 500 Littré; Mark 5: 25 (Luke 8: 43 and Matt. 9: 20 [αἱμορροοῦσα] are probably based on Mark).

[144] Cf. the reference to the non-figurative mythical flood (14. 10), on the anniversary of which Athens is said to have been taken; this coincidence of dates is paralleled in Lys. 15. 1, where the surrender of Athens is said to have taken place on the same date as the battle of Salamis (in Cyprus: Badian and Buckler 1975).

Archelaos, Sulla refers to Boiotia (22. 7) as being 'impassable because of the number of corpses' (ἄβατον . . . ὑπὸ νεκρῶν πλήθους). In the proscriptions, Catiline washes his hands of blood in the basin of Apollo (32. 4).

Likewise the image of disease recurs throughout the Sulla in contexts of brutality. So in 4. 6, the hostility between Marius and Sulla is described in words which continue the metaphor:

ἡ μὲν οὖν ἔχθρα βραχεῖαν οὕτω καὶ μειρακιώδη λαβοῦσα τὴν πρώτην ὑπόθεσιν καὶ ἀρχήν,[145] εἶτα χωροῦσα δι᾽[146] αἵματος ἐμφυλίου καὶ στάσεων ἀνηκέστων ἐπὶ τυραννίδα καὶ σύγχυσιν ἁπάντων πραγμάτων, ἀπέδειξε τὸν Εὐριπίδην σοφὸν ἄνδρα καὶ πολιτικῶν ἐπιστήμονα νοσημάτων, διακελευσάμενον φυλάττεσθαι τὴν φιλοτιμίαν, ὡς ὀλεθριωτάτην καὶ κακίστην δαίμονα τοῖς χρωμένοις.

The hatred between them had such a short and juvenile first foundation and beginning. Afterwards it led them through civil bloodshed and incurable discords to tyranny and the confusion of all affairs. This proved Euripides a wise man, and acquainted with the diseases of a state, when he advised men to beware of the love of honour as a deity most destructive and evil to those who deal with it.[147]

Plutarch here paraphrases Eur. Phoin. 531–4 where love of honour (φιλοτιμία) is described as the 'worst of deities' (τῆς κακίστης δαιμόνων). In 7. 3, ὀλεθριωτάτην and δαιμόνιον recur: Sulla's march on Rome and the events of 88 BC are thus tied into a nexus of events which have love of honour as their cause. Violence, bloodshed, and immorality continue to occur in conjunction with disease metaphors. In 6. 16 Sulla does not punish his troops for the murder of a legate, saying that his troops would be all the more enthusiastic as they tried to 'remedy' (ἰωμένοις) their wrong-doing. In 9. 4, the praetors Brutus and Servilius, ill-treated by Sulla's army, declare that the sedition cannot be checked but is 'incurable' (ἀνήκεστον). Later Aristion, the tyrant of Athens, whose soul is said to be full of licentiousness and cruelty, is described as having all the worst diseases and passions (νοσήματα καὶ πάθη) of Mithridates and as fixing himself like a 'fatal disease' (νόσημα

---

[145] Cf. *Them.* 3. 2: the enmity of Themistokles for Aristeides 'seems to have had a juvenile beginning' (δοκεῖ παντάπασιν ἡ πρὸς τοῦτον ἔχθρα μειρακιώδη λαβεῖν ἀρχήν); cf. *Arist.* 2. 3. For μειρακιώδης (literally, 'characteristic of a youth') as 'foolish' or 'irresponsible' cf. also Plato, *Rep.* 466b; Polyb. 2. 68. 2; 10. 33. 6; 11. 4. 7: with Eckstein (1995), 140–50.

[146] This unusual phrase is also found in *Mar.* 44. 4, also in the context of a disease metaphor; cf. Carney (1960), 25 n. 5. But analysis of Galen and Hippokrates produces no parallels for it.

[147] Cf. Stadter (1992a), 44.

θανατηφόρον) on Athens (13. 2). Here the metaphor is linked to violence and immorality: Aristion stands as a kind of parallel to Sulla (cf. 2. 3–8).

It is only towards the end of the Life, however, that the full significance of this disease and flood imagery becomes clear. In 36. 3–4, the disease which caused Sulla's death is described, after being introduced briefly at 2. 2 and 26. 4. It is said to have been exacerbated by his dissolute life-style; the ambiguity of 2. 6 now has extra significance: immorality and disease merge into one. Sulla's flesh is eaten by maggots (φθεῖρες); his clothes and food[148] are continually filled with blood (36. 3: ἀναπίμπλασθαι τοῦ ῥεύματος ἐκείνου καὶ τῆς φθορᾶς), and finally (37. 5–6) he dies by bursting a blood vessel through the excitement of having someone murdered in his bedroom (τὸ ἀπόστημα ῥήξας, πλῆθος αἵματος ἐξέβαλεν). Disease, blood, and violence culminate here. Sulla, the man who had lived by violence, meets a fitting death.[149] Immediately after the description of Sulla's death, Plutarch briefly lists some other figures who had died from the same disease, which he calls *phtheiriasis* (36. 5–6).[150] This list, probably derived from Aristotle,[151] has as its parallel Plutarch's discussion in the *Lysander* of those who had suffered from *melancholia* (*Lys.* 2. 5), where, as we have seen, Plutarch explicitly attributes his material to [pseudo-]Aristotle (*Problems* 30. 1, 953a10–32). The reminder of Lysander's tendency to anger is appropriate in the context of Sulla's death, itself brought about in a fit of anger (37. 5–6). Sulla's anger, the reader is reminded, is more extreme and more violent than Lysander's.[152]

---

[148] σιτίον. Or should we read, as Philip Stadter has suggested to me, σιτλίον (a bucket)?

[149] Compare the way Plutarch links Marius' death to his ambitious and discontented character: see above, pp. 120–1; on Cicero's death, see above, n. 73. Sulla dreams of his son and wife beckoning him to a life free of toil and troubles (37. 3): a strangely serene dream which, as Pelling (1999) argues, further complicates our picture of Sulla.

[150] Syphilis, according to Carney (1961a); scabies, according to Keaveney and Madden (1982). Africa (1982) is rightly sceptical about such attempts at diagnosis. The ultimate source for the tradition of Sulla's death by maggots (recorded also in Pliny, *NH* 7. 138; 11. 114; 26. 138; Paus. 1. 20. 7; 4. 33. 4) is probably anti-Sullan propaganda: death by maggots had become a *topos* by which wicked autocrats and the impious could be ascribed a morally satisfying end: e.g. Hdt. 4. 205; Paus. 9. 2–4; Acts 12: 23; cf. Lucian, *Alex.* 59; Memnon of Herakleia, *FGrH* 434 F 1. 2. 4–5. As Ziehen (1898) noted, the tradition of Sulla's death may have originated in a remark he made to the people of Rome (Appian, *BC* 1. 101), when he compared himself to a farmer bitten twice by maggots (φθεῖρες), who will burn them if bitten again.   [151] *Hist. Anim.* 5. 31, 556b–557a.

[152] It may be that Plutarch's mention of Eunous, leader of the Sicilian slave-revolt of 135–132 BC, as the final example of a victim of *phtheiriasis* is significant. Eunous, like Sulla, was thought to have desired to be king (Diod. 34/35. 2. 23). It is noteworthy that Appian, in *BC* 1. 101 (see above, n. 150), refers to the debate about whether Sulla desired kingship or not.

Not only is Sulla more violent, he is also more greedy. Lysander's financial incorruptibility is stressed throughout his Life. The importance of the theme of corruption in the *Life of Sulla* is signalled by the opening mention of Sulla's ancestor, P. Cornelius Rufinus (1. 1), who was expelled from the Senate in 275 BC for possessing too much silver plate. The prefiguring of traits which will be of significance to the subject of the Life by reference to an ancestor is a common Plutarchan practice.[153] According to Plutarch, Sulla, like Lysander, begins life poor;[154] but, as becomes clear, Lysander's financial honesty is not repeated in Sulla. He takes money from Delphoi (12), condemns people in the proscriptions because of their wealth (31. 10–12), and wastes money recklessly on dissolute living (2. 3–6; 36. 1–2).[155] Furthermore, the opening description of the corruption of Sulla's ancestor picks up the description at the end of the *Lysander* of the revelation of Lysander's poverty after his death. Two very different discoveries are made; the phrase in the *Sulla* (1. 1), 'his dishonour became more conspicuous than his honour' (τῆς τιμῆς ἐπιφανεστέραν γενέσθαι τὴν ἀτιμίαν), echoes the words several lines earlier at the end of the *Lysander* (30. 2), where the discovery of his poverty is said to have 'made his virtue more conspicuous' (φανερωτέραν ἐποίησε τὴν ἀρετήν); ἐκκαλυφθεῖσα in the former context is picked up by εὑρέθη in the latter. The mention of the tribune Sulpicius (*Sulla* 8) continues this theme. The reader is told that he passed a law forbidding senators to have debts of more than 2,000 *denarii*; after his death, however, it is discovered that he himself has debts of three million (8. 4). He functions as a contrast to Lysander, whose poverty, not greed, was discovered after death. He also serves once again to prefigure Sulla's greed. But paradoxically, as the 'formal' *synkrisis* will stress (3. 7–8), it is Lysander not Sulla whose behaviour introduces greed into his state.

---

[153] See below, Appendix 1.

[154] Reams (1984) has demonstrated that Sulla was not poor in his early years. He suggests that Plutarch misunderstood the evidence. Badian (1976), 37–8, suggests that the inaccuracy came from Sulla's own memoirs. At any rate, reports of Sulla's poverty suited Plutarch's comparison of the two men's attitude to wealth: both started from the same point.

[155] The Delphic oracle and the hero's dealings with it feature heavily in both Lives. Lysander's attempt to bribe the oracle is presented at length in Plutarch, whereas Diodoros gives no details (14. 13) and Nepos (*Lys.* 3) gives an account much less damning to Lysander. As Brenk points out (1977), 245–6, this prepares the reader for Sulla's contemptuous treatment of the oracle in *Sulla* 12. 6 ff. Plutarch seems to miss an opportunity to link Sulla further to Lysander by not recording an oracle given to Sulla and almost certainly originating from Delphoi: see Appian, *BC* 1. 97, with Balsdon (1951), 8–9. Perhaps Plutarch was simply unaware of Appian's source, but it remains unclear why he chooses certain features for comparison, and not others (see above, n. 22).

A similar paradox is emphasized by the close parallels between the descriptions of Lysander's naval victory at Aigospotamoi (*Lys.* 10–11) and of Sulla's land engagements in the vicinity of Chaironeia (*Sulla* 15–19). Although ancient battle narratives were often written to a kind of programme, with the result that certain standard features recur,[156] the correspondences of detail in Plutarch's accounts of Aigospotamoi and Chaironeia are nevertheless remarkable, particularly in view of the fact that the former was fought at sea and the latter on land.[157] Common features include the enemy's belittling of the general's forces (*Lys.* 10. 4; *Sulla* 16. 2–6), the enemy's indiscipline which leads him to scatter far from camp (*Lys.* 11. 7; *Sulla* 16. 6–8), and the contrast between the position of Sulla and Lysander as sole commanders, and the many generals on the enemy side (πολυαρχίαν in *Sulla* 16. 6 picks up μοναρχουμένῳ in *Lys.* 10. 6). Most noticeable is the way in which the description of Sulla's army crossing in its charge the space between it and the enemy (*Sulla* 18. 4: τὸ μέσον διάστημα τῷ τάχει συνελών) echoes the similar description of the Spartan fleet bearing down on the Athenians before they have time to put to sea (*Lys.* 11. 5: τὸ δὲ μεταξὺ τῶν ἠπείρων διάστημα . . . ταχέως . . . συνῄρετο).[158]

These similarities place the victories of Lysander at Aigospotamoi and of Sulla at Chaironeia as parallel moments in the lives of the two heroes. In the description of Sulla's victory at Chaironeia in Boiotia, however, the reader is reminded not only of Lysander's victory at Aigospotamoi, but also of his ignominious defeat and death at Haliartos, also in Boiotia. This time the effect of the reminiscences is not to stress the similarities between the two men but to bring out the differences—namely, that Lysander, having been raised by his victory to such heights of personal power, was, in contrast to Sulla, ultimately unsuccessful. Thus the sacking of Panopeus and Lebadeia by Archelaos' forces in *Sulla* 16. 8 recalls Lysander's sack of Lebadeia just before his defeat (*Lys.* 28. 2), and, more particularly, his burial at Panopeus (29. 4). Sulla twice manages to get troops inside a city ahead of the enemy (16. 11–13, Parapotamioi; 16. 14–15, Chaironeia). Lysander had failed to do this at Haliartos and had lost his life as a result (28. 5–10). Prophecies and oracles are a common feature of the *Sulla*, and several of these are reported which predict Sulla's victory (17. 1–4). These are very different from the oracles

---

[156] e.g. Gray (1987*b*).

[157] They are not noted in Hammond (1938), 188–201, which is largely based on *Sulla* 15–19.

[158] Holden (1886), on *Sulla* 18. 4, gives parallels for this phrase in *Luc.* 28. 2 and *Mar.* 8. 3.

narrated after the battle of Haliartos (29. 5–12), which had predicted Lysander's death there.

Especially unusual in the accounts of both battles are the detailed descriptions of the battlefields, which lead to mythological digressions based on the name of one of the features of each: for Lysander's defeat at Haliartos, the spring of Kissoussa where Dionysos was washed as a baby and where Rhadamanthys lived (*Lys.* 28. 7–9), and for Sulla's victory near Chaironeia, the temple of Apollo Thourios at Thourion (*Sulla* 17. 7–8). These digressions are doubtless to be attributed partly to Plutarch's special knowledge of the countryside around his native Chaironeia. Occurring at the same point, however, in both narratives, they serve to relate more obviously Lysander's defeat at Haliartos to Sulla's victory not far away at Chaironeia. The similarities between these two episodes emphasize the major difference between them: Sulla was victorious whereas Lysander, on ground close by, was killed and his forces defeated.

7. THE 'FORMAL' COMPARISON

The 'formal' comparison or *synkrisis*, finally, which follows the two Lives, does not solve the moral problem raised by them; in fact, the *synkrisis* contributes to the difficulties involved in a moralizing reading. As will later become clear, this is a recurrent feature of Plutarch's *synkriseis*, which often give a radically different version or interpretation of the past from the one implied or stated in the narrative itself.[159] The first three chapters of the *synkrisis* demonstrate that Lysander was more virtuous than Sulla. He held his offices by merit in a healthy state, unlike Sulla who seized and held on to power by force (*Lys.-Sulla* 1. 1–7); his planned change to the constitution was reasonable, in contrast to Sulla's illegal overthrow of the state (*Lys.-Sulla* 2. 1–4); he was milder in his acts of injustice (*Lys.-Sulla* 2. 5–7) and he did not enrich himself through his offices (*Lys.-Sulla* 3. 1–5). Surprisingly, we are told (3. 2) that Lysander performed no act of 'wantonness or of youthful irresponsibility' (οὐδὲν ἀκόλαστον οὐδὲ μειρακιῶδες) and 'avoided the saying *Lions at home but foxes abroad*', which alludes to the belief that, from Pausanias onwards, Spartan kings and commanders when serving overseas fell below the traditional standards of Spartan morality.[160] This statement is dis-

---

[159] See below, Ch. 8, esp. 263–86.

[160] On which, see Cartledge (1987), 49–50. The saying was evidently proverbial: cf. Aristoph. *Peace* 1189–90, with the comment of the scholiast.

concerting as Lysander is shown in the Life to apply this proverb to himself (7. 6). His conduct, furthermore, is here said to be 'sober, Lakonic, and restrained' (σώφρονα καὶ Λακωνικὴν καὶ κεκολασμένην).[161] Such a description does not agree at all with the picture of Lysander presented in the Life. This assessment is clearly in part motivated by the demands of the rhetorical structure of the *synkrisis*, which argues a case for each of the subjects in turn. And Plutarch does seem to have believed that Sulla's behaviour had more youthful irresponsibility about it than Lysander's: τὸ μειρακιῶδες, here denied for Lysander, had been used to describe the origins of Sulla's war with Marius (*Sulla* 4. 6). But to call Lysander's conduct 'Lakonic' raises a host of questions. Part of the interest of the Life has been to show how problematic Lysander's status as a Spartan was.

In the fourth chapter of the *synkrisis*, the scales tilt towards Sulla. We are reminded of the paradox that Sulla was politically successful whereas Lysander was not. Indeed, Sulla was successful in the affairs of state, partly because he was so ruthless, so unsuccessful morally. Furthermore, Lysander's more moral behaviour went much further in harming the state than Sulla's did. This paradox is at the heart of the *Lysander–Sulla*. As we have seen, the fact that Lysander's financial honesty resulted in the beginning of corruption in his own country is stated directly at the start of the Life (*Lys.* 2. 6) and is later illustrated by the attempted fraud of Gylippos (16. 2–4); the implications of this episode are made clear by the discussion which follows about the issue of wealth in Sparta and the bad effects of Lysander's introduction of foreign coinage (17. 1–10). In the formal *synkrisis* (*Lys.-Sulla* 3. 6–8) this paradox is again stated forcefully. Good moral traits have a bad effect on the hero's society, and vice versa.

Plutarch's concern to find material in favour of Sulla in this second half of the *synkrisis* adds to the sense of dissonance between narrative and *synkrisis*. First, Lysander is criticized at length (4. 1–5) for throwing away his life unnecessarily on the battlefield. Now the unnecessary death of a hero through reckless conduct seems to have been especially distasteful to Plutarch. Indeed, at the start of the *Pelopidas–Marcellus* pair Plutarch makes explicit his aversion for generals who die unnecessarily on the battlefield (*Pel.* 1. 1–2. 12). One of the reasons for his condemnation of such deaths is that he saw in them a failure to control the

---

[161] These positive views of Lysander may well derive from Theopompos' *Hellenika*, which appears to have been rather favourable to Lysander, though not (*pace* Momigliano 1931) to the empire which he set up. On Theopompos, and a possible emendation of *Lys.* 13. 8, see above, nn. 74 and 133, and Bruce (1987).

passions.[162] In the case of Pelopidas and Marcellus, however, credit is still given for their bravery (*Pel.-Marc.* 3. 8); no such credit is given here to Lysander. Furthermore, although so much space is given to the rather unfair criticism of Lysander's death, Sulla's is not mentioned at all. This is surprising as his death had been presented in the Life, as we have seen, as particularly foul. One would have expected this, more than Lysander's death, to be condemned by Plutarch; but not a word is said in comment on it. Surely the reader is not to prefer Sulla's unworthy end to Lysander's foolish but brave death in battle?

In the last chapter of the *synkrisis* Plutarch makes the point that Sulla's military successes were more to be commended than Lysander's, because they were achieved against the background of a hostile home government (*Lys.-Sulla* 5. 1–2). This analysis, weighing up the resources available to each hero from his country, is a common one in the *synkriseis*.[163] But in this case, Sulla's opposition to his government might certainly have been interpreted in a negative, rather than a positive, light. Furthermore, Sulla is commended for putting his state's broader interests before his own in defeating Mithridates soundly before turning towards his private enemies in Rome (5. 3). Such an interpretation, while not in itself unreasonable,[164] seems to contradict the suspicions raised in the preceding narrative that Sulla made peace with Mithridates in order to be able to turn quickly to the war with Fimbria and the government in Rome (e.g. *Sulla* 23. 3–5; 24. 7).[165]

The last part of the formal *synkrisis* deals with the way the two heroes treated Athens (*Lys.-Sulla* 5. 5). Here Sulla is commended for granting freedom to the city, whereas Lysander is criticized as the man who 'took away democracy and appointed the most brutal and lawless tyrants'. This is extremely puzzling. Plutarch's discussion flies in the face of historical fact and contradicts the emphasis of his own narrative. Lysander did install the Thirty Tyrants in Athens but he did not sack it like Sulla. Great play was made in the *Life of Sulla* of the slaughter which attended Sulla's taking of the city in 86 BC; the blood of those slaughtered deluged the Kerameikos and the suburb beyond and left a mark still visible in Plutarch's own day (*Sulla* 14. 5–7). Frederick Brenk argues that, for some reason unknown to us, Plutarch wanted to defend Sulla from

---

[162] See above, pp. 30 and 82.

[163] See pp. 98 and 263.

[164] It is shared, for example, by Velleius Paterculus (2. 24. 4).

[165] Elsewhere Plutarch records that Sulla's lieutenant Lucullus deliberately allowed Mithridates to escape when he had him in his power (*Luc.* 3. 4–8.). Cf. Badian (1958), 272 n. 3.

the worst criticisms which could be made against him.[166] We do know, for what it is worth, that one of Plutarch's friends, the speaker in the *On lack of anger* and *On the face which appears in the circle of the moon*, was a Sulla, perhaps a descendant of the dictator. If such was Plutarch's purpose, however, the job has not been done very effectively, as the narrative has already given a very full treatment to Sulla's brutality at Athens and degrading death; in fact, Plutarch's narrative gives much more emphasis to the violence of the sack than does Livy's epitome.[167] Perhaps, however, we can see the very dissonance itself as having an important function within the moral programme. The shocking contrast between Life and *synkrisis* forces the reader to assume a more active role in assessing the good and the bad. Such judgements are not always easy, and, in thus problematizing the moral status of Lysander and Sulla, the *synkrisis* picks up and continues a theme which had been important throughout the two Lives.

The final words of the *synkrisis*, and of the *Lysander–Sulla* pair as a whole, while in one sense providing a 'closed' ending to the book, highlight the unresolved moral dilemma at its heart: the conflict between the demands of success in virtue (in Greek terms, controlling oneself)[168] and success in politics (controlling others). The phrasing is significant:

Ὥρα δὴ σκοπεῖν, μὴ ⟨οὐ⟩ πολὺ τἀληθοῦς διαμαρτάνωμεν ἀποφαινόμενοι, πλέονα μὲν κατωρθωκέναι Σύλλαν, ἐλάττονα δ' ἐξημαρτηκέναι Λύσανδρον, καὶ τῷ μὲν ἐγκρατείας καὶ σωφροσύνης, τῷ δὲ στρατηγίας καὶ ἀνδρίας ἀποδιδόντες τὸ πρωτεῖον.

It is time to consider whether we shall not miss the truth by much if we declare that Sulla succeeded more but Lysander sinned less, and if we award to the latter the first prize for self-control and temperance and to the former the prize for generalship and bravery. (*Lys.-Sulla* 5. 6)

So the book ends. The invitation to the reader to assess Plutarch's final judgement, and the doubt implied, may well reflect that sense of

---

[166] Brenk (1977), 265–7; cf. above, p. 161.

[167] Though cf. Paus. 1. 20. 7; 9. 33. 6. In the epitome of Livy (Book 81), Athens is not said to be sacked; rather Sulla restores to it 'autonomy and property' (*libertatem et quae habuerat reddidit*); in Appian (*Mithridatic Wars* 38–9), Sulla sacks Athens but pardons the free citizens. In *Luc.* 19. 5 Plutarch has Lucullus, unable to save the captured city of Amisos from flames, envy Sulla for having been able to 'save' Athens. It is true, however, that Plutarch's picture of Sulla in this Life is more positive than it could have been. He is often shown as a good commander, with many of the traditional *topoi* applied to him. This picture (seen also in *Praec. Ger.* 806e) probably derives from Sulla's own *Memoirs*, on which, see *inter alia* Valgiglio (1975); Lewis (1991*b*); (1993), 665–6; Ramage (1991), 93–5.

[168] See below, p. 211.

provisionality and doubt which the *synkrisis*, and the book as a whole, encourage.[169] The reader has been encouraged throughout to make moral judgements, but, as the final sentence seems to suggest, no simple classification of actions and men as 'good' or 'bad' has emerged. In fact, the moral import of this pair is more challenging and in many ways more satisfying—at least to a modern reader—than a simple paradigm. Lysander, apparently the better of the two men, is unsuccessful politically; Sulla, through the greater use of violence, succeeds where Lysander had failed. Lysander's honesty in returning wealth to the Spartan state harmed it more than Sulla's greed harmed Rome. Two very important questions are raised. First, to what extent is service of the state a good in itself? What happens when the demands of personal virtue conflict with the good of one's state (τὸ τῇ πόλει συμφέρον)? Secondly, what happens to a moral programme when a good man harms his city by his very virtue, and when a bad man is shown to succeed because of his very wickedness?

[169] For similar wording, cf. *Phil.-Flam.* 3. 5, and my discussion below, on pp. 268–9. There seems also to be a pun on the compounds of the verb ἁμαρτάνειν.

7
The Lives of Coriolanus and Alkibiades

Two pairs of Lives have been examined where Plutarch seems to make it difficult for the reader to extract moral lessons. The third example is the *Coriolanus–Alkibiades*,[1] a pair which seems both to reinforce and to challenge moral norms: it is no surprise that Plutarch regarded both of these men as having 'great natures'. The *Coriolanus–Alkibiades* can, on the one hand, be read as a morality tale which underlines the importance of education (παιδεία) and the consequences for those who lack it: Coriolanus' poor education leaves him unable to control the passions which destroy him—in particular anger (ὀργή) and love of honour (φιλοτιμία). Furthermore, because of his very greatness, he falls victim, like so many other Plutarchan heroes, to the envy of the masses. Comparison with the account of Coriolanus' career by Dionysios of Halikarnassos (*Ant. Rom.* 6. 92–8. 62), which Plutarch probably used directly, reveals how Plutarch has reshaped his material to emphasize these themes.[2] On this reading, Alkibiades stands in stark contrast to Coriolanus. He receives an education at the hands of Sokrates, and this is implicitly linked to his greater success in handling the people.

However, the *Life of Alkibiades*, while reinforcing the moral norms, seems itself to challenge them. In part this is because this Life brings out the same clash between success and virtue which we have observed in the *Phokion–Cato Minor* and *Lysander–Sulla*: though possessing the virtues of education and affability which Coriolanus lacked, Alkibiades' fate is ultimately the same: both die as exiles in a foreign country. But there is a further difficulty: the impossibility of coming to an objective moral judgement of Alkibiades is a key theme of his Life, a life which seems to challenge the very notion of judgement. The *Alkibiades* is a much more complex Life than the *Coriolanus*, and it is probably for this reason that Plutarch has reversed the normal order of Lives by placing

---

[1] In fact, Plutarch refers to Coriolanus as Gaius Marcius. I have followed modern convention in using his *cognomen* Coriolanus.

[2] Peter (1865), 7–17; Russell (1963). Dionysios is cited once at *Cor.-Alk.* 2. 4.

the Greek Life after the Roman Life: Coriolanus provides the simple model against which the rather more challenging *Life of Alkibiades* is set.[3]

1. MORAL NORMS REINFORCED: CORIOLANUS

The *Life of Coriolanus* begins with a discussion of four ancestors of Coriolanus. Plutarch mentions that one was a king, two brought abundant water into Rome, while a fourth, Marcius Censorinus, after election twice to the office of censor, persuaded the people to make such re-election illegal (1. 1). As so often in Plutarch, ancestors are used to provide a paradigm through and against which the protagonist is to be measured.[4] As becomes clear in the pages that follow, Coriolanus did great services to his city, like his ancestors; but he also did great harm— itself a characteristic of men whose 'great natures' are not properly educated (Plato, *Rep.* 495b). Furthermore, he was conspicuously unable, unlike his ancestor Censorinus, to maintain good relations with the people: the key event in Coriolanus' Life is his failure to get elected to high office.

Plutarch continues by discussing Coriolanus' upbringing (*Cor.* 1. 2–3):

(1. 2) Γάιος δὲ Μάρκιος, ὑπὲρ οὗ τάδε γέγραπται, τραφεὶς ὑπὸ μητρὶ χήρᾳ πατρὸς ὀρφανός, ἀπέδειξε τὴν ὀρφανίαν ἄλλα μὲν ἔχουσαν κακά, πρὸς δὲ τὸ γενέσθαι σπουδαῖον ἄνδρα καὶ διαφέροντα τῶν πολλῶν οὐδὲν ἐμποδὼν οὖσαν, ἄλλως δὲ τοῖς φαύλοις αἰτιᾶσθαι καὶ ψέγειν παρέχουσαν αὐτὴν ὡς ἀμελείᾳ διαφθείρουσαν. (1. 3) ὁ δ' αὐτὸς ἀνὴρ ἐμαρτύρησε καὶ τοῖς τὴν φύσιν ἡγουμένοις, ἐὰν οὖσα γενναία καὶ ἀγαθὴ παιδείας ἐνδεὴς γένηται, πολλὰ τοῖς χρηστοῖς ὁμοῦ φαῦλα συναποτίκτειν, ὥσπερ εὐγενῆ χώραν ἐν γεωργίᾳ θεραπείας μὴ τυχοῦσαν.

(1. 2) Gaius Marcius, about whom what follows has been written, lost his father and became an orphan, and was brought up by his mother. He showed, however,

---

[3] The Roman Life stands first in the manuscripts of only the *Aem.-Tim., Sert.-Eum.* and *Cor.-Alk.* This seems to reflect the internal logic of these pairs. As Pelling suggests (1986b, 94–6; 1988b, 23–6), Plutarch has reversed the normal order out of a wish to have the less complex Life come first; this Life sets a pattern which is then exploited in the second Life. This seems a more likely solution than to propose that the unusual order in these pairs of Lives is the result of an error by later scribes or editors. See also Geiger (1981), 104; and the earlier discussion in Ziegler (1907), 26–32. The argument of Stiefenhofer (1914–16), 470–1 n. 24, that the naming of Alkibiades before Coriolanus throughout the formal *synkrisis* guarantees that the *Alk.* stood first in the pair, is mistaken: in pairs where there is no doubt as to the order of the Lives, the second Life is not seldom named first in the *synkrisis*: *Thes.- Rom.* 1. 1; *Lyk.-Num.* 1. 1; *Kim.-Luc.* 1. 1; *Ages.-Pomp.* 1. 2; *Pel.-Marc.* 1. 1; *Ag./Kleom.-Gracchi* 1. 2; cf. *Sert.-Eum.* 1. 1. On the order of the *Lives*, cf. also Van Der Valk (1982), 326–7; Valgiglio (1992), 4029.   [4] See below, Appendix 1.

that although being an orphan has many bad features in general, it is no impediment to becoming a serious man who surpasses the majority, but that the worthless accuse and censure their condition in vain, when they say that it ruins them by neglect. (1. 3) But the same man also bore witness to those who maintain that even if nature is noble and good but is deprived of education, it brings forth many bad fruits along with the good, just like rich farm land which has not received the proper care.

Coriolanus' nature, then, was good, and not ruined by being an orphan.[5] But, says Plutarch, his good nature was perverted by a lack of proper education. He is a paradigm of, he bore witness to (ἐμαρτύρησε), the evil consequences which a lack of education brings: a very Plutarchan theme.[6] But more than that, he is a paradigm of the man of 'great nature'. That this is intended is clear from the metaphor of plant life which Plutarch has re-used from its original context in Plato's discussion of 'great natures' in *Republic* 491d–492a. The more vigorous a seed, Plato had argued, the more it suffers from poor nurture; the 'best nature' fares the worst. In the same way, souls with the best natural endowment (εὐφυέσταται) suffer most from bad education. 'So I think,' Plato concludes (492a), 'that the nature which we posited for the philosopher, if it receives the proper teaching, must grow and reach complete virtue; but if it is sown, planted, and brought up in an unsuitable environment, the opposite will happen.'[7]

Coriolanus, then, is for Plutarch a man with a 'great nature': capable of both great good and great evil. The doctrine of the 'great nature' is given its fullest treatment in Plutarch in a passage in the treatise *On why the gods are so slow to punish*. Here Plutarch explains the fact that some evil-doers escape punishment by asserting that the god can see that they will also do great good. Human beings do not always allow the god's plan to work: one of the examples Plutarch chooses is, significantly, Alkibiades, who could, if he had lived, have done great good to his city, but, regrettably, was exiled by the Athenians for his apparent tyrannical leanings (552b). He continues:

οὐδὲν γὰρ αἱ μεγάλαι φύσεις μικρὸν ἐκφέρουσιν οὐδ' ἀργεῖ δι' ὀξύτητα τὸ σφοδρὸν ἐν αὐταῖς καὶ δραστήριον, ἀλλ' ἐν σάλῳ διαφέρονται, πρὶν εἰς τὸ μόνιμον καὶ καθεστηκὸς ἦθος ἐλθεῖν. ὥσπερ οὖν ὁ γεωργίας ἄπειρος οὐκ ἂν

---

[5] Alkibiades too loses his father at an early age: *Alk.* 1. 1–2. On such children in Plutarch, cf. Salvioni (1982).

[6] See above, pp. 73–8, and 108–10. See also Russell (1963), 23 and 27 (=1995, 361–2 and 370); Swain (1990b), 136–7; cf. Pelling (1989), 206–7.

[7] On this passage and on the doctrine of 'great natures' in general, above, pp. 47–9.

ἀσπάσαιτο χώραν ἰδὼν λόχμης ἔμπλεω δασείας καὶ φυτῶν ἀγρίων καὶ θηρία πολλὰ καὶ ῥεύματα καὶ πολὺν ἔχουσαν πηλόν, ἀλλὰ τῷ μεμαθηκότι διαισθάνεσθαι καὶ κρίνειν αὐτὰ ταῦτα τὴν ἰσχὺν καὶ τὸ πλῆθος ὑποδείκνυσι καὶ τὴν μαλακότητα τῆς γῆς, οὕτως ἄτοπα πολλὰ καὶ φαῦλα προεξανθοῦσιν αἱ μεγάλαι φύσεις, ὧν ἡμεῖς μὲν εὐθὺς τὸ τραχὺ καὶ νύττον οὐ φέροντες ἀποκόπτειν οἰόμεθα δεῖν καὶ κολούειν, ὁ δὲ βελτίων κριτὴς καὶ ἀπὸ τούτων τὸ χρηστὸν ἐνορῶν καὶ γενναῖον περιμένει λόγου καὶ ἀρετῆς συνεργὸν ἡλικίαν καὶ ὥραν, ᾗ τὸν οἰκεῖον ἡ φύσις καρπὸν ἀποδίδωσι.

> For great natures produce nothing small, and, because of their keenness, the vigour and activity within them do not lie inactive,[8] but they drift in the flood before they come to an abiding and settled character. Someone who is ignorant of agriculture would not embrace land when he saw it full of dense thicket and wild plants, and infested with wild animals and rivers and lots of mud. But for someone who has learnt discernment and judgement, these very things show the strength, the abundance and the softness of the land. In the same way great natures first put forth many strange and worthless shoots. We, unable to bear their roughness and thorns, think that we should immediately cut them off and prune them back. But a better judge actually sees in these things the land's good and noble nature, and waits for the maturity which works with reason and virtue, and for the season when its nature brings forth its proper fruit. (*De Sera Num.* 552c–d)

The agricultural imagery recalls the key passage of the *Republic*.[9] Characteristically in both this passage and in the *Coriolanus*, Plutarch associates the process of coming to maturity and producing good fruit with reason and education.[10] The emphasis of the passage from the *On why the gods are so slow to punish* is that, with proper nurture, and time, apparently bad men, like apparently poor land, may turn out well; indeed, the same qualities of greatness which make them particularly bad, may, with proper nurture, make them particularly good. Coriolanus is presented at the start of his Life as a negative proof of this doctrine. He had a 'good and noble nature' but lacked the proper education he needed; he is therefore like uncultivated and wild land.

Plutarch goes on to indicate the flaws in Coriolanus' character that this lack of education brings (*Cor.* 1. 4–5):

(1. 4) τὸ γὰρ ἰσχυρὸν αὐτοῦ πρὸς ἅπαντα τῆς γνώμης καὶ καρτερὸν ὁρμάς τε μεγάλας καὶ τελεσιουργοὺς τῶν καλῶν ἐξέφερε, θυμοῖς τε πάλιν αὖ χρώμενον

---

[8] The etymology of ἀργεῖν from ἀ-ἔργον is important: men with great natures always perform some sort of 'exploit', good or bad. For ἀργεῖν of land lying fallow, cf. Xen. *Kyr.* 1. 6. 11.

[9] The same imagery is used by the pig Gryllos in *Brut. Anim.* 987b; cf. *Dem.* 1. 3.

[10] For the emphasis on maturity (ἡλικία), cf. Plato, *Rep.* 487a.

ἀκράτοις καὶ φιλονικίαις ἀτρέπτοις οὐ ῥᾴδιον οὐδ᾽ εὐάρμοστον ἀνθρώποις συνεῖναι παρεῖχεν, ἀλλὰ τὴν ἐν ἡδοναῖς καὶ πόνοις καὶ ὑπὸ χρημάτων ἀπάθειαν αὐτοῦ θαυμάζοντες καὶ ὀνομάζοντες ἐγκράτειαν καὶ δικαιοσύνην καὶ ἀνδρείαν, ἐν ταῖς πολιτικαῖς αὖ πάλιν ὁμιλίαις ὡς ἐπαχθῆ καὶ ἄχαριν καὶ ὀλιγαρχικὴν ἐδυσχέραινον. (1. 5) οὐδὲν γὰρ ἄλλο Μουσῶν εὐμενείας ἀπολαύουσιν ἄνθρωποι τοσοῦτον, ὅσον ἐξημεροῦσθαι τὴν φύσιν ὑπὸ λόγου καὶ παιδείας, τῷ λόγῳ δεξαμένην τὸ μέτριον καὶ τὸ ἄγαν ἀποβαλοῦσαν.

(1. 4) The strength and endurance of his resolution in all things produced many great and effective impulses; but because he indulged unmixed passions and unbending rivalries, he did not make himself very easy or accommodating for men to be with. On the contrary, people admired his insensibility to pleasures, pain, and money, and called it self-control, justice, and manliness, but in political relations they were disgusted at it as being offensive, ungracious, and oligarchic. (1. 5) For men can enjoy no greater favour from the Muses than the taming of their nature by reason and education, having received moderation by means of reason and having got rid of excess.

It is these traits, his inability to control his 'unmixed passions' (θυμοῖς ἀκράτοις) and 'unbending rivalries' (φιλονικίαις ἀτρέπτοις), his obstinacy and his unapproachability, which will lead, later in the Life, to his taking up arms against his own country. It is not that Coriolanus was without virtue: his 'insensibility' (ἀπάθεια) to pleasure, pain, and the temptations of money is sufficient proof of that. But, as for Cato the Younger, such qualities make for dangerous extremism, and, while they may inspire grudging respect, do not, unlike true virtues, inspire love or a desire to imitate. In the *synkrisis* Plutarch declares that, because of his pride and aloofness, 'he was admired without being loved' (*Cor.-Alk.* 3. 6).[11] In the case of Cato the Younger, who did indeed inspire love,[12] extremism is tempered by education; in Coriolanus' case, this is emphatically not so. Nor can Coriolanus carry over his 'insensibility' (ἀπάθεια) into the rest of his life. He is, in fact, dominated by passion (πάθος): Plutarch seems almost to be punning on the literal meaning of ἀπάθεια (freedom from passions). This is all clear in Plutarch's description of his military training. He is by nature 'passionate' for war (2. 1: ἐμπαθὴς γεγονὼς πρὸς τοὺς πολεμικοὺς ἀγῶνας). He handles arms from boyhood, but lays special store by his ability to wrestle: his 'natural and native weapon' (τὸ σύμφυτον ὅπλον καὶ συγγενές). Coriolanus relies on nature before education, on innate strength and endurance rather than reason or anything taught. Plato considered that, without divine

---

[11] περιῆν θαυμαζομένῳ μὴ φιλεῖσθαι.
[12] *Cato Min.* 9. 9–10. See above, pp. 148–9; cf. p. 36.

intervention, it was impossible for a man to escape the ill effects of a bad environment (*Republic* 492a; 492e–493a). In Plutarch's *On why the gods are so slow to punish*, however, the god is said to be prepared to delay punishment for those 'to whom vice is not by nature unmixed or unbending' (551d: οἷς οὐκ ἄκρατος οὐδ' ἄτρεπτος ἡ κακία πέφυκε): for these men of 'great natures' there is hope of better things to come. For Coriolanus, ill-educated, unreasoning, and obstinate, there was no hope.[13]

In fact, Plutarch moderates his criticism slightly, arguing that, in the Rome of Coriolanus' time, only that part of virtue which was concerned with military matters was respected; as evidence of this he cites the fact that the Latin word for virtue (*virtus*) really meant manliness (ἀνδρεία), only one part of true virtue (1. 6). It is an insight which will have special significance for Coriolanus as the Life progresses. Coriolanus values manliness. This serves him well as a soldier: his 'untiring strength' (2. 2: τὴν . . . ῥώμην . . . ἄτρυτον)[14] is invincible. But it is also the reason for his downfall: as with Demetrios and Antony, two other men of 'great nature', the same traits are both strengths and weaknesses.

At first, Coriolanus' susceptibility to the passion of love of victory (φιλονικία) is, as is often the case for the young in Plutarch, a spur to great exploits (4. 1–4).[15] But the negative effects of this trait are soon clear when, after a notable military success, he is rejected in his bid for the consulship. Both he and the Senate react angrily. His anger is explicitly linked to his poor education:

(15. 4) αὐτὸς δ' ἐκεῖνος οὐ μετρίως ἔσχεν οὐδ' ἐπιεικῶς πρὸς τὸ συμβεβηκός, ἅτε δὴ πλεῖστα τῷ θυμοειδεῖ καὶ φιλονίκῳ μέρει τῆς ψυχῆς ὡς ἔχοντι μέγεθος καὶ φρόνημα κεχρημένος, τὸ δ' ἐμβριθὲς καὶ τὸ πρᾷον, οὗ τὸ πλεῖστον ἀρετῇ πολιτικῇ μέτεστιν, ἐγκεκραμένον οὐκ ἔχων ὑπὸ λόγου καὶ παιδείας, οὐδὲ τὴν ἐρημίᾳ σύνοικον, ὡς Πλάτων ἔλεγεν, αὐθάδειαν εἰδὼς ὅτι δεῖ μάλιστα διαφεύγειν ἐπιχειροῦντα πράγμασι κοινοῖς καὶ ἀνθρώποις ὁμιλεῖν, καὶ γενέσθαι τῆς πολλὰ γελωμένης ὑπ' ἐνίων ἀνεξικακίας ἐραστήν. (15. 5) ἀλλ' ἁπλοῦς τις ὢν ἀεὶ καὶ ἀτενής, καὶ τὸ νικᾶν καὶ κρατεῖν πάντων καὶ πάντως ἔργον ἀνδρείας ἡγούμενος, οὐκ ἀσθενείας καὶ μαλακίας, ἐκ τοῦ πονοῦντος καὶ πεπονθότος μάλιστα τῆς ψυχῆς ὥσπερ οἰδήμα τὸν θυμὸν ἀναδιδούσης, ἀπῄει ταραχῆς μεστὸς ὢν καὶ πικρίας πρὸς τὸν δῆμον.

---

[13] He is later (15. 5) described as ἀτενής (intense, unbending, stubborn). For such natures condemned, cf. *De Vit. Pud.* 529a: ἡ ἄτρεπτος καὶ ἀτενὴς διάθεσις; cf. *Sulla* 30. 4.
[14] One manuscript (Y) has ἄτρεπτον, making more explicit the link between Coriolanus' military virtues and his obstinacy.
[15] See above, pp. 84–7.

(15. 4) He himself did not act moderately or mildly in the face of what had happened, in that he greatly indulged the spirited and victory-loving part of his soul, as though this part had greatness and magnificence, but the weighty and self-restrained part of his soul, which is the chief component of political virtue, was not mixed in by reason and education. He did not know that one who tries to consort with affairs and people of state should most avoid stubbornness, which, as Plato says, is the companion of solitude, and should become a lover of forbearance, which is much laughed at by some. (15. 5) But he was always a simple and obstinate man. He considered that winning and triumphing over everyone in every way was a work of manliness, not of weakness and softness, which causes the spirit to break out like a swelling from the troubled and wounded part of the soul. So he went away full of agitation and bitterness towards the people. (*Cor.* 15. 4–5)

Many of the key terms of Plutarch's opening discussion of Coriolanus' character recur here. Lacking reason and education, he is unable to act with moderation ($\mu\epsilon\tau\rho\iota\omega s$), but instead becomes impassioned. The analysis is unmistakably Platonic: Coriolanus is an example of the 'spirited' ($\theta\upsilon\mu o\epsilon\iota\delta\eta s$) man. Plato, as we have noted, sees 'spiritedness', and its manifestation as anger, as a necessary quality for those involved in warfare and as an essential quality for bravery ($\dot{a}\nu\delta\rho\epsilon\dot{\iota}a$). But 'spiritedness' must be tempered by calmness or self-restraint ($\pi\rho\dot{a}\dot{o}\tau\eta s$), for which education and the reason are vital, so that anger can be used in the right way (*Rep.* 440d–442d).[16] Coriolanus' soul, owing to his lack of education, did not possess the proper admixture of self-restraint.[17] That Plutarch is working within a value-system drawn from Platonic philosophy is confirmed by the explicit reference which he makes to Plato's warning (*Epistle* 4, 321c) to flee stubbornness ($a\dot{\upsilon}\theta\dot{a}\delta\epsilon\iota a$), 'which, as Plato says, is the companion of solitude',[18] and to be prepared to mingle with men and not bear a grudge. Coriolanus, however, wrongly considered that manliness ($\dot{a}\nu\delta\rho\epsilon\dot{\iota}a$)—the only form of virtue which he understood (1. 6)—consisted only in 'winning and triumphing over everyone in every way' (15. 5). In fact, in much Greek thought, it is in mastery of oneself ($\kappa\rho a\tau\epsilon\hat{\iota}\nu$ $\dot{\epsilon}a\upsilon\tau o\hat{\upsilon}$ or $\ddot{a}\rho\chi\epsilon\sigma\theta a\iota$) that virtue lies.[19] The result of his attitude is, predictably, 'spirit' ($\theta\upsilon\mu\dot{o}s$), in this case the passion of anger

---

[16] Cf. Pelling (1996), p. xxviii.
[17] Cf. his 'unmixed passions' in 1. 4. Contrast Brutus in *Brut.* 1. 3. On mixing of character, see above, pp. 90–4.
[18] This saying is also quoted at *Alk.-Cor.* 3. 3. Plutarch uses it in its original context, Plato's advice to Dion to beware of pride, at *Dion* 8. 4; 52. 5; *Quomodo Adult.* 69f–70a.
[19] In particular: Xen. *Mem.* 5. 1–5; *Oik.* 12. 9–14; *Ages.* 10. 2; cf. also Plato, *Phaidros* 231d; 233c; *Gorgias* 527d; Isok. *Ad Nicocl.* 29; 39; Plut. *Alex.* 21. 7; *De Alex. Fort.* 337f; *De Pyth. Orac.* 404a; *Ad Princ. Inerud.* 780b–c. See Foucault (1985), 75–7 and 170–4.

(cf. 1. 4), which shows itself in the bitterness he displays towards the people as he leaves the forum.

Plutarch's train of thought and his expression here closely follow that of his treatise *On lack of anger*.[20] In fact the correspondence is so great that in writing these Lives Plutarch must have made use of material he had earlier employed for the treatise, whether directly or from memory. Coriolanus is to be seen as the concrete demonstration of the doctrine set out in the treatise. At *On lack of anger* 456f, Plutarch argues that the nature of θυμός (anger, spirit) is 'neither noble nor manly, nor containing any magnificence or greatness'.[21] Most people, Plutarch continues, mistake the confusion (τὸ ταρακτικόν) of anger for activity, its threatening behaviour (τὸ ἀπειλητικόν) for confidence, and its obstinacy (τὸ ἀπειθές) for strength. Some even mistake the cruelty (ὠμότης) of anger for greatness, its implacability (τὸ δυσπαραίτητον) for vigour, and its moroseness (τὸ δύσκολον) for hatred of evil. This will be the tragedy of Coriolanus. He thinks that his anger, bitterness, incivility, and intractability are marks of greatness and manliness. In fact, they reveal his thoroughly flawed character. People admire, Plutarch continues, angry people, but really their raging and bitterness declare their 'utter littleness and weakness' (cf. *Pel.* 21. 6): we have seen how Coriolanus' contemporaries admired him, while at the same time being disgusted with his ungraciousness (*Cor.* 1. 4). Anger (θυμός), Plutarch continues, results from sickness and weakness in the soul:

ὡς γὰρ οἴδημα μεγάλης ἐστὶν ἐν σαρκὶ πληγῆς πάθος, οὕτως ἐν ταῖς μαλακωτάταις ψυχαῖς ἡ πρὸς τὸ λυπῆσαι ἔνδοσις ἐκφέρει μείζονα θυμὸν ἀπὸ μείζονος ἀσθενείας.

For just as a swelling is the result [*pathos*] of a wound inflicted on the flesh, so, in the weakest souls, to succumb to the desire to inflict hurt produces anger which is proportional to the weakness of the soul from which it springs. (457a–b)

Those, Plutarch continues, whose souls are the weakest are most prone to anger: women, the sick, the old,[22] those suffering misfortune; also the man who seeks 'empty glory' (ὁ κενόδοξος), when he is maligned. But most susceptible of all are, he declares, quoting from Pindar (fr. 210

---

[20] Discussed on pp. 87–9.

[21] On anger as antithetic to manliness (ἀνδρεία) see also fr. 48. 19 Sandbach, from Plutarch's *On anger* (Lamp. Cat. 93). Nikolaidis (1991), 172, discusses these passages.

[22] Cf. 453b. Elsewhere Plutarch argues that the old are less susceptible to anger than the young: *De Virt. Moral.* 450f; *An Seni* 788f. See Nikolaidis (1991), 171–2.

Maehler), 'men who woo love of honour in cities; they cause obvious pain'. He continues:

οὕτως ἐκ τοῦ λυπουμένου μάλιστα τῆς ψυχῆς καὶ πάσχοντος ἀνίσταται μάλιστα δι' ἀσθένειαν ὁ θυμός, οὐχὶ νεύροις, ὥς τις εἶπε, τῆς ψυχῆς ἐοικώς, ἀλλ' ἐπιτάμασι καὶ σπάσμασιν ἐν ταῖς ἀμυντικαῖς ὁρμαῖς σφοδρότερον ἐξανισταμένης.

In this way anger arises most of all through weakness, from the most troubled and suffering part of the soul. Anger is not, as someone said, like the sinews of the soul, but like the strainings and convulsions of the soul when it rises up too vehemently in its impulses to defend itself. (457b–c)

It is unusual for Plutarch to disagree with Plato outright, and it is probably for this reason that he avoids mentioning him by name here.[23] But Plutarch seems to be referring to Plato's words in *Republic* 411b where, discussing the spirited man (ὁ θυμοειδής), Plato argues that some amount of 'spirit or anger (θυμός) is necessary for bravery, and calls the spirit the 'sinews (νεῦρα) of the soul'. But for Plutarch, at least in the *On lack of anger*, 'spirit' or anger has no place. Manliness (ἀνδρεία), he continues, is often thought, wrongly, to have no relation to calmness (πραότης): in fact, however, calmness, with its connotations of reasoned behaviour, and manliness go together. Anger may be hard to defeat, as he illustrates with a quotation from Herakleitos (fr. 70 Marcovich), a quotation which he will use in discussing Coriolanus (*Cor.* 22. 3).[24] But, in fact, to defeat anger in one's soul is the sign of 'great and victorious strength'; and this strength, Plutarch concludes, in a fine re-use of the earlier simile and correction of Plato, 'has the judgements (κρίσεις) as, truly, sinews and tendons against the passions' (457d). Manliness, then, the virtue on which Coriolanus prided himself, does not, for Plutarch, show itself in anger, which is rather a sign of a weak and troubled soul, and—by implication—one which does not possess correct judgements or reason.

Coriolanus' anger and obstinacy lead to his trial and condemnation to exile by a popular jury. The people are overjoyed, the Senate downcast. Plutarch continues (21. 1):

Πλὴν αὐτὸς ὁ Μάρκιος ἀνέκπληκτος καὶ ἀταπείνωτος καὶ σχήματι καὶ βαδίσματι καὶ προσώπῳ καθεστηκὼς ἐν πᾶσι τοῖς ἄλλοις ἐφαίνετο πεπονθόσιν ἀσυμπαθὴς ἑαυτῷ μόνος, οὐχ ὑπὸ λογισμοῦ καὶ πραότητος, οὐδὲ τῷ φέρειν μετρίως τὸ συμβεβηκός, ἀλλ' ἐμπαθὴς ὢν ὑπ' ὀργῆς καὶ βαρυφροσύνης.

---

[23] In fact, in the *De Virt. Moral.* Plutarch does agree that passion can be useful and necessary (see p. 75), quoting with approval (449f) and himself using (451d) the comparison of passions to sinews.   [24] Aristotle too alludes to it in *NE* 1105a7–8.

But Marcius himself was undaunted and undismayed, and composed in his demeanour, walk, and face. Amongst all the others who were affected, he appeared to be the only man who did not feel for himself: not because of reason or self-restraint, nor by bearing what had happened moderately, but because he was full of the passions of anger and indignation.

A 'fixed' face (καθεστηκὸς or συνεστηκὸς πρόσωπον) is often used by Plutarch as an indication of calmness (πρᾳότης).[25] The point here, however, is somewhat paradoxical: though showing all the symptoms of self-restraint, Coriolanus is in fact in the throes of passion.[26] We see again the link between his inability to obey reason (λογισμός) and the anger which leads him to turn against his own state. Once again, he is unable to 'bear what had happpened moderately' (φέρειν μετρίως τὸ συμβεβηκός). Plutarch's disapproval of Coriolanus is clear when, a few lines further on (21. 3), we read of him bidding his mother and wife 'to bear what had happened moderately' (φέρειν μετρίως τὸ συμβεβηκός): the very thing which he himself was unable to do (1. 5; 15. 4; 21. 1). Dionysios, Plutarch's source, had presented Coriolanus as really calm and unmoved (7. 67. 2); Plutarch emphasizes the anger which he sees as lying below the surface of his calm exterior.[27]

This emphasis on anger is one of the ways in which Plutarch departs from Dionysios in his treatment of Coriolanus throughout the Life.[28] His 'spiritedness' and anger (θυμός; ὀργή) breed the same qualities in others. First it is seen in the people, who become enraged against Coriolanus and the Senate (17. 4; 18. 2; 19. 1, 19. 4). Anger is the motivating force behind Coriolanus' approach to the Volsci, a people who are themselves filled with love of strife (φιλονεικία)[29] and anger (ὀργή) against the Romans (21. 5–6). Later the aristocrats too will become angry with Coriolanus (29. 4). Plutarch quotes in explanation (22. 3) a saying of Herakleitos which he had used in the relevant passage of the *On lack of anger* (457d): 'To fight passion is difficult; for whatever it wants, it buys

---

[25] *Fab.* 17. 7; *Arat.* 40. 4; *De Fort. Rom.* 317c; *Praec. Ger.* 800c. Mobility in the features of the face, especially change of colour, suggests that passions, such as fear (e.g. *Arat.* 29. 7–8) or anger (*Galba* 23. 5), are in control. Conversely, in *Mar.* 6. 6 a 'fixed' face is a proof of courage; cf. *De Sera Num.* 550d–e; 551a; 552c. For walk and look as indications of character, compare ps.-Aristotle, *Physiog.* 808a12–16; Sallust, *Cat.* 15. 5.

[26] Compare *Sulla* 30. 4, where Sulla's fixed face (ἀτρέπτῳ καὶ καθεστηκότι τῷ προσώπῳ) is an indication not of calmness but of insensibility to pity.

[27] Cf. Plutarch's claim to reveal what escapes 'the majority' in *Nik.* 1. 5, pp. 23–5.

[28] e.g. 30. 1; 30. 7; *Cor.-Alk.* 2. 4–6; 4. 4; 5. 1. See Russell (1963), 27–8 (=1995, 370–1); Pelling (1996), pp. xxii–xxxv.

[29] Ziegler prints φιλονικία (21. 6); but the combination with ὀργή suggests that the νεῖκος root is particularly in view here. See above, p. 83 n. 38.

at the price of soul' (Herakleitos fr. 70 Marcovich): an ominous forecast; eventually it is Coriolanus' life which will be forfeit to his passionate rage. For the moment, however, the result of this anger is suffering and defeat for Rome, and, equally reprehensible to Plutarch, an increase in the disharmony between Senate and people (27. 4–6). Significantly, when Coriolanus does finally give way to his mother's entreaties, he is not swayed by reason but by the emotion (πάθος) of the scene (34. 3):

ἐπιγνοὺς δὲ τὴν μητέρα πρώτην βαδίζουσαν, ἐβούλετο μὲν ἐμμένειν τοῖς ἀτρέπτοις ἐκείνοις καὶ ἀπαραιτήτοις λογισμοῖς, γενόμενος δὲ τοῦ πάθους ἐλάττων καὶ συνταραχθεὶς πρὸς τὴν ὄψιν, οὐκ ἔτλη καθεζομένῳ προσελθεῖν, ἀλλὰ καταβὰς θᾶττον ἢ βάδην καὶ ἀπαντήσας . . . μήτε δακρύων ἔτι μήτε τοῦ φιλοφρονεῖσθαι φειδόμενος, ἀλλ' ὥσπερ ὑπὸ ῥεύματος φέρεσθαι τοῦ πάθους ἑαυτὸν ἐνδεδωκώς.

When he recognized his mother walking first, he wanted to remain in those inflexible and implacable reasonings, but mastered by the passion and thrown into confusion at the sight, he could not endure them to approach while he himself remained seated, but jumped down quickly and ran to meet them . . . sparing neither his tears nor his embrace, he surrendered himself to be swept away, as it were, by a torrent of passion.

There is, of course, something of a paradox here. The reasonings to which Coriolanus is unable to remain faithful, are immoral and obstinate; the passion to which he gives in forces him, finally, to the right course.

2. MORAL NORMS REINFORCED: ALKIBIADES

Alkibiades is, in many ways, an utter contrast to Coriolanus. In nature, he is not dissimilar: like him he is a man of many passions, of which 'love of victory' (τὸ φιλόνικον) and 'love of being first' (τὸ φιλόπρωτον) are the strongest (2. 1). But he is also able to adjust his manner to suit and charm those he is with (23. 3–6). Alkibiades, then, is far from being the stubborn, unbending soldier which is Coriolanus. He is amenable in the extreme. But the most important difference between him and Coriolanus is that, unlike Coriolanus, Alkibiades receives an education—and not from any ordinary teacher. He is educated by the best teacher of all, the philosopher Sokrates. Although Alkibiades is repeatedly tempted away by his suitors and lovers, who are attracted by his beauty, it is Sokrates to whom he keeps returning (6. 1; cf. 1. 3). This contrast, between Sokrates and the other lovers, between pleasure and flattery at their hands and education at his, dominates the early chapters of the Life (3. 1–6. 5). Though Alkibiades' other lovers are struck by his beauty (4. 1), Sokrates sees Alkibiades' potential for virtue (τῆς πρὸς ἀρετὴν εὐφυΐας). The other lovers seek and offer pleasure; Sokrates is 'a lover who was not hunting[30] unmanly pleasure nor begging kisses and touches, but seeking to expose the weakness of his soul and to rebuke his vain and foolish pride' (4. 3). Plutarch states the moral clearly in a sentence the structure of which recalls his strictures (*Cor*. 1. 5) on Coriolanus' woeful lack of education:

οὐδένα γὰρ ἡ τύχη περίεσχεν ἔξωθεν οὐδὲ περιέφραξε τοῖς λεγομένοις ἀγαθοῖς τοσοῦτον ὥστ' ἄτρωτον[31] ὑπὸ φιλοσοφίας γενέσθαι καὶ λόγοις ἀπρόσιτον παρρησίαν καὶ δηγμὸν ἔχουσιν·

For fortune does not surround or fence off anyone with so many so-called good things that he is invulnerable to philosophy and impervious to words which have boldness and bite. (*Alk*. 4. 2)

Although Alkibiades' love of honour (φιλοτιμία) and love of glory (φιλοδοξία) make him vulnerable to the flattery of his lovers (6. 4), Sokrates rids him of vanity by means of reason (6. 5): 'pressing and crushing him with reason (πιέζων τῷ λόγῳ καὶ συστέλλων), he made him humble and fearful, as he learnt how much he lacked and how incomplete he was as regards virtue.' The wrestling metaphors here which describe Sokrates' educational influence on Alkibiades recall the wrestling matches which were such a feature of Coriolanus' purely physical and military training (2. 1).[32] Alkibiades' true philosophical education, gained from the philosopher *par excellence*, stands in marked contrast to Coriolanus' physical training.[33] These references to wrestling would probably also bring to mind Alkibiades' account in Plato's *Symposium* (217b–c) of his attempt to seduce Sokrates while wrestling. The influence of the *Symposium* is clear at numerous other points in the *Alkibiades*.[34] But Sokrates' wrestling bouts with Alkibiades, alluded to

[30] For lovers and sophists hunting the young, Russell (1997), 110 n. 16, refers to Plato, *Sophist* 221–2; 231d; *Laws* 831b, Xen. *Kyneg*. 13. 9.

[31] ἄτρωτον recalls Coriolanus' ῥώμην . . . ἄτρυτον (*Cor*. 2. 2).

[32] Cf. 4. 3: πιεζοῦντος; 6. 2: λαβὰς παρέχειν. Cf. also Alkibiades' real wrestling: *Alk*. 2. 2–3; 4. 4. Plutarch notes Xenokrates' comparison of philosophy to wrestling in *De Virt. Moral*. 452d (= Xenok. fr. 2 Heinze); cf. Diog. Laert. 4. 10.

[33] On the special value which Plutarch puts on the influence of a philosopher on a hero, see above, p. 150 n. 64.

[34] Cf. p. 143. Russell (1966*b*), 40 (=1995, 196), notes close parallels in *Alk*. 6–7 to the *Symposium* and to Plato, *Alk*. *I* 104a and 105b: e.g. *Alk*. 6. 1~*Symp*. 215e (cf. *Prof. in Virt*.

briefly at 4. 4, have been transformed into metaphors emphasizing Sokrates' educational influence on him. Plutarch has concentrated on the educational rather than on the erotic aspects of their relationship.[35] It is true, however, that Plutarch talks frequently of the 'love' (ἔρως) of Sokrates for Alkibiades.[36] This could be taken as metaphorical, but the language is certainly suggestive: ultimately, and perhaps, significantly Plutarch leaves the question unclear.[37]

Alkibiades, then, receives an education from Sokrates, and his character is very different from Coriolanus'. Coriolanus is rigid and unapproachable; Alkibiades is able to charm the people and win their support, and he does not give way to bitterness and anger. This is clear from a comparative reading of the two Lives, a reading which is encouraged by the basic similarity of their stories—both are turn-coats against their country—and by the numerous deliberate parallels which Plutarch has introduced between them. In particular, the same figure, Anytos son of Anthemion, occurs in both Lives: in *Alk*. 4. 4-6 he is one of the lovers who suffers outrageous treatment at Alkibiades' hands. In the *Coriolanus* (14. 6), he is mentioned in a discussion of electoral bribery at Rome as the first man to introduce this practice to Athens. As we shall see, many of these parallels serve, as often in Plutarch's *Lives*, to bring out the differences between the two subjects.

Very clear examples of this kind of paralleling are provided by the accounts of the two men's early military exploits.[38] The account of the actions of Alkibiades as a youth on campaign at Potidaia and Delion (*Alk*. 7. 3–6) is adapted from Plato's *Symposium* (219e–221c).[39] Plutarch follows Plato in showing Sokrates defending Alkibiades after the battle of Potidaia, but Alkibiades winning the crown for bravery because of the

84d), 216a–b; *Alk*. 6. 5~*Symp*. 216a; *Alk*. 7. 3–6~*Symp*. 219e–221c (see below). Cf. *Alk*. 4. 2 with Alkibiades' words in *Symp*. 218a: . . . πληγείς τε καὶ δηχθεὶς ὑπὸ τῶν ἐν φιλοσοφίᾳ λόγων. Jones (1916), 139–42, and Helmbold and O'Neil (1959), 61, note only 6. 1 and 7. 3–6 as Platonic allusions.

[35] As Littman argues (1970, 271–5), there is in fact no reason to think that the relationship between Sokrates and Alkibiades was not sexual.

[36] 4. 1; 4. 3; 6. 1; cf. τοῖς ἄλλοις ἐρασταῖς at 4. 4; 5. 1; cf. also 6. 2. But cf. *De Virt. Moral.* 448e, where pupils of good teachers are called 'lovers' (ἐρασταί), not beloved: plainly a metaphorical use.

[37] Plutarch's considered views on pederasty are difficult to pin down: see the ironic reading of the *Dialogue on love* by Goldhill (1995), 144–61.

[38] Plutarch refers to each of the men as 'still a youth' (ἔτι μειράκιον ὤν). This is an emphasis not shared by Livy who implies that Coriolanus was much older (2. 34. 10).

[39] Possibly influenced also by Antisthenes' *Alkibiades*: see fr. V A 200 Giannantoni, with Dittmar (1912), 83–90, and Giannantoni (1990), 348–9. Also by Isokrates' *On the team of four* 29: see Russell (1966b), 41 (= 1995, 197).

partiality of the judges. To pair with these exploits, Plutarch has imaginatively expanded a hint which he found in Dionysios, his main source (8. 29. 4). This shows the young Coriolanus fighting bravely to defend a fallen comrade at the battle of Lake Regillus against Tarquin (*Cor.* 3. 1–3) and, like Alkibiades, winning a garland for his conduct.[40] In Dionysios, this incident is mentioned only in passing in a speech made by Coriolanus in exile, but, for Plutarch, it provides the basis for a significant comparison: significant, that is, in the differences which he has built into the two accounts. Coriolanus wins his prize by bravery in defending a fellow citizen; Alkibiades is himself defended and wins the prize through his ability to get on with the right people. It is this antithesis, of course, which forms the heart of the Plutarchan pair: Coriolanus possesses immense military prowess but is unable to win the hearts of the people; Alkibiades, on the other hand, wins the support of all. This difference is made clear by the different tones of the quotations from Plato which Plutarch uses in his description of the two men. For Coriolanus, as we have seen, he quotes Plato's warning against stubbornness as the 'companion of solitude'; for Alkibiades, the quotation (from *Phaidros* 255d) refers to his love of Sokrates (4. 4).

These same differences underlie another parallel. Coriolanus' most important military success is the taking of Corioli (*Cor.* 8. 1–6). After driving the enemy back inside the city, Coriolanus and a few companions burst inside the gates; the enemy rallies, but he and his followers, cut off inside, overwhelm their foe. This incident finds its partner in Alkibiades' attack on Selymbria (*Alk.* 30. 3–10). Here Alkibiades is let in by treachery through the city gate and finds himself cut off with a few companions behind the enemy walls; he calls for a parley to allow his army time to arrive. Once again the differences are significant: Alkibiades wins the day not by force of arms but by a clever stratagem.

A further point of comparison underlines the difference in their fates after they have been exiled. Plutarch gives an account of an omen in Rome (*Cor.* 24–5), probably adapted from Dionysios 7. 68–73. A certain Titus Latinius has a dream in which Zeus (as Plutarch calls him) declares, enigmatically, that he is displeased with the dancer who led his

---

[40] Coriolanus' first military campaign (πρώτην στρατείαν) cannot, in fact, have been the battle of Lake Regillus as Plutarch says (3. 1): see Russell (1963), 23–4 (=1995, 362–3). Plutarch's transposition of the battle to an early date in Coriolanus' life makes his entry on to the military stage more impressive, and streamlines the narrative. On Plutarch's attitude to chronology, see below, Appendix 2.

procession. After an enquiry, it is concluded that the god is displeased because the procession held in his honour had met a slave undergoing a cruel whipping. The slave's master is punished and the procession repeated. This incident finds its parallel in the account of Alkibiades' celebration of the Eleusinian Mysteries in 407 BC (*Alk.* 34. 3–7), the first time since the fortification of Dekeleia that they are celebrated with a full procession by land. These two processions occupy parallel places in the two Lives, but their tone is very different. Though both men are exiled, Alkibiades, through a greater sociability with the *demos*, wins recall to his native city and leads a joyful march to Eleusis; his fall from grace, on accusations of parodying the mysteries at Eleusis, is truly over—for the moment. The procession in the *Coriolanus*, however, is performed while the latter is still at war with his country; it has no connection with Coriolanus himself but casts a dark shadow over the narrative.

Coriolanus' return to Rome is as an enemy leading a foreign army. The terror of his approach causes the people and Senate to be reconciled with each other and to send ambassadors to seek reconciliation with him (*Cor.* 30. 1–3). He, however (30. 7), utterly rejects their kind and moderate words (λόγους ἐπιεικεῖς καὶ φιλανθρώπους). His response is characteristic: 'he answered', Plutarch tells us, 'on his own behalf bitterly and angrily at what he had suffered (τὰ μὲν πικρῶς ὑπὲρ ἑαυτοῦ καὶ πρὸς ὀργὴν ὧν ἔπαθε), and on behalf of the Volsci he answered as general . . .'. Contrast Alkibiades' return to Athens. Crowds throng to see him (*Alk.* 32. 1–4). The people's regret at their past treatment of him is matched by his moderate speech in the Assembly, which recalls and contrasts that of Coriolanus (33. 2): 'Having bewailed and lamented his own sufferings (τὰ μὲν αὐτοῦ πάθη), and having made some small and moderate accusations against the people, he put down the whole affair to some evil fate and envious demon of his own.'

Alkibiades, then, is driven by ambition, but not by anger, as is stated explicitly in the *synkrisis* (*Cor.-Alk.* 2. 4–6). In contrast to Coriolanus' extreme ungraciousness to the people (*Cor.* 1. 4; 15. 4–5), stand Alkibiades' popularity with them, and his ability to inspire confidence and loyalty. Coriolanus is unbending; Alkibiades is a master at winning popularity and can assume more changes than a chameleon (23. 3–5). Coriolanus might be, like Alkibiades, a good orator, but he cannot bring himself to ingratiate himself with the people; Alkibiades' words, on the other hand, are full of charm (*Cor.* 39. 6; *Alk.* 10. 3–4). The contrast between them is brought out strongly in the *synkrisis* (3. 3–6; 4. 7–5. 1). It is this difference in character, partly a result of Coriolanus' defective education, which results in Alkibiades' being recalled from exile while Coriolanus is not.[41]

So this pair of Lives brings out forcefully the evil consequences of poor education and excessive anger: in this respect, Coriolanus stands as a negative paradigm, a warning of the dangers of potential without *paideia*. He is a great man, and it is, paradoxically, his exceptional qualities which lead to his fall. Coriolanus, then, seems to lend weight to the Platonic conception that 'great natures' produce great vices as well as great virtues. Alkibiades avoids many of Coriolanus' mistakes and forms a more positive paradigm. All the same, the moral lesson is not quite as clear as it might have been. As so often, although Plutarch treats the theme of education or the lack of it in both Lives of the pair, it is only in the Roman Life that he explores its effects.[42] Plutarch never makes it clear quite how Alkibiades benefits from his experience as a pupil of Sokrates.[43] Furthermore, Alkibiades is shown to be a particularly unwilling student. He wavers between the attractions of education and those of pleasure and ambition (4. 2; 6. 1–5); and is, after all, driven by ambition and lives a life notorious for its lawlessness ($\pi a \rho a \nu o \mu i a$) and unevenness ($\dot{a}\nu\omega\mu a\lambda i a$): 6. 3–4; 16. 1–9. There is, then, a moral lesson about education in these two Lives, but, as often in Plutarch, it is a far from straightforward one.

These Lives also reinforce some of Plutarch's more constant moral and political concerns. The first of these is the danger of strife within the state. For Plutarch, strife between people and council is a constant danger which the statesman must strive to reduce (*Praec. Ger.* 823f–825a); it is the reverse of the like-mindedness ($\delta\mu\delta\nu o\iota a$) which is one of the chief blessings which a good statesman can bring.[44] Both Coriolanus and Alkibiades fuel such strife. This is seen first in *Cor.* 5. 4, where Coriolanus opposes the relaxation of the harshness, literally 'the excessive intensity and prescriptiveness' ($\tau\grave{o}\ \sigma\acute{v}\nu\tau o\nu o\nu\ \ddot{a}\gamma a\nu\ \kappa a\grave{i}\ \nu\acute{o}\mu\iota\mu o\nu$), of the debt laws. The choice of words here recalls the discussion of

---

[41] There are several other points of comparison between the two Lives. Both arrive in the nick of time to win a victory: *Cor.* 9. 1–9, following Dionysios, *Ant. Rom.* 6. 93; *Alk.* 27. 2–6. The Romans are at first disheartened when they see Coriolanus, thinking that he has been defeated: a detail not in Dionysios but paralleling the despair Alkibiades' arrival initially brings to his own side. When in exile both men make war against their own country and engage in secret dealings. According to some, Coriolanus sends a false accuser ($\kappa a\tau\acute{\eta}\gamma o\rho o\nu$) to stir up the Romans against the Volsci (*Cor.* 26. 3; *Cor.-Alk.* 2. 4); Alkibiades too sends accusers ($\tau o\grave{v}s\ \ldots\ \kappa a\tau\eta\gamma o\rho\acute{\eta}\sigma o\nu\tau as$) against Phrynichos (25. 9).

[42] Swain (1990b), 129–45; partly summarized in (1996a), 140–4.

[43] Cf. Pelling (1990a), 232–5.

[44] On the $\delta\hat{\eta}\mu o s$–$\beta o \upsilon \lambda\acute{\eta}$ dichotomy in Plutarch, see pp. 302–3. On $\delta\mu\delta\nu o\iota a$ see pp. 89–90.

Coriolanus' education at 1. 5: he had a nature which was not educated by reason to 'take on moderation and cast off excess' (δεξαμένην τὸ μέτριον καὶ τὸ ἄγαν ἀποβαλοῦσαν). Thus the reader is invited to associate his opposition to the people with his defective education. Strife between people and council is a theme central to the *Coriolanus* (1. 1; 5. 1–7. 4; 12. 1–21. 6; 24. 1). Repeatedly, harmony returns only when there is a war on: perhaps natural in a state in which virtue is synonymous with manliness (ἀνδρεία: 1. 6; cf. 15. 7). In the *Alkibiades* likewise, though to a lesser extent, we see a divided state; Alkibiades at times exploits these divisions for his own ends, for example in 411 BC, when he plays off against each other the oligarchic and democratic elements in the fleet (25. 3–26. 6).

The second more general moral truth which these Lives reinforce is the danger of the people's envy, which can ruin a successful statesman. Plutarch shows in both Lives how the people can take on the characteristics of their statesmen: Coriolanus infects the Romans with his own anger;[45] Alkibiades gets a people as ambitious and inconsistent as he.[46] But, despite these differences, the motif of the people's envy (φθόνος) runs through both Lives. In the *Coriolanus* it has been introduced into situations where it does not occur in Dionysios;[47] it is this envy which leads to Coriolanus' failure to be elected consul (15. 1–3) and eventually, when the people are incited by the attacks of the tribunes, to his exile. Alkibiades also meets his downfall because of the envy of the people. Though exiled once, he manages, unlike Coriolanus, to win the people's support once again and his own return to favour; but ultimately, like Coriolanus, he falls foul of the popular leaders who stir up the people to anger and resentment against him (35. 3–4; 36. 1–4). Though superior to Coriolanus in education, and in charm and the ability to handle the masses, a superiority made very clear in the formal *synkrisis*, Alkibiades ultimately meets the same fate as Coriolanus. In fact, his very superiority to Coriolanus, and the very injustice of his treatment at the hands of the Athenians, make all the more obvious the dangers which the envy and passions of the mob pose to the political leader—a theme close to Plutarch's heart throughout the *Lives*. Coriolanus perhaps deserved what he got; Alkibiades' fate is a tragedy, but it is a tragedy which brings with it a lesson about the way the world, especially that of politics, works.[48]

---

[45] People: *Cor.* 17. 4; 18. 2; 19. 1; 19. 4; Senate: 29. 4.

[46] Pelling (1992), 21–4; (1996), pp. li–lvii. For the link between Alkibiades' ambition and the people's: cf. *Alk.* 17. 2.

[47] e.g. 10. 7; 13. 6; 31. 1; cf. 2. 2. See Russell (1963), 25 (= 1995, 366–7).

[48] The fate of Alkibiades can, then, be read as a form of 'descriptive moralism' (see

3. 'GREAT GOOD AND GREAT EVIL': PLUTARCH AND THE ALKIBIADES TRADITION

This pair of Lives, then, underlines and reinforces some of the values most central to Plutarch's thought: the importance of education, the need for reason to control the passions, especially anger, and the dangers of envy and disharmony within the state. Compared with Coriolanus, Alkibiades can be seen as functioning as a positive paradigm. But Plutarch's Alkibiades remains a deeply problematic figure. This is no surprise, as Alkibiades' problematic status is a constant in fifth- and fourth-century presentations of him. The question of how to regard him was central to late fifth-century Athenian politics: was he to blame for Athens' fall, or was the city to blame for sending him into exile? In Aristophanes' *Frogs*, this is the question which a poet who comes back from the dead will have to debate (1420–57). Thucydides' treatment of Alkibiades reveals this uncertainty about him: he suggests that the unconventionality of Alkibiades' private life, and his overblown personal ambition, led the Athenians to suspect that he wanted to become tyrant (6. 15. 3–4). But Thucydides also recognizes Alkibiades' services to Athens (e.g. 8. 86. 4), and even seems to suggest, by his digression on the Peisistratid tyranny (6. 53. 3–60. 1), that the Athenian people were foolish to rush to condemnation of Alkibiades for his tyrannical aims: tyranny need not be all bad.[49] Xenophon, writing in the early fourth century, represents the Athenian people debating the question of what to make of Alkibiades as he sails back into Athens from exile in 407 BC: some say he is the best of citizens, others that he is responsible for all Athens' troubles (*Hell.* 1. 4. 13–17).[50]

This debate around the figure of Alkibiades continued to be of political importance into the fourth century for various reasons. First, his son was involved in several legal cases in the early years of the century, cases in which the record of Alkibiades senior was utilized by both sides. Thus Isokrates' speech *On the team of four*, written on the

---

pp. 68–9): it teaches a truth about the human condition. For popular envy, cf. the *Per.-Fab.*

[49] Palmer (1982). For Thucydides' treatment of Alkibiades in general, see Westlake (1968), 9–10 and 212–60. It is not necessary to assume with Brunt (1952) that Thucydides actually met Alkibiades during the latter's second exile: see Westlake (1985b).

[50] The positive picture is given much more space (13–16); Canfora (1982) suggests that the text is corrupt.

son's behalf, praises Alkibiades' service to the state, and paints him as a defender of democracy.[51] This positive valuation of Alkibiades seems to have continued in the histories of Ephoros, as far as we can judge from Diodoros (Books 12–14). On the other hand, several attacks on Alkibiades—in order to denigrate his son—survive from this period:[52] the speech *Against Alkibiades* by Lysias (*Oration* 14; cf. frs. 30–1 Gernet-Bizos) and the speech of the same name which is preserved in the corpus of Andokides (*Oration* 4). The latter purports to have been delivered before the Assembly at an ostracism, but it is almost certainly either a fourth-century political pamphlet, possibly by Andokides, or a later rhetorical exercise.[53] At any rate, these two speeches paint Alkibiades as a would-be tyrant and associate of Kritias, one of the Thirty Tyrants; as a man who did both great good and great evil to his city.[54] It is not surprising that in this context Alkibiades' association with Sokrates could be seen as deeply embarrassing to the followers of Sokrates: the sophist Polykrates attacks Sokrates for just this reason.[55] Plato and other Sokratic writers, such as Antisthenes the Cynic and Aischines of Sphettos in their respective works entitled *Alkibiades*,[56] and Xenophon in his *Memorabilia*, aimed to disassociate Sokrates from a man who certainly could be presented as an anti-democratic figure. Xenophon sets this out as his aim in the first two chapters of his *Memorabilia* (especially 1. 2. 12).[57] By the mid-fourth century Alkibiades had achieved almost mythical status. Demosthenes in his speech *Against Meidias* (*Oration* 21, 143–50) uses Alkibiades, in passing, as an example of a man who combined arrogant behaviour ($ὕβρις$) with great services to the state:

---

[51] Plutarch certainly knew of this speech, to which he refers in *Alk.* 12. 3.

[52] Cf. Turchi (1984).

[53] See Burn (1954); Furley (1989); Prandi (1992), 258–60 and 269–70 n. 25; Gribble (1994), 119–40; Edwards (1995), 131–6. Plutarch may have read this speech; it may be this to which he refers in *Alk.* 13. 3, though he ascribes it to a certain Phaiax, possibly the Phaiax mentioned in Aristoph. *Knights* 1377–80 and Thuc. 5. 4–5, and named on ostraka. In the pseudo-Plutarchan *Life of Andokides* (835a) this speech seems to be referred to as a *Defence against Phaiax*. Burn (1954) argues that both it and Plutarch's *Alkibiades* are based on a common source.

[54] e.g. Lysias, *Against Alkibiades* 16, 30.

[55] Polykrates' work, called by Isokrates (*Busiris* 4) an *Attack on Sokrates* ($Σωκράτους κατηγορία$), is lost, but some of its arguments can be reconstructed from the replies to it in Xenophon's *Memorabilia* and in the 4th-c. AD reply by Libanios. See Dodds (1959), 28–9.

[56] On Antisthenes' *Alkibiades* (frs. V A 198–202 Giannantoni), see Giannantoni (1990), 347–9. Athenaios records that Antisthenes said (534c = fr. V A 198 Giannantoni) that Alkibiades was, significantly, uneducated ($ἰσχυρὸν αὐτὸν καὶ ἀνδρώδη καὶ ἀπαίδευτον καὶ τολμηρὸν καὶ ὡραῖον ἐφ' ἡλικίας ⟨πάσης⟩$). On Aischines, see Dittmar (1912); Giannantoni (1997).

[57] See Erbse (1961), 258–66.

Alkibiades has become a test-case figure, a notion to think with and to debate with.[58]

The most important influence on Plutarch's conception of Alkibiades was, of course, Plato, whose picture of Alkibiades is equally problematic.[59] The focus of Plato's presentation of Alkibiades in the *Gorgias* and *Symposium*, and in the *Alkibiades I*, if this was really written by Plato, is on showing Alkibiades' wavering between philosophy and the temptations of power.[60] He is a man of great natural ability, but he does not gain the philosophical education which he needs in order to use his ability properly: so, Plato implies, Sokrates could not be held responsible for his failings. But it is the picture of Alkibiades in the *Republic* that most clearly lies behind Plutarch's Alkibiades. We have seen that Plutarch's Coriolanus is explicitly assimilated to the Platonic type of a 'great nature'. In fact, it seems to have been Alkibiades whom Plato had particularly in mind in his discussion of great natures in *Republic* 491b–492a. He goes on to argue that the chief means by which young men are corrupted is by the inappropriate censure and praise of the mob (492a–493a). The mob cannot engage in philosophy; therefore they censure those who do (493e–494a). Plato now gives a picture of the sort of man who might thus be diverted from philosophy by his inappropriate environment. It is a picture which is unmistakably intended to bring Alkibiades to mind.[61] The traits of 'this sort of nature' are quickness to learn, a good memory, courage, and magnificence. Even as a boy he will be 'first', especially if his body 'is by nature' ($\phi v \hat{\eta}$) as excellent as his soul (494b).[62] As a youth he will be flattered and fawned upon by people who anticipate his future power ($\pi\rho o\kappa\alpha\tau\alpha\lambda\alpha\mu\beta\acute{\alpha}\nu o\nu\tau\epsilon\varsigma\ \kappa\alpha\grave{\iota}\ \pi\rho o\kappa o\lambda\alpha\kappa\epsilon\acute{u}o\nu\tau\epsilon\varsigma\ \tau\grave{\eta}\nu\ \mu\acute{\epsilon}\lambda\lambda o\upsilon\sigma\alpha\nu\ \alpha\grave{\upsilon}\tauo\hat{\upsilon}\ \delta\acute{\upsilon}\nu\alpha\mu\iota\nu$). How, Sokrates asks, would one expect a youth to behave in these conditions, especially if he is from a great city, and is wealthy and nobly-born, and also handsome and large (494b–c)? He answers the question himself:

ἆρ' οὐ πληρωθήσεσθαι ἀμηχάνου ἐλπίδος, ἡγούμενον καὶ τὰ τῶν Ἑλλήνων καὶ

---

[58] In the 3rd c. Douris of Samos and Satyros both wrote about Alkibiades; their works survive only in a few fragments. Plutarch knew both authors. On the ancient literary tradition on Alkibiades, see Gribble (1994) and the brief account in Prandi (1992), 257–81. Cf. also Hatzfeld (1951), 35–58.

[59] On the sources for Plutarch's *Alk.*, see Levi (1955), 218–27, and, more usefully, the brief discussions in Russell (1966*b*), 37–8 (= 1995, 191–2); (1973), 106–8.

[60] Gribble (1994), 228–47. On the authenticity of the *Alkibiades I*, cf. ibid. 260–3.

[61] Cf. Adam (1902), nn. to 494c, 494d, 495b (also to 519b, 239a); Gribble (1994), 238–40.

[62] Alkibiades' physical beauty was noted by Antisthenes (see above, n. 56).

τὰ τῶν βαρβάρων ἱκανὸν ἔσεσθαι πράττειν, καὶ ἐπὶ τούτοις ὑψηλὸν ἐξαρεῖν
αὑτόν, σχηματισμοῦ καὶ φρονήματος κενοῦ ἄνευ νοῦ ἐμπιπλάμενον;

Do you not consider that he will be filled with boundless hope, thinking that he is capable of managing the affairs of both Greeks and barbarians, and that he will exalt himself on this, filled with posturing and empty, senseless pride? (494c–d)

Alkibiades' pride and his dreams of overseas empire, particularly in Sicily or even Africa, are commonplaces of the fifth-century tradition. His posturing was satirized by Aristophanes. All these features are picked up by Plutarch in his Life.[63] 'Someone', Plato continues, may come and gently tell a man like this the truth: 'that he has no sense, and needs it, and that it is not obtainable unless one works like a slave to obtain it' (494d). But he will either refuse to listen, or, if he does, he will soon be drawn away from philosophy by his companions (494d–495a). That 'someone' is plainly Sokrates, and the picture fits the Alkibiades of the *Symposium* and *Alkibiades I*, and is taken up in Plutarch's Life. Plato's Sokrates concludes:

Ὁρᾷς οὖν, ἦν δ' ἐγώ, ὅτι οὐ κακῶς ἐλέγομεν ὡς ἄρα καὶ αὐτὰ τὰ τῆς φιλοσόφου
φύσεως μέρη, ὅταν ἐν κακῇ τροφῇ γένηται, αἴτια τρόπον τινὰ τοῦ ἐκπεσεῖν ἐκ
τοῦ ἐπιτηδεύματος, καὶ τὰ λεγόμενα ἀγαθά, πλοῦτοί τε καὶ πᾶσα ἡ τοιαύτη
παρασκευή; Οὐ γάρ, ἀλλ' ὀρθῶς, ἔφη, ἐλέχθη. Οὗτος δή, εἶπον, ὦ θαυμάσιε,
ὄλεθρός τε καὶ διαφθορὰ τοσαύτη τε καὶ τοιαύτη τῆς βελτίστης φύσεως εἰς τὸ
ἄριστον ἐπιτήδευμα, ὀλίγης καὶ ἄλλως γιγνομένης, ὡς ἡμεῖς φαμεν. καὶ ἐκ
τούτων δὴ τῶν ἀνδρῶν καὶ οἱ τὰ μέγιστα κακὰ ἐργαζόμενοι τὰς πόλεις
γίγνονται καὶ τοὺς ἰδιώτας, καὶ οἱ τἀγαθά, οἳ ἂν ταύτῃ τύχωσι ῥυέντες·
σμικρὰ δὲ φύσις οὐδὲν μέγα οὐδέποτε οὐδένα οὔτε ἰδιώτην οὔτε πόλιν δρᾷ.
Ἀληθέστατα, ἦ δ' ὅς.

'So do you see', I said, 'that we were not wrong in saying that the very qualities of the philosophical nature, when they get bad nurture, actually become responsible, in a way, for its falling away from the pursuit [of philosophy], as do the so-called good things—wealth and all such resources?' 'Yes,' he said, 'what we said was correct.' 'This,' I said, 'my good friend, is the way the best nature is destroyed and corrupted so completely as regards the best pursuit, a nature which is rare anyway, as we affirm. From these men come both those who do the greatest evil to their cities and to individuals—and those who do the greatest good, if they happen to flow in that direction. For a little nature never does anything great, either to an individual or to a city.' 'Quite true,' he said. (Plato, *Republic* 495a–b)

---

[63] Overseas ambitions: Thuc. 6. 90. 2 (cf. Plut. *Alk.* 15. 2); ps.-Plato, *Alk. II*, 141a–c. Pride (φρόνημα): Thuc. 5. 43. 2; 6. 16. 1–6. 17. 1; Plato *Alk. I*, 104a. Posturing: Aristoph., *Wasps* 44–6 (cf. Plut. *Alk.* 1. 6–8). On Alkibiades' possible tyrannical aspirations, see below, n. 81.

Thus Plato returns to the doctrine of the 'great nature', and it is now clear that he had Alkibiades particularly in mind. He, more than any other Athenian, can be said to have done 'the greatest evil and the greatest good to his city'. It is this ambiguity which lies at the heart of Plutarch's *Life of Alkibiades*, a truly Platonic text.

In other texts, Plutarch speaks of Alkibiades as a 'great nature'. This is the implication, as has been noted, of *On why the gods are so slow to punish* 552b (see above, p. 207). In the *Life of Nikias*, Alkibiades is compared (9. 1), significantly in view of the repeated agricultural metaphors associated with discussions of 'great natures', to the soil of Egypt which 'because of its excellence (δι' ἀρετὴν) produces together *many good drugs intermingled with many deadly ones*' (a quotation from Homer's *Odyssey* 4. 230). 'In the same way', Plutarch goes on, 'the nature of Alkibiades, flowing in full force and brightness to both sides (ἐπ' ἀμφότερα πολλὴ ῥυεῖσα καὶ λαμπρά), afforded cause for great innovations': a clear allusion to Plato, *Republic* 495b. But Plutarch gives his clearest indication that he is following this Platonic model when, towards the start of the *Life of Alkibiades* itself, he discusses Alkibiades' susceptibility to flattery and Sokrates' attempts to teach him philosophy. Though Alkibiades' other lovers are struck by his beauty (4. 1), Sokrates falls in love with, and therefore confirms, his potential for virtue (τῆς πρὸς ἀρετὴν εὐφυΐας; cf. 6. 1). Plutarch continues:

(4. 1) . . . φοβούμενος δὲ τὸν πλοῦτον καὶ τὸ ἀξίωμα καὶ τὸν προκαταλαμβάνοντα κολακείαις καὶ χάρισιν ἀστῶν καὶ ξένων καὶ συμμάχων ὄχλον, οἷος ἦν ἀμύνειν καὶ μὴ περιορᾶν ὥσπερ φυτὸν ἐν ἄνθει τὸν οἰκεῖον καρπὸν ἀποβάλλον καὶ διαφθεῖρον.

(4. 1) [Sokrates] . . . feared his wealth and public esteem and the mob of citizens, foreigners, and allies who were anticipating them with flatteries and fawnings. So he was inclined to protect him and not allow, as it were, a plant in flower to throw away and corrupt its natural fruit.

Alkibiades, because of his good nature (ὑπ' εὐφυΐας), chooses Sokrates and not his other lovers. 'He crouched,' says Plutarch in a tragic quotation, probably from Phrynichos, 'like a defeated cock, lowering his wings' (4. 3).[64] He recognized that Sokrates' work was 'really a service provided by the gods for the care and salvation of the young' (4. 4: τῷ ὄντι θεῶν ὑπηρεσίαν εἰς νέων ἐπιμέλειαν εἶναι καὶ σωτηρίαν). This,

---

[64] ἔπτηξ' ἀλέκτωρ δοῦλον [mss: δοῦλος Ziegler, following E] ὡς κλίνας πτέρον (*TrGF* II. 408a), also quoted by Plutarch at *Pel.* 29. 11 and *Amat.* 762e. For this use of δοῦλος, as the defeated bird in a cock-fight, cf. Aristoph. *Birds* 71–2, with Dunbar (1995), 158.

according to Plutarch in *To an uneducated ruler* (780d), is a quotation from the Academic philosopher Polemon and referred in its original context to love (ἔρως). Possibly the original context concerned the love of Sokrates for Alkibiades; the thought, at any rate, is probably derived ultimately from Sokrates' speech in Plato's *Symposium* (204c–2212b).[65] It is a fine tribute to Sokrates on Plutarch's part. It echoes Sokrates' own defence at his trial (*Apology* 30a),[66] but also assimilates Sokrates himself to the divine intervention which Plato said was the only way in which a man like Alkibiades might be saved from the corrupting influences of his society (*Rep.* 492a and 492e–493a).

Plutarch follows Plato, then, and the wider tradition, in making his Alkibiades a 'great nature': someone capable of both great good and great evil. Other 'great natures' in Plutarch, like Coriolanus, are great men turned bad; but Alkibiades' moral status is a little more problematic. The question of how to evaluate Alkibiades and his actions is constantly raised, not least because the reactions to him of others is such a central part of the Life. But Plutarch's treatment of Alkibiades seems to suggest the impossibility of coming to a satisfactory moral judgement: Plutarch's Alkibiades defies classification into the usual categories of virtue and vice, and seems to stand outside, and even to challenge, any moral schema. He is, Plutarch seems to suggest, outside of morality. The only explicit narratorial judgement which Plutarch makes in the Life itself is to point out his consistent inconsistency[67] and his susceptibility to ambition (2. 1; cf. *Nik.* 9. 1). It is probably significant that Aristotle (*Poetics* 9, 1451b10–11), to exemplify his contention that history is concerned with the particular (τὸ καθ' ἕκαστον) rather than with the universal (τὰ καθόλου), chooses the career of Alkibiades: he recognized the difficulty of drawing general truths from 'what Alkibiades did or what experiences he had'.

The Alkibiades of Plutarch's Life does, it is true, seem to invite comparison with the common Plutarchan types of, for example, the flatterer (cf. *Cor.-Alk.* 1. 3–4) or the 'friend of many'; indeed, in the *How to tell a flatterer from a friend* (52e) he is explicitly cited as an example of the

---

[65] It is quoted also in *Thes.-Rom.* 1. 6 to refer to Ariadne's love for Theseus. See Flacelière (1948), 101–2; Ampolo and Manfredini (1988), 342.

[66] ἐγὼ οἴομαι οὐδέν πω ὑμῖν μεῖζον ἀγαθὸν γενέσθαι ἐν τῇ πόλει ἢ τὴν ἐμὴν τῷ θεῷ ὑπηρεσίαν.

[67] Alkibiades' inconsistency is one of the few constants in Plutarch's picture of him: in Pelling's terminology, Alkibiades' character is 'integrated' around this trait (Pelling 1988a, 257–74; 1990a, 235–40). On Plutarch's refusal to make explicit judgements on Alkibiades, cf. Piccirilli (1989), 11–14.

flatterer (κόλαξ) and demagogue (δημαγωγός).⁶⁸ But, as we have seen, it is his very charm, versatility, and ability to flatter, on this model bad characteristics, which win him success. Charm (χάρις), a word which in Plutarch often carries the negative associations of flattery or gratification of subordinates (e.g. *Aem.* 3. 6; *Sulla* 31. 1), is indeed a key term to describe Alkibiades and his activities (*Alk.* 1. 6; 10. 3; 24. 5; *Cor.-Alk.* 3. 4; 5. 1), but only in the *synkrisis* does it seem to carry such negative connotations (*Cor.-Alk.* 1. 4). It is unclear, therefore, whether Alkibiades is a good or a bad example. This accounts for the difficulty of modern scholars in deciding whether Alkibiades is supposed to be an example to be followed or avoided.⁶⁹ In reality he is neither; and it is perhaps the fact that Plutarch here has not tried to fit Alkibiades into any 'typical' pattern that accounts for the strong sense of Alkibiades' personality with which the reader is left. Plutarch's Alkibiades, one of his most memorable characters, is above all an individual.⁷⁰ If there is any lesson here, it is that the moral categories do not always work—especially not for the great.

Plutarch's picture of Alkibiades owes much to the diverse literary tradition on the figure of Alkibiades and the opposing evaluations of his worth. But Plutarch has transformed the contradictory tradition into a vision of Alkibiades as a man of contradictions. He certainly found in his sources the first hints of this treatment of Alkibiades as a man of contradictions and an enigma. Satyros, for example, noted his ability to adapt himself to suit his circumstances (Athenaios 534b; cf. Plut. *Alk.* 23. 3–5). Nepos, who seems in his *Life of Alkibiades* to have used many of the same sources as Plutarch, shares this view—to an extent.⁷¹ At the beginning of Nepos' Life, Alkibiades' character is analysed as a mixture of abilities and vices, 'with the result that everyone was amazed that such differences and such a varied nature could exist in one man' (1. 4). Later on, Nepos comments again in the same vein, 'he not only filled them

---

⁶⁸ See Russell (1973), 95–6; 123–4. See below, p. 235.
⁶⁹ See above, p. 56.
⁷⁰ The interest in the *Alk.* is, to use Gill's initial terminology (see p. 13), in *personality* rather than in *character*. The *Alk.* is one of the few Lives with an extended treatment of the subject's childhood and education; the effect is more than just to prefigure adult traits: Alkibiades is individuated. See Pelling (1990a), esp. 224–31.
⁷¹ Nepos refers directly to Thucydides, Theopompos, and Timaios (11. 1–2). Plutarch used Nepos when writing some other Lives (he is cited at *Marc.* 30. 5, *Luc.* 43. 2, and *Gracchi* 21. 3; cf. Geiger 1985, 117–20; Moles 1993a, 77; 79), but he was probably not a source for the *Alk.*: some details in Nepos' much shorter Life are omitted in Plutarch's, inexplicably if the former was the direct source for the latter (e.g., concerning Alkibiades' stronghold in Thrace, Nepos, *Alk.* 7. 4–5: cf. Plut. *Alk.* 36. 5; the *hospes* from Arkadia who is present at his death, Nepos, *Alk.* 10. 5).

with the greatest hope, but also with fear, because he could both harm them greatly and help them' (3. 5). Nepos, like Plutarch and Satyros, notes Alkibiades' adaptability (11. 3–5). Furthermore, the important assessment of the reason for Alkibiades' failure—his own reputation—in Plut. *Alk.* 35. 3–5 is very similar to that in Nepos, *Alk.* 7. 2–3. The difference between the two accounts, however, is striking. After the opening characterization, the picture of Alkibiades in Nepos' *Life* is wholly favourable; he is ascribed virtues, but no vices.[72] Even Alkibiades' imitation of Persian and Thracian customs (11. 4–6; cf. Plut. *Alk.* 23. 3–6) is probably to be seen as unproblematic in Nepos, given his explicit support in the *Preface* and in the *Life of Epameinondas* (1. 1–2) for the doctrine of cultural relativism. This positive picture of Alkibiades results partly, at least, from the fact that Nepos has included none of the anecdotal material which plays such an important role in problematizing our reading of Plutarch's *Alkibiades*. Furthermore, he presents none of the complexities which are such a central feature of Plutarch's account and which prevent any simple moral conclusions. Thus Nepos is clear in his belief that, throughout his life, Alkibiades' motive was love of his country. This is particularly striking in 4. 6, where he argues that his reason for helping the Spartans was actually patriotism, as his own personal enemies were also the enemies of the state (cf. also 8. 1; 9. 4). The analysis is crude, but is what we would, after all, expect from a writer whose aim is to use Alkibiades as a moral exemplar. Nepos' account provides a model for us to see how far Plutarch has gone to work against any such simple reading: it is not easy to extract moral lessons from Plutarch's *Alkibiades*.

4. MORAL NORMS CONFUSED: ALKIBIADES

After an initial discussion of Alkibiades' family (1. 1–3), appearance (1. 4–5), and voice (1. 6–8), all usual features of the opening of a Plutarchan *Life*, Plutarch comments on the inconsistencies of his character, while picking out his 'love of honour' and 'love of being first' for special mention (2. 1):

Τὸ δ' ἦθος αὐτοῦ πολλὰς μὲν ὕστερον, ὡς εἰκὸς ἐν πράγμασι μεγάλοις καὶ τύχαις πολυτρόποις, ἀνομοιότητας πρὸς αὑτὸ καὶ μεταβολὰς ἐπεδείξατο. φύσει δὲ πολλῶν ὄντων καὶ μεγάλων παθῶν ἐν αὐτῷ τὸ φιλόνικον ἰσχυρότατον ἦν καὶ τὸ φιλόπρωτον, ὡς δῆλόν ἐστι τοῖς παιδικοῖς ἀπομνημονεύμασιν.

[72] Noted briefly by T. G. McCarty (1974), 388–9.

His character later displayed many inconsistencies and changes, as one might expect in the midst of great matters and varied fortunes. By nature, there were many great passions in him, but love of victory and love of coming first were the strongest, as is clear from his childhood anecdotes.

Alkibiades' passionate nature is supposedly illustrated by the anecdotes about his childhood ambition which follow (2. 2–7). But what is remarkable for the present analysis is that Plutarch draws attention to a contrast between Alkibiades' innate nature ($\phi\acute{v}\sigma\iota\varsigma$) and his developed character ($\mathring{\eta}\theta o\varsigma$). His ambitious and passionate nature, Plutarch maintains, is not always reflected in his character, that is, in the way he behaved. His character was totally unpredictable: its one point of consistency was its very inconsistency. Plutarch is on occasion prepared elsewhere, as here, to believe that character could change, usually as a result of great changes of circumstance ($\tau\acute{v}\chi\eta$).[73] In fact, at the close of the initial anecdotal section of the Life (16. 9), he declares that there was 'unevenness' ($\dot{a}\nu\omega\mu a\lambda\acute{\iota}a\nu$) in Alkibiades's *nature*: a much more shocking statement. He will return to the theme of Alkibiades' changeableness later in the Life (23. 3–6).[74]

Alkibiades, then, is inconsistent; it is difficult to tell what his real character or nature were. After this initial characterization, Plutarch continues with a long section recording anecdotes about Alkibiades as a boy, a youth, and as a man (1–16). The material here has been selected and arranged not to preserve chronology but, in the first instance, to reveal Alkibiades' character.[75] The first section of anecdotes, which relate to his childhood (2. 2–2. 7), are specifically introduced as illustrative of his love of victory and of pre-eminence (2. 1). In fact, the character they reveal is much harder to pin down than Plutarch's initial summary implies.[76] We see his ambition (2. 1–7; cf. 6. 4; 23. 8; 27. 6; 34. 3), his outrageousness (9. 1–2), his susceptibility to flattery (6. 1; cf. 4. 1; 6. 4), his bravery (2. 3–4; 7. 4), his extravagance (11. 1–12. 1), his political astuteness (13. 1–9), and his military and diplomatic skill (14. 1–15. 8); in particular we see how he was able to win friends and inspire loyalty (4. 1–6. 5; 7. 3–6; 10. 1–3)—his relationship with and treatment by the Athenian *demos* is a key concern later in the narrative (e.g. 17–22; 26. 1–27. 1; 32. 1–35. 4). But

---

[73] e.g. *Sert.* 10. 5–7. See especially Swain (1989*a*), 64–8, and above, p. 74.
[74] For 'unevenness', cf. below, pp. 270–1 on *Nik.-Cross.* 1. 4.
[75] Russell (1966*b*). On this tendency in Plutarchan narrative, see below, Appendix 2.
[76] Pelling (1996), pp. xliv–xlvii, sees this as an example of Plutarch's tendency to characterize a man with a very broad brush at the start of his Life (e.g. *Lys.* 2. 4), and then to progressively refine and nuance this characterization as the Life progresses. See also Pelling (1988*a*), 269–70; (1988*b*), 12–13; 25; 42–3.

more than anything this section, both by its arrangement and by its content, suggests the difficulty of making any kind of moral judgement about Alkibiades. The structure is loose and hard to follow; chronology is confused and a vast range of literary sources lies behind it; the reader has the impression of being confronted with a mass of unharmonized and often contradictory excerpts which seem to build no coherent picture of the man at the centre of them. The multiplicity and the contradictory nature of the sources reflect the contradictory nature of Alkibiades himself. The unevenness of the Life reflects the unevenness, the ἀνωμαλία, of Alkibiades, the man who could be, according to Plutarch, all things to all men. Form and content, medium and message, harmonize perfectly in what, paradoxically, appears at first to be such an ill-harmonized Life.

Alkibiades' amorality is clear from the start: in a wrestling match (2. 2) he is accused of biting his opponent 'just like women do' (καθάπερ αἱ γυναῖκες). He replies 'No . . . but as lions do' (οὐκ ἔγωγε, . . . ἀλλ' ὡς οἱ λέοντες). The incident, known only here and at ps.-Plut. Reg. et Imp. 186d,[77] not only indicates Alkibiades' desire to win, the explicit reason for its inclusion, but also shows him challenging the norms of acceptable behaviour. It is also slightly ambiguous: is the suggestion that Alkibiades fights in an underhand, female way? Or that his fighting has something of the erotic about it? Later in his life he will continue to use unorthodox methods to obtain his ends; this is seen clearly in his double-dealings in the period between his exile and his recall, and is stated explicitly in Cor.-Alk. 5. 2. His behaviour questions and redefines the boundaries between male and female and between human and animal. Alkibiades' tendency to confuse such boundaries is a feature which will recur (cf. 8. 1–2; 23. 6); in 2. 5–7, where he causes a reaction against flute playing, he redefines what is acceptable for a citizen and for a foreigner. The repetition of the image of the lion at the end of the anecdotal section (16. 3) not only provides a neat sense of closure, but also suggests the inapplicability to Alkibiades of any usual criteria by which human behaviour might be judged. Lions have different standards.[78]

One of the major facts which Plutarch chooses to emphasize about Alkibiades is the difficulty which his contemporaries have in coming to any moral estimate of him.[79] In other Lives, the judgements made by contemporaries often provide a key for the way in which Plutarch expects

---

[77] The same story is told of a nameless Spartan at Ap. Lac. 234d–e.
[78] And are often associated with monarchy or tyranny: Hdt. 5. 56; 5. 92; 6. 131. 2; Aristoph. Knights 1037. See Gribble (1994), 2.   [79] Noted also by Gribble (1994), 272–5.

the reader to react,[80] but in this Life all such judgements are explicitly contradictory and uncertain. This is especially clear in the important passage at 16. 1–9, but it is true throughout the whole opening, anecdotal section (1–16), where the focus is as much on the reactions Alkibiades elicits as on his own actions. No coherent picture of Alkibiades emerges, rather, a confusing sequence of snapshots of Alkibiades as seen from numerous different angles, in different lights and focuses. This must be the reason for the inclusion of the accusations of Antiphon (3. 1–2). They do indeed introduce the section on Alkibiades' lovers which follows; but why has Plutarch included what he explicitly believed to be abuse (λοιδορίαι) and therefore not worthy of credence? The answer is clear; the reader is given a number of conflicting views of Alkibiades drawn from a vast number of different sources. Plutarch avoids making explicit narratorial judgements; the anecdotes and judgements are presented on their own without comment, and form a contradictory and deeply problematic picture of Alkibiades. It is the very 'unevenness' of the picture which in Plutarch's view is the key to Alkibiades.

This is clear in the section on Sokrates and his other lovers (4. 1–7. 6). We have seen how, in comparison with Coriolanus' lack of education, Alkibiades' education with Sokrates is morally commendable. But matters are not so simple. Alkibiades continues to have other lovers (4. 4–5. 5; 6. 2–5). He is susceptible to flattery (4. 1) and even close association with Sokrates does not cure him, so that at times he runs away from Sokrates to his flatterers (6. 1). Even his treatment of his other lovers is contradictory and evokes contradictory reactions. He spurns the invitation of his lover Anytos, but then arrives drunk at the dinner and makes off with half of the gold and silver ware. Anytos' guests claim that Alkibiades has acted with insolence and arrogance (ὑβριστικῶς καὶ ὑπερηφάνως); Anytos himself, on the other hand, says he acted 'reasonably and with humanity' (ἐπιεικῶς . . . καὶ φιλανθρώπως) in not taking the lot (4. 5–6). Notably in Plutarch's version Alkibiades' behaviour is made to seem more outrageous than in Satyros' (Athenaios 534e–f), where Alkibiades gives the gold and silver cups he has taken to a needy friend. If Plutarch had followed this version of the incident, it could have been made to fit nicely with the following anecdote (5. 1–5) where Alkibiades helps a metic lover: the theme could have been 'generosity to friends', as well as unorthodox and outrageous behaviour. In fact, the two anecdotes are in stark contrast. One illustrates insolence (ὕβρις) to lovers, the other kindness.

[80] See above, p. 120 n. 67.

The theme of outrageous behaviour continues in the subsequent anecdotes. But in all of them there is a twist in the tail. Alkibiades assaults a school teacher (7. 1): but it is with the aim, for Plutarch commendable, of defending Homer, the central figure in Greek culture and education. He remarks that Perikles would do better to find a way not to render account to the people (7. 3). Perhaps the words of a would-be tyrant; but then it is unclear whether such a comment would seem immoral in the eyes of a Greek reader of the imperial period, for whom Classical Athens meant the rule of Perikles and not democracy.[81] He wins a prize for valour, but does not really deserve it (7. 4–6). He hits Hipponikos, but then goes and submits to assault himself (8. 1–2). Does this demonstrate commendable repentance, or the outrageous assumption by a male aristocrat of a position suitable only for a slave or woman? He consorts with courtesans, and carries his wife off by force when she attempts to obtain a divorce; she dies soon after. But, Plutarch explains, such violence ($\beta i\alpha$) was not at the time thought lawless or cruel (8. 5–6).[82] This rare intervention by Plutarch serves to confuse, not settle, the question of the morality of Alkibiades' action. The following chapters, showing some anecdotes from his entry into public life, demonstrate his ability to charm the *demos*. But what does the reader make of his cutting off his dog's tail (9. 1–2)? He wins great applause when, on making a contribution of money to the state, he lets a quail escape from under his cloak. People rush to catch the bird; its captor is 'Antiochos the helmsman, who became in consequence a great favourite of Alkibiades' (10. 1–2)—and the one who was to end Alkibiades' career by disobeying orders and attacking Lysander at Notion (35. 5–8). Alkibiades is a brilliant public speaker; his words have great charm ($\chi \acute{\alpha} \rho \iota s$); but he often stumbles over them (10. 3–4). Alkibiades' deception of the Spartan ambassadors (14. 1–12) does not seem to invite either praise or blame.[83] As we have seen, deception and guile ($\dot{\alpha} \pi \acute{\alpha} \tau \eta$ and $\delta \acute{o} \lambda o s$), the words with which Alkibiades' deception is described, need not carry a pejorative sense;[84] in fact, Plutarch goes on to stress, with what looks like admiration, how close Alkibiades came to defeating Sparta outright at

---

[81] Plutarch consistently brings out the themes of Alkibiades' hybristic personal life and the fear of tyranny which this instilled (*Alk.* 7. 3; 12. 1; 13. 3; 16. 2; 16. 7; 34. 6–35. 1; 39. 9), a feature of Alkibiades' image going back to the 5th c.: e.g. ps.-Plato, *Alk. II*, 141b–142d; cf. Seager (1967). See below on the quotation of Thuc. 6. 15. 4 at *Alk.* 6. 3.

[82] For pseudo-Andokides, Alkibiades' treatment of his wife is a straightforward example of *hybris* (*Against Alkibiades* 14–15).

[83] See Russell (1966b), 44 (= 1995, 202).

[84] See above, pp. 171–3.

Mantineia in the events which followed (15. 1–2; cf. *Cor.-Alk.* 2. 1–5). Later he will use guile to take for Athens the cities of Kyzikos, Selymbria, and Byzantion (28. 6–7; 30. 3–10; 31. 3–6).

The impossibility of judging Alkibiades is stated most clearly in the crucial chapter (16) which closes the introductory, anecdotal section on Alkibiades' childhood and entry into politics. Paradoxes abound. Combined with his masterly and successful statesmanship on Athens' behalf, of which some examples have been narrated in the previous chapters, are his luxury and effeminacy. Those of good repute (ἔνδοξοι) fear him, suspecting him of tyranny; the people experience varying emotions (16. 2–3). Plutarch quotes (16. 3) Aristophanes' words (*Frogs* 1425): 'It desires him, but hates him, and wants to have him' (ποθεῖ μέν, ἐχθαίρει δέ, βούλεται δ' ἔχειν). Thucydides had stated (6. 15. 4) that everyone (ἕκαστοι) became hostile to Alkibiades because of his life-style, and feared that he wanted to become tyrant. For Plutarch, things are more uncertain: different sections of the population have different views.[85] He leaves it unclear which view of Alkibiades, if any, is correct. The Athenians are said (16. 4) to have given his faults (ἁμαρτήματα) the mildest names, calling them pranks and self-aggrandisement (παιδιαί and φιλοτιμίαι). It is unclear whether the anecdotes told in illustration of this invite condemnation or not. He kidnaps the painter Agatharchos, then sends him away with a gift (16. 5). In the version of this story in pseudo-Andokides' *Against Alkibiades* 17, which Plutarch may have read or with which he may at least have shared a common source, the painter is not set free but has to escape; Plutarch's version clouds the issue: do we abhor the kidnap or applaud the gift?[86] Similar difficulties are encountered with the story of Alkibiades saving a Melian woman by making her his mistress (16. 5). For Plutarch continues (16. 6):

καὶ γὰρ τοῦτο φιλάνθρωπον ἐκάλουν, πλὴν ὅτι ⟨τοῦ⟩ τοὺς Μηλίους ἡβηδὸν ἀποσφαγῆναι τὴν πλείστην αἰτίαν ἔσχε, τῷ ψηφίσματι συνειπών.

In fact they called this an act of humanity—except for the fact that he was chiefly responsible for the slaughter of all the Melians from youth upwards, having lent his support to the decree.

The mood and tense of ἐκάλουν (rather than ἐκάλεσαν ἄν) keep the reader guessing as to whether Plutarch thought the inconsistency of

---

[85] Cf. Pelling (1992), 21–5. Contrast *Nik.* 11. 2, where Plutarch is happy to repeat Thucydides' judgement.

[86] Demosthenes (*Against Meidias* 147) is also ambivalent, suggesting ways in which Alkibiades' kidnap of Agatharchos, and his hitting of the *choregos* Taureas, also narrated in Plut. *Alk.* 16. 5, might be viewed less negatively.

Alkibiades' action, saving one prisoner but condemning to death all the rest, was noted at the time,[87] or is, as strict grammar would suggest, Plutarch's own retrospective opinion. His pose in a picture of Nemea is said explicitly to have elicited both delight and indignation in his contemporaries (16. 7). Timon congratulates Alkibiades on growing up (16. 9); but the reason is shocking: he will be a great evil (μέγα κακόν) to the Athenians. Plutarch again remarks on the different reactions this elicits, and sums up: 'So undecided was opinion (doxa) about him due to the unevenness of his nature' (οὕτως ἄκριτος ἦν ἡ δόξα περὶ αὐτοῦ διὰ τὴν τῆς φύσεως ἀνωμαλίαν).

In many ways, then, this Life is not about Alkibiades himself, but about his *doxa*—that is, his reputation and other people's opinion about him. This theme is introduced at the very start of the Life when Plutarch says (1. 3) that Alkibiades' *doxa* benefited from his association with Sokrates.[88] The anecdotes told about him focus on people's reactions to him. It is because people believe that Alkibiades was involved in the celebrated profanation of the Eleusinian Mysteries that he is forced into exile (19. 1–22. 5). Plutarch himself does not state whether Alkibiades was really involved or not, but he does point out an inaccuracy in some of the statements of the accusers (20. 8). Once in exile, Alkibiades goes to Sparta where he advises the Spartans on the war with Athens. There Plutarch picks out for mention his ability to mimic the customs and characters of his hosts, both good and bad, and compares him to a chameleon (23. 3–6), an animal used also by Aelian as a paradigm for human changeability (*On animals* 2. 14). Earlier Plutarch had highlighted Alkibiades' apparent changes of character and even nature. Here he explains further: while Alkibiades did change his behaviour, he did not, in fact, change his character (ἦθος) entirely. It was more that when he saw that his nature (φύσις) was likely to annoy his associates, he adopted 'the invented outward show that would be suitable for them'— the classic behaviour of a flatterer (κόλαξ).[89] Alkibiades' apparent character-changes are not forced on him by misfortune; rather, he is, chameleon-like, able to adjust his behaviour to suit his associates,

---

[87] The speech of ps.-Andokides notes the contradiction (*Against Alkibiades* 22–3), but its date is uncertain. Thucydides does not connect Alkibiades with the Athenian decision to slaughter the Melian men and sell the rest into slavery (5. 116. 4).

[88] For Alkibiades' *doxa*, cf. Isok. *De Bigis* 3.

[89] Cf. the very similar *Quomodo Adult*. 52e (with Paradiso 1996), where Alkibiades' changes of behaviour in Athens, Sparta, Thrace, and Ionia are used as evidence that he was a flatterer (κόλαξ) and demagogue (δημαγωγός). It is unclear whether the *Alk*. or the *Quomodo Adult*. was written first: see Jones (1966), 66–8 and 72.

whether Spartans, Ionians, Thracians, Thessalians, or even a Persian satrap (23. 3–6):

(23. 5) οὐχ αὑτὸν ἐξιστὰς οὕτω ῥᾳδίως εἰς ἕτερον ἐξ ἑτέρου τρόπον, οὐδὲ πᾶσαν δεχόμενος τῷ ἤθει μεταβολήν, ἀλλ' ὅτι τῇ φύσει χρώμενος ἔμελλε λυπεῖν τοὺς ἐντυγχάνοντας, εἰς πᾶν ἀεὶ τὸ πρόσφορον ἐκείνοις σχῆμα καὶ πλάσμα κατεδύετο καὶ κατέφευγεν. (23. 6) ἐν γοῦν τῇ Λακεδαίμονι πρὸς τὰ ἔξωθεν ἦν εἰπεῖν· "οὐ παῖς Ἀχιλλέως, ἀλλ' ἐκεῖνος αὐτὸς εἶ," οἷον ὁ Λυκοῦργος ἐπαίδευσε, τοῖς δ' ἀληθινοῖς ἄν τις ἐπεφώνησεν αὐτοῦ πάθεσι καὶ πράγμασιν· "ἔστιν ἡ πάλαι γυνή".

(23. 5) He did not change himself so easily from one disposition to another, nor did he receive every change in his character, but, because he was going to pain those he happened to be with, if he stuck to his nature, he used to put on and take refuge in whatever facade or fiction suited them. (23. 6) In Sparta, at any rate, as far as the exterior was concerned, one could say: '*You are not the son of Achilles, but Achilles himself*', a man such as Lykourgos trained. But as regards his true passions and affairs, someone might have declared: '*he is the same woman as always*'.

As Plutarch continues, Alkibiades' seduction of Timaia, the wife of the Spartan king Agis, proves that he was the same outrageous self (23. 7–9).

The quotations from tragedy are important here. In claiming that Alkibiades behaved like an archetypal Spartan, Plutarch uses a quotation about Achilles from an unknown tragedy (*TrGF* II. 363).[90] The reference to Achilles, with whom Alkibiades was certainly compared by Antisthenes (fr. V A 199 Giannantoni) and perhaps by others, sits somewhat uneasily with the mention of Lykourgos and the Spartan context as a whole. But the point becomes clear with the quotation from Euripides' *Orestes* (129), '*he is the same woman as always*'. The quotation in its Euripidean context is about Helen, whom Elektra accuses of putting on only an outward show of mourning for Klytaimnestra; it therefore suits Plutarch's theme of Alkibiades' ability to change his outward behaviour, not his character. But more significant is the use of the feminine, which suggests sexual ambiguity, that Alkibiades crossed or confused the boundaries of gender. This might suggest his licentious private life, amply demonstrated in the illustrative anecdote of his seduction of Timaia, which itself might suggest a tyrannical nature: sexual excess was associated with both a female nature and a tyrant's lusts.[91] Alkibiades'

---

[90] Possibly from Sophokles' *Philoktetes at Troy* or *Skyrians*. The quotation is attested only here and in *Quomodo Adult*. 51c, where it is used of the flatterer who is able to adapt his manner and pursuits to those of people whom he wants to 'attack through imitation'.

[91] Antisthenes makes the connection between Alkibiades' sexual behaviour and a desire for tyranny in his *Kyros or on Kingship*: fr. V A 141 Giannantoni.

effeminacy has been central to Plutarch's Life from the start, and forms a contrast with Coriolanus' exclusive attachment to manliness (ἀνδρεία): from the section on his appearance and lisp (1. 4–8); to the accusation that he bites likes women (2. 3); to the anecdotes about his lovers (chs. 3–6). Clearest is the description in 16. 1 of his 'wanton life-style, outrages in drink and sex (περὶ πότους καὶ ἔρωτας ὑβρίσματα), feminities (θηλύτητας) of purple clothing sweeping through the market place, arrogant expense, cutting away of the decks in triremes so that he could sleep more softly (μαλακώτερον), his bed made up on cords not on planks, the making of a gold shield with no ancestral device but with an Eros bearing a thunderbolt'.[92]

These associations of Alkibiades with the feminine make clear the point of the reference to Achilles in the tragic quotation of 23. 6. A well-known story about Achilles concerned his behaviour on the island of Skyros. Dressed in women's clothing, he hid amongst the daughters of king Lykomedes, in order to avoid going to the Trojan war: an archetypal story of disguise, changeability, and the crossing of gender distinctions.[93] Plutarch elsewhere quotes twice from a lost tragedy which dealt with this incident, possibly Euripides' *Skyrians*.[94] The hypothesis of this play records, as do other versions of the story, that while in hiding Achilles seduced Deidameia, one of the daughters of Lykomedes. Later, after Achilles had left, Deidameia gave birth to a son, Neoptolemos. It is of course to Neoptolemos that the first tragic quotation must have been addressed in its original context: 'You are not the son of Achilles, but Achilles himself.' Alkibiades can, like Achilles, change his outward manner of life; like the youthful Achilles, he can cross boundaries of gender, but his character, like Achilles', stays the same: before leaving Sparta, he impregnates the wife of king Agis.[95]

Moral terms are absent from the narrative of his desertion to Sparta, his aiding of Sparta against Athens, and his imitation of foreign customs (22. 1–24. 2); what Plutarch does stress is the effectiveness of his operations against Athens (22. 1; 23. 2; 24. 2). Moral judgements are not encouraged; Alkibiades is simply the subject of the narrative. In this respect, Tissaphernes' admiration for his cunning (24. 5–6) could be a

[92] An audacious and unparalleled design: see Blanckenhagen (1964).
[93] For an exploration of the feminine in Greek conceptions of masculinity, see Loraux (1995).
[94] *De Aud. Poet.* 34d; *Quomodo Adult.* 72e (= Nauck, *TrGF* Adesp. 9). For the various versions of the incident, see Roussel (1991), 123–41.
[95] Cf. ps.-Bion of Smyrne on Achilles' seduction of Deidameia: θυμὸν δ' ἀνέρος εἶχε καὶ ἀνέρος εἶχεν ἔρωτα (*Epithalamios* 21).

paradigm for the reader. When Alkibiades returns to favour with the Athenian fleet at Samos in 411, issues of right and wrong seem particularly clouded. He engineers the suppression of the democracy (25. 5; 26. 1); Plutarch tells us that this was done not out of political principle but out of self-interest; indeed, Alkibiades' claim to the oligarchs that he does not seek to gratify the masses is plainly a short-term pose, given his largely successful attempts to do just this throughout the Life. The only moral term employed in this narrative is that of traitor ($\pi\rho o\delta \acute{o}\tau\eta s$), which is applied, significantly, to Phrynichos—the oligarchic general who sees Alkibiades' real motives (25. 7; 25. 11).[96]

Finally, Alkibiades is recalled to Athens. Before returning home, he wins some notable military successes. In one of them, he appears unexpectedly with a squadron of ships when fighting between the Spartan and Athenian fleets had already begun off the city of Abydos. Alkibiades' intervention leads to an Athenian victory, but Plutarch is able to use this incident to pursue further the theme of Alkibiades' *doxa*: he states that initially Alkibiades instilled in both sides a 'contradictory opinion' ($\dot{\epsilon}\nu\alpha\nu\tau\acute{\iota}\alpha\nu$ $\delta\acute{o}\xi\alpha\nu$), as he is presumed by both to be an enemy (27. 4).[97] In the end, it is the impossibility of seeing the real 'Alkibiades' which leads to his downfall. Plutarch states this very clearly (35. 3): 'It seems', he says, 'that more than anyone else Alkibiades was undone by his own *doxa*.' The Athenians thought, Plutarch continues, that Alkibiades could do anything; they did not give him proper resources, and blamed him for reverses (35. 3–4). When one of his subordinates loses a battle, while he is away raising the money which the Athenian state had not supplied him (35. 5–8), his enemies accuse him of negligently entrusting his command to his drinking partners and of debauchery and drunkenness (36. 1–3), typical vices associated with tyranny. Plutarch's narrative shows that the charges are unfair, but what is important is that the Athenians 'believe' them ($\pi\epsilon\iota\sigma\theta\acute{\epsilon}\nu\tau\epsilon s$), and strip Alkibiades of his command; he goes into exile again, this time never to return (46. 4–5). The underlying reason for their distrust of Alkibiades is, Plutarch has already stated, their fear that he wanted to become tyrant (35. 1). Whether he really did or not, Plutarch tells us, is uncertain ($\ddot{a}\delta\eta\lambda\acute{o}\nu$ $\dot{\epsilon}\sigma\tau\iota$). But it is, as always, what people believe about Alkibiades that matters.[98] Suspicions that Alkibiades

---

[96] In Thucydides, Phrynichos is accused of treachery by his enemies (8. 51. 2; 54. 3); Plutarch states it as a fact.

[97] A detail not in either Xen. *Hell.* 1. 1. 2–7 or Diod. 13. 45. 1–47. 2: see Westlake (1985a), 319.

[98] Cf. 37. 3, where before the battle of Aigospotamoi he claims that he would have been able to force the Spartans into an unfavourable engagement, had his help not been

had tyrannical aspirations had dogged him all his career, due in large part, as Plutarch has already stated explicitly, to his luxurious and unconventional life-style (16. 2; 16. 7). Early in the Life, Plutarch had quoted a phrase of Thucydides on this unconventional life-style (6. 3: Thuc. 6. 15. 4). As Christopher Pelling has pointed out, Plutarch's reader is expected to call to mind the context from which the quotation is drawn: Thucydides is linking Alkibiades' dissolute life-style with a popular belief that he was aspiring to become tyrant.[99] In a very real sense, then, Plutarch's narrative shows Alkibiades falling from power as a result of his *doxa*: the Athenians believe he can win battles against the odds; when he fails, they believe it is because he has indulged in the vices of a tyrant, a belief which his own life-style had done much to nurture. It is a typically Plutarchan analysis, showing that the things which make a protagonist successful are the same ones which lead to his downfall. Usually it is character-traits that are the cause of both a man's rise and his fall. But here it is Alkibiades' very success at creating a reputation for himself which will ruin him.[100]

Later it is his reputation, and the hopes and fears which this excites, that leads to his assassination (38. 3–6). The Athenians, now that they have capitulated, 'recognized the reasonings which they would not take when salvation was in their power': they regretted their anger against Alkibiades which had led them, through no fault of his, to exile him and deprive Athens of their greatest and most warlike general. A vague hope remained, however, that Alkibiades might somehow return to help his native city. But, as so often in this Life, it is the very hopes and fears which Alkibiades excites that determine his fate. Aware of Athenian longing for Alkibiades, the Spartans arrange his murder in Phrygia.

Plutarch closes the Life with two accounts of Alkibiades' death in exile, one more commendable than the other (39. 4–9). He gives no explicit preference for either. Both agree that he dies bravely resisting the attacks of a party of assassins who set fire to the house he was living in. But in the first version, his murder has been arranged by the satrap Pharnabazos, on Lysander's bidding, because Alkibiades is considered a dangerous focus of democratic Athenian resistance and has to be

refused: 'it seemed to some that he was merely boasting, but to others his claim seemed reasonable'.

[99] Pelling (1992), 18–19. Cf. Russell (1966b), 40–1 (= 1995, 196–7).
[100] Compare the way Pompey's power causes his fall, when it is used to help his rivals: *Pomp.* 46. 3–4. Pompey's willingness to gratify his friends, introduced in *Pomp.* 1. 4, finally ruins him (e.g. 39. 6; 47. 4–10; 67. 1–68. 1). On the same character-traits leading to a man's success and downfall, see above, p. 123 n. 79.

removed for reasons of state. Even into this rather glamorous picture, a note of doubt is introduced. The authorities in Sparta authorize Alkibiades' murder (38. 6) 'either because they too feared the cleverness and enterprise of the man (τὴν ὀξύτητα καὶ μεγαλοπραγμοσύνην τοῦ ἀνδρός), or because they wanted to do Agis a favour (τῷ Ἄγιδι χαριζομένων)'. The theme of his extravagant life-style is recalled by the presence at his death of Timandra, a famous courtesan, his only companion in exile. She buries him λαμπρῶς καὶ φιλοτίμως (39. 7). Rather unusually, Plutarch draws here on an association, common in Greek more generally, of φιλοτιμία with benefaction.[101] The 'honour' involved is that done by Timandra to Alkibiades: in death, as in life, Alkibiades seeks, and gets, glory. In the second version of Alkibiades' death, the cause of his death is 'not Pharnabazos, nor Lysander, nor the Spartans, but Alkibiades himself'. He has, according to this account, seduced a local girl, whose brothers murder him in revenge for this outrage (ὕβρις). It is with this alternative version that the *Life of Alkibiades* ends. Even in death, the truth about Alkibiades is hard to ascertain. Hard to define, harder to judge, it is impossible to draw simple moral lessons from this Life. And this is, perhaps, the great strength of Plutarch's Life; after all, how could Alkibiades, the individualist *extraordinaire*, be a paradigm for anything—except individuality itself?

[101] See Frazier (1988a), 115–16.

PART III
Writing in Parallel

8
Synkrisis and the *Synkriseis* in the *Parallel Lives*

A recurrent theme of the previous chapters has been the importance of parallelism, of the paired structure of the *Parallel Lives*. Each book consists of two Lives, often preceded by a common prologue and usually followed by a closing 'comparison' or *synkrisis* (σύγκρισις). This parallel structure encourages the reader to compare the two Lives, to do, in other words, his own act of *synkrisis*. The cultural implications of this paralleling of Greek and Roman figures will be discussed in the final chapter. In this chapter, we shall examine the literary background for the parallel structure of Plutarch's *Lives* and the way in which Plutarch uses and discusses *synkrisis* in his other works. Most importantly, we shall examine the formal *synkriseis* which end many pairs of Lives. Are they unconvincing afterthoughts, summaries of the content of the Lives themselves, or are they, as will be argued, designed to make the reader ask new and rather challenging moral questions?

1. *SYNKRISIS*: LITERARY BACKGROUND

Synkritic modes of thought seem to have run deep in the Greek mentality. The tendency to conceive the world in polarized terms is strong in pre-Sokratic and Hippokratic writings; Hippokratic medical treatises, for example, conceive the body in terms of a series of opposites, such as hot and cold, wet and dry, which should be in balance for good health.[1] The Greeks of the fifth and fourth centuries BC constructed their own identity by means of a set of mutually exclusive polarities: Greek–barbarian, male–female, citizen–alien, free–slave.[2] *Synkrisis* became an important means of moral characterization. It features heavily in praise speeches (*enkomia*) such as Isokrates' *Evagoras* and Xenophon's *Agesilaos*, where the subjects are compared, to their advantage, with a past or contemporary Persian king.[3] This use of

---
[1] See Lloyd (1966), 15–26. [2] Cartledge (1993).
[3] Xen. *Ages.* 9. 1–5; Isok. *Evag.* 37–9; cf. *Panathen.* 39–40.

comparison in *enkomia* is recommended by Aristotle and Quintilian, and later by Menander Rhetor.[4] Comparison is included in the collections of rhetorical 'elementary exercises' (προγυμνάσματα) of, amongst others, Libanios and Aphthonios.[5] Aphthonios defines *synkrisis* as 'a speech of comparison (λόγος ἀντεξεταστικός), which brings into juxtaposition with the object of comparison something greater or equal' (*Progym.* 10, Spengel, ii. 42. 21–2).[6]

The Greek tendency to evaluate by means of contrast also manifests itself in the rhetorical *agon*: both real, paired speeches given in the law-court, and 'staged' literary contests which allow the dramatization of conflicting choices, philosophies, or literary schools.[7] Many examples survive of works which consist of two speeches arguing opposing theses. This technique can be seen as early as the fifth century BC in the Tetralogies ascribed to Antiphon (*Orations* 2–4) and in the twin speeches probably by Antisthenes, which put forward fictional arguments of first Ajax and then Odysseus in their contest over the arms of Achilles.[8] In the second century AD Maximos of Tyre wrote paired speeches, such as the pair entitled in some manuscripts *Which life is better: the practical or the theoretical?* (*Or.* 15–16 Hobein).[9] There are also examples of single speeches which present, in turn, two sides of the same argument. This technique can be seen in the pseudo-Plutarchan *Is water more useful than fire?*[10] In the *Controversiae* of the elder Seneca, particular legal cruces and

---

[4] Aristotle, *Rhet.* 1368a19–26; Quint. *Inst. Orat.* 2. 4. 21; Menander Rhetor II. 372. 21–5; 376. 31–377. 9.

[5] Libanios, *Progym.* 10 (Förster[b], viii. 334–60); Hermogenes, *Progym.* 8 (Spengel, ii. 14–15); Aphthonios, *Progym.* 10 (Spengel, ii. 42–4); Theon, *Progym.* 9 (Spengel, ii. 112–15); Nikolaos, *Progym.* 10 (Spengel, iii. 485–8). Cf. Focke (1923), 328–39; Clark (1957), 198–9.

[6] See Leo (1901), 149–51; Stiefenhofer (1914–16), 463–4; Focke (1923), 339–51. Historians regularly use *synkrisis* to characterize or to pass judgements. On Thucydides, see Cairns (1982); Xenophon's *Hellenika*: Lévy (1990), 136–8 and 156–7; Livy: Walsh (1961), 86–7; Velleius: Woodman (1977), 42; Tacitus' *Agricola*: M[c]Ging (1982); *Annals*: Goodyear (1972), 32–4; Paladini (1984). Other examples are given by Valgiglio (1992), 4022–3. On New Comedy: Wilner (1930), 56–66; cf. the 'types of life' comparisons mentioned by Quintilian (*Inst. Orat.* 2. 4. 24; cf. Tibullus 1. 1; Ovid, *Amores* 1. 9), with McKeown (1989), 259–60.

[7] Most famously, the argument in Aristophanes' *Clouds* (889–1114) between the Just and Unjust Case, and in the *Frogs* (830–1481) between Aischylos and Euripides. *Synkrisis* became an important vehicle for literary criticism: e.g. Cicero on L. Licinius Crassus and M. Antonius (*Brutus* 161–5), Kaikilios and others on Demosthenes and Cicero (see below, n. 20), the fragmentary and probably pseudo-Plutarchan *Comparison of Aristophanes and Menander*.

[8] Frs. V A 53–4 Giannantoni. On the question of their authenticity, see Giannantoni (1990), 257–64.

[9] Cf. Dion of Prousa's speeches *On law* (Περὶ νόμου) and *On custom* (Περὶ ἔθους), *Or.* 75–6, perhaps to be regarded as a pair.

[10] On the structure of this text, see Milazzo (1991), who also argues, against the con-

the moral issues which they raise are explored by amassing arguments on one side and then on the other.

2. PLUTARCHAN *SYNKRISIS*: THE *MORALIA*

Plutarch's own tendency towards synkritic thought can be seen in many of his non-biographical works. Plutarchan enkomiastic display speeches use *synkrisis*, one of the most important rhetorical devices of *enkomia*. The two extant declamations on Alexander the Great each compare the roles of fortune ($\tau\acute{v}\chi\eta$) and virtue ($\mathring{a}\rho\epsilon\tau\acute{\eta}$) in Alexander's life (*On the fortune or virtue of Alexander*). The aim is to praise Alexander by demonstrating that his success was due to his own qualities not to chance: a standard rhetorical argument.[11] Plutarch also in these speeches makes use of another sort of *synkrisis* common to *enkomia*: comparison with other great figures. In the first speech, Alexander is compared with the philosophers Sokrates, Plato, and others to show that he is the best philosopher of all (e.g. 328a–329d and 333a–c). In the second, he is compared with other monarchs whom he outstrips in patronizing the arts (333e–334d), and, later, with numerous statesmen whom he outstrips in virtue (343a–e). In another declamation, *On the fortune or virtue of the Romans*, Plutarch compares the roles of fortune and virtue in the success of the Roman state. In this case, fortune is given a positive role in Rome's success, probably to be contrasted with its continual hindering of Alexander in the similarly named *On the fortune or virtue of Alexander*: a thought-provoking and perhaps disturbing implicit *synkrisis*.[12]

This tendency to use *synkrisis* to provoke thought and raise questions is particularly and distinctively Plutarchan. He often uses *synkrisis* not to demonstrate the superiority of one side of the equation over the other, but rather to explore the issues raised as a whole.[13] A good example is his treatise *On superstition*, which consists of a comparison between the superstitious man ($\acute{o}$ $\delta\epsilon\iota\sigma\iota\delta a\acute{\iota}\mu\omega\nu$) and the atheist ($\acute{o}$ $\ddot{a}\theta\epsilon os$). Both are criticized, but the atheist is deemed less reprehensible than the superstitious man. However, the purpose of the treatise is not so much the hierarchical rating of the two ways of life against one another as an exploration of the dangers of departing from the moderate position of traditional piety (171f: $\mathring{\epsilon}\nu$ $\mu\acute{\epsilon}\sigma\omega$ $\kappa\epsilon\iota\mu\acute{\epsilon}\nu\eta\nu$ $\tau\grave{\eta}\nu$ $\epsilon\mathring{v}\sigma\acute{\epsilon}\beta\epsilon\iota a\nu$). Provocative

---

[11] See below, p. 263.　　[12] See pp. 300–1.　　[13] See Swain (1992b), 104–6.

contrast both engages the reader and provides an avenue for the discussion of key issues of religious practice.[14]

This use of *synkrisis* as a tool of discussion rather than as a means of grading is even clearer in the work entitled *Which are cleverer: land animals or sea animals?* This work begins with a dialogue between one Autoboulos, probably to be thought of as Plutarch's father, and his comrade Soklaros. Autoboulos argues that animals do indeed possess reason, and that Stoic arguments to the contrary are wrong (959a–965e). This is the main thesis of the work, but the bulk of it is given over to two staged speeches in which the superiority of first land animals (965e–975c) and then sea animals (975c–985c) is argued in turn. The purpose of the work is not the demonstration that one side is superior, but the demonstration of the central thesis: all animals have intelligence. By elucidating the differences between the two sorts of animals, their possession of common qualities and shared intelligence becomes clear. Autoboulos says as much in his initial exposition. The fact that some animals are more intelligent than others proves, he argues, that they all possess intelligence in some measure (962d–963a). 'The present argument which has brought about our young men's debate proves the point', he maintains. 'It is because they assume there is some difference (διαφορά) that one side can argue that land animals, the other that sea animals, are by nature more advanced towards virtue' (962d). After the two speeches in which arguments are put on both sides, Soklaros sums up with a quotation from Sophokles: '*How well the speech of those who strive against each other welds both together in the middle.* For when you combine what you have just said against each other, you will both be able to struggle well together against those who deprive animals of reason and intelligence' (985c).[15]

In fact, Plutarch's name appears to have been specifically associated with this kind of argumentation in which two sides of an issue are put and the audience is invited to chose the best. This method of exploring issues appears to have been advocated in a work by the sophist Favorinus of Arles (AD c.90–154) entitled *On the Academic disposition* (Περὶ τῆς Ἀκαδημαϊκῆς διαθέσεως). Favorinus' work was, significantly, also called *Plutarch* (Πλούταρχος). Another work by Favorinus, the *Against Epiktetos*, presented the Stoic philosopher Epiktetos debating with,

---

[14] In fact, Plutarch could also argue the case the other way around. In *Non posse*, he seems to consider superstition the lesser of the two evils. See Babut (1969b), 523; Nikolaidis (1991), 164–7.

[15] For *synkrisis* in other Plutarchan texts, see the brief survey in Valgiglio (1992), 4023–4.

significantly, Plutarch's slave Onesimos. Once again, the audience is invited to judge the best; Epiktetos appears to have emerged the loser from the debate.[16]

It is this use of *synkrisis* as a means to explore common qualities, as a means not of grading but of understanding, which is so central to the moralism of the *Parallel Lives* and is one of Plutarch's most original contributions to historiography. Plutarch will certainly have been influenced by the work of Cornelius Nepos, who placed whole books of Lives of Roman figures and non-Roman figures in parallel. Unfortunately, only the book *On eminent foreign leaders*, and two short Lives from the book *On Latin historians* (Cato the Elder and Atticus) survive. It is therefore impossible to gauge how, if at all, Nepos used this parallel structure as a literary tool. It seems likely that the use to which Plutarch puts *synkrisis* in the *Parallel Lives* as the defining structural principle for a historical work, and the sophistication with which he uses it to demonstrate and deconstruct morality, were unparalleled.[17]

It is surprising that Plutarch gives no explicit justification for his decision to write the Lives of Greeks and Romans in parallel. Perhaps the lost *Lives of Epameinondas and Scipio* contained such a programmatic statement. We do, however, possess one extant justification for the use of a synkritic structure in history at the start of another of his works the treatise *Virtues of women*:

Καὶ μὴν οὐκ ἔστιν ἀρετῆς γυναικείας καὶ ἀνδρείας ὁμοιότητα καὶ διαφορὰν ἄλλοθεν καταμαθεῖν μᾶλλον, ἢ βίους βίοις καὶ πράξεσι πράξεις ὥσπερ ἔργα μεγάλης τέχνης παρατιθέντας ἅμα καὶ σκοποῦντας, εἰ τὸν αὐτὸν ἔχει χαρακτῆρα καὶ τύπον ἡ Σεμιράμεως μεγαλοπραγμοσύνη τῇ Σεσώστριος . . . · ἐπειδὴ διαφοράς γέ τινας ἑτέρας ὥσπερ χροιὰς ἰδίας αἱ ἀρεταὶ διὰ τὰς φύσεις λαμβάνουσι καὶ συνεξομοιοῦνται τοῖς ὑποκειμένοις ἔθεσι καὶ κράσεσι σωμάτων καὶ τροφαῖς καὶ διαίταις· ἄλλως γὰρ ἀνδρεῖος ὁ Ἀχιλλεὺς ἄλλως ὁ Αἴας· καὶ φρόνησις Ὀδυσσέως οὐχ ὁμοία τῇ Νέστορος, οὐδὲ δίκαιος ὡσαύτως Κάτων καὶ Ἀγησίλαος, οὐδ᾿ Εἰρήνη φίλανδρος ὡς Ἄλκηστις οὐδὲ Κορνηλία μεγαλόφρων ὡς Ὀλυμπιάς. ἀλλὰ μὴ παρὰ τοῦτο πολλὰς καὶ διαφόρους ποιῶμεν ἀνδρείας καὶ φρονήσεις καὶ δικαιοσύνας, ἂν μόνον τοῦ λόγου τοῦ οἰκείου μηδεμίαν αἱ καθ᾿ ἕκαστον ἀνομοιότητες ἐκβιβάζωσι.

In fact it is not possible to learn better the similarity and difference between men's virtue and women's virtue in any other way than by setting lives beside

---

[16] These works are known from Galen's *On the best instruction* (Περὶ ἀρίστης διδασκαλίας: 1. 40–52 Kühn = Favorinus fr. 28 Barigazzi), an attack on the supposed inconsistency in the position of Favorinus and of Academics in general on the doctrine of 'suspension of judgement'. See Bowie (1997), 2–3; Opsomer (1997), esp. 18–23; Swain (1997), 177–9.

[17] On *synkrisis* in Nepos, see Geiger (1985), 94–5 and 118–19. See also below, p. 290–1.

lives and deeds beside deeds, like works of great art, and considering whether the magnificence of Semiramis has the same stamp and pattern as that of Sesostris ... For the virtues acquire certain other differences, as it were their own colours, because of the natures of the individuals concerned, and they assimilate themselves to the habits in question, their physical temperaments, upbringing, and way of life. For Achilles is brave in one way, Ajax in another. The wisdom of Odysseus is not the same as that of Nestor, nor is Cato just in the same way as Agesilaos, nor Eirene devoted to her husband in the same way as Alkestis, nor Cornelia high-minded in the same way as Olympias. But let us not on this account create many different braveries, wisdoms, and justices, provided only that their individual dissimilarities do not prevent any of them from attaining its proper estimation. (*Mul. Virt.* 243 b–d)

The language and thought allude to Plato's *Menon* (71e–73c), where Sokrates argues that different people may display different manifestations of virtue but that the essential quality of virtue remains the same. Here Plutarch adapts this Platonic, and by now uncontroversial, doctrine to formulate a justification for his use of *synkrisis* of the virtuous acts of women which will follow. Virtues like bravery, wisdom, and justice have different manifestations in different individuals; an understanding of these differences, attained through a comparative examination of these qualities as manifested in different figures, leads one, Plutarch claims, to a better understanding of the central meaning of the qualities themselves.[18] Comparison (*synkrisis*), or, as Plutarch puts it, 'setting lives beside lives and deeds beside deeds', is an important means to understanding both the nature of virtue as a whole and its manifestation in individual figures.[19] The series of narratives which follows provides numerous examples of bravery manifested in different ways. By comparing one with another, Plutarch implies, and in particular by comparing the examples of women's bravery with more well-known examples of men's bravery, a better understanding of the nature of bravery itself will be attained.

---

[18] For exploration of differences as a key to understanding what is shared, cf. *De Virt. Moral.* 449d–f and *Quaest. Conv.* 732b–c with Swain (1992*b*), 105.

[19] On this passage, see Stadter (1965), 9–12; Desideri (1992*b*), 4475–6. Cf. *Phok.* 3. 6–8, where Plutarch claims that, although the same quality manifests itself in different ways in different men, in the case of Phokion and Cato these differences are particularly difficult to find.

3. PLUTARCHAN *SYNKRISIS*: THE *PARALLEL LIVES*

Plutarch's use of *synkrisis* reaches its most pronounced form in the *Parallel Lives*, a collection structured, as the title implies, around large-scale *synkrisis* of Greeks and Romans. The rationale behind his choice of which figures to compare with which is not wholly clear. Sometimes the pairing will have been rather obvious, as in the case of Demosthenes and Cicero, Alexander and Caesar, and the unusual double pair Agis/Kleomenes and the Gracchi, who had already been brought together before Plutarch.[20] A few figures he had already compared in essays which predate the *Lives*.[21] It seems that in the case of six of the late-Republican Roman Lives, which Plutarch seems to have composed as a group, and towards the end of the collection, he must have started with the Roman subject and chosen the Greek to match.[22] But for most pairs we cannot be sure which Life was chosen first or how Plutarch arrived at the pairing.[23] What does seem clear, though, is that Plutarch thought that the two men chosen had enough similarities, combined with some significant differences, for their Lives, when told side-by-side, together to demonstrate or explore a common moral issue or set of issues. Similarity in the external circumstances of the two men certainly seems to have been a factor. Plutarch appears to begin the *Nikias–Crassus* with a reference to the parallel disasters which befell them: 'Since it seems to me to be reasonable to compare Nikias with Crassus and the Parthian

---

[20] On Cicero and Demosthenes, see Cic. *De Opt. Gen.* 13. Plutarch himself refers to a comparison of their style by the first-century BC critic Kaikilios of Kale Akte (Plut. *Dem.* 3. 2; cf. Lammert 1916). They are also compared by Quintilian (10. 1. 105–12) and by ps.-Longinos, *On the Sublime* (12. 4–5). See Geiger (1995a), 294–7. Agis/Kleomenes and the Gracchi are compared by Cicero (*De Off.* 2. 80). The coupling of Caesar and Alexander as world conquerors became a commonplace in the literature of the early principate: e.g. Strabo 13. 1. 27, C 594–5; Velleius 2. 41. 1–2; Lucan, *BC* 10. 20–48; cf. Livy 9. 16. 19–9. 19. 17, and the anecdotes which connected the two figures: Suet. *Div. Jul.* 7. 1; Plut. *Caes.* 11. 5–6. On Roman conquerors regularly compared to Alexander, see Michel (1976); P. Green (1978); Samsaris (1990).

[21] Aristeides and Cato Major (*De Cohib. Ira* 463e); Themistokles and Camillus (*De Lat. Viv.* 1129b–c); Lykourgos and Numa (fr. 47 Sandbach).   [22] See p. 21 n. 22.

[23] Some of Plutarch's statements seem at first sight to indicate that in some cases he chose the Roman subject first, and the Greek to match (e.g. *Thes.* 1. 4–5; *Ag./Kleom.* 2. 7–9; *Kim.* 3. 1; *Sert.* 1. 11), others the reverse (*Pub.* 1. 1; *Nik.* 1. 1; *Phil.* 21. 12–*Flam.* 1. 1). It seems probable, however, that in these statements Plutarch intended to do no more than point to some of the similarities which led him to pair the two subjects, not indicate which he chose first. On the whole question of Plutarch's choice and pairing of subjects, see Ziegler (1949), 261–2 (=1951, 898–9); Geiger (1981), esp. 85–99; Frazier (1987); Desideri (1992b), 4478–81; Valgiglio (1992), 4028–30.

disaster with the Sicilian ...' (1. 1).[24] But for Plutarch, analysis of a man's deeds is the chief way to understand and evaluate his character. Similarity in the circumstances of life facilitates this comparison of character, as the reader observes the different reactions of two men to similar trials.

The case studies of this book have demonstrated the importance of reading the two Lives of a pair together. Recent attention has been focused on the examination of individual pairs of Lives to demonstrate the way in which the pairing affects our understanding of them.[25] Important here is the principle of pattern and variation: the first Life sets a pattern which is then exploited and varied in the second.[26] As Plutarch had claimed in the *Virtues of women*, by placing in parallel different examples of the same virtue or vice, a clearer understanding of the nature of that quality is attained. The concern in the *Parallel Lives* is less to evaluate which protagonist was better than to explore the issues raised by both Lives. An appreciation of the importance of the synkritic structure of the *Parallel Lives* is vital if we are to understand the rationale behind Plutarch's selection and deployment of the source material at his disposal; as we have seen, very often Plutarch is moulding one incident to form a parallel with an incident in the paired Life. Furthermore, an appreciation of the synkritic structure is vital for our understanding of the way in which moral truth is conveyed or moral questions raised across paired Lives. By placing alongside each other Lives of two individuals, drawn from different periods and different cultures, attention is focused on the constants: the character and moral status

---

[24] Something may be lost from the text before this point: see p. 22.
[25] The seminal discussion of the effect of *synkrisis* between paired Lives is Erbse (1956). Other theoretical analyses of this kind of *synkrisis* include: Bucher-Isler (1972), 74–8; Pelling (1986b); Brenk (1992), 4375–80; Desideri (1992b); Larmour (1992), 4154–74. Studies of *synkrisis* in particular pairs of Lives include: on the *Thes.-Rom.*: Larmour (1988); *Them.-Cam.*: Stadter (1983–4); Larmour (1992), 4174–4200; *Kim.-Luc.*: Fuscagni (1989), 43–52; Swain (1992c); *Per.-Fab.*: Stadter (1975); *Nik.-Crass.*: Scardigli (1987a); *Dem.-Cic.*: Erbse (1956), 406–13 (=1979, 487–94); Moles (1988), 19–26; Geiger (1995a), 297–300; *Alex.-Caes.*: Erbse (1956), 405–6 (=1979, 486–7); Hamilton (1969), p. xxxiv; Harris (1970), 193–7; *Lys.-Sulla*: Stadter (1992a); *Ages.-Pomp.*: Hillman (1994); Harrison (1995), 99–102; *Pel.-Marc.*: Georgiadou (1992a); *Aem.-Tim.*: Talbert (1974), 19–21; Geiger (1981), 97–102; Swain (1989c); Desideri (1989); *Dion.-Brut.*: Erbse (1956), 413–16 (=1979, 494–7); *Phok.-Cato Min.*: Geiger (1988), 254–6 (=1993, 315–19); Bearzot (1993), 85–8; *Demetr.-Ant.*: Harris (1970), 197–9; Pelling (1986b), 89–96; (1988b), 18–26; Brenk (1992), 4380–4402; Harrison (1995), 95–9; *Sert.-Eum.*: Bosworth (1992); *Phil.-Flam.*: Pelling (1986b), 84–9; (1989), 208–13; Swain (1988); Walsh (1992); cf. Pelling (1997c). On the *Ag./Kleom.-Gracchi*: Magnino (1991), 55–72. On the interaction between the *Caius Gracchus* and *Tiberius Gracchus* (but not between the *Gracchi* and the *Ag./Kleom.*): Ingenkamp (1992a).
[26] Pelling (1986b), 93–6.

of the two subjects.²⁷ This is brought out most clearly in the formal prologues which precede about half of the extant pairs and which tend to focus on the similarities between the characters of the two men, revealed in their reactions to sometimes similar events.²⁸ One of the main themes of this book has been to demonstrate how *synkrisis* across paired Lives assists Plutarch's exploration of moral themes and sometimes, as in the case of most of the texts we have examined, contributes to a destabilizing of the ideal boundaries between virtue and vice, to a questioning and re-evaluation of simple moral assumptions. The encouragement to compare the second Life with the first is, as has been seen, one of the key strategies by which Plutarch explores ethical issues.

Within individual Lives, it is true, *synkrisis* is often used on a small scale to bring out the characteristics of the subject, usually to his favour: a rhetorical technique.²⁹ Thus, in a strikingly enkomiastic section of the *Life of Caesar*, Julius Caesar is explicitly compared with numerous past and contemporary Roman generals, to all of whom he is superior (*Caes.* 17. 3–5). Sertorius' skills as a general, and his bad luck, are brought out by explicit comparison with the greatest generals before him (*Sert.* 1. 8–10). At other times the encouragement to compare is implicit. Thus Sertorius' skill as a general is brought out by an implicit comparison with Metellus (*Sert.* 13. 1–3), and Perikles' military sureness (ἀσφάλεια) is implicitly contrasted with Tolmides' foolhardiness in undertaking the Koroneia campaign (*Per.* 18. 1–3). Fabius is compared briefly with Diogenes for his ability to undergo ridicule (*Fab.* 10. 1). Phokion is set against Demades, who disgracefully flatters the Macedonians.³⁰ Pausanias' treason, arrogance, and severity throw into relief the mildness and justice of Kimon (*Kim.* 6. 1–7). On a larger scale, an implicit comparison with his Macedonian opponent Perseus brings out the virtue and superiority of Aemilius. In particular, the miserliness of Perseus (12. 3–13. 3), itself contrasted with the willing use of money by his ancestors Philip and Alexander (12. 9–11), brings out by contrast the generosity of Aemilius towards the Greeks, and his financial rectitude (28. 1–13). More importantly, Perseus functions as an example of the instability of

---

[27] Jones (1971), 103–9; cf. Deremetz (1990), 54–62. Brenk (1992), 4377–9, suggests that the use of *synkrisis* is linked to a Platonic belief in the reincarnation of the soul; at any rate, it implies a belief that the same patterns in history recur.

[28] Most noticeably in the *Phok.-Cato Min.* Cf. *Aem.* 1. 6; *Dem.* 3. 1; *Pel.-Marc.* 1. 2–3.

[29] On internal *synkrisis*, see Leo (1901), 151–2; Russell (1966a), 150–1; Wardman (1974), 27–34; Frazier (1992), 4512–14; Valgiglio (1992), 4024. Georgiadou (1992b), 4620, also sees synkritic tendencies in Plutarch's description of appearance.

[30] See above, pp. 135–6.

fortune; when the two men meet, Aemilius sees Perseus' fate as a warning to himself (27. 1–6). When disaster does strike Aemilius, in the form of the death of his sons, he bears it calmly (36. 1–9), as he had urged Perseus to do (26. 8–12).[31]

Internal Plutarchan *synkrisis*, then, owes much to rhetoric, especially to speeches of praise and blame. But it is also used in a much more subtle way, where the effect is not to demonstrate superiority but to encourage reflection. We have noticed how implicit comparison between Lysander and Kallikratidas functions to raise and explore moral issues.[32] Similarly, Plutarch uses *synkrisis* between episodes as well as between people to demonstrate character or encourage reflection. So, for example, Plutarch may construct a Life with two major climaxes or focuses which are implicitly compared. Thus, by describing the Parthian campaign of Antony at length (*Ant.* 37–52) and compressing the intervening narrative, he creates a parallel for the Aktion campaign (59–69). In both campaigns, Antony's love for Kleopatra causes disaster. In Parthia his skills as a general allow him to retrieve matters. His flight from Aktion stands in contrast.[33] In a similar way, Pompey's two returns to Rome in 71 and 62 BC are implicitly contrasted with each other (*Pomp.* 21–3; 43–9).[34] In both, Pompey returns to celebrate a triumph, and scotches popular fears that he will take power by force (21. 5–8; 43. 1–5). There are hints in the first episode of his inability to deal with political life (23. 1–6), and of conflict with colleagues. But he maintains his dignity and leaves Rome successful. On his next return, these hints have become reality, as his domination by Crassus and Caesar demonstrates. How much better it would have been, Plutarch muses in a rare first-person intervention, if Pompey had died at the height of his power (46. 1–4).

4. THE 'FORMAL' *SYNKRISEIS*

The most striking aspect of Plutarch's adaptation of the synkritic tendencies of previous and contemporary Greek thought is in the concluding *synkriseis* which follow most pairs of *Parallel Lives*.[35] Little has

---

[31] Swain (1989c), 324–5. Cf. Aigeus as a contrast with Theseus in the *Thes.* (esp. 3. 5–7; 12. 2–6; 17. 1–4): Pérez Jiménez (1994).
[32] Especially *Lys.* 5. 7–8; 6. 2–3; 7. 5–6. See pp. 164, 168–72, and 180–1.
[33] Pelling (1988b), 220–1.
[34] Hillman (1992), 137; (1994), 259–60.
[35] The term σύγκρισις is used by Plutarch when he introduces some of these closing

been said so far about these so-called 'formal' *synkriseis*, partly because they are missing from two of the four pairs (*Pyrrhos–Marius, Phokion–Cato Minor*) which we have discussed in detail. It is to these formal *synkriseis* that we now turn. Here, in a short closing section, the subjects of the preceding two Lives are explicitly compared and assessed in relation to each other. The influence of contemporary rhetorical practice is clear, especially the tradition of writing two speeches which argue opposing theses in turn, or a single speech which presents in turn two sides of the same argument. Most Plutarchan *synkriseis* are structured around arguments in favour of each of the two subjects in turn. Many of them have a transition roughly half way through, where the direction of the argument changes:[36] each figure in turn has a case argued on his behalf. Some of Suetonius' *Caesars*, such as *Tiberius, Caius*, and *Nero*, share this rhetorical structure, containing as they do a distinct turning point: in the early part of these Lives the presentation is fairly positive; after the transition, material is marshalled for the purpose of denigration.[37]

Formal *synkriseis* are to be found at the end of most, but not all, pairs of *Parallel Lives*. There are no formal *synkriseis* to the *Themistokles–Camillus, Pyrrhos–Marius, Phokion–Cato Minor*, and *Alexander–Caesar*. The reason why these pairs lack a formal *synkrisis* is unclear. The most likely explanation is that the *synkriseis* to these Lives have simply been lost.[38] Previous ages, which like ours have tended to regard the *synkriseis*

comparisons (e.g. *Arist.-Cato Maj.* 1. 2; *Nik.-Crass.* 1. 1; *Lys.-Sull.* 1. 1; *Flam.* 21. 15; *Sol.-Pub.* 1. 1). The cognate verb (συγκρίνειν) can mean no more than 'put side by side', but it may be that Plutarch draws on the associations of the root verb κρίνειν, to distinguish or judge. At any rate, σύγκρισις seems to imply exploration of differences, whereas παραβάλλειν or its cognates, which often occur in the openings of the Lives themselves (e.g. *Thes.* 1. 5; *Pub.* 1. 1; *Nik.* 1. 1; *Phok.* 3. 6; *Ag./Kleom.* 2. 9; *Gracch.* 1. 1), as well as in the formal *synkriseis* (e.g. *Thes.-Rom.* 1. 4; *Kim.-Luc.* 3. 5; *Ages.-Pomp.* 3. 1; *Phil.-Flam.* 1. 1), implies sameness and equality (cf. *Kim.-Luc.* 1. 5: ὁμοιῶσαι). Cf. Costanza (1956), 130–2. But cf. *Per.-Fab.* 3. 7, where παραβάλλειν and ἀσύγκριτος are used in the same context, and *Lys.* 7. 5 and *Cato Min.* 3. 10 where παραβάλλειν implies recognition of differences. Discussions of the formal *synkriseis* include Prieth (1908); Stiefenhofer (1914–16); Focke (1923); Costanza (1956); Larmour (1992), 4154–62; Swain (1992b); Boulogne (1994), 62–9.

[36] e.g. *Thes.-Rom.* 3. 3.–4. 1; *Arist.-Cato Maj.* 4. 1; *Kim.-Luc.* 2. 6–3. 1; *Dion-Brut.* 3. 6; *Lys.-Sull.* 3. 8–4. 1.

[37] *Tib.* 42. 1; *Cal.* 22. 1; *Nero* 19. 3. Suetonius' *Caesars* have much in common with rhetorical speeches of attack or defence, as *exempla* are marshalled to support a case, either to denigrate or to praise the subject. Enkomiastic treatments are given, for example, to Augustus (Wallace-Hadrill 1983, 110–12) and Titus (Luck 1964). The *Nero*, on the other hand, includes many of the standard Roman *topoi* of invective: Lounsbury (1991); Barton (1994).

[38] Costanza (1956), esp. 134–53, on the *Alex.-Caes.*

as at an inferior literary level to the preceding narrative, may have been less careful in their transmission of these sections. A strong argument for this can be made in the case of the *Alexander–Caesar*. There is good reason to think that the end of the *Alexander* and the start of the *Caesar* are lost. The text of the *Caesar* seems to begin in mid-sentence, with no connective particle, and is therefore almost certainly corrupt.[39] Furthermore, the text as it stands unusually gives no treatment to Caesar's family or boyhood. The ending of the *Alexander*, which stood immediately before the opening of the *Caesar* in the codices, is probably also lost.[40] The twelfth-century Byzantine writer Zonaras seems to have made use of an epitome of Plutarch's *Alexander–Caesar*;[41] part of the lost ending of the Alexander seems to be paraphrased in Zonaras 4. 14.[42] It is therefore quite plausible that the *synkrisis* to this pair shared the fate of the other lost parts of the book of which it would once have formed the concluding element.

It is, however, possible that for some reason Plutarch avoided writing a comparison to these particular four pairs.[43] It is clear that on the question of the order of Lives in a pair he was prepared occasionally to vary his usual pattern: in three pairs, the *Coriolanus–Alkibiades*, *Aemilius–Timoleon*, and *Sertorius–Eumenes*, the usual order of Lives is reversed so that the Roman comes before the Greek. This should caution us against assuming that in the case of the formal *synkriseis* Plutarch could not break out of the structure he himself had imposed. Chistopher Pelling has suggested that the endings of three of the four pairs which lack *synkriseis* are in some sense unusual. The presence of a long reflective passage at the end of the *Marius* (46. 1–5), which has relevance to Pyrrhos as well as Marius, may suggest one reason for the lack of a

---

[39] Pelling (1984a), 33. The absence of δέ in the first line of the *Caesar*, which commonly marks the transition from the first to the second Life of a pair, would support this conclusion, although it should be noted that *Rom*. 1. 1, *Alk*. 1. 1, *Mar*. 1. 1, and *Ant*. 1. 1 also lack this particle: see Watkins (1984), 1–2.

[40] Cf. Ziegler (1935), 387–90.

[41] Manfredini (1992b and 1993).

[42] Pelling (1973). Curiously, the opening of Suetonius' *Divus Julius*, which may have contained a dedication to Septicius Clarus, is probably also lost: see Townend (1959), 285.

[43] It is possible that a lost Plutarchan *synkrisis* may have influenced the lengthy comparison of Alexander and Caesar at the end of Appian's second book of the *Civil Wars* (*BC* 2. 149–54). Cf. *BC* 2. 14~*Caes*. 14. 8 (forms of διαμαστροπεύομαι occurs in both); *BC* 2. 27~*Caes*. 30. 2 (ὥσπερ ἀθλητὴν ἀνθοβολοῦντες). But the coupling of Alexander and Caesar was itself not uncommon. Furthermore, if Appian's decision to compare Alexander and Caesar was influenced by Plutarch's text, he may have been as much aiming to make up for the lack of a formal *synkrisis* as influenced by an existing one. Cf. Gabba (1956), 226–8, who is rightly sceptical.

formal *synkrisis* to the *Pyrrhos–Marius*. This passage is, unusually, explicitly critical of Marius and by implication Pyrrhos, a feature usually reserved for the *synkrisis*.[44] The final chapters of the *Cato Minor* are unusually dramatic and contain a strong implicit *synkrisis* with the ending of the *Phokion*: Cato, despite his philosophical ideals, does not die as calmly as Phokion. Both Lives end with some details about the children of the subjects. Here the tables are turned: Phokion's son was worthless and known only for buying a prostitute from a brothel (*Phok.* 38. 3–4); Cato's son, though equally debauched, dies fighting at Philippoi, and his daughter becomes the wife of Brutus—who killed Cato's enemy Caesar; she likewise dies bravely (*Cato Min.* 73. 1–7). The contrast threatens the superiority of Phokion over Cato which the Lives have suggested: a destabilization which is so characteristic of the formal *synkriseis* themselves. The *Alexander–Caesar* ends with Caesar's 'great guardian spirit' (ὁ μέγας αὐτοῦ δαίμων) tracking down and taking vengeance on all Caesar's murderers (*Caes.* 69. 2–14). If, as Pelling suggests, the end of the *Alexander* is preserved in Zonaras 4. 14, then the end of the *Caesar* forms a strong implicit contrast with it. In the endings of both Lives as preserved, death is in the air, an atmosphere of portents and the supernatural. Alexander, in the Zonaras fragment, attempts on his death-bed to exploit this by drowning himself in the Euphrates in order to foster a myth of his own ascension to heaven. His wife prevents him and deflates both his pretensions and the daimonic atmosphere. In contrast, at the end of the *Caesar* the divine atmosphere is deflated by Caesar himself, but erupts in omens and portents and in the activity of the supernatural which avenges his death. As Pelling suggests, the contrast is 'open and thought-provoking'.[45]

These four cases are exceptional. In all others, the *synkriseis* form an integral part of the Plutarchan book: many books begin with a 'formal' prologue which introduces some of the themes relevant to both Lives,[46] and end with a 'formal' *synkrisis*, which weighs the two subjects against

[44] See above, pp. 107–9.
[45] Pelling (1997a), 244–50. The reason for the lack of the formal *synkrisis* for the *Them.-Cam.* is, as Pelling admits, rather harder to explain (though see next n.). The explanations for these four cases offered by Erbse (1956), 403–6 (= 1979, 484–7) are unconvincing; cf. also Van der Valk (1982), 329; Larmour (1992), 4174–6.
[46] For the term book (βιβλίον), see *Per.* 2. 5; *Dion* 2. 7. Formal prologues begin only 13 of the surviving 22 books: see Stadter (1988), esp. 283–93. There is some reason for thinking that the *Them.-Cam.* may have originally possessed a formal introduction which has since been lost. As Costanza (1956), 133, points out, the connective particle δέ stands as its second word; no other book begins in such a way. The loss of its formal prologue perhaps makes the loss of its *synkrisis* more plausible.

each other. The *synkrisis* and the formal prologue knot together the two strands of the Plutarchan book, which for the course of the two Lives had run separately. The transitions from formal prologue to first Life, from first Life to second, and from second Life to *synkrisis* are usually clearly signalled, but there is some evidence that the titles which appear in modern texts to mark such transitions may not be authentic.[47] At any rate, Plutarchan books must be read as a whole. In general, where they exist, formal prologues bring out the similarities between the two subjects; *synkriseis* bring out the differences, though there is considerable variation from this pattern.[48] The interest within the *synkriseis* is ethical, in the ancient sense of the word. That is, the focus is on the analysis and evaluation of the character of the two subjects, and on the deeds by which their character revealed itself, rather than on the circumstances of their lives.[49]

The *synkriseis*, then, assess and compare the subjects of the two Lives, and encourage the reader, often explicitly, to make judgements on the subjects' conduct. Modern readers have often been rather unimpressed by the *synkriseis*, though attempts to dispute their authenticity have proved unsuccessful.[50] Explicit moralizing, at least in historiography or biography, is not highly regarded in our age. But speeches, or literary works purporting to record speeches, or, as here, written in the form of speeches, were common forms of literature in the age of Plutarch. Historical personages were often the subjects of these orations: the elder Seneca in his book of *Suasoriae* records numerous such exercises, in which the declaimer purports to give advice to a historical character regarding some decision or future event. Many Greek authors composed speeches on topics drawn from history and purporting to be for delivery to audiences contemporary with the events.[51] So Plutarch's original readers would certainly not have had the same prejudices to overcome against rhetoric as their modern counterparts, although it must be

---

[47] Ziegler (1907), 128–32; Stiefenhofer (1914–16), 480–5. Notably, only one poor manuscript (Paris. 1675) includes titles between second Life and *synkrisis*. Photios, furthermore, (*Biblioth. Cod.* 245, 396b22–5) quotes from *Sert.-Eum.* 2. 5 simply as 'from the *Eumenes*' (ἐκ τοῦ Εὐμένους).

[48] Notably, where there is no formal prologue the *synkrisis* sometimes brings out similarities too: see Stiefenhofer (1914–16), 468–73, with the criticism of Swain (1992b), 106–10. On the relationship between formal prologue and *synkrisis*, see also Erbse (1956), 398–403 (=1979, 478–84); Larmour (1992), 4157–8.

[49] But similarities of circumstance are sometimes mentioned in the formal prologue: *Nik.* 1. 1; *Dion* 2. 1–2; *Dem.* 3. 3–5; *Sert.* 1. 1–12.

[50] e.g. by Hirzel (1912), 70–3: refuted by Stiefenhofer (1914–16); cf. also Costanza (1956).

[51] e.g. Ailios Aristeides, Libanios, Sopratos. See Russell (1983), 106–28.

admitted that the combination of historiographical narrative and rhetorical analysis in one text was, even for its time, unusual and has remained virtually unique.

Modern critics, however, have often regarded the *synkriseis* as simplistic reductions of the two preceding narratives into a rigid scheme which does not do justice to the complexities and subtleties of what had gone before.[52] It is certainly the case that the *synkriseis* do not provide a good summary of the themes and issues explored in the Lives: there is often a marked divergence between the themes and interests which had emerged in the preceding narratives and those which appear in the *synkrisis*. Sometimes, indeed, there are even contradictions in substance between *synkrisis* and Life. It is these divergences and contradictions between Life and *synkrisis* which will be the focus of the rest of this chapter. The lack of 'fit' between the *synkrisis* and the Lives which it follows serves an important function within the book, and within Plutarch's moral purpose as a whole. The *synkriseis* are not intended as closing summaries; that is not the way Plutarch himself presents them. For him, the *synkrisis* brings out the 'differences' between the two subjects, just as the prologue had brought out the 'similarities'. To regard them simply as naïve, or even failed, summaries of the moral import of the narrative is to miss the point, and to do them and Plutarch an injustice. The past is constructed in the *synkrisis* in a way different from that in the narrative. The reader sees the past from two different angles: it is the divergences and differences which make the *synkriseis* so thought-provoking, and which cause the reader to reflect on issues of right and wrong.

5. ARGUING A CASE IN TURN: EQUALITY IN THE 'FORMAL' *SYNKRISEIS*

We now turn to the text of the *synkriseis* themselves. As we have noted, many *synkriseis* are structured, like paired speeches, around arguments in favour of each of the two subjects. Towards the middle comes a distinct turning-point in which the direction of the argument changes.[53] This structure can be seen particularly clearly in the *synkrisis* to the *Theseus–Romulus*. An initial sentence marks the transition from narrative to *synkrisis* (1. 1): 'Such are the noteworthy things about Romulus

[52] e.g. Moles (1988), 20 and 25; Pelling (1988*b*), 19–20.
[53] Cf. Van der Valk (1982), 329–30; Walsh (1992), 221–5; Boulogne (1994), 62–9.

and Theseus which I have happened to learn.' Plutarch then begins arguing the case for Theseus with a series of clearly signalled points (πρῶτον ... ἔπειτα ...). Then comes the transition to arguments in favour of Romulus. Plutarch flags the change clearly: 'So one would give these votes to Theseus. But for Romulus, first, there is this great thing in his favour ...' (3. 3.–4. 1). Plutarch goes on to cast doubt as to whether Romulus was really responsible for the death of his brother Remus, adding that he saved his mother and helped his grandfather. In contrast, he fixes on Theseus the blame for the death of his father, Aigeus, much more firmly than he had done in the narrative, actually here accusing him of parricide and dismissing alternative explanations (5. 1–2; cf. *Thes.* 22. 1–4). The *synkrisis* ends by suggesting that Theseus' birth may have been unfavourable to the gods (6. 7).[54] There is no general summing-up: the reader is left to make the final valuation.

In other cases, the transitions from arguments in favour of one subject to arguments in favour of the other are handled more subtly, often by means of a reassessment of a particular moral judgement. This is the case, for example, in the *synkrisis* to the *Lysander–Sulla*. Lysander is initially preferred. The transition occurs in the discussion of the two men's attitude to money (3. 8): Lysander was much more commendable, but then his honest handing over of war-booty to the state actually led to the corruption of his country's morals. From this point on, Sulla is now preferred. The *synkrisis* to the *Kimon–Lucullus* begins by favouring Kimon. The transition occurs after a discussion of Lucullus' bad relations with his soldiers. 'Or is this factor', Plutarch asks, 'shared by Kimon too?' (2. 6). Kimon, he goes on, also had bad relations with his citizens; perhaps, he continues, such bad relations are inevitable. Plutarch concludes, 'So both should equally be cleared of guilt in this respect' (2. 7). At this point the section favouring Lucullus begins.[55]

This balanced structure of the *synkriseis* provides a key to understanding the inclusion of incidents or interpretations which do not occur at all in the narrative. In the *synkrisis* to the *Nikias–Crassus*, Plutarch seems to label one such new detail as an 'afterthought'. He is discussing

---

[54] On the *synkrisis* to the *Thes.-Rom.* see Larmour (1988); Pérez Jiménez (1994), 230.

[55] Cf. also the *synkrisis* to the *Arist.-Cato Maj.* (below), and the similar transitions at *Dion-Brut.* 3. 6 (ἢ τοῦτ' ἀντιστρέφει πρῶτον;), where the issue is that Brutus was a friend of Caesar. Some *synkriseis* do not contain such a clear division, and preference for each of the two subjects is intermingled: e.g. *Lyk.-Num.*, *Sol.-Pub.*, *Per.-Fab.*, *Aem.-Tim.*, and *Pel.-Marc.* The first two *synkriseis* are somewhat unusual cases anyway. That of the *Lyk.-Num.* is as much about the states which they created as about themselves as individuals. On the *synkrisis* to the *Solon-Pub.*, see below, p. 260.

the two men's political conduct (2. 1: τὰ πολιτεύματα). Nikias, Plutarch tells us, did no acts of wickedness: rather, he was himself deceived by Alkibiades. Crassus, on the other hand, was faithless and violent. Among the incidents which Plutarch mentions to support this argument is Crassus' punching in the mouth of a senator who was speaking against him: a fact, he explains, 'which had passed us by in our narrative' (*Nik.- Crass.* 2. 3).[56] Plutarch's explanation may well be true, but there is more to it than that. The rhetorical nature and structure of the *synkrisis* demand that ammunition is used in favour of, or against, each of the protagonists in turn. Anecdotes which have not been selected for inclusion in the narrative may now gain a function in the *synkrisis*.

We can now, therefore, understand a little better the two instances where new details are introduced into the *synkrisis* to the *Lysander–Sulla*. In the first, Plutarch quotes three examples of Sulla's brutality to his friends after he had seized supreme power. Two of them—his stripping Pompey of his military command and his attempted removal of Dolabella's naval command—are not mentioned in Sulla's Life (2. 7). In the second instance, to illustrate Sulla's lack of temperance (σωφροσύνη), especially concerning money, Plutarch uses an incident, hitherto unknown, from the time of the proscriptions. When at an auction of confiscated property someone outbids one of Sulla's cronies, he is shown, with some irony, to cry out how unfair it is, if he is not to be allowed to dispose of his 'spoils' as he wants (3. 5).[57] Both instances are introduced into that part of the *synkrisis* which is arguing Lysander's case against Sulla. To fulfil this aim, Plutarch is using new material which contributes to the blackening of Sulla's character.

As these last examples will have made clear, Plutarch did not always try in the *synkriseis* to see the best qualities of his subjects, or to present their shortcomings with the same sympathy as he had done in the narratives. This is a harder-edged, more critical analysis. We can relate this to the generic origins and identity of the *synkriseis*. We have seen that the writer of historical narrative was expected to be no more critical than absolutely necessary. He should display no malice (κακοήθεια).[58] But the speaker in a rhetorical display speech was expected ruthlessly to marshal all the possible arguments which would prove his case. So in the

[56] ὅπερ ἡμᾶς ἐν τῇ διηγήσει παρελήλυθε. Pelling (1988b), 20, regards these anecdotes as afterthoughts. He lists seven such episodes: *Nik.-Crass.* 2. 3 (cited as 4. 4); *Phil.-Flam.* 2. 6; *Dem.-Cic.* 4. 4; *Lys.-Sulla* 2. 7; 3. 5; *Lyk.-Num.* 1. 10–11; *Pel.-Marc.* 1. 7–8. Cf. Erbse (1956), 416–19 (=1979, 497–500); Pelling (1986b), 88–9; Larmour (1992), 4161–2.

[57] Δεινά γ'... καὶ τυραννικὰ πάσχω: possibly echoing Xen. *Hell.* 1. 7. 12.

[58] See pp. 56–9.

synkriseis often both subjects are criticized, and actions or character-traits which had been passed over with little comment in the narrative are singled out for censure. But, despite this greater willingness to criticize, the two subjects emerge, on the whole, fairly equal.[59] This equality is one of the most striking features of the Plutarchan *synkriseis*, although it is perhaps not altogether surprising. The contemporary rhetorician Theon, in his discussion of *synkrisis* as a rhetorical exercise, argues that there must be no great imbalance between the objects of a comparison. 'The man who wondered whether Achilles or Thersites was braver would be ridiculous' (*Progym.* 9, Spengel, ii. 112. 27–9).[60] In fact none of the *synkriseis* comes down without reservation in favour of one subject or another overall. There are only a few cases where any general assessment is made at the end of a *synkrisis*, but even in these cases it is not clear whether one subject is to be preferred over the other.[61] Occasionally, it is true, an overall preference for one subject over the other does seem to be implicit in the discussion. The most obvious example is the *synkrisis* to the *Solon–Publicola*, where Publicola seems to emerge as morally superior to Solon.[62] But these are the exceptions; normally no overall preference is either expressed or discernible. Most striking, as we shall see, is the *synkrisis* to the *Coriolanus–Alkibiades*, where, although Alkibiades has been consistently preferred, in the final summary Plutarch suddenly turns the tables and praises Coriolanus.

Equality of treatment is particularly clear in the comparison of Kimon and Lucullus. Here Plutarch tries hard to give the luxury-loving Lucullus as favourable a treatment as Kimon. In the Life, as we have seen, Plutarch had presented Lucullus' retirement into luxury and pleasure as a form of philosophical retreat. His house became a centre for Greek learning.[63] In the *synkrisis* Plutarch is prepared to be much more critical, and uses Lucullus' behaviour in old age as ammunition against him in the first half of the *synkrisis*. But he also suggests a possible way in which an issue which condemned Lucullus (his extravagance in old age) might be reinterpreted more to his favour: if Lucullus, like Kimon, had died at the height of his power, he might have seemed as good as Kimon

---

[59] A fact noted by Montaigne in his 'Defence de Seneque [*sic*] et de Plutarque' (*Essais* 2. 32).
[60] See above p. 244. Cf. Focke (1923), 330–2; Swain (1992*b*), 102.
[61] *Phil.-Flam.* 3. 5; *Cor.-Alk.* 5. 2; *Lys.-Sulla* 5. 6; *Ag./Kleom.-Gracchi* 5. 7.
[62] Less obvious is the preference for Flamininus in the *synkrisis* to the *Phil.-Flam.*, for Nikias in that to the *Nik.-Cras.*, and for Demetrios in that to the *Demetr.-Ant.*
[63] See above, p. 60.

did (*Kim.-Luc.* 1. 7–8). This particular argument has something of the unexpected or paradoxical about it, as so often in these sections; the ingenuity of the argument is part of their attraction. The first half of the *synkrisis*, then, favours Kimon, and so in the second half Plutarch argues that Lucullus had more success in war (3. 1–5). The argument is rather dubious, partly resting as it does on the *scale* of the achievements rather than on their significance or on the skill required to do them. But it is a form of argument which recurs in many *synkriseis*, where the Roman is often judged superior in military matters.[64] The effort which Plutarch makes here to show Lucullus as equal to Kimon may, it is true, be related to Lucullus' links with Plutarch's home town of Chaironeia (cf. *Kim.* 1. 1–2. 5). But it has much more to do with the need for equality of treatment within the *synkrisis*. This equality is most clearly expressed in the closing words of this *synkrisis*, and of the book: 'The result is that, if one looks at all sides of the argument, it is difficult to judge between them (δυσδιαίτητον εἶναι τὴν κρίσιν), since even the divine seems to have been well-disposed to both, making it clear in advance what one should perform and what the other should avoid. So even the vote of the gods seems to have gone to them both as men by nature good and god-like' (3. 6). The final sentence asserts not only their equality, but gives a surprisingly positive twist to the *synkrisis*.[65] This kind of closural dissonance is something we shall meet again.

Equality of treatment is also clear in the comparison of Aristeides and Cato the Elder. The first half of the *synkrisis* argues in favour of Cato. Plutarch plainly struggled to find arguments in Cato's favour and so, as often in the *synkriseis*, sees what advantages or disadvantages were provided by the circumstances in which the two men lived. On this analysis, Cato can be rated superior because he had much greater competition in obtaining high office than did Aristeides (*Arist.-Cato Maj.* 1. 2–4). More surprisingly, Cato's minor military action at Thermopylai in 191 BC is rated superior to Aristeides' successes at Marathon, Salamis, and Plataia, on the grounds that Cato, unlike Aristeides, achieved his success without the help of others (2. 1–3). Furthermore, Cato, thanks to his eloquence, was never disgraced in all his numerous court cases, unlike Aristeides who suffered ostracism (2. 4–5). Then the discussion turns to household management, and once again Cato is commended: he left his family well-provided for, unlike Aristeides (3. 1–5). It is within this discussion of household management that the transition occurs. 'Or does this first

[64] e.g. *Lys.-Sulla* 4. 1; *Ages.-Pomp.* 3. 1.
[65] Cf. Lavery (1994), 272.

point', Plutarch asks, 'invite discussion?' (4. 1);[66] he goes on to show that Aristeides' self-sufficient poverty could be seen as more commendable than Cato's eagerness to make money (4. 1–7). The transition within the discussion of this individual point turns out to function as a transition within the whole *synkrisis*: Aristeides is consistently preferred from this point on. Now Plutarch reinterprets the two men's military actions. In the first half of the *synkrisis*, Cato had come out better, because he achieved his military success without the help of others. In contrast, in the second half, Aristeides' victories are said to be greater, and his co-operation with Themistokles—in contrast to Cato's rivalry with Scipio—is singled out for special commendation (5. 1–4). In the final chapter of the *synkrisis*, Plutarch returns to the theme of the two men's households, and now criticizes Cato for marrying a low-born woman late in his life (6. 1–3). Once again, Plutarch shows himself capable of looking at the same themes—in this case the two men's military successes and their households—and interpreting or reinterpreting them as the rhetorical structure of the *synkrisis* requires.

Why does Plutarch put such weight on equality of treatment in the *synkrisis*? One possible answer to this is to see it as part of some sort of cultural programme. The desire to show Roman and Greek subjects as equal could be seen as part of an attempt to demonstrate the equality of Roman and Greek culture in general and to reconcile the two parts of the Roman Empire to each other.[67] Or it could be seen as a means of asserting Greek cultural superiority. At stake would be not so much the comparative worth of individual Greek or Roman figures, but the supremacy of the Greek values by which both are judged. We shall explore this issue in the next and final chapter. But the more important reason for equality is surely that it focuses the reader's attention not so much on the individual subjects—which was a better man?—as on the virtues and vices, or more subtly on the choices and ambiguities, revealed by their two lives. Plutarch's refusal in the *synkriseis* to come down in favour of either figure, therefore, prevents the *synkriseis* becoming a mere exercise in grading or ranking, a ritual prize-giving to whichever of the subjects might be judged superior. The emphasis is not so much on the differences between the two protagonists as on the qualities which the two men had in common and which they manifested within their own particular *milieu*. Through reading the *synkriseis* our understanding of virtue, vice, and morality is broadened.

[66] ἢ τοῦτο πρῶτον ἀμφιλογίαν ἔχει;
[67] Asserted by Boulogne (1994), 57–71, but see the review by Swain (1996*b*).

6. CLOSURAL DISSONANCE: CONTRADICTIONS BETWEEN *SYNKRISEIS* AND LIVES

What aspects of the two protagonists are analysed and compared? The *synkriseis* have their own programme of themes which is not always closely related to the concerns of the Life. This programme usually covers two broad categories, that is, military and political achievements.[68] These are assessed for their own sake, in terms of success or failure, and as indices of character more generally. There are often also comments on other aspects of a subject's life,[69] though usually most are presented as having a bearing on either his political or military achievements. Once again we can see the influence of rhetoric here. Menander Rhetor (II. 372. 25–7), for example, recommends a similar division into deeds in war and deeds in peace when composing an *enkomion*.

The most common concern of the *synkriseis* is to show the extent to which the subject was responsible for his own political or military success or failure: what advantages did his city or family give him;[70] did he have the aid of colleagues;[71] or did he have powerful rivals or enemies?[72] Plutarch's interest in these questions corresponds to his interest, seen elsewhere, in the relationship between fortune ($\tau\acute{\upsilon}\chi\eta$) and virtue ($\mathring{\alpha}\rho\epsilon\tau\acute{\eta}$).[73] It is an interest which is seen at its clearest in another not unrelated context: the display speeches *On the fortune or virtue of the Romans* and *On the fortune or virtue of Alexander*. The attempt to distinguish between successes for which the subject can truly be held responsible and those in which chance played a part, has a long history: it was an axiom of ancient rhetorical theory since Aristotle that the good things which a man possesses by chance, though they may be mentioned in an *enkomion*, are not themselves worthy of praise.[74]

---

[68] This two-fold interest broadly corresponds to the division into activities in war and in peace which operates in many of the Lives. On this, see De Blois (1992), 4583–4.

[69] e.g. the discussion of the 'life-style' ($\delta\acute{\iota}\alpha\iota\tau\alpha$) of Kimon and Lucullus, that is, criticism of Lucullus' dissipation (*Kim.-Luc.* 1. 1–8).

[70] e.g. *Aem.-Tim.* 1. 2–2. 7; *Kim.-Luc.* 2. 2; *Lys.-Sulla* 5. 1–2; *Phil.-Flam.* 2. 2–5; *Sert.-Eum.* 1. 3–5; *Demetr.-Ant.* 1. 1–3; *Ag./Kleom.-Gracchi* 1. 3–5. Plutarch admits at *Lyk.-Num.* 2. 1–4 and *Sol.-Pub.* 4. 4–5 that the different countries in which the protagonists lived necessitated different conduct. Cf. also, p. 98 above.

[71] *Sol.-Pub.* 3. 3; *Pel.-Marc.* 2. 2–3; *Per.-Fab.* 1. 1–5; *Arist.-Cato* 2. 1–3; *Demetr.-Ant.* 5. 5; *Nik.-Crass.* 5. 1–2.

[72] *Arist.-Cato Maj.* 1. 2–4; *Nik.-Crass.* 2. 4; *Lys.-Sulla* 1. 2–7; *Dion-Brut.* 4. 1–4; *Sert.-Eum.* 1. 6–9.   [73] *Sol.-Pub.* 3. 5; *Phok.* 1. 4–6; 3. 1–4; *Dion* 1. 3.

[74] e.g. *Rhet.* 1368a2–5; cf. *Per.* 2. 3. In practice, and especially in orators of the Second Sophistic, the favour of $\tau\acute{\upsilon}\chi\eta$, in this context rather destiny than chance, can be presented

Another concern of the *synkriseis* is to assess how important a subject's success or failure was: how important were his military campaigns;[75] how long did the laws which he passed or the constitution which he founded last?[76] In this respect, Plutarch is interested, as we have noted in the Lives themselves, in the morally paradoxical possibility that actions which are virtuous in themselves may in fact harm the state as a whole,[77] and bad actions contribute to its well-being.[78] Another important theme is the subject's temperance (σωφροσύνη) and self-control (ἐγκράτεια) as regards both sex and money:[79] in particular, did he accept bribes;[80] and did he use his wealth to benefit his country?[81] Other themes include his manner of death: did he throw away his life;[82] did he die bravely?[83] Also, what was his attitude to power (in particular to tyranny);[84] did he perpetrate any violence against his fellow-citizens?[85]

These themes are not always the ones which have been emphasized in the narrative: there is in many books of *Parallel Lives* a marked dichotomy between the themes which emerge as important in the narratives and those which receive attention in the *synkrisis*. Perhaps the most striking example of this concerns education or culture (παιδεία). The extent of a subject's education and his commitment to Greek culture, despite its centrality to the value-system of the narratives, is not a major theme of the *synkriseis*. The fact that little is made of the subject's childhood is perhaps unsurprising. The *synkrisis* compares the two men as men, as fully formed adults: character-development and the educational process within childhood naturally have little place.[86] If education functioned in

as itself praiseworthy. See Pernot (1983). For τύχη as both chance and destiny in Plutarch, see above, Ch. 4, n. 81.

[75] *Kim.-Luc.* 3. 1–5; *Lys.-Sulla* 4. 1–9.
[76] *Sol.-Pub.* 3. 1–5; *Lyk.–Num.* 4. 8–12.
[77] *Lys.-Sulla* 3. 6–8; *Cor.-Alk.* 2. 1–3.
[78] *Thes.-Rom.* 6. 2–5; cf. *Ages.-Pomp.* 2. 3–4.
[79] *Arist.-Cato Maj.* 3. 1–4. 7; 6. 1–3; *Cor.-Alk.* 5. 2; *Lys.-Sulla* 3. 1–8; *Aem.-Tim.* 2. 8–9; *Ag./Kleom.-Gracchi* 1. 3–8; *Demetr.-Ant.* 3. 1–4. 6.
[80] *Cor.-Alk.* 3. 1–2; *Dem.-Cic.* 3. 5–7; *Per.-Fab.* 3. 5–6; *Nik.-Crass.* 1. 1–3; *Aem.-Tim.* 2. 1–9.
[81] *Sol.-Pub.* 1. 7–8; *Kim.-Luc.* 1. 5–6; *Per.-Fab.* 3. 5; *Nik.-Crass.* 1. 4; *Dion-Brut.* 1. 5; *Ag./Kleom.-Gracchi* 1. 7–8.
[82] *Lys.-Sulla* 4. 3–5; *Pel.-Marc.* 3. 1–8; *Phil.-Flam.* 1. 7.
[83] *Nik.-Crass.* 5. 4; *Dem.-Cic.* 5. 1–2; *Sert.-Eum.* 2. 6–8; *Ag./Kleom.-Gracchi* 3. 1; *Demetr.-Ant.* 6. 3–4.
[84] *Thes.-Rom.* 2. 1–3; *Sol.-Pub.* 2. 4–6; *Lyk.-Num.* 1. 1–5; *Aem.-Tim.* 2. 1–7; *Dion-Brut.* 1. 6–4. 8.
[85] *Lyk.-Num.* 4. 15; *Demetr.-Ant.* 5. 3–4; *Ag./Kleom.-Gracchi* 4. 1–5. 6; *Lys.-Sulla* 2. 1–7; *Nik.-Crass.* 2. 1–3. For an analysis of themes treated in the *synkriseis*, see also Prieth (1908), 4–16; Scardigli (1987a), 19–22.
[86] Cf. Prieth (1908), esp. 8–26, on the freedom of Plutarch in the *synkrisis* to discuss character without the need to mention the deeds from which that character is deduced.

the *Lives* only as an explanation of why the adult character was as it was, then the absence of this theme from the *synkrisis* would be entirely explicable. But in fact within the narrative education and culture function not only as an explanation but also as a key yardstick by which character is evaluated. Plutarch's silence, then, on this theme in the *synkriseis* is striking.

In fact, it is not uncommon for the *synkriseis* to concentrate on very different themes from those which emerge in the preceding narratives. A good example is the *Perikles–Fabius*. Here the themes which have been so important in the Life—the calmness ($\pi\rho\alpha\acute{o}\tau\eta s$) of the two men, their ability to endure the stupidity of the masses and the attacks of their demagogic opponents—are not picked up in the *synkrisis*. In fact the main concern of this *synkrisis* is in their military activities. Other changes are made in the emphasis of those themes which do recur in the *synkrisis*. The case of the Periklean programme of temple-building in Athens is particularly interesting. In the narrative two whole chapters had been devoted to enthusiastic description of the buildings on the Akropolis (*Per.* 12. 1–13. 13), proof that, even if Perikles' methods were demagogic, they did indeed benefit Athens. But the extent of the description makes clear that this is more than a simple defence of Perikles' policies, but also a glorification of the achievements of Perikles and of Perikles' Athens, the high point of the Classicism to which Plutarch and his contemporaries were so attached.[87] It is only this last aspect which is in prospect in the *synkrisis*. Perikles' building programme is introduced as the last item and is now presented as the climax of all Perikles' achievements (*Per.-Fab.* 3. 7). Any discussion of Perikles' motives, or any possible criticisms, have been banished. Furthermore, the *synkrisis* ignores another, contradictory way of looking at the building programme which has emerged in the prologue to the *Perikles–Fabius* pair. There works of art are denigrated in comparison with works of virtue; the Periklean building programme is implicitly included in this denigration by the mention of Pheidias, one of its chief designers (2. 1). The Life thus seems to allow a possible reading of Perikles' building programme as a superficial distraction from the real job of the statesman, which is to practise and teach virtue, a distraction all the more dangerous in the case of one prone to demagogy. The criti-

[87] The long description should be seen as a rhetorical *auxesis*: Stadter (1987), 265–6. In *Bellone an Pace*, where Plutarch argues for the superiority of action over art, Perikles' building programme is included amongst his *military* exploits (348c; 349d; 351a); clearly, the building programme was important in Plutarch's conception of the achievements of Classical Athens.

cisms made of the use for the building programme of revenue extracted from the Athens' supposed allies (12. 1–2; 14. 1) might encourage such a reading.[88] This possibility is not reflected in the *synkrisis*.

So, where the narrative allows several different interpretations of the same event, Plutarch may select just one for the *synkrisis*. Occasionally these new interpretations actually contradict the narrative in substantive terms. An example of this occurs at *Sol.-Pub.* 4. 1, where, arguing in favour of Publicola, Plutarch explicitly questions his own narrative in the Life that precedes, and prefers to refer the reader to the account of Daïmachos of Plataia, not narrated in the Life, which denied Solon any part in the war with Megara (contrast *Sol.* 8. 1–11. 1). Most often, though, the contradictions between *synkrisis* and narrative are at the level of interpretation, of the valuation which should be given to particular acts or character-traits. The same action or character-trait receives a very different moral assessment in the *synkrisis* from its treatment, implicit or explicit, in the preceding narrative; one subject's conduct may be preferred in the *synkrisis*, when the implication of the two Lives themselves was that the other's was preferable. We have already noticed examples of such contradictions between narrative and *synkrisis* in the *Lysander–Sulla*. But it is a wider phenomenon.

Consistency with the preceding narratives, either in points of detail or in implied moral judgements, is not a priority.[89] This lack of consistency serves an important function within the Plutarchan book in forcing the reader to reassess and reconsider the lives in question and how they might be judged. Now it is true that Plutarch does not seem elsewhere in his works to have regarded consistency as an overriding goal. He is quite prepared to argue for and against the same proposition in two different works. Thus, Plutarch is capable of both attacking and making use of the Herodotean dictum that women take off their modesty along with their underwear.[90] Similarly, he argues both for and against the notion of passion as necessary for the human soul, quoting Plato's description of 'spirit' as 'the sinews of the soul' with both approval and disapproval.[91]

---

[88] But cf. Moles (1992), 293: Perikles' buildings are unique in that they 'transcend the limitations of ordinary works of art' as set out in the prologue; they 'can themselves be categorized as moral/political ἔργα'. Moles links this to the view of Ameling (1985), esp. 61–3, that the *Per.* contains an implied plea for contemporary euergetism.

[89] A few contradictions were noticed also by Pelling (1986b), 88–90; (1988b), 19–20.

[90] Hdt. 1. 8. 3. Attacking the dictum: *Con. Praec.* 139c; using it: *De Aud. Poet.* 37d. For this and many more examples of contradictions across different texts, see Nikolaidis (1991); Casertano (1992); Bannon (1995), 42–3.

[91] See pp. 75 and 213.

In other words, Plutarch's paramount aim is to prove the point that he is arguing; in doing this he is prepared in one text to make use of arguments with which he may disagree in another text. This willingness to argue for different purposes in different texts is perhaps most clearly seen in Plutarch's treatment of Alexander the Great. The two speeches *On the fortune or virtue of Alexander* are wholly positive about Alexander, who is presented as the philosopher and the leader *par excellence*. Negative features of the tradition on Alexander are simply ignored, or refuted. In the *Life of Alexander*, however, the picture is distinctly less positive.[92] So persuasiveness within a given text can be more important than consistency across texts. An understanding of Plutarch's method of argumentation can, then, go some of the way towards explaining the contradictions between Life and *synkrisis*: the rhetorical demands of the moment lead him to argue different sides of the same coin. But this can only be part of the answer. After all, these contradictions occur within the *same* text. They would be glaringly obvious even to the most casual reader. Such contradictions serve to problematize the moral status of the two subjects and to make more difficult a moralizing reading of their lives.[93]

Philopoimen and Flamininus

Take, for example, the *Philopoimen–Flamininus*. The opening chapter of the *synkrisis* puts arguments in favour of Flamininus. The chapter does, it is true, emphasize one of the main concerns of the narrative, the question of benefaction to Greece, in which Flamininus emerges much the superior (1. 1–3; cf. 3. 4). Furthermore, this section of the *synkrisis* does seem to offer a good explicit formulation of what had been implicit in the preceding Lives, when, in analysing their errors or sins (ἁμαρτήματα), it draws a distinction (1. 4) between Flamininus' love of honour (φιλοτιμία) and Philopoimen's love of strife (φιλονεικία).[94] But Plutarch goes on in the next lines to take this contrast beyond what the narrative supports. Along with 'love of strife' he stresses anger as a defining characteristic of Philopoimen. As Christopher Pelling has

[92] This difference in approach can be related to the genre and purpose of the two sets of texts. The two works *De Alex. Fort.* are rhetorical display speeches, more specifically, *enkomia*; the Life is biographical narrative. See Rubina Cammarota (1992).
[93] Thus the assumption made by, for example, Larmour (1992), 4176–7; Hamilton (1992), 4206–7, and Bosworth (1992), 59–61, that the *synkriseis* are a good guide to the themes which Plutarch wished to bring out in the two Lives, is unsound.
[94] For suggestions of disapproval of Philopoimen's wars against other Greeks, cf. *Phil.* 3. 1; 17. 7; *Flam.* 11. 3–7. See Pelling (1986b), 85–8.

argued, this leads Plutarch to reinterpret Philopoimen's destruction of Sparta's constitution and his rash attack on Messene as acts of anger (1. 6), an interpretation at odds with the *Life of Philopoimen* itself (*Phil.* 16. 4–8; 18. 1–14).[95] He also represents Philopoimen's death, after he allows himself to be captured by the Messenians, as the result of 'throwing away his life through anger and contentiousness' (ὀργῇ καὶ φιλονικίᾳ [or φιλονεικίᾳ?]): it contrasts him with Flamininus, who always managed military matters 'with reasoning and for safety' (*Phil.-Flam.* 1. 6–7). This judgement of Philopoimen's death has not occurred in the narrative, although it is perhaps not surprising given Plutarch's views expressed elsewhere on generals who die in battle.[96]

Until now, Flamininus has been preferred. Much the rest of the *synkrisis* is concerned with the standard rhetorical themes of how responsible the subjects were for their own successes (2. 1–3. 3). It is not surprising that, in the interests of equality, Philopoimen is rated more the sole architect of his own success than is Flamininus, given Plutarch's harsh words on Philopoimen's anger and contentiousness in the earlier sections. In order to tip the scales in Philopoimen's favour, a rather unfair accusation against Flamininus by an Aitolian named Archedamos is included, that Flamininus had been a coward at the battle of Kynoskephalai (*Phil.-Flam.* 2. 6). No suggestion of this has been made in the narrative, but here it serves to bolster the arguments in favour of Philopoimen.[97]

This *synkrisis*, then, is a good example of the way in which *synkriseis* can state explicitly and make clearer the important ethical focuses of a pair, such as that of contentiousness and ambition. It also shows how Plutarch can draw out of an incident, such as Philopoimen's death, an interpretation which was not stated in the narrative, but nevertheless sits comfortably with it. On the other hand, it shows, with its concentration on the question of responsibility, how little connection there may be between a *synkrisis* and its narrative: the *synkrisis* may introduce new ethical prisms through which to view the past. More significantly, this *synkrisis* shows how Plutarch can make a thorough-going and striking reinterpretation of an event, such as the taking of Sparta, an interpretation which may sit far from comfortably with the narrative.

But it is the final sentence of this *synkrisis*, where Plutarch offers a rare final judgement, which is the most interesting and most revealing. 'After

---

[95] Pelling (1986*b*), 88–99. On this *synkrisis*, see now Pelling (1997*c*).
[96] See pp. 30 and 82.
[97] Compare *Flam.* 7. 4–9. 8; 15. 4. See Walsh (1992), 223–4.

this examination', Plutarch tells us, 'since the difference is hard to define (δυσθεώρητος), consider (σκόπει) whether we shall not be fair arbitrators if we award the Greek the crown for military skill and generalship, and the Roman the crown for justice and goodness' (3. 5). This judgement, as in the other cases where a final judgement is given, is crude and disappointing. It also, as often in these judgements, has something of the paradoxical about it: Philopoimen, the champion of the conquered nation, is praised for his military skill above the conqueror himself.[98] But more significant than the crudity of the judgement is its provisional nature. The invitation to the reader to take part in the judgement, and the use of first-person verbs, establish a sense of complicity and cooperation between reader and narrator. Plutarch has already in these Lives demonstrated how the same event—Rome's conquest of Greece—might be looked at from two different angles. The ending of the *synkrisis*, with its invitation to the reader to verify for himself the crude and surprising final judgement, adds to this sense of provisionality and complicates, rather than simplifying, the book of which it forms the final part. We have already noted the possibility of a similar open reading of the end of the *Lysander–Sulla*.[99]

Nikias and Crassus

The *synkrisis* of Nikias and Crassus provides another case-study for the sort of reassessment which Plutarch undertakes in the *synkriseis*.[100] The opening sentence signals clearly the transition from narrative to *synkrisis* and gives an impression of the clearly signposted, evaluative mode of argument which will follow: 'In the *synkrisis*, first of all, the wealth of Nikias, when compared (παραβαλλόμενος) with that of Crassus, was acquired in a more blameless (ἀμεμπτοτέραν) manner.'[101] After dealing with the way the two men acquired and used their wealth, Plutarch declares 'So much concerning wealth. But in their political lives (πολιτεύμασι) . . .' (2. 1), thus introducing a discussion of their statesmanship in both war and peace. Another transition is marked with the phrase 'In their actual periods of generalship (στρατηγίαις) . . .' (5. 1)—

---

[98] In general, it is the Roman protagonist who is commended for military skill and success, often partly because his campaigns were on a larger scale and against more dangerous opponenets.
[99] See above, pp. 203–4. For similar thought-provoking endings, cf. *Cor.-Alk.* 5. 2 (see below) and, *Ag./Kleom.-Gracchi* 5. 7.
[100] On this *synkrisis*, cf. Nikolaidis (1988), 329–33.
[101] Cf. 4. 1 for the key terms 'praise' (ἐπαινεῖν) and 'blame' (ψέγειν).

introducing a section on their personal conduct on expedition as opposed to their strategy. After a discussion of their attitude to divination, from which Nikias emerges superior (5. 3), the final section is introduced thus (5. 4): 'But concerning their end, Crassus was more blameless (ἀμεμπτότερος).' The phrasing echoes that of the opening and provides an internal signal of closure.

It seems fairly clear in this *synkrisis* that Plutarch's instincts were to prefer Nikias. This is most evident in his praise for Nikias' ending of the first phase of the Peloponnesian War, an attitude which is consistent with his own deep commitment to the unity of the Hellenic world. 'His love of peace', Plutarch declares, 'was truly divine, and his ending of the war was a particularly Greek political act (ἑλληνικώτερον πολίτευμα), and because of this deed it is not right to compare (παραβαλεῖν) Crassus with Nikias—not even if Crassus had brought the Caspian Sea or the Indian Ocean and added them to the Roman Empire' (2. 7). Plutarch uses cognates of the word ἐπιεικής ('reasonable') several times to mitigate criticisms of Nikias and his conduct (*Nik.-Crass.* 1. 1; 3. 6; 5. 3). In fact it is only in the discussion of their military activities, and in the final section on their deaths, that the 'scales' tilt towards Crassus.[102]

However, it is noticeable that, in the sections which favour Nikias, Plutarch is still prepared to find material to moderate these judgements, and to be reasonably critical of both men. So in the initial section on wealth, Plutarch declares that 'no one would approve' (οὐκ ἄν τις δοκιμάσειε) of Nikias' manner of making his fortune—owning mines worked by forced labour; but, in comparison (παραβαλλομένη), it is better than Crassus' profiteering from political confiscations and fires (1. 1). Plutarch then lists various other accusations against Crassus. Although these may have been false, he says, they were still made, whereas Nikias was never accused of malpractice. But, Plutarch continues, in a sly side-sweep, Nikias achieved his honest reputation by spending vast sums on informers, 'out of cowardice'; he was as Plutarch puts it, 'not naturally courageous' (1. 2: οὐκ εὖ πεφυκότι πρὸς τὸ θαρρεῖν). Nikias was 'more statesman-like' (πολιτικώτερος: that is, he benefited his city more) in the way he spent his money, but Crassus, Plutarch says, in a rather feeble attempt to even things up, had more of it to spend on his citizens (1. 4). Plutarch now makes a significant comment: 'So I am amazed,' he says, 'if it has escaped anyone's notice that vice (κακίαν) is a sort of unevenness (ἀνωμαλίαν) and inconsistency (ἀνομολογίαν) of character,

---

[102] The metaphor of scales (ῥοπὴν ποιεῖν or ἔχειν) in fact occurs several times in the *synkriseis*: *Cor.-Alk.* 1. 1; *Lys.-Sulla* 5. 5; cf. *Praec. Ger.* 801c.

when he sees people gaining wealth shamefully and then pouring it out uselessly' (1. 4). There are two things at stake here. On the one hand, Plutarch appears to be suggesting that, in judging Nikias and Crassus, the reader should be sympathetic, remembering that vice is a warp of character, a deficiency. Plutarch retains his *persona* of understanding for human nature, his φιλανθρωπία. But, on the other hand, Nikias' and Crassus' conduct is here explicitly called 'vice' (κακία). This passage should be contrasted with Plutarch's claim in the prologue to the *Kimon–Lucullus*, where he asks that mistakes be classed as 'shortcomings in a particular virtue rather than the wickednesses of vice' (*Kim.* 2. 5). The contradiction reveals an important factor in the moralism of the *synkriseis*. Plutarch is prepared in this part of the text to be much more critical, to speak much more in the black-and-white terms of virtue and vice.

In the next chapter, Plutarch continues in this highly critical tone. He admits that Nikias' statesmanship 'involved no trickery, injustice, violence, or harshness. But instead', he continues, 'he was deceived by Alkibiades and approached the people with caution' (2. 1). The point is basically a positive one, but it carries with it hints of a more negative treatment of Nikias' unworldly virtue which will come to the fore a little later. Crassus' record is, according to Plutarch, wholly to be censured: it is at this point that the extra detail of Crassus' violent behaviour is introduced (2. 2–3).[103] But Nikias is not to escape so lightly: 'Just as in these matters Crassus was violent and tyrannical, so, on the other hand, Nikias' timidity and cowardice in public life, and his surrendering of the most important matters to the worst of men, is worthy of censure' (2. 4).[104] Plutarch probably has in mind Nikias' surrendering of the command at Pylos to Kleon, a fact with which he will deal more fully in the next section, as well as his fear of the masses which in the Life was one of his main characteristics.[105] In contrast to Nikias' timidity, Crassus' boldness in competing with Caesar and Pompey is praised: opponents whom, Plutarch implies, were far more worthy than 'Kleons and Hyperboloi' (2. 4).[106] 'For in the most important matters (ἐπὶ μεγίστοις)

---

[103] See above, pp. 258–9.

[104] οὕτως αὖ πάλιν ἐκείνου τὸ ψοφοδεὲς ἐν τῇ πολιτείᾳ καὶ ἄτολμον καὶ τοῖς κακίστοις ὑφιέμενον τῶν μεγίστων ἐπιλήψεως [Ziegler: ἐπιλήψεων codices] ἄξιον. For ἐπίληψις, cf. *De Aud. Poet.* 35d. Nikias' timidity is literally 'fear of noise', as at *Nik.* 2. 6: for a statesman's fear of the noise of the popular assembly, cf. *Mar.* 28. 1–3.

[105] See above, p. 56 n. 16.

[106] As Nikolaidis (1988), 329–30, points out, Nikias' most formidable political opponent, Alkibiades, has been ignored.

one should not adopt a course which will not be envied, but one which is brilliant in statesmanship and which by the size of its power obscures envy' (2. 5).[107]

So far, Crassus has fared worse than Nikias. When we reach the sections on the two men's military activities it seems that Plutarch has cast around for material which could favour Crassus, or, more accurately, show Nikias in an even worse light than him. The point seems to be once again the desire for equality of treatment—unsurprising given the rhetorical expectation that comparison is most revealing when equals are compared. Nikias is criticized for surrendering his command at Pylos to Kleon, which, Plutarch argues, he did out of cowardice and fear for his own safety (3. 1–6). He is compared unfavourably with two other characters, Themistokles and Cato the Younger—a use of *synkrisis* well-known in rhetorical speeches of praise or, of more relevance here, denigration: these men understood, unlike him, the importance of keeping bad men out of public office (3. 4).[108] Plutarch mentions at this point an incident which he has not mentioned in the Life: the capture of Melos (3. 5).[109] This, together with two incidents which have been mentioned in the Life—the captures of Minoa and Kythera (cf. *Nik*. 6. 4)—is used as an example of a fairly easy military undertaking which Nikias does perform, to be contrasted with his reluctance to accept the more difficult command at Pylos. Plutarch has chosen here to present Nikias' role in the Pylos affair in the worst possible light. It is true that in the Life, after Kleon's success in the ensuing campaign, Plutarch discusses the harm that Nikias did to his own reputation; people considered, he tells us, that what he had done was worse than throwing away his shield. He also laments the way Nikias facilitated Kleon's rise to power (*Nik*. 8. 1–6). But the Life has also suggested other, less negative, ways of reading the incident. The emphasis in the actual narrative is on Kleon's brash boasting, and his embarrassment by the unexpected suggestion, made in the first instance by the people, that he himself take the command (*Nik*. 7. 3–6). It is also implied in the narrative that Nikias' reluctance to prosecute the war results from his policy of peace with Sparta (*Nik*. 7. 2), a policy praised in the *synkrisis* (2. 7). Such arguments might have been taken up here.

---

[107] δεῖ γὰρ ἐπὶ μεγίστοις οὐ τὸ ⟨ἀν⟩επίφθονον, ἀλλὰ τὸ λαμπρὸν ἐν πολιτείᾳ λαμβάνειν, μεγέθει δυνάμεως ἐξαμαυροῦντα τὸν φθόνον.

[108] See above, p. 153.

[109] Thucydides treats the capture and its preliminaries at length (5. 84–116), but does not mention Nikias' involvement.

But instead the Pylos affair is used as proof of Nikias' preference for his own safety rather than for that of the state.

Furthermore, to make the point that Crassus' military undertakings were greater than Nikias', Plutarch chooses to compare Crassus' Parthian campaign not with Nikias' command of the important Sicilian expedition, which he had declared at the start of the Life to be particularly comparable, but with three minor campaigns of Nikias: the capture of Thyrea on the Peloponnesian coast from its Aiginetan settlers, and the captures of Skandeia on Kythera and of Mende in Thrace (4. 3). These minor operations, drawn from Book Four of Thucydides, are mentioned very briefly in the Life, in rather vague terms, amongst a larger list of examples, drawn from Books Three and Four,[110] of the many military successes which Nikias enjoyed (*Nik.* 6. 4–7); they are contrasted with the defeats suffered by other, contemporary, Athenian generals. In the *synkrisis*, however, Plutarch ignores all Nikias' other successes and actively plays down the importance of these. In the Life Plutarch says, paraphrasing Thucydides, 'he captured Kythera, an island well-suited for action against Lakonia and having Lakedaimonian settlers, and he captured in addition many places in Thrace, which had revolted, and brought them back.' But in the *synkrisis*, the capture of Kythera and campaigns against revolting allies in Thrace have been reduced to the sackings of two towns. The different presentations of Nikias' campaigns plainly relate to the different rhetorical purpose of the two sections in which they occur. In the Life, Plutarch is demonstrating Nikias' great good fortune and uses his military successes, in comparison to the defeats suffered by other generals, as proof of this. In the *synkrisis* Plutarch is trying to play down Nikias' military successes in a section of comparison from which Nikias must emerge inferior to Crassus. Here Nikias' military successes are marshalled to make the point that Crassus had greater aims than Nikias. As we have noted, the Sicilian expedition—an enterprise of great size and daring—is, at this point, conveniently ignored.

But there is one serious objection that could be made to any attempt to make Crassus' military activities superior to Nikias', particularly if the Sicilian expedition is played down: Crassus' one major spell as general, when he invaded Parthian territory, was a complete disaster. To deal with this, Plutarch argues that Crassus should not be condemned for the Parthian defeat, as he was only trying to do the kind of thing for which Pompey, Caesar, and Alexander were praised (*Nik.-Crass.* 4. 1–4). The point is a perceptive one, as it recognizes that where judgements of

[110] Skandeia (Thuc. 4. 54. 1); Thyrea (4. 56. 2–4. 57. 5); Mende (4. 129–30).

military actions are concerned, it is normally, and perhaps unfairly, only by the success or failure of the venture which people, Plutarch included, judge. He quotes a couplet from Euripides to lend authority to the point. In Euripides' *Phoenician Women* (524–5), Eteokles had declared, 'For if injustice must be done (εἴπερ γὰρ ἀδικεῖν χρή), it is most noble to do it for the sake of being tyrant'. Plutarch recasts and expands this to compare Crassus' large undertaking with, once again, some of Nikias' most minor ones: '*For if injustice must be done*, as Euripides says, by people who cannot stay quiet and do not know how to enjoy the good things which they have at hand, they should not lay waste to Skandeia or Mende, nor hunt out Aiginetan fugitives who have abandoned their own land and hidden themselves in another like birds. Rather, the act of injustice should be valued highly; people should not give up justice easily on any terms which come along, as though it were something insignificant or small' (4. 3). This is a particularly clear case of special pleading. On two occasions elsewhere in his work, Plutarch specifically disapproves of this sentiment and these lines from Euripides.[111] It is true that Plutarch is elsewhere concerned to investigate how easy or difficult a general's task was, and certainly wars against barbarians are regarded more favourably than those which, like Nikias' Sicilian campaign, were fought against Greeks.[112] But nowhere else are large defeats presented as preferable to small victories.

So Plutarch is working hard to defend Crassus. His surprisingly favourable attitutude to Crassus' Parthian campaign may well spring also, partly at least, from a willingness, when arguing in favour of the Roman Crassus, to adopt a more militaristic attitude which glories in war for its own sake and which Plutarch perhaps sees as more characteristic of Romans (cf. *Lyk.-Num.* 4. 10–13). In arguing in favour of the Roman figure, then, Plutarch may be more prepared to adopt Roman values. But the issue is more complex than that. Plutarch chooses to characterize the motives of the two men in setting out on military adventures with the language of discontent, familiar to us from the *Pyrrhos–Marius*. Neither, it is implied, should have gone to war at all, though, it is argued perversely, once going to war one may as well do it on a big scale. This is, of course, a grave misrepresentation of the motives of Nikias as presented in the Life.

The new emphasis on the preference of Nikias for his own safety, which appears to contradict the Life, occurs also in the comparison of the

---

[111] *De Aud. Poet.* 18d–e; *De Tuenda Sanit.* 125d–e: cf. Nikolaidis (1991), 158–9.
[112] e.g. *Ages.* 14. 2–4; *Pomp.* 70. 3–6; *Kim.* 13. 1.

deaths of the two men. This is perhaps the most surprising example of an attempt to find a point in Crassus' favour. It is true that in the Life, to explain Nikias' refusal to contemplate retreat from Syracuse while there was still time, Plutarch lays even stronger emphasis than Thucydides did on Nikias' fear of conviction in Athens, and his superstition. He seems to disapprove of Nikias' avowed preference to die at the hands of the enemy rather than of his own citizens (22. 2–3).[113] But once the retreat begins, Plutarch expounds on Nikias' great dedication to his own men: 'Despite his illness he did and endured what many of the strong could scarcely bear. It was obvious to all that he was sticking at his labours not for himself nor through love of life, but for their sake, not wishing to give up their hope of salvation' (26. 4). Similarly, Nikias' final words in the Life (27. 5) are, as in Thucydides (7. 85. 1), to beg salvation not for himself but for his men: 'You are the victors, Gylippos. Have pity—not on me, who for my great successes have gained reputation and glory—but on the other Athenians.'[114] In the final words of the *synkrisis*, however, Crassus is commended for surrendering only as a result of the entreaties of his friends and the deception of his enemies, whereas Nikias is criticized for surrendering in the hope of personal safety (*Nik.-Crass.* 5. 4).

In fact, reassessment of a subject's manner of death occurs in other *synkriseis*. There is a similar contradiction in the way the death of Eumenes is treated. In the Life (*Eum.* 17–19), Eumenes is taken captive by his own mutinous troops, and in a fine speech asks them to kill him rather than surrender him to the enemy. After he is handed over, Plutarch puts into his mouth words which seem to stand as a final judgement on him: he asks why his death is delayed; his guard taunts him that he has not faced death bravely in battle and he replies: 'Yes, by Zeus, I did at that time too. Ask the men who fought me. I know that no one whom I met was better than me' (*Eum.* 18.8). In the *synkrisis*, however, Eumenes is criticized for wanting to escape, for being willing to live on after capture, and for supplicating his captor for his life (*Sert.-Eum.* 2. 6–8).[115]

Agesilaos and Pompey

Such surprising and thought-provoking contradictions between Life and *synkrisis* can be seen too in the *Agesilaos–Pompey*. In their Lives both Agesilaos and Pompey had been treated fairly positively. The first half of

[113] Nikolaidis (1988), 327–8. But cf. the comments of Pelling (1992), 20–1.
[114] Cf. Scardigli (1987a), 19; Nikolaidis (1988), 330–3.
[115] On Antony's death, see below.

each Life shows both men as successful and virtuous; indeed, the first half of the *Agesilaos* takes up Xenophon's enkomiastic treatment wholesale. Both men meet disaster in the second half of their Lives, partly because of their inability to control their own friends and their own passions. Agesilaos, however, at the end of the Life is able to put aside his love of honour and save Sparta; Pompey, on the other hand, is ultimately incapable in politics, a fact hinted at in the early parts of the Life, and is brought down by his own power. Agesilaos, then, is perhaps the superior of two generally virtuous men.[116]

The *synkrisis* begins by clearly signalling the transition from the narrative, and the new aim of this section of text: comparative analysis of the differences between the two protagonists. 'Now that the Lives lie before us, let us summarize quickly the matters that make differences, gathering them side by side. They are the following. First, . . .' (1. 1). The use of a first-person verb, and the clearly pointed structure of the succeeding pages, betray traces of the generic origin of the *synkrisis* in the rhetorical display speech. There follows a series of numbered points detailing ways in which first Pompey and then Agesilaos might be seen as superior. What is most noticeable is that the two men are presented in a rather different manner from the way they had been presented in the preceding Lives. First of all, the *synkrisis* is much more critical of both. Secondly, as so often, Plutarch is concerned to present them as equal. The *synkrisis* begins by favouring Pompey, who is superior in what we might call 'moral' matters—dealing with friends, rivals, enemies, how he came to power (1. 2–2. 2)—and in both the scale and the morality of his military campaigns (3. 1–3). Then Agesilaos is shown to be a more skilful general and politician (2. 3–6; 3. 4–4. 11).

This leads to a few surprising twists. First, the non-military matters. Pompey's loyalty to Sulla is presented as a good point, in contrast to Agesilaos' behaviour to Lysander. But in the Life, Pompey has been shown committing murder in the service of Sulla (*Pomp.* 10. 2–10; 16. 6–7). Furthermore, Pompey is excused some of his later political wrongdoings on the grounds that he acted because of his marriage ties; that is, Plutarch explains (*Ages.-Pomp.* 1. 7), he acted 'out of deference or ignorance' ($\delta\iota$' $\alpha\grave{\iota}\delta\hat{\omega}$ . . . $\mathring{\eta}$ $\mathring{\alpha}\gamma\nu o\iota\alpha\nu$). In the Life, though, it is this very trait—Pompey's inability to stand up to his friends, the way he allowed others to push him to actions against his own judgement—which is his biggest failing.[117] Furthermore, the defence of having acted to help

---
[116] Hillman (1994).
[117] e.g. *Pomp.* 39. 6; 46. 1–47. 10; 61. 4; 67. 1–10.

his friends could just as much have been made concerning Agesilaos' support of Sphodrias and Phoibidas for their treacherous attacks on Athens and Thebes respectively. Instead Plutarch highlights the erotic element in the Sphodrias affair and attributes Agesilaos' assistance of Phoibidas to 'anger and love of strife' ($\theta v\mu\hat{\omega}$ καὶ φιλονεικίᾳ) (1. 5–7). To even the scales a little, Plutarch now turns to commend Agesilaos: first, for his 'remedy' of suspending the law concerning those who fled in battle, 'thus demonstrating his great power to his friends' (2. 3). He continues, 'I also attribute the following inimitable (ἀμίμητον) deed to the political virtue of Agesilaos: that, having received the message-roll, he abandoned his exploits in Asia' (2. 5). Pompey, however, is criticized for helping the state 'only as he made himself great' (2. 6); his disbanding of his troops on his return to Italy in 60 BC has been forgotten (*Pomp.* 43. 1–5).

Moving to their military exploits, Plutarch makes the fair point that Pompey's achievements were on a scale vastly different from Agesilaos'. Not even Xenophon, he says, would have compared Agesilaos' victories with Pompey's (3. 1). The fact that Agesilaos had been presented in the Life as a proto-Alexander (e.g. 15. 4) is forgotten. Pompey is also commended for reasonableness (ἐπιείκεια) to enemies, in contrast to Agesilaos' desire to 'enslave Thebes and depopulate Messene, of which the latter was founded by the same colonists as his country, the former was the mother city of his family' (3. 2). This alludes to the mythical ancestry of the Spartan kings, who were believed to be the descendants of the Theban-born Herakles, who supposedly also founded Messene along with Argos and Sparta.[118] The argument that Agesilaos' hostilities against Messene broke bonds of common blood is particularly unconvincing: Spartan foreign policy had for several centuries consistently opposed Messenian independence. It is clearly brought in as a weak attempt to bolster the attack on Agesilaos in this section.[119]

Now comes the transition (3. 4): 'However, if it is for the greatest and most important acts and reasonings in war that the first prize for a commander's virtue is to be given, the Spartan has left (ἀπολέλοιπε) the Roman a long way behind.' Pompey is now condemned for leaving Rome behind (3. 5: ἐξέλιπεν)[120] when he could have beaten Caesar, and then for being driven by the complaints of his friends 'from his safest

---

[118] In fact, Messene was re-founded in c.369 BC as Plutarch notes in *Ages.* 34. 1.

[119] But it has a serious point too: Agesilaos fought wars against other Greeks, a crime which Plutarch is always quick to condemn.

[120] One manuscript (V) continues the pun with ἀπολιπών in 3. 7.

reasonings' and so fighting at the wrong time (4. 3; cf. 4. 8). In the later sections of the *synkrisis* Plutarch's argument is much more what one might have expected from reading the two Lives, and much more unfavourable to Pompey.

At the end of the *synkrisis*, Plutarch addresses the two men's deaths in Egypt and finds in favour of Pompey (5. 1–2). But the treatment is given a novel twist as Plutarch records that the Egyptians blamed their murdering of Pompey on Agesilaos, whom they had trusted and who had deserted them. A similar kind of real, historical link between paired figures is argued for at the start of the *synkrisis* to the *Solon–Publicola*. Here Plutarch claims that in this pair, uniquely, the second figure, Publicola, imitated the first, Solon, and the first 'bore witness to' the second: that is, as Plutarch explains at length, Publicola fulfilled more than any man of Solon's age Solon's own criteria for whether a man should be judged happy (*Sol.-Pub.* 1. 1–8). Plutarch concludes: 'So if Solon is the wisest of all, Publicola is the happiest. For the good things which Solon prayed for as the greatest and finest of blessings, Publicola was able to win and to keep enjoying until the end' (1. 8, alluding to Hdt. 1. 30–3). Plutarch goes on to argue that in his reform of Roman society Publicola actually imitated and carried further Solon's 'democratic' reforms in Athens (2. 1–6). These ingenious links between paired figures seem to carry with them the implication that the pairing of subjects is not simply intellectually satisfying or revealing of character, but actually relates to some reality beyond the author's literary construction. It implies that paired subjects—Solon and Publicola, Agesilaos and Pompey—are, somehow, in themselves linked as representatives of the same features in both Greek and Roman society: history does indeed repeat itself.[121]

Demetrios and Antony

The *Demetrios–Antony* provides another interesting example of the way in which Plutarch was prepared to bend the facts as narrated in preceding Lives to support the argumentation of the *synkrisis*. The *synkrisis* here is not a good summary of the themes which had been of importance in the Life; indeed, scholars have been rather puzzled by the contradictions between narrative and *synkrisis*.[122] This *synkrisis* is, like many, rather

---

[121] Desideri (1992c), 74–7 and 86–7.

[122] e.g. Pelling (1986b), 89–90; (1988b), 19–20, who suggests that the discordant elements in the *synkrisis* are simply afterthoughts.

negative in its treatment of both subjects, as one might perhaps expect from one dealing with two men who were introduced as examples of the vices which 'great natures' produce. The *synkrisis* begins by favouring Antony, making the point that his rise was due to his own efforts, unlike that of Demetrios, who inherited his position (1. 1–6). In the middle section of the *synkrisis*, the scales tilt more in favour of Demetrios (2. 1–4. 2). Here we encounter one of the points in which the *synkrisis* diverges from the narrative. We are told that 'though both were insolent in good fortune (ὑβρισταὶ . . . εὐτυχοῦντες) and abandoned to luxury and pleasures, no one would say opportunity for action escaped Demetrios because he was engaged in merry-making and parties; on the contrary, it was when leisure was abundant that he brought in his pleasures . . .' (3. 2). This statement is indeed in accord with several important passages in the body of the Life itself, which characterize Demetrios by drawing a clear line between his energetic conduct of wars and his luxurious life-style in peacetime.[123] But it seems to contradict a story related in the Life, and preserved only in Plutarch (*Demetr.* 9. 5–7). Here Demetrios abandons his army while it is besieging Megara and goes off with only a small guard for an assignation with the famous beauty Kratesipolis. As a result, he almost loses his life in a surprise attack. Plutarch concludes the incident (*Demetr.* 9. 7): 'he narrowly escaped being made captive in a most disgraceful way because of his lack of self-control (ἐξ ἀκρασίας).'[124] The phrasing underlines the contrast between Demetrios' fine political and military deeds—he has just liberated Athens and laid siege to Megara—and his irresponsible eagerness for pleasure which almost ruins everything. In the *synkrisis*, however, this incident is forgotten in the interests of a contrast between Demetrios and Antony, in which Demetrios must come out better.

The discussion continues in Demetrios' favour until we reach the section on their sexual conduct, at which point the treatment becomes more equal. One might expect Antony to be favoured at this point, but, in fact, the final sections of the *synkrisis* are remarkably mixed in their judgements. Antony's marriages did him great harm, whereas Demetrios' did not. Here Plutarch shows a notable sensitivity to differences of culture and period, in arguing that Demetrios' dynastic marriages were quite acceptable, but Antony's two marriages were not. To balance this, Plutarch then discusses Demetrios' sexual debaucheries on the Athenian Akropolis (4. 3–5). His conclusions on the sexual

[123] 2. 3; 19. 4–5; 19. 10; 44. 8; cf. Diod. 20. 92. 4. Cf. Andrei (1989), 58–9 and 82–3.
[124] Pelling (1986b), 92–3, notes the contradiction.

conduct of the two men are that both suffered from lack of self-control (ἀκρασία), but whereas Demetrios harmed others by this trait, Antony harmed himself (4. 6).

The equal, though critical, treatment of the two men continues. Demetrios treated his family better than Antony (5. 1–2). But whereas both men violated oaths of friendship (5. 3–4), Antony had some excuse in arresting Artavasdes of Armenia, in that he had deserted him in Media (cf. *Ant.* 39. 1; 50. 3–7).[125] Demetrios, however, Plutarch maintains, had no excuse for murdering Alexander of Macedon. This is a surprising reinterpretation of the events presented in the Life (*Demetr.* 36. 1–12). There, Demetrios' murder of Alexander is presented as a forestalling of Alexander's plot against him. In other authors, however, the murder is seen in a much more negative light, and this is the way it is presented in the *synkrisis*: as a simple violation of trust by Demetrios.[126] It seems that in the Life Plutarch has tried, as so often, to present events in a way most sympathetic to the protagonist. In the *synkrisis*, on the other hand, he is free to adopt another more critical interpretation. The contrast between these two opposing versions forces the reader to reconsider the incident and its morality, and indeed the possibility that different interpretations might be offered of the same event.

Plutarch seems, then, to be challenging and subverting his own narrative for no other end than to destabilize the reader's judgements on these two men. This is the case in the closing words of the *synkrisis*. The ways in which the two subjects meet their deaths, a standard topic of the *synkriseis*, are compared (6. 3–4). 'It is possible to praise the death of neither', Plutarch declares, 'but Demetrios' is more to be criticized' (ψεκτὸς δ' ὁ Δημητρίου μᾶλλον). But, though preferred over Demetrios', Antony's death is still presented in a very negative light. In the narrative, there has been no hint of any criticism of his death; it was brave and noble, and ended with fine last words: he reviews the blessings of his life, not least of which was that he died 'not ignobly, a Roman overcome by a Roman' (*Ant.* 77. 7).[127] In the *synkrisis*, however, we find his death

---

[125] In the *synkrisis*, Plutarch wrongly styles Artavasdes by the name Artabanos. This is presumably a simple mistake, but it has the effect of increasing the impression of distance and lack of fit between Life and *synkrisis*.

[126] Andrei (1989), 72–4, arguing that Demetrios' responsibility is played down in the Life in order to show him as the victim of fortune, responding to, rather than initiating events: a theme of the pair as a whole.

[127] On Antony's last words, see Pelling (1988*b*), n. on 77. 7. The fact that Antony dies like a Roman is significant given his earlier un-Roman behaviour (e.g. 54. 5: μισορρώμαιον); cf. Swain (1990*a*).

described in rather different terms: 'Antony made his exit in a cowardly, pitiful and dishonourable way, though at least it was before the enemy became master of his person' (6. 4). There is here, it is true, a contrast with Demetrios, who did allow himself to be captured, and died a slave to food and drink. But Plutarch has still chosen a surprisingly negative way to present Antony's death.

One way to approach these different treatments of Antony's death is to see them as reflecting the variations in moral register within the *Demetrios–Antony*. As has been noted already, the moral register is largely closed in the second part of the *Antony*; Antony and Kleopatra are more like heroes in a novel or protagonists in a tragedy than *exempla* for moral instruction.[128] Plutarch returns to explicit moralizing in the *synkrisis*, a moralizing prefigured in the closing words of the *Antony* itself, where Antony's descendants are traced down to Nero. 'He reigned in our time (ἐφ' ἡμῶν) and killed his mother and almost destroyed the Roman empire with his stupidity and madness, having become fifth in number in the succession (διαδοχῆς) from Antony' (*Ant.* 87. 9).[129] But variations in the moral register cannot wholly explain the very real contradiction in the way Antony's death is described. Plutarch provides us with two different ways of looking at the same event, and shows us that moral evaluation is not always easy, and is, to an extent, capable of revision, dependent on point of view.[130]

Coriolanus and Alkibiades

Finally, we return to the *Coriolanus–Alkibiades*. Here too the *synkrisis* provides a surprising reinterpretation of events as presented in the narrative—though this time the reinterpretation is of a rather different kind. The tone of the *synkrisis* is negative, which fits well with the proposed status of these figures as 'great natures' gone wrong. Alkibiades consistently fares better, as indeed one might have expected from reading the preceding Lives. For example, in assessing their military

[128] See pp. 61–2 and 69–70.
[129] This passage finds its parallel in *Demetr.* 53. 8–9, where Demetrios' descendants are traced down in succession (ταῖς διαδοχαῖς) to Perseus, 'in whose time (ἐφ' οὗ) the Romans subdued Makedonia'. Brenk (1992), 4374–5, sees the cowardliness of Antony's death in the *synkrisis* as related to the association of Antony with Nero (on Plutarch's view of whom, see Brenk 1987 and 1992, 4356–75). The parallel with the *Demetrios* passage serves to associate Nero also with Perseus, a Hellenistic king, and for Plutarch a figure of distaste, and a contrast to the virtuous Aemilius (e.g. *Aem.* 19. 3–10; 23. 1–11; 26. 1–12). On Plutarch and Hellenistic kings, see above, pp. 115–16.
[130] Cf. Pelling (1988b), 19–26 and 325.

record, both are declared great generals, but Alkibiades greater, because he won victories by sea as well as on land (1. 2). There follows a section on their statesmanship (πολιτεία), where Alkibiades is condemned for flattering the people, and Coriolanus for pride and ungraciousness (1. 3–4); Plutarch concludes that neither character-trait is to be praised (ἐπαινετέον), but Alkibiades is 'more blameless' (ἀμεμπτότερος). This is what one might expect from the Lives themselves. This *synkrisis* is largely a comparison of bad traits or actions, and Plutarch explicitly raises the problem of how one compares extremes: Alkibiades' unprincipled affability and Coriolanus' principled pride and aloofness. Alkibiades comes off best.

But, in fact, the scales seem to be weighted against Coriolanus even more than one might have expected. Plutarch reports criticisms of Alkibiades' deception of the Spartan ambassadors (2. 2), but, as in the Life (*Alk.* 15. 1–2), he stresses that it had a good result for Athens (2. 3). Coriolanus, on the other hand, is condemned for deceit. The incident to which Plutarch refers concerns the Roman decision to expel the Volsci from Rome, and the subsequent war. In the Life, Plutarch had mentioned that 'some' had seen Coriolanus as responsible for the Roman action, because, it was alleged, he had sent to Rome a deceitful message that the Volsci were planning a surprise attack (*Cor.* 26. 3). In the *synkrisis*, however, Plutarch accepts without question that Coriolanus was to blame and puts it down to his anger (2. 4–5). This time he names his authority, Dionysios, thus lending more credibility to the negative tradition. This passage in the *synkrisis* should, perhaps, be seen as a reinterpretation, a choice of the more negative of two alternatives, rather than an outright contradiction of the Life.[131] But it is striking all the same that whereas Alkibiades' deception is not condemned, the parallel episode in Coriolanus' career is.

The rest of the *synkrisis* continues this hostility to Coriolanus, who is repeatedly condemned for pride and unsociability. All possible arguments are mustered against him. For example, Plutarch claims that Coriolanus, unlike Alkibiades, did not obtain any success for his city, only against it (4. 1); this seems to go against the implication of the early chapters of his Life, where many military successes on behalf of Rome are recounted. It might also be thought to go against what was said in the earlier part of the *synkrisis*, where *both* men are said to have harmed their country as much as they helped it (1. 2). But the most shocking example of reinterpretation comes in the closing words of the *synkrisis* and of

[131] Russell (1963), 21 (= 1995, 358–9).

the book as a whole. Here Plutarch seems to undercut and to challenge the whole preceding presentation which had consistently condemned Coriolanus. Plutarch concludes by saying of him: 'These are the things of which one might accuse the man. But all the rest are brilliant. For temperance (σωφροσύνης) and financial self-control (χρημάτων ἐγκρατείας), it is right to compare him with the best and purest of the Greeks—not with Alkibiades who, by Zeus, became in these matters the most audacious of men and who most despised what is good' (5. 2). This judgement is, in the first instance, about the two men's financial and probably sexual behaviour. But Alkibiades' conduct in neither had been condemned or presented in a negative light in the Life. It is true that earlier in the *synkrisis* Alkibiades was condemned for getting money 'not well' by taking bribes, and for spending it on 'luxury and wantonness' (εἰς τρυφὴν καὶ ἀκολασίαν). But Coriolanus' conduct in not accepting gifts is condemned much more (3. 1–2). So this judgement, coming at the end of the book as a whole, is a striking about-face. We could see this sudden vote in favour of Coriolanus as an attempt, at the end of a *synkrisis* which had swung consistently in favour of Alkibiades, to even the scales a little. But such a formalistic answer does not lessen the contrast of this final judgement with all that has gone before. Whatever the reason for it, this final contrast causes the reader to reassess the moral assumptions which the preceding Lives and the preceding *synkrisis* had encouraged. Who is better? How should one rate 'purity' against affability, stubbornness against deception? In the final analysis— in the final sentence—the *Coriolanus–Alkibiades* poses more questions than it answers.

7. CONCLUSION

Perhaps, then, we can see the very dissonance between Life and *synkrisis* as having an important function within the moral programme. The striking contrast forces the reader to assume a more active role in assessing the men he has read about and the moral issues their Lives raise. This destabilizing of moral certainties has been a feature of most pairs of *Parallel Lives* examined in this book. The *synkriseis* perform, then, a double function. On the one hand, they provide a strong 'closed' ending to the texts they follow; they provide explicitly a way of making sense of and evaluating the events which have been narrated. Moral categories are invoked, judgements made, an end is signalled. But there is also a sense in which the *synkriseis* work against a strong ending to the Plutarchan book. The dissonance between narrative and comparison, between life (or Life) with its uncertainties and conflicts and the simple moral evaluations of the *synkrisis*, forces us to reassess all that we have read before. Furthermore, far from simply rounding off the preceding Lives with a rhetorical *tour de force*, the *synkriseis* invite the reader's renewed attention to the moral questions which had been raised in the narrative, and raise new and disturbing ones.[132] The endings of the Lives themselves tend to avoid moral issues and close the narrative on a note of calm; discordant themes are avoided. If difficult moral questions have been raised or the subject criticized in the course of the Life, such themes are generally eschewed in the final chapters.[133] The *synkriseis* reopen these difficult questions. The *Life of Brutus*, for example, consistently avoids opening up moral questions over issues such as Brutus' political allegiances, the murder of Caesar, and his own suicide.[134] Some of these, in particular the question of whether it was right to kill Caesar, are raised in the *synkrisis*.[135]

One might compare the similar effect at the end of some tragedies. For example, the final lines of the *Oidipous Tyrannos* (1524–30), if genuine, present Oidipous as a paradigm of the common *topos* 'call no man happy until he is dead' (cf. Hdt. 1. 32. 1–9). As Burton puts it: 'Thus at the end of this play we have the final presentation of the παράδειγμα [paradigm] Oedipus as he has been depicted passing from happiness to misery; and the παράδειγμα is followed by gnomic comment, traditional and expected.'[136] But after the intensity and pathos of the play which has preceded it, this evaluation has seemed to some readers, both ancient and modern, platitudinous and therefore inappropriate. Paradoxically, this final closural gnomic utterance is as thought-provoking as anything else in Sophokles. Compare also the similarly 'conclusive' and yet disturbing final line of the *Trachiniai*: 'And there is none of this which is not Zeus' (1278: κοὐδὲν τούτων ὅ τι μὴ Ζεύς).[137]

Examples can be cited of historiographical works whose endings, like the Plutarchan *synkriseis*, seem to open new questions as they close

[132] Though, undoubtedly, final comparison does function as a means of closure; cf. also the end of each of the surviving *Lives of the Caesars* (*Galba* 29. 4–5; *Otho* 18. 3). Cf. Appian's *BC* 2. 149–54 (see above, n. 43).
[133] Pelling (1997a), 232–6.
[134] Pelling (1989), 222–8.
[135] Pelling (1997a), 242–3.
[136] Burton (1980), 184; cf. 182–5. Cf. D. H. Roberts (1987) and (1988).
[137] Pelling (1997a), 236–7, points to the discordant endings of the other Sophoklean tragedies.

others down: for example, Curtius Rufus' summing-up of Alexander's character (Curtius 10. 5. 26–10. 5. 37), Tacitus' of Tiberius (*Annals* 6. 51. 1–3), and Dio Cassius' of Augustus' reign (Dio 56. 43–5). The endings of these narratives offer a final, evaluative perspective on the events which have preceded and provide, in one sense, a strong, and closed, ending to the narrative. But their evaluations sit uneasily with the preceding narrative. Dio Cassius' summing-up seems more favourable to Augustus than his narrative has led us to expect. In particular, his statement—given as the thoughts of the Romans after Augustus' death—that Augustus mixed monarchy with democracy (56. 43. 4) seems to contradict his consistent assertions that Augustus' restoration of the Republic was a sham (e.g. 53. 11. 1–12. 3; 16. 1).[138] Tacitus seems to imply in his obituary of Tiberius that the influence of Seianus was both of less importance and more benign than his narrative in Books 4–6 has suggested. In particular, at the start of Book Four he had placed much of the blame for Tiberius' moral decline on Seianus (4. 1–2); the obituary suggests that Seianus' presence had a retraining effect.[139] Similarly, the obituary seems to suggest that Tiberius' character remained unchanged, but that his vice was in the early part of his life concealed. But earlier passages, notably Arruntius' speech in *Annals* 6. 48. 2, just a few chapters earlier, suggest that Tiberius' character did actually change for the worse (also *Hist.* 1. 50. 4). Koestermann suggests that Tacitus deliberately presents the reader with alternative pictures of Tiberius from which to chose.[140] Curtius Rufus' summing-up of Alexander is comparable. It bears resemblance to the Plutarchan *synkriseis* in its weighing up of good and bad points. But the tone of the preceding narrative had on the whole been critical of Alexander: he was presented as corrupted by power. In the summing-up, the evaluation is much more evenly balanced; bad points, such as his drinking, are played down (10. 5. 32, 34).[141] The discord of this final section with what went before serves to raise rather than settle questions about how Alexander should be judged: great leader, or tyrant?

A similar sense of discord with what has gone before informs the end of Xenophon's *Education of Kyros*. The final chapter (8. 8), coming after a description of Kyros' death, discusses the degeneracy of present-day

---

[138] Though see Rich (1989), 104–8; cf. also Manuwald (1979), 140–62. I am indebted to Pelling (1997a), 237, for this example.

[139] Cf. Martin (1981), 139–43. For an attempt to reconcile the narrative to the obituary, see Woodman (1989).

[140] Koestermann (1963), 38.

[141] On Alexander's drinking, cf. Curt. 6. 2. 1–2; 8. 1. 22, 1. 43; 2. 1; 4. 29–30; 6. 14.

Persia—a striking contrast with the idealization of Kyros' Persia which had gone before, and one which contains several contradictions in substance with the preceding narrative.[142] The effect of the epilogue is to raise implicitly some important questions about the passing nature of all things: great men die and with them their achievements. It is a disturbing messsage, but one which is not inconsistent with a work which sets out to explore the nature of power. It ends with an appeal to the reader to verify the facts of Persian degeneration for himself.[143]

To conclude, the *synkriseis* do not give the reader a summary of the content or the moral issues raised in the preceding narratives. Rather they give a new and often different view of the protagonists from the one given in the narrative. This is partly a result of the rhetorical structure of the *synkriseis*: the two different ways of constructing the past inevitably give different pictures. But the dissonace between narrative and *synkrisis* seems deliberate. Sometimes, furthermore, the text actually draws attention to the dissonance by means of unresolved contradictions between Life and *synkrisis*. The reader gets a double presentation of the protagonists, he sees the past through two different lenses.[144] The question of which is right is left open for the reader, the jury in the rhetorical *agon* of the *synkrisis*,[145] whose complicity in making the final decision is encouraged by the intimate and co-operative tone established in the *synkriseis* by the frequent use of first-person verbs. This chapter confirms the earlier findings of this book; where questions of ethics are concerned, Plutarch is more ready to ask questions than to provide simple answers.

---

[142] Hirsch (1985), 92–5.
[143] The authenticity of the final chapter has, as one might expect, been disputed. See Hirsch (1985), 91–7; Due (1989), 16–22; Tatum (1989), 215–25.
[144] For this technique of double presentation, see also above, pp. 133–5, and below, pp. 307–8.
[145] For court-room metaphors in the *synkriseis*, cf. 'votes': *Thes.-Rom.* 3. 3; *Kim.-Luc.* 3. 6; the 'first place' (πρωτεῖον): *Per.-Fab.* 3. 7; *Lys.-Sulla* 5. 6; *Ag./Kleom.-Gracchi* 5. 7; 'crowns': *Phil.-Flam.* 3. 5. Court-room metaphors abound also in the *De Fort. Rom.* : 317c; 318a; 318d; 320a; 323e; see Swain (1989*d*), 508.

9

The Politics of Parallelism
Greeks and Romans in the Parallel Lives

εἰ δὲ καὶ τὸ περὶ τοὺς εἵλωτας ἀναγκάσει τις ἡμᾶς εἰς τὴν Λυκούργου θέσθαι πολιτείαν, ὠμότατον ἔργον καὶ παρανομώτατον, μακρῷ τινι τὸν Νομᾶν ἑλληνικώτερον γεγονέναι νομοθέτην φήσομεν, ὅς γε καὶ τοὺς ὡμολογημένους δούλους ἔγευσε τιμῆς ἐλευθέρας.

If we must ascribe to the state of Lykourgos the treatment of the helots, a most savage and lawless practice, we shall declare that Numa was far more Greek a lawgiver, in that he gave acknowledged slaves a taste of the dignity of freedom.   (*Lyk.-Num.* 1. 10)

In this chapter, I shall attempt to analyse the way in which Plutarch constructs Greek and Roman identities in the *Parallel Lives*. Central to this construction is his use of *synkrisis*, one of his most original contributions to the writing of the past. Much of this study has been concerned with the literary effects of *synkrisis*. As we have seen, Plutarch uses the two parallel Lives of a pair, with their prologue and *synkrisis*, to explore a set of moral themes which run across the whole Plutarchan 'book'. By putting together two figures from two different backgrounds and two different periods, Plutarch is able to focus attention on the moral issues which their Lives raise rather than simply on the historical details of each Life. Furthermore, *synkrisis* contributes to Plutarch's moral programme not simply by the similarities between two Lives of a pair, but by the differences: a moral issue is often explored in one Life, then complicated or approached in a different way in the second. The destabilizing effect of *synkrisis* is most striking in the formal *synkriseis* themselves, which, as the last chapter argued, sometimes break away from the moral pattern established in the preceding Lives and suggest a new way of looking at the actions narrated.

But Plutarchan *synkrisis* has cultural implications. Behind the idea of *synkrisis* lies the belief, central to ancient theories of the usefulness of history, that the past repeats itself: one of the benefits of studying history is in the identification of these repeated patterns. The comparative structure of the *Parallel Lives* suggests that not only does history repeat itself, but events in Greek history have parallels in events in Roman history. The histories of the two cultures are presented as mirror images of one another, as parallel examples of the same underlying patterns. Such a presentation of the history of Greece and Rome has important implications for contemporary second-century discourse concerning Greek culture and Roman power. Both Roman and Greek heroes are described and judged on the same terms—a fact which makes possible comparison of individual paired subjects, and of Greek and Roman culture and history as a whole, while at the same time exposing the contrasts and irreducible differences between them.

At stake, then, in Plutarch's use of *synkrisis* is the construction of identity and culture. Cultural identity in any age is not fixed, but malleable and variable, subject to contestation and construction; in the second century AD Greek and Roman identities were being fashioned, tested, and appropriated not least through the writing of history. The malleability of images of Greece under Roman rule is demonstrated by Plutarch's own Delphic dialogues which give two contrasting pictures of the contemporary prosperity of Delphoi and of Greece as a whole: the *On the obsolescence of oracles* gives a picture of impoverishment, while the *Why does the Pythia no longer give oracles in verse?* gives a picture of affluence.[1] The past, moreover, was a prime site for the construction of culture. As we shall see, Plutarch shows himself very much aware of the potential importance of the past within this debate when he warns the contemporary Greek statesman not to invoke the glories of the Classical Greek past in the wrong context (*Praec. Ger.* 814a–c). The *Parallel Lives*, through their construction of a parallel history of Greece and Rome, a history projected through the focal lens of *synkrisis*, are key documents in this continuing debate over the meaning of Greekness and Romanness.

The notion of Greek and Roman identities as being open for contestation might be seen to be confirmed by prosopographical studies of Plutarch's circle of friends and associates—those individuals who are mentioned in his work, or whom we have other reasons to link with him.[2] Q. Sosius Senecio, the dedicatee of the *Lives* as well as of the *Table talk* and the essay *How to recognize that one is making progress in virtue*, is an interesting case. He was plainly an important figure in the imperial

---

[1] For an attempt to find a reality, cf. Alcock (1993).
[2] The most thorough-going is Puech (1992). Cf. also Flacelière (1951); Ziegler (1951), 665–96 (= 1964, 30–60); Jones (1967; 1970; 1972); Follet (1972); Puech (1981); Donini (1986).

administration, holding the 'ordinary' consulship in both 99 and 107. His origins are probably in the Latin-speaking West, but he may well have had family connections in the Greek world and is implicitly presented by Plutarch as a man well-versed in Greek literary culture.[3] His career, and in particular Plutarch's construction of his *persona*, shows one way in which Romanness might be presented. Similarly, the career of Favorinus of Arles in Gaul, who was a friend of Plutarch, and also on good terms with the Roman Aulus Gellius, shows how Greek identity could be appropriated and constructed. Favorinus' most famous saying that 'although a Gaul, he spoke/was Greek' neatly captures the sense in which cultural identity was neither unitary nor fixed.[4] In a similar way the presence of some Greeks in the Roman administration in the second century should not be taken, as it has been by some, as evidence for an increasingly unifed élite, of the breakdown of separate Greek and Roman identities.[5] The careers of these men are certainly not typical and say nothing about the attitudes of such office-holders to the societies and cultures in which they move.[6] But, more importantly, they demonstrate the complexity of cultural identity, how it varies according to context: Plutarch, like many members of the Greek élites, was a Roman citizen and able presumably in some contexts—though not in his literary work—to present himself as Roman; in other contexts, however, and certainly in his literary work, Greek and occasionally local *polis* identity is stressed.[7]

Plutarch's decision to set Greek and Roman history in parallel was radical. There was indeed a long tradition before him of Greek writers who dealt with Roman history, attempting to account for the dominant

---

[3] Senecio is now thought to be the subject of the acephalous inscription *CIL* vi 1444 = *ILS* 1022. Other evidence shows that he had clients in Sparta, and that his daughter and son-in-law had connections in Phrygia. Jones (1970) argues for a Greek origin. Contrast Halfmann (1979), 211, who argues rather for an Italian or African origin, and, in particular, Swain (1996a), 144–5 and 426–7.

[4] Γαλάτης ὢν ἑλληνίζειν (Phil. *Vit. Soph.* 1. 8. 489). On Favorinus, see Holford-Strevens (1988), 72–92; Gleason (1995), esp. 3–20.

[5] Greeks in the Roman government: Syme (1963, and especially the 1982 revision); Hopkins (1983), 184–93. Cf. the Julii Quadrati of Pergamon: Halfmann (1979), 112–15; Habicht (1969), 43–53; Arrian: Syme (1982); Bosworth (1988), 16–24. Unified élite: Jones (1971), 39–64, 107–9, 122–30, with Babut (1975), 210; Dihle (1989), 205–6.

[6] Cf. Barnish (1994), 173–4 on the limits of prosopography.

[7] On variable identities, cf. Millar (1964), 182–92. The 8th-c. historian Georgos Synkellos (659 Dindorf) claims, unconvincingly, that Plutarch himself held a procuratorship under Hadrian. The *Souda* (s.v. Πλούταρχος) claims that he received consular powers under Trajan (interpreted by Jones 1971, 29–30, as *ornamenta consularia*); this is even less likely. For the details, see Swain (1996a), 171–2.

position which Rome had come to assume in the world. In the second century BC Polybios charted Rome's rise to power and paid special attention to Rome's constitution. In the first century Cornelius Alexander 'Polyhistor' and his pupil Iulius Hyginus both wrote about Rome.[8] Under Augustus, Dionysios of Halikarnassos wrote his *Roman Antiquities*, tracing Rome's early history down to the First Punic War. But their work did not set Roman history side by side with Greek history. Other Greek historians, perhaps the majority, preferred to ignore Rome and either look back to the days of Greek political independence before the death of Alexander, or to write purely local histories.[9] Plutarch departs from both these models in his direct confrontation of Roman history with Greek history.

Perhaps it is to the Roman tradition of Universal History that we must look for a precedent for the paralleling of the histories of Greece and Rome.[10] At any rate, it is certain that in this undertaking Plutarch was influenced by the *Lives of illustrious men* of the Roman Cornelius Nepos (published c.35–31 BC), which had brought into parallel Lives of Roman and non-Roman figures, treated in separate books.[11] The figures whom Nepos dealt with seem to have been mainly literary figures, and in this respect Nepos can be viewed as an expression of the contemporary Roman desire to assert their *literary* equality with Greece: it is probable that only the two books on generals dealt with political or military history.[12] At any rate, Nepos' work betrays a Romano-centric conception

---

[8] See Wiseman (1979), 160–1. Juba (1st c. BC to 1st c. AD) wrote in Greek a work entitled Ὁμοιότητες (Athenaios 170e) or Περὶ Ὁμοιοτήτων (Hesychios s.v. καρτή), probably a comparison of Greek and Roman customs and institutions. See Jacoby (1916), 2394. The *Souda* (s.v. Charax) records that the Pergamene historian A. Claudius Charax (*FGrH* 103), suffect consul in AD 147, wrote thirteen books of *Greek and ?Roman histories* (Ἑλληνικῶν τε καὶ ⟨Ῥωμαικῶν Jacoby⟩ ἱστοριῶν βιβλία μ΄.). For his career, see Habicht (1959–60), 109–25; more generally on Charax, Andrei (1984). Cf. also the pseudo-Plutarchan *Collection of parallel Greek and Roman histories*, of uncertain date, though this may be a parody of, or at least influenced by, Plutarch's *Parallel Lives*: see Babbitt (1936), 253–5.

[9] Cf. Bowie (1970).

[10] e.g. Nepos' *Chronica* and Atticus' *Liber Annalis* (both 1st c. BC), and Velleius Paterculus (1st c. AD). Cf. Desideri (1992b), 4482–4. On universal history, see Starr (1981); also Momigliano (1982); Alonso-Núñez (1990); Sacks (1981) 96–121; Wiseman (1979), 154–66. On Nepos' *Chronica*, see Geiger (1985), 68–78; on Velleius, Woodman (1975), 282–7.

[11] The non-Romans seem to have been mainly Greeks, but not exclusively: Hannibal and Hamilcar occur in the only book to survive in full, the *On eminent foreign leaders*. See Geiger (1985), 84–115. On Nepos' influence on Plutarch, see id. (1981), 95–8; (1985), 119–20, with the reservations of Moles (1989), 232–3.

[12] Roman attempts to place Latin and Greek literature in parallel are best exemplified in Quint. *Inst. Orat.* 10. 1. 46–131. Cf. Lucret. 1. 926–30; Virgil, *Eclogues* 6. 1–2; Catullus 95. 1–2; Propert. 4. 1. 64; 2. 34. 65–6; 3. 1. 1–2; cf. Cic. *Brut.* 26–52. See Kroll (1924), 12–16. On the content of the lost books of Nepos, see Geiger (1979a); (1985), 88–92.

of the world (cf. *pref.*; *Pel.* 1. 1; *Hann.* 13. 4). Plutarch's *Parallel Lives*, on the other hand, are written from a Helleno-centric viewpoint: the decision to place individual Greeks and Romans in parallel, a much more thorough-going parallelism than that of Nepos, suggests a confidence that Greek political and military history could stand side by side with that of the ruling power, that Greek heroes were the match of the Roman. For Plutarch, the past provides a protected space, shielded from the unpleasant realities of Greek political weakness, a space where Roman history might be appropriated into a Greek world-view and Greek culture championed freely.

Plutarchan *synkrisis*, then, has a significance beyond the literary structure and moral message of each pair of Lives. Plutarch's choice of Romans and Greeks as the objects of his comparison carries implications for his understanding of Greek and Roman identities. How are the two cultures presented in relation to each other? Was Plutarch's purpose, as has often been claimed, to reconcile the two peoples, to demonstrate to Romans that the Greeks had a history and heroes comparable to their own, and to demonstrate to Greeks that Romans were their equals in the finer arts of civilization?[13] Do the *Lives* reflect a belief in the essential unity of Greek and Roman culture?[14] Or, on the other hand, is the act of comparison one of resistance, an appropriation of Roman history into a Greek framework, a subtle demonstration of the inferiority of Rome when measured against the virtues and standards of the classical past, a past soon to be renascent in the Greek cities of the second century? What, in short, did it mean for a Greek living under the Roman Empire to write *Parallel Lives*?

2. PLUTARCH AND ROME: THE *POLITICAL PRECEPTS*

It is within the context of the contestation and construction of identities that Plutarch's explicit remarks on Roman government and culture should be seen. His criticism of gladiatorial combat, made also by other Greek writers of this period, is a criticism also made by contemporary Romans and early Christians and so is not to be interpreted in the black

[13] Trench (1873), 31–2; followed more recently by Gabba (1959), 369; Hommeyer (1963), 156–7; Russell (1966a), 140; (1982), 29–30; Bucher-Isler (1972), 89; Valgiglio (1992), esp. 4047–50. *Contra*: Jones (1971), 103–9; Babut (1975), 208–9; cf. Dihle (1956), 103; Barrow (1967), 57–9. Wardman (1974), esp. 39–41, sees Plutarch's purpose as the encouragement of a Greek readership to engage in local politics.

[14] As argued by Barigazzi (1984), esp. 284–5; (1994), esp. 33–54 and 149–53.

and white colours of an attack by a Greek on Roman culture, rather it is part of an attempt to delimit of what these cultures consisted: the boundaries and components of Greekness and Romanness are themselves up for contestation in this period.[15] Similarly, Plutarch's criticism of the emperor Nero on no account shows him as anti-Roman; rather it shows him as sharing the same attitudes to the recent past as his near contemporaries Tacitus and Suetonius.[16] It has been suggested that his consistently negative treatment of the divine honours paid to Hellenistic kings in their lifetime might be taken as a criticism of contemporary imperial cult.[17] But emperors, significantly, were not deified in their lifetime, and when dealing with the posthumous deification of Romulus, a key figure for the imperial cult, Plutarch agrees that, after death, the souls of some virtuous men may, like that of Romulus, ascend to 'to the gods' (*Rom.* 28. 10). Perhaps the most we may say is that, in those passages where Plutarch criticizes the deification of kings, he is using the past to explore an issue which has relevance to the present.[18]

Several passages have been taken as expressions of Plutarch's acquiescence in or happiness with Roman rule. At the end of the dialogue *Why does the Pythia no longer give oracles in verse?*, the speaker Theon appears to admit to happiness with present conditions. 'There is profound peace and tranquillity; war has stopped; there are no migrations and civil strifes, nor tyrannies nor any other diseases and ills of Greece, requiring special or elaborate remedies' (408b–c). The assumption is sometimes made that Theon is expressing Plutarch's own considered views. But this pronouncement must instead be seen in its literary context. The point is not contentment with Roman rule, but rather the reason why responses from Greek oracular shrines are no longer given in verse: Greece is more peaceful than in past ages, and so the questions asked of oracles are no longer of sufficient importance to merit verse replies. Significantly, Romans are not mentioned as the authors of this peace. Furthermore,

---

[15] Plut. *Terrest. an Aquat.* 959c; *De Esu Carn.* 997b–c. Other Greeks: e.g. Dion of Prousa, *Or.* 21. 121–2; Phil. *Apoll.* 4. 22. Romans: Cic. *Ad Fam.* 7. 1. 3; Seneca, *Ep.* 7. 2–5. Cf. Swain (1996a), 174 n. 118. For the criticisms of gladiatorial combat, see also Wiedemann (1992), 128–64.

[16] For Suetonius and Plutarch on Nero, see above, Ch. 8, nn. 37 and 129. Cf. *De Frat. Amore* 487e–488a for an emperor, probably Domitian, as a 'tyrant'.

[17] e.g. *Arist.* 6. 2–5; *Demetr.* 10. 3–13. 3; 24. 1–12; 30. 6–8; 42. 8–11. Scott (1929) claims such criticisms would be associated with the imperial cult; against: Jones (1971), 123–4, and Bowersock (1973), 187–91. Cf. Swain (1996a), 182 n. 146.

[18] Compare Dio Cassius' exploration of contemporary cult through his fictional account, set safely in the past, of Maecenas' speech to Augustus in 52. 35–6. Cf. Bowersock (1973), 202–6; Reinhold (1988), 207–8.

the massive impact of Roman predation and benefaction at Delphoi is not mentioned in either this dialogue or in the earlier *On the obsolescence of oracles*. The Delphic dialogues of Plutarch, like Pausanias' *Guide to Greece*, suggest not passive acceptance of the *pax romana* but a studied indifference to Roman intrusion.[19]

This sense of resistance to Roman influence is seen most clearly in the *Political precepts*. Here Plutarch deals explicitly with contemporary political life, and confronts the question of how the Greek past can and cannot be deployed within the context of Roman political domination.[20] The *Political precepts*, written at roughly the same time as the *Parallel Lives*, is an essay of advice, addressed in the first instance to Plutarch's friend Menemachos, a Greek from Sardis who is apparently about to embark on a political career in his own city. The wider readership is constructed as élite and Greek.[21] The focus of the *Political precepts* is entirely on the local Greek city-state and its political life: how the aspiring politician should address the people, how he should enter politics and with what motive, how he should deal with political friends and enemies, how harmony should be maintained at all levels within the city. In fact one of the most notable features of this essay is the general lack of reference to Rome. In discussing the daring actions with which a young man may launch his political career, Plutarch notes, without spelling out why, that city affairs no longer embrace warfare and alliances. Serving on embassies to the emperor, he continues, is a possible means of becoming known; but preferable are court cases or the limiting of a faction's power within one's own city, or, even better, the support of a powerful patron (804c–806f).

[19] On Pausanias' silence on Roman monuments, and his construction of Greek identity, see Elsner (1992), 17–20; (1994), 244–52; Bowie (1994). Flacelière (1971) argues that in *De Pyth. Orac.* 409c Plutarch makes a cryptic reference to the Emperor Hadrian in ascribing recent benefaction at Delphoi to 'the leader in this policy' (τὸν καθηγεμόνα ταύτης τῆς πολιτείας). It is more likely, however, as Swain (1991) argues, that the reference is to Plutarch himself.

[20] For the date (between AD 96 and 114), see Jones (1966), 72. The *Praec. Ger.*, which exercised an influence on Machiavelli (Desideri 1995*b*), is among the most intensely studied works of Plutarch. Most accessible and most recent is Swain (1996*a*), 162–83. Earlier studies include: Renoirte (1951); Carrière (1977); Panagopoulos (1977); Pavis d' Escurac (1981); Desideri (1986; 1991); Caiazza (1993); Masaracchia (1995); Tirelli (1995). Less useful are Lavagnini (1992); Massaro (1995). There is a commentary (largely linguistic) by Valgiglio (1976).

[21] Menemachos is not known outside the *Praec. Ger.* It is unlikely that he is a literary construct, given Plutarch's practice elsewhere of addressing works to real individuals. See Renoirte (1951), 69–81. Menemachos may be the recipient of *De Exil.*, identified as an exiled Sardian (600a; 601b), and an exemplar of the precariousness of political life as propounded in the *Praec. Ger.*

Towards the middle of the essay, Plutarch returns to the theme of the limited power of the city-state. Here he is a little more explicit about the reason for this limitation:

εἰσιόντα δ' εἰς ἅπασαν ἀρχὴν οὐ μόνον ἐκείνους δεῖ προχειρίζεσθαι τοὺς λογισμούς, οἷς ὁ Περικλῆς αὑτὸν ὑπεμίμνησκεν ἀναλαμβάνων τὴν χλαμύδα "πρόσεχε, Περίκλεις· ἐλευθέρων ἄρχεις, Ἑλλήνων ἄρχεις, πολιτῶν Ἀθηναίων·" ἀλλὰ κἀκεῖνο λέγειν πρὸς ἑαυτὸν "ἀρχόμενος ἄρχεις, ὑποτεταγμένης πόλεως ἀνθυπάτοις, ἐπιτρόποις Καίσαρος· 'οὐ ταῦτα λόγχη πεδιάς', οὐδ' αἱ παλαιαὶ Σάρδεις οὐδ' ἡ Λυδῶν ἐκείνη δύναμις." εὐσταλεστέραν δεῖ τὴν χλαμύδα ποιεῖν, καὶ βλέπειν ἀπὸ τοῦ στρατηγίου πρὸς τὸ βῆμα, καὶ τῷ στεφάνῳ μὴ πολὺ φρονεῖν μηδὲ πιστεύειν, ὁρῶντα τοὺς καλτίους ἐπάνω τῆς κεφαλῆς·

πολὺ φρονεῖν μηδὲ πιστεύειν Koraes: πολὺ φρόνημα πιστεύειν

When entering upon any office whatsoever, you must not only have at hand those reasonings of which Perikles used to remind himself when he assumed the general's cloak: 'Take care, Perikles; you are ruling free men, you are ruling Greeks, Athenian citizens.' You must also say to yourself, 'You who rule are yourself ruled, you rule a city subject to proconsuls, the agents of Caesar. *These are not the spearmen of the plain* [Soph. *Trach.* 1058], nor is this ancient Sardis, nor the famed Lydian power.' You should arrange your cloak more decently and look at the orator's platform from the standpoint of the governor's office[22] and not have great pride or confidence in your crown, since you see his boots above your head. (*Praec. Ger.* 813d–e)

Above the head of the Greek statesman, Plutarch reminds Menemachos, in a powerful image of suppressed violence, stand the military boots of the Roman governor. Rome and Roman power must form the mental backdrop to the Greek statesman's policy and conduct. He should, Plutarch continues, imitate an actor, not over-stepping 'the rhythms and metres (τοὺς ῥυθμοὺς καὶ τὰ μέτρα) of the power given by the rulers' (813e–f).[23] The Greek statesman must, then, be aware of the place of the Greek *polis* within the wider Roman empire; he may indeed see himself as the heir of Perikles, but he is also a subject of the emperor. For 'being booed off the stage' (ἔκπτωσις), Plutarch continues, brings not the jeers of the audience but, in the words of a tragedy unknown to us, 'the terrible chastiser, the axe that cuts the neck' (δεινὸς κολαστὴς πέλεκυς

---

[22] βλέπειν ἀπὸ τοῦ στρατηγίου πρὸς τὸ βῆμα. The text is probably corrupt. My translation follows Russell (1993), 164. Swain (1996a), 166, following Jones (1971), 133, translates 'look out of your headquarters to the governor's tribunal'. The word στρατηγός could be used of a local magistrate (reference in Swain) or of the Roman governor (Mason 1974, 155–8). Jones argues for the manuscript reading πολὺ φρόνημα πιστεύειν citing *Cato Min.* 11. 8 as a parallel; but Ziegler emends the latter.

[23] On comparison of statesmen to actors, see Becchi (1995); Swain (1996a), 178–9.

αὐχένος τομεύς): whether this image is to be taken literally or not remains ominously unclear. The word ἔκπτωσις is selected for its theatrical associations: ἐκπίπτειν is used of an actor or speaker being hissed off the stage or rostrum. But in addition it conveys the very real dangers which aggravation of the ruling power might bring: ἐκπίπτειν regularly means to be exiled. Such a fate, Plutarch goes on, whatever exactly this may be, befell Menemachos' fellow-Sardian Pardalas when he 'forgot the limits' (ἐλαθομένοις τῶν ὁρίων).[24]

The statesman, Plutarch continues (814a), should not, as some do, stir up the common people 'by urging them to imitate the deeds, the confidence, the exploits of their ancestors, which are not fitting to the present times and conditions (ἀσυμμέτρους τοῖς παροῦσι καιροῖς καὶ πράγμασιν)'. To do this is laughable, but the punishment, Plutarch warns darkly (814a), is 'far from laughable' (γέλωτά τε ποιοῦντες οὐκέτι γέλωτος ἄξια πάσχουσιν). The Greek past is a powerful totem, not to be invoked rashly or in the wrong context. Examples from the past which can safely be used in addressing the people, Plutarch goes on, are those which encourage harmony and moderation within the city: such as the amnesty declared in Athens in 403 BC for those who had taken part in the oligarchic revolution. 'But Marathon, Eurymedon, Plataia, and all other examples which make the many swell and snort with pride should be left in the schools of the sophists' (814c), that is, should be left for formal declamation amongst the élite, not for mass gatherings of the common people. The advice is striking, given Plutarch's emphasis in the *Lives* and elsewhere on the importance of imitating the men of the past, especially so as it is the military deeds of the past on which Plutarch so often concentrates.[25] The composition of the audience, that is, the context in which the past is evoked, is obviously vital: stirring up the crowd with tales of past glories might lead to riots and Roman intervention; retelling and idealizing the classical past in the context of a literary salon or work of history is, Plutarch suggests, a different matter. The same past, the same events, may have different meanings in different contexts.

Plutarch now moves on to address the issue of personal contacts with members of the Roman élite, contacts of the sort that some prosopographical studies have brought to light. 'The statesman,' he says, 'should always have a friend amongst the most powerful people up there (τῶν ἄνω δυνατωτάτων), like a firm bulwark of his administration (πολιτεία);

---

[24] Cf. 825b–d below, p. 298.
[25] See above, Chs. 1–2 and pp. 97–8.

for the Romans themselves are most eager in the political interests of their friends' (*Praec. Ger.* 814c). The use of ἄνω in this sentence seems to assimilate the Roman Empire to the Persian Empire:[26] an ambiguous tactic, suggesting both the otherness and menace of Rome but perhaps also dulling the implied criticism by momentarily shifting it to the distant past. Personal links, then, can be of the utmost importance in protecting or gaining benefit for one's city (814c–d). But this should be the limit of involvement with the Roman administration: Plutarch goes on to criticize those who seek office in the imperial administration, a practice which leads, he claims, to neglect of their duties 'at home' (τὰ οἴκοι), that is, in their own city (814d–e).[27] He also criticizes those who appeal 'to the rulers' (τοῖς κρατοῦσιν) to adjudicate disputes which should have been solved without outside intervention (814e–815c), though, of course, the statesman should stand firm when 'storms' fall on the state, by which he evidently means when unrest brings Roman disfavour. 'Such were the troubles', he explains, 'which befell the Pergamenes under Nero, and the Rhodians recently under Domitian, and the Thessalians earlier under Augustus after they had burnt Petraios alive' (815d).[28] It is this awareness of the potential for violent Roman intervention that lies behind Plutarch's pleas in the remaining sections of the work for the maintenance of concord and harmony within the city, both between politicians and amongst the common people. The maintenance of this harmony is the chief job of the Greek statesman. Plutarch sums up in his final chapter:

κράτιστον δὲ προνοεῖν, ὅπως μηδέποτε στασιάζωσι, καὶ τοῦτο τῆς πολιτικῆς ὥσπερ τέχνης μέγιστον ἡγεῖσθαι καὶ κάλλιστον. ὅρα γάρ, ὅτι τῶν μεγίστων ἀγαθῶν ταῖς πόλεσιν, εἰρήνης ἐλευθερίας εὐετηρίας εὐανδρίας ὁμονοίας, πρὸς μὲν εἰρήνην οὐδὲν οἱ δῆμοι τῶν πολιτικῶν ἔν γε τῷ παρόντι χρόνῳ δέονται, πέφευγε γὰρ ἐξ ἡμῶν καὶ ἠφάνισται πᾶς μὲν Ἕλλην πᾶς δὲ βάρβαρος πόλεμος· ἐλευθερίας

---

[26] Jones (1971), 113 n. 22; Swain (1996a), 176–7.

[27] See Swain (1996a), 168–71. Service in the Roman adminstration could be presented in different ways for different rhetorical purposes. At *De Tranq. An.* 470c desire for such office is used as an example of lack of tranquillity (εὐθυμία). The *De Cap. ex Inim.* is addressed to Cornelius Pulcher, a Greek who held high office in the imperial administration (ibid. 163). At the start of the tract his political conduct is praised, although, significantly, his imperial offices are not mentioned (86b). At 92d–e, however, Plutarch adopts a critical tone giving 'dishonourable and slavish power in courts and governments' (αἰσχρὰς καὶ ἀνελευθέρους δυνάμεις ἐν αὐλαῖς ἢ πολιτείαις) as possible rewards for flatterers; he goes on, however, to mitigate the criticism by suggesting it is the *Persian* empire he has in mind (eunuchs, concubines, satrapies).

[28] For the events at Pergamon, cf. Tac. *Ann.* 16. 23. 1. Petraios was the leader of the pro-Caesarian party in Thessaly and was executed after Caesar's death (Caes. *BC* 3. 35. 2; Cic. *Phil.* 13. 33). The events at Rhodes are otherwise unknown.

δ' ὅσον οἱ κρατοῦντες νέμουσι τοῖς δήμοις μέτεστι καὶ τὸ πλέον ἴσως οὐκ ἄμεινον· εὐφορίαν δὲ γῆς ἄφθονον εὐμενῆ τε κρᾶσιν ὡρῶν, καὶ τίκτειν γυναῖκας "ἐοικότα τέκνα γονεῦσι" σωτηρίαν ⟨τε⟩ τοῖς γεννωμένοις εὐχόμενος ὅ γε σώφρων αἰτήσεται παρὰ θεῶν τοῖς ἑαυτοῦ πολίταις.

But the best thing is to see to it in advance that factional discord shall never arise and to regard this as the greatest and finest part of, as it were, the art of statesmanship. For observe that of the greatest blessings for states—peace, freedom, prosperity, abundance of men, and concord—so far as peace is concerned, the peoples have, at the present time at least, no need of statesmen; for all war, both Greek and barbarian, has fled from us and has disappeared. And of freedom the peoples have as great a share as the rulers grant them, and perhaps more would not be better; but bountiful productivity of the land, kindly temperament of the season, the birth of *children like their parents* [Hesiod, *Works and Days* 235], and safety for their offspring, these are the things the sensible statesman will pray to the gods to grant his citizens. (*Praec. Ger.* 824b–e)

This passage has been interpreted by some as a statement of acquiescence in, even happiness with, the fact of Roman rule. But it is not Plutarch's purpose to express such sentiments here. Rather his purpose is to make clear that the only sphere of activity left to the statesman of the Greek *polis* is the maintenance of internal order. And the maintenance of this order is vital because without it Roman intervention is assured.[29] As so often, the Romans are not named: they stand threateningly in the shadows, ready to intervene violently if private élite rivalries cause unrest in the city.

The statesman, Plutarch continues, will try to reconcile those in dispute:

ἔπειτα καὶ καθ' ἕνα καὶ κοινῇ διδάσκοντα καὶ φράζοντα τὴν τῶν Ἑλληνικῶν πραγμάτων ἀσθένειαν, ἧς ἐν ἀπολαῦσαι ἄμεινόν ἐστι τοῖς εὖ φρονοῦσι, μεθ' ἡσυχίας καὶ ὁμονοίας καταβιῶναι, μηδὲν ἐν μέσῳ τῆς τύχης ἆθλον ὑπολελοιπυίας. τίς γὰρ ἡγεμονία, τίς δόξα τοῖς περιγενομένοις; ποία δύναμις, ἣν μικρὸν ἀνθυπάτου διάταγμα κατέλυσεν ἢ μετέστησεν εἰς ἄλλον, οὐθὲν οὐδ' ἂν παραμένῃ σπουδῆς ἄξιον ἔχουσαν;

Then he should teach them individually and all together and make reference to the weakness of Greek affairs, in which it is better for wise men to enjoy one thing, to live out their lives in quiet and harmony, since fortune has left us no prize for open competition. For what leadership, what glory is there for those who are successful? What sort of power is it, which a small edict of the proconsul

---

[29] Cf. the pleas for internal harmony in the speeches of Dio of Prousa (e.g. *Or.* 34; 38), and the emphasis on ὁμόνοια in contemporary inscriptions (Sheppard 1984–6). Cf. Ailios Aristeides, *On Rome* 67–71.

may abolish or transfer to another and which, even if it lasts, has in it nothing worthwhile? (824e–f)

Greece is weak; Roman power potentially arbitrary. Roman intervention must be avoided. Small rivalries, Plutarch goes on, may lead to larger unrest. To illustrate this, Plutarch cites two examples drawn from Greek history: revolution ($\nu\epsilon\omega\tau\epsilon\rho\iota\sigma\mu\acute{o}s$) in Delphoi in the fourth century, caused by rivalry between two noble families, and a case of erotic jealousy in Syracuse, probably to be dated to 485 BC, which led to factionalism ($\sigma\tau\acute{a}\sigma\iota s$) and the overthrow of the government. Both incidents are taken from, or based on a source common to, *Politics* 1303b17–1304a4, where Aristotle warns of the dangers of factional conflict.[30] Plutarch's choice of examples from the past is significant: tales from the days of the independent Greek cities are useful and instructive and might in the right circumstances be used even before the people. But they must be matched to context. Plutarch ends, as he puts it, with examples which are for Menemachos 'close to home' ($o\mathit{i}\kappa\epsilon\hat{i}a$ $\pi a\rho a\delta\epsilon\acute{i}\gamma\mu a\tau a$): the enmity of Pardalas and Tyrrhenos in Sardis, his own *polis*, which resulted in rebellion and war, and—though Plutarch does not spell it out—Roman retribution (825b–d).[31]

Rome, then, in the context of the *Political precepts*, is an external and potentially threatening power. There is no sense here of the parallel existence of two equal cultures. This fact makes clearer the striking nature of Plutarch's programme in the *Parallel Lives*. It also cautions against assuming a simple link between Plutarch's use of a parallel structure there and his 'real' views on the relationship of Roman and Greek culture. Context, is as ever, vital. The dark picture of Rome which emerges in the *Political precepts* prepares us for a more problematizing, combative reading of the *Parallel Lives*, which can be seen, on one level, as a statement of cultural resistance.

3. WRITING IN PARALLEL: *MORALIA*

Plutarch's presentation in the *Lives* of Roman and Greek culture in parallel is foreshadowed in two sets of texts drawn from his non-biographical works. The first of these are the *Greek questions* and the *Roman questions*. Here, however, Roman and Greek cultures are not

---

[30] See Newman (1902), 319–21. On the events at Delphoi, see Parke (1939), 234–5.

[31] The precise events to which Plutarch refers, their date and the identity of Pardalas, are now unknown: see Hanfmann (1983), 144.

portrayed as the twin poles of the human cosmos: there also existed a third parallel strand, the lost *Barbarian questions* (Lamp. Cat. 139). The presence of this third strand itself suggests a more problematic and negative presentation of Roman culture, as somewhere between Greek and barbarian. Plutarch is, then, in these texts, far from assuming that Greek and Roman are two constituents of a single, broad, civilized culture. Furthermore, although the two cultures are presented in parallel, Plutarch presents himself and his audience as firmly Greek, as insiders in one culture and outsiders, albeit informed and educated, in the other. The *Greek questions* (Αἴτια Ἑλληνικά) plainly owe much to Kallimachos' *Aitia*, as the title indicates, as well as to the long Greek aetiological tradition.[32] Such Greek 'antiquarian' enquiries were particularly in vogue in the second century, as we see in the *Sophists at Dinner* of Athenaios and, indeed, in Plutarch's own *Table talk* (Συμποσιακά), a series of topics for discussion (προβλήματα). The mode of narration of the *Greek questions* is *inclusive*; the narrator presents himself as an insider. The questions generally concern local issues, of the sort: 'Who are the *Koliadai* among the people of Ithake and what is the *phagilos*?' (14, 294c). Occasionally the concern is one of more general Greek culture, such as (10, 293a) 'What is the sheep-escaper?' (τί τὸ φυξίμηλον;). Narrator and audience are bonded, by the very act of enquiry into the aetiology of local Greek customs, as members of the same wider Hellenic community, a community from which the Romans are excluded. In the *Roman questions*, the mode of narration is *exclusive*; Plutarch projects himself and the audience as outsiders. Questions are framed with a vague 'they' as subject. For example: 'Why do they [the Romans] not marry women who are closely related to them?' (108, 289d). Notably, when recording Roman criticisms of Greek athletics, Plutarch feels himself obliged to intervene to mitigate the criticism (274d-e). Roman customs are explained and Latin words and names translated;[33] the Greeks are occasionally referred to in the first person.[34]

[32] Boulogne (1992), 4683–7.
[33] e.g. 13, 266f; 62, 279b; 72, 281a.
[34] e.g. 40, 274b; 57, 278c–d. Of course, in other contexts Plutarch might equally represent himself as Roman. The Latin writers Sallust (e.g. *Cat.* 6. 5) and Seneca (*Ep.* 89. 7), for example, both also use the third person of Romans: Bowersock (1968), 262. Dio Cassius who regularly explains Roman institutions (54. 24. 7–8; 54. 26. 16–17; 55. 8. 6–7), could also present himself as Roman (e.g. 39. 38, 1). Lucian, on the other hand, whose *persona* is consistently Greek, can refer to Roman soldiers, engaged in fighting barbarians, as 'our men' (*Alex.* 48). Similarly, Byzantine historiographers like Prokopios who explain Christian practices cannot be assumed to be either pagan themselves or writing for a pagan audience: cf. Alan and Averil Cameron (1964); Averil Cameron (1966), 470–2; (1985), 113–19.

With the *Roman questions* we might contrast Ovid's *Fasti*; here narrator, addressee, and reader are all linked as insiders, members of a community, for whom the ritual calendar, linking past and present, provides a way of understanding their own identity.[35] The *Greek questions* and *Roman questions*, then, present Greek and Roman cultures as different, a difference exposed by placing them side by side. Roman customs are selected for comment where they differ from Greek, and Rome is shown to have derived its customs from Greece: Greek culture provides the yardstick by which Roman is measured.[36]

Another set of texts which foreshadow the parallelism of the *Parallel Lives* are the display speeches on Rome and on Alexander. The first of these, probably to be entitled *On the fortune or virtue of the Romans*, may have been intended to be read or heard alongside one or both of the speeches *On the fortune or virtue of Alexander*.[37] If this is so, then Alexander's Empire would be set against that of Rome, an example of the parallelism which would later reach its apogee in the *Lives*. It is a thought-provoking comparison. In a notable passage in the speech on Rome (316e–317c), Plutarch likens the imposition by Rome of order and stability on the world to the establishment of the ordered universe of Plato's *Timaios*.[38] This passage cannot be read as an uncomplicated acceptance of Roman rule in Greece. Most obviously, the speech is an *epideixis*; perhaps an *enkomion*; the original audience and occasion are unknown, but praise of Rome is unsurprising in a speech on the topic of the virtue and fortune of the Romans. The comparison may indeed have been conventional; Ailios Aristeides employs it in his laudatory speech *On Rome* (103–5).[39] Significantly, the language with which the Roman Empire is praised is that of classical Greek philosophy; Rome is praised, but it is on Greek terms. Furthermore, the emphasis on Rome as providing stability to a world in chaos plainly relates to the Greek world *after*

---

[35] e.g. at 1. 277–88; 529–38; 587–616. On this aspect of the *Fasti*, see Beard (1987).

[36] Cf. Boulogne (1994), 115–24.

[37] Those manuscripts which give the former a title list it as *On the fortune or virtue of the Romans* (Περὶ τῆς Ῥωμαίων τύχης ἢ ἀρετῆς) or *Does the Roman state belong to fortune or virtue?* (Πότερον τὰ Ῥωμαίων πράγματα τύχης ἢ ἀρετῆς;). In the Lamprias Catalogue, however, it is listed simply as *On the fortune of the Romans* (Περὶ τῆς Ῥωμαίων τύχης). On the *synkrisis* between the two speeches, cf. Swain (1989d), 504 n. 2. Schröder (1991) suggests, less convincingly, that each of Plutarch's speeches on Alexander was originally paired with a speech arguing the opposite case.

[38] Dillon (1997), 236–8. Cf. *De Sera Num.* 550d–e, where God creates order in the cosmos in order to inspire men to create order in their souls.

[39] See Oliver (1953), 874–8, 883–4, and 946, with the criticisms and bibliography of Swain (1996a), 275.

Alexander. In the *Lives* too, Plutarch presents Hellenistic history as a period of decline and disorder, even likening it, as here, to the chaos of a disordered cosmos (*Demetr.* 5. 1).[40] In fact, Plutarch avoids discussing either Rome's conquest of Greece or Roman dominion over the Greek cities; reference is limited to two brief mentions of the defeats of the Hellenistic kings Philip V and Antiochos (323f; 324c–d).[41] The speech on Rome does not, then, present Rome as more powerful than Greece: rather, seen in its context alongside the Alexander speeches, it expresses a comparability between the two cultures—a comparability which reveals, or at least suggests, some essential differences. The emphasis on the civilizing mission of Alexander's Empire, the bringing of *paideia* to barbarians, is by comparison notably absent in the treatment of Rome, where the stress is more on military virtue, as well as the favour of providence ($\tau \acute{v} \chi \eta$).[42] The speech closes with a vision of the imagined clash between the armies of Alexander and of Rome, forestalled only by Fortune's intervention in removing Alexander (326a–c). It is a remarkable end, briefly making an explicit parallel between the two empires and subversively suggesting that Rome's victory was won by mere chance.[43]

In the speeches on Alexander and Rome, as in the *Greek questions* and *Roman questions*, Plutarch places Roman history and culture alongside Greek, thereby encouraging comparison and exposing difference. But it is a Greek framework within which such comparison is made. This strategy reaches its most developed form in the *Parallel Lives*, where Roman history is placed alongside Greek and where both are explained and judged in the language of Greek political and philosophical discourse.

4. WRITING IN PARALLEL: THE *PARALLEL LIVES*

The synkritic structure of the *Parallel Lives*, the placing of Roman subjects alongside Greek, throws the spotlight onto the issue of identity. How are Greek and Roman to be constructed? By adopting this radically new approach to the writing of history, Plutarch is able to explore issues

---

[40] See above, p. 115.
[41] Swain (1989d), 516. Contrast the *Phil.-Flam.*, where Plutarch does talk of providence willing the conquest of Greece (see below, p. 307). On providence and the conquest of Greece in the *Lives*, see Swain (1989b), 279–98.
[42] On the meaning of *tyche* in this treatise see Swain (1989d), 506–7; cf. above, Ch. 4, n. 81.
[43] Contrast the vehement denial of this in Livy 9. 16. 19–9. 19. 17. Cf. Breitenbach (1969).

of identity within the protected, safe space of the distant past. His Romans are not, like those of Dionysios of Halikarnassos, descended from Greeks. Dionysios presented Rome as a Greek *polis*, founded by Greeks and growing to success because of its adherence to Greek virtue:[44] the fact of Roman domination of the world was made more palatable by emphasizing its Greek origins. Plutarch's Romans, though, are not barbarians either: they are set side by side with, and are in one sense the equals of, the Greeks. Certainly in the *synkriseis*, as we have noted, Romans emerge in no way inferior to Greeks. But it is from a Hellenocentric position that Plutarch's Romans are seen: Plutarch uses Greek political and ethical models to provide the conceptual framework by which Roman conduct is described and the standard against which it is judged. As in the *Greek questions* and *Roman questions*, so in the *Parallel Lives* author and audience are constructed as Greek, as knowledgeable insiders as far as Greek history is concerned, and as outsiders in Roman history: Plutarch takes much more care to explain Roman institutions and Latin words than he does for their Greek counterparts.[45] The synkritic structure makes more obvious this appropriation of Roman history: each Roman subject is judged and analysed according to the standards and themes set out in the Greek Life which preceded it. In this sense, the order in which the two Lives of a pair are usually placed has a cultural significance: the Greek Life establishes the evaluative norms against which the Roman must stand. The moral categories applied to both Roman and Greek figures are unmistakably Greek: Romans are assessed on Greek criteria, and figures from Roman history re-used as exempla of Greek moral and political imperatives.

The effect of this use of a Greek lens through which to project his Romans is both at times to misrepresent the motives of Roman statesman and the workings of Roman politics, and to suggest—albeit subtly—the universality of Greek cultural and political models. Thus, as Christopher Pelling has demonstrated, Plutarch presents Roman politics in terms of 'the few' and 'the many': the complexities of late Roman Republican politics are thus recast into a simple dichotomy. This leads him to blur the complexities of the various Roman popular assemblies with their different compositions and different political characteristics. In Plutarch's projection, what is important is the contrast

---

[44] See Hartog (1991); Gabba (1991), 109–10.
[45] Most markedly in *Thes.-Rom*. Cf. *Crass*. 7. 1, where he explains the meaning of Pompey's soubriquet Magnus. Also *Aem*. 3. 2; *Caes*. 37. 3; *Cam*. 13. 1; *Cato Maj*. 16. 1–3; *Cor*. 19. 1; *Sulla* 1. 7; 37. 7. More examples are given by Cerezo Magán (1992), 16–18.

between the Senate, presented as the Council (βουλή) of a Greek *polis*, and the people (δῆμος), presented as a potentially unruly mob: a contrast central to much Greek political thought. This framework leads him to assimilate the struggles between the *populares* and the 'optimates', rival groups *within* the Roman Senate, to the struggle of people *against* Senate. Similarly, Plutarch plays down the role of the Italian peasantry and of the *equites*, groups which do not fit into his political framework, in the conflicts of the late Republic. Contrast Appian, whose interpretation is much less influenced by classical Greek models. For Plutarch, Roman dynasts are seen as aiming for tyranny; motivations such as the desire for *gloria* or the concern for *dignitas* are not developed.[46] Similarly, Roman concepts such as *mos maiorum* or *pietas* are ignored.

The distinctly Greek lens through which Plutarch projects his vision of Roman history can be seen clearly at work in the *Life of Caesar*. Here Julius Caesar's career is made to fit a model familiar from Greek political thought: he is a popular leader, who comes to power through demagogic means and uses that power to install himself as a tyrant. His murder takes place when the people turn against his hybristic ways. He is, then, identified with two 'types' drawn from Greek literature: the demagogue and the tyrant, both of which have distinctly negative connotations.[47] In his rise to power, Caesar is presented as a typical Greek demagogue: stirring up the mob against more moderate and legitimate leaders within the Senate. Hints of his tyranny occur early,[48] and culminate in his appointment to the dictatorship for life, which Plutarch describes (57. 1) as 'an acknowledged tyranny' (ὁμολογουμένη τυραννίς), a clear reference to Plato's discussion in *Republic* 562a–576b of the career of the tyrant, who begins as a popular champion and ends up enslaving the people in an 'acknowledged tyranny'.[49]

Not only are Roman politics redrawn to a Greek template, but Greek virtues, often taken from Plato or from the philosophical *koine*, form the standards against which individual conduct is measured. The psychology of Roman heroes is described in terms of the standard Greek bipartite, and occasionally the Platonic tripartite, division of the soul. The control of passions, the importance of education, the qualities of *douceur*: Roman heroes are measured against and provide exemplars of these very

---

[46] Pelling (1979), 78; (1980), 137; (1985), 325–6; (1986a), 163–87.
[47] On the demagogue and the tyrant as types in Plutarch, see Wardman (1974), 49–57. Plutarch seems to have taken the picture of Kleon in Aristophanes, especially the *Knights*, as the archetype for all demagogues (cf. *Demetr.* 11. 2). See above, Ch. 5, n. 61.
[48] e.g. 4. 8; cf. 6. 3; 6. 6; 29. 5; 30. 1. Cf. his words in 35. 8.
[49] Pelling (1997b), 221.

Greek ethical concerns. Marius is a negative paradigm of the dangers of discontent (μεμψιμοιρία) and greed (πλεονεξία). Cato cannot live up to the ideals of moderation and of the mixing of hard and soft embodied in his parallel Phokion. Coriolanus is an example of a spirited man (θυμοειδής), who cannot control his anger (ὀργή). Sulla is a brutal demagogue. Fabius Maximus is a model of a wise leader who resists the attacks of such populist leaders: what stands out in the Lives of Perikles and Fabius is not so much the details of the two Lives, as the shared, Greek, politico-moral themes: the calmness and rationality (πραότης) of the great leader in the face of an unruly mob and troublesome demagogues.[50] In the Galba and Otho, the events of the 'Year of Four Emperors' are used as exemplars of the dangers of passions out of control.[51] By applying Greek values to Roman history, Plutarch appropriates the past of Rome into the Greek cultural tradition.

This use of Greek values by which to judge Roman subjects is at its most clear where the issue of Hellenic education is concerned. In the Pyrrhos (16. 7) and the Flamininus (5. 6–7) Plutarch is careful to point out that Greek expectations that the Romans would be barbarians were disappointed. Like almost all Greek writers from Polybios onwards, he does not call Romans barbarians (βάρβαροι); 'barbarian', is now applied only to those neither Greek nor Roman: thus both Plutarch and Dionysios describe the non-Greeks with whom the Romans come into contact as barbarians,[52] making them at some level the parallel of the 'barbarian' Persians against whom the Greeks fought.[53] Romans may not be barbarians, but that is because they have adopted the civilized standards of the Greek world, and it is by the standards of the Greek world that Romans are judged.[54] As has been demonstrated by Simon Swain, the level of Hellenization which a Roman attained is always an issue, in a way it is not for Greeks for whom Hellenic educa-

[50] See Stadter (1975; 1987).
[51] See Ash (1997).
[52] e.g. Dion. Ant. Rom. 1. 16. 1; 1. 20. 1; Plut. Aem. 4. 3; Mar. 14. 1; Sert. 14. 1.
[53] Cf. the parallel denouncements of the Korinthian War of 395 BC and of the war of Pompey and Caesar as distractions from conquering the East (Ages. 15. 2–4; Pomp. 70. 1–7). The use of Greek and barbarian as moral terms (e.g. Nik.-Crass. 2. 7; Lys. 27. 7; Phil. 8. 1; Caes. 2. 4: ἀπαιδεύτους καὶ βαρβάρους; Art. 6. 8) goes back to the 5th c. and before (e.g. Thuc. 1. 77. 6). This associative framework was still very much alive in Plutarch's day (e.g. Chariton 5. 2. 6; 6. 4. 10; 6. 5. 8): Bowie (1991); Scobie (1973). On Plutarch's use of the Greek–barbarian polarity, see Nikolaidis (1986). Cf. also the Souda's gloss of Ἕλλην as φρόνιμος, and Hesychios' of Ἕλληνες as φρόνιμοι ἤτοι σοφοί.
[54] Cf. Dion of Prousa who avoids classifying the Romans as barbarians (though cf. Or. 32. 40 and 45. 1), but does regard Greek culture as superior (cf. Bowie 1991, 194–201). On Ailios Aristeides, see Swain (1996a), 279–80.

tion is assumed. Some Romans, such as Coriolanus, the elder Cato, or Marius, reject the influence of Hellenism and come perilously close to barbarism.[55]

This subtle championing of Greek cultural models is clear in two Lives or pairs of Lives where Plutarch explores Rome's conquest of Greece. The first is the *Life of Marcellus*, the Roman conqueror of Syracuse. Plutarch's treatment of him is in no sense 'anti-Roman'. He stresses in the opening words of the Life Marcellus' bellicose nature but also his early love of Greek literary culture: 'he was such a lover of Greek education (παιδείας) and literature (λόγων) that he honoured and admired (τιμᾶν καὶ θαυμάζειν) those who excelled in it' (1. 3). Marcellus was, however, prevented, Plutarch tells us, by the continual wars which the Romans were fighting at this period, from developing this education further.

A key moment in the *Life of Marcellus* for examining Plutarch's valuations of the relationship of Greek and Roman culture is Marcellus' sacking and despoiling of the Greek city of Syracuse. This could so easily have been presented as an act of brutality.[56] Plutarch instead places the blame on unruly soldiers, and shows Marcellus sad and in tears at the fate of the city and the death of Archimedes (19. 1–12). Up to this date, Plutarch goes on, the Romans were feared for their military skill, 'but had given no examples of gentleness (εὐγνωμοσύνης), humanity (φιλανθρωπίας), and, in a word, political virtue (πολιτικῆς ἀρετῆς)'. Marcellus, however, because of his clemency and beneficence, 'seems at that time to have been the first to demonstrate to the Greeks that the Romans were particularly just' (20. 1).[57] With the spoils which he brings back from Syracuse he 'variegated the city with sights which possessed Hellenic pleasure, charm, and persuasiveness'—a city until that time 'full of barbarian arms and bloody spoils' from Rome's previous wars (21. 2–4). This Hellenization of the city is unpopular, Plutarch tells us, with some Romans. 'But nevertheless, Marcellus spoke with pride of it even to the Greeks, claiming that he had taught ignorant Romans to honour and admire (τιμᾶν καὶ θαυμάζειν) the beautiful and wonderful things of Greece' (21. 7). Marcellus, then, as an individual, comes out rather well. Far from being a vicious despoiler, he is a man of humanity and virtue. But the implications of this narrative for the relative worths

---

[55] Swain (1990b): partly summarized in id. (1996a), 140–4; cf Pelling (1989). See above, pp. 76–7; 108–10 (Marius); 206–12 (Coriolanus).

[56] As by Livy 25. 40. 1–3. See Wardman (1974), 130; Pelling (1989), 201–5.

[57] ὑποδεῖξαι τοῖς Ἕλλησι δικαιοτάτους [C Reiske: δικαιοτέρους] 'Ρωμαίους.

of Greek and Roman culture are striking. At this early date in their history Romans knew no arts except that of war, a result of their lack of knowledge of Greek culture or appreciation of either literary or visual art. Marcellus surprises the Greeks by showing that Romans can be just, and teaches some, though not all, of the Romans to appreciate Greek culture. All of this is the result, significantly, of Marcellus' own early training in Greek language and literature. But as Plutarch emphasized at the start of the Life, Marcellus' Greek education is limited, and it is precisely his bellicosity, for Plutarch a characteristic of Marcellus and of Romans at this period generally, insufficiently tempered by Hellenic education, which will indeed finally lead Marcellus, overcome by passion (ἔρως; πάθος), to a rash and fatal attack on Hannibal (28. 3–6; cf. *Pel.-Marc.* 3. 3).[58] The considerable virtues of Marcellus' parallel Greek subject, Pelopidas, need, of course, no such explanation: he is Greek.[59]

The supremacy of Greek culture is also clear in Plutarch's treatment of the Greek mathematician Archimedes in the same Life (*Marc.* 14–17). Archimedes manages to keep the large Roman army at bay for some time by his feats of military engineering.[60] Plutarch stresses, however, probably wrongly, that Archimedes undertook engineering merely as a by-product of his real study, geometry (*Marc.* 14. 7–8; 17. 5–12). He quotes approvingly Plato's view of the superiority of geometry over mechanics (14. 9–11), and even describes Archimedes in very Platonic language.[61] This denigration of engineering in favour of pure mathematics is one well embedded in Greek philosophical tradition, and, significantly, one which devalues a field of Roman expertise and promotes one of Greek expertise. Plutarch also seems to contrast the true glory (δόξα) which Archimedes won for his 'inspired' knowledge (17. 5), with the apparently lesser glory of Marcellus, the subject of the Life (14. 3), and with false opinion (δόξα) about Archimedes' discoveries (17. 10).[62] The fact that the Roman Marcellus did actually take Syracuse is played down and attributed to the seizing of a tower during a festival (18. 3–5). Archimedes 'kept himself and Syracuse unconquered, so far as

---

[58] Pelling (1989), 205–8.
[59] Swain (1990b), 131–2 and 140–2 (=1995, 239–40 and 254–6), notes some of this.
[60] For the details of what follows, see Culham (1992). Plutarch's treatment of the siege of Syracuse is, as she rightly claims, not 'anti-Roman', but it does assert the supremacy of Greek conceptions of engineering.
[61] Ibid. 184–6. *Marc.* 14. 9: Archimedes is the creator (δημιουργός); cf. Plato, *Tim.* 29d–30c; 17. 3: he is the soul (ψυχή) of the Syracusans' body (σῶμα); cf. Plato, *Phaidr.* 245c–246a; *Laws* 896e–897b.
[62] Ibid. 186–9.

it was in his power' (18. 1). Greek seems to win a victory, if only a cultural one, over Roman here, even though it is a Roman who is the subject of the Life and the victor in the military engagement.

The *Philopoimen–Flamininus* provides, finally, a particularly interesting example of Plutarch's construction of Greek and Roman cultures.[63] Here, for the only time in the extant Lives, Plutarch pairs a Greek and a Roman who lived at the same period, the period of Rome's conquest of Greece in the late third and early second centuries BC. Furthermore, Philopoimen and Flamininus actually fought each other. This might be thought to force Plutarch to express an opinion about the Roman conquest. But, in fact, he manages to have sympathy, in their respective Lives, with both men and their policies. This double presentation absolves Plutarch from the need to judge, while at the same time allowing him to explore an issue which could undoubtedly have strong implications for contemporary attitudes to Roman domination.[64] Conclusions are left to the reader—a very Plutarchan strategy, as this book has so often emphasized. This is at its clearest in *Phil.* 17. 2–3, where Plutarch seems both to suggest that Rome's conquest of Greece was willed by the gods,[65] and also to admire Philopoimen's personal courage in defence of the liberty of Greece:

ἐπεὶ δὲ νικήσαντες οἱ Ῥωμαῖοι τὸν Ἀντίοχον ἐνεφύοντο τοῖς Ἑλληνικοῖς μᾶλλον ἤδη, καὶ περιεβάλλοντο τῇ δυνάμει τοὺς Ἀχαιούς, ὑποκατακλινομένων αὐτοῖς τῶν δημαγωγῶν, ἡ δ' ἰσχὺς ἐπὶ πάντα πολλὴ μετὰ τοῦ δαίμονος ἐχώρει, καὶ τὸ τέλος ἐγγὺς ἦν εἰς ὃ τὴν τύχην ἔδει περιφερομένην ἐξικέσθαι, καθάπερ ἀγαθὸς κυβερνήτης πρὸς κῦμα διερειδόμενος ὁ Φιλοποίμην, τὰ μὲν ἐνδιδόναι καὶ παρείκειν ἠναγκάζετο τοῖς καιροῖς, περὶ δὲ τῶν πλείστων διαφερόμενος, τοὺς τῷ λέγειν καὶ πράττειν ἰσχύοντας ἀντισπᾶν ἐπειρᾶτο πρὸς τὴν ἐλευθερίαν.

The Romans, having defeated Antiochos, were now clinging more closely to Greek affairs, and were surrounding the Achaians with their power, since the demagogues were secretly inclining to them. Their power was going forward, with the help of the divine, in great strength in all directions, and the end to which fortune in its instability had to come, was near. But Philopoimen, like a good helmsman striving against the waves, was forced sometimes to give in and yield to the times (τοῖς καιροῖς), but in most matters he endured and tried in response to draw to freedom those who were good in word or deed.

(Phil. 17. 2–3)

[63] On *Phil.-Flam.* in this context, see Swain (1996a), 145–50; cf. Pelling (1986b), 84–9.

[64] For similar double presentatations, see p. above, pp. 133–5 and 286. Plutarch avoids drawing out the contemporary implications too clearly: see pp. 67–8.

[65] As also at *Flam.* 12. 10. See Swain (1989b), 284–5; (1996a), 151–61.

Philopoimen is admired; the same metaphor, a helmsman fighting against a rough sea, is used of the struggles of Cato the Younger against an irresistible fate (*Phok.* 3. 3–4).[66] Both Phokion and Philopoimen, though not Cato, also knew when to compromise, to give in to the times (τοῖς καιροῖς). It is this to which Menemachos is urged in the *Political precepts* (814a). To this extent, Philopoimen could stand as a model of independence combined with pragmatism for contemporary Greeks in their dealings with Rome.[67]

Plutarch avoids suggesting that either Philopoimen or Flamininus was superior, or the policies of either better. This sense of carefully crafted equality is at its clearest in the final words of the *synkrisis* (*Phil.-Flam.* 3. 5).[68] It is true that at the end of his Life Flamininus' pursuit of Hannibal is presented as motivated by an excessive love of glory and as cruel (*Flam.* 20. 2–3; 21. 1). But there is no sense of uncomplicated Roman inferiority. Indeed, Plutarch has already suggested that it was Greek 'love of strife' (φιλονεικία) which led to, and partly justified, the Roman conquest. He presents this contentiousness as a particularly Greek weakness (*Flam.* 11. 3–7).[69] Philopoimen himself is criticized, in contrast to Flamininus, for his susceptibility to this quality (*Phil.-Flam.* 1. 4); Philopoimen's own final years have been marred by this peculiarly Greek failing (e.g. *Phil.* 18. 1–3). So Plutarch is prepared to admit that the Greeks were more susceptible to some faults than the Romans. But significantly the moral framework for the analysis is Greek. The synkritic structure of the *Parallel Lives* encourages the reader to compare Greek subject and Roman subject; attention is focused on the virtues and vices revealed by their lives, rather than on the details of time and place. But in judging both heroes, Greek values are used: it is an uncompromisingly Greek value system which underlies Plutarch's reworking of both Greek and Roman history. It is Greek virtues by which Roman heroes are judged, and in this way the universality of Greek culture is—subtly— proclaimed. The highest compliment which Plutarch pays to a Roman is, significantly, when he calls the Roman Numa, paradoxically, 'more Greek' (ἑλληνικώτερον) a lawgiver than the Spartan Lykourgos (*Lyk.-Num.* 1. 10).[70]

---

[66] See p. 140.

[67] At the end of the *synkrisis* Plutarch declares that both Flamininus' kindness to the Greeks, and Philopoimen's bravery in defending their freedom are to be commended (*Phil.-Flam.* 3. 4). [68] See pp. 268–9.

[69] See Walsh (1992), esp. 221–6; cf. Jones (1971), 100–2.

[70] Cf. *Nik.-Crass.* 2. 7: Nikias' ending of the Archidamian War was a 'most Greek political act' (ἑλληνικώτατον πολίτευμα).

Plutarch does not in the *Parallel Lives* preach a message of Greco-Roman cultural unity or reconciliation. Rather, he explores the meaning of Hellenism and Romanness. If his work has a cultural message, it lies in the imposition, helped along by the device of *synkrisis*, of a Greek perspective onto Roman history. To this extent, the *Parallel Lives* can be seen as a Greek response to Roman power, a statement of resistance. Plutarch's refusal to preach, to declare an authorial view on Greek or Roman superiority or equality, is characteristic of his stance in general. This book has emphasized throughout ways in which Plutarch's texts resist simplistic univocal presentations of the past, but are complex, exploratory, and challenging: they invite the reader to challenge and to ponder. For this, if for nothing else, they are worthy of their place alongside the best products of the Classical Greek literature of which Plutarch himself was so fond.

APPENDIX ONE
Plutarch and Ancestors

The mention of a subject's ancestors was perhaps a traditional feature of *enkomion* or biography. But for Plutarch, such material is deployed for clear literary ends. Thus he often uses a figure mentioned in the opening lines of the Life, particularly an ancestor, to provide a paradigm or contrast to the subject, or to alert the reader to a theme which will become important as the Life progresses.

Kleisthenes, Perikles' great-grandfather, is said (*Per.* 3. 2) to have ended the Peisistratid tyranny and set up a 'constitution mixed in the best way for harmony and safety' (πολιτείαν ἄριστα κεκραμένην πρὸς ὁμόνοιαν καὶ σωτηρίαν). This raises the question of the nature of Perikles' leadership, the subject of the first fifteen chapters of the Life.[1] Like that of his ancestor Kleisthenes, Perikles' constitution (πολιτεία) was 'aristocratic' (9. 1; 15. 1: ἀριστοκρατική); it brought internal harmony as, like a doctor, he cured the ills of the state with 'life-saving drugs' (15. 1: φάρμακα σωτήρια). His expedition to the Thracian Chersonesos (19. 1) is likewise life-saving (σωτήριος), as he walled off the isthmos with 'bulwarks' (ἐρύμασι). After his death, Perikles' own power is recognized to be neither monarchical nor tyrannical but (39. 4) a 'saving bulwark of the constitution' (σωτήριον ἔρυμα τῆς πολιτείας).

A similar prefiguring of important traits or themes in the brief descriptions of ancestors can be seen at the start of other *Lives*. The theme of the relationship between virtue (ἀρετή) and chance (τύχη) which is central to the *Aemilius–Timoleon* (e.g. *Aem.* 1. 6)[2] is prefigured in Aemilius' ancestors, who are said (*Aem.* 2. 3) to have 'had good fortune through virtue' (δι' ἀρετὴν . . . εὐτύχησαν).[3] The specific example of L. Aemilius Paullus (*Aem.* 2. 3), whose wisdom and courage were revealed by 'the misfortune at Cannae' (τὸ περὶ Κάννας ἀτύχημα) has special relevance to Aemilius, whose great successes are followed by great reversals of fortune (cf. *Aem.* 36. 3–9). There are many other examples. Pyrrhos is linked to his ancestor Achilles at the opening of his Life (*Pyrrh.* 1. 2–3; cf. 2. 8); throughout the Life allusions to Achilles are used to bring out his valour and give him heroic status.[4] Solon's father is said to have reduced his estate in acts of kindness and generosity (2. 1: εἰς φιλανθρωπίας τινας . . . καὶ χάριτας). This serves as

---

[1] Cf. Breebaart (1971); Stadter (1987), 258–60.
[2] Swain (1989c).
[3] Cf. *Tim.* 36. 4: ἀρετῆς εὐτυχούσης. On ἀρετὴ εὐτυχοῦσα as a theme of this pair, cf. Ingenkamp (1997).
[4] Mossman (1992).

a paradigm for Solon's own extravagance[5] and, more importantly, for his sympathetic identification with the poor in his society (3. 1–3). L. Junius Brutus the tyrannicide opens the *Brutus* (1. 1–2), thus providing an implicit paradigm for his descendant Marcus, who goes on to kill Caesar. Lucullus' father was convicted of theft and his mother had a reputation for intemperance (*Luc.* 1. 1): characteristics which raise the question of Lucullus' notorious dissipation at the end of his Life.[6] The ancestors of Lysander and Sulla also provide paradigms for their lives.[7]

Sometimes ancestors provide a negative paradigm, a contrast with the subject of the Life. Kimon had the reputation of taking after his grandfather of the same name, a man famed for stupidity (4. 4); in fact, Kimon was superior in intelligence to Themistokles (5. 1). Pompey's father, Strabo, was hated by the Roman people; he is explicitly contrasted with his son, who is ever popular (*Pomp.* 1. 1–4). But there is an irony. Pompey's father, Plutarch tells us, is so hated that his body is maltreated after his death. But Pompey will in the end fare no better: murdered as he comes ashore in Egypt, his head is cut off, and his body left naked on the beach (79. 4–80. 2). Such a negative paradigm is provided also by the ancestors of Coriolanus.[8]

The use to which Plutarch puts a subject's ancestors is perhaps more than simply literary technique: he seems to have been prepared to believe the notion that children did inherit part of their father's nature (*De Sera Num.* 559c–e). Thus at the beginning of the *Antony* (1. 1–3), an anecdote illustrating the generosity of Antony's father to his friends prefigures Antony's own generosity, a trait which will be important in the Life as a whole;[9] but this trait may also prefigure Nero—who was indeed descended from Antony, a fact of which the reader is explicitly reminded at the end of the Life (*Ant.* 87. 1–9).[10]

[5] Albini (1997), 64.
[6] *Luc.* 39. 1–42. 4; *Kim.-Luc.* 1. 2–8. See pp. 59–60 and 260–1.
[7] *Lys.* 2. 1; *Sulla* 1. 1–2. See pp. 177–8 and 198.
[8] *Cor.* 1. 1. See pp. 206.
[9] Pelling (1988*b*), 117; Brenk (1992), 4369.
[10] Cf. Brenk (1992), 4348–75.

APPENDIX TWO
Plutarch and Chronology

Plutarch certainly was capable on occasion of sound chronological argumentation (e.g. *Them.* 2. 5–7 and 27. 1–2) and had a good knowledge of, for example, the Attic dating system and the Archon lists (e.g. *Arist.* 5. 9–10).[1] But chronological exactitude was not always his first priority: he is sometimes prepared to forgo such exactitude in the interest of character portrayal. In some cases such prioritization of character over date is blatant. The explicit preference in *Sol.* 27. 1 for a version of events (Solon's meeting with Kroisos) which supported his conception of the subject's character over clear chronological evidence to the contrary is striking:[2]

τὴν δὲ πρὸς Κροῖσον ἔντευξιν αὐτοῦ δοκοῦσιν ἔνιοι τοῖς χρόνοις ὡς πεπλασμένην ἐξελέγχειν. ἐγὼ δὲ λόγον ἔνδοξον οὕτω καὶ τοσούτους μάρτυρας ἔχοντα καὶ (ὃ μεῖζόν ἐστι) πρέποντα τῷ Σόλωνος ἤθει καὶ τῆς ἐκείνου μεγαλοφροσύνης καὶ σοφίας ἄξιον, οὔ μοι δοκῶ προήσεσθαι χρονικοῖς τισι λεγομένοις κανόσιν, οὓς μύριοι διορθοῦντες, ἄχρι σήμερον εἰς οὐδὲν αὑτοῖς ὁμολογούμενον δύνανται καταστῆσαι τὰς ἀντιλογίας.

As to his meeting with Kroisos, some think to prove by chronology that it is fictitious. But when a story is so famous and has so many witnesses and, more importantly, fits Solon's character and is worthy of his magnanimity and wisdom, I do not think it right to reject it on the grounds of some so called chronological rules, which to this day tens of thousands are correcting but can never bring their contradictions into general agreement.   (*Sol.* 27. 1)

Similarly in the *Lykourgos*, Plutarch rejects apparent evidence that the establishment of the *krypteia* dated from Lykourgos' times, on the grounds that it did not accord with his character (*Lyk.* 28. 1–2, 12–13).[3]

Plutarch's view that accuracy was more difficult to obtain in the period of the

---

[1] On the dating system, see Badian and Buckler (1975), esp. 227–8 and 238–9. Cf. *Per.* 27. 4.

[2] For a more detailed discussion of both *Sol.* 27. 1 and *Them.* 27. 2, cf. Pelling (1990*b*), 19–21.

[3] Of course, the development of the *krypteia* is much more complex: cf. Vidal-Naquet (1968), 953–5 (=1981, 153–5); Cartledge (1987), 30–2; as is the relationship of a historical Lykourgos to any reforms ascribed to him. For more arguments based on coherence of character, a rhetorical argument (e.g. Aristotle, *Ath. Pol.* 6. 3), see *Per.* 10. 7; *Dem.–Cic.* 3. 5–7. Cf. also Barbu (1934), 139–43; Lombardi (1996).

early Lives (*Thes.* 1. 5), and that the chronology for this period was unreliable (*Num.* 1. 1–6; *Cam.* 22. 2), may go part of the way towards explaining these examples.[4] It is itself significant, however, that Plutarch chose to extend his biographical interest back into these periods, even writing a free-standing *Life of Herakles*; his practice is in accord with ancient theory, which tended to class narrative both of events which actually happened and of events which were traditionally held to have happened within the orbit of 'history'.[5] But the privileging of moral over chronological considerations is common, though not constant, throughout all the *Lives*. Most often Plutarch is simply organizing his material on thematic rather than chronological grounds, a strategy employed extensively by Suetonius, and familiar from rhetoric.[6] In *Cato Min.* 25, for example, Plutarch discusses the bizarre incident of Cato giving his wife to his friend Hortensius. At the end of the chapter (25. 13) he is explicit that he has presented this incident out of chronological sequence because it was relevant to his analysis of Cato's dealings with his womenfolk, itself presented by Plutarch as a 'small indication of character' (24. 1).

But often Plutarch is not so explicit, and the chronological relationship of events described is difficult to recover. There are two main sections of a Life where Plutarch is particularly prone to place the revelation of character before chronogical narration. The first is when he describes a subject's early years until his entry on to the stage of politics. Thus, it is difficult to construct a chronological sequence of events from the *Perikles* before chapter 22,[7] from the *Alkibiades* before chapter 16,[8] and from the *Phokion* before chapter 12.[9] Secondly, Plutarch often suspends chronological narration to give a portrait of the subject at the height of his political career—a timeless image which will remain in the reader's mind.[10] To construct this portrait, events may be deployed out of chronological sequence or without reference to chronology, as at *Them.* 19–22.[11] It is extremely difficult, for example, to construct a narrative of Lysander's movements between autumn 405 BC and autumn 404 from *Lysander* 15–18,[12] which rather presents a picture of Lysander's power and arrogance at the height of his career. In *Lys.* 19. 3, furthermore, Plutarch appears to narrate again and out of chronological sequence an incident, the murder of democrats at Miletos, which

---

[4] Paratore (1993).
[5] See pp. 18–19.
[6] e.g. in *enkomia* such as Isok. *Evag.* and Xen. *Ages.* Cf. Plutarch's use of poetic quotations, where Plutarch cares more for what the quotation can reveal about the subject than about the chronological relationship between it and the context in which it is placed. See Frazier (1988b).
[7] Steidle (1951), 152–66.
[8] Russell (1966b) and above, pp. 230–1. See also, on *Cor.* 3. 1–3, id. (1963), 23–4 (=1995, 362–3).
[9] See pp. 135–6.
[10] Polman (1974).
[11] Stadter (1983–4), 361–2
[12] Andrewes (1971), 217–26.

he had already narrated in 8. 1–3. Earlier he had used it as an illustration of Lysander's use of trickery; here he uses it to illustrate (19. 2) his haughtiness (ὑπεροψία) and severity (βαρύτης), which reveal themselves in violence.[13] In the *Alexander*, the theme of the great leader's descent into increasingly autocratic behaviour, a theme central to the *Alexander–Caesar*, as a whole,[14] dominates chapters 48–55, where Plutarch seems to have grouped several incidents indicating Alexander's tyrannical behaviour. He gives the impression that they happened in quick succession, presenting, for example, Antipatros' treasonable negotiations with Aitolia as though they were a result of, and followed after, the execution of Parmenion (330 BC), implying a chronological and causative link; in fact the negotiations took place six years later in 324 (*Alex.* 49. 14–15).[15] Similarly, the murder of Kleitos took place in 328, two years after the death of Parmenion, despite Plutarch's 'not much later' (50. 1: οὐ πολλῷ δ' ὕστερον).

[13] See p. 189. The murder in Miletos took place in early 405 BC (Bommelaer 1981, 80). In fact, the incident described in 19. 3 may be a confused rendering of a different event which took place on the island of Thasos (Diod. 13. 104. 7, with Piccirilli 1993a, 25–7; Nepos, *Lys.* 2. 2–3; Polyainos 1. 45. 4; see Bommelaer 1981, 157), though Plutarch seems to have thought it was the event in Miletos. See also pp. 182–3 on *Lys.* 2. 7–8.
[14] Harris (1970), 193–7.
[15] Hamilton (1969), n. ad loc. Cf. Moles (1988), 37, on Plutarch's 'frequent chronological liberties' in the *Cic.* On logical connections presented as though they were chronological, cf. *Cato Min.* 51. 6 and Pelling (1980), 127–9, with the bibliography he cites.

Bibliography

The following is a list of all modern works cited in the footnotes. Editions of ancient authors are listed in the preface. Abbreviations of journal titles follow those of *L' Année Philologique*.

Bibliographic surveys of scholarship on the *Lives* include: Garzetti (1953); Averincev (1964); Alsina (1990); Tsagas (1990); Podlecki and Duane (1992); Titchener (1992). On the *Lives* and *Moralia*: Del Re (1953); Alsina (1961–2); Flacelière (1968). On the *Moralia* alone: Harrison (1992a).

Aalders, G. J. D. (1968), *Die Theorie der gemischten Verfassung im Altertum* (Amsterdam).
—— (1982), *Plutarch's Political Thought* (Verhandelingen der Koninklijke Nederlandse Akademie van Wetenschappen, Afd. Letterkunde, N.R. 116: Amsterdam, Oxford, and New York).
Adam, J. (1902), *The Republic of Plato*, 2 vols. (Cambridge).
Affortunati, M., and Scardigli, B. (1992), 'La vita "plutarchea" di Annibale: Un imitazione di Donato Acciaiuoli', *A&R* NS 37: 88–105.
Africa, T. (1982), 'Worms and the Death of Kings: A Cautionary Note on Disease and History', *ClAnt* 1: 1–17.
Aguilar, R. M. (1990–1), 'La mujer, el amor y el matrimonio en la obra de Plutarco', *Faventia* 12–13: 307–25.
Ahl, F. (1984), 'The Art of Safe Criticism in Greece and Rome', *AJPh* 105: 174–208.
Albini, F. (1997), 'Family and the formation of character in Plutarch'. In Mossman (1997), 59–71.
Alcock, S. E. (1993), *Graecia Capta: The Landscapes of Roman Greece* (Cambridge).
Alessandrì, S. (1985), 'Le civette di Gilippo (Plut., *Lys.*, 16–17)', *ASNP* ser. 3, 15: 1081–93.
Alfinito, L. (1992), 'Sull' epicureismo di Cassio in Plutarco, *Vita di Bruto*, 37', *Vichiana*, ser. 3, 3: 227–36.
Allen, W. S. (1987, 3rd edn.; 1st edn. 1968), *Vox Graeca: A Guide to the Pronunciation of Classical Greek* (Cambridge).
Alonso-Núñez, J. M. (1990), 'The Emergence of Universal Historiography from the 4th to the 2nd Centuries B.C.'. In Verdin, Schepens, and De Keyser (1990), 173–92.
Alsina, A. (1961–2), 'Ensayo de una bibliografía de Plutarco', *EClás* 6: 515–33.
—— (1990), 'Bibliografía de Plutarco'. In *La Historiografía Griega* (*Anthropos* Supplement 20: Barcelona), 128–31.
Ambrosini, R. (1991), 'Funzione espressiva della sintassi nella lingua di Plutarco'. In D'Ippolito and Gallo (1991), 19–34.
Ameling, W. (1985), 'Plutarch, Perikles 12–14', *Historia* 34: 47–63.

Ampolo, C. (1990), 'Inventare una biografia: Note sulla biografia greca ed i suoi precedenti alla luce di un nuovo documento epigrafico', *Quaderni Storici* 25: 213–24.
—— and Manfredini, M. (1988) (eds.), *Plutarco: Le Vite di Teseo e di Romolo* (Fondazione Lorenzo Valla: Milan).
Amyot, J. (1559), *Plutarchus: Les vies des hommes illustres grecs et romains*, 2 vols. (Antwerp).
Anderson, G. (1976), *Lucian: Theme and Variation in the Second Sophistic* (*Mnemosyne* Supplement 41: Leiden).
—— (1993), *The Second Sophistic. A Cultural Phenomenon in the Roman Empire* (London and New York).
Andrei, O. (1984), *A. Claudius Charax di Pergano: Interessi antiquari e antichità cittadine nell' età degli Antonini* (Bologna).
—— (1989), 'Demetrio Poliorcete secondo Plutarco: da una "grande" natura a "grandi" vizi'. In Andrei and Scuderi (1989), 35–93.
—— and Scuderi, R. (1989) (eds.), *Plutarco. Vite parallele: Demetrio–Antonio* (Biblioteca Universale Rizzoli: Milan).
Andrewes, A. (1971), 'Two Notes on Lysander', *Phoenix* 25: 206–26.
Angeli Bertinelli, M. G., Carena, C., Gabriella, M., Manfredini, M., and Piccirilli, L. (1993) (eds.), *Plutarco: Le Vite di Nicia e di Crasso* (Fondazione Lorenzo Valla: Milan).
Annas, J. (1993), *The Morality of Happiness* (Oxford).
Ash, R. (1997), 'Severed heads: Individual portraits and irrational forces in Plutarch's *Galba* and *Otho*'. In Mossman (1997), 189–214.
Aulotte, R. (1965), *Amyot et Plutarque: La tradition des Moralia au XVIe siècle* (Geneva).
Avenarius, G. (1956), *Lukians Schrift zur Geschichtsschreibung* (Meisenheim am Glan).
Averincev, S. S. (1964), 'Biograficheskie sochineniya Plutarkha v zarubezhnoi nauke XX veka' (The Biographical works of Plutarch in foreign scholarship in the twentieth century), *VDI* 89: 202–12 (in Russian).
—— (1965), 'Podbor geroev v "Paralel'nykh Zhizneopisaniyakh" Plutarkha i antichnaya biograficheskaya traditsiya' (The Choice of Heroes in Plutarch's 'Parallel Lives' and Ancient Biographical Tradition), *VDI* 92: 51–67 (in Russian).
Babbitt, F. C. (1936), *Plutarch's Moralia iv* (London and Cambridge, Mass.).
Babut, D. (1969*a*), *Plutarque de la vertu éthique* (Bibliothèque de la Faculté des Lettres de Lyon 15: Paris).
—— (1969*b*), *Plutarque et le Stoicisme* (Paris).
—— (1975), '῾Ιστορία οἷον ὕλη φιλοσοφίας: histoire et réflexion morale dans l'oeuvre de Plutarque', *REG* 88: 206–19.
—— (1981), 'A propos des enfants et d' un ami de Plutarque: essai de solution pour deux énigmes', *REG* 94: 47–62.

Bacon, F. (1605), *De dignitate et augmentis scientarum*, 9 vols. (London). Trans. G. Wats (1639) as *Of the advancement and proficiencie of learning: or the partition of sciences* (Oxford).
Badian, E. (1958), *Foreign Clientelae (264–70 BC)* (Oxford).
—— (1976), 'Lucius Sulla: The Deadly Reformer'. In A. J. Dunston (ed.), *Essays on Roman Culture (The Todd Memorial Lectures*, 35–74: Toronto and Sarasota).
—— (1981), 'The Deification of Alexander the Great'. In H. J. Dell (ed.), *Ancient Macedonian Studies in honor of Charles F. Edson* (Thessaloniki), 27–71.
—— and Buckler, J. (1975), 'The Wrong Salamis?', *RhM* 118: 226–39.
Balsdon, J. P. V. D. (1951), 'Sulla Felix', *JRS* 41: 1–10.
Bannon, C. J. (1995), 'Fraternal and Political Ethics in Plutarch's *Lives*'. In Gallo and Scardigli (1995), 41–50.
Barbu, N. I. (1934), *Les Procédés de la peinture des caractères et la vérité historique dans les biographies de Plutarque* (Paris). Reprinted Rome, 1976 (Studia Philologica 19).
Barigazzi, A. (1984), 'Plutarco e il corso futuro della storia', *Prometheus* 10: 264–86. Reprinted in *Studi su Plutarco* (Studi e testi 12: Florence), 303–30.
Barnes, J. (1989), 'Antiochus of Ascalon'. In Griffin and Barnes (1989), 51–96.
Barnish, S. J. B. (1994), 'Late Roman Prosopography Reassessed', *JRS* 84: 171–7.
Barrett, C. K. (1961), *Luke the Historian in Recent Study* (London).
Barrow, R. H. (1967), *Plutarch and his Times* (London).
Barthelmess, J. A. (1977), 'Recent Studies on the Influence of Plutarch', *CLS* 14: 186–91.
—— (1986), 'Recent Work on the *Moralia*'. In Brenk and Gallo (1986), 61–81.
Barton, T. S. (1991), 'Power and Knowledge: Studies in Astrology, Physiognomics and Medicine under the Roman Empire'. Dissertation, Cambridge.
—— (1994), 'The *inventio* of Nero: Suetonius'. In J. Elsner and J. Masters (eds.), *Reflections of Nero: Culture, History & Representation* (Chapel Hill, NC, and London), 48–63.
Beard, M. (1987), 'A Complex of Times: No More Sheep on Romulus' Birthday', *PCPhS* 33: 1–15.
Bearzot, C. (1984), 'Focione φίλος τοῦ βασιλέως: il tema dell' amicizia con Alessandro nella tradizione biografica focioniana'. In Sordi (1984), 75–90.
—— (1985), *Focione tra storia e trasfigurazione ideale* (Milan).
—— (1993), 'Il confronto tra Focione e Catone' and 'Introduzione' to *Focione*. In Bearzot, Geiger, and Ghilli (1993), 85–8 and 91–152. Contains much material published in ead. 1985.
—— Geiger, J., and Ghilli, L. (1993) (eds.), *Plutarco. Vite Parallele: Focione–Catone Uticense* (Bibliotec a Universale Rizzoli: Milan).
Becchi, F. (1975), 'Aristotelismo ed antistoicismo nel 'De virtute morali' di Plutarco', *Prometheus* 1: 160–80.

Becchi, F. (1978), 'Aristotelismo funzionale nel 'De virtute morali' di Plutarco', *Prometheus* 4: 261–75.
—— (1981), 'Platonismo medio ed etica plutarchea', *Prometheus* 7: 125–45 and 263–84.
—— (1990a), 'La nozione di ὀργή e di ἀοργησία in Aristotele e in Plutarco', *Prometheus* 16: 65–87.
—— (1990b) (ed.), *Plutarco: La virtù etica* (Corpus Plutarchi Moralium 5: Naples).
—— (1995), 'La saggezza del politico e la saggezza dell' attore: una questione di *Quellenforschung*'. In Gallo and Scardigli (1995), 51–63.
Bellemore, J. (1995), 'Cato the Younger in the East in 66 BC', *Historia* 44: 376–9.
Benediktson, D. T. (1994), 'Plutarch on the Epilepsy of Julius Caesar', *AncW* 25: 159–64.
Berardi, E. (1990), 'Plutarco e la Religione: L' εὐσέβεια come giusto mezzo fra δεισιδαιμονία e ἀθεότης', *CCC* 11: 141–70.
Bergen, K. (1962), *Charakterbilder bei Tacitus und Plutarch* (Inaugural-Dissertation zur Erlangung des Doktorgrades der Philosophischen Fakultät der Universität zu Köln: Cologne).
Bergua Cavero, J. (1995), *Estudios sobre le tradución de Plutarco en España (siglos XIII–XVII)* (Saragossa).
Bernini, U. (1985), 'Il "progetto politico" di Lisandro sulla regalità spartana e la teorizzazione critica di Aristotele sui re spartani', *SIFC* ser. 3, 3 (year 78): 205–38.
—— (1988), 'Λυσάνδρου καὶ Καλλικρατίδα σύγκρισις. Cultura, etica e politica spartana fra quinto e quarto secolo a. c.', *Memorie dell' Istituto Veneto di Scienze, Lettere ed Arti* 41. 2: 1–247.
Berry, E. G. (1961), *Emerson's Plutarch* (Cambridge, Mass.).
Birley, R. A. (1988) (ed.), *Ronald Syme: Roman Papers iv* (Oxford).
Blanckenhagen, P. H. von (1964), 'The Shield of Alcibiades'. In L. F. Sandler (ed.), *Essays in Memory of Karl Lehmann* (New York), 38–42.
Blignières, A. de (1851), *Essai sur Amyot et les traducteurs français au XVIe siècle: précédé d'un éloge d'Amyot* (Paris). Reprinted Geneva, 1968.
Bloesch, H. (1943), *Agalma: Kleinod, Weihgeschenk, Götterbild: Ein Beitrag zur frühgriechischen Kultur- und Religionsgeschichte* (Berne).
Blomqvist, K. (1997), 'From Olympias to Aretaphila: women in politics in Plutarch'. In Mossman (1997), 73–97.
Bommelaer, J-F. (1981), *Lysandre de Sparte: Histoire et Traditions* (Bibliothèque des écoles françaises d'Athènes et de Rome 240: Athens and Paris).
Borzsák, I. von (1973), 'Spectaculum: Ein Motiv der "tragischen Geschichtsschreibung" bei Livius und Tacitus', *ACD* 9: 57–67.
Boswell, J. (1791), *The Life of Samuel Johnson, LL.D: comprehending an account of his studies and numerous works* (London). Numerous editions.

Bosworth, A. B. (1980), *A Historical Commentary on Arrian's History of Alexander, i, Commentary on Books I–III* (Oxford).
—— (1988), *From Arrian to Alexander: Studies in Historical Interpretation* (Oxford).
—— (1992), 'History and Artifice in Plutarch's *Eumenes*'. In Stadter (1992*b*), 56–89.
Boulogne, J. (1992), 'Les "Questions Romaines" de Plutarque', *ANRW* 2. 33. 6, 4682–4708.
—— (1994), *Plutarque: Un aristocrate grec sous l'occupation Romaine* (Lille).
—— (1996), 'Plutarque et la médicine', *ANRW* 2. 37. 3, 2762–92.
Bowersock, G. W. (1968), review of D. Nörr (Munich, 1966), *Imperium und Polis in der hohen Prinzipatszeit*. In *JRS* 58: 261–2.
—— (1969), *Greek Sophists in the Roman Empire* (Oxford).
—— (1973), 'Greek Intellectuals and the Imperial Cult in the Second Century AD'. In W. den Boer (ed.), *Le Culte des souverains dans l'empire romain* (Fondation Hardt pour l'Étude de l'antiquité classique. Entretiens 19: Geneva), 177–212.
—— (1994), *Fiction as History: Nero to Julian* (Berkeley).
Bowie, E. L. (1970), 'The Greeks and their Past in the Second Sophistic', *P&P* 46: 3–41. Reprinted in M. I. Finley (ed.), *Studies in Ancient Society* (London and Boston, 1974), 166–209.
—— (1991), 'Hellenes and Hellenism in Writers of the Early Second Sophistic'. In Saïd (1991), 183–204.
—— (1994), 'Past and Present in Pausanias'. In J. Bingen (ed.), *Pausanias historien* (Fondation Hardt pour l'Étude de l'antiquité classique. Entretiens 41: Geneva), 207–30.
—— (1997), 'Hadrian, Favorinus, and Plutarch'. In Mossman (1997), 1–15.
Bowra, C. M. (1940), 'The Fox and the Hedgehog', *CQ* 34: 26–9.
Bradford, A. S. (1977), *A Prosopography of Lacedaemonians from the Death of Alexander the Great, 323 BC, to the Sack of Sparta by Alaric, AD 396* (Vestigia. Beiträge zur alten Geschichte 27: Munich).
—— (1994), 'The duplicitous Spartan'. In A. Powell and S. Hodkinson (eds.), *The Shadow of Sparta* (London and New York), 59–85.
Bradley, K. R. (1985), 'Ideals of marriage in Suetonius' *Caesares*', *RSA* 15: 77–95.
Braund, D. (1993), 'Dionysiac Tragedy in Plutarch, *Crassus*', *CQ* NS 43: 468–74.
Breebaart, A. B. (1971), 'Plutarch and the Political Development of Pericles', *Mnemosyne*, ser. 4, 24: 260–72.
Breitenbach, H. R. (1969), 'Der Alexanderexkurs bei Livius', *MH* 26: 146–57.
Brenk, F. E. (1975), 'The Dreams of Plutarch's Lives', *Latomus* 34: 336–49.
—— (1977), *In Mist Apparelled: Religious Themes in Plutarch's Moralia and Lives* (Leiden).
—— (1987), 'From Rex to Rana: Plutarch's Treatment of Nero'. In A. Ceresa-Gastaldo (ed.), *Il Protagonismo nella storiografia classica* (Pubblicazioni del

Dipartimento di Archeologia e Filologia Classica e Loro Tradizioni, Università di Genova, NS 108: Genoa), 121–42.

Brent, F. E. (1988), 'Plutarch's *Erotikos*: The Drag Down Pulled Up', *ICS* 13: 457–71.

—— (1992), 'Plutarch's Life "Markos Antonios": A Literary and Cultural Study', *ANRW*, 2. 33. 6, 4347–4469 and (indices) 4895–4915.

—— (1995a), 'The Boiotia of Plutarch's *Erotikos* beyond the shadow of Athens'. In Christopoulu (1995), 1109–17.

—— (1995b), 'Heroic Anti-Heroes. Ruler Cult and Divine Assimilations in Plutarch's "Lives" of Demetrius and Antonius'. In Gallo and Scardigli (1995), 65–82.

—— and Gallo, I. (1986) (eds.), *Miscellanea Plutarchea (Atti del I convegno di studi su Plutarco, Roma, 23 novembre 1985*, Quaderni del Giornale Filologico Ferrarese 8: Ferrara).

Brożek, M. (1963), 'Noch über die Selbstzitate als chronologischen Wegweiser in Plutarchs Parallelbiographien', *Eos* 53: 68–80.

Bruce, I. A. F. (1987), 'Theopompus, Lysander and the Spartan Empire', *AHB* 1: 1–5.

Brunt, P. A. (1952), 'Thucydides and Alcibiades', *REG* 65: 59–96.

—— (1979), 'Cicero and Historiography'. In M. J. Fontana (ed.), φιλίας χάριν: *miscellanea di studi classici in onore di Eugenio Manni* (Rome), i. 309–40. Reprinted in *Studies in Greek History and Thought* (Oxford, 1993), 181–209.

—— (1994), 'The Bubble of the Second Sophistic', *BICS* 39: 25–52.

Bucher-Isler, B. (1972), *Norm und Individualität in den Biographien Plutarchs* (Noctes Romanae 13: Berne and Stuttgart).

Buckler, J. (1992), 'Plutarch and Autopsy', *ANRW* 2. 33. 6, 4788–4830.

—— (1993), 'Some Thoughts on Ploutarkhos' Approach to History'. In J. M. Fossey (ed.), *Boeotia Antiqua 3. Papers in Bioitian History, Institutions and Epigraphy in Memory of Paul Roesch* (Amsterdam), 69–77.

Bultmann, K. R. (1921), *Geschichte der synoptischen Tradition: Forschungen zur Religion und Literatur des Alten und Neuen Testaments* (Göttingen). Revised edns. 1931, 1958, 1961. English trans. of the 2nd edn. by J. Marsh as *The History of the Synoptic Tradition* (Oxford, 1963): this trans. revised and supplemented, 1972.

Burke, P. (1966), 'A survey of the popularity of ancient historians 1450–1700', *H&T* 5: 135–52.

Burn, A. R. (1954), 'A Biographical Source on Phaiax and Alkibiades? ([Andokides] IV and Plutarch's *Alkibiades*)', *CQ* NS 4: 138–42.

Burridge, R. A. (1992), *What are the Gospels? A Comparison with Graeco-Roman Biography* (Society for New Testament Studies. Monograph Series 70: Cambridge).

Burton, R. W. B. (1980), *The Chorus in Sophocles' Tragedies* (Oxford).

Caiazza, A. (1993) (ed.), *Precetti Politici* (Corpus Plutarchi Moralium 14: Naples).

Cairns, F. (1982), 'Cleon and Pericles: A suggestion', *JHS* 102: 203–4.
Calero Secall, I. (1990), 'Las *Bacantes* de Euripides en Plutarco'. In A. Pérez Jiménez and G. del Cerro Calderon, *Estudios sobre Plutarco: Obra y Tradición* (*Actas del I Symposion Español sobre Plutarco, Fuengirola 1988*: Malaga), 159–65.
Cameron, Alan (1995), *Callimachus and His Critics* (Princeton).
—— and Cameron, Averil (1964), 'Christianity and Tradition in the Historiography of the Later Roman Empire', *CQ* NS 14: 316–28.
Cameron, Averil (1966), 'The "Scepticism" of Procopius', *Historia* 15: 466–82.
—— (1985), *Procopius and the Sixth Century* (London).
Canfora, L. (1982), 'L' "Apologie" d'Alcibiade', *REG* 95: 140–4.
—— Garzetti, A., and Manetti, D. (1987) (eds.), *Plutarco. Vite parallele: Nicia–Crasso* (Biblioteca Universale Rizzoli: Milan). Second edn. 1991.
Carena, C., Manfredini, M., Piccirilli, L. (1990) (eds.), *Plutarco: Le Vite di Cimone e di Lucullo* (Fondazione Lorenzo Valla: Milan).
Carney, T. F. (1958), 'The death of Marius', *AClass* 1: 117–22.
—— (1960), 'Plutarch's Style in the *Marius*', *JHS* 80: 24–31.
—— (1961*a*), 'The Death of Sulla', *AClass* 4: 64–79.
—— (1961*b*), 'The Flight and Exile of Marius', *G&R* NS 8: 98–121.
—— (1962), *A Biography of C. Marius; An Inaugural Lecture* (*Proceedings of the African Classical Associations* Supplement 1).
—— (1967), 'The Changing Picture of Marius in Ancient Literature', *Proceedings of the African Classical Associations* 10: 5–22.
Carr, E. H. (1961), *What is History?* (The George Macaulay Trevelyan Lectures delivered in the University of Cambridge January–March 1961). Second edn., ed. R. W. Davies (London, 1986).
Carrière, J.-C. (1977), 'A propos de la *Politique* de Plutarque', *DHA* 3 (Centre de recherches d'histoire ancienne 25): 237–51.
Carsana, C. (1990), *La teoria della "costituzione mista" nell' età imperiale romana* (Biblioteca di Athenaeum 13: Como).
Cartledge, P. A. (1987), *Agesilaos and the crisis of Sparta* (London).
—— (1993), *The Greeks: A Portrait of Self and Others* (Oxford). Revised edn. 1997.
Casabona, J. (1966), *Recherches sur le vocabulaire des sacrifices en grec des origines à la fin de l'époque classique* (Aix-en-Provence).
Casertano, G. (1992), 'Un discorso plutarcheo sull' amore tra ideologia e moralismo', *Vichiana*, ser. 3, 3: 220–6.
Cerezo Magán, M. (1992), 'Plutarco y Polibio: Problemática de un bilingüismo activo', *Sintagma* 4: 15–21.
Cesa, M., Prandi, L., and Raffaelli, L. M. (1993) (eds.), *Plutarco. Vite parallele: Coriolano–Alcibiade* (Biblioteca Universale Rizzoli: Milan).
Chamoux, F. (1974), 'La prophétesse Martha'. In *Mélanges d'histoire ancienne offerts à William Seston* (Paris), 81–5.
Cherniss, H. (1976), *Plutarch's Moralia xiii Part ii* (Loeb Classical Library: Cambridge, Mass., and London).

Chitty, S. C. (1859), *The Tamil Plutarch: A Summary Account of the Lives of the Poets and Poetesses of Southern India and Ceylon from the earliest to the present times with Select Specimens of their Compositions* (Colombo). Second edn. 1946 with notes by T. P. Meenakshisundaram. Reprinted New Delhi, 1982.

Christopoulou, A. C. (1995), Επετηρίς της Εταιρείας Βοιωτικών Μελετών, τόμος Β΄, τεύχος Β΄. Β΄ Διεθνές Συνέδριο Βοιωτικών Μελετών, Λιβαδειά, 6–10 Σεπτεμβρίου 1992 (Athens).

Citti, V. (1983), 'Plutarco, *Nic.* 1, 5: storiografia e biografia'. In A. Mastrocinque (ed.), *Omaggio a P. Treves* (Padua), 99–110.

Clark, D. L. (1957), *Rhetoric in Greco-Roman Education* (New York and London).

Clay, D. (1972), 'Epicurus' Κυρία Δόξα xviii', *GRBS* 13: 59–66.

Collingwood, R. G. (1946), *The Idea of History* (Oxford). Revised edn. (1993) with Lectures 1926–1928, edited and with an introduction by J. van der Dussen.

Conquest, R. (1991), *Stalin: Breaker of Nations* (London).

Corbellini, C. (1976), 'La presunta guerra tra Mario e Cinna e l'episodio dei Bardiei', *Aevum* 50: 154–6.

Cornford, F. M. (1907), *Thucydides Mythistoricus* (London).

Costanza, S. (1956), 'La synkrisis nello schema biografico di Plutarco', *Messana: Studi diretti da Michele Catalano* 4: 127–56.

Cournos, J. (1928), *A Modern Plutarch: being an account of Some Great Lives in the Nineteenth Century, together with Comparisons between the Latin and Anglo-Saxon Genius* (London).

Criniti, N. (1979), 'Per una storia del plutarchismo occidentale', *NRS* 63: 187–203.

Culham, P. (1992), 'Plutarch on the Roman siege of Syracuse: The primacy of science over technology'. In Gallo (1992*b*), 179–97.

De Blois, L. (1992), 'The Perception of Politics in Plutarch's Roman "Lives"', *ANRW* 2. 33. 6, 4568–4615.

—— and Bons, J. A. E. (1992), 'Platonic Philosophy and Isocratean Virtues in Plutarch's *Numa*', *AncSoc* 23: 159–88.

—— —— (1995), 'Platonic and Isocratean Political Concepts in Plutarch's *Lycurgus*'. In Gallo and Scardigli (1995), 99–106.

Decker, J. de (1951), 'Semantische Beschouwing', *Hermeneus* 22: 142–6.

De Lacy, P. (1952), 'Biography and Tragedy in Plutarch', *AJPh* 73: 159–71.

—— (1974), 'Plato and the Intellectual Life of the Second Century AD'. In G. W. Bowersock (ed.), *Approaches to the Second Sophistic: Papers Presented at the 105th Annual Meeting of The American Philological Association* (Pennsylvania), 4–10.

Della Corte, F. (1967), *Suetonio: eques romanus* (Florence). First edn. 1958.

Del Re, R. (1953), 'Gli studi plutarchei nell' ultimo cinquantennio', *A&R* ser. 3, 3: 187–96.

Delvaux, G. (1988), 'Retour aux sources de Plutarque', *LEC* 56: 27–48.

—— (1993), 'Valère Maxime, cité par Plutarque, via Paetus Thraséa', *Latomus* 52: 617–22.

Den Boer, W. (1985), 'Plutarch's Philosophic Basis for Personal Involvement'. In Eadie and Ober (1985), 373–85.
Denniston, J. D. (1966), *The Greek Particles* (Oxford). First edn. 1934; 2nd edn. 1954. Reprinted with corrections 1959 and 1966.
Denton, J. (1993), 'Plutarco come lo leggeva Shakespeare: la traduzione delle *Vite Parellele* di Thomas North (1579)'. In Cesa, Prandi, and Raffaelli (1993), 57–78.
Deremetz, A. (1990), 'Plutarque: histoire de l'origine et genèse du récit', *REG* 103: 54–78.
de Romilly, J. (1977), *The Rise and Fall of States According to Greek Authors* (Ann Arbor).
—— (1979), *La Douceur dans la pensée grecque* (Collection des Universités de France: Paris).
—— (1988*a*), 'Plutarch and Thucydides or the Free Use of Quotations', *Phoenix* 42: 22–34.
—— (1988*b*), 'Rencontres avec Plutarque', *ICS* 13. 2: 219–29.
Desideri, P. (1984), 'Il *De Genio Socratis* di Plutarco un esempio di "storiografia tragica"?', *Athenaeum* NS 62 (year 72), 569–85.
—— (1985), 'Ricchezza e vita politica nel pensiero di Plutarco', *Index* 13: 391–405.
—— (1986), 'La vita politica cittadina nell' impero: lettura dei *Praecepta gerendae rei publicae* e dell' *An seni res publica gerenda sit*', *Athenaeum* NS 64 (year 74), 371–81.
—— (1989), 'Teoria e prassi storiografica di Plutarco: una proposta di lettura della coppia Emilio Paolo–Timoleonte', *Maia* 41: 199–215.
—— (1991), 'Citazione letteraria e riferimento storico nei "Precetti politici" di Plutarco'. In D'Ippolito and Gallo (1991), 225–33.
—— (1992*a*), 'I Documenti di Plutarco', *ANRW* 2. 33. 6, 4536–67.
—— (1992*b*), 'La formazione delle coppie nelle "Vite" plutarchee', *ANRW* 2. 33. 6, 4470–86.
—— (1992*c*), 'Scienza nelle *Vite* di Plutarco'. In Gallo (1992*b*), 73–89.
—— (1995*a*), '"Non scriviamo storie, ma vite" (Plut. *Alex*. 1. 2): la formula biografica di Plutarco', *Testis Temporum: Aspetti e problemi della storiografia antica* (*Incontri del Dipartimento di Scienze dell' Antichità dell' Università di Pavia* 8), 15–25.
—— (1995*b*), 'Plutarco e Machiavelli'. In Gallo and Scardigli (1995), 107–22.
Detienne, M., and Vernant, J.-P. (1974), *Les Ruses de l'intelligence: La mètis des grecs* (Paris). English trans. by J. Lloyd (1978), *Cunning Intelligence in Greek Culture and Society* (Sussex and New Jersey).
Devillers, Q. (1993), 'Le Rôle des passages relatifs à Germanicus dans les *Annales* de Tacite', *AncSoc* 24: 225–41.
Dibelius, M. (1919), *Die Formgeschichte des Evangeliums* (Tübingen). Second edn. 1933; 3rd edn., reprinted with a supplement by G. Iber, 1966. English trans. of the 2nd edn. by B. L. Woolf as *From Tradition to Gospel* (London, 1934).

Di Gregorio, L. (1979), 'Lettura diretta e utilizzazione di fonti intermedie nelle citazioni pluarchee dei tre grandi tragici. I', *Aevum* 53: 11–50.

—— (1980), 'Lettura diretta e utilizzazione di fonti intermedie nelle citazioni pluarchee dei tre grandi tragici. II', *Aevum* 54: 46–79.

Dihle, A. (1956), *Studien zur griechischen Biographie* (Abhandlungen der Akademie der Wissenschaften in Göttingen. Philologische-historische Klasse 3, Folge 37: Göttingen).

—— (1989), *Die griechische und lateinische Literatur der Kaiserzeit: Von Augustus bis Justinian* (Munich).

Dillery, J. (1995), *Xenophon and the History of his Times* (London and New York).

Dillon, J. (1997), 'Plutarch and the end of History'. In Mossman (1997), 233–40.

Dionisotti, A. C. (1988), 'Nepos and the Generals', *JRS* 78: 35–49.

D'Ippolito, G., and Gallo, I. (1991) (eds.), *Strutture formali dei "Moralia" di Plutarco* (*Atti del III Convegno plutarcheo, Palermo, 3–5 maggio 1989*: Naples).

Dittmar, H. (1912), *Aischines von Sphettos: Studien zur Literaturgeschichte der Sokratiker* (Berlin).

Dodds, E. R. (1959), *Plato: Gorgias* (Oxford).

Donini, P. L. (1974), *Tre studi sull' aristotelismo nel II secolo d. C.* (Historica, Politica, Philosophica. Il Pensiero Antico. Studi e testi 7: Turin).

—— (1986), 'Plutarco, Ammonio e l'Academia'. In Brenk and Gallo (1986), 97–110.

Dorey, T. A. (1967) (ed.), *Latin Biography* (London).

Döring, K. (1979), *Exemplum Socratis: Studien zur Socratesnachwirkung in der kynisch-stoischen Popularphilosophie der frühen Kaiserzeit und im frühen Christentum* (*Hermes* Einzelshriften 42: Wiesbaden).

Dover, K. J. (1968), *Aristophanes: Clouds* (Oxford).

—— (1988), 'Anecdotes, Gossip and Slander'. In *The Greeks and their Legacy: Collected Papers, ii. Prose Literature, History, Society, Transmission, Influence* (Oxford), 45–52.

Dryden, J. (1684–8), *Plutarch's Lives. Translated from the Greek by several hands*, 5 vols. (London).

Ducrey, P. (1968), *La Traitement des prisonniers de guerre dans la Grèce antique des origines à la conquête romaine* (Paris).

Due, B. (1987), 'Lysander in Xenophon's *Hellenica*', *C&M* 38: 53–62.

—— (1989), *The Cyropaedia: Xenophon's aims and methods* (Aarhus).

Dunbar, N. (1995), *Aristophanes: Birds* (Oxford).

Dunkle, J. R. (1967), 'The Greek Tyrant and Roman Political Invective of the Late Republic', *TAPhA* 98: 151–71.

—— (1971–2), 'The Rhetorical Tyrant in Roman Historiography: Sallust, Livy and Tacitus', *CW* 65: 12–20.

Durling, R. J. (1993), *A Dictionary of Medical Terms in Galen* (Leiden, New York, and London).

Dušanić, S. (1996), 'Plato and Plutarch's Fictional Techniques: The Death of the Great Pan', *RhM* 139: 276–94.
Eadie, J. W., and Ober, J. (1985) (eds.), *The Craft of the Ancient Historian: Essays in Honour of Chester G. Starr* (Lanham, NY, and London).
Eckstein, A. M. (1995), *Moral Vision in* The Histories *of Polybius* (Berkeley).
Edwards, C. (1993), *The Politics of Immorality in Ancient Rome* (Cambridge).
Edwards, M. J. E. (1995) (ed.), *Greek Orators, iv. Andocides* (Warminster).
Elsner, J. A. S. (1992), 'Pausanias: a Greek Pilgrim in the Roman World', *Past and Present* 135: 3–29.
—— (1994), 'From the pyramids to Pausanias and Piglet: monuments, travel and writing'. In S. Goldhill and R. Osborne (eds.), *Art and Text in Ancient Greek Culture* (Cambridge), 224–54.
Erbse, H. (1956), 'Die Bedeutung der Synkrisis in den Parallelbiographien Plutarchs', *Hermes* 84: 398–424. Reprinted in id. (1979), 478–505.
—— (1961), 'Die Architektonik im Aufbau von Xenophons Memorabilien', *Hermes* 89: 257–87. Reprinted in id. (1979), 308–40.
—— (1979), *Ausgewählte Schriften zur klassischen Philologie* (Berlin and New York).
Evans, E. C. (1935), 'Roman Descriptions of Personal Appearance in History and Biography', *HSPhh* 46: 43–84.
—— (1941), 'The Study of Physiognomy in the Second Century AD', *TAPhA* 72: 96–108.
—— (1945), 'Galen the Physician as Physiognomist', *TAPhA* 76: 287–98.
—— (1969), 'Physiognomics in the Ancient World', *TAPhS* 59. 5: 1–101.
Ewbank, L. C. (1982), 'Plutarch's Use of Non-literary Sources in the "Lives" of Sixth- and Fifth-Century Greeks'. Dissertation, University of North Carolina at Chapel Hill.
Fairweather, J. A. (1974), 'Fiction in the Biographies of Ancient Writers', *AncSoc* 5: 231–75.
—— (1984), 'Traditional Narrative, Inference and Truth in the *Lives* of the Greek Poets'. In F. Cairns (ed.), *Papers of the Liverpool Latin Seminar, Fourth Volume, 1983* (ARCA Classical and Medieval Texts, Papers and Monographs 11), 315–69.
Fantham, E. (1972), *Comparative Studies in Republican Latin Imagery* (Toronto).
Federici, F. (1828), *Degli scrittori greci e delle italiane versioni delle loro opere: Notizie* (Padua).
Fenik, B. (1968), *Typical Battle Scenes in the Iliad. Studies in the Narrative Techniques of Homeric Battle Description* (*Hermes* Einzelschriften 21: Wiesbaden).
Ferrarese, P. (1974), 'La spedizione di Pericle nel Ponto Eusino'. In M. Sordi (ed.), *Propaganda e persuasione occulta nell' antichità* (*Contributi dell' Istituto de storia antica* 2: Milan), 7–19.
—— (1975), 'Caratteri della tradizione antipericlea nella "Vita di Pericle" di Plutarco'. In M. Sordi (ed.), *Storiografia e propaganda* (*Contributi dell' Istituto de storia antica* 3: Milan), 21–30.

Ferrari, F. (1996), 'La teoria delle idee in Plutarco', *Elenchos* 17: 121–42.
Fisher, N. R. E. (1992), *Hybris: A Study in the Values of Honour and Shame in Ancient Greece* (Warminster).
Flacelière, R. (1946), 'Plutarque et les Oracles Béotiens', *BCH* 70: 199–207.
—— (1948), 'Sur quelques passages des *Vies* de Plutarque. 1. Thésée–Romulus II. Lycurge–Numa', *REG* 61: 67–103 and 391–429.
—— (1951), 'Le poète stoïcien Sarapion d'Athènes, ami de Plutarque', *REG* 64: 325–7.
—— (1968), 'État présent des études sur Plutarque'. In *Actes du VIIIe Congrès Budé (Paris, 5–10 avril 1968)* (Paris), 483–505.
—— (1970), 'Héraclès ou Héraclite'. In *Hommages à M. Delcourt* (Collection Latomus 114) (Brussels), 207–10.
—— (1971), 'Hadrien et Delphes', *CRAI* 1971: 168–85.
—— (1974), 'La Théologie selon Plutarque'. In *Mélanges de philosophie, de littérature et d'histoire ancienne offerts à Pierre Boyancé* (Rome), 273–80.
—— (1980), 'Tacite et Plutarque'. In *Mélanges de littérature et d'épigraphie latines, d'histoire ancienne et d'archeologie: Hommages à la memoire de P. Wuilleumier* (Paris), 113–19.
—— and Irigoin, J. (1987), 'Introduction Générale'. In *Plutarque: Oeuvres Morales Tome I, 1re partie* (Collection des Universités de France: Paris).
Focke, F. (1923), 'Synkrisis', *Hermes* 58: 327–68.
Follet, S. (1972), 'Flavius Euphanès d'Athènes, ami de Plutarque'. In *Mélanges de linguistique et de philologie grecques offerts à Pierre Chantraine* (Paris), 35–50.
Fornara, C. W. (1983), *The Nature of History in Ancient Greece and Rome* (Berkeley).
Foucault, M. (1985), *The Use of Pleasure* (*The History of Sexuality*, ii: New York). Trans. R. Hurley. First published as *L' Usage des plaisirs* (Paris, 1984).
—— (1986), *The Care of the Self* (*The History of Sexuality*, iii: New York). Trans. R. Hurley. First published as *Le Souci de soi* (Paris, 1984).
Fowler, A. (1982), *Kinds of Literature: An Introduction to the Theory of Genres and Modes* (Oxford).
Fowler, D. P. (1989), 'First Thoughts on Closure: Prospects and Problems', *MD* 22: 75–122.
Fox, M. (1993), 'History and Rhetoric in Dionysius of Halicarnassus', *JRS* 83: 31–47.
Fraenkel, E. (1957), *Horace* (Oxford).
Franco, C. (1991), 'Trittico plutarcheo (*Nicia* 1. 5; *Demetrio* 27. 5–7; *Artaserse* 1. 2)', *Prometheus* 17: 125–31.
Fraser, P. M., and Matthews, E. (1997) (eds.), *A Lexicon of Greek Personal Names*, iiiA. *The Peloponnese, Western Greece, Sicily, and Magna Graecia* (Oxford).
Frazier, F. (1987), 'A propos de la composition des couples dans les "Vies parallèles" de Plutarque', *RPh* 61: 65–75.

Frazier, F. (1988a), 'A propos de la "philotimia" dans les "Vies": quelques jalons dans l'histoire d'une notion', *RPh* 62: 109–27.

—— (1988b), 'Remarques à propos de l'usage des citations en matière de chronologie dans les *Vies*', *ICS* 13. 2: 297–309.

—— (1990), 'Introduction' to 'La gloire des Athéniens (De gloria Atheniensium)'. In F. Frazier and C. Froidefond (eds.), *Plutarque: Oeuvres Morales. Tome V, 1re partie: La Fortune ou la vertu d'Alexandre, La gloire des Athéniens* (Collection des Universités de France: Paris), 159–84.

—— (1992), 'Contribution à l'étude de la composition des "Vies" de Plutarque: l'élaboration des grandes scènes', *ANRW* 2. 33. 6, 4487–4535.

—— (1995), 'Principes et décisions dans le domaine politique d'après les *Vies* de Plutarque'. In Gallo and Scardigli (1995), 147–71.

Frézouls, E. (1991), 'L' hellénisme dans l'épigraphie de l'Asie Mineure romaine'. In Saïd (1991), 125–47.

Friedrich, W. H. (1938), 'Cato, Caesar und Fortuna bei Lucan', *Hermes* 73: 391–421.

Frost, F. J. (1980), 'Plutarch and Clio'. In S. M. Burstein and L. A. Okin (eds.), *Panhellenica: Essays in Ancient History and Historiography in honor of Truesdell S. Brown* (Lawrence, Kans.), 155–70.

Fuhrmann, F. (1960), 'Das Vierkaiserjahr bei Tacitus: Über den Aufbau der Historien Buch I–III', *Philologus* 104: 250–78.

—— (1964), *Les Images de Plutarque* (Paris).

Furley, W. D. (1989), 'Andokides IV ("Against Alkibiades"): fact or fiction?', *Hermes* 117: 138–56.

Fuscagni, S. (1989), 'Introduzione' to *Cimone*. In Fuscagni, Mugelli, and Scardigli (1989), 35–134.

—— Mugelli, B., and Scardigli, B. (1989) (eds.), *Plutarco. Vite parallele: Cimone–Lucullo*. (Biblioteca Universale Rizzoli: Milan). Second edn. 1993.

Gabba, E. (1956), *Appiano e la storia delle guerre civili* (Florence).

—— (1959), 'Storici greci da Augusto ai Severi', *RSI* 71: 361–81.

—— (1991), *Dionysius and The History of Archaic Rome* (Berkeley).

Galinski, K. (1988), 'The Anger of Aeneas', *AJPh* 109: 321–48.

Gallo, I. (1967), 'La *Vita di Euripide* di Satiro e gli studi sulla biografia antica', *PP* 22: 134–60.

—— (1992a), 'Ecdotica e critica testuale nei "Moralia" di Plutarco'. In id. (1992c), 11–37.

—— (1992b) (ed.), *Plutarco e le scienze* (*Atti del IV Convegno plutarcheo, Genova–Bocca di Magra, 22–25 aprile 1991*: Genoa).

—— (1992c) (ed.), *Ricerche plutarchee* (Università degli Studi di Salerno. Quaderni del dipartimento di scienze dell' antichità 12: Naples).

—— and Scardigli, B. (1995) (eds.), *Teoria e prassi politica nelle opere di Plutarco* (*Atti del V Convegno plutarcheo, Certosa di Pontignano, 7–9 giugno 1993*: Naples).

Gallotta, B. (1987), *Germanico* (Centro ricerche e documentazione sull' antichità classica. Monografie 10: Rome).
Gamberale, L. (1995), 'Un probabile errore di latino in Plutarco, *Tib. Gracch.* 13, 6', *RFIC* 123: 433–40.
García Valdés, M. (1994) (ed.), *Estudios sobre Plutarco: Ideas Religiosas* (*Actas del III Simposio Internacional sobre Plutarco, Oviedo 30 de abril a 2 de mayo de 1992*: Madrid).
Garoufalias, A. P. (1979; 1st edn., in Greek, Athens 1946), *Pyrrhus King of Epirus* (London).
Garzetti, A. (1953), 'Plutarco e le sue "Vite Parallele": Rassegna di studi 1934–1952', *RSI* 65: 76–104.
—— (1954) (ed.), *Plutarchi Vita Caesaris* (Florence). Second edn. 1968.
Gehrke, H.-J. (1976), *Phokion: Studien zur Erfassung seiner historischen Gestalt* (Zetemata 64).
Geiger, J. (1971), 'A Commentary on Plutarch's Cato Minor'. Dissertation, Oxford.
—— (1975), 'Zum Bild Julius Caesars in der römischen Kaiserzeit', *Historia* 24: 444–53.
—— (1979a), 'Cornelius Nepos, *De Regibus Exterarum Gentium*', *Latomus* 38: 662–9.
—— (1979b), 'Munatius Rufus and Thrasea Paetus on Cato the Younger', *Athenaeum* NS 57 (year 67), 48–72.
—— (1981), 'Plutarch's Parallel Lives: The Choice of Heroes', *Hermes* 109: 85–104. Reprinted in Scardigli (1995a), 165–90.
—— (1985), *Cornelius Nepos and Ancient Political Biography* (*Historia* Einzelschriften 47: Stuttgart).
—— (1988), 'Nepos and Plutarch: From Latin to Greek Political Biography', *ICS* 13: 245–56.
—— (1993), 'Introduzione' to *Catone* (Italian trans. by M. Grottanelli). In Bearzot, Geiger, and Ghilli (1993), 273–319.
—— (1995a), 'Introduzione' to *Cicerone* (Italian trans. by M. Grottanelli). In Geiger, Ghilli, Mugelli, and Pecorella Longo (1995), 293–313.
—— (1995b), 'Plutarch on Hellenistic Politics: the case of Eumenes of Cardia'. In Gallo and Scardigli (1995), 173–85.
—— Ghilli, L., Mugelli, B., and Pecorella Longo, C. (1995) (eds.), *Plutarco. Vite Parallele: Demostene–Cicecro* (Biblioteca Universale Rizzoli: Milan).
Gentili, B., and Cerri, G. (1978), 'L' idea di biografia nel pensiero greco', *QUCC* 27: 7–27. English trans. in id. (1988), 61–85.
———— (1988), *History and Biography in Ancient Thought* (London Studies in Classical Philology 20: Amsterdam). First published (1983) as *Storia e biografia nel pensiero antico* (Bibl. di Cult. Mod. 878: Rome and Bari).
Georgiadou, A. (1988), 'The *Lives of the Caesars* and Plutarch's Other *Lives*', *ICS* 13. 2: 349–56.

Georgiadou, A. (1992a), 'Bias and Character-portrayal in Plutarch's Lives of Pelopidas and Marcellus', *ANRW* 2. 33. 6, 4222–57.
—— (1992b), 'Idealistic and Realistic Portraiture in the Lives of Plutarch', *ANRW* 2. 33. 6, 4616–23.
Giachetti, A. F. (1910), 'Contributo alla storia del volgarizzamento del sec. XIV delle *Vite Parallele* di Plutarco', *Rivista delle Biblioteche e degli Archivi* 21: 1–18.
Gianakaris, C. J. (1970), *Plutarch* (Twayne's World Authors Series 111: New York).
Giangrande, G. (1988), 'Problemi testuali nei "Moralia"'. In A. Garzya, G. Giangrande, and M. Manfredini (eds.), *Sulla tradizione manoscritta dei "Moralia" di Plutarco* (Quaderni del Dipartimento di Scienze dell' Antichità dell' Università di Salerno 2: Salerno), 55–101.
—— (1991), 'Linguaggio e struttura nelle "Amatoriae narrationes"'. In D'Ippolito and Gallo (1991), 273–94.
—— (1992a), 'La lingua dei *Moralia* di Plutarco: normativismo e questioni di metodo'. In I. Gallo and R. Laurenti (1992) (eds.), *I Moralia di Plutarco tra Filologia e Filosofia. Atti del giornata plutarchea di Napoli, Istituto Suor Orsola Benincasa, 10 aprile 1992* (Strumenti per la ricerca plutarchea: Naples), 29–46.
—— (1992b), 'Testo e lingua nel *De Alexandri fortuna aut virtute* plutarcheo'. In Gallo (1992c), 39–84.
Giannantoni, G. (1990), *Socratis et Socraticorum Reliquiae*, iv (Elenchos. Collana di testi e studi sul pensiero antico diretta da Gabriele Giannantoni 18: Naples).
—— (1997), 'L' *Alcibiade* di Eschine e la letteratura socratica su Alcibiade'. In G. Giannantoni and M. Narcy (eds.), *Lezioni Socratiche* (Elenchos. Collana di testi e studi sul pensiero antico diretta da Gabriele Giannantoni 26: Naples), 349–73.
Gill, C. (1983), 'The Question of Character Development: Plutarch and Tacitus', *CQ* NS 33: 469–87.
—— (1985), 'Plato and the Education of Character', *AGPh* 67: 1–26.
—— (1986), 'The Question of Character and Personality in Greek Tragedy', *Poetics Today* 7: 251–73.
—— (1990), 'The Character-Personality Distinction'. In C. B. R. Pelling (ed.), *Characterization and Individuality in Greek Literature* (Oxford), 1–31.
—— (1994), 'Peace of Mind and Being Yourself: Panaetius to Plutarch', *ANRW* 2. 36. 7, 4599–4640.
—— (1996), *Personality in Greek Epic, Tragedy, and Philosophy: The Self in Dialogue* (Oxford).
Gleason, M. W. (1995), *Making Men: Sophists and Self-Presentation in Ancient Rome* (Princeton).
Goar, R. J. (1987), *The Legend of Cato Uticensis from the First Century BC to the Fifth Century AD with an Appendix on Dante and Cato* (Collection Latomus 197: Brussels).
Goldhill, S. (1995), *Foucault's Virginity: Ancient Erotic Fiction and the History of Sexuality* (Cambridge).

Gomme, A. W. (1945) (ed.), *A Historical Commentary on Thucydides*, i. *Introduction and Commentary on Book I* (Oxford).
—— and Sandbach, F. H. (1973), *Menander: A Commentary* (Oxford).
González González, M. (1994), 'Ecos de Plutarco en los versos de Cavafis'. In García Valdés (1994), 651–8.
Goodyear, F. R. D. (1970), *Tacitus* (Greece and Rome New Surveys in the Classics 4: Oxford).
—— (1972) *The Annals of Tacitus, Books 1–6, edited with a Commentary*, i. *Annals 1. 1–54* (Cambridge).
Gossage, A. J. (1967), 'Plutarch'. In Dorey (1967), 45–77.
Gould, J. (1955), *The Development of Plato's Ethics* (Cambridge).
Gray, V. J. (1986), 'Xenophon's "Hiero" and the Meeting of the Wise Man and Tyrant in Greek Literature', *CQ* NS 36: 115–23.
—— (1987a), 'Mimesis in Greek Historical Theory', *AJPh* 108: 467–86.
—— (1987b), 'The Value of Diodorus Siculus for the Years 411–386 BC', *Hermes* 115: 72–89.
—— (1989), *The Character of Xenophon's* Hellenica (London).
Green, D. C. (1978), *Plutarch "revisited": eine Studie über Shakespeares lezte Römertragödien und ihre Quelle*. English trans. (Salzburg, 1979), *Plutarch Revisited: A Study of Shakespeare's Last Roman Tragedies and their Source*.
Green, P. (1978), 'Caesar and Alexander: Aemulatio, Imitatio, Comparatio', *AJAH* 3: 1–26.
Gribble, D. (1994), 'Alcibiades and Athens: a Study in Literary Presentations'. Dissertation, Oxford.
Griffin, M. T., and Barnes, J. (1989) (eds.), *Philosophia Togata: Essays in Philosophy and Roman Society* (Oxford).
Grossman, G. (1950), 'Politische Schlagwörter aus der Zeit des Peloponnesischen Krieges' (Inaugural Dissertation, Basle: Zurich).
Grube, G. M. A. (1961), *A Greek Critic: Demetrius on Style* (*Phoenix* Supplement 4: Toronto).
Guerrini, R., Santoni, A., and Stadter, P. A. (1991) (eds.), *Plutarco. Vite parallele: Periclo–Fabio* (Biblioteca Universale Rizzoli: Milan).
Guthrie, W. K. C. (1969), *A History of Greek Philosophy*, iii. *The Fifth-Century Enlightenment* (Cambridge).
Habicht, Chr. (1959–60), 'Zwei neue Inschriften aus Pergamon', *Istanbuler Mitteilungen* 9–10: 109–27.
—— (1969), *Altertümer von Pergamon*, viii. 3. *Die Inschriften des Asklepieions* (Deutsches Archäologisches Institut: Berlin).
—— (1970), *Gottmenschentum und griechische Städte*, 2nd edn., with a supplement (Munich). First edition 1956 (Zetemata 14).
Halfmann, H. (1979), *Die Senatoren aus den östlichen Teil des Imperium Romanum bis zum Ende des 2. Jahrhunderts n. Chr.* (Hypomnemata 58: Göttingen).

Hamilton, C. D. (1992), 'Plutarch's "Life of Agesilaus"', *ANRW* 2. 33. 6, 4201–21.
—— (1994), 'Plutarch and Xenophon on Agesilaus', *AncW* 25: 205–12.
Hamilton, J. R. (1969), *Plutarch: Alexander. A Commentary* (Oxford).
Hammond, N. G. L. (1938), 'The two battles of Chaeronea (338 BC and 86 BC)', *Klio* 31: 186–218.
Hanfmann, G. M. A. (1983), *Sardis from Prehistoric to Roman Times: Results of the Archaeological Exploration of Sardis 1958–1975* (Assisted by W. E. Mierse) (Cambridge, Mass., and London).
Hardy, E. G. (1890) (ed.), *Plutarch's Lives of Galba and Otho with introduction and explanatory notes* (London and New York). Pages ix–lx of the introduction are reprinted as 'Plutarch, Tacitus and Suetonius, on Galba and Otho', in *Studies in Roman History* (London, 1906), 295–334.
Harris, B. F. (1970), 'The Portrayal of Aristocratic Power in Plutarch's *Lives*'. In id. (ed.), *Auckland Classical Essays presented to E. M. Blaiklock* (Auckland and Oxford), 185–202.
Harrison, G. W. M. (1992a), 'The Critical Trends in Scholarship on the Non-Philosophical Works in Plutarch's "Moralia"', *ANRW* 2. 33. 6, 4646–81.
—— (1992b), 'Plutarch, *Vita Antonii* 75. 3–4: Source for a Poem by Kavafis', *A&R* NS 37: 207–9.
—— (1995), 'The Semiotics of Plutarch's Συγκρίσεις: The Hellenistic Lives of Demetrius–Antony and Agesilaus–Pompey', *RBPh* 73: 91–104.
Harrison, J. E. (1922, 3rd edn.; 1st edn. 1903), *Prolegomena to the Study of Greek Religion* (Princeton). Reprinted Cambridge, 1991.
Hartog, F. (1980), *Le Miroir d'Hérodote: Essai sur la représentation de l'autre* (Paris). English trans. by J. Lloyd (1988), *The Mirror of Herodotus: The Representation of the Other in the Writing of History* (Berkeley).
—— (1991), 'Rome et la Grèce: Les choix de Denys d'Halicarnasse'. In Saïd (1991), 149–67.
Hatzfeld, J. (1951; 1st edn. 1940), *Alcibiade: Étude sur l'histoire d'Athènes à la fin du Ve siècle* (Paris).
Heinze, R. (1890), 'Ariston von Chios bei Plutarch und Horaz', *RhM* 45: 497–523.
Helmbold, W. C., and O'Neil, E. N. (1959), *Plutarch's Quotations* (Philological Monographs published by the American Philological Association 19: Baltimore).
Herbert, K. B. J. (1957), 'The Identity of Plutarch's Lost *Scipio*', *AJPh* 78: 83–8.
—— (1958), 'Ephorus in Plutarch's Lives: A source Problem'. Resumé of Harvard Dissertation, 1954, *HSPh* 63: 510–13.
Hershbell, J. P. (1982), 'Plutarch and Democritus', *QUCC* NS 10: 81–111.
—— (1992), 'Plutarch and Stoicism', *ANRW* 2. 36. 5, 3336–52.
—— (1993), 'Plutarch and Herodotus—The Beetle in the Rose', *RhM* 136: 143–63.
Hesk, J. (1997), 'Deception, Democracy and Ideology: The Rhetoric of Self-Representation in Classical Athenian Culture'. Dissertation, Cambridge.

Hillard, T. W. (1987), 'Plutarch's Late-Republican Lives: Between The Lines', *Antichthon* 21: 19–48.
Hillman, T. P. (1992), 'Plutarch and the First Consulship of Pompeius and Crassus', *Phoenix* 46: 124–37.
—— (1994), 'Authorial Statements, Narrative, and Character in Plutarch's *Agesilaus–Pompeius*', *GRBS* 35: 255–80.
Hirsch, S. W. (1985), *The Friendship of the Barbarians: Xenophon and the Persian Empire* (Hanover and London).
Hirzel, R. (1912), *Plutarch* (Leipzig).
Holden, H. A. (1886), Πλουτάρχου Σύλλας: *Plutarch's Life of Lucius Cornelius Sulla with introduction, notes and lexicon* (Cambridge).
Holford-Strevens, L. (1988), *Aulus Gellius* (London).
Hommeyer, H. (1963), 'Beobachtungen zu den hellenistischen Quellen der Plutarch-Viten', *Klio* 41: 145–57.
Hopkins, K. (1983), *Death and Renewal: Sociological Studies in Roman History*, ii (Cambridge).
Hopkinson, N. (1988), *A Hellenistic Anthology* (Cambridge).
Hornblower, J. (1981), *Hieronymus of Cardia* (Oxford).
Howard, M. W. (1970), *The Influence of Plutarch in the Major European Literatures of the Eighteenth Century* (University of North Carolina Studies in Comparative Literature 50: Chapel Hill).
Huart, P. (1968), *Le Vocabulaire de l'analyse psychologique dans l'oeuvre de Thucydide* (Paris).
Humbert, S. (1991), 'Plutarque, Alexandre et l'Hellénisme'. In Saïd (1991), 169–82.
Hunter, R. L. (1983), *A Study of Daphnis & Chloe* (Cambridge).
Hunter, V. J. (1973), *Thucydides the Artful Reporter* (Toronto).
Hyde, W. W. (1921), *Olympic Victor Monuments and Greek Athletic Art* (Washington).
Immerwahr, H. R. (1960), '*Ergon*: History as a Monument in Herodotus and Thucydides', *AJPh* 81: 261–90.
Ingenkamp, H. G. (1971), *Plutarchs Schriften über die Heilung der Seele* (Hypomnemata 34: Göttingen).
—— (1988), 'Der Höhepunkt der deutschen Plutarchrezeption: Plutarch bei Nietzsche', *ICS* 13: 505–29.
—— (1992*a*), 'Plutarchs "Leben der Gracchen": Eine Analyse', *ANRW* 2. 33. 6, 4298–4346.
—— (1992*b*), 'Plutarch und die konservative Verhaltensnorm', *ANRW* 2. 33. 6, 4624–44.
—— (1997), Ἀρετὴ εὐτυχοῦσα (Plut, Tim. 36) und die Last der Leichtigkeit', *RhM* 140: 71–89.
Irigoin, J. (1982–3), 'La Formation d'un *corpus*: un problème d'histoire des textes dans la tradition des *Vies parallèles* de Plutarque', *RHT* 12–13: 1–12.

—— (1986), 'Le Catalogue de Lamprias: Tradition manuscrite et éditions imprimées', *REG* 99: 318–31.
Jacoby, F. (1916), 'Iuba II', *RE* 9, coll. 2384–95.
Jannaris, A. N. (1897), *An historical Greek grammar chiefly of the Attic dialect as written and spoken from classical antiquity down to the present time founded upon ancient texts, inscriptions, papyri and present popular Greek* (London).
Jones, C. P. (1966), 'Towards a Chronology of Plutarch's Works', *JRS* 56: 61–74. Reprinted in Scardigli (1995a), 75–123.
—— (1967), 'Julius Naso and Julius Secundus', *HSPh* 72: 279–88.
—— (1970), 'Sura and Senecio', *JRS* 60: 98–104.
—— (1971), *Plutarch and Rome* (Oxford).
—— (1972), 'Two Friends of Plutarch', *BCH* 96: 263–7.
—— (1982), 'Plutarch, Lucullus 42, 3–4', *Hermes* 110: 254–6.
Jones, R. M. (1916), *The Platonism of Plutarch* (Menasha, Wis.). Reprinted in *The Platonism of Plutarch and selected papers* (New York and London, 1980).
Jouanna, J. (1978), 'Le Médecin modèle du législateur dans les *Lois* de Platon', *Ktèma* 3: 77–91.
Kane, J. (1990), 'Greek Values in Xenophon's *Hellenica*'. In A. Loizou and H. Lesser (eds.), *Polis and Politics: Essays in Greek Moral and Political Philosophy* (Aldershot), 1–11.
Keaveney, A., and Madden, J. A. (1982), 'Phthiriasis and its Victims', *SO* 57: 87–99.
Kebric, R. B. (1977), *In the Shadow of Macedon: Duris of Samos* (Historia Einzelschriften 29: Wiesbaden).
Keen, A. G. (1996), 'Lies about Lysander'. In F. Cairns and M. Heath (eds.), *Papers of the Leeds International Latin Seminar, ix. Roman Poetry and Prose, Greek Poetry, Etymology, Historiography* (Leeds), 285–96.
Kelly, T. (1985), 'The Spartan Scytale'. In Eadie and Ober (1985), 141–69.
Kerényi, K. (1962), '$\mathring{A}\gamma\alpha\lambda\mu\alpha$, $\epsilon\mathring{\iota}\kappa\acute{\omega}\nu$ $\epsilon\mathring{\iota}\delta\omega\lambda o\nu$'. Italian trans. by O. M. Nobile in *Demitizzazione e Immagine* (*Archivio di Filosofia* 1–2: Padua), 161–71.
Klibansky, R., Panofsky, E., and Saxl, F. (1964), *Saturn and Melancholy: Studies in the History of Natural Philosophy, Religion and Art* (London).
Klotz, A. (1934), 'Die Quellen der plutarchischen Lebensbeschreibung des Marcellus', *RhM* 83: 289–318.
—— (1935a), 'Über die Quelle Plutarchs in der Lebensbeschreibung des Q. Fabius Maximus', *RhM* 84: 125–53.
—— (1935b), 'Die Quellen Plutarchs in der Lebensbeschreibung des Titus Quinctius Flamininus', *RhM* 84: 46–53.
—— (1938), 'De Plutarchi vitae Caesarianae fontibus', *Mnemosyne* ser. 3, 6: 313–19.
—— (1941), 'Zu den Quellen der plutarchischen Lebensbeschreibung des Camillus', *RhM* 90: 282–309.
Knox, P. E. (1985), 'Wine, Water, and Callimachean Polemics', *HSPh* 89: 107–19.

Koestermann, E. (1963), *Cornelius Tacitus: Annalen*, i. *Buch 1–3* (Heidelberg).
Kokolakis, M. (1960), 'Lucian and the tragic performances in his time', *Platon* 12: 67–109.
Konstantinovic, I. (1989), *Montaigne et Plutarque* (Travaux d'humanisme et Renaissance 231: Geneva).
Korus, K. (1977), 'Plutarch wobec greckiej Tradycji Wyksztalcenia Ogólnego' (Polish with German summary: 'Plutarchs Stellung in der Tradition der griechischen Allgemeinbildung'), *Eos* 65: 53–76.
Krenkel, W. A. (1980), 'Sex und politische Biographie', *Wissenschaftliche Zeitschrift der Wilhelm-Pieck-Universität Rostock, Gesellschaft- und Sprachwissenschaftliche* 29. 5: 65–76.
Krentz, P. (1989) (ed.), *Xenophon: Hellenika I–II. 3. 10* (Warminster).
Krevans, N. (1993), 'Fighting against Antimachus: the *Lyde* and the *Aetia* Reconsidered'. In M. A. Harder, R. F. Regtuit, and G. C. Wakker (eds.), *Callimachus* (Hellenistica Groningana. Proceedings of the Groningen Workshops on Hellenistic Poetry: Groningen), 149–60.
Kroll, W. (1924), *Studien zum Verständnis der römischen Literatur* (Stuttgart). Reprinted 1964.
Kuhn, R. (1976), *The Demon of Noontide: Ennui in Western Literature* (Princeton).
Kühner, R. (1904), *Ausführliche Grammatik der griechischen Sprache* (3rd edn., ed. B. Gerth), ii (Hanover and Leipzig).
Lammert, F. (1916), 'Appian, Plutarch und Cäcilius von Kale Akte', *Berliner PhilologischeWochenschrift* 36, coll. 477–80.
Larmour, D. H. J. (1988), 'Plutarch's Compositional Methods in the *Theseus* and *Romulus*', *TAPhA* 118: 361–75.
—— (1992), 'Making Parallels: *Synkrisis* and Plutarch's "Themistocles and Camillus"', *ANRW* 2. 33. 6, 4154–4200.
Lasso de la Vega, J. S. (1961–2), 'Traducciones españolas de las "Vidas" de Plutarco', *EClás* 6: 451–514.
Lattimore, R. (1939), 'The Wise Adviser in Herodotus', *CPh* 34: 24–35.
Lausberg, H. (1960), *Handbuch der literarischen Rhetorik: Eine Grundlegung der Literaturwissenschaft*, 2 vols. (Munich).
Lavagnini, B. (1989), 'In Plutarco, *Vita Luculli* 29, 16–20 la fonte di una poesia di Kavafis', *A&R* NS 33: 144–6. Reprinted as 'In Plutarco, *Vita Luculli* XXIX, 16–20 l'ispirazione di una poesia di Kavafis', in *Studi di filologia classica in onore di Giusto Monaco* (Palermo, 1991), iv. 1805–7.
—— (1992), 'Il fascino discreto di Plutarco', *A&R* NS 37: 1–5.
Lavery, G. B. (1994), 'Plutarch's *Lucullus* and the Living Bond of Biography', *CJ* 89: 261–73.
Le Corsu, F. (1981), *Plutarque et les femmes dans les* Vies parallèles (Paris).
Leo, F. (1901), *Die griechisch-römische Biographie nach ihrer litterarischen Form* (Leipzig).

Levene, D. S. (1992), 'Sallust's *Jugurtha*: An "Historical Fragment"', *JRS* 82: 53–70.
Lévêque, P. (1957), *Pyrrhos* (Paris).
Levi, M. A. (1955), *Plutarco e il V secolo* (Milan).
Lévy, E. (1990), 'L'Art de la déformation historique dans les *Helléniques* de Xénophon'. In Verdin, Schepens, and De Keyser (1990), 125–57.
Lewis, R. G. (1991*a*), 'Suetonius' "Caesares" and their Literary Antecedents', *ANRW* 2. 33. 5, 3623–74.
—— (1991*b*), 'Sulla's Autobiography: Scope and Economy', *Athenaeum* NS 69 (year 79), 509–19.
—— (1993), 'Imperial Autobiography, Augustus to Hadrian', *ANRW* 2. 34. 1, 629–706.
Lieberich, H. (1898), *Studien zu den Proömien in der griechischen und byzantinischen Geschichtschreibung*, i. *Die griechischen Geschichtschreiber* (Programm des Kgl. Realgymnasiums München). Reprinted (1899) as dissertation, Munich.
Littman, R. J. (1970), 'The Loves of Alcibiades', *TAPhA* 101: 263–76.
Lloyd, G. E. R. (1966), *Polarity and Analogy: Two Types of Argumentation in Early Greek Thought* (Cambridge). Reprinted Bristol, 1987 and 1992.
Lombardi, M. (1996), 'Il principio dell' εἰκός nel racconto biografico plutarcheo', *RCCM* 38: 91–102.
Loraux, N. (1995), *The Experiences of Tiresias: The Feminine and the Greek Man*, trans. Paula Wissing (Princeton).
Lotze, D. (1964), *Lysander und der Peloponnesische Krieg* (Abhandlungen der sächsischen Akademie der Wissenschaften zu Leipzig. Philologisch-historische Klasse 57. 1: Berlin).
Lounsbury, R. C. (1991), '*Inter quos et Sporus erat*: The Making of Suetonius' "Nero"', *ANRW* 2. 33. 5, 3748–79.
Luce, T. J. (1971), 'Design and Structure in Livy: 5. 32–55', *TAPhA* 102: 265–302.
—— (1989), 'Ancient Views on the Causes of Bias in Historical Writing', *CPh* 84: 16–31.
—— (1991), 'Tacitus on "History's Highest Function": *praecipuum munus annalium* (Ann. 3. 65)', *ANRW* 2. 33. 4, 2904–27.
Luck, G. (1964), 'Über Suetons "Divus Titus"', *RhM* 107: 63–75.
McCarty, T. G. (1974), 'The Content of Cornelius Nepos' *De Viris Illustribus*', *CW* 67: 383–91.
McCarty, W. (1989), 'The Shape of the Mirror: Metaphorical Catoptrics in Classical Literature', *Arethusa* 22: 161–95.
McGing, B. L. (1982), '*Synkrisis* in Tacitus' *Agricola*', *Hermathena* 132: 15–25.
McKeown, J. C. (1989), *Ovid: Amores. Text, Prolegomena and Commentary in four volumes*, ii. *A Commentary on Book One* (Leeds).
Mader, G. (1993), 'Ἀννίβας ὑβριστής: Traces of a "Tragic" Pattern in Livy's Hannibal Portrait in Book XXI?', *AncSoc* 24: 205–24.

Magnino, D. (1991) (ed.), *Plutarco: Vite parallele: Agide e Cleomene–Tiberio e Caio Gracco* (Biblioteca Universale Rizzoli: Milan).

—— and La Penna, A. (1987) (eds.), *Plutarco: Vite parallele: Alessandro–Cesare* (Biblioteca Universale Rizzoli: Milan). Seventh edn. 1995.

Malkin, I. (1990), 'Lysander and Libys', *CQ* NS 40: 541–5.

Manfredini, M. (1987), 'La tradizione manoscritta delle *Vite*'. In Canfora, Garzetti, and Manetti (1987), 25–35; Magnino and La Penna (1987), pp. x–xx. Reprinted in Andrei and Scuderi (1989), 16–26; Fuscagni, Mugelli, and Scardigli (1989), 16–26; Magnino (1991), 73–83; Guerrini, Santoni, and Stadter (1991), 51–61; Cesa, Prandi, and Raffaelli (1993), 79–89; Bearzot, Geiger, and Ghilli (1993), 57–67; Geiger, Ghilli, Mugelli, and Pecorella Longo (1995), 57–67; Pelling (1997*c*), 57–67.

—— (1992*a*), 'Il Plutarco di Planude', *Studi Classici e Orientali* 42: 123–5.

—— (1992*b*), 'Due codici di *excerpta* plutarchei e l'*Epitome* di Zonara', *Prometheus* 18: 193–215.

—— (1993), 'Due codici di *excerpta* plutarchei e l'*Epitome* di Zonara (II parte)', *Prometheus* 19: 1–25.

—— and Piccirilli, L. (1980), *Plutarco: le Vite di Licurgo e di Numa* (Milan).

Manuwald, B. (1979), *Cassius Dio und Augustus: Philologische Untersuchungen zu den Büchern 45–56 des dionischen Geschichtswerkes* (Palingenesia 14: Wiesbaden).

Marasco, G. (1976), *Plutarco: Vita di Nicia* (Rome).

—— (1983), 'Note ellenistiche', *Prometheus* 9: 221–31.

Marinatos, N. (1980), 'Nicias as a Wise Advisor and Tragic Warner in Thucydides', *Philologus* 124: 305–10.

Marincola, J. M. (1994), 'Plutarch's Refutation of Herodotus', *AncW* 25: 191–203.

Martin, H. M. (1960), 'The Concept of Prāotēs in Plutarch's *Lives*', *GRBS* 3: 65–73.

—— (1961), 'The Concept of *Philanthropia* in Plutarch's *Lives*', *AJPh* 82: 164–75.

—— (1992), review of Stadter (1989). In *AJPh* 113: 297–300.

—— (1995), 'Moral Failure Without Vice in Plutarch's Athenian *Lives*', *Ploutarchos* 12. 1: 13–18.

Martin, R. H. (1981), *Tacitus* (London). Reprinted 1989 and, with corrections, 1994.

—— and Woodman, A. J. (1989), *Tacitus: Annals, Book IV* (Cambridge).

Masaracchia, A. (1995), 'Tracce aristoteliche nell' *An seni res publica gerenda sit* e nei *Praecepta gerendae rei publicae*'. In Gallo and Scardigli (1995), 227–34.

Mason, H. J. (1974), *Greek Terms for Roman Institutions: A Lexicon and Analysis* (American Studies in Papyrology 13: Toronto).

Massaro, D. (1995), 'I *Praecepta gerendae rei publicae* e il realismo politico di Plutarco'. In Gallo and Scardigli (1995), 235–44.

Mayor, J. B. (1910; 1st edn. 1892), *The Epistle of Saint James: The Greek Text, with introduction, notes and comments* (London). Reprinted 1913 with a supplement.

Mazzarino, S. (1966), *Il pensiero storico classicso, ii. 2*. Reprinted as vol. iii, 1983 (Biblioteca Universale Laterza: Rome and Bari).
Meichsner, I. (1983), *Die Logik von Gemeinplätzen: Vorgeführt an Steuermannstopos und Schiffsmetapher* (Bonn).
Meijering, R. (1987), *Literary and Rhetorical Theories in Greek Scholia* (Groningen).
Mewaldt, J. (1907), 'Selbstcitate in den Biographieen Plutarchs', *Hermes* 42: 564–78.
Meyer, E. (1899), *Forschungen zur alten Geschichte, ii* (Halle).
—— (1921–3), *Ursprung und Anfänge des Christentums*, 3 vols. (Stuttgart and Berlin).
Michel, D. (1967), *Alexander als Vorbild für Pompeius, Caesar und Marcus Antonius* (Collection Latomus 94: Brussels).
Milazzo, A. M. (1991), 'Forme e funzioni retoriche dell' opuscolo "Aqua an ignis utilior" attribuito a Plutarco'. In D'Ippolito and Gallo (1991), 419–33.
Millar, F. (1964), *A Study of Dio Cassius* (Oxford).
—— (1988), 'Cornelius Nepos, "Atticus", and the Roman Revolution', *GR* NS 35: 40–55.
Miola, R. S. (1983), *Shakespeare's Rome* (Cambridge).
—— (1985), '*Julius Caesar* and the Tyrannicide Debate', *RenQ* 38: 271–89.
Mittelstadt, M. C. (1967), 'Tacitus and Plutarch: some interpretive methods', *Rivista di Studi Classici* 15: 293–304.
Moles, J. L. (1985*a*), 'The Interpretation of the "Second Preface" in Arrian's "Anabasis"', *JHS* 105: 162–8.
—— (1985*b*), 'Plutarch, Brutus and the Ghost of Caesar', *PCA* 82: 19–20.
—— (1988) (ed.), *Plutarch: The Life of Cicero* (Warminster).
—— (1989), review of Geiger (1985). In *CR* NS 39: 229–33.
—— (1992), review of Stadter (1989). In *CR* NS 42: 289–94.
—— (1993*a*), 'On Reading Cornelius Nepos with Nicholas Horsfall', *LCM* 18, 76–80.
—— (1993*b*), 'Truth and Untruth in Herodotus and Thucydides'. In C. Gill and T. P. Wiseman (eds.), *Lies and Fiction in the Ancient World* (Exeter), 88–121.
—— (1994), 'Xenophon and Callicratidas', *JHS* 114: 70–84.
Momigliano, A. (1931), 'Sulla storiografia greca del IV secolo a. C. 1: Teopompo', *RFIC*, NS 9: 230–42 and 335–54. Reprinted in *Terzo Contributo alla Storia degli Studi Classici e del Mondo Antico* (Rome, 1966), i. 367–92.
—— (1971*a*), *The Development of Greek Biography* (Cambridge, Mass.). Reprinted in an expanded edition, 1993.
—— (1971*b*), *Second Thoughts on Greek Biography* (Mededelingen der Koninklijke Nederlandse Akademie van Wetenschappen, Afd. Letterkunde, nieuwe reeks, deel 34, no. 7: London and Amsterdam). Reprinted in *Quinto Contributo alla Storia degli Studi Classici e del Mondo Antico* (Rome, 1975), i.

33–47, and in id. (1993), *The Development of Greek Biography* (see previous item), 105–21.

Momigliano, A. (1982), 'The origins of universal history', *ASNP*, ser. 3, 12: 533–60. Reprinted in *Settimo Contributo alla Storia degli Studi Classici e del Mondo Antico* (Rome, 1984), 77–103, and in *On Pagans, Jews, and Christians* (Middletown, Conn., 1987), 31–57.

Montaigne, M. E. de (1580), *Essais* (Bordeaux). Numerous editions.

Montano, A. (1991), '*Ἁρμονία* e *ὁμολογία* nei *Coniugalia Praecepta* di Plutarco', *Elenchos* 12: 331–8.

Moreno, L. A. G. (1992), 'Paradoxography and Political Ideals in Plutarch's *Life of Sertorius*'. In Stadter (1992*b*), 132–58.

Morgan, M. G. (1979), 'Catullus 112: A *Pathicus* in Politics', *AJPh* 100: 377–80.

Mossman, J. M. (1988), 'Tragedy and epic in Plutarch's *Alexander*', *JHS* 108: 83–93. Reprinted in Scardigli (1995*a*), 209–28.

—— (1991), 'Plutarch's Use of Statues'. In M. A. Flower and M. Toher (eds.), *Georgica: Greek Studies in Honour of George Cawkwell* (*BICS* Supplement 58), 98–119.

—— (1992), 'Plutarch, Pyrrhus and Alexander'. In Stadter (1992*b*), 90–108.

—— (1997) (ed.), *Plutarch and his Intellectual World: Essays on Plutarch* (London).

Muecke, F. (1982), 'A Portrait of the Artist as a Young Woman', *CQ* NS 32: 41–55.

Mueller, H.-F. (1995), 'Images of Excellence: Visual Rhetoric and Political Behavior'. In Gallo and Scardigli (1995), 287–300.

Murray, P. (1996) (ed.), *Plato on Poetry. Ion; Republic 376e–398b9; Republic 595–608b10* (Cambridge).

Neu, J. (1971), 'Plato's Analogy of State and Individual: The *Republic* and the Organic Theory of the State', *Philosophy* 46: 238–54.

Newman, W. L. (1902), *The Politics of Aristotle, iv. Essays on Constitutions Books VI–VIII—Text and Notes* (Oxford).

Nikolaidis, A. G. (1980), '*Γύρω ἀπὸ τὴν ὀρθογραφία τῶν λέξεων πρᾶος (πρᾷος) καὶ φιλόνικος (φιλόνεικος)*', *Hellenica* 32: 364–70.

—— (1982), 'Aristotle's Treatment of the Concept of *πραότης*', *Hermes* 110: 414–22.

—— (1982–4), '*Ὁ σκοπός τῶν Βίων τοῦ Πλουτάρχου καί οἱ διάφορες συναφεῖς θεωρίες*', *Archaiognosia* 3: 93–114.

—— (1986), '*Ἑλληνικός—βαρβαρικός*: Plutarch on Greek and Barbarian Characteristics', *WS* 119, n.f. 20: 229–44.

—— (1988), 'Is Plutarch Fair to Nikias?', *ICS* 13. 2: 319–33.

—— (1991), 'Plutarch's contradictions', *C&M* 42: 153–86. A shorter version appears in *AncW* 25 (1994), 213–22.

—— (1995), 'Plutarch's Heroes in Action: Does the End Justify the Means?' In Gallo and Scardigli (1995), 301–12.

Nisbet, R. G. M., and Hubbard, M. (1970), *A Commentary on Horace: Odes Book I* (Oxford).
Nock, A. D. (1930), 'Σύνναος Θεός', *HSPh* 41: 1–62. Reprinted in Stewart (1972), 202–51.
—— (1933), 'The Vocabulary of the New Testament', *JBL* 52: 131–9. Reprinted in Stewart (1972), 341–7.
Norden, E. (1898), *Die Antike Kunstprosa vom VI. Jahrhundert v. Chr. bis in die Zeit der Renaissance* (Leipzig).
North, T. (1579), *The Lives of the noble Grecians and Romanes, compared together by that grave, learned Philosopher and Historiographer Plutarke of Chaeronea: translated out of Greeke into French by I. Amyot and into Englishe by T. North* (London).
Norton, G. (1906), *Le Plutarque de Montaigne: Selections from Amyot's translation of Plutarch arranged to illustrate Montaigne's essays* (Boston).
Oakley, S. P. (1985), 'Single Combat in the Roman Republic', *CQ* NS 35: 392–410.
Ogilvie, R. M., and Richmond, I. (1967) (eds.), *Cornelii Taciti De Vita Agricolae* (Oxford).
Oliver, J. H. (1953), 'The Ruling Power: A Study of the Roman Empire in the Second Century after Christ through the Roman Oration of Aelius Aristides', *TAPhS* NS 43. 4: 870–1003.
Opsomer, J. (1994), 'L'Âme du monde et l'âme de l'homme chez Plutarque'. In M. García Valdés (1994), 33–49.
—— (1997), 'Favorinus versus Epictetus on the philosophical heritage of Plutarch: A debate on epistemology'. In Mossman (1997), 17–39.
Padel, R. (1995), *Whom Gods Destroy: Elements of Greek and Tragic Madness* (Princeton).
Paladini, M. L. (1984), 'A proposito del parallelo Alessandro Magno–Germanico Cesare in Tacito'. In Sordi (1984), 179–93.
Palmer, M. (1982), 'Alcibiades and the Question of Tyranny in Thucydides', *Canadian Journal of Political Science* 15: 103–24.
Panagopoulos, C. (1977), 'Vocabulaire et mentalité dans les *Moralia* de Plutarque', *DHA* 3 (Centre de recherches d'histoire ancienne 25): 197–235.
Paradiso, A. (1996), 'Plut. Alc. 23,3 e *Quom. adul. ab amico internoscatur* 52E', *RhM* 139: 373–5.
Paratore, E. (1993), 'Il giudizio sulla tradizione nelle *Vite* plutarchee di Teseo e Romolo'. In R. Pretagostini (ed.), *Tradizione e innovazione nella cultura greca da Omero all' età ellenistica: Scritti in onore di Bruno Gentili*, 3 vols. (Rome), iii. 1077–87.
Parke, H. W. (1939), *A History of the Delphic Oracle* (Oxford).
Patterson, C. (1992), 'Plutarch's "Advice on Marriage": Traditional Wisdom through a Philosophic Lense', *ANRW* 2. 33. 6, 4709–23.
Pauw, D. (1980), 'Impersonal Expressions and Unidentified Spokesmen in Greek and Roman Historiography and Biography', *AClass* 23: 83–95.

Pavis d'Escurac, H. (1981), 'Périls et chances du régime civique selon Plutarque', *Ktèma* 6: 287–300.

Pecorella Longo, C. (1995), 'Introduzione' to *Demostene*. In Geiger, Ghilli, Mugelli, and Pecorella Longo (1995), 87–150.

Pédech, P. (1951), 'Polybe et l'"Éloge de Philopoemen"', *REG* 64: 82–103.

—— (1964), *La Méthode Historique de Polybe* (Paris).

Pelling, C. B. R. (1973), 'Plutarch, "Alexander" and "Caesar": Two New Fragments', *CQ* NS 23: 343–4.

—— (1979), 'Plutarch's method of work in the Roman Lives', *JHS* 99: 74–96. Reprinted with a postscript (312–18) in Scardigli (1995a), 265–318.

—— (1980), 'Plutarch's adaptation of his source-material', *JHS* 100: 127–40. Reprinted in Scardigli (1995a), 125–54.

—— (1984a), 'Notes on Plutarch's *Caesar*', *RhM* 127: 33–45.

—— (1984b), 'Plutarch on the Gallic Wars', *CB* 60: 88–103.

—— (1985), 'Plutarch and Catiline', *Hermes* 113: 311–29.

—— (1986a), 'Plutarch and Roman Politics'. In I. S. Moxon, J. D. Smart, and A. J. Woodman (eds.), *Past Perspectives. Studies in Greek and Roman Historical Writing* (Cambridge), 159–87. Reprinted in Scardigli (1995a), 319–56.

—— (1986b), 'Synkrisis in Plutarch's Lives'. In Brenk and Gallo (1986), 83–96.

—— (1988a), 'Aspects of Plutarch's Characterisation', *ICS* 13. 2: 257–74.

—— (1988b) (ed.), *Plutarch: Life of Antony* (Cambridge).

—— (1989), 'Plutarch: Roman Heroes and Greek Culture'. In Griffin and Barnes (1989), 199–232.

—— (1990a), 'Childhood and Personality in Greek Biography'. In id. (ed.), *Characterization and Individuality in Greek Literature* (Oxford), 213–44.

—— (1990b), 'Truth and Fiction in Plutarch's *Lives*'. In Russell (1990), 19–52.

—— (1992), 'Plutarch and Thucydides'. In Stadter (1992b), 10–40.

—— (1993), 'Tacitus and Germanicus'. In T. J. Luce and A. J. Woodman (eds.), *Tacitus and the Tacitean Tradition* (Princeton), 59–85.

—— (1995a), 'The Moralism of Plutarch's *Lives*'. In D. Innes, H. Hine, and C. B. R. Pelling (eds.), *Ethics and Rhetoric: Classical Essays for Donald Russell on his Seventy-Fifth Birthday* (Oxford), 205–20. Also published in Italian, as 'Il moralismo delle *Vite* di Plutarco', in Gallo and Scardigli (1995), 343–61.

—— (1995b), 'Plutarch's Method of Work in the Roman Lives'. Reprinted with a postscript in Scardigli (1995a), 265–318 (Oxford). Originally published without postscript in *JHS* 99: 74–96.

—— (1996), 'Prefazione'. In F. Albini (ed.), *Plutarco: Vita di Coriolano; Vita di Alcibiade* (I grandi libri Garzanti: Milan), pp. xx–lviii.

—— (1997a), 'Is Death the End? Closure in Plutarch's *Lives*'. In D. H. Roberts, F. M. Dunn, and D. Fowler (eds.), *Classical Closure: Reading the End in Greek and Latin Literature* (Princeton), 228–50.

—— (1997b), 'Plutarch on Caesar's fall'. In Mossman (1997), 215–32.

Pelling, C. B. R. (1997c) (ed.), *Plutarco: Vite Parallele: Filopemene–Tito Flaminino* (Biblioteca Universale Rizzoli: Milan). Italian trans. by F. Albini and E. Melandri.
—— (1999), 'Modern Fantasy and Ancient Dreams'. In C. Sullivan and B. White (eds.), *Writing and Fantasy* (London and New York), 15–31.
Pérez Jiménez, A. (1992), 'Alle frontiere della scienza: Plutarco e l'astrologia'. In Gallo (1992b), 271–86.
—— (1994), 'Plutarch: The Irresponsibility of Aegeus', *AncW* 25: 223–31.
—— (1995), '*Proairesis*: las formas de acceso e la vida pública y el pensiamento politico de Plutarco'. In Gallo and Scardigli (1995), 363–81.
Pernot, L. (1983), 'Chance et destin dans la rhétorique épidictique grecque à l'époque impériale'. In F. Jouan (ed.), *Visages du destin dans les mythologies: Mélanges Jacqueline Duchemin* (*Actes du colloque de Chantilly 1er–2 mai 1980*: Paris), 121–9.
Perrin, B. (1916), *Plutarch's Lives*, iv. *Alcibiades and Coriolanus; Lysander and Sulla* (Loeb Classical Library: Cambridge, Mass., and London).
—— (1918), *Plutarch's Lives*, vi. *Dion and Brutus; Timoleon and Aemilius Paulus* (Loeb Classical Library: Cambridge, Mass., and London).
Peter, H. (1865), *Die Quellen Plutarchs in den Biographieen der Römer* (Halle). Reprinted Amsterdam, 1965.
Piccirilli, L. (1977), 'Cronologia relativa e fonti della *Vita Solonis* di Plutarco', *ASNP* ser. 3, 7: 999–1016.
—— (1980), 'Cronologia relativa alle fonti delle *Vitae Lycurgi et Numae* di Plutarco'. In φιλίας χάριν: *miscellanea di studi classici in onore di Eugenio Manni* (Rome), v. 1751–64.
—— (1985), 'Le *Vite* dello storico Tucidide: Un terzo tipo di biografia greca', *AALig* 42: 133–44.
—— (1989), 'La tradizione "nera" nelle biografie plutarchee degli Ateniesi del sesto e del quinto secolo'. In A. Ceresa-Gastaldo (ed.), *Gerolamo e la biografia letteraria* (Pubblicazioni del Dipartimento di Archeologia, filologia, classica e loro tradizioni, Nuova Serie 125: Genoa), 5–21.
—— (1990a), 'Introduzione'. In Carena, Manfredini, and Piccirilli (1990), pp. ix–xl.
—— (1990b), 'Nicia in Filisto e in Timeo', *RFIC* 118: 385–90.
—— (1990c), 'Nicia in Plutarco', *AALig* 47: 351–68.
—— (1993a), 'In margine alla plutarchea "Vita di Lisandro"', *CCC* 14: 25–9.
—— (1993b), 'Introduzione' to *Nicia*. In Angeli Bertinelli *et al.* (1993), pp. ix–xxviii.
Podlecki, A. J. (1988), 'Plutarch and Athens', *ICS* 13. 2: 231–43.
—— and Duane, S. (1992), 'A Survey of Work on Plutarch's Greek Lives, 1951–1988', *ANRW* 2. 33. 6, 4053–4127.
Polman, G. H. (1974), 'Chronological Biography and *Akmē* in Plutarch', *CPh* 69: 169–77.

Powell, C. A. (1972), '*Deum Ira, Hominum Rabies*', *Latomus* 31: 833–48.
Prandi, L. (1992), 'Introduzione' to *Alcibiade*. In Cesa, Prandi, and Raffaelli (1993), 255–317.
Prieth, K. (1908), 'Einige Bemerkungen zu den parallelen Biographien Plutarchs mit besonderer Berücksichtigung der συγκρίσεις', *VII. Jahresbericht des Städt. Gymnasiums in Wels für das Schuljahr 1907/08*, 1–36.
Proctor, D. (1980), *The Experience of Thucydides* (Warminster).
Puech, B. (1981), 'Soclaros de Tithorée, ami de Plutarque, et ses descendants', *REG* 94: 186–92.
—— (1992), 'Prosopographie des amis de Plutarque', *ANRW* 2. 33. 6, 4831–93.
Quet, M.-H. (1979), 'Rhétorique, culture et politique: Le fonctionnement du discours idéologique chez Dion de Pruse et dans les *Moralia* de Plutarque', *DHA* 4 (Centre de recherches d'histoire ancienne, vol. 28): 51–117.
Ramage, E. S. (1991), 'Sulla's Propaganda', *Klio* 73: 93–121.
Ramón Palerm, V. (1992), *Plutarco y Nepote: Fuentes e interpretación del modelo biográfico plutarqueo* (Saragossa).
—— (1994), 'El "Cato" de Cornelio Nepote y los orígenes de la biografía política grecolatina', *QS* 39: 279–87.
Rawlings, H. R. (1981), *The Structure of Thucydides' History* (Princeton).
Rawson, E. (1972), 'Cicero the Historian and Cicero the Antiquarian', *JRS* 62: 33–45. Reprinted in *Roman Culture and Society. Collected Papers* (Oxford, 1991), 58–79.
—— (1985), *Intellectual Life in the Late Roman Republic* (London).
Reams, L. E. (1984), 'Sulla's Alleged Early Poverty and Roman Rent', *AJAH* 9: 158–74.
Reardon, B. P. (1971), *Courants littéraires grecs des IIe et IIIe siècles après J.-C.* (Paris).
Reinhold, M. (1975) (ed.), *The Classick Pages: Classical Reading of Eighteenth-Century Americans* (Pennsylvania).
—— (1984), 'Plutarch's Influence in America from Colonial Times to 1890'. In *Classica Americana: The Greek and Roman Heritage in the United States* (Detroit), 250–64.
—— (1988) (ed.), *From Republic to Principate: An Historical Commentary on Cassius Dio's* Roman History Books 49–52 (36–29 BC) (Atlanta).
Renehan, R. (1981), 'Plutarch *Lysander* 2: An Addendum', *CPh* 76: 206–7.
Renoirte, T. (1951), *Les "Conseils politiques" de Plutarque: une lettre ouverte aux Grecs à l'époque de Trajan* (Louvain).
Resta, G. (1962), *Le epitomi (delle Vite parallele) di Plutarco nel Quattrocento* (Padua).
Rich, J. W. (1989), 'Dio on Augustus'. In Averil Cameron (ed.), *History as Text: The Writing of Ancient History* (London), 86–110.
Ritzenstein, R. (1906), *Hellenistische Wundererzählungen* (Leipzig). Reprinted Stuttgart, 1963.

Robert, L. (1927), 'Études d'épigraphie grecque', *RPh*, ser. 3, 1: 97–132. Reprinted in *Opera Minora Selecta: Épigraphie et antiquités grecques,* ii (Amsterdam, 1969), 1052–87.
—— (1940), *Les gladiateurs dans l'Orient grec* (Limoges). Reprinted Amsterdam, 1971.
—— (1967), 'Sur des inscriptions d'Éphèse; fêtes, athlètes, empereurs, épigrammes', *RPh*, ser. 3, 41: 7–84. Reprinted in *Opera Minora Selecta: Épigraphie et antiquités grecques,* v (Amsterdam, 1989), 347–424.
Roberts, D. H. (1987), 'Parting Words: Final Lines in Sophocles and Euripides', *CQ* NS 37: 51–64.
—— (1988), 'Sophoclean Endings: Another Story', *Arethusa* 21: 177–96.
Roberts, J. T. (1987), 'Paradigm Lost: Tritle, Plutarch and Athenian Politics in the Fourth Century', *AHB* 1. 2: 34–5.
Robertson, A., and Plummer, A. (1911), *A Critical and Exegetical Commentary on the First Epistle of St Paul to the Corinthians* (The International Critical Commentary: Edinburgh). Second edn. 1914.
Rohde, E. (1876), *Der griechische Roman und seine Vorlaüfer* (Leipzig). Third edn. 1914. Fourth edn. with foreword by K. Kerényi, Hildesheim, 1960.
Rosalia, A. De (1991), 'Il latino di Plutarco'. In D'Ippolito and Gallo (1991), 445–59.
Rose, H. J. (1924), *The Roman Questions of Plutarch* (Oxford).
Rose, J. J. (1988), 'The Concept of *Arete* in Plutarch's *Parallel Lives*'. Dissertation, University of New Jersey, New Brunswick.
Rosenmeyer, T. G. (1992), 'Beginnings in Plutarch's *Lives*'. In F. M. Dunn and T. Cole (eds.), *Beginnings in Classical Literature* (*YClS* 29: Cambridge), 205–30.
Ross, D. (1951), *Plato's Theory of Ideas* (Oxford).
Roussel, M. (1991), *Biographie légendaire d'Achille* (Amsterdam).
Rubina Cammarota, M. (1992), 'Il *De Alexandri Magni fortuna aut virtute* come espressione retorica: il panegirico'. In Gallo (1992*c*), 105–24.
Rudd, N. (1966), *The Satires of Horace* (Cambridge).
Russell, D. A. (1963), 'Plutarch's Life of Coriolanus', *JRS* 53: 21–8. Reprinted in Scardigli (1995*a*), 357–72.
—— (1966*a*), 'On Reading Plutarch's *Lives*', *G&R* NS 13: 139–54. Reprinted in Scardigli (1995*a*), 75–94.
—— (1966*b*), 'Plutarch, "Alcibiades" 1–16"', *PCPhS* 192: 37–47. Reprinted in Scardigli (1995*a*), 191–207.
—— (1973), *Plutarch* (London).
—— (1981), *Criticism in Antiquity* (London).
—— (1982), 'Plutarch and the Antique Hero', *The Yearbook of English Studies* 12 (Heroes and the Heroic: Special Number), 24–34.
—— (1983), *Greek Declamation* (Cambridge).
—— (1990) (ed.), *Antonine Literature* (Oxford).

Russell, D. A. (1993), *Plutarch: Selected Essays and Dialogues* (The World's Classics: Oxford).
—— (1997), Plutarch, *Amatorius* 13–18. In J. Mossman (ed.), *Plutarch and his Intellectual World: Essays on Plutarch* (London), 99–111.
—— and Wilson, N. G. (1981) (eds.), *Menander Rhetor: Edited with Translation and Commentary* (Oxford).
Rutherford, R. B. (1994), 'Learning from History: Categories and Case-Histories'. In R. Osborne and S. Hornblower (eds.), *Ritual, Finance, Politics: Athenian Democratic Accounts Presented to David Lewis* (Oxford), 53–68.
Sacks, K. (1981), *Polybius on the Writing of History* (University of California Publications, Classical Studies 24: Berkeley).
—— (1990), *Diodorus Siculus and the First Century* (Princeton).
—— (1994), 'Diodorus and his Sources: Conformity and Creativity'. In S. Hornblower (ed.), *Greek Historiography* (Oxford), 213–32.
Saïd, S. (1991) (ed.), *ἙΛΛΗΝΙΣΜΟΣ. Quelques jalons pour une histoire de l'identité grecque* (*Actes du Colloque de Strasbourg 25–7 octobre 1989*: Leiden).
Ste Croix, G. E. M. de (1975), 'Aristotle on History and Poetry (*Poetics* 9, 1451a36–b11)'. In B. Levick (ed.), *The Ancient Historian and his Materials. Essays in honour of C. E. Stevens on his seventieth birthday* (Farnborough), 45–58. Reprinted in A. O. Rorty (ed.), *Essays on Aristotle's* Poetics (Princeton, 1992), 23–32.
Saller, R. P. (1980), 'Anecdotes as Historical Evidence for the Principate', *G&R* ns 27: 69–83.
Salvioni, L. (1982), 'Le "madri dell' ira" nelle *Vite* di Plutarco', *Quaderni del Giornale Filologico Ferrarese* 5: 83–92.
Samsaris, D. K. (1990), 'Ὁ Μέγας Ἀλέξανδρος ως πρότυπο Ρωμαίων στρατηγών και αυτοκράτορων. Μια πρώτη αποτίμηση του φαινομένου της ρωμαϊκής *imitatio Alexandri*', *Dodone* 19: 253–62.
Sandbach, F. H. (1969) (ed.), *Plutarch's Moralia, xv. Fragments* (Loeb Classical Library: Cambridge, Mass., and London).
—— (1982), 'Plutarch and Aristotle', *ICS* 7: 207–32.
Sanders, L. J. (1991), 'Dionysius I of Syracuse and the Origins of the Ruler Cult in the Greek World', *Historia* 40: 275–87.
Sansone, D. (1980), 'Plutarch, Alexander and the Discovery of Naphtha', *GRBS* 21: 63–74.
—— (1981), 'Lysander and Dionysius (Plut. *Lys.* 2)', *CPh* 76: 202–6.
—— (1988), 'Notes on Plutarch: *Pericles and Fabius*', *ICS* 13: 311–18.
Scardigli, B. (1977), 'Echi di atteggiamenti pro e contro Mario in Plutarco', *CS* 14: 185–253.
—— (1979), *Die Römerbiographien Plutarchs* (Munich).
—— (1987*a*), 'Il confronto fra Nicia e Crasso'. In Canfora, Garzetti, and Manetti (1987), 13–22.
—— (1987*b*), 'La fortuna di Plutarco e le *Vite*'. In Canfora, Garzetti, and Manetti

(1987), 5–13. Reprinted in Fuscagni, Mugelli, and Scardigli (1989), 5–13; Magnino and La Penna (1987), pp. i–ix; Andrei and Scuderi (1989), 5–13; Guerrini, Santoni, and Stadter (1991), 39–47.

Scardigli, B. (1995a) (ed.), *Essays on Plutarch's Lives* (Oxford).

—— (1995b), 'Introduction'. In Scardigli (1995a), 1–46. A revised and expanded version of her general introduction to Magnino (1991), 5–54. Reprinted in Cesa, Prandi, and Raffaelli (1993), 5–55; Bearzot, Geiger, and Ghilli (1993), 5–55; Geiger et al. (1995), 5–55; Pelling (1997c), 5–55.

Schaefer, H. (1957), 'Das Eidolon des Leonidas'. In K. Schauenburg (ed.), *Charites: Studien zur Altertumswissenschaft* (Bonn), 223–33.

Schenkeveld, D. M. (1964), *Studies in Demetrius On Style* (Amsterdam).

Schmid, W. (1887–97), *Der Atticismus in seinem Hauptvertretern von Dionysius von Halikarnass bis auf den zweiten Philostratus*, 5 vols. (Stuttgart). Reprinted Hildesheim, 1964.

Schmidt, L. (1882), *Die Ethik der Alten Griechen*, 2 vols. (Berlin).

Schneeweiss, G. (1979), 'History and Philosophy in Plutarch: Observations on Plutarch's *Lycurgus*'. In G. W. Bowersock, W. Burkert, and M. C. J. Putnam (eds.), *Arktouros: Hellenic Studies presented to B. M. W. Knox on the occasion of his 65th birthday* (Berlin and New York), 376–82.

—— (1985), 'τὴν τοῦ ἀρίστου καὶ δοκιμωτάτου μνήμην ὑποδεχόμενος ἀεὶ τῇ ψυχῇ . . . Gegenstand und Absicht in den Biographien Plutarchs'. In W. Suerbaum and F. Maier (eds.), *Festschrift . . . Fr. Egermann* (Munich), 147–62.

Schoppe, C. (1994), *Plutarchs Interpretation der Ideenlehre Platons* (Münsteraner Beiträge zur klassischen Philologie 2: Münster and Hamburg).

Schröder, St. (1991), 'Zu Plutarchs Alexanderreden', *MH* 48: 151–7.

Scobie, A. (1973), 'Barbarians in the Greek Romances'. In id., *More Essays on the Ancient Romance and its Heritage* (Beiträge zur Klassischen Philologie 46: Meisenheim am Glan), 19–34.

Scott, K. (1929), 'Plutarch and the Ruler Cult', *TAPhA* 60: 117–35.

—— (1938), 'Ruler Cult and Related Problems in the Greek Romances', *CPh* 33: 380–9.

Seager, R. J. (1967), 'Alcibiades and the Charge of Aiming at Tyranny', *Historia* 16: 6–18.

—— and Tuplin, C. J. (1980), 'The freedom of the Greeks of Asia: on the origins of a concept and the creation of a slogan', *JHS* 100: 141–54.

Sellers, M. N. S. (1994), *American Republicanism: Roman Ideology in the United States Constitution* (Basingstoke and London).

Shackford, M. H. (1929), *Plutarch in Renaissance England, with Special Reference to Shakespeare*. Reprinted Folcroft, Pa., 1973, and Norwood, Pa., 1977.

Sheppard, A. R. R. (1984–6), '*Homonoia* in the Greek Cities of the Roman Empire', *AncSoc* 15–17: 229–52.

Sherman, N. (1989), *The Fabric of Character: Aristotle's Theory of Virtue* (Oxford).

Shochat, Y. (1981), 'Tacitus' attitude to Galba', *Athenaeum* NS 59 (year 69), 199–204.
Simpson, P. (1988), 'Aristotle on Poetry and Imitation', *Hermes* 116: 279–91.
Smith, B. H. (1968), *Poetic Closure: A Study of How Poems End* (Chicago and London).
Smith, R. E. (1940), 'Plutarch's Biographical Sources in the Roman Lives', *CQ* 34: 1–10.
—— (1944), 'The Sources of Plutarch's Life of Titus Flamininus', *CQ* 38: 89–95.
Smits, J. (1939) (ed.), *Plutarchus' Leven van Lysander: Inleiding–tekst–commentaar* (Amsterdam).
Sordi, M. (1984) (ed.), *Alessandro Magno tra storia e mito* (Ricerche dell' Istituto di Storia Antica dell' Università Cattolica di Milano 1: Milan).
—— (1991), 'L'ultimo Mario e la sua immagine'. In ead. (ed.), *L'immagine dell' uomo politico: vita pubblica e morale nell' antichità* (Contributi dell' Istituto di storia antica 17: Milan), 151–8.
Spanneut, M. (1994), '*Apatheia* ancienne, *apatheia* chrétienne, Ière partie: L' *apatheia* ancienne', *ANRW* 2. 36. 7, 4641–4717.
Spawforth, A. J. (1994), 'Symbol of Unity? The Persian-Wars Tradition in the Roman Empire'. In S. Hornblower (ed.), *Greek Historiography* (Oxford), 233–47.
—— and Walker, S. (1985), 'The World of the Panhellenion. I. Athens and Eleusis', *JRS* 75: 78–104.
Spence, J. (1759), *A Parallel in the Manner of Plutarch: between a most celebrated Man of Florence; and One, scarce ever heard of, in England* (2nd edn., London).
Spencer, T. J. B. (1964), *Shakespeare's Plutarch* (Harmondsworth).
Stadter, P. A. (1965), *Plutarch's Historical Methods: An Analysis of the* Mulierum Virtutes (Cambridge, Mass.).
—— (1975), 'Plutarch's Comparison of Pericles and Fabius Maximus', *GRBS* 16: 77–85. Reprinted in Scardigli (1995*a*); 155–64.
—— (1983–4), 'Searching for Themistocles: a review article'. Review of F. J. Frost (ed. 1980, Princeton), *Plutarch's Themistocles: A Historical Commentary*. In *CJ* 79: 356–63.
—— (1987), 'The Rhetoric of Plutarch's *Pericles*', *AncSoc* 18: 251–69.
—— (1988), 'The Proems of Plutarch's *Lives*', *ICS* 13. 2: 275–95.
—— (1989) (ed.), *A Commentary on Plutarch's* Pericles (Chapel Hill, NC, and London).
—— (1992*a*), 'Paradoxical Paradigms: Lysander and Sulla'. In id. (1992*b*), 41–55.
—— (1992*b*) (ed.), *Plutarch and the Historical Tradition* (London and New York).
Stanton, G. R. (1973), 'Sophists and Philosophers: Problems of Classification', *AJPh* 94: 350–64.
Starr, R. J. (1981), 'The Scope and Genre of Velleius' History', *CQ* NS 31: 162–74.

Steidle, W. (1951), *Sueton und die antike Biographie* (Zetemata 1: Munich).
—— (1990), 'Zu Plutarchs Biographien des Cicero und Pompeius', *GB* 17: 163–86.
Stein, R. H. (1991), *Gospels and Tradition: Studies on Redaction Criticism of the Synoptic Gospels* (Grand Rapids, Mich.).
Stephanus, H. (1572), *Plutarchi Chaeronensis quae extant opera, cum latina interpretatione*, 13 vols. (Geneva).
Stewart, Z. (1972) (ed.), *Arthur Darby Nock: Essays on Religion and the Ancient World*, i (Oxford).
Stiefenhofer, A. (1914–16), 'Die Echtheitsfrage der biographischen Synkriseis Plutarchs', *Philologus* 73, n.f. 27: 462–503.
Stolz C. (1929), *Zur relativen Chronologie der Parallelbiographien Plutarchs* (Lund).
Strachey, G. L. (1918), *Eminent Victorians* (London). Numerous editions.
Strasburger, B. H. (1938), *Caesars Eintritt in die Geschichte* (Munich). Reprinted Darmstadt, 1965, and in id., *Studien zur alten Geschichte I* (ed. W. Schmitthenner and R. Zoepffel) (Hildesheim and New York, 1982), i. 181–327.
Stuart, D. R. (1928), *Epochs of Greek and Roman Biography* (Berkeley).
Süss, W. (1910), *Ethos: Studien zur älteren griechischen Rhetorik* (Leipzig and Berlin).
Swain, S. C. R. (1988), 'Plutarch's *Philopoemen* and *Flamininus*', *ICS* 13. 2: 335–47.
—— (1989*a*), 'Character Change in Plutarch', *Phoenix* 43: 62–8.
—— (1989*b*), 'Plutarch: Chance, Providence and History', *AJPh* 110: 272–302.
—— (1989*c*), 'Plutarch's Aemilius and Timoleon', *Historia* 38: 314–34.
—— (1989*d*), 'Plutarch's *De Fortuna Romanorum*', *CQ* NS 39: 504–16.
—— (1990*a*), 'Cultural Interchange in Plutarch's *Antony*', *QUCC* NS 34: 151–7.
—— (1990*b*), 'Hellenic culture and the Roman heroes of Plutarch', *JHS* 110: 126–45. Reprinted in Scardigli (1995*a*), 229–64.
—— (1990*c*), 'Plutarch's Lives of Cicero, Cato and Brutus', *Hermes* 118: 192–203.
—— (1991), 'Plutarch, Hadrian, and Delphi', *Historia* 40: 318–30.
—— (1992*a*), 'Novel and Pantomime in Plutarch's *Antony*', *Hermes* 120: 76–82.
—— (1992*b*), 'Plutarchan Synkrisis', *Eranos* 90: 101–11.
—— (1992*c*), 'Plutarch's Characterization of Lucullus', *RhM* 135: 307–16.
—— (1996*a*), *Hellenism and Empire. Language, Classicism and Power in the Greek world AD 50–250* (Oxford).
—— (1996*b*), review of Boulogne (1994). In *Ploutarchos* 12. 2: 16–20.
—— (1997), 'Plutarch, Plato, Athens, and Rome'. In J. Barnes and M. Griffin (eds.), *Philosophia Togata*, ii. *Plato and Aristotle at Rome* (Oxford), 165–87.
Sweet, W. E. (1951), 'Sources of Plutarch's *Demetrius*', *Classical Weekly* 44: 177–81.
Syme, R. (1958), *Tacitus*, 2 vols. (Oxford).
—— (1963), 'The Greeks under Roman Rule', *Proceedings of the Massachusetts Historical Society* 72, 1957–60, 3–20. Reprinted in E. Badian (ed.), *Ronald Syme:*

Roman Papers, ii (Oxford, 1979), 566–81. A revised version appeared as *Greeks Invading the Roman Government* (The Seventh Stephen J. Brademas, Sr., Lecture: Brookline, Mass., 1982), reprinted in Birley (1988), 1–20.

Syme, R. (1982), 'The Career of Arrian', *HSPh* 86, 181–211. Reprinted in Birley (1988), 21–49.

Talbert, R. J. A. (1974), *Timoleon and the Revival of Greek Sicily 344–317 BC* (Cambridge).

Tarn, W. W. (1913), *Antigonos Gonatas* (Oxford).

Tatum, W. J. (1989), *Xenophon's Imperial Fiction: On* The Education of Cyrus (Princeton).

—— (1991), 'Lucullus and Clodius at Nisibis (Plutarch, *Lucullus* 33–34)', *Athenaeum* NS 69 (year 79), 569–79.

—— (1996), 'The Regal Image in Plutarch's *Lives*', *JHS* 106: 135–51. First published in shorter form, as 'The Image of the King in Plutarch's *Lives*', in Gallo and Scardigli (1995), 423–31.

Taylor, W. C. (1846), *The Modern British Plutarch, or Lives of Men Distinguished in the Recent History of England for their Talents, Virtues or Achievements*. Reprinted Freeport, NY, 1972.

Teza, E. (1902–3), 'Plutarco nella traduzione italiana di B. A. Jaconello', *AIV* 62, 1–15.

Theander, C. (1951), *Plutarch und die Geschichte* (Årsberättelse. Bulletin de la Société Royale des Lettres de Lund, 1950–1: Lund).

—— (1958), 'Zur Zeitfolge der Biographien Plutarchs', *Eranos* 56: 12–20.

—— (1959), 'Plutarchs Forschungen in Rom: Zur mündlichen Überlieferung als Quelle der Biographien', *Eranos* 57: 99–131.

Thévenaz, P. (1938), *L' Ame du monde: Le Devenir et la matière chez Plutarque avec une traduction du traité "De la Genèse de l'Ame dans le* Timée*" (1re partie)* (Collection d'études anciennes: Neuchâtel and Paris).

Tigerstedt, E. N. (1965), *The Legend of Sparta in Classical Antiquity*, i (Stockholm Studies in History of Literature 9: Stockholm).

Tirelli, A. (1995), 'L' intelletuale e il potere: pedagogia e politica in Plutarco'. In Gallo and Scardigli (1995), 439–55.

Titchener, F. B. (1991), 'Why did Plutarch Write About Nicias?', *AHB* 5. 5: 153–8.

—— (1992), 'Critical Trends in Plutarch's Roman Lives, 1975–1990', *ANRW* 2. 33. 6, 4128–53.

Toohey, P. (1987), 'Plutarch, *Pyrrh*. 13: ἄλυς ναυτιώδης', *Glotta* 65: 199–202.

—— (1988), 'Some Ancient Notions of Boredom', *ICS* 13: 151–64.

—— (1990), 'Some Ancient Histories of Literary Melancholia', *ICS* 15: 143–61.

Torraca, L. (1998), 'Problemi di lingua e stile nei "Moralia" di Plutarco', *ANRW* 2. 34. 4, 3487–3510.

Tosh, J. (1991; 1st edn., 1984), *The Pursuit of History: Aims, Methods and New Directions in the Study of Modern History* (London and New York).

Townend, G. B. (1959), 'The Date of Composition of Suetonius' *Caesares*', *CQ* NS 9: 285–93.
—— (1964), 'Cluvius Rufus in the *Histories* of Tacitus', *AJPh* 85: 337–77.
—— (1967), 'Suetonius and his Influence'. In Dorey (1967), 79–111.
—— (1987), 'C. Oppius on Julius Caesar', *AJPh* 108: 325–42.
Trapp, M. B. (1990), 'Plato's *Phaedrus* in Second-Century Greek Literature'. In Russell (1990), 141–73.
Trench, R. C. (1873), *Plutarch: His Life, His Lives and His Morals* (four lectures) (London).
Tritle, L. A. (1987), 'Leosthenes and Plutarch's View of the *Strategia*', *AHB* 1. 1: 6–9.
—— (1992), 'Plutarch's "Life of Phocion": An Analysis and Critical Report', *ANRW* 2. 33. 6, 4258–97.
Tsagas, N. M. (1990), *Mise à jour bibliographique des 'Vies parallèles' de Plutarque* (Athens).
Tsekourakis, D. (1983), Οἱ Λαϊκοφιλοσοφικὲς πραγματεῖες τοῦ Πλουτάρχου. Ἡ σχέση τους μὲ τὴ "διατριβὴ" καὶ μὲ ἄλλα παραπλήσια γραμματειακὰ εἴδη (Ἀριστοτέλειο Πανεπιστήμιο Θεσσαλονίκης, Ἐπιστημονικὴ Ἐπετηρίδα Φιλοσοφικῆς Σχολῆς 34: Thessaloniki).
—— (1989), 'Die Ursachen von Krankheiten bei Plutarch', *Hellenica* 40: 257–69.
Tucker, R. A. (1988), 'What actually happened at the Rubicon?', *Historia* 37: 245–8.
Tuplin, C. J. (1984), 'Pausanias and Plutarch's *Epaminondas*', *CQ* NS 34: 346–58.
Turchi, M. (1984), 'Motivi della polemica su Alcibiade negli oratori attici', *PP* 39: 105–19.
Valgiglio, E. (1975), 'L' autobiografia di Silla nelle biografie di Plutarco', *StudUrb (B)* 49: 245–81.
—— (1976), *Plutarco: Praecepta Gerendae Reipublae* (Testi e documenti per lo studio dell' antichità 52: Milan).
—— (1987), 'Ἱστορία e βίος in Plutarco', *Orpheus* NS 8: 50–70.
—— (1991), 'Dall' ἴστωρ omerico al βίος plutarcheo'. In A. Buttita *et al.* (eds.), *Studi di filologia classica in onore di Giusto Monaco* (Palermo), i. 17–35.
—— (1992), 'Dagli "Ethicà" ai "Bioi" in Plutarco', *ANRW* 2. 33. 6, 3963–4051.
Van der Stockt, L., (1990), 'L' expérience esthétique de la mimèsis selon Plutarque', *QUCC* NS 36: 23–31.
—— (1992), *Twinkling and twilight: Plutarch's reflections on literature* (Verhandelingen van de Koninklijke Academie voor Wetenschappen, Letteren en Schone Kunsten van België, Klasse der Letteren, Jaargang 54, 1992, Nr. 145: Brussels).
Van der Valk, M. (1982), 'Notes on the Composition and Arrangement of the Biographies of Plutarch'. In M. Naldini (ed.) *Studi in onore di Aristide Colonna* (Perugia), 301–37.
Vander Waerdt, P. A. (1985), 'Peripatetic Soul-Division, Posidonius, and Middle Platonic Moral Psychology', *GRBS* 26: 373–94.

Verdin, H., Schepens, D., and De Keyser, E. (1990) (eds.), *Purposes of History: Studies in Greek Historiography from the 4th to the 2nd Centuries BC* (Studia Hellenistica 30: Leuven).

Vessey, D. W. T. C. (1971), 'The Reputation of Antimachus of Colophon', *Hermes* 99: 1–10.

Vidal-Naquet, P. (1968), 'Le chasseur noir et l'origine de l éphébie athénienne', *Annales (ESC)* 23: 947–64. Trans. (1968) by J. Lloyd as 'The Black Hunter and the origin of the Athenian Ephebeia', *PCPhS* 194, NS 14: 49–64. Reprinted in R. L. Gordon (ed.), *Myth, Religion and Society: Structuralist Essays by M. Detienne, L. Gernet, J.-P. Vernant and P. Vidal-Naquet* (Cambridge, 1981), 147–62. An Italian trans. of a revised version appeared as 'Il Cacciatore nero' in M. Detienne (ed.), *Il Mito: Guida storica e critica* (Bari, 1975), 53–72 and 245–52. French version reprinted in revised form in *Le chasseur noir. Formes de pensée et formes de société dans le monde grec* (Paris 1981; 1983), 151–75. This version appeared in an English trans. by A. Szegedy-Maszak in *The Black Hunter: Forms of Thought and Forms of Society in the Greek World* (Baltimore and London, 1986), 106–28.

Vukobrat, S. (1995), 'The Plutarchan anecdotal principle in modern English biography'. In Christopoulou (1995), 1131–4.

Walbank, F. W. (1951), 'The Problem of Greek Nationality', *Phoenix* 5: 41–60. Reprinted in *Selected Papers: Studies in Greek and Roman History and Historiography* (Cambridge, 1985), 1–19.

—— (1967) (ed.), *A Historical Commentary on Polybius,* ii (Oxford).

—— (1972), *Polybius* (Berkeley, Los Angeles, and London).

—— (1990), 'Profit or Amusement: Some Thoughts on the Motives of Hellenistic Historians'. In Verdin, Schepens, and De Keyser (1990), 253–66.

Walcot, P. (1977), 'Odysseus and the Art of Lying', *AncSoc* 8: 1–19.

Wallace-Hadrill, A. (1983), *Suetonius: The Scholar and his Caesars* (London; New Haven, 1984).

Walsh, J. J. (1992), 'Syzygy, Theme and History: A Study in Plutarch's *Philopoemen* and *Flamininus*', *Philologus* 136: 208–33.

Walsh, P. G. (1961), *Livy: His Historical Aims and Methods* (Cambridge).

Wardman, A. E. (1955), 'Plutarch and Alexander', *CQ* NS 5: 96–107.

—— (1967), 'Description of Personal Appearance in Plutarch and Suetonius: The use of Statues as Evidence', *CQ* NS 17: 414–20.

—— (1971), 'Plutarch's Methods in the *Lives*', *CQ* NS 21: 254–61.

—— (1974), *Plutarch's Lives* (London).

Watkins, O. D. (1984), 'A commentary on Plutarch's *Life of Pompey*, chapters 1–46. 4'. Dissertation, Oxford.

Weiss, R. (1953), 'Lo studio di Plutarco nel Trecento', *PP* 8: 321–42. Reprinted in *Medieval and Humanist Greek* (Padua, 1977), 204–26.

Weissenberger, B. (1895), *Die Sprache Plutarchs von Chaeronea und di pseudo-plutarchischen Schriften* (Straubing). Italian trans. by G. Indelli, with preface by I. Gallo, *La lingua di Plutarco di Cheronea e gli scritti pseudoplutarchei* (Naples, 1994).

Weizsäcker, A. (1931), *Untersuchungen über Plutarchs biographische Technik* (Problemata. Forschungen zur Klassischen Philologie 2: Berlin).

Westlake, H. D. (1938), 'The Sources of Plutarch's Timoleon', *CQ* 32: 65–74.

—— (1939), 'The Sources of Plutarch's *Pelopidas*', *CQ* 33: 11–22.

—— (1968), *Individuals in Thucydides* (Cambridge).

—— (1985a), 'Abydos and Byzantium: The Sources for Two Episodes in the Ionian War', *MH* 42: 313–27.

—— (1985b), 'The Influence of Alcibiades on Thucydides, Book 8', *Mnemosyne* 38: 95–108.

—— (1985c), 'The Sources for the Spartan Debacle at Haliartus', *Phoenix* 39: 119–33.

Wheeler, E. L. (1988), *Stratagem and the Vocabulary of Military Trickery* (*Mnemosyne* Supplement 108: Leiden).

White, H. V. (1978), 'The Historical Text as Literary Artifact'. In R. H. Canary and H. Kozicki (eds.), *The Writing of History: Literary Form and Historical Understanding* (Madison and London), 41–62.

Whitehead, D. (1983), 'Competitive Outlay and Community Profit: φιλοτιμία in Democratic Athens', *C&M* 34: 55–74.

Wiedemann, T. (1992), *Emperors and Gladiators* (London and New York).

Wilamowitz-Moellendorf, U. von (1926), 'Plutarch als Biograph', *Reden und Vorträge* 2: 247–79. Reprinted in an Italian trans. by L. La Penna in Guerrini, Santoni, and Stadter (1991), 5–38. Also in an English trans. by Juliane Kerkhecker in Scardigli (1995a), 47–74.

Wilner, O. L. (1930), 'Contrast and Repetition as Devices in the Technique of Character Portrayal in Roman Comedy', *CPh* 25: 56–71.

Wiseman, T. P. (1979), *Clio's Cosmetics: Three Studies in Greco-Roman Literature* (Leicester).

Wolman, H. B. (1972), 'The Philosophical Intentions of Plutarch's Roman *Lives*'. In *Studi Classici in onore di Quintino Cataudella* (Catania), ii. 645–78.

Woodhead, A. G. (1960), 'Thucydides' Portrait of Cleon', *Mnemosyne* ser. 4, 13: 289–317.

Woodman, A. J. (1975), 'Questions of Date, Genre and Style in Velleius: Some Literary Answers', *CQ* NS 25: 272–306.

—— (1977) (ed.), *Velleius Paterculus: The Tiberian Narrative (2. 94–131)* (Cambridge).

—— (1989), 'Tacitus' Obituary of Tiberius', *CQ* 39: 197–205.

Yaginuma, S. (1992), 'Plutarch's Language and Style', *ANRW* 2. 33. 6, 4726–42.

Ziegler, K. (1907), *Die Überlieferungsgeschichte der vergleichenden Lebensbeschreibungen Plutarchs* (Leipzig). Reprinted Aalen, 1974.

—— (1908), 'Plutarchstudien', *RhM* 63: 239–53.

—— (1927), 'Plutarchstudien', *RhM* 76: 20–53.

Ziegler, K. (1935), 'Plutarchstudien', *RhM* 84: 369–90.
—— (1949), *Plutarchos von Chaironeia* (Stuttgart). Second edn. 1964. Reprinted (1951) as 'Plutarchos 2', *RE* 21. 1, coll. 636–962.
—— (1973, 2nd edn.; 1st edn., 1926), *Plutarchus Vitae Parallelae,* iii. 2 (Teubner: Leipzig).
Ziehen, J. (1898), 'Sullas Phthiriasis', *Philologus* 57: 189–91.
Zimmerman, R. (1930), 'Die Quellen Plutarchs in der Biographie des Marcellus', *RhM* 79: 55–64.

I regret that the following items appeared too late for me to consult:

Angeli Bertinelli, M. G., Manfredini, M., Piccirilli, L., and Pisani, G. (1997) (eds.), *Plutarco: Le Vite di Lisandro e di Silla* (Fondazione Lorenzo Valla: Milan).
Cerezo Magán, M. (1996), *Plutarco: Virtudes y vicios de sus héroes biográficos* (Edicions de la Universitat de Lleida, Studi generali 5: Lleida).
Fernández Delgado, J. A., and Pordomingo Pardo, F. (1996) (eds.), *Estudios sobre Plutarco: Aspectos formales* (*Actas del IV Simposio Español sobre Plutarco, Salamanca, 26 a 28 de Mayo de 1994:* Madrid).
Frazier, F. (1996), *Histoires et morale dans les* Vies parallèles *de Plutarque* (Collection d'études anciennes 124: Paris).
Gallo, I. (1995) (ed.), *Seconda miscellanea filologica* (Università degli Studi di Salerno. Quaderni del dipartimento di scienze dell' antichità 17: Naples).
—— (1996) (ed.), *Plutarco e le religione* (*Atti del VI Convegno plutarcheo, Ravello 29–31 maggio 1995:* Naples).
Luppino Manes, E., and Marcone, A. (1996) (eds.), *Plutarco. Vite Parallele: Agesilao–Pompeo* (Biblioteca Universale Rizzoli: Milan).
McGrail, M. A. (1997) (ed.), *Shakespeare's Plutarch* (*Poetica* 48: Tokyo).
Marincola, J. M. (1997), *Authority and Tradition in Ancient Historiography* (Cambridge).
Porter, S. E. (1997) (ed.), *Handbook of Classical Rhetoric in the Hellenistic Period 330 BC–AD 400* (Leiden).
Strobach, A. (1997), *Plutarch und die Sprachen: ein Beitrag zur Fremdsprachenproblematik in der Antike* (Palingenesia 64: Stuttgart).
Van der Stockt, L. (1996) (ed.), *Plutarchea Lovaniensia: A Miscellany of Essays on Plutarch* (Studia Hellenistica 32: Leuven).

Index Locorum

Note: extended discussions, which in some cases make up whole chapters, are in bold type. Individual passages within such extended discussions are not cited separately.

ACTS OF THE APOSTLES (see also
    LUKE–ACTS)
    12:23: 197 n. 150

AELIAN
On animals
    2. 14: 235
    6. 24: 175 n. 63
V. H.
    1. 25: 136 n. 19
    4. 3: 17 n. 11
    11. 9: 136 n. 19

AGATHIAS SACHOLASTIKOS
Palatine Anthology
    16. 331: vii

AILIOS ARISTEIDES
    10, 77, 256 n. 51, 304 n. 54
Panath.
    225–31: 77
On Rome
    67–71: 297 n. 29
    103–5: 300

PS.-AILIOS ARISTEIDES
Orations
    35. 1–2: 21 n. 26

AINEIAS TAKTIKOS
On how to withstand a siege
    39–40: 172 n. 44
    fr. 52, 56–8 Schöne: 172 n. 44

AISCHINES OF SPHETTOS
Alkibiades
    223

AISCHYLOS
Persians
    181–99: 191
Fragments
    TrGF III F 393: 32 n. 56

AISOP
Fab.
    6: 175 n. 69
    119: 175 n. 68
    192: 175 n. 63

ANAXANDRIDES (or -AS)
    FGrH 404 F 3–5: 165 n. 19

ALKAIOS
    fr. 333 Page: 32 n. 56

ANDOKIDES
Orations
    3. 33–34: 171 n. 43

PS-ANDOKIDES
Against Alkibiades (=Andokides, *Or.*
    4) 223
    14–15: 233 n. 82
    17: 234
    22–23: 235 n. 87

ANTIPHON:
Orations
    2–4 Blass: 244
    fr. 66 Blass: 232

ANTISTHENES (Giannantoni)
    frs. V A 53–4: 172 n. 47, 244

Alkibiades
(frs. V A 198–202): 223 n. 56
fr. V A 198: 223 n. 56, 224 n. 62
fr. V A 199: 236
fr. V A 200: 217 n. 39

Kyros or on Kingship
fr. V A 141 Giannantoni: 236 n. 91

APHTHONIOS
Progymn.
1, Spengel, ii, 21, 2–3: 163 n. 9
2, Spengel, ii, 22, 6–7: 19 n. 16
10, Spengel, ii, 42–4: 244

APPIAN 303
BC
1. 73: 128 n. 98
1. 97: 198 n. 155
1. 101: 197 nn. 150, 152
2. 14: 254 n. 43
2. 27: 254 n. 43
2. 99: 137 n. 24
2. 110: 79 n. 26
2. 149–54: 254 n. 43, 284 n. 132
4. 16: 26 n. 39

BM
38–9: 203 n. 167

ARCHILOCHOS
fr. 174, 185, 201 West: 175 n. 69:

ARISTOPHANES
Ach.
307–8: 172 n. 49
410–13: 56 n. 20

Birds
71–2: 226 n. 64

Clouds 174 n. 62
102–4: 143 n. 45
362–363: 143 n. 45
559: 163 n. 8
889–1114: 244 n. 7

Frogs
830–1481: 56 n. 20, 244 n. 7
905–6: 163 n. 8
1420–57: 222
1425: 234

Knights
134: 149 n. 61, 303 n. 47
193: 149 n. 61
249: 174 n. 57
304–7: 149 n. 61
637: 149 n. 61
1037: 231 n. 78
1377–80: 223 n. 53

Lysistrata
629: 172 n. 49
1269–70: 175 n. 63

Peace
622–4: 172 n. 49
1063–7: 172 n. 49
1189–90: 200 n. 160

Thesm.
149–50: 56 n. 20
773, scholia on: 170 n. 37

Wasps
44–6: 225

Wealth
249, scholia on: 165 n. 19

ARISTOPHANES OF BYZANTION
249 Nauck = Syrian, *In Hermog.* 2.
23. 10–11 Rabe[a]: 34 n. 62

ARISTOTLE
7, 29, 39–40, 43–5, 67, 72 nn. 1–2, 73,
85, 87, 90, 92, 152, 178, 196, 244,
263

Ath. Pol.
6. 3: 312 n. 3
34. 2–3: 186 n. 108
58. 1: 127 n. 96

EE
1220a38–1220b7: 74 n. 6

Ethics
1095a14–1102a4: 103
1104b4–1105b13: 44 n. 96
1104b12–13: 44
1105a10–12: 44

Hist. Anim.
488b20–1: 175 n. 68
556b–557a: 197 n. 151
631b2: 110 n. 30

MM
   1185b38–1186a8: 74 n. 6

NE 39 n. 78, 72 n. 2
   1095a14–1102a4: 103
   1103a11–b25: 74 n. 6
   1104a2: 28 n. 46
   1105a7–8: 213 n. 24
   1107b14–16: 28 n. 46
   1107b21–1108a2: 83 n. 39
   1111b4–1112a17: 39 n. 78
   1125b1–25: 83 n. 39
   1125b26: 87
   1150b25–8: 178 n 76

Poetics
   1447a13–1148a25: 44
   1447a16–18: 45 n. 98
   1450a15–22: 45
   1450a27–9: 17 n. 11
   1450b8–10: 39 n. 78
   1451a16–35: 45
   1451b4–11: 19 n. 16, 29
   1451b5–7: 44
   1451b10–11: 227
   1454b8–10: 44

Politics
   1237b37–8: 92 nn. 80, 81
   1269b41: 195
   1288b1–2: 90 n. 72
   1293b30–1294a25: 90 n. 72
   1296a2–3: 92 n. 81
   1303b17–1304a4: 298
   1312b35–6: 92 n. 81
   1314b30–6: 95 n. 96
   1339b11–1340b19: 44
   1340a15–16: 44 n. 96
   1340a32–5: 16 n. 8
   1388b12 and 30–1: 175 n. 63

Prior An.
   707b1–37: 93 n. 84

Rhetoric
   1368a2–5: 263 n. 74
   1368a19–26: 244 n. 4
   1393a23–1393b4: 50 n. 108
   1402a23: 174 n. 62

Lost works
   '*Fondations and Constitutions*' 19

PS.-ARISTOTLE
Problems
   953a10–954a40: 178–9, 197
   953a10–31: 48 n. 108
   955a32: 37 n. 79

Physiog.
   806a30: 17 n. 11
   808a12–16: 214 n. 25
   812a13–21: 166, 175 n. 68
   812b3–4: 166
   814b1–9: 17 n. 11

Rhet ad Alex.
   1462b7: 185 n. 101

ARISTOXENOS 19

ARRIAN 10
Anabasis
   6. 13. 4: 82 n. 34
Discourses of Epiktetos
   2. 14. 7: 156 n. 85
   2. 14. 21: 32
   3. 24. 106: 156 n. 85
   3. 26. 8: 156 n. 85

ARULENUS RUSTICUS 142 n. 41

ASKLEPIADES OF MYRLEIA
apud Sextos Empeirikos, *Adv. Gramm.*
   1. 252–3: 18–19

ASKLEPIADES OF SAMOS
Anth. Pal.
   9. 63: 190

ATHENAIOS
Deipnosophistai 3, 299
   168e: 19 n. 18
   170e: 290 n. 8
   274c: 19 n. 18
   274e–f: 60 n. 28
   534b: 228
   534c: 223 n. 56
   534e–f: 232

543a: 60 n. 28
543b–c: 178 n. 74

AULUS GELLIUS 3, 289
Attic Nights
2. 8. 1: 3
3. 6. 1–3: 3
4. 11. 12–13: 3
7. 8. 1: 83 n. 38

BIAS
apud, Stobaios *Flor.* 21. 11 (1, 317 Meineke): 32

BION OF BORYSTHENES 104

PS.-BION OF SMYRNE
Epithalamios
21: 237 n. 95

CATULLUS
95. 1–2: 290 n. 12

CAVAFY
King Demetrios 125 n. 91

CHARITON
Chaireas and Kallirrhoe
1. 1. 1–2: 170 n. 38
5. 2. 6, 6. 4. 10, 6. 5. 8: 304 n. 53

CICERO
De Opt. Gen.
13: 249 n. 20
De Inv.
1. 27: 19 n. 16
Par. Stoic.
2: 155
Brutus
26–52: 290 n. 12
112: 19
191: 190
161–5: 244 n. 7
In Ver.
1. 14: 95 n. 96
2. 1. 82: 95 n. 96

Pro Mur.
31: 95 n. 97
61–2: 157 n. 88
Pro Arch.
30: 16 n. 9
Dom. Sua:
49, 92: 95 n. 97
Harr. Resp.
9, 38, 42: 95 n. 97
Pro Sest.
16–17: 95 n. 97
Prov. Cons.
6: 95 n. 96
Phil.
13. 13: 296 n. 28
Republic
2. 45–6: 95 n. 96
2. 69: 32, 92 n. 80
De Fin.
1. 10, 36: 52 n. 3
1. 17–19, 57–63: 107 n. 21
5. 7, 20: 156 n. 8
Tusc.
1. 71–2: 142 n. 41
5. 95: 107 n. 21
De Offic.
1. 84: 170 n. 40
2. 80: 249 n. 20
Ad Fam.
1. 9. 16: 128 n. 100
5. 12. 4: 52 n. 3
7. 1. 3: 292 n. 15
Ad Att.
2. 1. 8: 140
apud Donatus, *De Com.*
5: 33 n. 61

PS.-CIC.
Rhet. ad Herenn.
1. 8, 13: 19 n. 16
4. 28, 39: 42 n. 86
4. 53, 67: 16 n. 7

CIL
vi. 1444: 289 n. 43

A. CLAUDIUS CHARAX (*FGrH* 103)
Greek and ⟨?Roman⟩ histories 290 n. 8

CLEM. ALEX.
Paid.
1. 88, 150 Potterius: 33 n. 56
Stromata
7. 45. 3, 858 Potterius: 157 n. 88

CORINTHIANS, FIRST EPISTLE TO
15:10: 38 n. 77

CORNELIUS ALEXANDER 'POLYHISTOR' 290

CORNELIUS NEPOS
De viris illustribus 7, 20, 228–9, 247, 290–1
Preface to the book 'On eminent foreign leaders': 96 n. 101, 229, 291
Lys.
2. 2–3: 314 n. 13
3: 198 n. 155
Alk.
3. 5. 1–4, 7. 2–5, 8. 1, 9. 4, 10. 5, 11.1, 11. 3–6: 228–9
Thras.
1. 1–2: 53 n. 6:
Pel.
1. 1: 20 n. 21, 291
Epam.
1. 1–2: 229
Eum.
8. 1–3: 53 n. 6, 67 n. 52
Phok. 133
Hann.
13. 4: 291
Atticus
2. 3: 20 n. 21
Chronica 290 n. 10

CURTIUS RUFUS 65, 284–5
6. 2. 1–2: 285 n. 141
8. 1. 22, 8. 1. 43, 8. 2. 1, 8. 4. 29–30, 8. 6. 14: 285 n. 141
10. 5. 26–37: 284–5

DEMETRIOS OF PHALERON 134 n. 11, 142, 149 n. 63

PS.-DEMETRIOS OF PHALERON
On Style
171, Spengel, iii, 299–300: 16 n. 7
227, Spengel, iii, 311, 26–7: 164 n. 10

DEMOKRITOS
On tranquillity of mind 105
frs. 68 [55] B 166 Diels-Kranz: 31
frs. 68 [55] B 191 and 202 Diels-Kranz: 107 n. 21
apud Diog. Laert. 9. 45: 106 n. 20

DEMOSTHENES
Orations
18. 26 (*On the crown*): 38 n. 76
21. 143–50 (*Against Meidias*): 223–4
21. 147 (*Against Meidias*): 234 n. 86
23. 197 (*Against Aristokrates*): 16 n. 9
60. 15 (*Funeral Speech*): 21 n. 26

DIO CASSIUS
37. 52. 2: 80 n. 29
39. 38. 1: 299 n. 34
43. 11. 6: 137 n. 24
52. 35–36: 292 n. 18
53. 11. 1–12. 3: 285
53. 16. 1: 285
54. 24. 7–8: 299 n. 34
54. 26. 16–17: 299 n. 34
55. 8. 6–7: 299 n. 34
56. 43–5: 284–5
57. 19. 4: 20 n. 20
69. 4. 6: 190

DIODOROS 9 n. 39
1. 1. 4: 52 n. 2
1. 5. 2: 28 n. 46
4. 5: 26 n. 39
4. 31. 1: 158 n. 92

5. 31. 1: 125 n. 89
10. 9. 1: 186 n. 103
12–13 (on Nikias): 26
12–14 (on Alkibiades): 223
13. 45. 1–47. 2: 238 n. 97
13. 104. 7: 314 n. 13
14. 3. 4–7: 186 n. 103
14. 10. 2–3: 183
14. 10. 12: 183 n. 96
14. 13: 198 n. 155
14. 70. 2: 183 n. 96
16–18 (on Phokion): 133, 142
17. 15: 146 n. 51
19. 81. 4: 125 n. 90
20. 17. 5: 173
20. 92. 3: 125 n. 90
20. 92. 4: 279 n. 123
26. 1. 1: 17 n. 11
34/35. 2. 23: 197 n. 152

DIODOROS THE PERIEGETE
(*FGrH* 372): 192 n. 131

DIOGENES LAERTIOS
1. 33: 108 n. 22
4. 10: 216 n. 32
6. 84: 19
9. 45: 106 n. 20
9. 68: 106 n. 20
10. 37: 106 n. 20

DION OF PROUSA
10, 77, 90 n. 70, 304 n. 54

Orations
4. 16–32: 84
4. 123: 84 n. 47
4. 130–1: 84 n. 47
21. 121–2: 292 n. 15
32. 3: 77
32. 40: 304 n. 54
45. 1: 304 n. 54
48. 8: 77
74. 15: 176
75–76: 244 n. 9

DIONYSIOS OF HALIKARNASSOS
9, 57–8, 290, 302, 304

Ad Amm.
4: 186 n. 105

Ad Pomp.
3. 6: 57–8
3. 15: 52 n. 3
6: 28 n. 47
6. 7: 24

Ant. Rom.
1. 1. 2–4: 56–7
1. 1. 2: 26 n. 39
1. 2. 1: 33
1. 4. 1–6. 2: 25 n. 36
1. 5. 4: 28 n. 46
5. 48. 1: 18 n. 15
6. 70. 2: 125 n. 89
6. 92–8. 62: 205, 214, 221, 282
6. 93: 220 n. 41
7. 66. 5: 28 n. 46
7. 67. 2: 214
7. 68. 73: 218
8. 29. 4: 218
11. 1. 5: 26 n. 39, 28 n. 46
16: 115 n. 50

Lysias
7, 1. 14. 17 Us.-Rad: 42 n. 84

Thucydides 57

Lost works

De Imit. 57

DIONYSIOS OF HERAKLEIA
On exercise (Περὶ ἀσκήσεως): 157 n. 89

DIONYSIOS THRAX, scholia on
449. 11 Hilgard: 19 n. 16
173. 3–4 Hilgard: 34 n. 62

DONATUS
De Com.
5: 33 n. 61

DOURIS OF SAMOS
42 n. 85, 101, 113 n. 34, 125, 224 n. 58
FGrH 76 F 1: 40 n. 80
FGrH 76 F70: 125 n. 93

ENNIUS
fr. 99, 195–202 Jocelyn: 112 n. 42

EPHOROS
40 n. 80, 57, 184 n. 97, 223
FGrH 70 F 71: 172

EPIKOUROS:
Ad Herod.
p. 4 Usener: 106 n. 20
p. 32 Usener: 106 n. 20
fr. 210 Usener: 33 n. 60
fr. 422 Usener: 109 n. 23
fr. 496 Usener/103 Diano: 112 n. 42
fr. 108 Diano: 110 n. 32

EPIKTETOS
Discourses (by Arrian)
2. 14. 7: 156 n. 85
2. 14. 21: 32
3. 24. 106: 156 n. 85
3. 26. 8: 156 n. 85
Ench.
8: 156 n. 85
s. v. also Favorinus, *Against Epiktetos*

EUDOXOS OF RHODES 19

EURIPIDES
Alk.
1, scholia on: 165 n. 19
766: 174 n. 56
Andr.
445–53: 172 n. 57
Her.
357–8: 170 n. 37
Hipp.
428–30: 33 n. 56
1400: 174 n. 57
Orestes
129: 236
Phoen.
524–5: 274
531–4: 196
Supp.
447–55: 95 n. 96

Lost plays of (?) Euripides
Skyrians
fr. Adesp. 9 Nauck TrGF: 237

FAVORINUS 246–7, 289
On the Academic disposition (or *Plutarch*): 246–7
Against Epiktetos: 246–7
apud Philostratos, *Vit. Soph.* 1. 8. 489: 289 n. 4

FGrH 1 F 1: 25 n. 36
FGrH 70 F 71: 172
FGrH 76 F 1: 40 n. 80
FGrH 76 F70: 125 n. 93
FGrH 115 F 20: 178 n. 74
FGrH 115 T 20a: 24, 27, 28 n. 47, 57–8
FGrH 115 F 24: 25 n. 36
FGrH 115 F 74–5: 167 n. 28
FGrH 115 F 192: 176 n. 71, 183 n. 96
FGrH 372: 192 n. 131
FGrH 373: 192 n. 131
FGrH 404 F 3–5: 165 n. 19
FGrH 434 F 1. 2. 4–5: 197 n. 150

GALEN 93, 196 n. 146
De Opt. Doct.
1. 40–52 Kühn: 247 n. 16
De Plac. Hipp. et Plat.
5. 5 Kühn: 93 n. 84
5. 464 Kühn: 93 n. 84
De Morb. Temp.
7. 424. 3 Kühn: 195
De Typis
7. 463. 9 Kühn: 195

HEKATAIOS
FGrH 1 F 1: 25 n. 36

HELIODOROS
2. 35. 2: 127 n. 87

HELIODOROS THE PERIEGETE (FGrH 373) 192 n. 131

HERAKLEIDES PONTIKOS
fr. 91 Voss: 190

HERAKLEITOS (THE PRE-SOKRATIC)
fr. 70 Marcovich: 213, 214–15

HERAKLEITOS
Hom. Prob. 61. 5: 110 n. 32

HERILLOS OF CARTHAGE
On exercise (Περὶ ἀσκήσεως) 157 n. 89

HERMIPPOS OF SMYRNE 142

HERODOTOS 19, 52, 53 n. 4, 57–8
preface: 47, 36 n. 69
1. 8. 3: 266
1. 30–3: 113, 278
1. 32. 1–9: 284
1. 51. 3: 36 n. 68
1. 82. 7–8: 164 n. 15
1. 93. 2: 36 n. 68
2. 44. 5: 127 n. 97
3. 41. 1: 36 n. 68
3. 80. 5: 95 n. 96
4. 205: 197 n. 150
5. 56: 231 n. 78
5. 75: 187 n. 107
5. 92: 231 n. 78
6. 58. 3: 168 n. 30
6. 98. 2: 187 n. 109
6. 103. 2: 190 n. 122
6. 131. 2: 231 n. 78
7. 10–18: 113
7. 10. ϵ. 2: 113 n. 44
7. 16. α. 2: 113 n. 44
7. 18. 2–4: 113 n. 44
7. 24: 112 n. 29
7. 182: 110 n. 30
8. 3. 1: 89–90 n. 67
8. 28: 112 n. 29
8. 144. 2: 89–90 n. 67
9. 54. 1: 172 n. 50

HERMOGENES
Progymnasmata
8, Spengel, ii, 14–15: 244 n. 5
9, Spengel, ii, 15: 37 n. 74

HESIOD
Theogony
933–7: 92 n. 82
975–7: 92 n. 82
Works and Days
235: 297
705: 110 n. 29

HESYCHIOS
s. v. καρτή 290 n. 8
s. v. Ἕλληνες 304 n. 53

HIPPOKRATES 196 n. 146, 243
Seventeenth Letter
IX, 362, 8–11 Littré: 104
Aphor.
3. 27. 5= IV, 500 Littré: 195 n. 143

PS.-HIPPOKRATES
De Morb. Sacro
18. 1=VI, 394 Littré: 178 n. 76

HOMER
13 n. 3, 19, 26, 44, 121, 190, 233
Iliad
6. 506: 191–2
11. 482: 175
12. 243: 124
13. 516: 143 n. 47
15. 263–8: 191–2
22. 373: 88
23. 175–6: 127 n. 97
Odyssey 33 n. 61
3. 163: 175
4. 230: 226
13. 293: 175
15. 357: 110 n. 29
Hymn to Aphrodite
262–3: 168 n. 29

HORACE
Ep.
1. 8, 1. 11: 112 n. 42
Odes
2. 1. 12: 143 n. 45

Satires
  1: 104
IG
  v. 1432, 33: 181 n. 88
  xii. 5, 278: 181 n. 88
ILS
  1022: 289 n. 43

ISOKRATES 185
Areop.
  18: 110 n. 30
De Bigis 222–3
  3: 235 n. 88
  22: 28 n. 46
  29: 217 n. 39
  39: 21 n. 26
Busir.
  4: 223 n. 54
Ad Demon.
  34: 44 n. 93
Evag.
  37–9: 243 n. 3
  47–50: 185
  73: 16 n. 9
  77: 68 n. 56
Ad Nicocl.
  29: 211 n. 19
  35: 44 n. 93
  36: 16 n. 9
  39: 211 n. 19
Panathen. 185 n. 102
  39–40: 243 n. 3
Paneg.
  81: 89–90 n. 67
  86: 185 n. 102
Phil.
  127: 89–90 n. 67
Ad Phil.
  46: 28 n. 46
  146: 38 n. 76

JAMES, EPISTLE TO
  1:23: 33 n. 56

JEROME
Comm. in Zach.
  3. 14. 47, 1522 Migne: 19

JOHN, GOSPEL OF
  12:44: 38 n. 77
  20:30: 21 n. 26
  21:25: 21 n. 26

JOSEPHUS
Jewish Antiquities
  1. 11 (203): 19
  13. 3. 3 (72): 19
  13. 5. 9, (173): 19, 28 n. 47
  13. 10. 6 (298): 19
  17. 3. 3 (60): 52 n. 2
Life
  65 (339): 58
  74 (412): 19

JUBA
Likenesses 290 n. 8

JULIAN
Orations
  1. 1 Spanheim: 21 n. 26

JULIUS CAESAR
Anticato 143 n. 46, 152 n. 79
BC
  3. 35. 2: 296 n. 28

JULIUS HYGINUS 290

JUSTIN
  Preface 4: 52 n. 2

KALLIMACHOS
Aitia 229
Epigrams
  28 Pfeiffer: 23 n. 30
Hymn to Apollo
  105–12: 23 n. 30
  fr. 398 Pfeiffer: 190

KORINTHIANS, *see* CORINTHIANS

KTESIAS 30

LAMPRIAS CATALOGUE
  1–2, 20 n. 19, 300 n. 37. *See also*
    PLUTARCH, lost works

LIBANIOS 256 n. 51
  Progym. 10, Förster[b] viii, 334–60: 244
  Antiochikos 6, Förster[b] i, 439: 21 n. 26
  Defence of Sokrates, Förster[b] v, 13–121:
    223 n. 55

LIVY 26, 244 n. 6
  Preface 10: 52 n. 2
  1. 35. 2: 186 n. 106
  1. 55. 5: 186 n. 106
  2. 34. 10: 217 n. 38
  5. 32. 6–55. 5: 54
  9. 3. 9: 186 n. 106
  9. 16. 19–19. 17: 249 n. 20, 301 n. 43
  21. 1–3: 26 n. 40
  21. 3: 113
  21. 10: 113
  22. 43. 4: 186 n. 106
  25. 40. 1–3: 305 n. 56
  30. 23–30: 113
  Epitome of Book 81: 203

PS.-LONGINOS
  On the Sublime 40 n. 80
  12. 4–5: 249 n. 20
  15. 2: 42 n. 84

LONGOS
  4. 17. 2: 125 n. 88

LUCAN 138 n. 28
  1. 185–203: 80
  2. 380–91: 155
  10. 20–48: 249 n. 20

LUCIAN 10
  Alex. 60
  3: 16 n. 10
  48: 299 n. 34
  59: 197 n. 150
  61: 21 n. 26
  Demon.
  67: 21 n. 26

De Hist.
  51: 33 n. 61
  59: 58 n. 24

Gall.
  10: 125 n. 88
  24: 125 n. 89

Imag. 163 n. 8
  3: 16 n. 10
  6: 17 n. 11

Jup. Trag.
  41: 125 n. 89

Peregr.
  1: 86 n. 55
  33: 109 n. 28
  38: 86 n. 28

LUCRETIUS
DNA
  1. 926–30: 290 n. 12
  3. 1060–67: 112 n. 42

LUKE-ACTS: 9 n. 39

LUKE, GOSPEL OF
  8:43: 195 n. 143

LYKOURGOS OF BOUTADAI
  Against Leokrates
    40: 126 n. 94

LYSIAS
  Orations
    12. 71–6: 168 n. 109
    12. 78: 115 n. 49
    14: 223
    14. 16, 30: 223 n. 54
    frs. 30–1 Gernet-Bizos: 223

MARK, GOSPEL OF
  5:25: 195 n. 143
  9:37: 38 n. 77

MATTHEW, GOSPEL OF
  9:20: 195 n. 143
  10:20: 38 n. 77

MAXIMOS OF TYRE
Orations
  15–16 Hobein: 244
  15. 1a–d Hobein: 104

MENANDER 32 n. 56, 34 n. 62, 244 n. 7
Epitrep.
  535: 174 n. 58

MENANDER RHETOR
  2. 368. 10–12: 21 n. 26
  2. 368. 23–369. 2: 21 n. 26
  2. 372. 21–5: 244
  2. 372. 25–7: 263
  2. 376. 31–377. 9: 244
  2. 378. 17–26: 185
  2. 392. 28–31: 3, 13

MEMNON OF HERAKLEIA
  FGrH 434 F 1. 2. 4–5: 197 n. 150

MUNATIUS RUFUS 142

NIKOLAOS OF MYRA
Progymn.
  1, Spengel, iii, 453, 19–20: 163 n. 9
  10, Spengel, iii, 485–488: 244 n. 5

OGIS
  220, 5–8: 181 n. 88

OPPIAN
Halieutika
  2. 107–19: 175

OPPIUS
Life (?) of Casear: 7 n. 31, 80 n. 29, 86 n. 52, 98 n. 107

OVID
Amores
  1. 9: 244 n. 6
Fasti 300
Met.
  90–9: 167 n. 28

PANAITIOS
On tranquillity of mind 105

PAUSANIAS
Guide to Greece 293
  1. 20. 7: 197 n. 150, 203 n. 167
  2. 10. 1: 127 n. 97
  2. 11. 7: 127 n. 97
  4. 33. 4: 197 n. 150
  7. 17. 3: 49 n. 105
  8. 34. 3: 127 n. 97
  9. 2–4: 197 n. 150
  9. 33. 6: 203 n. 167

PETRONIUS
Sat.
  88: 17 n. 11

PHAINIAS OF ERESOS 20

PHILEMON COM.
  fr. 74 Kassel-Austin: 112 n. 41

PHILISTOS 22–26

PHILO
De Vit. Cont.
  78 (pp. 483–4 M): 33 n. 56

PHILOSTRATOS
Life of Apollonios
  1. 2–3: 23 n. 32
  4. 22: 292 n. 15
  5. 2: 195
  5. 9: 125 n. 89
  5. 32: 47 n. 99, 195
  6. 27: 167 n. 28
  8. 7. 6: 164 n. 15
Vit. Soph.
  1. 8. 489: 289 n. 4

PHOTIOS
Bibliotheca
  161, 104a23–b33: 3 n. 10
  176, 121a41–b3: 40 n. 80
  245, 396b22–25: 256 n. 47

PHRYNICHOS (?)
  TrGF II. 408a: 226

PINDAR
Isthmian
  4. 45–7: 174–5
Nem.
  5. 1 ff: 16 n. 9
  7. 14: 33 n. 56
Pyth.
  3. 19–23: 115 n. 49
Fragments
  fr. 205 Maehler: 128
  fr. 210 Maehler: 212–3

PLATO 36–7, 40, 43–5, 47–9, 72–98,
  179 n. 81, 192 n. 131, 206–13,
  217–18, 223–7, 251 n. 27, 303
Alkibiades I 224–5
  104a: 216 n. 34, 225 n. 63
  105b: 216 n. 34
  133c ff: 35 n. 64
Apology
  30a: 227
Epistles
  4, 321c: 211, 218
Euthydemos 174 n. 62
Gorgias 224
  493d–494c: 109 n. 24
  494d: 163 n. 8
  503d–505b: 93 n. 86
  509d–510a: 35 n. 54
  525e: 48 n. 103
  527d: 211 n. 19
Hippias Minor 172 n. 47
  365b: 172 n. 47
  375e: 48 n. 103
Kratyllos
  408c: 125 n. 88
Kriton
  43b–c: 144
  44d: 48 n. 103
Laws
  644c: 163 n. 8
  649d–652: 15 n. 6
  692e–693a: 185 n. 100
  711d–712a: 90 n. 68
  736c: 117
  761e: 152 n. 72
  792e: 74 n. 6
  831b: 216 n. 30
  863e: 175 n. 66
  896e–897b: 306 n. 61
  905b: 33 n. 61
Menexenos
  238c–d: 90 n. 72
Menon
  71e–73c: 248
Phaidon 144, 152
  58a–c: 144
  116b–118a: 143–4
  255d: 218
Phaidros 79 n. 25
  231d: 211 n. 19
  233c: 211 n. 19
  233e: 38 n. 76
  245c–246a: 306 n. 61
  247c: 110 n. 33
  253c–254e: 78–9, 85, 88–9, 110 n. 33
  255d: 33 n. 61, 218
  255e–256a: 79, 110 n. 33
Protagoras
  337d: 60 n. 20
Republic 43–5, 73, 140, 150 n. 64, 156
  n. 85, 224–7
  349b–350c: 104
  365c: 175 nn. 63, 69
  374d–417b: 76
  375b–c: 87
  382c: 171 n. 43
  382d: 176 n. 70:
  387d–388a: 82 n. 33
  392c–398b: 43 n. 90
  410b–412a: 87 n. 58
  410d: 92 n. 81
  411b: 75 n. 10, 213, 266
  412a: 92 n. 79
  419b–c: 173 n. 52
  429b–430b: 76 n. 13
  435 ff: 91 n. 73
  439e–441c: 87
  439e–440d: 73
  439e: 87 n. 57

440d–424d: 211
441e–444a: 76 n. 13
441e–442a: 87 n. 58
442a–c: 73
443d–444a: 92 n. 79
445d: 90 n. 72
466b: 196 n. 145
470b–471c: 89–90 n. 67
473c–e: 90 n. 68
478e–480a: 37 n. 72
487a: 208 n. 10
491b–492a: 47–9, 60–1, 156, 207–9, 220, 224
491c: 92 n. 81
492a: 210, 227
492e–493a: 209, 210, 224, 227
493e–494a: 224
494b–495b: 224–6
495b: 49, 206, 226
526a–576b: 303
540d: 90 n. 72
544e: 90 n. 72
545a: 83, 92 n. 81
548a: 171 n. 43
548b–c: 76 n. 13
548c: 83
549a–b: 76 n. 13
549b: 92 n. 79
562c–d: 193 n. 134
573d: 95 n. 96
580d–583a: 36 n. 66
587c–d: 90 n. 72
588b–d: 167 n. 27
588e–591d: 78 n. 24
591c–d: 92 n. 79
598d–602b: 97 n. 104
602c–605b: 43
603e–604d: 82 n. 33
606a: 76 n. 13

Sophist:
221–2: 216 n. 30
231d: 216 n. 30

Symposium: 143, 157, 216–18, 224
174a: 143 n. 45
204c–221b: 227
215a: 163 n. 8
215e: 216 n. 34

216a–b: 216 n. 34
217a–219d: 143
217b–c: 216
218c: 175 n. 66
219e–221c: 217–18
220a–221b: 143
223b–d: 143 n. 46

Timaios: 2, 91, 300
21b–d (Proklos' comment on): 190
28b: 115 n. 55
29d–30c: 306 n. 61
31b–32b: 115 n. 55
69b–71d: 93 n. 84
88b: 93 n. 84

PS.-PLATO
Alkibiades II
141a–c: 225 n. 63
141b–142d: 233 n. 81

PLAUTUS
Epidic. 383–6: 33 n. 56

PLINY THE ELDER
NH
7. 138: 197 n. 150
11. 114: 197 n. 150
26. 138: 197 n. 150
34. 16: 163 n. 8
34. 58: 17 n. 11
34. 70: 17 n. 11
35. 100: 17 n. 11

PLINY THE YOUNGER
Epistles
3. 13: 143 n. 46
5. 5. 3: 142 n. 41
8. 12. 4: 142 n. 41

PLUTARCH
Parallel Lives
Theseus and Romulus: 2, 2 n. 6, 4, 250 n. 25, 302 n. 45
Thes.
1. 1–5: 18
1. 1: 2 n. 5, 23 n. 30
1. 2: 33 n. 58

1. 4–5: 249 n. 23
1. 4: 18 n. 14
1. 5: 253 n. 35, 313
3. 5–7: 252 n. 31
6. 8–9: 51, 84
12. 2–6: 252 n. 31
12. 5: 186 n. 106
17. 1–4: 252 n. 31
17. 1–2: 120 n. 67
22. 1–4: 258
25. 5: 51, 84
36. 1–6: 137 n. 25

Rom.
1. 1: 254 n. 39
17. 2: 186 n. 106
18. 6: 186 n. 106
21. 5: 186 n. 106
28. 10: 292

Thes.-Rom. synk. **257–8**
1. 1: 26 n. 39, 206 n. 3
1. 4: 253 n. 35
1. 6: 227 n. 65
2. 1–3: 264 n. 85
3. 1: 25 n. 95
3. 3.-4. 1: 253 n. 36
3. 3: 286 n. 45
6. 2–5: 264 n. 78
6. 2–3: 132

Lykourgos and Numa 2 n. 6, 54
Lyk.
4. 4: 93 n. 86, 186 n. 106
4. 12: 109 n. 26
5. 11: 92 n. 80
7. 1: 92 n. 80
7. 5: 92 n. 80
14. 1: 77 n. 15
15. 8: 187 n. 108
16. 10: 185 n. 102
17. 5–6: 174, 185 n. 102
22. 1: 191 n. 125
25. 5: 75 n. 11
28. 1–2: 312
28. 12–13: 312
30. 4: 90 n. 68
31. 3: 77 n. 15
31. 10: 142 n. 43

Num.
1. 1–6: 313
1. 1: 142 n. 13
3. 6–7: 90
4. 12: 131 n. 3
8. 10: 126 n. 95
16. 4: 37 n. 34
20. 7–12: 90 n. 68
20. 8–12: 90 n. 72, 150
22. 1: 137. n. 25

Lyk.-Num. synk. 258 n. 55
1. 1–5: 264 n. 84
1. 1: 206 n. 3
1. 10–11: 259 n. 56
1. 10: 287, 308
2. 1–4: 263 n. 70
4. 8–12: 264 n. 76
4. 9: 76 n. 13
4. 10–13: 274
4. 15: 89, 264 n. 85

Solon and Publicola
Sol.
2. 1–3. 3: 310–1
5. 5: 186 n. 106
7. 2: 186 n. 106
7. 5–6: 82 n. 33
8. 1–11: 266
15. 1: 94 n. 92
15. 2: 174 n. 60
18. 1: 92 n. 80
20. 8: 187 n. 108
21. 1: 76
22. 1–3: 131
27. 1–9: 113
27. 1–3: 184 n. 99
27. 1: 312, 312 n. 2

Pub.
1. 1: 249 n. 23, 253 n. 35
23. 4–5: 137 n. 25

Sol.-Pub. synk. 258 n. 55, 260
1. 1–8: 278
1. 1: 253 n. 35
1. 7–8: 264 n. 81
2. 4–6: 264 n. 84
3. 1–5: 264 n. 76
3. 2: 93 n. 86

3. 3: 263 n. 71
3. 5: 263 n. 75
4. 1: 266
4. 4–5: 263 n. 70

Themistokles and Camillus 2 n. 6, 103, 250 n. 25, 253, 255 nn. 45, 46

Them.
  2. 1–3: 20 n. 20
  2. 2: 97
  2. 5–7: 312
  2. 7: 62
  3. 2: 196 n. 145
  3. 4–5: 51, 84
  6. 1–2: 153 n. 76
  6. 5: 89 n. 67
  10. 1: 126 n. 95
  11. 1: 89 n. 65
  19–22: 313
  19. 1–3: 173–4 n. 55
  21. 7: 175 n. 63
  22. 3: 164 n. 11, 170 n. 38
  27. 1–2: 312
  27. 2: 312 n. 2
  31. 5: 109 n. 28
  32. 1–4: 42 n. 85
  32. 1–3, 6: 137 n. 25
  32. 4–6: 137 n. 25
  32. 6: 137 n. 25

Cam.
  7. 1: 190 n. 119
  9. 3: 93 n. 86
  13. 1: 302 n. 45
  19. 6: 187 n. 110
  22. 2: 313
  40. 1: 83 n. 38

Perikles and Fabius Maximus 2 n. 4, 14 n. 5, 64–5, 66, 81–2, 222 n. 48, 250 n. 25, 304

Per. 42 n. 85, 64, 67 n. 53, 77 n. 19, 90, 265–6
  1–2: 31 n. 53, **34–45** *passim*, 46 n. 99, 148, 169, 266
  1. 4: 169 n. 36
  2. 1: 265
  2. 3: 263 n. 74

  2. 5: 2 n. 4, 33 n. 58, 90 n. 68, 110 n. 31, 225 n. 46
  3. 2: 92 n. 80, 310
  3. 3–4: 164 n. 11
  4. 6: 190 n. 118
  5. 1: 78 n. 22
  6. 1: 188
  6. 2–5: 188 n. 113
  7–14: 90
  7. 4: 154 n. 77
  7. 6: 190 n. 118
  7. 7: 93 n. 86:
  7. 8: 192 n. 129, 194 n. 134
  9. 1: 90, 310
  10. 7: 312 n. 3
  12. 1–13. 3: 265
  13. 16: 18 n. 14
  15. 1–3: 90
  15. 1: 25 n. 35, 310
  15. 3: 184 n. 99
  18. 1–3: 251
  19. 1: 310
  22. 4: 63 n. 39
  27. 4: 312 n. 1
  28. 2: 42 n. 35
  30. 1–32. 6: 64
  30. 1: 186 n. 106
  30. 2: 186 n. 106
  31. 1: 83 n. 38
  33. 6: 81–2
  36. 7–9: 82 n. 33
  39. 4: 310

Fab.
  1. 1: 18 n. 14, 26 n. 39
  3. 6: 81
  4. 3: 190 n. 18
  4. 4–5. 1: 131 n. 3
  5. 4: 81, 174 n. 60
  5. 5: 109 n. 24
  5. 7: 82
  10. 1: 251
  16. 6: 20 n. 21
  16. 8: 82
  17. 7: 78 n. 22, 214 n. 25
  19. 3: 82
  25. 3: 83 n. 37
  27. 3–4: 137 n. 25

Per.-Fab. synk.: 250 n. 25, 258 n. 55, **265–6**
1. 1–5: 98 n. 108, 263 n. 71
1. 1: 18 n. 14
1. 4: 192 n. 129
1. 5: 82
3. 5–6: 184 n. 99, 264 n. 80
3. 5: 264 n. 81
3. 7: 253 n. 35, 265, 286 n. 145

Coriolanus and Alkibiades: 9, 56, 62–5, 70–1, 103, **chapter 7** *passim*, 254

Cor. 3, 77, 89, 96, 110, 121, **chapter 7** *passim*, 304, 305
1. 1: 311
1. 3–2. 2: 121 n. 68
1. 3: 48 n. 102
1. 4: 121 n. 69
1. 6: 63–4
4. 1–2: 84 n. 42
11. 2–6: 130 n. 105, 187 n. 111
11. 6: 187 n. 108
12. 5: 93 n. 87
14. 2–6: 187 n. 111
15. 4–7: 121 n. 69
15. 4: 83 n. 40, 92 n. 76, 92 n. 78, 94 n. 91
21. 7: 77
26. 3: 282
31. 5: 109 n. 24
32. 4–8: 187 n. 111
32. 5–8: 39–40
34. 3: 80 n. 30, 195 n. 142
38. 1–7: 187 n. 111

Alk. 25 n. 37, **chapter 7** *passim*, 313
1. 1: 254 n. 39
2. 1–7: 20 n. 20
4. 1: 164 n. 11
14. 6–15. 2: 173 n. 55
15. 1–2: 282
16. 1–9: 187 n. 111
21. 6: 83 n. 38
23. 2: 125 n. 93
23. 3–9: 187 n. 111
23. 3–6: 175 n. 66
31. 8: 181

Cor.-Alk. synk. 206 n. 3, 260, **281–3**
1. 1: 26 n. 39, 270 n. 102
2. 1–3: 264 n. 77
2. 1–5: 173 n. 55
2. 4–6: 214 n. 28
2. 4: 205 n. 3, 220 n. 41
3. 1–2: 264 n. 80
4. 2: 205 n. 2
4. 4: 214 n. 28
5. 1: 214 n. 28
5. 2: 260 n. 61, 264 n. 79, 269 n. 99

Aemilius Paulus and Timoleon
14 n. 5, 64, 206 n. 3, 250 n. 25, 254

Aem. 6 n. 27, 139, 251–2, 310
1. 1–6: 28, 30–4, 35–6, 45, 65
1. 1: 18 n. 14
1. 5: 18 n. 14
1. 6: 2 n. 5, 251 n. 28, 310
3. 2: 302 n. 45
3. 6: 228
4. 3: 304 n. 52
4. 4: 92 n. 80
5. 10: 18 n. 14, 55
12. 3–13. 3: 251
17. 1–13: 131 n. 3
17. 7–13: 188
19. 3–10: 281 n. 129
22. 4: 83 n. 37
23. 1–11: 281 n. 129
26. 1–12: 281 n. 129
26. 8–28. 13: 251–2
36. 1–9: 82 n. 33, 252
39. 11: 142 n. 43

Tim. 4, 6 n. 27, 32 n. 54, 132
1. 1: 142 n. 23
3. 5: 91 n. 75
6. 1–5: 137 n. 27
6. 1: 81
8. 1–8: 188
15. 1: 187 n. 108
15. 11: 27 n. 45, 33 n. 58
24. 3: 32 n. 54
28. 2–4: 188
35. 1: 185 n. 100
36. 3: 190

Indexes

36. 4: 310 n. 3
37. 4: 32 n. 54

Aem.-Tim. synk. 258 n. 25
1. 1–5: 98 n. 108
1. 1: 18 n. 14
1. 2–2. 7: 263 n. 70
2. 1–9: 264 n. 80
2. 1–7: 264 n. 84
2. 8–9: 184 n. 99, 264 n. 79
2. 10: 82 n. 33

Pelopidas and Marcellus 250 n. 25

Pel.
1. 1–2. 12: 201
1. 1: 20 n. 21
2. 2–3: 170 n. 40
4. 5–8: 98 n. 105
7. 2: 51
19. 1–5: 92
19. 2: 94 n. 91
19. 5: 51
21. 6: 212
29. 8: 126
29. 11: 226 n. 64
30. 8–13: 184 n. 99
31. 3–4: 188 n. 113
31. 5–6: 84 n. 43
32. 9–11: 84 n. 43
32. 9: 82
35. 1–12: 137 n. 25

Marc. 305–7
1. 3: 305
14. 1–18. 5: 306–7
19. 1–21. 7: 305
21. 7: 64 n. 41
24. 2: 93 n. 86
28. 3–6: 306
28. 6: 84 n. 42
30. 5: 228 n. 71

Pel.-Marc. synk. 258 n. 314
1. 1: 18 n. 14, 206 n. 3
1. 2–3: 251 n. 28
1. 4–2. 3: 98 n. 108
1. 6: 173 n. 55
1. 7–8: 259 n. 56
2. 2–3: 263 n. 71

3. 1–8: 264 n. 82
3. 3: 306
3. 6–8: 82 n. 34
3. 8: 202

Aristeides and Cato Major 54

Arist.
2. 3–4: 97
2. 3: 196 n. 145
2. 6–7. 7: 132
5. 9–10: 312
6. 1–5: 55, 116 n. 56, 292 n. 17
13. 2: 132
22. 3–4: 132
23. 1: 78 n. 21
24. 1–7: 184
25. 1–3: 132–3
25. 10: 16 n. 8

Cato Maj. 6 n. 27
7. 3: 9
8. 12–14: 116 n. 60
10–14: 98
23. 1–3: 77
27. 3: 192 n. 129
27. 7: 137 n. 25

Arist.-Cato Maj. synk. 258 n. 55, **261-2**
1. 1: 26 n. 39, 141 n. 38
1. 2: 253 n. 35
2. 1–3: 263 n. 72
3. 2–5: 184
3. 1–4. 7: 264 n. 79
4. 1: 253 n. 36
4. 4: 187 n. 108

Philopoimen and Flamininus 56, 63, 67–8, 121, 134–5, 250 n. 25, 301 n. 41, 307–8

Phil. 22 n. 27
2. 1–6: 164 n. 11
3. 1–5: 121 n. 68
3. 1: 51, 83 n. 37, 267 n. 94
8. 1: 77, 304 n. 53
8. 3: 92 n. 80
13. 9: 173
15. 6–12: 184 n. 99
16. 2–17. 7: 67–8, 267–8
17. 2–3: 134, 307–8

17. 7: 83 n. 38, 267 n. 94
18. 1–3: 308
18. 2: 93 n. 87
20. 3: 78 n. 22
21. 3–9: 137 n. 25
21. 12–*Flam.* 1. 1: 249 n. 23

Flam. 6 n. 27
1. 1: 249 n. 23
1. 4: 121 n. 68
5. 6–7: 77, 304
7. 4–9. 8: 268 n. 97
7. 4: 109 n. 24
11. 3–7: 67, 89 n. 67, 115, 120 n. 67, 308
12. 10: 134, 307 n. 65
15. 4: 268 n. 97
17. 3–8: 16 n. 6
20. 1–2: 84 n. 42
20. 2–21. 1: 308
21. 15: 18 n. 14, 253 n. 35

Phil.-Flam. synk. 260 n. 62, **267–9**
1. 1: 253 n. 35
1. 2: 89 n. 67
1. 4: 308, 83 n. 37
1. 7: 82 n. 34, 264 n. 82
2. 1–6: 98 n. 108
2. 2–5: 263 n. 70
2. 2: 139 n. 33
2. 4: 173
2. 6: 259 n. 56
3. 4: 134–5, 308 n. 67
3. 5: 204 n. 169, 260 n. 61, 286 n. 145, 308

Pyrrhos and Marius 9–10, 56, 62–63, 65, 70, **chapter 4** *passim*, 131, 253–5, 274

Pyrrh. **chapter 4** *passim*,
1. 1: 18 n. 14
1. 2–3: 310
1. 4: 77
2. 8: 310
4. 7: 154 n. 77
14. 14: 80
16. 7: 304

Mar. 62 n. 35, 77, 96, **chapter 4** *passim*, 304, 305

1. 1: 254 n. 39
2. 1: 78 n. 22, 92 n. 76, 92 n. 78, 164 n. 11
2. 4: 84 n. 42
6. 6: 214 n. 39
8. 3: 199 n. 158
14. 1: 304 n. 52
24. 2: 93 n. 86
28. 1–3: 271 n. 104
28. 2: 81 n. 31
32. 4: 167 n. 26
34. 6: 84 n. 42
35. 8–40. 14: 62 n. 35
42. 4: 132
44. 4: 196 n. 146
45. 10–12: 84 n. 42, 197 n. 149
46. 1–5: 254–5

Lysander and Sulla 2 n. 6, 9, 62–3, 70–1, 129, 131, **chapter 6** *passim*, 205, 250 n. 25

Lys. 84, **chapter 6** *passim*
2. 1: 311 n. 7
2. 2–4: 84 n. 44
2. 4: 84 n. 45, 230 n. 76
2. 5: 49 n. 105
2. 7–8: 314 n. 13
5. 7–7. 6: 252
7. 5: 253 n. 35
8. 1–3: 313
15–18: 313
17. 11: 63 n. 39
19. 1–2: 84 n. 45
19. 2–3: 313–14
22. 1–5: 16 n. 6
23. 3: 55, 84 n. 45, 89 n. 66
23. 7: 84 n. 45
25. 2: 126 n. 95
26. 6: 126 n. 92
27. 7: 304 n. 53
30. 2: 58 n. 24
30. 5–6: 137 n. 25
30. 8: 18 n. 14, 142 n. 43

Sulla **chapter 6** *passim*, 304
1. 1–2: 311
1. 1: 142 n. 43
1. 7: 302 n. 45

4. 6: 89 n. 66
12. 11: 90 n. 72
21. 8: 63 n. 39
30. 4: 210 n. 13, 214 n. 26
30. 5–6: 25 n. 35
31. 1: 228
37. 7: 302 n. 45

Lys.-Sulla synk. **200-4**, 258–9, 266, 269
1. 1: 253 n. 35
1. 2–7: 263 n. 70
2. 1–7: 264 n. 86
2. 7: 259 n. 56
3. 1–8: 264 n. 79
3. 5: 259 n. 56
3. 6–8: 264 n. 77
3. 8–4. 1: 253 n. 36
4. 1–9: 264 n. 75
4. 1: 261 n. 64
4. 3–5: 82 n. 34, 264 n. 86
5. 1–2: 263 n. 70
5. 5: 270 n. 102
5. 6: 260 n. 61, 286 n. 145

Kimon and Lucullus 59–60, 250 n. 25
Kim. 6 n. 26
1. 1–2. 5: 261
1. 1–2. 2: 59
2. 2–3: 16 n. 9
2. 2: 16 n. 7, 33 n. 58
2. 3–5: 31 n. 53, 55–6, 59–60, 96, 159, 162, 271
2. 3: 28 n. 46
2. 5: 18 n. 14
3. 1: 89 n. 67, 249 n. 23
3. 3: 110 n. 67
4. 4: 311
5. 1: 311
6. 1–7: 251
10. 7: 60 n. 30
13. 1: 274 n. 112
15. 12: 92
17. 9: 84 n. 46, 89 n. 65
18. 1: 89 n. 67
19. 3–4: 89 n. 64
19. 5: 143 n. 43
Luc. 7 n. 7
1. 1: 143 n. 43, 311

1. 5–6: 77
2. 4–5: 185
3. 4–8: 202 n. 165
6. 4: 154 n. 77
19. 5: 203 n. 167
28. 2: 60 n. 30, 199 n. 158
38. 3–4: 110 n. 30, 118 n. 64, 189 n. 117
39. 1–42. 4: 60, 260, 311
42. 3: 60 n. 30
43. 2: 228 n. 71
43. 3–4: 137 n. 25

Kim.-Luc. synk. **258, 260-1**
1. 1–8: 263 n. 69
1. 1: 134 n. 14, 206 n. 3
1. 2–8: 311 n. 6
1. 5–6: 264 n. 81
1. 5: 253 n. 35
2. 2: 263 n. 70
2. 6–3. 1: 253 n. 36
2. 6–7: 258
2. 7: 93 n. 86
3. 1–5: 264 n. 75
3. 5: 253 n. 35
3. 6: 286 n. 145

Nikias and Crassus 2 n. 6, 14 n. 5, 54, 56, 62–3, 250 n. 25
Nik. 56 n. 15, 96
1. 1: 23 n. 28, 249 n. 23, 249–50, 253 n. 35, 256 n. 49
1. 5: 18 n. 14, **22–30**, 57, 214 n. 27
2. 2–3: 180 n. 84
2. 3: 149 n. 61
2. 4: 94 n. 92
2. 6: 271 n. 104
6. 4–8. 6: 272–3
8. 5–6: 153 n. 76, 180 n. 84
9. 1: 226, 227
11. 2: 234 n. 85
17. 4: 139 n. 32
22. 2–3: 275
23. 1–9: 188 n. 113
26. 4–6: 120 n. 67
26. 4: 275
27. 5: 275

Crass. 123 n. 83
  2. 8: 90 n. 72
  3. 3: 169 n. 31
  7. 1: 302 n. 45
  19. 5: 170 n. 40
  27. 6: 23 n. 30, 120 n. 67

Nik.-Crass. synk 260 n. 62, **269-75**
  1. 1-3: 264 n. 80
  1. 1: 253 n. 35
  1. 2: 56 n. 16
  1. 4: 264 n. 81
  2. 1-3: 258-9, 264 n. 85
  2. 3: 259 n. 56
  2. 4-3. 6: 153 n. 76
  2. 4: 56 n. 16, 263 n. 72
  2. 6: 56 n. 16
  2. 7: 304 n. 53, 308 n. 70
  3. 4: 153 n. 76
  3. 5: 180 n. 84
  3. 6: 56 n. 16
  4. 1-2: 105 n. 19
  4. 3-4: 132
  5. 1-2: 263 n. 71
  5. 1: 56 n. 16
  5. 4: 264 n. 83

Sertorius and Eumenes 30 n. 50, 206 n. 2, 250 n. 25

Sert. 138-9
  1. 1-12: 256 n. 49
  1. 1-8: ix
  1. 1-2: 53 n. 4
  1. 8-10: 139, 173, 251
  1. 11: 249 n. 23
  10. 3: 173 n. 55, 174
  10. 5-7: 230 n. 73
  11. 2: 126 n. 95, 173 n. 55, 174 n. 61
  13. 1-3: 251
  14. 1: 304 n. 52
  18. 3: 140 n. 35
  20. 1: 126 n. 95
  27. 6-7: 137 n. 25

Eum. 101 n. 2
  1. 1: 18 n. 14, 101 n. 2
  8. 1-3: 53 n. 6
  8. 2-3: 67 n. 52
  9. 1-2: 25 n. 35

  13. 5-6: 116 n. 60
  17-19: 275
  19. 3: 137 n. 25

Sert.-Eum. synk.
  1. 1: 26 n. 39, 206 n. 3
  1. 3-5: 263 n. 70
  1. 6-9: 263 n. 72
  2. 1-5: 105 n. 19
  2. 5: 256 n. 47
  2. 6-8: 264 n. 83, 275

Agesilaos and Pompey 2 n. 6, 250 n. 25, 275-6

Ages. 84-5, 96 n. 100
  1. 2-3: 191
  2. 1-3. 9: 164 n. 11
  2. 3: 84 n. 45
  5. 5-7: 84
  5. 5: 188 n. 114
  6. 6-9: 176 n. 73
  7. 1-8. 7: 85
  7. 4: 84 n. 45
  8. 5-7: 89 n. 66
  8. 5: 55, 84 n. 45
  9. 2: 85
  9. 3: 173
  10. 1: 173 nn. 52-3
  10. 2: 211 n. 19
  11. 6: 85
  11. 6-10: 96
  14. 2-4: 274 n. 112
  15. 2-4: 89 n. 67, 96 n. 100, 115, 304 n. 53
  15. 4: 277
  17. 4-5: 187
  23. 11-24. 3: 85
  28. 1-8: 85
  30. 2-6: 131-2
  30. 2: 93 n. 86
  34. 1: 277 n. 118
  37. 9-11: 180-1
  40. 3: 176 n. 73

Pomp. 69, 252
  1. 1-4: 311
  1. 4: 239 n. 100
  2. 1: 78 n. 22, 90 n. 72
  8. 7: 24

10. 2–10: 276
16. 6–7: 276
21–23: 252
23. 6: 110 n. 31
23. 5–6: 121
28. 4–7: 181 n. 90
29. 1–31. 13: 85. n. 48
29. 4: 89 n. 66
31. 1: 25 n. 35
37. 4: 19 n. 18
38. 2: 60 n. 30
39. 6: 239 n. 100, 276 n. 117
40. 3: 176 n. 73
43–49: 252
43. 1–5: 252, 277
46. 1–47. 10: 276 n. 117
46. 1–4: 121 n. 69
46. 4: 110 n. 31
46. 8: 149 n. 61
47. 4–10: 239 n. 100
48. 8: 149 n. 61
53. 10: 116 n. 59
55. 4: 93 n. 86
61. 4: 81, 276 n. 117
67. 1–68. 1: 239 n. 100
67. 1–10: 276 n. 117
67. 5: 176 n. 73
67. 7: 81
69. 7: 109 n. 24
70. 1–7: 120 n. 67, 304 n. 53
70. 1–3: 116 n. 59
70. 3–6: 274 n. 112
79. 4–80. 2: 311

Ages.-Pomp. synk. **275-8**
1. 2: 206 n. 3
2. 1–2: 164 n. 11
2. 3–4: 131–2, 264 n. 78
2. 3: 93 n. 86, 174 n. 60
3. 1: 253 n. 35, 261 n. 64
3. 2–3: 181 n. 90
4. 3–11: 81
4. 8: 81 n. 32

Alexander and Caesar 2 n. 6, 14 n. 5, 86 n. 51, 85–7, 96 n. 100, 103, 249, 250 n. 25, 253–5, 314

Alex. 16 n. 6, 64, 65, 76, **85-6**, 98 n. 107, 102, 120 n. 83, 267 n. 92
1. 1–3: 5 n. 24, **14-22**, 24, 25, 26, 29, 94, 96, 135
2. 2: 186 n. 106
2. 3: 88 n. 62, 187
3. 5–6: 88 n. 62, 187
4. 1–7: 17 n. 11
4. 1–3: 164 n. 11
4. 5–7: 88 n. 62, 93, 187
4. 7–9. 4: 85
4. 10: 16 n. 6
5. 1–6: 20 n. 20
5. 4: 16 n. 6
5. 7–8: 65 n. 47
6. 1–8: 20 n. 20
6. 6: 85, 109 n. 24
7. 1–8. 5: 65 n. 47
7. 1–2: 85
13. 2: 85
14. 5: 16 n. 6
21. 1–22. 6: 96
21. 1–7: 98 n. 107
21. 6: 186 n. 106
21. 7: 211 n. 19
21. 11: 170 n. 38
24. 10–14: 98 n. 107
26. 1–7: 65 n. 47
26. 14: 83 n. 40, 85
35. 1–16: 187
35. 16: 187 n. 108
38. 4–8: 88 n. 62, 187
39. 1–13: 98 n. 107
42. 3–4: 86
42. 5–10: 98 n. 107
43. 5–7: 98 n. 107
44. 3–5: 98 n. 107
47. 6: 65 n. 47
48. 3: 190 n. 119
48–55: 314
49. 14–50. 1: 314
51. 10: 86
59. 1–5: 98 n. 107
59. 6–7: 175
60. 14–15: 98 n. 107
72. 4: 127 n. 97
75. 2: 109 n. 24
75. 5: 42 n. 85

Caes. 3, 4, 6 n. 27, 16 n. 61, 21, 67, 85–7, 94–5, 97, 135 n. 16, 303
  1. 1: 254
  2. 4: 304 n. 43
  3. 2–3: 86
  4. 7–8: 86
  4. 8: 303 n. 48
  4. 9: 17 n. 11
  5. 8–9: 86
  5. 9–6. 3: 86 n. 54
  6. 3: 303 n. 48
  6. 6: 303 n. 48
  7. 1–4: 86
  8. 3–4: 186 n. 106
  9. 1–10. 11: 135 n. 17
  9. 2: 149 n. 61
  11. 3–6: 86
  11. 5–6: 249 n. 20
  12. 4: 98 n. 107
  14. 8: 254 n. 43
  15–27: 21, 67, 98
  15–17: 186 n. 106, 187 n. 111
  17. 2: 17 n. 11, 79 n. 26, 86
  17. 3–5: 251
  18. 5: 98 n. 107
  22. 6: 86
  23. 2: 86
  28. 6: 93 n. 86, 149
  29. 5: 303 n. 48
  30. 1: 303 n. 48
  30. 2: 254 n. 43
  32. 6–8: 79–80, 114 n. 48
  33. 6: 81
  34. 7–8: 98 n. 107
  35. 8: 303 n. 48
  37. 3: 302 n. 45
  43. 3–6: 188
  48. 3–4: 98 n. 107
  53. 6: 79 n. 26
  54. 4: 98 n. 107
  57. 1: 303
  57. 8: 98 n. 107
  58. 4–5: 86
  60. 1: 86
  66. 3: 81 n. 31
  69. 2–14: 137 n. 25, 255
  69. 4–5: 188

Phokion and Cato Minor 2 n. 6, 9, 63, 70, 129, **chapter 5** *passim*, 162, 205, 248 n. 19, 250 nn. 25 and 28, 253, 255, 304, 308

Phok. 94, **chapter 5** *passim*, 251, 304
  1–12: 313
  1–3: 63
  1. 4–6: 263 n. 73
  2. 6–9: 90 n. 68, 93, 188 n. 114
  3. 1–4: 263 n. 73
  3. 3–4: 308
  3. 6–8: 248 n. 19
  3. 6: 253 n. 36
  5. 1: 164 n. 11
  5. 10: 15 n. 6
  6. 1: 92 n. 76
  6. 2: 82 n. 34
  9. 1–10: 16 n. 6
  18. 1–8: 184 n. 99
  37. 1–2: 120 n. 67
  38. 3–4: 255

Cato Min. 4, **chapter 5** *passim*, 209
  1. 3–3. 10: 20 n. 20
  3. 10: 253 n. 35
  9. 5: 90 n. 72
  9. 9–10: 209 n. 12
  9. 10: 32, 36 n. 64
  11. 8: 294 n. 22
  12. 2: 41 n. 83
  20. 1: 93 n. 86
  23. 1: 78 n. 21
  24. 1: 15 n. 6, 16, 135, 163–4, 164 n. 10, 313
  25. 1–13: 313
  26. 5: 120 n. 67
  37. 10: 15 n. 6, 135
  46. 1: 92 n. 77
  47. 2: 93 n. 86
  51. 6: 314 n. 15
  55. 4: 80 n. 30
  68. 6: 80 n. 30
  73. 1–7: 255

Agis and Kleomenes and Tiberius and Caius Gracchus 249, 250 n. 25

Ag./Kleom.
  1. 1–2. 8: 84

Indexes

1. 1–2: 84 n. 47
1. 3–4: 90 n. 68
2. 5–6: 90 n. 68
2. 7–9: 249 n. 23
2. 9: 2 n. 5, 110 n. 31, 253 n. 35
23(2). 2–6: 155–6
23(2). 3–5: 84 n. 44
23(2). 6: 49 n. 105
31(10). 7: 93 n. 86
34(13). 2–3: 116 n. 56
34(13). 3: 90 n. 72, 116 n. 58
34(13). 9: 90 n. 72
37(16). 7: 116 n. 58, 125
37(16). 8: 56 n. 15
45(24). 3: 90 n. 72
60(39). 1: 139 n. 32

Gracchi 250 n. 25
1. 1: 18 n. 14, 143 n. 43, 253 n. 35
2. 2: 78 n. 22
4. 5–6: 98 n. 105
4. 5: 36 n. 64, 51
21. 3: 228 n. 71
23(2). 1–3: 98 n. 105

Ag./Kleom.-Gracchi synk.
1. 1: 253 n. 35
1. 2: 206 n. 3
1. 3–8: 264 n. 79
1. 3–5: 263 n. 70
1. 7–8: 264 n. 81
3. 1: 264 n. 83
4. 1–5. 6: 264 n. 85
4. 2–3: 131 n. 1
4. 3: 93 n. 86
5. 7: 260 n. 61, 269 n. 99, 286 n. 145

Demosthenes and Cicero 2 n. 4, 133 n. 7, 249, 250 n. 25

Dem. 133–4
1. 1: 2 n. 5
1. 3: 36 n. 67, 208 n. 9
2. 1–4: 1 n. 1
2. 1–2: 23
2. 1: 18 n. 14
2. 2–4: 8 n. 35
3. 1: 2 n. 4, 33 n. 58, 133 n. 7, 251 n. 28
3. 2: 249 n. 20

3. 3–5: 53 n. 4, 256 n. 49
4. 1: 18 n. 14
5. 1–5: 51
11. 3: 23 n. 30
11. 7: 15
13. 1–14. 1: 133
14. 1: 134 n. 11
14. 3–6: 90
23. 4–6: 146 n. 51
25. 1–26. 4: 184 n. 99
30. 5–31. 6: 137 n. 25
30. 5: 137 n. 25
31. 7: 2 n. 5, 142 n. 43

Cic. 4, 76 n. 13, 176 n. 73, 314 n. 15
1. 1: 142–3 n. 43
1. 6: 187 n. 108
2. 1–5: 20 n. 20
32. 4: 188
32. 5–7: 77, 128 n. 100
32. 7: 76 n. 13
48. 2: 176 n. 73, 186 n. 106
49. 2–6: 137 n. 25
49. 2: 164 n. 10

Dem.-Cic. synk.
1. 1: 18 n. 14, 26 n. 39
1. 4: 15 n. 6
3. 2–4. 1: 184 n. 99
3. 2: 25 n. 35
3. 5–7: 264 n. 80, 312 n. 3
4. 4: 259 n. 56
5. 1–2: 264 n. 83

Demetrios and Antony: 2, 2 n. 6, 14 n. 5, 45–9, 55–6, 60–5, 162, 210, 250 n. 25, 280 n. 126, 281

Demetr. 3, 101–2, **116–18**, **125**
1. 1–8: 45–9, 55, 60–5, 101
1. 1–3: 31 n. 53, 34
1. 4: 36 n. 67
1. 5–7: 33 n. 58
1. 6: 18 n. 14, 162
1. 7–8: 116
1. 7: 79 n. 25
1. 8: 97 n. 102, 116
2. 2: 164 n. 11
2. 3: 116 n. 62, 279 n. 123
4. 5: 49 n. 104

5. 1: 115, 188 n. 114, 301
6. 4: 116
8. 1: 116
9. 5–7: 97 n. 102, 116 n. 62, 279
9. 7: 125
10–13: 292 n. 17
10. 1–2: 116
10. 2–13. 3: 116 nn. 56 and 58
11. 2: 180 n. 84, 303 n. 47
11. 5: 149 n. 61
11. 11–13: 125
14. 4: 61 n. 34
17. 10: 116 n. 62
18. 1–7: 116 n. 57
18. 1–5: 116–17
18. 5: 125
18. 6–7: 117 n. 63
19–20: 187 n. 111
19. 4–5: 116 n. 62, 279 n. 123
19. 10: 116 n. 62, 279 n. 123
20. 2: 49 n. 104
21. 4–5: 170 n. 40
24: 292 n. 17
25. 4–5: 117
25. 6–8: 116 n. 56
30: 292 n. 17
32. 7: 117
32. 8: 79 n. 25, 117
35. 3–6: 117
36. 1–12: 280
41. 1: 117
41. 5–7: 116 n. 57, 125, 125 n. 89
41. 5–8: 164 n. 11
42: 292 n. 17
42. 8–11: 55, 117 n. 63
44. 7: 80 n. 30
44. 8: 279 n. 123
44. 9: 125, 164 n. 11
45. 3–4: 163 n. 8
52. 2–4: 117–18
52. 3–4: 113 n. 44
53. 8–9: 281 n. 12
53. 10: 143 n. 43

Ant. 3, 61–2, 69–70, 125, 252
1. 1–3: 311
1. 1: 254 n. 39
2. 6: 149 n. 61

4. 7–9: 187 n. 111
6. 6–7: 61
9. 5: 23 n. 30
14. 4–5: 61
14. 5: 78
19. 4: 61
24. 1–12: 187 n. 111
25. 1: 61
26. 1–3: 125 n. 93
29. 1: 79 n. 25
36. 1–7: 97 n. 102
36. 1–2: 78, 79 n. 25, 96–7
37–52: 252
37. 6: 79
39. 1: 280
50. 3–7: 280
50. 5: 79
53. 5–11: 97 n. 102
54. 5: 280 n. 127
56. 6: 134 n. 14
59–69: 252
68. 6–8: 1 n. 1
70. 1–8: 187 n. 111
77. 7: 280
87. 1–9: 137 n. 25, 311
87. 9: 281

Demetr.-Ant. synk. 260 n. 62, 278–81
1. 1–3: 263 n. 70
1. 4: 61 n. 34
2. 3: 116
3. 1–5: 97 n. 102
3. 1–4. 6: 264 n. 79
3. 1–2: 116
5. 3–4: 264 n. 85
5. 5: 263 n. 71
6. 3–4: 264 n. 83

Dion and Brutus 2 nn. 4 and 6, 134, 137, 150 n. 64, 250 n. 25

Dion 4, 132
1. 1: 2 n. 5
1. 3–2. 6: 138
1. 3: 48 n. 102, 263 n. 73
2. 1–2: 256 n. 49
2. 1: 39 n. 78
2. 2–6: 188 n. 113

2. 7: 2 n. 4, 33 n. 58, 187 n. 108, 255 n. 46
8. 4: 211 n. 18
14. 5: 154 n. 77
21. 9: 27 n. 45, 187 n. 108
24. 1–10: 188 n. 113
24. 10: 131 n. 3
32. 8: 48 n. 102
37. 7: 93 n. 86
52. 5: 211 n. 18
52. 6: 91 n. 75
53. 4: 92 n. 80
55. 1–4: 80 n. 29

Brut. 3, 4, 156 n. 86, 192 n. 127, 284
1. 1–2: 311
1. 3: 91 n. 75, 92 n. 78, 94 n. 91, 211 n. 17
12. 3: 149 n. 63
15. 5–9: 82 n. 33
23. 3–7: 192 n. 127
36. 1–7: 188 n. 113
37. 7: 188 n. 113
47. 7: 134 n. 14
48. 2–5: 188 n. 113
55. 2: 93 n. 86

Dion-Brut. synk.
1. 5: 264 n. 81
1. 6–4. 8: 264 n. 84
2. 2: 93 n. 86, 134 n. 14, 149
3. 6–11: 134
3. 6: 253 n. 36, 258 n. 55
4. 1–4: 263 n. 72
5. 2: 163 n. 8

Lives of the Caesars (esp. *Galba–Otho–Vitellius*) 2, 4, 6 n. 27, 19–20, **28–9**, 93 n. 8, **159–60**, 284 n. 132, 304

Galba
1. 1–7: 93 n. 88
1. 3: 93 n. 90, 94 n. 91
1. 4: 48 n. 102
1. 7–8: 125 n. 89
2. 5: 28–9
3. 4: 158
6. 4: 79 n. 25, 93 n. 88
15–19: 159 n. 95

16. 1–5: 158
19–21: 20
21. 2: 158
22. 7–23. 1: 20
23. 5: 214 n. 25
27. 1: 158
29. 1–5: 158–9
29. 4–5: 284 n. 132

Otho
18. 3: 284 n. 132

Other *Lives*
Arat. 2 n. 7, 68
1. 3–5: 68
4. 1: 93 n. 90
10. 5: 110 n. 31
15. 3: 125 n. 89
24. 5–6: 89 n. 67
29. 7–8: 214 n. 25
40. 4: 214 n. 25
54. 7–8: 68

Art. 2 n. 7, 29–30, 68
6. 8: 304 n. 53
8–11: 29–30
8. 1: 42 n. 84
8. 4: 80

Moralia
De Aud. Poet.
15d–16a: 44
17e–18f: 42
18d–e: 274 n. 111
25b–d: 56 n. 15
26a: 56 n. 15
28a: 174 n. 58
31d: 79 n. 25
34d: 237 n. 94
35d: 271 n. 104
37d: 266 n. 90
42b: 32
44b: 41 n. 83

Quomodo Adult. 235 n. 89
49e: 92 n. 76
51a–53b: 119
51c: 119, 236 n. 90
52e: 227–8, 235 n. 89
58b: 42 n. 36

69f–70a: 211 n. 18
72e: 237 n. 94
73e: 31 n. 52

Prof. in Virt. 155
  75a: 288
  79b–d: 36 n. 65
  79c–e: 31–2
  79c: 31 n. 52
  81a: 96
  81f–82a: 178 n. 76
  83a–b: 79 n. 25
  84b–c: 51, 84
  84b: 32
  84d: 216–17 n. 34
  84e–85a: 32
  84f–85a: 136
  85c–d: 33 n. 60

De Cap. ex Inim.
  86b: 296 n. 27
  91b–c: 171 n. 43
  92d–e: 296 n. 27

Consol. ad Apoll.
  119d: 33 n. 59

De Tuenda Sanit.
  125b: 79 n. 25
  125d–e: 274 n. 111

Con. Praec. 50, 94
  139c: 266 n. 90
  142b: 92 n. 76

De Superstit. 138, 245
  171f: 245

Ap. Lac.
  229a: 183
  229f: 174 n. 59, 183 n. 95
  234d–e: 231 n. 77

Mul. Virt.
  242f–243e: 36 n. 65
  243a-b: 36 n. 67
  243b–d: 247–8, 250
  243d: 23

Quaest. Rom. 187, 298–300, 301, 302
  266f: 299 n. 33
  274b: 299 n. 34
  278c–d: 299 n. 34
  279b: 299 n. 33
  281a: 299 n. 33

Quaest. Graec. 187, 298–300, 301, 302
  292f–293a: 165 n. 19

De Fort. Rom. 245, 263, 300
  316e–317c: 115 n. 55, 188 n. 114, 300
  317c: 214 n. 25, 286 n. 145
  318a: 286 n. 145
  318d: 286 n. 145
  320a: 286 n. 145
  320e: 174 n. 60
  323e: 286 n. 145
  323f: 301
  324c–d: 301
  326a–c: 301
  326a–b: 189

Alex. Fort. 65, 185 n. 100, 245, 263, 267, 300
  328d–e: 44 n. 92
  330e: 15 n. 6
  333c: 124 n. 84
  333d–335e: 190
  334b: 46 n. 99
  334d: 35 n. 64
  335b: 164 n. 11
  335f: 36 n. 67
  336f–337a: 116 n. 60
  337d–e: 116 n. 57, 125 n. 89
  337f: 211 n. 19
  338a–c: 116 n. 58
  344b: 58 n. 26

Bellone an Pace 66, 97–8
  346f–347a: 45 n. 98
  346f: 42 n. 86
  348c: 265 n. 87
  349d: 265 n. 87
  350d: 185 n. 102
  351a: 265 n. 87

De Is. et Osir.
  360d: 116 n. 58
  369c: 88 n. 63

De Pyth. Orac. 288, 293
  397f: 166 n. 22
  398b: 88 n. 63
  401c–d: 89 n. 67

404a: 211 n. 19
408b–c: 292
409c: 293 n. 19
De Defect. Orac. 288
   410b: 50 n. 106
   416d: 163 n. 8, 188 n. 114
   419a–e: 79 n. 25
   419e–420c: 189
   419e: 41 n. 83
   420b: 88 n. 63
   421c: 189
   426d: 88 n. 63
   435e: 88 n. 63
An Virt. Doc. 36 n. 67
   440a–b: 36 n. 67
De Virt. Moral. 13 n. 2, 72–6, 155
   440d–444c: 72–4
   440d: 91 n. 74
   441d–442a: 91 n. 74
   442d: 79 n. 25
   442e–f: 94 n. 93
   444e: 91
   445b–c: 79 n. 25
   446c–d: 94
   446d: 91, 106 n. 20
   446f–448c: 80
   448d: 87
   448e: 217 n. 36
   449d–f: 248 n. 18
   449f: 75 n. 10, 213 n. 23
   450e–451b: 92
   450f: 37 n. 73, 212 n. 22
   451b–452d: 75, 84 n. 42, 157
   451d–f: 91 n. 74
   451d: 213 n. 23
   451f: 94
   452d: 84 n. 44, 216 n. 32
De Cohib. Ira 2, 74 n. 8, **87–9**, 203, 212–13
   453a–454a: 74 n. 8, 88–9
   453c: 79 n. 25
   455b: 78 n. 22
   456f: 158, 212
   457a–d: 213
   457d: 178 n. 76, 214–15
   458d–e: 89

458e: 178 n. 76
459a–460c: 151 n. 69
459b: 79 n. 25
462e–f: 158
462e: 34 n. 63
463e: 249 n. 21
De Tranq. An. 50, **105–9**
   465a–473d: 105–7
   465c–466a: 66 n. 50
   467d–e: 50
   469d: 108
   470b: 116
   470c: 299 n. 27
   473b–c: 107, 109
   474d: 107
   475a: 109 n. 25
De Frat. Amore
   478f–479b: 93
   481b–c: 87
   482c: 158
   487e–488a: 292 n. 16
De Garrul.
   511e: 74 n. 6
   513a–b: 190
De Cup. Divit.
   523d–524a: 159
   525b–c: 136 n. 19
   527a–f: 159
De Vit. Pud.
   529a: 94 n. 91, 210 n. 13
   532d: 83 n. 37
De Ipsum Laud. 50
   542e–543a: 131 n. 3
   545e: 56 n. 15
De Sera Num. 136
   550d–e: 214 n. 25, 300 n. 38
   551a: 214 n. 25
   551d–555d: 49 n. 105, 60
   551d: 74 n. 7, 210
   551e: 39 n. 78
   552b–d: 207–8
   552b: 226
   552c: 214 n. 25
   559c–e: 311
   562b: 74 n. 7

De Gen. Soc. 42 n. 85, 43, 141–2
   575b–c: 43, 49 n. 105, 139
   588f: 79 n. 25
De Exil.
   600a: 293 n. 21
   601b: 293 n. 21
Quaest. Conv. 288, 299
   632c–d: 46 n. 99
   642d: 18 n. 14
   673f: 174 n. 58
   697e: 110 n. 31
   724b: 83 n. 38
   732b–c: 248 n. 18
   748a: 42 n. 36
Amat. 79 n. 25, 94, 217 n. 37
   749a: 79 n. 25
   751d–e: 79 n. 25
   754d–e: 158 n. 92
   762e: 226 n. 64
   764a: 79 n. 25
Max. cum Princ. 66, 150 n. 64
   776b: 170 n. 39
   776c: 40 n. 79
   778a–b: 170 n. 39
Ad Princ. Inerud. 2
   780a–b: 109 n. 26
   780b–c: 211 n. 19
   780d: 227
   780f: 116
   799f–780b: 116 n. 56
An Seni 66 n. 50, 156 n. 85
   785c–d: 84 n. 42
   785e: 110 n. 32
   785f–786a: 60 n. 28
   788f: 88 n. 62, 212 n. 22
   791c: 84 n. 42
   792b–c: 60 n. 28
   793d: 84 n. 42
   794a: 84 n. 42
Praec. Ger. 2, 50, 67, 89, **293–8**
   799a–b: 37 n. 73
   800c: 214 n. 25
   801c: 270 n. 102
   802e–803b: 147 n. 54
   803b: 190

   804b–c: 147 n. 54
   804c–806f: 293
   805a: 67
   806e: 203 n. 167
   809b–810a: 89 n. 65
   811c: 1 n. 1
   813d–815d: 294–6
   813d–814c: 67
   814a–c: 288
   814a: 308
   814b: 37 n. 73
   814e–815b: 67
   815a–b: 93 n. 87
   816a–817c: 89 n. 65
   816e: 131 n. 3
   818b: 93 n. 87
   818d–e: 93 n. 87
   819f: 38 n. 77, 60 n. 32, 84 n. 46
   820b–f: 16 n. 9
   823f–825f: 89
   823f–825a: 220
   824b–825d: 296–8
   824c–d: 67
   825d: 93 n. 87
De Herod. Malig. 58
   855b: 149 n. 61
   855c–856d: 59
   857a: 58
De Facie 203
Terrest. an Aquat. **246**
   959c: 292 n. 15
   962d–963a: 246
   964d–e: 56 n. 15
   964e: 166 n. 23
   967d: 33 n. 61
   971a: 175 n. 68
   985c: 246
Brut. Anim. (also known as *Gryllos*) 172
   987b: 208 n. 9
   987c: 172
   989b–f: 109 n. 23
   989c: 106 n. 20
De Esu Carn.
   997b–c: 292 n. 15

Plat. Quaest. 72 n. 1
  1001c–d: 163 n. 8
  1001e: 37 n. 72
  1008c–d: 79 n. 25
  1009b: 79 n. 25

De Procr. An. 2, 72 n. 1, 91
  1023c: 37 n. 72
  1025a–c: 91 n. 74
  1026a–c: 91 n. 74

De Stoic. Repugn. 155 n. 82
  1045a: 158 n. 92
  1047c: 18 n. 14
  1053d: 37 n. 73

Stoicos absurdiora poetis dicere 155 n. 82

Non Posse 66 n. 50, 246 n. 14
  1092e–f: 49 n. 105
  1093b–c: 19
  1093b: 195 n. 142
  1095f: 46 n. 99
  1101d: 23 n. 30, 131 n. 3
  1102d: 23 n. 30
  1104a–b: 131 n. 3

Adv. Col.
  1115e: 163 n. 8
  1123b: 178 n. 76

De Lat. Viv. 66 n. 50
  1129b–c: 35 n. 64, 50 n. 106, 249 n. 21

De Prim. Frig. 2

De Am. Prol. 34 n. 63

De Comm. Not. 155 n. 82

Lost works: in order of their occurrence in the Lamprias Cataloque (s.v.), fr. nos. are those of Sandbach.

Epameinondas–Scipio (Lamp. Cat. 7, frs. 1–2): 4 n. 19, 14 n. 4, 247

Tiberius (Lamp. Cat. 27, frs. 6–8): 20 n. 20

Herakles (Lamp. Cat. 34, frs. 6–8): 2 n. 7, 313

Hesiod (Lamp. Cat. 35): 2 n. 7, 193–4 n. 137

Pindar (Lamp. Cat. 36, fr. 9): 2 n. 7, 193–4 n. 137

Krates (Lamp. Cat. 37, fr. 10): 2 n. 7, 193–4 n. 137

Daïphantos (Lamp. Cat. 38, fr. 11): 2 n. 7

Aristomemes (Lamp. Cat. 39, fr. 12): 2 n. 7

To Chrysippos on Justice (Lamp. Cat. 59): 155 n. 82

Where are the Forms? (Lamp. Cat. 67): 37 n. 72

How has matter participated in the Forms, that it makes the first bodies? (Lamp. Cat. 68) 37 n. 72

On common usage, against the Stoics (Lamp. Cat. 78): 155 n. 82

On anger (Lamp. Cat. 93, fr. 148): 212 n. 21
  fr. 148. 19: 212 n. 21

On the three names, which is most important? (Lamp. Cat. 100): 130 n. 105

How to judge true history (Lamp. Cat. 124): 18 n. 14

Barbarian questions (Lamp. Cat. 139): 299

On days (Lamp. Cat. 150, fr. 142): 187 n. 110

Selections from and refutations of Stoics and Epicureans (Lamp. Cat. 148): 155 n. 82

Causes of current Stoic doctrines (Lamp. Cat. 149): 155 n. 8

To Chrysippos on the first consequent (Lamp. Cat. 152): 155 n. 8

To the Stoics on what lies in our power (Lamp. Cat. 154): 155 n. 8

On the descent into the cave of Trophonios (Lamp. Cat. 181): 193–4 n. 137

Defence of Sokrates (Lamp. Cat. 189):
    141–2
On the condemnation of Sokrates
    (Lamp. Cat. 190): 141–2
On the Festival of Images at Plataia
    (Lamp. Cat. 201, frs. 157–8):
    193–4 n. 137
    fr. 157. 2: 178 n. 76
Other fragments
On Hesiod's Works and Days
    fr. 47: 249 n. 21

PSUEDO-PLUTARCH
De Lib. Educ.
    2f–3b: 74 n. 86
    5b: 110 n. 30
    14a: 32
Reg. et Imp.
    172d: 15 n. 6, 33 n. 56
    186d: 231
    188f: 136 n. 19
    218e: 183
Aquane an ignis 244
Inst. Lac.
    238a–b: 75 n. 11
Consol. ad Apoll.
    119d: 33 n. 59
Vitae dec. orat.
    835a (Andokides): 223 n. 53:
Com. Aristoph. et Men. 244 n. 7
Parallel. Graec. et Rom. 290 n. 8
De Vita et Poesi Homeris
    2. 216 Bernardakis: 42 n. 86
    7. 460 Bernardakis: 42 n. 86

POLEMON OF ATHENS 227

POLEMON OF LAODIKAIA 93
    i, 244 Förster[a]: 166
    i, 246 Förster[a]: 166

POLYAINOS
    1. 45. 3: 186 n. 103
    1. 45. 4: 314 n. 13
    3. 9. 32: 173

POLYBIOS: 290, 304
Histories
    1. 35. 1–10: 53 n. 6
    2. 14. 7: 33 n. 57:
    2. 68. 2: 196 n. 145
    3. 57. 4: 28 n. 47
    4. 8. 3: 173 n. 54
    5. 75. 2: 174
    6. 5. 2: 28 n. 47
    6. 7. 7–8: 95 n. 96
    7. 1. 1: 110 n. 30
    9. 2. 4: 28 n. 47
    9. 2. 5–6: 53
    9. 14. 1–4: 33 n. 57
    9. 25. 2: 33 n. 57
    10. 21. 2–8: 21–2
    10. 21. 4: 36 n. 64
    10. 33. 6: 196 n. 145
    11. 4. 7: 196 n. 145
    12. 3. 1–16. 14: 25 n. 36
    12. 23. 1–28a10: 25 n. 36
    12. 28. 1–28a10: 33 n. 57
    12. 28. 2: 90 n. 68
    15. 36. 3–7: 35 n. 64
Philopoimen 21–2

POLYKRATES
Attack on Sokrates: 223

POSEIDONIOS: 101 n. 1
    fr. 153 E–K (= Galen, *De Plac. Hipp.
    et Plat.* 5. 464 Kühn): 93 n. 84
    fr. 287 E–K (= Diog. Laert. 9. 68):
    106 n. 20

PROKLOS
Comm. on Plato's Timaios
    1. 90. 21–24 Diehl, on 21b–d
    (=Herakleid. Pont. fr. 91 Voss):
    190

PROKOPIOS 299 n. 34

PROPERTIUS
    2. 34. 65–6: 290 n. 12
    3. 1. 1–2: 290 n. 12
    4. 1. 64: 290 n. 12

QUINTILIAN
Inst. Orat.
  2. 4. 21: 244
  2. 4. 24: 244 n. 6
  3. 5. 11: 158 n. 91
  6. 2. 29: 42 n. 84
  8. 2. 11: 16 n. 7
  8. 3. 83: 16 n. 7
  9. 2. 58: 37 n. 74
  10. 1. 31: 47 n. 101
  10. 1. 105–12: 249 n. 20
  10. 1. 46–131: 290 n. 12

RUTILIUS RUFUS
Histories 19 n. 18, 101, 128 n. 100

SALLUST 128 n. 100
Jugurtha 54
  95. 4: 54
Catiline 54, 128 n. 100
  6. 15: 299 n. 34
  15. 5: 214 n. 25
Histories 128 n. 100

SATYROS 224 n. 58
Life(?) of Euripides (*P. Oxy.* IX 1176 and XXVII 2465): 7
  apud Athenaios 534b: 228–9
  apud Athenaios 534e–f: 232

SCHOLIA
On Aristoph. *Wealth* 249: 165 n. 19
On Aristoph. *Thesm.* 773: 170 n. 37
On Aristoph. *Peace* 1189–90: 200 n. 160
On Dionysios Thrax 173. 3–4 Hilgard: 34 n. 62
On Dionysios Thrax 449. 11 Hilgard: 19 n. 16
On Euripides, *Alk.* 1: 165 n. 19
On Lucian, *Gall.* 24 (94. 8–9, Rabe[b]): 125 n. 89

SCRIPTORES HISTORIAE AUGUSTAE
Vita Hadriani
  16. 2: 190
SEG
  37. 320: 174 n. 59

SENECA THE ELDER
Suasoriae 256
Controversiae 244–5

SENECA THE YOUNGER 65, 260 n. 59
De Clem.
  1. 1: 32
De Const. Sap.
  2. 1: 155
  7. 1: 155
De Ira 88
  3. 5. 4: 151 n. 69
De Tranq. An.
  1. 9: 143 n. 46
  17. 4: 143 n. 46
Ep. Moral.
  7. 2–5: 292 n. 15
  11. 8–10: 33 n. 60
  24. 22: 112 n. 42
  24. 26: 112 n. 42
  67. 7: 142 n. 41
  71. 16–17: 142 n. 41
  89. 7: 299 n. 34
  98. 12: 142 n. 41
  104. 27–33: 142 n. 41
NQ
  1. 17. 4: 32 n. 56

SERVIUS
Comm. in Verg. Ecl.
  6. 13: 167 n. 28

SEXTOS EMPEIRIKOS
Adv. Dogm.
  2. 148–158: 16 n. 8
Adv. Eth. (=*Adv. Math.* 33)
  141: 106 n. 20
Adv. Gramm
  253: 18
  263: 19 n. 16

Pyrrh.
2. 99–101: 16 n. 8
SGDI
4. 36. 34–5, p. 690: 174 n. 59
*SIG*³
829A: 1 n. 1

SIMONIDES
fr. 111 Page: 191
apud *Bellone an Pace* 346f and *Quaest. Conv.* 748a: 42 n. 86

SOLON
11. 5–8 West: 175 n. 63

SOPHOKLES
Ant. 69
 36: 144 n. 49
OT 123
 1524–30: 284
Phil.
 442: 190 n. 120
Trach.
 1058: 294
 1278: 284

Fragments
TrGF IV 867: 246
TrGF IV 869: 85

SOPRATOS
Orations 256 n. 51

SOUDA
s.v. Ἕλλην: 304 n. 53
s.v. Ζηνόβιος: 128 n. 10
s.v. πανοῦργος: 174
s.v. Πλούταρχος: 289 n. 7
s.v. Χάραξ: 290 n. 8:

STEPHEN OF BYZANTION
s.v. Ὠκεανός: 115 n. 50

STOBAIOS
Flor.
 21. 11 (i, 317 Meineke): 32
 55. 5 (ii, 332–3 Meineke): 112 n. 41

STRABO
7. 3. 7, C 301: 175 n. 66
13. 1. 27, C 594–5: 249 n. 20

SUETONIUS
De vita Caesarum: 7–8, 20, 21, **94–6**, **98**, 253, 313
Divus Iulius 67
 1. 1: 254 n. 42
 2: 94
 7. 1: 86, 249 n. 20
 7. 2: 80 n. 29
 24. 3–25. 2: 98 n. 106
 31–3: 80
 34. 1–36: 98 n. 106
 45. 1: 79 n. 26
 49. 1–52. 3: 94
 50: 95
 57–70: 98 n. 106
Divus Augustus 253 n. 37
 9. 17. 3: 98 n. 106
 19. 1–2: 98 n. 106
 20–23. 2: 98 n. 106
 21. 1–3: 98 n. 106
 24. 1–25. 4: 98 n. 106
 68–69. 2: 94
 71. 1: 94
Tiberius 253
 16. 1–17. 1: 198 n. 106
 18. 1–19: 198 n. 106
 42. 1: 253 n. 37
 43. 1–45: 94
Caius 253
 22. 1: 253 n. 37
 43–47: 98 n. 106
Divus Claudius
 17. 1–3: 98 n. 106
Nero 60, 125, 253, 292
 18: 98 n. 106
 19. 3: 253 n. 37
 28–9: 96 n. 99
Galba 20, 159–60
 4. 1: 20 n. 20
 12. 1–13: 159
 20. 1: 159

Otho 20
  12. 1: 95 n. 97
Divus Vesp.
  8. 4: 98 n. 106
Divus Titus 253 n. 37
Otho
  12. 1: 95 n. 97

SVF
  1. 246: 112 n. 42
  1. 409: 157 n. 89
  1. 422: 157 n. 89
  2. 158: 157 n. 87
  3. 140 ff: 157 n. 87
  3. 639: 157 n. 88
  3. 728: 158 n. 92
  3. 743–56: 158 n. 92

SYNKELLOS
  659 Dindorf: 289 n. 7

SYRIAN
In Hermog.
  2. 23. 10–11 Rabe[a]: 24 n. 62

TACITUS 19, 95–6, 159–60, 161 n. 4, 292
Ann.
  3. 65: 47, 52 n. 2, 244 n. 6
  4. 1–2: 285
  4. 20: 158 n. 94
  4. 32–3: 26–7
  5. 31: 192 n. 129
  6. 10. 3: 158 n. 94
  6. 20: 20 n. 20
  6. 27. 4: 158 n. 94
  6. 48. 2: 285
  6. 51. 1–3: 284–5
  13. 30. 2: 95 n. 97
  15. 37. 4: 96 n. 99
  15. 64: 142 n. 41
  16. 22: 142 n. 41
  16. 23. 1: 296 n. 28
  16. 34–5: 142 n. 41
Hist.
  1. 2: 26
  1. 3: 52 n. 2
  1. 18: 159
  1. 20: 159
  1. 41: 159
  1. 50. 4: 285
  3. 51: 52 n. 2
Agric. 244 n. 6
  2. 1: 142 n. 41
  10–17: 21 n. 22
  42. 4: 158 n. 94
  46. 3: 16 n. 9

TELES
On self-sufficiency 104
  6. 13–15 Hense: 104
  7. 7–8 Hense: 104
  12–13 Hense: 105 n. 18
  32. 5 ff Hense: 113 n. 44
  43 Hense: 105 n. 18

THALES
  fr. A. 1. 33 Diels–Kranz: 108 n. 22

THEOKRITOS
Idylls
  10. 8: 115 n. 49

THEON
Progym.
  1, Spengel, ii, 59, 21–2: 163 n. 9
  9, Spengel ii, 112–15: 244 n. 5
  9, Spengel, ii, 112. 27–9: 260

THEOPHRASTOS
Characters 69
  17: 103–4
On Style
  139 Mayer: 16 n. 7
  fr. 136 Wimmer: 132

THEOPOMPOS COM.
  fr. 33. 3 Kassel–Austin: 32 n. 56
  fr. 66 Kassel–Austin: 193

THEOPOMPOS 40 n. 80, 193 n. 133, 194 n. 137, 201 n. 161, 223, 228 n. 71
  FGrH 115 T 20a: 24, 27, 28 n. 47, 57–8
  FGrH 115 F 20: 178 n. 74

FGrH 115 F 24: 25 n. 36
FGrH 115 F 74–75: 167 n. 28
FGrH 115 F 192: 176 n. 71, 183 n. 96

THRASEA PAETUS 142, 158

THUCYDIDES 22–6, 52, 53 n. 4, 56 n.
  16, 57, 69 n. 58, 110–11, 115, 222,
  228 n. 71, 244 n. 6
  1. 1. 1–3: 26, 186
  1. 1. 3: 41 n. 83
  1. 20–21: 25 n. 36
  1. 20. 3: 164 n. 15
  1. 21. 1: 41 n. 83
  1. 22. 1: 26, 28 n. 46
  1. 22. 2–3: 41 n. 83
  1. 22. 4: 18, 41 n. 83, 53
  1. 23. 1–3: 186–7
  1. 42. 2–4: 111 n. 36
  1. 77. 6: 304 n. 53
  1. 78. 1–84. 2: 111
  1. 95. 3: 176
  1. 120. 3–4: 111 n. 36
  1. 138. 2–3: 186
  2. 4. 7: 69 n. 58
  2. 35: 21 n. 26
  2. 39. 1: 172 n. 49
  2. 63. 2: 115 n. 53
  2. 65. 6–9: 90 n. 71
  2. 65. 10: 180 n. 84
  3. 36. 6: 180 n. 84
  3. 37. 2: 115 n. 53
  3. 39. 3–4: 111
  3. 45. 1–7: 111
  3. 45. 5–6: 111 n. 37
  3. 82: 69 n. 58, 174 n. 57
  3. 86: 186 n. 104
  4. 17–65: 111 n. 38
  4. 27–8: 180
  4. 28. 2: 180 n. 83
  4. 28. 5: 180 n. 84
  4. 54–7: 273 n. 110
  4. 108. 7: 165
  4. 129–30: 273 n. 110
  5. 4–5: 223 n. 53
  5. 9. 5: 174 n. 60
  5. 43. 2: 225 n. 63
  5. 84–116: 272 n. 109

  5. 116. 4: 235 n. 87
  6. 6–15: 113 n. 44, 115 nn. 49, 51
  6. 13. 1: 112 n. 39
  6. 15. 3–4: 222, 233 n. 81
  6. 15. 4: 234, 239
  6. 16. 1–17. 1: 225 n. 63
  6. 24. 3–4: 115 n. 51
  6. 30. 2: 115 n. 51
  6. 45. 5: 115 n. 51
  6. 53. 3–60. 1: 222
  6. 90. 2: 115 n. 51, 225 n. 63
  7. 85. 1: 275
  7. 87: 186 n. 104
  8. 38. 1: 170 n. 4
  8. 51. 2: 238 n. 96
  8. 54. 3: 238 n. 96
  8. 86. 4: 222

TIBERIUS RHETOR
De Fig.
  14, Spengel iii, 65, 28–9: 16 n. 7

TIBULLUS
  1. 1: 244 n. 6

TIMAIOS: 22, 25 n. 36, 26, 58 n. 24, 228
  n. 71

TIMON
  fr. 63–4 Di Marco (=Sext. Empeir.
  Adv. Math. 11. 141): 106 n. 20

PS.-TRYPHON
  746–7, Spengel iii, 199, 15–20: 16 n.
  7

TrGF II F 363: 236
TrGF II F 408a: 226
TrGF III F 393: 32 n. 56
TrGF IV F 867: 246
TrGF IV F 869: 85
TrGF fr. Adesp. 9 Nauck: 237

VALERIUS MAXIMUS 47, 53, 124
  3. 1. 2–3. 2. ext. 9: 53

VELLEIUS PATERCULUS 244 n. 6, 290
  n. 10
  2. 24. 4: 202 n. 164
  2. 33. 4: 60 n. 28

2. 41. 1–2: 249 n. 20
2. 45. 5: 152 n. 73

VIRGIL
Eclogues
6. 1–2: 290 n. 12
6. 13–26: 167 n. 28

XENOKRATES
fr. 2 Heinze: 216 n. 32

XENOPHON
Agesilaos 249, 276–7, 313 n. 6
1. 1: 21 n. 26
1. 12: 173
1. 17: 173
1. 29: 173 n. 52
6. 5: 173
9. 1–5: 243 n. 3
10. 2: 211 n. 19
Anabasis
1. 2. 13: 167 n. 28
1. 8. 1–29: 29–30
1. 8. 26–27: 29–30
2. 6. 7: 173 n. 51
Hellenika 9 n. 39, 57, 169, 244 n. 6
1. 1. 2–7: 238 n. 97
1. 4. 13–17: 222
1. 5. 2–7: 180
1. 6. 3: 180 n. 83
1. 6. 7: 169 n. 33
1. 6. 33: 170 n. 40
1. 7. 12: 259 n. 57
1. 7. 35: 137 n. 23
2. 1. 15: 186 n. 103
2. 1. 26: 180 n. 83
2. 1. 28: 186 n. 103
2. 1. 31: 181 n. 89
2. 2. 23: 193
2. 3. 2: 186 n. 103
2. 3. 7: 186 n. 103
2. 3. 56: 26 n. 39
3. 1. 8: 172 n. 50
3. 4. 11–12: 173 n. 52

4. 8. 1: 26 n. 39
5. 1. 4: 27 n. 44
5. 2. 32: 181, 181 n. 87
5. 4. 1: 53 n. 6
5. 4. 32: 181, 181 n. 87
5. 4. 48: 173 n. 52
7. 2. 1: 26 n. 39
7. 5. 21: 26 n. 39
Hieron 113 n. 44
Hipparch.
4. 7–5. 15: 171
Kyneg.
13. 9: 216 n. 30
Kyropaidia 19, 285–6
1. 6. 1–2. 1. 1: 171–2
1. 6. 11: 208 n. 8
1. 6. 27–40: 171 n. 43
8. 8: 285–6
Lak. Pol.
4. 1–6: 83 n. 98
Memorabilia 223
1. 1–2: 223 n. 55
1. 2. 1: 143 n. 45
1. 2. 12: 223
1. 3. 5–13: 143 n. 45
1. 6. 2: 38 n. 76, 143 n. 45
3. 10. 1–8: 17 n. 11
4. 1. 4: 48 n. 103
4. 2. 15–17: 171 n. 43
5. 1–5: 211 n. 19
Oik.
12. 9–14: 211 n. 19
21. 10: 90 n. 72
Symposium
1. 1: 15 n. 6

ZENO
SVF i, 246: 112 n. 42

ZONARAS
Epitome of Histories 3
4. 14: 254–5

Index of Greek Words

ἄγαλμα 168, 170
ἄγαν 209, 220–1
ἀγωγή 21
ἀγωγός 34, 40, 148 n.
ἀγών 15–16, 138, 145–6, 209
ἀγωνίζεσθαι 152
ἀδικεῖν 146, 274
ἄθεος 245
αἷμα 194–7, 202
αἴσθησις 34, 45, 107, 149 n.
αἰσχρός 46, 158, 164, 182, 296 n.
αἴτιος 185
ἄκαμπτος 157
ἀκμή 22, 139 n., 189 n.
ἀκολασία 283
ἀκόλαστος 200
ἀκρασία 92 n., 178 n., 195 n., 279–80
ἄκρατος, esp. 91–2; also 48, 160, 166, 193 n., 208–10
ἀκρίβεια 129, 132
ἀκριβῶς 28 n.
ἀκύμων 105–6
ἀλογιστία 106
ἄλογον, τὸ 75
ἄλογος 73–4, 105, 172 n.
ἅλυς 112
ἀλωπεκῆ 171
Ἀλώπεκον 176
ἁμαρτάνειν and compounds of 204
ἁμάρτημα 234, 267
ἁμαρτία 59, 142
ἄμεμπτος 269–70, 282
ἀμεμφής 59
ἀμίμητος 277
ἀμνήμων 108
ἀνάγκη 59, 131 n.
ἀνάγκη πολιτική 59
ἀναλογίζεσθαι 80

ἀναλογισμός 117
ἀνδρεία and ἀνδρία, esp. 209–13; also 83 n., 87, 91, 170, 203, 221, 237
ἀνδριάς 162, 166, 170 n.
ἄνεσις 195
ἀνήκεστος 196
ἀνθεῖν 140
ἀνόητος 106–8, 118
ἀνομοιότης 229, 247
ἀνομολογία 270
ἀντίταγμα, ἀντιτάττεσθαι 60 n.
ἀντίχειρ 181 n.
ἀνυπεύθυνος 152
ἀνυπόδητος 143
ἄνω 295–6
ἀνωμαλία 60 n., 220, 230–1, 235, 270
ἀνώμαλος 167
ἀξιόλογος 26–7, 34
ἄξιος ἀκοῆς 23
ἄξιος γέλωτος 295
ἄξιος ἐπιλήψεως 271
ἄξιος λόγου 28–9
ἄξιος μνήμης 26 n., 34, 257–8
ἄξιος σπουδῆς 34–5, 297
ἄξιος τῆς Λακεδαίμονος 170
ἄξιος τιμῆς 137
ἀξίωμα 119, 129, 152, 226
ἀοργησία 87–9
ἀπάθεια 72, 74, 76, 156–7, 209
ἀπαθής 156
ἀπαίδευτος 304 n.
ἀπάτη 171–4, 233
ἀπληστία 106, 110 n.
ἁπλοῦς 168, 171–3, 210–11
⟨ἀπο⟩καλύπτεσθαι 25
ἀπομιμεῖσθαι 175
ἀπόντα, τὰ, 105–7, 114–15
ἀργεῖν 207–8

ἀρετή, esp. 13–14; also 15, 24, 31, 34–5,
    43, 47–8, 50 n., 51 n., 59, 84, 91,
    98, 118, 137, 140, 148, 149 n., 152,
    168, 184, 198, 208, 210–11, 216,
    226, 245, 247, 263, 300 n., 310
    see also πολιτικὴ ἀρετή, ἠθικὴ
    ἀρετή
ἀριθμός, ἀριθμητός 194
ἀριστοκρατικός 90, 119, 310
ἀρκεῖν 104 n., 121
ἁρμονία 92–3
ἀρχαιοτροπία 140, 160
ἄρχειν 191, 210–11, 294
ἀρχή 25 n., 40
ἀσθένεια 210, 212–13
ἀσθενής 48, 79, 137
ἄσκησις 157
ἀσύγκριτος 253 n.
ἀσύμμετρος 140, 195
ἀσφάλεια 251
ἀτενής 157, 210–11
ἄτοπος 158 n.
ἀτρεμεῖν 112, 178 n.
ἄτρεπτος 149–50, 156, 157 n., 209–10,
    214 n., 215
αὐθάδεια 154, 210–11
αὐλή 105, 296 n.
αὔξησις 88, 265 n.
αὐστηρός 141, 145
αὐτομάτως 88 n.
αὐτονομία 192 n.
ἀφανίζεσθαι 170 n.
ἄφετος 192
ἀφίεσθαι 192
ἄφυκτος 123, 128, 130
ἄχρηστος 27 n.

βάδην 143 n., 215
βαρβαρικός 305
βάρβαρος 90, 296, 304
βασιλικός 90
βάσκανος 57
βέβαιος 128, 156
βέλτιστοι, οἱ 120
βῆμα 294 n.
βία 90, 233
βιβλίον 14, 47, 255 n.

βίος 2, 13–15, 17–22, 30, 33, 46–7, 66,
    105, 118, 247
βουλή 220 n., 303

γαληνισμός, γαληνός, ἐγγαληνίζειν
    106 n.
γέλως 295
γενναῖος 134, 171–3, 206, 208
γεύειν, γεῦμα 193, 287
γῆρας 109–10, 120
γλαυκός 166
γράμματα 109

δαιμόνιον 188
δαίμων 53 n., 196, 255, 307
δαμασίμβροτος 191
δέ 142, 254–5 n.
δεινότης 173, 178–9, 186
δεισιδαίμων 245
δημαγωγός 228, 235 n., 303, 307
δημιουργός 35, 306 n.
δῆμος 118–19, 154, 192 n., 210, 220 n.,
    296, 303
δημόσιος φόνος 144 n.
διάθεσις 22, 57
δίαιτα 263 n.
διακριβοῦν 187
διαποικίλλειν 175
διαφεύγειν 23
διάφορος 166–7
διήγησις 259 n.
δίκαιος 46, 129, 132–3, 141, 147 n., 152,
    168, 173, 247, 305 n.
δικαιοσύνη 46, 146, 157 n., 170, 209,
    247, 269
δοκιμάζειν 270
δόλος 171–3, 233
δόξα, esp. 238, 306; also 78, 86–7, 105,
    110 n., 118, 120, 137, 148, 158 n.,
    235, 297
    see also κενὴ δόξα
δοξομανία 83
δοῦλος 226 n.
δρᾶμα 126
δυναστεία 111
δυσδιαίτητος 261
δυσθεώρητος 269

δυσμίμητος 152
Δώριος 168

ἐγγαληνίζειν, see γαληνισμός
ἐγκεκραμένος 140, 210–11
ἐγκράτεια 92 n., 96, 203, 209, 264, 283
ἐγκώμιον 22
ἐγχαλινοῦν 192 n.
ἔθος 39, 73–4, 244 n., 247
εἰδοποιεῖν 15, 17
εἴδωλον 31, 84 n., 168
εἰκάζειν 167
εἰκονίζειν 163 n.
εἰκονικός 163
εἰκών 16, 163–4, 167, 170 n.
ἐκβαρβαροῦν, 185
ἐκκαλύπτειν 24
ἐκνευρίζειν 75 n.
ἐκπίπτειν 294
ἔκπτωσις 294
ἐλευθερία 192 n., 193, 202, 296–7, 307
ἐλλείμματα ἀρετῆς 59–60, 271
Ἕλλην 296, 304 n.
ἑλληνίζειν 289 n.
ἑλληνικός 270, 287, 297, 305, 308
ἐλπίς 103, 106, 108–9, 111, 113–15, 117–18, 224–5
ἐμμελής 92–3, 139–40
ἐμμένειν 128, 215, 275
ἐμπαθής 29, 147, 209, 213–14
ἔμφασις 16, 57 n.
ἐμφύλιος 89 n., 196
ἐναγισμός 127
ἐνάργεια 29, 41
ἐναργῶς 107
ἐνδεής 206
ἐνέδρα 171 n.
ἐνεργάζεσθαι 148
ἐνεργός 31, 88
ἐνθουσιασμός 152
ἐξανθεῖν, 166 n.
ἐξαπατᾶν 175
ἐξετασμός 24
ἕξις 74, 89
ἐξοκέλλειν 109–10, 123 n.
ἐξουσία 25 n., 46
ἐξυβρίζειν 192 n.

ἐπαινεῖν 46, 51–2, 134 n., 269 n.
ἐπαινετέος 282
ἔπαινος 81, 118–19
ἐπαίρειν 111, 113 n., 114, 117–18
ἐπανόρθωσις 31, 46
ἐπιείκεια 277
ἐπιεικής 93, 114, 139, 219, 232, 270
ἐπιθεῖναι τελευτήν 109
ἐπιθυμητικόν, τό 73
ἐπίληψις 271 n.
ἐπιφανής 46
ἐραστής 143, 210–11, 217 n.
ἔργον 29, 36, 39, 41, 266 n.
ἔρως 78, 86, 111, 114–15, 121, 217, 227, 237, 306
ἔρως βασιλείας 86
ἔρως δόξης 86
ἔρως τῶν ἀπόντων 114–15
ἐρωτικός 47
ἔσοπτρον 30, 32
εὐδαιμονία 103
εὐήνιος 88
εὐθυμία 105, 296 n.
εὐτυχεῖν, εὐτυχία 111 n., 114, 120, 138, 279, 310
εὐφυής 48, 207
εὐφυΐα 49 n., 88, 216, 226
εὐχέρεια 175, 195
ἐφίεσθαι 106, 114, 115 n.

ζῆλος 31, 34, 38, 50 n., 51, 75, 86, 148, 163
ζηλοῦν 32
ζηλωτής 51
ζωγραφία 42
ζωγράφοι 15

Ἠθικά, τά, 1
ἠθικὴ ἀρετή 13–14, 72, 74
ἠθοποιεῖν 39
ἠθοποιΐα 37
ἦθος, esp. 13–14, 39, 73–4; also 16, 17 n., 44, 54, 90–1, 119 n., 128, 135, 140, 156 n., 163–4, 173, 207–8, 229–30, 235–6, 312
ἡλικία 208 n., 223 n.
ἡρωικός 168

ἡσυχία 112, 120, 297

θαῦμα 149 n.
θαυμάζειν 32, 35, 51, 140, 148, 168, 209, 305
θαυμαστής 143
θεατής 38, 41, 43, 47
θεατρικῶς 180
θεῖος 186
θεραπεία 75, 89, 118–19, 170, 206
θεραπεύειν 88, 178 n.
θεραπευτικός 177
θεωρητικὸς βίος 66
θρασύνεσθαι 192 n.
θρασύς 145, 192
θρασύτης 149 n., 192 n.
θυμοειδές, τό 73, 76, 83, 85, 88, 92
θυμοειδής 93, 210–11, 304
θυμός, esp. 73, 87–89; also 75, 80, 82, 85, 109–10, 126–7, 145, 208–14, 237 n., 266, 277

ἰᾶσθαι 196
ἱστορεῖν 18 n., 23 n., 34, 127, 177
ἱστορία 13–14, 17–23, 33–4, 37, 41–2, 50 n., 290 n., 313
see also πραγματικὴ ἱστορία
ἱστορικόν, τό 17–22
ἱστορικός, ὁ 23 n.

κάθαρσις 44
καθεστώς 140, 207–8, 214
καθηγεμών 293 n.
καινὰ πράγματα, see πράγματα καινά
καιροί 140, 295, 307–8
κακία 15, 24, 46–7, 59–61, 210, 270–1
κακοήθεια 58–9, 259
καλός 164
καλόν, τό 37, 118, 133, 151·
καλύπτεσθαι 25
καρπός 140, 208, 226
καταμεμειγμένος 166
κατανόησις ἤθους 24
καταπραΰνειν 144 n.
κατειργασμένος 88
κεκολασμένος 201
κεκραμένος 91, 310

κενόδοξος 212
κενός 107–8, 180, 225
κενὴ δόξα 118
κενότης 116 n.
κεραννύναι 156 n.
κηλίς 175
κλέπτειν 171 n.
κολακεία 226
κολακεύειν 169 n.
κόλαξ 227–8, 235
κοσμεῖν 312
κρᾶσις 91, 93, 139–40, 247, 297
κρατεῖν ἑαυτοῦ 210–11
κρατοῦντες, οἱ 296–7
Κρητικός 173
κρίσις 40 n., 46, 81, 213, 261
κυβερνήτης 307

Λακωνικός 172 n., 175, 201
λέγεται, λέγουσι 186 n.
λιμήν 110
λογισμός, esp. 78–82; also 30, 75, 88, 114, 152, 195 n., 213–15, 239, 294
λόγος 45, 73–5, 81, 85, 88, 90, 105–6, 108–9, 172 n., 208–11, 216, 219, 305
λόγος ἀντεξεταστικός 244
λόγος ἐπιβατήριος 185

μακεδονίζειν 134 n.
μαλακία 210
μαλακός 88, 212, 237
μαλακότης 208
μανία 104, 152
see also δοξομανία
μαρτυρεῖν 48, 206–7, 278
μεγάλαι φύσεις 47, 177, 206–8, 226
μεγάλα πράγματα 46, 103, 111, 114
μεγαλαυχία 83
μεγαλοψυχία 179 n.
μέγεθος 16–17
μειρακιώδης 196, 200
μελαγχολία 176–9, 197
μελαγχολικός 177–9
μεμιγμένος 141
μεμορμένον, τό 124
μεμψιμοιρία 103–4, 123 n., 304
μέν 142

μεσότης 73-4, 87
μεταβολή 188-9, 229, 236
μετακόσμησις 189
μετάπτωσις 188
μετέωρος 188
μετριοπάθεια 72 n.
μέτριος 58 n., 209-11, 214, 221
μετριότης 147, 153
μέτρον 294
μηχανή 171 n., 172
μικρολογία 159
μιμεῖσθαι 42, 50-1, 68, 148
μίμησις 37-44, 50-1, 236 n.
  see also δυσμίμητος
μισοπονηρία 158
μισορρώμαιος 280 n.
Μοῦσαι 109
μῦθος 17-19, 163 n.
μυθώδης 17-19

ναυτιώδης 112
νεανικῶς 85
νεῖκος 83 n., 84, 214 n.
νεμεσητός 124 n., 127
νέμεσις 53 n., 124, 127
νεῦρον 213, 266
νεωτερισμός 298
Νίκαι 167 n.
νίκη 83 n.
νομή 191-2
νόμος 75
νομός 191
νόσημα 194-7
νοῦς 34

ὄγκος 118-19, 129, 190-1
οἴδημα 210-12
οἰκεῖος 45, 68, 81, 112, 156 n., 208, 226, 247, 298
οἶκοι 296
ὀλέθριος 188, 196
ὁμοιότης 15, 47, 247, 290 n.
ὁμόνοια 111 n., 220, 296-7, 310
ὀξύς 166
ὀξύτης 145, 207, 240
ὀργή 79, 82, 87-9, 114, 151, 205, 213-14, 219, 268, 304

ὀργιλότης 87
ὀρέγεσθαι 111 n., 113, 118-19
ὁρίζειν 112, 171
ὅριον 295
ὁρμή 35, 38-40, 145, 157 n., 208-9, 213
ὅρμος 110
ὅρος 74, 112 n., 115, 120
οὐκ ... ἀλλά 38
οὐκέτι 173 n.

παθεῖν, see πάσχειν
παθητικός 73, 105
πάθος, esp. 24-5, 72-5, 79; also 22,
   28-9, 81, 84 n., 86, 90, 97, 151,
   212, 215, 219, 229, 236, 306
παιδαγωγία 48, 74-5
παιδεία, esp. 75-7; also 62, 65, 90-1,
   108-9, 177, 185 n., 205-6, 209-11,
   264, 305
παιδιά 14, 234
πανουργία 172
πανοῦργος 172-5
παραβάλλειν 171, 253 n., 269-70
παράδειγμα 31, 32, 46, 50-2, 68, 90 n.,
   284, 298
παράλληλοι βίοι 33 n.
παρελθεῖν 22, 28-9, 259
παρόν, τό, παρόντα, τά, 104-8, 111 n.,
   112-14, 117, 120
πάσχειν 29, 48, 108, 127, 140, 210, 213,
   219, 259 n., 295
περιττός 159, 179
πικρία 130, 210-11
πικρός 166, 193, 219
πίστις 23 n., 137
πλάσμα 17-19, 236
πλάστης 167
πλάττειν 73, 167 n., 168, 312
πλεῖστοι, οἱ 191
πλέον, τό 111 n., 115 n.
πλεονεξία, esp. 104; also 90, 93, 103-5,
   109-12, 116, 120, 304
πλήρης 108-9
ποθεῖν 168
ποικιλομήτης 175
ποικίλος 175
πολιτεία 19, 90, 92, 109, 119, 134 n.,

140, 271 n., 272 n., 282, 287,
  293 n., 295, 296 n., 310
πολίτευμα 259, 269–270, 308 n.
πολιτικός 46, 158 n., 270
  πολιτικὴ ἀρετή 210, 305
  πολιτικὴ δεινότης 178–9
  πολιτικὴ τέχνη 296
  see also ἀνάγκη πολιτική
πολλοί, οἱ 23
πολύτροπος 172 n.
ποτικός 47, 93
ποτόν 193
πράγματα καινά 103, 112, 117, 120
πραγματεία 19
πραγματικὴ ἱστορία 19 n., 28–9
πρακτικός 35, 40
  πρακτικὸς βίος 66
πράξεις 14–15, 18–19, 21, 23–5, 28 n.,
  31, 35, 81, 88, 109, 114–15, 121, 247
πρᾶξις 45
πρᾷος 88, 146, 151, 156 n., 210–11
πραότης (and πραότης), esp. 77–8;
  also 87–8, 114, 210–11, 213–14, 304
πρέπειν 57, 109, 312
πρεσβευτής 183
προαίρεσις 37–40, 138
προαιρετικός 40
πρόβλημα 158 n., 300
προβληματώδης 158
πρόθυμος 146
προτρέπειν 68
πρυτανεῖον 60 n.
πρωτεῖον 203, 286 n.
πρῶτος 86, 114, 121, 127, 224, 258 n.,
  262 n.

ῥεῖν, 225–6
ῥεῦμα 194–7, 208, 215
ῥοπή 270 n.
ῥυθμός 139–40, 294
ῥύσις 195

σεμνός 93, 139
σημεῖον 16, 163–4
σίδηρον 131 n.
σιτίον 197 n.
σιτλίον 197 n.

σκηνή 125
σκοπεῖν 41
σκυτάλη 164 n.
σοφία 173, 312
σοφιστής 174
σοφιστικῶς 174 n.
στασιάζειν 296
στάσις 93, 111 n., 196
στέγειν 108 n.
στέφανος 286 n.
στρατηγεῖν 180
στρατηγία 109, 203, 269
στρατήγιον 294
στρατηγός 175, 294 n.
συγκρίνειν 253 n.
σύγκρισις 243, 252–3 n.
συζυγία 46
συμμετρία 74
συμφέρει 132
συμφέρον, τό 129 n., 131–3, 180–1, 204
συνεστηκώς 214
συνυποκρίνεσθαι 126
σχολή 112, 118
σῶμα 82, 306 n.
σωτηρία 181, 310
σωφροσύνη 46, 77–8, 147, 203, 259,
  264
σώφρων 178 n., 201, 297
  σώφρονες, οἱ 23 n.

ταμιεῖον 106, 108 n.
ταράττειν 115
τέρψις 35 n., 52
τέχνη 36, 42–3, 45–6, 171 n., 185, 247,
  296
τις 190 n.
τραγικός 124–5
τραγῳδία 125 n.
τράξ 124, 167
τραχύς 166–7
τρόπος 22, 24, 54, 154, 168, 236
τυραννικός 259 n., 271
τυραννίς 115 n., 196, 303
τύραννος 82, 175, 292 n., 303
τύχη, esp. 123, 137–8; also 35, 47, 85,
  108, 111–12, 114, 121, 124, 229–30,
  245, 263, 297, 300 n., 307, 310

ὕβρις 53 n., 63, 111, 112 n., 116, 124, 167, 192 n., 223, 232, 233 n., 240
ὕβρισμα 237
ὑβριστής 47, 279
ὑβριστικός 175, 232
ὑγρός 118–19
ὑπέκκαυμα 84, 86
ὑπεκρεῖν 107–8
ὑπελθεῖν 153–4
ὑπεραγαπᾶν 157
ὑπερβολή 152

φαντασία 39
φασί 186 n.
φάτνη 191
φθεῖρες 197
φθόνος 221, 272 n.
φιλανθρωπία, esp. 77–8; also 56, 59, 271, 305, 310
φιλάνθρωπος 46, 141, 145, 147 n., 151, 154, 219, 232, 234
φιλαρχία 109–10, 121
φιλαυτία 106
φιλοβάρβαρος 58
φιλοδοξία 83–4, 118–20, 216
φιλονεικία, esp. 83; also 56 n., 97, 110 n., 111 n., 116 n., 134, 214, 267, 268, 308
φιλόνεικος 84
φιλονικία, esp. 83; also 85–6, 110 n., 111 n., 177–80, 208–10, 214 n., 268, 277
φιλόνικος 177, 210–11, 215, 229
φιλόπρωτος 83, 215, 229
φιλοσοφεῖν 77 n.
φιλοσοφία 50 n., 81, 91, 216, 217 n.
φιλόσοφος 90 n., 147
φιλόστοργος 147 n.
φιλοτιμία, esp. 83, 86; also 75, 80, 110 n., 120, 155, 167, 177–80, 194, 196, 205, 216, 234, 240, 267
φιλότιμος 43, 84, 86, 177, 240
φοβερός 126, 147, 163, 166

φονεύειν 128
φόνος 127, 194
φρονεῖν 86, 294, 297
φρόνημα 117, 190–1, 210–11, 225, 294
φρόνιμος 106, 304 n.
  φρόνιμοι, οἱ 153
φυσικὸς λόγος 188
φύσις, esp. 74, 229–30; also 48–9, 62, 74, 118–19, 156 n., 158 n., 177, 206, 208–9, 224–5, 235–6, 247
  see also μεγάλαι φύσεις

χαρακτήρ 140, 247
χάρις, esp. 140, 228; also 58 n., 92, 118–19, 129–30, 137, 147, 148 n., 154, 157 n., 180, 226, 228, 233, 305, 310
Χάριτες 109
χειμών 123
χείρ 181 n.
χειροήθης 75 n., 88
χλαμύς, χλαμύδιον 125–6, 294
χολή 178 n.
χρεία 169 n., 171, 177
χρειῶδες, τό 168
χρήσιμος 34, 36
χωρεῖν δι' αἵματος 196

ψέγειν 47, 52, 206, 269 n.
ψεκτός 280
ψεύδεσθαι, ψευδής, ψεῦδος 171–4
ψῆφος 286 n.
ψόγος 81, 119, 137
ψοφοδεής 271 n.
ψυχή 15–16, 24, 40, 44, 48, 78, 90, 105, 163–4, 210–13, 266, 306 n.

Ὠκεανός 115 n.
ὦμός 109–10, 287
ὠμότης 130, 212
ὠφέλεια 35 n., 52
ὠφέλιμος 40 n., 46

Index nominum

Note: Names both of ancient authors, and of the subjects of Plutarch's *Lives* and of other eponymous texts, are not generally here included. References to these figures can be traced through the index locorum. Names of modern authors can likewise be traced through the index of authors.

Abydos, battle of 238
Academy 143
Acciaivoli, Donato 4 n.
Achaian League 68, 89 n.
Achilles 112, 121–2, 124, 127 n., 172 n., 179 n., 236–7, 244, 248, 260, 310
Adeimantos 48
Aegeus 258
Aemilius = Aemilius Paullus, L. (cos. 182 BC):
  in *De Tranq. An.* 50
  see also index locorum
Aemilius Paullus, L. (cos. 219, 216 BC) 82, 310
Africa 4, 121, 127, 154, 176, 197, 225, 289
Agamemnon 176 n.
Agatharchos (painter) 234
Agesilaos = Agesilaos II of Sparta:
  and Lysander 176, 186 n., 194
  as a proto-Alexander 96 n., 277
  in *Mul. Virt.* 248
  in *Prof. in Virt.* 32
  in *De Ipsum Laud.* 50
  prone to φιλοτιμία 84
  see also index locorum
Agis II of Sparta 236–7, 240
Agis = Agis IV of Sparta, esp. 106
  in *De Tranq. An.* 50
  see also index locorum
Agis/Kleomenes and the Gracchi, early *synkriseis* of 249 n.
Aigina 273–4
Aigospotamoi, battle of 180 n., 181, 186–7, 199, 238 n.

Aischylos:
  in Eur. *Frogs* 56 n., 244 n.
  see also index locorum
Ajax 172 n., 244, 248
  and *melancholia* 179
Akanthians, treasury of 163
Akropolis
  Demetrios on 279
  Periklean buildings on 265
Aktion, battle of 252
Aldine edition 30n., 109
Alexander = Alexander III ('the Great') of Macedon, esp. 65, 76, 85–6, 144 n., 189, 245, 251; *see also* index locorum
  and Phokion 135, 146
  compared with Crassus 273
  compared with Sokrates and Plato 245
  Greek history ends with 290
  in Curtius Rufus 284–5
  in *De Ipsum Laud.* 50
  in *De Tranq. An.* 50
Alexander and Caesar:
  compared in Appian 254 n.
  early *synkriseis* of 249 n.
Alexander of Pherai 82, 84
Alexander V of Macedon 280
Alexandria (in Egypt) 1
Alkestis 248
Alkibiades, chapter 7 *passim*
  assimilated to Achilles 236–7
  and Lysander 185
  and Nikias 259, 271 n.
  and Sokrates 143

Alkibiades, (*cont.*):
  deception of Spartan ambassadors 233, 282
  in earlier literature 49, 222–6
  in *De Sera Num.* 207
  tyrannical aspirations of 207, 222, 231, 233, 236, 238–9
  see also index locorum
Alkibiades, son of Alkibiades 222–3
Amisos 203
Ammon 191
Amyot, Jacques 3
Anaxagoras 187–8, 190
Androkleides 175
Annius, P. (murderer of M. Antonius) 130
Antigone, wife of Pyrrhos 122 n.
Antigonos Gonatas 122
Antigonos Monophthalmos 117, 122
Antilochos (poet) 190
Antioch (in Syria) 152
Antiochos III ('the Great') of Syria 67, 301
Antiochos (helmsman of Alkibiades) 233
Antipatros of Macedon 133, 144, 146, 314
Antipatros of Tarsos 106–8, 128
Antipatros of Tyre 157
Antonius Creticus, M. (father of Antony) 311
Antonius, M. (cos. 99 BC) 129–30, 244 n.
Antony = Mark Antony (cos. 44 BC), esp. 96–7
  see also Parthian Campaign; index locorum
Anytos 217, 232
Aphrodite 92
Apollo Thourios 200
Apollodoros of Phaleron 143
Apollonides the Stoic 149 n.
Archedamos (not Archedemos) of Aitolia 268
Archelaos (general of Mithridates) 195–6, 199
Archidamos II of Sparta 111

Archidemos (speaker in *De Gen. Soc.*) 43
Archimedes 306–7
Ares 92, 130 n.
Aretes, corruption of Aristas 183 n.
Arginousai, battle of 137 n., 170
Argos 115, 123–4, 163, 277
Ariadne 227 n.
Aristas 183 n., 186
Aristeides:
  in *Prof. in Virt.* 32
  and Cato Major, early *synkriseis* of 249 n.
  see also index locorum
Aristion (tyrant of Athens) 196–7
Aristoboulos (historian of Alexander) 102 n.
Aristokletos (father of Lysander) 177–8
Aristonous of Korinth (harpist) 190
'Aristos', corruption for Aristas 183 n.
Aristotle, influence on Plutarch, esp. 73, 85
  see also index locorum, index of themes
Aristoxenos 19
Arkadia 173, 228 n.
Armenia 280
Artabanos 113
  mistake for Artavasdes 280 n.
Artavasdes 79, 280
Artaxerxes = Artaxerxes II of Persia, esp. 29, 243
  see also index locorum
Aspasia 97
Athenodoros 148, 157
Athens 106, 131–3, 136, 138, 142, 146–7, 150, 173 n., 181, 186 n., 189, 192–3, 195–7, 202–3, 217, 219, 222, 233, 238, 275, 277–9, 282, 295
  Agesilaos and 277
  Demetrios and 279
  Periklean building programme 67 n., 265
  Plutarch and 9, 67 n., 97–8, 142 n., 192 n., 233, 265 n.
  victories over 188, 192–4, 202–3

Atossa 191
Attike, invasions of 81
Attius Varus, P. 154
Augustus 20 n., 34, 284–5, 290, 296
Aulus Gellius 289
Autoboulos (father of Plutarch) 246
Autolykos 193

Bacon, Francis 4 n.
Bakkhiadai 163
Bellerophon 179
Berenike I of Egypt 122 n.
Biblioteca Universale Rizzoli 10 n.
Black Sea 120
Bocchus I of Mauretania 167
Boiotia 195–6, 199
 Plutarch and 193–4
Boswell, James 4
Boukephalas 85
Brasidas 163, 165
Britain 21 n.
Brutus = M. Iunius Brutus:
 and Caesar 258 n.
 maries Cato Minor's daughter 255
 see also index locorum
Brutus, L. Junius (the tyrannicide) 311
Brutus, M. Iunius (father of Brutus) 196
Byzantion:
 Alkibiades and 234
 Phokion and 146, 148

Caepio (brother of Cato Minor) 147
Caesar = C. Julius Caesar, esp. 94–5, 98, 255
 and Brutus 284
 and Cato Minor 135–7, 149–55, 158
 and Crassus 271, 273
 and Pompey 252, 277
 as demagogue and tyrant 303
 his monarchy as divinely ordained 134, 149
 see also Gallic Wars; index locorum
Calpurnius Piso Frugi Licinianus (adopted son of Galba) 159
Camillus = M. Furius Camillus:
 compared with Galba 160
 in *Non Posse* 50 n.
 see also index locorum
Campus Martius 120
Cannae, battle of 82, 310
Capitol 167
Carthage 114, 124
Caspian Sea 270
Catiline 54, 136, 151, 196
Cato Major = M. Pocius Cato Censorinus:
 in *De Ipsum Laud.* 50
 in *Mul. Virt.* 248
 see also index locorum
Cato Minor = M. Porcius Cato Uticensis, chapter 5 *passim*
 see also index locorum
Cato (son of Cato Minor) 255
Catulus, Q. Lutatius (cos. 102 BC) 127–8
Cavafy 4 n., 125 n.
Chabrias 145
Chaironeia 1, 23 n., 59, 199–200, 261
 battle of (338 BC) 146, 200
 battle of (86 BC) 199
Chaldean 166
Chares 146
Chersonesos, Thracian 310
Cicero = M. Tullius Cicero (cos. 63):
 and Cato Minor 154 n.
 see also index locorum
Cinna, Cornelius L. (cos. 86 BC) 126, 128, 132
Clodius Pulcher, P. (aed. 56 BC) 95, 149 n., 153
Coriolanus = Cn. Marcius Coriolanus, chapter 7 *passim*
 see also index locorum
Corioli 218
Cornelia (mother of the Gracchi) 248
Cornelius Lentulus, Cn. (cos. 201 BC) 82
Cornelius Nepos (biographer), esp. 290–1
 see also index locorum, index of themes

Cornelius Pulcher, Cn. (addressee of *De Cap. ex Inim.*) 296 n.
Cornelius Rufinus, P. (cos. 290, 277 BC, ancestor of Sulla) 198
Cossutianus Capito 142 n.
Crassus = M. Licinius Crassus:
  compared with Caesar, Pompey, and Alexander 273
  dominates Pompey 252
  see alos index locorum; Parthian Disaster
For L. Licinius Crassus, *see* Licinius
Cretan character 173
Cruserius 178 n.
Cures 91
Cyprus 195 n.
  Cato Minor and 152

Daïmachos of Plataia 266
Deidameia (daughter of Lykomedes) 237
Dekeleia 219
Delian League, transfer of treasury 133
Delion, battle of 143, 217
Delos 144, 187 n.
Delphoi 1, 176 n., 194, 288, 292–3, 298
  Akanthian treasury at 162
  Lysander and 162, 165
  Sulla robs 194, 198
Demades 135, 146 n., 251
Demetrios = Demetrios I ('Poliorketes') of Maecdon, esp. 116–18, 125
  see also index locorum
Demetrios of Phaleron 137 n., 149 n.
Demosthenes:
  and Cicero, early *synkriseis* of 244 n., 249 n.
  in *De Ipsum Laud* 50
  see also index locorum
Derkylidas 172–3
Derkylos (not Derkyllos) 146
Diodotos 111
Diogenes 251
Dionysios I of Syracuse 57, 176 n., 182, 184

Dionysos 200
Diophanes 67
Dioskouroi 186–7
Dolabella, Cn. Cornelius (cos. 81 BC) 259
Domitian 2, 296
Dorian 172–3
Douris of Samos 101, 125
Dryden, J. 4
Dyrrachion 188

Egypt
  Agesilaos and Pompey in 181, 278
  Egyptian land compared with Alkibiades 226
Eirene 248
Elektra 236
Eleusis 219
  see also Mysteries
Empedokles 179
Epameinondas 2, 51, 106
  in *Non Posse* 50 n.
  in *Prof. in Virt.* 32
  see also index of themes s.v. Plutarch, lost works
Ephesos 182, 185
Ephoros:
  in Dionysios of Hallikarnassos 57
  see also index locorum
Eros 237
Eteokles 274
Etruscan 189
Eualkos of Sparta 127
Euboia 135, 145–6
Eudoxos 19
Eunous 197 n.
Euphrates, river 255
Euripides, esp. 7, 56 n., 244 n.
  see also index locorum
Eurymedon, battle of 295
Euthydemos 174 n.

Fabricius Luscinus, C. (cos. 282, 278 BC) 50, 106, 129, 160
Favonius, M. (admirer of Cato Minor) 143
Fimbria 202

Flamininus = T. Quinctius
  Flamininus, (cos. 198 BC), esp. 67
  see also index locorum
Fondazione Lorenzo Valla 10 n.
Fonteius Capito, C. (suff. cos. 33 BC) 78
Fundanus (speaker in *De Cohib. Ira*) 88

Galba, esp. 20, 159–60
  see also index locorum
Gallic sack of Rome 54
Gallic Wars of Caesar 21, 67, 98
German Wars of Marius 118, 122–3, 128–9
Graces 109–10
Gryllos 208 n.
Gylippos 184, 201, 275

Hades 24
Hadrian 190, 289 n., 293 n.
Haliartos, battle of 176, 178 n., 199–200
Hamilcar 290 n.
Hannibal 4 n., 81–2, 113–14, 122, 290 n., 306, 308
Hanno 113–14
Harmony (daughter of Ares and Aphrodite) 92
Harpalos 184 n.
Hektor 124, 191
Helen 236
Helots 46
Hephaistion 127 n.
Hera 84 n.
Herakleidai 177–8
Herakles 51, 158 n., 277
  and *melancholia* 177–9
Herodotos, *see* index locorum, index of themes
Hieronymos of Kardia 122 n.
Hipparete (wife of Alkibiades), 233
Hippias 172 n.
Hipponikos (uncle of Alkibiades), 233
Homer:
  Alkibiades and 233
  Plutarch's views of 44

  see also index locorum
Hortensius Hortalus, Q. (cos. 69 BC) 158, 313
Hyperbolos 271

Idomeneus 143 n.
Indian Ocean 270
Iolaos (assistant of Herakles) 158 n.
Ionia:
  Alkibiades and 235–6
  Lysander's arrival in 184
Ipsos, battle of 121
Ismenias (flute player) 46 n.
Ithake 299
Ixion 84 n.

Jugurtha 54, 118
Julii Quadrati 289 n.
Junius, *see* Brutus
Justus of Tiberias 58

Kallikratidas 164, 168–72, 181, 252
Kallirhoe 170 n.
Kallistratos 51
Kambyses of Persia 172
Kappadokia 120
Kassandros 146
Kerameikos 202
Kilikia 106
Killes (general of Ptolemy I) 116
Kineas 112–14, 118, 123
Kissoussa, spring of 200
Klearchos 30, 80
Kleisthenes 310
Kleitarchos 102 n.
Kleitos 314
Kleombrotos (speaker in *De Defect. Orac.*) 50 n., 189
Kleon 111, 149 n., 153 n., 180, 271–2, 303 n.
Kleon of Halikarnassos 174
Kleopatra 61–2, 78, 96–7, 252, 281
Klytaimnestra 236
Koliadai 299
Koraes, Adamantios 10
Korinth 111 n., 163
Korinthian War 304 n.

Koroneia, battle of 251
Kotyrta, in Lakonia 174 n.
Kounaxa, battle of 29
Kratesipolis 125, 279
Kratidas 174
Kritias 223
Kriton 144
Kroisos 113, 312
Kynoskephalai, battle of 268
Kyros I of Persia 243, 285–6
Kyros, brother of Artaxerxes II 30, 82, 171–2, 180, 185, 194
Kythera 272–3
Kyzikos 234

Lakonic 200
Lake Regillus, battle of 218
Lamprias Catalogue 1–2
  see index locorum
Lebadeia 194 n., 199
Leuktra, battle of 131–2, 166 n.
Lex Apuleia 128
Libya, as object of desire 114–15
Licinius Crassus, L. (cos. 95 BC) 244 n.
Licinius Murena, L. (cos. 62 BC) 147
Loeb edition 30 n.
Lucullus = L. Licinius Lucullus (cos. 74 BC), esp. 59–60
  Pompey's rivalry with 85 n.
  see also index locorum
Lydia 294
Lykomedes 237
Lykourgos:
  and Numa, early *synkriseis* of 249 n.
  compared to Solon 131
  in *Alk.* 236
  in *Lys.* 163–4, 166
  in *Prof. in Virt.* 32
  see also index locorum
Lysander, chapter 6 *passim*
  and murder of Alkibiades 239–40
  prone to φιλοτιμία 84
  see also index locorum
Lysimachos 112

Machiavelli 293 n.
Maecenas 292 n.
Makedonia:
  Cato Minor in 148
  Phokion's struggle with 133, 138
  Pyrrhos' wars in 114–15
Mantineia, battle of 233–4
Marathon, battle of 51, 261, 295
Marcellus = M. Claudius Marcellus (cos. 222, 210, 208 BC):
  in *Fabius* 82
  see also index locorum
Marcia, wife of Cato Minor 157–8
Marcius Censorinus (ancestor of Coriolanus) 206
Marius = C. Marius (cos. 107, 104–10, 86 BC), chapter 4 *passim*
  and Sulla 167, 188, 196, 201
  in Sallust 54
  see also German Wars, index locorum
Marius, C. (son of Marius) 127–30
Mars 130 n.
Martha (prophetess of Marius) 126
Media 280
Megara 64, 266, 279
Melian Dialogue 57
Melos 234–5, 272
Mende 273
Menelaos, Harbour of 176 n.
Menemachos 293–5, 298, 308
Messene 268, 277
Mestrius Florus, L. (cos. AD 67/8, patron of Plutarch) 1
Metellus Creticus, Q. Ceacilius (cos. 69 BC) 85 n.
Metellus Nepos, Q. (cos. 57 BC) 149, 152
Metellus Numidicus, Q. Caecilius (cos. 109 BC) 54, 105 n., 119–20, 122 n., 128–9
Metellus Pius, Q. Caecilius (cos. 80 BC) 251
Metellus Pius Scipio, Q. Caecilius (cos. 52 BC) 150 n., 151, 154
Miletos 175, 313
Miltiades the Elder 190 n.

Miltiades the Younger 51
Minoa 272
Minturnae 124, 129
Minucius Rufus, M. (cos. 221) 82
Mithridates VI of Pontos 120, 195–6, 202
Montaigne, Michel de 4 n., 260 n.
Munatius Rufus (friend of Cato Minor) 152
Muses 109–10
Mysteries, Eleusinian 219, 235
Mytileneans 111

'Navarchs Monument' 165 n.
Nemea 235
Neoptolemos (son of Achilles) 237
Neoptolemos of Epeiros (son of Alketas) 111
Nero 157, 160, 281, 292, 296, 311
Nestor 248
Nietzche 4 n.
Nikanor (general of Kassandros) 133, 146
Nikeratos of Herakleia 190
Nikias, esp. 25–6, 56
　as wise advisor 115
　compared with Kallikratidas 180
　Peace of 270
　see also index locorum; Sicilian Expedition
Nikomedes of Bithynia 94
North, Thomas 3
Notion, battle of 185, 233
Numantia 121
Nymphs 168

Octavius, (cos. 87 BC) 129, 132
Odysseus 106 n., 172, 175, 244, 248
Olympias (mother of Alexander the Great) 248
Olympic Games 190 n.
Onesimos (?slave of Plutarch) 247
Orchomenos, battle of (86 BC) 63 n., 195
Ostia 127
Otho, esp. 20, 159
　see also index locorum

Oxford World Classics 10 n.

Panopeus 199
Pantauchos 121
Papirius Carbo, Cn. (cos. 85, 84, 82 BC) 176
Parapotamioi 199
Pardalas 295, 298
Paris 191
Parmenion 314
Parthian campaign of Antony 79, 252
Parthian disaster of Crassus 132, 249–50, 273–5
Patroklos 127 n.
Pausanias (King of Sparta 445–426 and 408–395 BC) 192
Pausanias (Regent of Sparta) 59, 200, 251
Peisistratidai 222, 310
Pellene 68
Peloponnese 115, 124, 173
Peloponnesian War 26, 187, 270
Penguin Classics 10 n.
Pergamon 290 n., 296
Perikles:
　his demagogic period 90
　in *De Ipsum Laud.* 50
　in *Praec. Ger.* 294
　see also index locorum
Peripatos 66
Perseus of Macedon 251–2, 281 n.
Persia:
　Alkibiades and 229, 236
　as barbarian 304
　in *Kyropaidia* 285–6,
　Roman Empire assimilated with 296
Petraios 296
Phaiax 223 n.
Pharax 176 n., 183 n.
Pharnabazos 176, 190, 239–40
Pharsalos, battle of 116 n., 154, 188
Pheidias 265
Philip II of Macedon 59, 85, 117, 133, 135, 146, 251
Philip V of Macedon 59, 68, 301
Philippoi, battle of 144, 255

Philistos:
    in Dionysios of Halikarnassos 57
    see also index locorum
Philokles 181
Philologos (freedman of Cicero)
    176 n.
Phoibidas 181, 277
Phokion, chapter 5 *passim*
    in *De Ipsum Laud.* 50
    in *Prof. in Virt.* 32
    see also index locorum
Phrygia:
    Alkibiades' death in 239
    Sosius Senecio's possible
        connections with 289 n.
Phrynichos (Athenian general) 220
    n., 238
Piso, see Calpurnius
Planoudes, Maximos 3
Plataia 194 n.
    battle of 261, 295
Plato, influence on Plutarch, esp.
    72–4, 76
    and *melancholia* 177, 179
    compared with Alexander 245
    contrasted with Marius 107, 128
    in *Non Posse* 50 n.
    in *Prof. in Virt.* 32
    see also index locorum, index of
        themes
Ploutarchos of Eretria 145
Polydamas 124
Polykrates of Samos 175
Polykrates of Sikyon 68
Pompeius Strabo, Cn. (cos. 89 BC,
    father of Pompey) 259, 311
Pompey = Cn. Pompeius Magnus
    (cos. 70, 55 BC), esp. 81, 252,
    275–8
    and Cato Minor 135, 138, 149, 152–3
    and Lucullus 60 n.
    compared with Crassus 273
    see also index locorum
Pompeius Magnus, Cn. (elder son of
    Pompey) 144 n.
Porcia (daughter of Cato Minor, wife
    of Brutus) 255

Porcius, see Cato
Potidaia 217–18
Praeneste 129
Protagoras 174 n.
Ptolemy I (Soter) 116
Ptolemy (King of Cyprus) 152
Ptolemy (son of Pyrrhos) 127
Pylos 180, 271–3
Pyrrhos of Epeiros, chapter 4 *passim*
    see also index locorum
Pythagoras 73

Quirites 91

Remus 258
Rhadamanthys 200
Rhodes 296
Rome 21, 26–7, 50, 54, 67, 89, 106, 115,
    122, 127–9, 132, 139, 148–9, 152–4,
    188, 196–7, 202, 206, 210, 217–19,
    252, 277, 282, 289–90, 300, 302,
    305–6, 308
    conquest of Greece 134, 269
    Plutarch and 1, 4, 9, 66, 245, 288
    see also general index
Romulus, 'dregs of' 140
Roxane, wife of Alexander 255

Sabines 91, 132
Salamis (in Cyprus):
    battle of 195 n.
    Evagoras' return to 185
Salamis (in Saronic Gulf), battle of
    261
Samos 165, 238
Sardis 293–5, 298
Saturninus, Appuleius, L (trib. pleb.
    103 BC) 120, 128
Satyrs 167–8
Scipio Africanus (the Elder), P.
    Cornelius (cos. 205 BC) ?2, 4 n.,
    160, ?247, 262
Scipio Africanus (the Younger) = P.
    Cornelius Scipio Aemilianus
    Africanus (Numantinus) (cos.
    147 BC) ?2, 51, 118, 121–2, ?247
For Metellus Scipio *see* Metellus

Scribonius Curio, C. (cos. 76 BC) 152
Second Sophistic 10, 263 n.
Seianus 285
Seleukos I 117
Selymbria 218, 234
Septicius Clarus 254 n.
Servilius (praet. 88 BC) 196
Sesostris (legendary king of Egypt) 248
Shakespeare 3–4
Sicilian expedition 25, 111, 115, 273–5
Sicily:
  Alkibiades and 225
  associations with *hubris* 111, 115, 225
  associations with excess 176 n.
  Pyrrhos and 114–15, 122, 132
  Timoleon's conquest of 188
  tyrants of 20
Sidon 117
Silenoi 167–8
Sisyphos 172 n.
Skandeia 273–4
Skyros 237
Social War (91–87 BC) 143
Soklaros 246
Sokrates:
  Alkibiades and 205, 215–20, 223–7, 232, 235
  as a sophist 174 n.
  compared with Alexander 245
  in *Prof. in Virt.* 32
  melancholia and 177, 179,
  Phokion and Cato Minor and 141–5
  Plutarch's interest in 141–2, 248
Solon 113
Sosius Senecio, Q. (cos. AD 99, 107) 2, 66, 288–9
Sparta 46, 77 n., 163–5, 172–6, 179–81, 183–4, 187 n., 191, 200–1, 273, 276–7, 289 n.
  Alkibiades and 235–7
  krypteia 173 n., 312
  Philopoimen and 268
  prone to φιλοτιμία 83–5, 155
  Sosius Senecio's connection with, 289 n.

Spartiates 176 n., 177–8
Sphairos of Borysthenes 155
Sphakteria 153 n.
Sphodrias 277
Stalin 5 n.
Statyllios (or Statilius?) (friend of Cato Minor) 149, 150 n., 157 n.
Stephanus (= Étienne), H. 3
Stesilaos of Keos 97
Stilpo 106
Stoic Paradoxes 144, 155 n. 157
Strachey, Lytton 5
Stratokles 149 n.
Sulla = L. Cornelius Sulla Felix, chapter 6 *passim*
  Pompey and 276
  in Sallust 54
  see also index locorum
Sulla (speaker in *De Cohib. Ira* and *De Facie*) 88–9, 203
Sulpicius Rufus, P. 188, 198
Syracuse 275, 298, 305–7
  sack of 64 n., 77 n.
Syria 78

Tarentum 112
Tarquinius Superbus 218
Taureas 234 n.
Thasos 314 n.
Theban Sacred Band 92
Thebes 85, 92, 181
  Agesilaos and 277
  liberation of 43, 51, 173 n.
Themistokles:
  and Aristeides 132, 262
  and Camillus, early *synkiseis* of 249 n.
  as 'great nature' 62
  compared with Kimon 311
  in *De Ipsum Laud.* 50
  in *Non Posse* 50 n.
  in *Prof. in Virt.* 51
  inspired by Miltiades 51, 84
  see also index locorum
  Thucydides on 186
Theon (speaker in *De Pyth. Orac.*) 292

Theopompos:
  in Dionysios of Halikarnassos 57
  see also index locorum
Theramenes 181, 193
Thermopylai, battle of (191 BC) 98, 261
Thersites 260
Thessaly 296
  Alkibiades and 235–6
Thibron 192 n.
Thirty Tyrants 202, 223, 295
Thourion 200
Thrace 147, 273, 310
  Alkibiades and 228 n., 229, 236
Thrasyboulos 51
Thucydides
  and moralism 69 n.
  in Dionysios of Halikarnassos 57
  see also index locorum, index of themes
Thyrea 273–4
Tiberius 20 n., 284–5
Timaia (wife of Agis II) 236–7
Timandra 240
Timon of Athens 235
Timophanes (tyrant of Korinth) 81

Tissaphernes 173, 237
Titus Latinius 218
Tolmides 251
Trajan 67 n., 289 n.
Trebia, battle of 81
Trojan War 237
Trophonios 194 n.
Tydeus (Athenian general) 181 n.
Tyre 117
Tyrrhenos 298

Utica 137, 149

Vercellae, battle of 127
Vespasian 47 n.
Vitellius 20
Volsci 214, 219, 220 n., 282

Xenokrates 143, 150, 156
Xenophon
  in Dionysios of Halikarnassos 57
  see also index locorum, index of themes
Xerxes 113

Zenobios 128 n.

Index of modern authors

Aalders, G. J. D. 56, 89, 90, 92, 116, 193
Adam, J. 10, 83, 224
Affortunati, M. 4
Africa, T. 197
Aguilar, R. M. 94
Ahl, F. 16
Albini, F. 311
Alcock, S. E. 288
Alessandrì, S. 184
Alfinito, L. 81
Allen, W. S. 83
Alonso-Núñez, J. M. 290
Alsina, A. 315
Ambrosini, R. xiii
Ameling, W. 266
Ampolo, C. 18, 227
Amyot, J. 3–4, 35, 41
Anderson, G. 77, 125
Andrei, O. 62–4, 101–2, 116, 125, 279–80, 290
Andrewes, A. 313
Annas, J. 103
Ash, R. 304
Aulotte, R. 3
Austin, C. 32, 112
Avenarius, G. 52
Averincev, G. 13, 315

Babbitt, F. C. xiii, 290
Babut, D. 1, 8, 39, 72, 75–6, 93, 149, 155–7, 246, 289, 291
Badian, E. 165, 195, 198, 202, 312
Balsdon, J. P. V. D. 198
Bannon, C. J. 266
Barbu, N. I. 312
Barigazzi, A. 247, 291

Barnes, J. 60
Barnish, S. J. B. 289
Barrett, C. K. 9
Barrow, R. H. 4, 155, 291
Barthelmess, J. A. 4–5
Barton, T. S. 93, 96, 253
Beard, M. 300
Bearzot, C. 133, 135–7, 142, 144, 147, 250
Becchi, F. 72, 87–8, 294
Bellemore, J. 152
Benediktson, D. T. 79
Berardi, E. 126, 131, 188
Bergen, K. 74
Bergua Cavero, J. 3
Bernardakis, G. N. 183
Bernini, U. 164, 168
Berry, E. G. 4
Bizos, M. 223
Blanckenhagen, P. H. von 237
Blignières, A. de 3
Bloesch, H. 170
Blomqvist, K. 97, 164
Bommelaer, J.-F. 163, 165, 178, 180, 182, 314
Bons, J. A. E. 90, 185
Borzsák, I. von 42
Bosworth, A. B. 250, 267, 289
Boulogne, J. 93, 253, 257, 262, 299, 300
Bowersock, G. W. 19, 192, 292, 299
Bowie, E. L. 77, 192, 247, 290, 293, 304
Bowra, C. M. 175
Bradford, A. S. 174
Bradley, K. R. 95
Braund, D. 123

Breebaart, A. B. 90, 310
Breitenbach, H. R. 301
Brenk, F. E. xiii, 50, 65, 74, 79–80, 94, 110, 123–4, 137, 161, 188–9, 198, 202–3, 250–1, 281, 311
Brożek, M. 2
Bruce, I. A. F. 201
Brunt, P. A. 52, 174, 222
Bucher-Isler, B. 54, 83, 190, 250, 291
Buckler, J. 8, 23, 193, 195, 312
Bultmann, R. K. 6
Burke, P. 3
Burn, A. R. 223
Burridge, R. A. 6, 17
Burton, R. W. B. 284

Caiazza, A. 293
Cairns, F. 244
Cameron, Alan 190, 299
Cameron, Averil 299
Canfora, L. 222
Carney, T. F. 103, 122, 130, 196, 197
Carr, E. H. 8, 293
Carrière, J.-C. 90
Carsana, C. 92
Cartledge, P. A. ix, 165, 173, 180, 187, 200, 243, 312
Casabona, J. 127
Casertano, G. 266
Cerezo Magán, M. 302
Cerri, G. 17, 40, 42, 44, 52
Chamoux, F. 126
Cherniss, H. xiii, 155
Chitty, S. C. 5
Citti, V. 23
Clark, D. L. 244
Clay, D. 106
Cobet, C. G. 167
Collingwood, R. G. 8
Conquest, R. 5
Corbellini, C. 101, 128
Cornford, F. M. 112
Costanza, S. 103, 253, 255–6
Cournos, J. 5
Criniti, N. 3
Cruserius, H. 178
Culham, P. 306

De Blois, L. 90, 119, 132, 178, 185, 263
Decker, J. de 175
De Lacy, P. xiii, 62, 79, 123, 125, 164, 180
Della Corte, F. 159
Del Re, R. 315
Delvaux, G. 8, 142
Den Boer, W. 30
Denniston, J. D. 38
Denton, J. 3
Deremetz, A. 251
de Romilly, J. 8, 77–8, 111
Desideri, P. 17, 23, 30, 42–3, 50, 139, 184, 188, 248–50, 278, 290, 293
Detienne, M. 175
Devillers, Q. 161
Diano, C. 110, 112
Dibelius, M. 6
Diels, H. 107
Dihle, A. 74, 289, 291
Dillery, J. 90
Dillon, J. 300
Di Marco, M. 106
Dindorf, W. 289
Dionisotti, A. C. 67
Dittmar, H. 217, 223
Dodds, E. R. 93–4, 223
Donini, P. L. 72, 288
Döring, K. 142
Dover, K. J. 174, 183
Duane, S. 315
Ducrey, P. 181
Due, B. 169, 286
Duff, J. N. ix
Dunbar, N. 226
Dunkle, J. R. 95
Durling, R. J. 195
Dušanić, S. 79

Eckstein, A. M. 196
Edelstein, L. 93, 106
Edwards, C. 95
Edwards, M. J. E. 223
Elsner, J. A. S. 293
Erbse, H. 8, 10, 102–3, 223, 250, 255–6, 259
Evans, E. C. 17, 93, 166

Ewbank, L. C. 23

Fairweather, J. A. 183
Fantham, E. 32
Federici, F. 3
Fenik, B. 121
Fernández Delgado, J. A. x
Ferrarese, P. 6
Ferrari, F. 37
Fisher, N. R. E. 95, 111
Flacelière, R. 1–2, 8, 50, 178, 193, 227, 288, 293, 315
Focke, F. 244, 253, 260
Follet, S. 288
Fornara, C. W. 40, 42, 47, 52
Förster, R. 166, 244
Foucault, M. 94, 211
Fowler, A. 53
Fowler, D. P. 186
Fox, M. 9, 57, 174, 176
Fraenkel, E. 104
Franco, C. 24
Fraser, P. M. 174
Frazier, F. 51, 80, 83, 86, 97, 114, 131–2, 135, 153, 180, 192, 240, 249, 251, 313
Frézouls, E. 77, 84
Friedrich, W. H. 138
Frost, F. J. 13
Fuhrmann, F. 6, 79, 93, 192
Furley, W. D. 223
Fuscagni, S. 60, 250

Gabba, E. 254, 291, 302
Galinski, K. 87
Gallo, I. xiii, 7
Gallotta, B. 161
Gamberale, L. 8
Garoufalias, A. P. 113
Garzetti, A. 315
Gehrke, H.-J. 142
Geiger, J. 2, 7–8, 17, 20, 31, 96, 116, 141–2, 147, 157–8, 206, 228, 247, 249–50, 290
Gentili, B. 17, 40, 42, 44, 52
Georgiadou, A. 17, 20, 164, 250–1
Gernet, L. 223
Giachetti, A. F. 3

Gianakaris, C. J. 4
Giangrande, G. xiii
Giannantoni, G. 172, 217, 223, 236, 244
Gill, C. 13, 70, 73–4, 76, 92, 105, 107, 228
Gleason, M. W. 93, 289
Goar, R. J. 155
Goldhill, S. 94, 217
Gomme, A. W. 7–8, 133, 174
González González, M. 4
Goodyear, F. R. D. 21, 244
Gossage, A. J. 4, 67
Gould, J. 36
Gray, V. J. 9, 40, 113, 199
Green, D. C. 3
Green, P. 249
Gribble, D. 223–4, 231
Grossman, G. 172
Grube, G. M. A. 16
Guthrie, W. K. C. 174

Habicht, Chr. 165, 289–90
Halfmann, H. 289
Hamilton, C. D. 194, 267
Hamilton, J. R. 16–17, 250, 314
Hammond, N. G. L. 199
Hanfmann, G. M. A. 298
Hardy, E. G. 8
Harris, A., ix
Harris, B. F. 86, 250, 314
Harrison, G. W. M. 3–4, 250, 315
Harrison, J. E. 127
Hartog, F. 168, 302
Hatzfeld, J. 224
Heinze, R. 105, 216
Helmbold, W. C. xiii, 143, 185, 217
Hense, O. 104–5, 113
Herbert, K. B. J. 14, 172
Hershbell, J. B. 58, 105, 155
Hesk, J. 171–2, 175–6
Hilgard, A. 19, 34
Hillard, T. W. 2, 6
Hillman, T. P. 85, 110, 121, 250, 252, 276
Hirsch, S. W. 286
Hirzel, R. 4, 256

Hobein, H. 104, 244
Holden, H. A. 8, 195, 199
Holford-Strevens, L. 289
Hommeyer, H. 291
Hopkins, K. 23, 289
Hopkinson, N. 23
Hornblower, J. 122
Howard, M. W. 4
Huang, T.-T. ix
Huart, P. 111
Hubbard, M. 122
Humbert, S. 65, 185
Hunter, R. L. ix, 125
Hunter, V. J. 111
Hyde, W. W. 163

Immerwahr, H. R. 36
Ingenkamp, H. G. 4, 54, 88, 250, 310
Irigoin, J. 2

Jacoby, F. 290, see also index locorum, *FGrH*
Jocelyn, H. D. 112
Jones, C. P. 1–2, 8, 14, 22, 25, 38, 60, 63, 66, 88–9, 96, 105, 133–4, 193, 235, 251, 288–9, 291–4, 296, 308
Jones, R. M. 72, 143–4, 217
Jouanna, J. 93

Kane, J. 172
Kassel, R. 32, 112
Keaveney, A. 197
Kebric, R. B. 42, 101, 125
Keen, A. G. 186
Kelly, C. M. ix
Kelly, T. 164
Kerényi, K. 170
Klibansky, R. 179
Klotz, A. 8
Knox, P. E. 190
Koestermann, E. 285
Kokolakis, M. 125
Konstantinovic, I. 4
Koraes, A. 10, 294
Korus, K. 44
Kranz, W. 107
Krenkel, W. A. 95

Krentz, P. 186
Krevans, N. 190
Kroll, W. 290
Kuhn, R. 103, 112
Kühn. C. G. 38, 93, 195, 247
Kühner, R. 38

Lammert, F. 249
Larmour, D. H. J. 250, 253, 255–6, 258–9, 267
Lasso de la Vega, J. S. 3
Lattimore, R. 113
Lausberg, H. 16
Lavagnini, B. 4, 293
Lavery, G. B. 60, 261
Le Corsu, F. 164
Leo, F. 6–7, 126, 146, 187, 244, 251
Levene, D. S. 54
Lévêque, P. 113
Lévy, E. 9, 244
Lewis, R. G. 8, 203
Lieberich, H. 25
Lindskog, Cl. xiii
Littman, R. J. 217
Littré, E. 104, 178, 195
Lloyd, G. E. R. 243
Lombardi, M. 312
Loraux, N. 237
Lotze, D. 165
Lounsbury, R. C. 253
Luce, T. J. 47, 54, 58
Luck, G. 253

McCarty, W. 32
McCarty, T. G. 229
McGing, B, J. C. 244
McKeown, J. C. 244
Madden, J. A. 197
Mader, G. 114
Maehler, H. 213
Magnino, D. 250
Malkin, I. 191
Manfredini, M. 3, 185, 227, 254
Manuwald, B. 285
Marasco, G. 56, 113
Marcovich, M. 213, 215
Marinatos, N. 115

Marincola, J. M. 58
Martin, H. M. 37, 55–6, 60, 64, 77–8
Martin, R. H. 25–7
Masaracchia, A. 293
Mason, H. J. 294
Massaro, D. 293
Matthews, E. 174
Mayer. A. 16
Mayor, J. B. 32
Mazzarino, S. 18
Meichsner, I. 122
Meijering, R. 19, 34
Meineke, A. 32, 112
Mewaldt, J. 2
Meyer, E. 6
Michel, D. 249
Michelakis, P. ix
Migne, J.-P. 19
Milazzo, A. M. 244
Millar, F. 67, 289
Miola, R. S. 3–4
Mittelstadt, M. C. 6
Moles, J. L. ix, 7, 15, 21, 25, 36, 41, 53, 67, 76, 128, 137, 169, 176, 188, 228, 250, 257, 266, 290, 314
Momigliano, A. 7, 66, 201, 290
Montano, A. 94
Moreno, L. A. G. 128
Morgan, M. G. 95
Mossman, J. M. x, 62, 65, 103, 112, 121, 123, 125, 127, 163–5, 310
Muecke, F. 56
Mueller, H.-F. 42
Murray, P. 44

Nauck, A. 34, 237
Neu, J. 91
Newman, W. L. 298
Nikolaidis, A. G. 13, 56, 77, 83, 87, 132, 212, 246, 266, 269, 271, 274–5, 304
Nisbet, R. G. M. 122
Nock, A. D. 170
Norden, E. 21
Norton, G. 4

Oakley, S. P. 122
Ogilvie, R. M. 21

Oliver, J. H. 300
O'Neil, E. N. 143, 185, 217
Opsomer, J. ix, 72, 79, 88, 91, 247

Padel, R. 179
Page, D. L. 32, 191
Paladini, M. L. 244
Palmer, M. 222
Panagopoulos, C. 293
Panofsky, E. 179
Paradiso, A. 235
Paratore, E. 313
Parke, H. W. 298
Patterson, C. 94
Pauw, D. 186
Pavis d' Escurac, H. 293
Pecorella Longo, C. 184
Pédech, P. 22, 28
Pelling, C. B. R. ix, 2–3, 8, 10, 16, 21–2, 25, 56, 60–2, 67–9, 77, 83, 102, 120, 123, 126, 135–7, 139, 149–50, 153, 156, 161–2, 164, 169–70, 176, 178–9, 186–7, 197, 206–7, 211, 214, 220–1, 227–8, 230, 234, 239, 250, 252, 254–5, 257, 259, 266–8, 275, 278–81, 284–5, 302–3, 305–7, 311–12, 314
Pérez Jiménez, A. 39, 188, 252, 258
Pernot, L. 264
Perrin, B. xiii, 30, 195
Peter, H. 128, 205
Pfeiffer, R. 23, 190
Piccirilli, L. 2, 7–8, 21, 26, 56, 62–4, 174, 185, 227, 314
Plummer, A. 38
Podlecki, A. J. 23, 192, 315
Pohlenz, M. xiii
Polman, G. H. 7, 189, 313
Pordomingo Pardo, F., x
Prandi, L. 223–4
Preston, R. ix
Prieth, K. 253, 264
Proctor, D. 111
Puech, B. 288

Quet, M.-H. 93

Rabe, H. 34, 125

Radermacher, L. 42
Ramage, E. S. 203
Ramón Palerm, V. 7
Rawlings, H. R. 53
Rawson, E. 187
Reams, L. E. 198
Reardon, B. P. 77
Reinhold, M. 4, 292
Reiske, J. J. 35
Renehan, R. 182–3
Renoirte, T. 293
Resta, G. 3
Rich, J. W. 285
Richmond, I. 21
Ritzenstein, R. 19
Robert, L. 181, 190
Roberts, D. H. 284
Roberts, J. T. 140
Robertson, A. 38
Rosalia, A. De 8
Rose, H. J. 8
Rose, J. J. 13
Rosenmeyer, T. G. 7
Ross, D. 37
Roussel, M. 237
Rubina Cammarota, M. 102, 267
Rudd, N. 104
Russell, D. A. xiii, 4, 8, 41, 44, 47, 56, 74, 162, 205, 207, 214, 216–18, 221, 224, 228, 230, 233, 239, 251, 256, 282, 291, 294, 313
Rutherford, R. B. 69

Sacks, K. 9, 16, 28, 40, 42, 290
Ste Croix, G. E. M. de 44
Saller, R. P. 183
Salvioni, L. 207
Samsaris, D. K. 249
Sandbach, F. H. xiii, 2, 14, 39, 174, 178, 194, 212, 249
Sanders, L. J. 165
Sansone, D. 3, 17, 93, 178, 182–3, 187
Saxl, F. 179
Scardigli, B. 4, 39, 101, 142, 250, 264, 275
Schaefer, H. 168
Schenkeveld, D. M. 16

Schmid, W. xiii
Schmidt, L. 83
Schneeweiss, G. 13, 77
Schöne, R. 172
Schoppe, C. 37
Schröder, St. 300
Scobie, A. 304
Scott, K. 170, 292
Seager, R. J. 95, 193, 233
Sellers, M. N. S. 4
Shackford, M. H. 3
Sheppard, A. R. R. 89, 297
Sherman, N. 39
Shochat, Y. 159
Simpson, P. 45
Sintenis, C. xiii
Smith, B. H. 186
Smith, R. E. 6
Smits, J. 169, 172
Sordi, M. 101
Spanheim, E. F. 21
Spanneut, M. 76
Spawforth, A. J. 192
Spence, J. 5
Spencer, T. J. B. 3
Spengel, L. 16, 19, 37, 163–4, 244, 260
Stadter, P. A. ix, 2, 8, 14, 36–7, 77, 90, 103, 161–2, 164–5, 167, 170, 193, 196–7, 248, 250, 255, 265, 304, 310, 313
Stanton, G. R. 174
Starr, R. J. 290
Steidle, W. 2, 87, 313
Stein, R. H. 9
Stiefenhofer, A. 206, 244, 253, 256
Stoltz, C. 2
Strachey, G. L. 5
Strasburger, B. H. 6
Strobard, A. 8
Stuart, D. R. 8
Süss, W. 95
Swain, S. C. R. 1, 7, 31, 60, 62, 64, 74, 76–7, 105, 123, 129, 134, 139, 150, 188, 192, 207, 220, 230, 245, 247–8, 250, 253, 256, 260, 262, 265, 280, 286, 289, 292–4, 296, 300–1, 304–7, 310
Sweet, W. E. 101

Syme, R. 142, 289

Talbert, R. J. A. 31, 250
Tarn, W. W. 113
Tatum, W. J. 117, 164, 286
Taylor, W. C. 5
Terkourafi, M. x
Teza, E. 3
Theander, C. 2, 8
Thévenaz, P. 106
Tigerstedt, E. N. 172
Tirelli, A. 293
Titchener, F. B. 56, 315
Toohey, P. 112, 178
Torraca, L. xiii
Tosh, J. 8
Townend, G. B. 6–8, 86, 98, 159, 186, 254
Trapp, M. B. 79
Trench, R. C. 291
Tritle, L. A. 140, 142
Tsagas, N. M. 315
Tsekourakis, D. 93, 105, 113
Tucker, R. A. 80
Tuplin, C. J. 14, 193
Turchi, M. 223

Usener, H. 33, 42, 106, 109, 112

Valgiglio, E. 5, 18–19, 21, 37, 41, 50–1, 147, 203, 206, 244, 246, 249, 251, 291, 293
Van der Stockt, L. x, 42, 45
Van der Valk, M. 2, 187, 206, 255, 257
Vander Waerdt, P. A. 73
Vernant, J.-P. 175
Vessey, D. W. T. C. 190
Vidal-Naquet, P. 173, 312

Voss, O. 190
Vukobrat, S. 5

Walbank, F. W. 22, 36, 40, 90
Walcot, P. 172
Walker, S. 192
Wallace-Hadrill, A. 8, 95–6, 98, 253
Walsh, J. J. 8, 56, 83, 134, 250, 257, 268, 308
Walsh, P. G. 244
Wardman, A. E. ix, 21, 39, 65, 74, 83, 89, 92, 121, 150, 164, 184, 192, 251, 291, 303, 305
Watkins, O. D. 254
Weiss, R. 3
Weissenberger, B. xiii
Weizsäcker, A. 7
West, M. L. 175
Westlake, H. D. 6, 194, 222, 238
Wheeler, E. L. 171
White, H. V. 8
Whitehead, D. 180
Whitmarsh, T. ix, 169
Wiedemann, T. 292
Wilamowitz-Moellendorf, U. von 8
Wilner, O. L. 244
Wiseman, T. P. 290
Wolman, H. B. 13
Woodhead, A. G. 180
Woodman, A. J. 25–7, 244, 285, 290

Yaginuma, S. xiii

Ziegler, K. xiii, 1–3, 8, 13, 20, 35, 77, 83, 108, 206, 214, 226, 249, 254, 256, 271, 288, 294
Ziehen, J. 197
Zimmerman, R. 8

Index of themes

Academy 146
  see also Plato; Platonism, contemporary
Actors 116, 125, 293–4
After-thoughts 257, 278
Agesilaos–Pompey synkrisis 275–8
  see also index locorum
Agriculture, see Plant metaphors
Alexander–Caesar prologue 14–21
  see also index locorum
Alexander the Great, presentations of 65, 76, 85–6, 102, 267, 300–1, 314
  see also index locorum
Ambiguity, moral, *esp.* 70–1, 83–7, 131–4, 161–2; *also* 129, 154, 164–5, 168–71, 174, 177–84, 189–91, 193, 197, 222, 226, 228, 231, 236, 239–40, 262, 296, and chapters 5–8 *passim*
Ambition, *esp.* 83–7, 267, 308; *also* 110–11, 116, 162, 179–80, 194, 205, 210, 212–16, 219, 227, 229–30
Ancestors, Plutarch's use of, *esp.* 310–11; *also* 178, 198, 206, 254
Anecdotes, *esp.* 5, 15–16, 182–4; *also* 34, 85, 94–8, 108, 135, 190–3, 230–7, 259, 311
Anger, *esp.* 87–9; *also* 74, 78, 151, 158, 178–9, 197, 205, 210–15, 219, 267–8, 282, 304
Animals 34, 48, 75, 78, 92, 108, 172, 208, 231, 235, 246
  see also Chameleons; Foxes; Horses; Lions
Antiquarianism 187, 299
Antony, not wholly bad 61–2

  see also index locorum
Apatheia 72, 74, 156–7, 209
Apophthegms, see Sayings, reveal character
Aporia, see Hesitation, scenes of
Appearance as guide to character, *esp.* 16, 164; *also* 78, 125–6, 145, 166–7, 251 n.
  see also Clothes; Statues
Appropriateness as a criterion for the historian 57, 312
Aratos prologue 68
  see also index locorum
Aristocracy 90, 310
Aristotle, Plutarch's relation to 39 n., 44–5, 72 n., 74 n.
  see also index locorum
Art, works of 35–8, 43, 97–8, 169–70, 265–6
Assemblies, Roman 302
Astronomical phenomena, see Eclipses, Portents
Athenian Empire 132–3, 265–6
Athletes, athletics 190, 299
Atticism, xiii n., 83 n., 174
Audience:
  constructed as Greek 293, 299–300, 302
  expectations of 53, 185–6, 234–5
Authorial intervention 53–5, 148–9, 176, 203, 232, 251, 299, 309
  see also Onlookers as mouthpiece for author

Barbarians 146, 169, 185, 274, 298–9, 301–2, 304–5
Battle-narratives 199

see also Generals; Warfare,
    Plutarch's interest in
Benefaction 67, 240, 266–7, 305
Bereavement 82, 127, 147, 151, 252
Bile, see Humoural theory
Biography:
    blurred boundaries of 17–22, 96
    of philosophers and literary men 7,
        66, 82, 290
    Plutarch's influence on the modern
        genre 4–5
Bios, see Biography; Life (Βίος),
    multiple meanings of
Boredom 112
Bribery 129, 194, 198 n., 217, 264, 283
Brothers 81, 93, 147, 151, 240, 258
Burial 199, 240
    see also Posthumous honour or
        dishonour
Bystanders, see Onlookers

Caesar:
    his monarchy as divinely ordained
        134, 149, 153–4
    Plutarch's presentation of, esp.
        79–80, 86–7, 303
    see also index locorum
Calendar 187–9, 300, 312
Calmness, esp. 77–8; also 81, 87, 143–6,
    211, 213–14, 251–2, 265, 304
Career, natural pattern of 189, 293,
    303, 313
    see also Characterization; Entry into
        politics or adult life; Patronage
Caution, cautiousness 31, 141, 251, 271
    see also Calmness; Generals, dying
        in battle
Chameleons 175 n., 219, 235
Chance, see Fortune
Character:
    ancient conceptions of 13–15, 73–4,
        119, 256
    moulding or formation of 37, 39,
        73–4
    Plutarch's concern with 5, 14–17,
        24–8, 30, 54, 256 and passim
Character- and personality-
    viewpoint, 13 n., 69–70, 228 n.
Character-change, esp. 230; also 25 n.,
    119, 154, 228–30, 235–7, 285
Characterization:
    at height of power 189, 313
    by reaction, see Onlookers, as
        mouthpiece for the author
    indirect 7, 16 n.
    initial 110, 177–8, 206–11, 229–30
Charm, and the lack of it, esp. 228;
    also 90, 129–30, 140, 147, 154, 209,
        211–12, 215–21, 233, 282, 305
    see also Flattery, Flatterers
Childhood 85, 151, 157 n., 228 n., 230,
    254, 264, 313
    see also Education; Entry into
        politics or adult life
Children of the subject, esp. 130,
    182–4; also 127–8, 136–7, 144 n.,
    222–3, 255
    see also Ancestors, Plutarch's use
        of; Bereavement
Choice of subjects 58–9, 249
Chronology:
    of Plutarch's works, esp. 2, 63, 65;
        see also 88 n., 105, 128 n., 133
    not the highest priority, esp. 312–14;
        see also 50, 135, 175, 182–3
Civil war, esp. 89; also 194, 196, 218,
    230, 249, 267 n., 298
Classicism, Plutarch's, esp. 58–9, 265;
    also 55, 89, 97–8, 192–3, 233
    see also Atticism
Clemency 181 n., 277, 305
Closure, esp. 136–7, 283–6; also 130,
    184, 186, 231, 270
Clothes 116–17, 124–6, 143, 181
Co-operation, esp. 89–90; also 111 n.,
    215, 219–20, 261, 293, 296–8
    see also Rivalry
Coincidence ix, 53 n., 139
Commemoration, a function of
    history 47
Compromise 131–4, 139–41, 154–6,
    160, and chapter 5 passim,
    307–8
Conflation of episodes 218 n., 313 n.

Conflation of episodes (*cont.*):
  see also Chronology, not the
  highest priority
Conquest of Greece, Roman 115,
  134–5, 269, 301, 305–8
Constitutional debate 90
Contemplative Life 66, 75
Contemporary relevance 66–8, 288,
  307–8
Contentiousness, see Rivalry
Contradictions within Plutarchan
  corpus 75, 213, 246, 266–7, 274
  see also Discordant endings;
  Synkrisis, 'formal'; Variation
Coriolanus–Alkibiades Lives, chapter
  7 *passim*
  synkrisis 281–3
  see also index locorum
Corn Dole 152
Cornelius Nepos, Plutarch's use of
  228–9, 247, 290–1
Cosmic imagery, see Universe, comparisons with and metaphors of
Council–People dichotomy 213–15,
  220–1, 302–3
  see also Demagogues; Roman
  History, distortions of; Tyrants
Court-room metaphors 286
Creativity, Plutarch's 5–9, 101–2, 161
Criteria for inclusion 26–30, 56–60,
  312
  see also Selectivity; Sources
Cultural identity, chapter 9 *passim*
Cunning, see Deception
Cyclical nature of history 53, 96 n.,
  250–1, 277, 287–8
Cynicism 103–5

Dates, see Calendar
Death:
  of a relative, see Bereavement
  of the subject, *esp.* 136–7, 264; also
  32, 120–1, 129, 142–4, 157, 176, 184,
  188, 197, 201–3, 239–40, 255, 268,
  270, 274–5, 278, 280–1, 311; see
  also Posthumous honour or
  dishonour; Burial

  place or manner of, linked to
  character 176, 197, 202
Deception, *esp.* 171–6; also 154 n.,
  233–4, 237, 271, 282
Dedication to Sosius Senecio 2
Deeds:
  revealing character 5, 13–15, 21–2,
  25–7, 110, 118, 249–50, 264 n.
  the stuff of history 15, 18–19, 21–2,
  54
Deification, *esp.* 116, 292; also 86, 165,
  170, 186, 189, 255
Delusions 86–7, 120–1
Demagogues 81, 90, 119–20, 149,
  227–8, 265, 303–4
Demetrios–Antony
  prologue 45–9
  synkrisis 278–81
  see also index locorum
Democracy, *esp.* 92, 133–4; also 51, 173,
  194, 202, 221–3, 233, 238–9, 278,
  285, 314
Depression 178 n.
  see also Boredom; *Melancholia*
Descendants, see Children of the
  subject; Posthumous honour or
  dishonour
Descriptive moralism 68–70, 161,
  221 n.
Deterrent Lives 45–9, 55–65, 101,
  148–9, 208
Dialogue 7, 112–14
Diatribes 103–5, 113 n.
Dictatorship 303
Digressions, *esp.* 186–7; also 92, 164,
  200, 222
Dionysios of Halikarnassos:
  as a source for Plutarch 92, 115 n.,
  205, 214, 218, 220 n., 221, 282
  his views on the historian 56–8
  see also index locorum
Discontent, *esp.* 103–7; also chapter 4
  passim, 274, 296 n., 304
Discordant endings 137, 155 n., 255,
  257, 260–1, 263–86.
Disease, literal and metaphorical
  194–7

see also Medicine, metaphors of
Display speeches 97–8, 245–7, 259–60,
   263, 267, 276, 300
   see also Enkomion
Distortions, see Greek history; Roman
   history
Divine retribution 136–7, 207, 210
   see also Gods, intervention into
   history
Divine worship, see Deification
Divorce 104, 157, 233
Double-presentation 133–5, 286, 307
   see also Synkrisis, 'formal'; Paired
   or double speeches
Douceur 77–8, 303
Dramatic irony, see Tragic irony and
   patterning
Dreams and visions 80 n., 188 n., 197
Dress, see Clothes
Drunkenness:
   Plutarch's treatment of 93, 117, 143,
   167, 238, 178 n., 285
   reveals character 15 n., 32 n.
Dying words, see Last words

Earthquakes 187–8
Eclipses 187–8
Editions of Plutarch xiii, 3–4
Education, esp. 73–7, 90–2, 264–5; also
   62–5, 85, 108–10, 121, 128, 150,
   205–11, 215–17, 220–1, 223 n.,
   232–3, 301
   see also Hellenism
Eidologische–chronologische
   distinction 7
Elections 119, 151–4, 206, 210
Emperors 94–6, 142 n., 159–60, 292–3
   see also Caesar, his monarchy as
   divinely ordained
Emulation of predecessors, see
   Predecessors
Engineering 306
Enkomion:
   overlap with and influence on
   biography, esp. 17, 19, 21–2; also
   31, 96, 98, 134, 158–9, 161–2, 185–7,
   265, 310–11, 313

influence on Plutarchan synkrisis
   243–4, 251–3, 263, 267, 272, 276
   see also Display speeches; Paired or
   double speeches
Entry into politics or adult life 184–5,
   217–18, 233–4, 293, 313
   see also Childhood; Patronage
Envy:
   by one's peers 104, 131 n., 165,
   271–2
   by the gods 113, 138
   by the people 87, 205, 221–2
Ephors 174, 191
Epic associations 121–2, 124, 127, 143
   n., 191–2, 197, 310
   see also index nominum, s.v.
   Achilles, Hektor
Epicureanism 81, 88 n., 105, 107
Epideixis, see Display speeches
Epilepsy as a πάθος 79 n.
Episodic nature of Plutarch's
   narrative 135–6
Equites 303
Erotic imagery 143, 216–17, 226–7, 231,
   236–7
   see also Sex
Euergetism, see Benefaction
Examples, Plutarch's use of 31–2,
   50–4, 56, 64–5, 68, 90 n., 110 n.,
   117, 223–4, 227–8, 234, 248, 250,
   288, 295, 298
Exempla literature 53–4
Exile 43, 51, 62 n., 76 n., 128, 184 n.,
   205, 207, 213, 218–19, 220–2, 231,
   235, 238–40, 293 n., 295
Expediency, esp. 131–5; also 129, 146–7,
   152–4, 159, 162, 180–2, 192, 202–4,
   264, 272–3, 277, 281, and chapters
   5 and 6 passim
Extremism, to be avoided 155–60
   see also Compromise; Inflexibility;
   Stoicism
Eyes, reveal character 17 n., 166

Face, mobility of the features 214
   see also Appearance as guide to
   character

Families 93
  see also Ancestors; Brothers;
    Children of the subject; Fathers;
    Mothers
Fate, esp. 123–4, 137–9; also 85, 103–4,
  115, 121, 128–30, 149, 219, 245, 297,
  307–8
Fathers 32, 206–7, 246, 258, 310–11
  see also Ancestors; Children of the
    subject
Femininity, constructions of, esp.
  95–7; also 164 n., 231, 236–7, 243,
  247–8, 266
  see also Masculinity, constructions
    of
Fiction, relationship to history 18–19,
  168
Fire, see Heat, linked with passions or
  spirit (θυμός)
First-person verbs 35–6, 61, 252, 269,
  276, 286, 299
Flattery, Flatterers, esp. 119, 178–9,
  226–8; also 57, 68, 71, 128–9,
  135–6, 140 n., 153–4, 167, 169–70,
  190, 194, 216, 224, 230, 232, 235–6,
  251, 282, 296 n.
Flood imagery, see Water imagery
Flute-playing 46, 92, 231
Forgetfulness 106–7
Forms, doctrine of 37 n., 43
Fortune, esp. 123, 263; also 35, 43, 48,
  58 n., 75, 85, 106, 108, 114, 116 n.,
  117, 120, 127, 137–9, 142, 154, 212,
  216, 245, 263, 273, 279, 300–1, 310
  changes of 32, 42 n., 50, 107, 117,
    123–4, 179 n., 230, 251–2, 280 n.,
    310
  see also Fate
Foxes 174–6, 200–1
Freedom 67, 134–5, 192–3, 202, 287,
  297, 307–8
Friendship, esp. 135, 239 n., 276–7; also
  85–6, 88, 119, 143–4, 146, 152–3,
  157–9, 227–8, 230–2, 258–9, 275–6,
  280, 295–6, 311, 313
  see also Flattery, Flatterers;
    Plutarch, his circle

Frugality 55, 135, 179, 182–4, 198, 261–2
  see also Wealth

Galba-Otho prologue 28–9
  see also index locorum
Generals:
  dying in battle 30, 82, 170, 201–2,
    264, 268, 306
  problems adapting to civilian life
    119–21, 252, 276
  topoi associated with 148, 171–3,
    203
Genitive, use of 190
Genres:
  blurred boundaries of 17–22
  function of 53, 187
Gentleness, see Calmness
Gladiators 291–2
Glory 83–87, 108–9 n., 119–20
Gods, intervention into history, esp.
  39–40, 136–8, 149, 255, 307; also
  53 n., 131, 134, 152, 186–9, 207,
  209–10, 227, 261
  see also Fortune; Miracles; Nemesis;
    Portents; Spirits; Superstition
Good, the (τὸ καλόν) 37–8, 40
Gospels 6
Great natures, esp. 47–9, 60–5, 205–8,
  224–8; also 70, 116, 121, 155–6, 162,
  179, 278–9, 281
Greed, esp. 104, 110–12; also 116–17,
  120, 136 n., 198, 278–9, 281, 303–4
  see also Discontent; Wealth
Greek history, distortions of 146,
  312–14
  see also 263–83 passim
Grief, see Bereavement

Habituation, role of 39, 73–5, 89
Hair 126, 164
Happiness, theme of much
  philosophical debate 102–3
Harmony, see Co-operation; Music,
  metaphors of
Heat, linked with passions or spirit
  (θυμός) 88, 93, 187

Hellenism:
  influence in Rome 63–4, 77 n., 210, 305–6
  high valuation of, *esp.* 76–7, chapter 9 *passim*; also 58–60, 65, 85, 89, 109–10, 142, 176, 185, 192–3, 233, 260, 262, 270, 274
Hellenistic biography 6–8
Hellenistic kings, Plutarch's presentations of, *esp.* 115–17; also 63, 122, 189, 281 n., 292, 300–1
Herodotos:
  corrections of 164 n., 187 n., 266
  Dionysios' favourable presentation of 57
  Plutarch's unfavourable presentation of 58
Heroes, deified 168–70
Hesitation, scenes of 79–80, 113–14
Historia (ἱστορία), two meanings of 33, 41
Historiography, overlap of Plutarchan biography with 20–1, 52–3
History:
  ancient conceptions of, *esp.* 17–22, 52–3, 57–9; also 47, 96, 259, 313
  periods and themes traditionally covered 63–4, 289–90
Homosexuality, *see* Sex
Honour, love of, *see* Ambition
Horses:
  metaphor for the passions, *esp.* 62, 78–9, 85, 167
  metaphor for rivalry 51
  Spartans compared to 191–2
Hubris:
  in Plutarch 113–14, 116, 124, 167, 232–3, 240, 279, 303
  in Thucydides 110–11
Human nature, never wholly good 56, 59, 64
Humanity, *see* Philanthropia
Humoural theory 92–3, 178–9, 243

Imitation, *see* Mimesis
Imperial cult, *see* Deification
Inconsistency of character 119, 167, 220–1, 227–31, 235, 270–1
  see also Character-change
Incorruptibility, *see* Wealth
Inflexibility 150, 156–7, 209–15
  see also Compromise
Inherited characteristics, *see* Ancestors
Intermediate sources, Plutarch and 6–8
Invitations to audience 9, 27, 33, 53, 64, 69–71, 133, 173, 203–4, 221, 227, 246–7, 262, 268–9, 284, 286, 309
  see also First-person verbs
Irrational, the, *esp.* 73–5; also 43, 78–9, 83, 87, 91–2, 94, 104–6, 108, 131
  see also Passions; Reason; Reasonings
Irresolution 79–82
  see also Hesitation, scenes of
Isokrates, Plutarch's use of 185, 222–3
  see also index locorum
It is said, see Unnamed sources

Jokes 15–16, 234

Katharsis 44
Kimon–Lucullus prologue 59, 159, 271
  see also index locorum
Kings, kingliness 90 n., 116–17
  see also Hellenistic kings, Plutarch's presentations of; Kingship, desire for; Philosopher-kings
Kingship, desire for 86–7, 168 n., 178, 187 n., 197 n.

Lack of fit, *see* Contradictions within Plutarchan *corpus*; Discordant endings; *Synkrisis*, 'formal'
Lamprias Catalogue 1–2
  see also index locorum
Last words 159, 275, 280–1
Latin, Plutarch's knowledge of 8, 128 n., 299, 302
Life (βίος), multiple meanings of 17, 33–4, 283–4
  see also Biography
Lions 174–6, 200–1, 231

Literature, benefits of 31–2, 42–5
Lives of the Caesars 19–20, 28–9
   see also index locorum
Lost works of Plutarch 2
   see also index locorum
Lucullus, Plutarch's favourable
   presentation of 59–60, 260–1
Luxury 60, 95, 104, 118, 176 n., 178 n.,
   194, 234, 239, 260, 279, 283
   see also Wealth
Lysander–Sulla, chapter 6 passim
   see also index locorum

Madness 152, 178–9
   see also Delusions
Maggots 197
Malice, accusations of 56–9, 97, 259
Manuscripts of Plutarch 3–4
   see also Text, corruptions and
   emendations of
Marriage:
   no cure for discontent 104, 106
   Plutarch's presentation of 157–8,
   184, 262, 299; see also Sex
   political and dynastic 122 n., 135,
   153, 276, 279–80
Masculinity, constructions of, esp.
   95–7, 209–13; also 91, 221, 231, 233,
   237, 243
   see also Femininity, constructions
   of
Mathematics 306
Mean, the 145
   see also Moderation
Meanness, see Parsimony
Medicine, metaphors of, esp. 92–4,
   194–7; also 88–9, 131, 149, 153, 277,
   292, 310
Melancholia 177–9, 197
Meteorites 187–9
Military achievements, revealing of
   character? 15–17, 98
   see also Warfare, Plutarch's interest
   in
Mimesis, esp. 37–45, 50–1, 148–9, 209;
   also 33–4, 47, 161, 235–6
Miracles 129

Mirrors 32–4
Mistakes of Plutarch 8 n., 280 n.,
   314 n.
Mixed constitution 92 n.
Mixing, metaphorical and real, esp.
   89–94; also 139–41, 145–7, 160,
   211, 304, 310
Moderation 58, 75, 133, 139–40, 145,
   147, 152–4, 209, 211, 214, 219, 221,
   245–6, 295, 304
   see also Compromise; Mixing
Moralia:
   unity with the Lives 5
   use of historical examples in 50
Moralism:
   in ancient historiography, esp.
   52–55
   not a transcultural term 13, 69; see
   also Character
   Plutarch's concern with 5 and
   passim
Mothers 80 n., 206, 214–15, 258, 281
   see also Ancestors; Children of the
   subject
Music:
   Aristotle on 44
   metaphors of 91–4
Mysticism 31
Myth, relationship to history 18–19,
   313
Mythology, Plutarch's use of 2, 167,
   195 n., 200, 277, 312–13

Names 130, 205 n., 302
Naphtha 187
National Interest, see Expediency
Nature ($\phi\acute{u}\sigma\iota\varsigma$), distinct from
   character ($\mathring{\eta}\theta o\varsigma$) 74, 119, 179, 230,
   235
   see also Character-change; Great
   natures
Negative examples 45–9, 56, 60–1,
   63–4, 101, 228, 251–2
   see also Deterrent Lives
Nemesis 124, 127–8
Nepos, see Cornelius Nepos

Nikias–Crassus
  prologue 22–28, 30
  synkrisis 269–75
  see also index locorum
Nikias, Plutarch's negative portrait of
  25–6, 56
Novels, similarity of some Lives with
  62, 69–70, 281

Oaths 175–6, 186 n.
Old, the 84, 110, 118, 120, 123, 212
Omens 124, 126–7
Onlookers as mouthpiece for author,
  esp. 55, 120; *also* 114, 116 n., 138,
  144, 152–3, 191, 227, 231–5, 285
Openings of Lives, *see* Prologues
Optimates 303
Oracles 199–200
Order of Lives within a pair 30 n.,
  205–6, 249, 254, 302
Orphans 206–7
Orthography 77 n., 83
Ostracism 223, 261

Painting, painters 15–17, 42–3, 167, 234
Paired or double speeches 243–7, 253,
  257–62
Panhellenism 89
Paradox 25 n., 26–7, 162, 168 n., 172,
  179, 183, 194, 198–9, 201, 214–15,
  220, 231, 234, 259–60, 264, 269,
  308
Parallel Lives, composition and publication of 2, 249
  see also Chronology of Plutarch's
  works; Order of Lives within a
  pair
Parsimony 159
Passions:
  necessary for the exercise of virtue
  73, 75–6, 87, 213, 266
  Plutarch's presentation of, chapter
  3 *passim*; *also* 29–30, 39, 43, 59,
  69–70, 108–10, 147, 151, 209,
  211–15, 303–4
Patronage 122, 293, 295–6
People, the, *esp.* 89–90, 220–1, 302–4;
  also 69, 81–82, 97, 115, 119, 265,
  271, 31
  see also Demagogues
Perikles, Plutarch's presentation of
  64, 81, 90, 97, 265–6
  see also index locorum
Perikles–Fabius prologue 34–45
  see also index locorum
Peripatetic:
  biography 6–8
  school 72 n., 87
Persian Empire, as code for Roman
  295–6
Personality-viewpoint, *see* Character-
  and personality-viewpoint
Phaidros, allusions to 78–9, 85, 88–9
  see also index locorum
Philanthropia:
  Plutarch's construction of, *esp.*
  77–8
  Plutarch's *persona* of 56–60, 78,
  94–7, 271
  see also index of Greek words
Philopoimen–Flamininus synkrisis
  267–9
  see also index locorum
Philosopher-kings, 90 n., 150 n., 156 n.
Philosophical biography,
  see Biography of philosophers
  and literary men
Philosophy 31, 40 n., 48–9, 50 n., 60
  n., 66, 72–3, 76 n.-77 n., 103, 106,
  128, 141, 144–5, 147, 149–51, 155–8,
  216, 224–6, 245, 267, 300–1
  see also Epicureanism; Platonism;
  Stoicism
Phtheiriasis, *see* Maggots
Phokion–Cato Minor, chapter 5
  passim
  see also index locorum
Physiognomics 17 n., 93, 166
Piccirilli, Luigi, his tripartite
  classification of the *Lives* 62–3
Pigs 106 n., 208
Plans, *see* Reasonings
Plant metaphors 48–9, 140, 207–8,
  226

Plato:
  Plutarch's criticisms of 43–5, 245, 266
  Plutarch's relation to, *esp.* 72–7, and chapter 3 *passim*; also 2, 32, 36–7, 40, 43–5, 117, 143–4, 211, 213, 216–18, 223–7, 248, 251 n., 266, 300, 303, 306
  see also Great natures; index locorum
Platonism, contemporary 72 n., 247
Pleasure, contrasted with utility 31–2, 35–7, 41, 46, 52–3
Plutarch:
  his circle 203, 288–9, 293
  life and works 1–2, 289 n.
Poetry, Plutarch's views of 42–5
Poets 190
Polarities 243
Political analysis, not the highest priority 90, 135–6
Political Precepts, *esp.* 293–8
  see also index locorum
Politics, the true calling of the philosopher 66, 75
Populares 303
Portents 123–4, 187–9, 255
  see also Eclipses
Posthumous honour or dishonour 136–7, 168 n., 184, 240, 311
Poverty 169, 198, 261–2, 310–11
  see also Wealth
Power, reveals character 25 n.
Pragmatic history 28–9
Predecessors:
  literary, polemic against and corrections of 22–3, 25, 164 n.
  of Plutarchan subjects, emulation of 51, 84, 86
Private life 15–16, 263, 280, 313
  see also Sex
Programmatic statements, chapter 1 *passim*
Prologues 14 and chapter 1 *passim* 102–3, 243, 251, 255–6
Pronunciation 83
Prophecies and predictions 20 n.
  see also Omens; Portents
Protreptic moralism 68
Pyrrhos–Marius, chapter 4 *passim*
  see also index locorum

Quotations 313

Rashness, Plutarch's criticisms of, *see* Generals, dying in battle
Reason, the rational, *esp.* 73–82 and chapter 3 *passim*, 105–6, 108–110; also 18, 29–30, 39–41, 43, 45, 47, 62, 69–70, 117, 131, 140, 148, 152, 178 n., 208–9, 211, 213–16, 221–2, 246, 253
Reasonings (λογισμοί), *esp.* 30, 78–82; also 91, 114, 152, 215, 239, 268, 277, 294
Reception of the *Lives* 1–9, 253–4
Recusatio 21
Reincarnation 251 n.
Relativism 131–4, 229, 233, 263 n., 279
  see also Ambiguity, moral
Reputation 61, 120, 128, 132, 148, 180, 229, 235, 238–40, 272, 275, 306, 311
Research 18, 24, 33, 41–2, 108
Revelation of character 15, 24–8, 214
Rhetoric:
  its influence on biography 95–6, 256–7.
  modern distrust of 256–7
  Plutarch's recommendations on 147 n.
  schools of 95, 185, 223, 243–4, 251, 260, 263, 276
  techniques of, used by Plutarch 16 n., 185, 201, 243–5, 251–86 *passim*, 312 n., 313
  see also Display Speeches; *Enkomion*; Paired or double speeches; *Synkrisis*; Vituperation
Ring-composition 130, 231
  see also Closure
Rivalry, *esp.* 83–5; also 51, 89, 97, 111 n., 116 n., 121, 127–8, 134, 151, 214, 263, 297–9, 308
  see also Ambition; Co-operation

Roman administration, careers in
  288–9, 295–6
Roman Empire 66–7, 270, 281, 300–1,
  and chapter 9 *passim*
Roman history, distortions of 119,
  218, 220–1, 263–83 *passim*, 302–3
Roman intervention in Greece 67–8,
  294–8
  see also Conquest of Greece,
  Roman
Romans:
  and education 76–7, 176 n., 220–21,
  303–6; *see also* Education
  not barbarians 289–9, 302
Rome:
  origins of 302
  Plutarch and, chapter 9 *passim*

Sacrifice 109, 127, 191
Sayings, reveal character 15–16, 32 n.,
  135, 174–6, 192
Scales, metaphors of 270
Scientific history 6
Secretaries, Plutarch and 8
Selectivity 4–5, 8–9
  see also Criteria for inclusion;
  Sources
Self-control 49, 91–2 n., 94–7, 132,
  147, 157, 203, 209, 211, 264,
  279–80, 283
  see also Calmness; Passions;
  Reason, the rational; Sex
Series of biographies 2, 19–20
Sex 94–7; *also* 116, 144 n., 167–8, 178
  n., 194–7, 216–17, 236–7, 240, 264,
  277, 279–80, 283, 298
Shakespeare, Plutarch's influence on
  3–4
Ship imagery 122, 307–8
  see also Water imagery
Single combat 121–2, 127
Skytale 164, 277
Sophists 3, 174, 216 n., 223, 246, 263–4
  n., 295, 299
Soul, bi- and tri-partite division of,
  esp. 72–6, 83–9, 303; *also* 40, 43,
  105–6, 211–15

Sources:
  claim to superior sources 23, 29–30
  non-literary 23
  Plutarch's use of, *esp.* 6–9, 101–2,
  161; *also* 86, 108, 113, 122, 125,
  128 n., 133–4, 142, 158–9, 173,
  178 n., 180, 184–6, 193–4, 198,
  201 n., 203, 205, 212, 214, 217–19,
  222–9, 231–2, 234, 238–9, 266, 273,
  278, 282
  see also Unnamed sources
Source-criticism 6–9
Spartan character 84–5, 155, 169,
  172–4, 176, 179–81, 191, 200–1
Spartan tradition 164–5, 181
Spectators:
  metaphor for readers 38–9, 41, 43
  as mouthpiece for author, *see*
  Onlookers
Spirit (Θυμός), spirited (Θυμοειδής)
  73, 76, 83, 85, 87–9, 93, 211–13, 304
Spirits 31, 138, 219, 255
Stage imagery, *see* Tragic imagery and
  language
Statesmanship 89–90, 97
Statues 16, 162–70
Stoic Opposition 142 n., 157
Stoicism, *esp.* 155–8; *also* 72–3, 75–6,
  88, 105, 151, 246
Strife, love of, *see* Ambition; Rivalry
Style, Plutarch's xiii, 184–5
  see also Atticism; Tautology
Success and failure, linked to same
  traits 123, 210, 220, 239, 276
  see also Great natures
Suetonius:
  compared with Plutarch 20–1, 67,
  80, 94–8
  Suetonian biography 6–8
Suicide 142, 151, 157, 284
Superlatives 186, 189
Superstition 126, 131, 187–8, 245, 255
Synkrisis:
  in the *Moralia* 245–9
  between paired Lives, *esp.* 249–51;
  also 10, 102–3, 141–3, 147, 243,
  287–8 and chapters 4–8 *passim*;

see also Order of Lives within a pair
Synkrisis (*cont.*):
  'formal' 200–3, 243, 252–87 *passim*
  'formal', missing ones 102–3, 107, 252–5
  internal, *esp.* 251–2; *also* 98, 107–8, 128–30, 135–6, 145–6, 160, 164, 168–71, 183–4, 198
  literary background to 243–5, 247, 259–60, 276
  missed opportunities for 166 n., 198 n.
Syphilis 197

Tacitus, programmatic statements 26–27
  see also index locorum
Tautology 110 n.
Text, corruptions and emendations of 22, 25, 38, 43, 109, 139, 167 n., 174, 178 n., 182–3, 193 n., 197, 206 n., 210 n., 214, 226, 249–50, 253–6, 294, 300, 305 n.
Texts of Plutarch, *see* Editions of Plutarch
They say, *see* Unnamed sources
Third-person verbs 299
Thucydides:
  and *hubris*, *see* Hubris
  Plutarch's use of 23, 25–6, 180, 187; *see also* index locorum
Titles of Plutarchan texts 256, 300
Tragedy, similarity of some Lives with 9, 61–2, 69–70, 123–4, 221, 281, 284, 309
Tragic:
  imagery and language 62, 65, 116–17, 123–6, 158, 176, 180, 294–5
  irony and patterning 123–4
Tragic History 41–2, 125
Translations of Plutarch xiii, 3–4
Transliteration xiii–xiv
Trickery, *see* Deception
'Types' of character, Greek 54, 119, 227–8, 303

see also Demagogues; Flattery, Flatterers; Tyrants
Tyrants:
  Alkibiades' tyrannical ambitions 207, 222, 231, 233, 236, 238–9
  a Plutarchan 'type', *esp.* 303; *also* 154, 264, 285, 292, 310, 314
  sexual lusts of 95–6, 236
  tyrannicide 284, 310–11
  wise men and 112–15

United States, Plutarch's influence in 4
Universal History 66, 290–1
Universe
  comparisons with and metaphors of 115, 139–40, 150, 188, 300–1
  soul as microcosm of 91
Unnamed sources 186
Utility of history 27–8, 31–2, 35–7, 41, 43–4, 46, 52–3

Variation
  across different works 65, 98, 102, 298; *see also* Contradictions within Plutarchan *corpus*
  within *Parallel Lives* 20–1, 54, 135
Vengeance, *see* Posthumous honour or dishonour
Vice, as 'shortcoming in virtue' 59–60, 271
Victory, love of, *see* Ambition
Virtue, as an art 36, 45
Visions, *see* Dreams and visions
Vituperation (negative biographies or speeches) 60, 96, 222–3, 253, 272
  see also Deterrent Lives; Negative examples
Vividness 29, 36, 41–2
Vulgate tradition (on Alexander) 102 n.

Walk, as indication of character 214
War-crimes 175, 181, 194–6, 234–5
Warfare, Plutarch's interest in, *esp.* 97–8, 263–4; *also* 67, 237–8, 251, 261–2, 272–3, 295

see also Deception; Expediency;
Military achievements, revealing
of character?
Water imagery 105–10, 122–3, 194–7,
225–6
Wealth 135–6, 179, 182–4, 201, 251, 258,
261–2, 264, 269–71, 283, 311
see also Bribery; Poverty
Wine, comparisons with 145
see also Drunkenness; Mixing,
metaphorical and real
Wise Man and Tyrant 112–15
Women 95, 104, 132, 158 n., 163 n.,
164 n., 168 n., 191, 212, 231, 234,
247–8, 262, 266, 299, 313
see also Femininity, constructions of

Word-play 83 n., 124–5, 131 n., 138 n.,
164, 172 n., 182, 203–4, 209,
216 n., 277
Words, *see* Sayings, reveal character
Worms, *see* Maggots
Wrestling 216–17, 231

Xenophon, Plutarch's use of 19,
29–30, 169, 180, 186, 193, 276
see also index locorum

Yoke 191
Young, the 44, 50–1, 55, 84, 179, 210

Zoroastrianism 138